GROWTH OF THE
ROMAN EMPIRE
44 B.C. - 300 A.D.

Scale of Miles

0   100   200   300   400   500

The Empire in 44 B.C.
Additions under Augustus, 31 B.C. - 14 A.D.
Later Annexations
Temporary Occupation (Colored Borders)
Losses in the Third Century

ATLANTIC OCEAN

IRELAND

Wall of Antoninus

82 A.D.

Hadrian's Wall

NORTH SEA

BALTIC SEA

BRITAIN
43 A.D.

Londinium

9 B.C.

9 B.C. - 9 A.D.

Cologne

GERMAN

LOWER GERMANY

Belgica

Lugdunensis

GAUL

Lugdunum

UPPER GERMANY

73 - 155 A.D.

RAETIA
15 B.C.

Danube

NORICUM
15 B.C.

UPPER PANNONIA
9 B.C.

Aquitania

Narbonensis

8 B.C.

Milano

LOWER
11 B.C.

SPAIN

19 B.C.

Tarraconensis

Lusitania

Baetica

Gades

New Carthage

BALEARIC IS.

SARDINIA

CORSICA

DALMATIA

ILLYRICUM

ADRIATIC SEA

ITALY

Rome

Ostia

Naples

MEDITERRANEAN

MAURETANIA
40 A.D.

NUMIDIA

AFRICA

Carthage

SICILY

MALTA

SAHARA

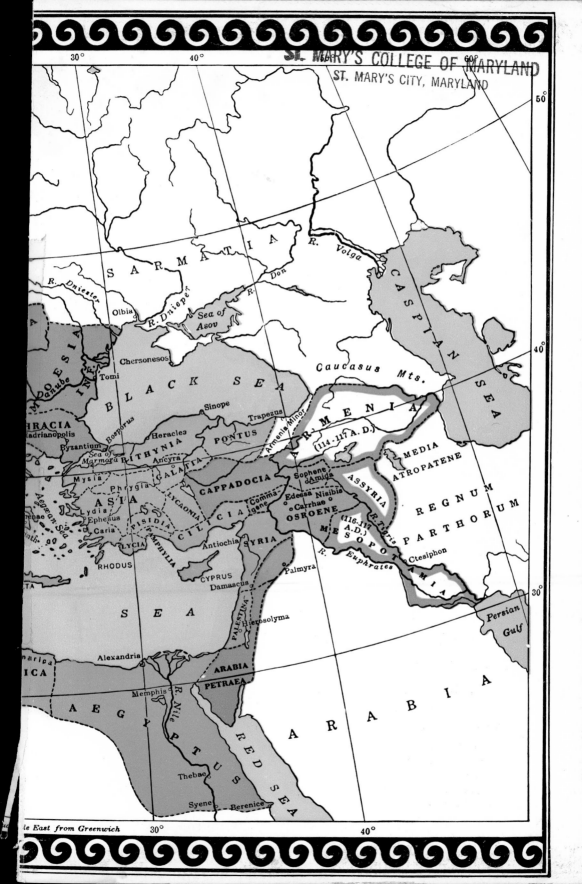

50°

30° 40° 50° 60°

S A R M A T I A

R. Volga

R. Dniester

Olbia

R. Dnieper

Sea of Asov

R. Don

CASPIAN SEA

50°

40°

MOESIA INF.

Danube

Tomi

Chersonesos

B L A C K   S E A

Caucasus Mts.

40°

THRACIA

Hadrianopolis

Byzantium

Bosporus

Sea of Marmora

Heraclea

Sinope

Trapezus

A R M E N I A

(114-117 A.D.)

MEDIA ATROPATENE

BITHYNIA

PONTUS

Ancyra

Armenia Minor

Mysia

GALATIA

CAPPADOCIA

Sophene

Amida

ASSYRIA

R E G N U M

ASIA

Phrygia

LYCAONIA

Commagene

Edessa   Nisibis

Lydia

Ephesus

PISIDIA

CILICIA

OSROENE

Carrhae

R. Tigris

P A R T H O R U M

Caria

Aegean Sea

Corinth

PAMPHYLIA

LYCIA

Antiochia

SYRIA

ME

(116-117 A.D.)

SO PO

Ctesiphon

RHODUS

CYPRUS

Palmyra

TA

R. Euphrates

MIA

30°

CRETA

S E A

Damascus

PALESTINA

Hierosolyma

Persian Gulf

Alexandria

ARABIA

PETRAEA

ICA

Memphis

R. Nile

A R A B I A

A E G Y P T U S

RED SEA

Thebae

Syene

Berenice

A HISTORY OF ROME TO A.D. 565

The Capitoline Wolf (Fifth Century B.C.)

A HISTORY OF ROME TO A.D. 565

FIFTH EDITION

Arthur E. R. Boak, Ph.D.
Late Richard Hudson Professor
of Ancient History
in the University of Michigan

William G. Sinnigen, Ph.D
Associate Professor of History
in Hunter College of the
City University of New York

THE MACMILLAN COMPANY, NEW YORK
COLLIER—MACMILLAN LIMITED, LONDON

Second Printing 1965

Earlier editions, entitled A HISTORY OF ROME TO 565 *A.D.*,
© copyright 1921, 1929, 1943 and 1955 by The Macmillan Company.
Copyright renewed 1949 and 1957 by Arthur E. R. Boak.

Library of Congress catalog card number: 65-11481

THE MACMILLAN COMPANY, NEW YORK

COLLIER-MACMILLAN CANADA, LTD., TORONTO, ONTARIO

PRINTED IN THE UNITED STATES OF AMERICA

PREFACE TO THE
FIFTH EDITION

FACED with the possibility of declining health in the fall of 1961, Professor Boak asked me to aid in the preparation of the fifth edition of his textbook, in particular to be responsible for the revision of those chapters dealing with the Late Empire. A year later, the state of his health becoming increasingly precarious, he requested me to take over all revisions of the Imperial period and to be responsible for the work as a whole if he were not able to finish the earlier parts.

By the time of his death on December 16, 1962, he had revised to the bottom of page 97 of the fourth edition. Although I disagree with some of his interpretations of early Roman history and am less critical than he was of literary tradition, I have not drastically changed his revision of the first chapters, whose viewpoint remains essentially his. All revisions following page 97 of this edition are my own responsibility. Before his death, Professor Boak had also decided on an expanded set of illustrations. The selections I have made follow his wishes, with the exception of the mosaics from Piazza Armerina and the Basilica at Trèves, which are my own choices. Professor Boak's original Preface to the new edition is given below.

I should like to thank members of the editorial staff of The Macmillan Company for their kindnesses during the preparation of the revision, and my friend Mr. John S. Widdicombe for his encouragement and criticism. The entire manuscript has benefited by criticism of Professor Henry C. Boren of The University of North Carolina, who has saved me from numerous errors. Lastly, I should like to express my indebtedness to Mrs. Boak for placing in my hands certain of Professor Boak's papers and notes and for much else besides.

Naturally, errors of fact and judgment that may remain in the following pages as a result of revisions made by me are my own responsibility.

WILLIAM G. SINNIGEN

New York City
March 8, 1964

* * *

[v]

PREFACE TO THE
FIFTH EDITION

FEW of the reading public have been oblivious of the tremendous advances in human knowledge made during the past eight years, but many of them have been blind to the fact that this expansion has been true of the social as well as of the physical sciences, and of history as well as of some more widely publicized humanistic studies. Some of the most spectacular achievements have been in the field of Ancient History; and Roman History can claim its share of these. New and striking archaeological discoveries in all parts of the Roman World, including many important inscriptions, new papyrological publications, and new and sounder interpretations of previously known historical materials of all sorts, have necessitated a fresh appraisal of many phases of the Roman experience, even though in its main outlines older evaluations maintain their validity. In the light of these considerations, a new edition of this text seems highly desirable.

The author wishes to express his thanks to The Macmillan Company for its kindness in permitting him to rewrite much of the text, to enlarge greatly the number of illustrations, and to change radically the list of suggested collateral readings. He is also deeply indebted to Professor Paul J. Alexander of the University of Michigan for pointing out typographical errors in the fourth edition and to Professor William G. Sinnigen of Hunter College for his suggestions for improving many aspects of the work.

A. E. R. B.

Ann Arbor, Michigan
October, 1962

*   *   *

PREFACE TO THE
FOURTH EDITION

ALTHOUGH I regret that the high cost of printing has prevented my making any substantial revisions of the parts of the book devoted to the Roman Republic and Principate, I am grateful to The Macmillan Company for the opportunity of rewriting most of the chapters dealing with the Autocracy, of making changes in Chapters 2 to 4 which reflect new interpretations of the early Italian period, of correcting typographical errors that appeared in the third edition and of improving the maps in Part IV. I have also been able to revise and enlarge the Supplementary Readings in order to take account of some of the more significant books printed in English during the past twelve years.

For the continued use of the illustrations which appeared in the third edition I wish to express my thanks to those who previously granted me the privilege of using them. The view of St. Sophia which has been added to Chapter 26 I owe to the kindness of Dr. E. E. Peterson, Director of the Kelsey Museum of Archaeology at the University of Michigan. I am also deeply indebted to Professor C. W. McDermott of the University of Pennsylvania for suggesting desirable emendations of the text of the previous edition.

A. E. R. B.

Ann Arbor, Mich.
September, 1954.

*   *   *

PREFACE TO THE
THIRD EDITION

THE passing of thirteen years alone would seem to justify the revision of an historical text that makes any pretence of keeping in touch with the results of current research in its field. But, in this case, since the appearance of the first revision, notable advances have been scored in the study of Roman history, owing both to the discovery of new and important evidence and the fruitful reassessment of the old. The completion of the monumental *Cambridge Ancient History* and the publication of the *Economic Survey of Rome,* to say nothing of less extensive studies, have stimulated and in fact compelled students of Roman civilization to re-evaluate their interpretation of its character and significance. In preparing this new edition, I have tried not only to make generally available the results of recent scholarly research but also to modify or discard in the light of more mature consideration what previously appeared to me to be sound conclusions. This has necessitated the complete rewriting of considerable portions of the text, and I have taken the opportunity thus offered to try to present a clearer, more readable, and, at the same time in some cases, a more detailed narrative. I have omitted the former Introduction on "The Sources for the Study of Early Roman History" and replaced it with brief discussions of the historical materials available for our knowledge of the successive periods of Roman history. Thanks to the kindness of the editors, I have been able to improve the quality of some of the maps and to add some new illustrations.

In addition to my continued indebtedness to the persons and authorities who permitted the use of older illustrations retained in this edition, I wish to express my appreciation of the permission given by the Metropolitan Museum of Art to reproduce the terra cotta statue of an Etruscan warrior and the Roman marble head, and also of the generosity of the Smithsonian Institution in allowing the use of the photograph of the fourth century Sassanian silver bowl. I desire also to acknowledge my general obligation to the reviewers and others who have pointed out defects in the earlier editions of the text, and my special debt to my colleague, Professor Clark Hopkins, who hase given me the benefit of helpful criticism on the treatment of the early Italic cultures.

A. E. R. BOAK

Ann Arbor, Michigan
July, 1942

*   *   *

PREFACE TO THE
SECOND EDITION

MY PURPOSE in preparing this second edition of *A History of Rome to A.D. 565* has been in part to add some new material bearing on the social and economic aspects of Roman History, to take into account the results of recent archaeological research on the prehistoric period, and to alter a few of the opinions and interpretations given in the first edition. I have also tried to make the book more serviceable to students by the insertion of new maps, four genealogical tables, and a list of additional readings. This latter addition has been made in response to numerous requests for recommendations of collateral readings and has been substituted for the Bibliographical Note of the previous edition. Owing to the kindness of the publishers, it has been possible to insert a number of plates which may serve to illustrate various phases of ancient Roman art and architecture. I am greatly indebted to Dr. L. D. Caskey and the authorities of the Boston Museum of Fine Arts for permission to use the portrait head of Augustus

and to Dr. G. F. Hill of the British Museum for help in selecting and secur-
ing casts of the coin portraits of Roman Emperors. The illustrations of
Roman Monuments have been selected from views taken by Mr. G. R.
Swain for the University of Michigan.

I wish to express my thanks to all those who by means of reviews or
private communications have indicated possibilities of improving the text,
and in particular to Professor Frank B. Marsh of the University of Texas for
his helpful criticisms.

A. E. R. BOAK

Ann Arbor, Michigan
March, 1929

* * *

PREFACE TO THE
FIRST EDITION

THIS SKETCH of the History of Rome to A.D. 565 is primarily intended
to meet the needs of introductory college courses in Roman History. However, it is hoped that it may also prove of service as a handbook for students
of Roman life and literature in general. It is with the latter in mind that
I have added the Bibliographical Note. Naturally, within the brief limits
of such a text, it was impossible to defend the point of view adopted on
disputed points or to take notice of divergent opinions. Therefore, to
show the great debt which I owe to the work of others and to provide those
interested in particular problems with some guide to more detailed study,
I have given a list of selected references, which express, I believe, the prevailing views of modern scholarship upon the various phases of Roman
History.

I wish to acknowledge my general indebtedness to Professor W. S. Fer-
guson of Harvard University for his guidance in my approach to the study
of Roman History, and also my particular obligations to Professor W. L.
Westermann of Cornell, and to my colleagues, Professors A. L. Cross and
J. G. Winter, for reading portions of my manuscript and for much helpful
criticism.

A. E. R. B.

University of Michigan
October, 1921

TABLE OF CONTENTS

PART III

PRINCIPATE OR EARLY EMPIRE: 27 B.C.–A.D. 285

LIST OF ILLUSTRATIONS

LIST OF MAPS

I

THE EARLY PEOPLES
OF ITALY

GEOGRAPHY OF ITALY

Italy, ribbed by the Apennines, girdled by the Alps and the sea, juts out like a long boot from Europe toward the North African coast. It includes two regions of widely differing physical characteristics: the northern, continental; the southern, peninsular. The peninsula is slightly larger than the continental portion; together their area is about 91,200 square miles.

CONTINENTAL ITALY. Continental Italy consists of the southern watershed of the Alps and the northern watershed of the Apennines with the intervening lowland plain. East to west this region measures about 320 miles; its width from north to south does not exceed 70 miles. On the north, the Alps extend in an irregular crescent of over 1,200 miles from the Mediterranean near Nice to the Adriatic near Trieste. On the Italian side they rise abruptly like a lofty wall, but on the northern faces the slope is gradual and river valleys afforded gradual ascents to passes leading over the divide to the plain below. From the west, there is an easy approach at the end of the Alpine chain along the Riviera coast, and at its eastern approaches, a low pass facilitates access from the basin of the middle Danube. Thus the Alps formed no serious barrier to landward migration into Italy. The lowland plain is occupied largely by the valley of the river Po, the greatest of Italian rivers, which rises in the western Alps and flows eastward for 360 miles to the Adriatic, receiving many tributaries along its route. Since the plain has been built up by the deposit of silt from the rivers, it has a rich alluvial soil. But much of the silt is carried down to the sea, where it chokes the river mouths and continuously extends the coastline. Thus it has formed the marshy delta of the Po and the lagoons where the city of Venice has been built. The Alpine rivers furnish an abundant supply of water throughout the year, however, and thus enhance the agricultural possibilities of the north Italian plain. In its natural state this region was covered with swamps and forests, and many centuries of patient human effort were required before it was cleared, drained, and cultivated.

THE PENINSULA. The southern portion of Italy consists of a long, narrow peninsula, running northwest and southeast between the Mediterranean and Adriatic seas and terminating in two promontories, which form the toe and heel of the Italian boot. The length of the peninsula is 650 miles; its breadth is nowhere more than 125 miles. In striking contrast to the plains of the Po, peninsular Italy is traversed by the parallel ridges of the Apennines, which give it an endless diversity of hill and valley. The average height of these mountains, which form a sort of vertebrate system along the peninsula (*Apennino dorso Italia dividitur,* Livy xxxvi, 15), is about 4,000 feet, and even their highest peaks (9,500 feet) are below the line of perpetual snow. Throughout central Italy the loftiest ranges of the Apennines lie close to the Adriatic, leaving only a narrow coast land, intersected by numerous short mountain torrents. On the west the mountains are lower and recede farther from the sea, leaving the wide lowland areas of Etruria, Latium, and Campania. On this side, too, are rivers of considerable length, navigable for small craft: the Volturnus, the Liris, the Tiber, and the Arno, whose valleys link the coast with the interior highlands. In the south, however, the mountain chain swings over to the western coast where it terminates in the rugged promontory of Calabria, the "toe" of Italy. To the north and east lie the lowlands of Apulia, which include the "heel" of Italy.

The west coast of Italy with its adjacent islands has always been the scene of considerable volcanic activity. Both north and south of the Tiber River there are extinct volcanoes. Farther south are three peaks active since ancient times: Vesuvius, near the Bay of Naples; Stromboli, on one of the Lipari islands; and Etna, in Sicily, the largest volcano in Europe. Although violent volcanic eruptions have caused considerable temporary damage, their effects have been beneficial in the long run. Volcanic ash and weathered volcanic rock form excellent soils particularly adapted to the cultivation of vineyards.

THE ISLANDS: SICILY, SARDINIA, CORSICA. The location of the three large islands, Sicily, Sardinia, and Corsica, permits them to be considered as a third region of Italy, with which their history has been closely linked. Sicily forms a large triangle (9,930 square miles) separated from the southern extremity of Italy by the narrow Strait of Messina and from the African coast by a shallow stretch of sea about 80 miles wide. It is really a prolongation of the Apennine chain and in early geologic times formed part of a land bridge between Italy and Africa. The small islands of Malta and Pantelleria south of Sicily and the Lipari group to the north are mountain tops projecting from the submerged portion of the broken bridge. Sardinia (9,299 square miles) and Corsica (3,376 square miles), lying to the west of the Tyrrhenian Sea, are rugged, mountainous offshoots of the Italian mountain system.

THE COASTLINE. In comparison with Greece, the Italian coastline is remarkably regular. Throughout a coastal length of over 2,000 miles it has remarkably few deep bays or good harbors, and these few are almost all on the southern and western shores. On the Adriatic, the chief harbor was at Brundisium (Brindisi), far down in the heel of Italy; on the southern shore there was Tarentum (Taranto), at the head of the gulf of that name; on the west, the Bay of Naples; and on the Gulf of Genoa the excellent ports of Genoa and Lunae Portus (Spezia), which, however, became important only late in Roman history. Sicily offered several good harbors for vessels of shallow draught; in particular, Syracuse on the east coast, Panormus (Palermo) on the north, and Drepanum on the west. Since the seagoing ships of ancient times did not require deep-water harbors, they found adequate accommodation in river mouths wherever the current was not too swift or the shoals too dangerous. For this reason many cities, like Rome itself, grew up a few miles from the sea, at the head of navigation rather than directly on the coast. The character of the Mediterranean coast of Italy, with its fertile lowlands, its rivers, its harbors, and its general southerly aspect, made it more inviting and accessible to approach from the sea than the Adriatic shore and determined its leadership in the cultural and material advancement of the peninsula.

CLIMATE. Although the climate of Italy, like that of Europe and North Africa, underwent great fluctuations in prehistoric times, since the fifth millennium B.C. at least, it has been approximately the same as today. In general, it is of the Mediterranean type, characterized by a high average temperature, an absence of extremes of heat and cold, and rainy winters followed by dry summers. Nevertheless, it varies greatly in different localities, according to their northern or southern situation, their elevation, and their proximity to the sea. In the Po valley there is a close approach to the continental climate of central Europe, with a wide difference between summer and winter temperatures and clearly marked transitional periods of spring and autumn. Here there are frequent winter snows, abundant rains in spring and fall, and moderate ones in the summer months. Farther south through the peninsula, the winters become much, and the summers slightly, warmer. Annual rainfall decreases, summers are drier, in south Italy and Sicily almost rainless, and there is a rapid transition between the wet and the dry seasons. Even in the rainy seasons there is a great deal of sunshine, and the Italian climate is not only healthful but for the most part stimulating.

MALARIA. . Both in antiquity and in modern times the disease from which Italy has suffered most has been the dreaded malaria. The explanation is to be found in the presence of extensive marshes in the river valleys and along the coast, generally formed by the blocking of channels of streams and rivers with soil washed down from the hills, and furnishing breeding grounds for the malarial mosquito. The ravages of this disease have varied as the progress of civilization has brought about the cultivation and drainage of the affected areas or as its decline has caused the undoing of this beneficial work.

FORESTS. Italy was much more thickly forested than most other Mediterranean countries. The southern slopes of the Alps and the Po valley were well wooded, the former being noted for their larch and bird's-eye maple, the latter for its oaks, beeches, and chestnuts. Great forests flourished on the Apennines, particularly along the Ligurian coast, in southern Etruria, and in the valleys of the Tiber and its tributaries. Latium was also well-wooded and produced fir, pine, and beech in large quantities.

The forests of Corsica were especially famous, and even the mountains in the toe of Italy were covered with a heavy growth of timber. It was there that a single pine furnished the mast for the largest ship of ancient times, built for King Hiero of Syracuse in the second half of the third century B.C. Besides the true forests, there were extensive thickets of laurel, myrtle, and similar shrubs and small trees. Italian timber was in great demand for shipbuilding among Carthaginians, Etruscans, Greeks, and Romans. It was not used extensively in household architecture owing to the preference for brick, stone, and cement, but was employed for roof and floor beams. Many articles of furniture, however, were made from the choicer woods. Coniferous forests supplied pitch and resin; oak, beech, and chestnut groves provided rich fodder for herds of swine. At the beginning of the Christian era, Italy was still considered to be well wooded, although much of the forest growth had disappeared long before. This deforestation was due to the activities of woodcutters, charcoal-burners, and farmers who cleared land for tillage or pasturage. Once they had been cut down, the forests were seldom replaced. The need for reforestation was not recognized, and the thin soil, exposed to the action of the winter rains, was washed off the hillsides before a new growth could establish itself. Even where seedlings managed to take root, they were devoured by herds of goats pastured in the clearings, which then, as now, were destructive to vegetation.

MINERALS.   The mineral wealth of Italy has never been very great. In ancient times the chief minerals mined were copper and iron, copper extensively in Etruria, Liguria, and Sardinia, iron on the island of Elba off the coast of Etruria. For a time, the gold washings in the valleys of the Graian Alps were worked. Tin was found in Etruria, and some silver in Sardinia. Obsidian, much in demand before the age of metals, was quarried in Sardinia and elsewhere. Salt was mined in Sicily and was also obtained from the salt marshes at the mouth of the Tiber and along the west coast of central Italy. Building stone of various sorts, including marble of excellent quality, has always been abundant. Latium, Etruria, and many other parts of Italy had excellent clays for making bricks, tiles, and pottery.

AGRICULTURE.   In ancient times Italy was essentially an agricultural and pastoral country. The lowland yielded large crops of grain of various sorts—millet, maize, wheat, and barley—while peas, beans, and other vegetables were raised in abundance everywhere. Campania was especially fertile and is reported to have yielded three successive crops annually. The island of Sicily was for a long time one of the chief granaries of the Mediterranean world. The vine, olive, and fig flourished, and their cultivation eventually became even more profitable than the raising of grain. Apples, pears, and other fruits, as well as nuts, were raised, but lemons and oranges, like rice, were not introduced from the East until long after the fall of the Roman Empire.

During the rainy season the coastal lowlands, and in summer the mountain slopes and upland meadows, afforded excellent pasturage for sheep, goats, cattle, and horses. Stock raising ranked next in importance to agriculture among the occupations of the people of Roman Italy. The Italians, unlike the Greeks and Phoenicians, never became a race of seafarers.

HISTORICAL SIGNIFICANCE OF ITALY'S CONFIGURATION AND LOCATION. The configuration of the Italian peninsula, long, narrow, and traversed by mountain ridges, hindered its political unification. Yet the Apennine chain, running parallel to the length of the peninsula, offered no such serious barrier to unification as did the network of mountains and the long inlets that intersect Greece. Once Italy had been welded into a single state by Rome, its central position greatly facilitated the extension of the Roman dominion over the whole Mediterranean basin. Because Italy was further removed than Greece from the older centers of civilization in Egypt and the Near East, it was less exposed to their cultural influences, and consequently its development lagged behind that of Greece and the Aegean area.

THE NAME ITALY. The name Italy is the ancient *Italia*, derived from the word *Fitalia* which probably means "land of cattle." It was applied by the Greeks as early as the fifth century B.C. to the southwestern extremity of the peninsula, adjacent to the island of Sicily. It rapidly acquired a much wider significance until, before the end of the first century B.C., *Italia* in a geographical and political sense denoted the whole country as far north as the Alps.

PREHISTORIC CULTURES IN ITALY

ACCESSIBILITY OF ITALY TO EXTERNAL INFLUENCES. The long coastline of Italy rendered it peculiarly accessible to influences from overseas, for the sea united rather than divided ancient peoples. Thus Italy was constantly subjected to immigration by sea and to cultural stimuli from the lands whose shores bordered the same seas as her own. Nor did the Alps and the forests and swamps of the Po valley oppose any effectual barrier to migrations and cultural influences from central Europe. Italy was the meeting ground of peoples coming by sea from east and south and coming overland from the north, each bringing a new ethnic, linguistic, and cultural element to enrich the life of the peninsula. These movements had been going on since remote antiquity, until, at the beginning of the historic period, Italy was occupied by peoples of different races, speaking different languages and living under widely different political and cultural conditions.

Our knowledge of this prehistoric age is derived almost wholly from archaeology, supplemented by studies of the languages of the peoples inhabiting Italy at the beginning of the historic period. On this basis we can do little more than trace the early cultural development of Italy and indicate the course and approximate date of the more important migrations. The chronology of these movements is very uncertain, and there are many other problems that can be solved only by new discoveries. We may regard the main outlines of the story as reasonably accurate.

I. Old Stone Age

ITALY IN THE GLACIAL AGE. The geologic and climatic development of Italy was similar to that of the neighboring parts of Europe and North Africa. During the Pleistocene or Glacial Age, which is also the Age of Man in Europe, there were four periods of glaciation in the Northern Hemisphere. These were characterized by a cold, moist climate during which ice fields formed in the mountains of Scandinavia and Switzerland and spread widely over the lowlands of northern and central Europe. Under these conditions, the plants and animals of warmer zones were replaced by those of a northern or arctic character. Then as each glacial wave receded under the influence of moderating climatic conditions, the arctic flora and fauna retreated to give place to those of more temperate climes. In Italy, as in North Africa, there was no glaciation, but each glacial period brought a colder climate and increased rainfall, which greatly affected conditions of life for plants and animals.

OLD STONE AGE PEOPLES OF ITALY.   The presence of man in Italy can be traced with certainty to the period between the third and fourth glaciations (third interglacial period), when the climate was warm and the hippopotamus, elephant, rhinoceros, and other types of tropical wild life roamed its forests and meadows along with the stag, bison, and horse of the more northerly zone. Evidence of the human occupation of Italy at this time comes chiefly from the discovery of the tools and weapons of flint, shaped by flaking or chipping in the fashion characteristic of the Old Stone or Palaeolithic Age. These artifacts are mostly hand axes, awls, gravers, and scrapers, found in river gravels and caves in association with the bones of animals. Parts of human skeletons have also come to light in the same geologic strata, and these have been identified as belonging to the so-called Neanderthal race. This primitive type of man, once widespread in Palaeolithic times over Europe and the Mediterranean lands, was more apelike and probably less intelligent than modern man. It was predominant in Europe between 170,000 and 35,000 B.C.

The last glacial period set in about 70,000 B.C. and lasted, with temporary recessions and advances, until about 9,000 B.C. During this period new types of men entered Europe from Asia and Africa, some of whom made their way into Italy.

The presence of late Palaeolithic men in Italy is attested by the discovery of their caves and rock-shelter abodes. The oldest of these date from about 10,000 B.C. They are a cave on the island of Livanzo off the western tip of Sicily, the rock shelters of Mt. Pellegrino on the northern coast of that island, the rock shelter of del Ramito in Calabria, and the grotto Polesini near Tivoli. Not much later are the Romanelli cave near Otranto in the extreme southeast of Italy and the long known Grimaldi caves at Balzi Rossi on the Italian Riviera in the northwest.

The del Ramito grotto, the Romanelli cave, and that of Polesini reveal the naturalistic animal art of the hunting peoples who decorated the caves of southern France and the Spanish peninsula in the late Palaeolithic Age. This cultural affinity is confirmed by later burials in the Grimaldi caves that contained skeletons of the Cro-Magnon type of modern men, who were one of the dominant peoples in southwestern Europe at this time. The burial accessories, such as stone tools and ornaments of seashells, also show affinities with the Magdalenian culture of southern France.

Like their predecessors, the late Palaeolithic inhabitants of Italy were food gatherers. They lived by hunting, fishing, and gathering wild fruits and edible plants. They had no domestic animals and raised no crops. They knew the use of fire, but their only durable habitations were rock shelters and caves. Under these conditions, Italy had only a small and widely scattered population which contributed little if anything to the ethnic elements in the historic population of the peninsula.

II. Middle and New Stone Ages

MESOLITHIC AGE. In the centuries that followed the retreat of the last glacial wave in Europe, the climate of Italy together with its vegetation and animal life gradually assumed its present characteristics. Since about 5000 B.C. climatic conditions in Italy have remained relatively constant. In the transitional period new peoples entered the peninsula bringing with them so-called Middle Stone, or Mesolithic, cultures. The various Mesolithic cultures were all characterized by the use of finely made small flint implements and by the extensive manufacture of bone tools and weapons. Their greatest contribution to human development, however, was the introduction of the bow and arrow as major implements of hunting and warfare. This weapon gave to people who had entered a Mesolithic stage of development greater mastery over wild animals and over those tribes that had remained at the Palaeolithic level, which latter they exterminated or absorbed. Mesolithic peoples also lived the lives of food gatherers, however, and consequently could not have been very numerous in Italy.

NEW STONE (NEOLITHIC) AGE. Beginning about 3500 B.C. the inhabitants of Italy entered a new and revolutionary period of their cultural development, the New Stone Age. This epoch marked the transition from a food-gathering to a food-producing economy and so laid the foundation for a new era in human history—ancient civilization. This transition was the result of the introduction of agriculture—that is, the cultivation of food-producing plants and the taming and raising of various animals as a source of food supply. So far as is known at present, these developments took place first in the Near East where the earliest village communities of farmers and herdsmen appeared about 7000 B.C. From this area the food-producing economy spread westward slowly along the shores of the Mediterranean and northwestward across the European continent. It underwent modifications as it was passed from one people to another or was carried by groups of immigrants, such as were filtering into Italy from North Africa by way of Sicily, from southern France into the northwest, and into the northeast from around the head of the Adriatic. It is probable that it reached Sicily and south Italy by 3500 B.C. and had spread over the whole of the peninsula, the Po Valley, Sardinia, and Corsica, by 2500 B.C. Adoption of an agricultural economy had three very important consequences. It led to the rise of settled village communities surrounded by clearings for fields and pastures; it made possible a greatly enlarged population by providing a regular and more abundant supply of food; and it led to conditions producing a more complicated division of labor.

NEW NEOLITHIC TECHNIQUES AND INDUSTRIES. As the name "Neolithic" implies, the age was characterized by the use of a new technique in the manufacture of stone implements, namely that of polishing or grinding suitable stones into the required forms, although the older processes of chipping and flaking flints continued in use and reached a high degree of perfection. Characteristic products of polished stone were hammer, axe, and club heads usually with holes bored to receive wooden handles, adzes, chisels and, later, stone hoes that could be fitted into similar handles. These tools made by the new grinding and polishing technique were commonly of much denser stone than that previously used and were therefore much more useful in a developing agricultural economy. The forms of these Neolithic implements set the pattern for the commoner metal tools of later times. Knives, spearheads, and arrowheads were usually made of flint or obsidian.

Apart from the manufacture of polished stone tools and weapons, the New Stone Age peoples introduced the making of pottery and the weaving of cloth. Pottery wares were hand formed and baked in open fires. They were fashioned in many shapes and sizes to satisfy domestic needs and burial requirements. In the decoration of these wares with incised and painted patterns, largely of geometric designs, the artistic instincts of the age found their chief expression.

AGRICULTURE AND STOCK RAISING. Several varieties of grain —chiefly wheat and barley—and flax were the chief products of Neolithic agriculture in Italy. Neolithic man's superior tools made it relatively easy for him to make clearings for his villages and cultivated fields. His domestic animals were goats, sheep, and dogs—which latter may have attached themselves even to Mesolithic settlements—and possibly pigs. Cattle were introduced later. Wild fruits and nuts were still eaten, but there were as yet no domesticated varieties. Hunting continued to be an important source of food. The chief game animals were deer, wild pigs, and hares; bears and wolves were killed in defense of the domestic animals.

NEOLITHIC CULTURE GROUPS. Archaeological discoveries from the Neolithic period in Italy reveal the presence of several different culture groups by 2000 B.C. The people of Liguria in the northwest were still living in caves, in which they also buried their dead. In the eastern Po Valley to the south of that river, however, many open villages are evidenced by the remains of their hut foundations (*fonde di capanne*). These contain ashes from the open hearths in which are embedded the charred remains of food, discarded utensils, and pottery, all of which reveal the cultural level of the villagers. From the foundations we can reconstruct the appearance of the huts. They were mainly round or elliptical, with walls made of a framework of wooden poles interlaced with small branches, reeds, or straw and plastered with mud. The wall poles curved inwards until they met, forming the framework of the roof. The floors of the huts usually were excavated to about a yard below ground level.

In southern Italy also we can distinguish two culture areas. In Sicily there was extensive use of cave dwellings but also communities of villagers living in the open. Unfortunately, the presence of the latter is attested only by their cemeteries. In the southeastern part of the peninsula, the Neolithic people also lived in caves and hut villages.

BURIAL CUSTOMS. Numerous cemeteries constitute one great source of information regarding the Neolithic period. In spite of local variations, there is a general uniformity of burial customs throughout Italy. Nearly always the dead were buried in a contracted position with the arms folded across the chest and the knees drawn up to the body. Inhumation was either in the floors of caves or in trenches or pits excavated in the open. It was also customary to strip the bones of their flesh, or to rebury them after the flesh had decayed, and to paint them with red ochre. Besides the corpses, which were usually interred with their clothing and ornaments, the graves contained weapons and pottery jars filled with food and drink. Graves were lined and covered with stone slabs or were filled with heaps of stone to protect the bones.

NAVIGATION. Apparently the Neolithic peoples of Italy were familiar with the use of seagoing vessels propelled by oars and sails. This explains migration from Africa to Sicily and Italy, and the occupation of Sardinia and Corsica, which seem to have been uninhabited in the Old Stone Age. Their ability to use the sea enabled them to establish contacts abroad, while at the same time seafarers from other Mediterranean lands were beginning to make voyages to Italy. Thereby trade began to develop, and with it an exchange of ideas and practices which led to continued cultural progress.

NEOLITHIC PEOPLES OF ITALY. Very little is known about the peoples of Italy in the Neolithic period, apart from the aspects of their culture revealed in the remains of their habitations and graves. They do not seem to have had a common name and almost certainly were divided into many small political units. Their language has not survived, although there are good reasons for believing that it was different from the later Indo-European languages of Italy. Physically, they probably belonged to the so-called Mediterranean type of the white race which from Neolithic times has been established in the Mediterranean Basin. The characteristics of this type are a dark complexion, dark hair, narrow head, and medium to short stature. It is the type that remains dominant in Italy and other Mediterranean countries, having assimilated both the round headed Alpine and the blond, long-headed Nordic types introduced by later migrations.

At the close of the Neolithic period, however, certainly after 2000 B.C., a new people entered Italy from the north by way of the central Alpine passes and settled near the Italian Lakes. Their intrusion is marked by the introduction of a new burial rite, that of cremating the dead and burying their ashes and bones in pottery urns. They also brought into Italy the practice of building villages on the marshy shores of lakes with the houses elevated on piles or stakes to insure their safety in times of high water. Centuries later a rise in the levels of these lakes submerged the villages, and they remained unknown until a lowering of the water in the nineteenth century revealed their remains. The term *palafitte* (sing. *palafitta*), an Italian word for piles, is usually applied to these communities, their builders, and their culture.

The earliest *palafitte* settlement was found in the vicinity of Lake Maggiore. Its remains are purely Neolithic, but later sites belong to the Age of Metals, and a description of the *palafitte* culture in general will be reserved until later. These northern intruders probably introduced the first Indo-European dialect into Italy.

III. Copper-Stone Age

From contacts abroad Neolithic peoples of Italy acquired a knowledge of copper, the first metal used as a substitute for and an improvement upon stone. Copper was probaly first brought to Italy by sea from Cyprus along a trade route which led through Crete and the Aegean to southern Italy, Sicily, Sardinia, Corsica, and Liguria. Northern Italy was in touch with the central Danubian valley, and there was communication between the islands and the Spanish peninsula, so that these regions, which are rich in copper, were supplementary sources of supply. Local copper ores were unworked. Stone implements were not discarded upon the introduction of copper, since the supply of that metal was limited and for some purposes it was not as satisfactory as stone. Hence the new period has been called the Chalcolithic, Aeneolithic, or Copper-Stone Age. The chief metal objects were daggers and chisels of pure copper. Not only did stone implements remain in use, but the technique of stoneworking reached its height in this period. Its finest products were axe and hammer heads, pierced for the insertion of wooden handles.

There is no evidence of any extensive immigration into peninsular Italy during the Copper-Stone Age. Cultural conditions developed gradually from the preceding period, so that at times it is almost impossible to distinguish between the Neolithic and Chalcolithic remains. In central and southern Italy and on the islands, the use of natural caves as tombs induced the inhabitants to excavate artificial ones in cliffs and hillsides. From the stone-lined trench graves developed the great stone tombs built above ground in south Italy, Sicily, and Sardinia. Some of these are dolmens or chambers, each of the sides and the roof being formed by a single huge block of stone. Associated with the dolmens are monuments called menhirs —single great stones set upright in the ground. Most of the megalithic tombs like the larger rock tombs were collective burial places in use for many generations. This is particularly true of the so-called "giants' graves" of Sardinia, long chambers built somewhat like the dolmens with stone sides and roofs of flat stone slabs.

THE PALAFITTE CULTURE. In northern Italy there was a reinforcement of the *palafitte* peoples from beyond the Alps, and they gradually spread southward and eastward in the Po Valley. *Palafitte* villagers were hunters, fishermen, and agriculturalists. They made wooden dugout canoes for use on the lakes and cleared the shores for their fields and pastures. Wheat and millet were their main crops, and among their domestic animals were oxen, sheep, dogs, and later horses. Their handmade pottery was gray in color and was ornamented with incised horizontal bands of circles and zigzags. Spindle whorls and traces of woven cloth attest their activities as weavers. They used stone axes with perforated heads, but also tools and weapons of copper, and later of bronze. There is some evidence for the use of wheeled carts.

IV. Bronze Age

BRONZE AGE IN NORTHERN ITALY. In northern and southern Italy alike, the transition from the Copper-Stone to the Bronze Age, begun about 1800 B.C., was accomplished by about 1300 B.C. The technique of mixing melted copper with tin to form the alloy called bronze was discovered in the Near East before 3000 B.C., but many centuries elapsed before the use of bronze made its way westward to Italy, where it was introduced both by way of trade routes and by the arrival of new immigrants who were familiar with it in their homelands. Tools and weapons of bronze were superior to those of copper because they were harder and could be given a sharper cutting edge. In the Bronze Age the use of stone implements virtually disappeared. In the Po valley, the Bronze Age was marked by the appearance of new groups of immigrants from beyond the Alps who brought with them a fully developed Bronze Age culture from central Europe. They did not arrive in large tribes to cause a violent displacement of the older population, but in a succession of small units which formed several culture groups. The best known of these is that of the so-called *Terramaricoli*, who settled in the central part of the valley and spread southeast. Their arrival was contemporary with the later *palafitte* settlements.

VILLAGES OF THE TERRAMARICOLI. Remains of these villages have been discovered in recent times in deposits of rich black earth which had accumulated on their sites as the result of prolonged human occupation. This earth was known in the local Italian dialect as *terramara* (plu.

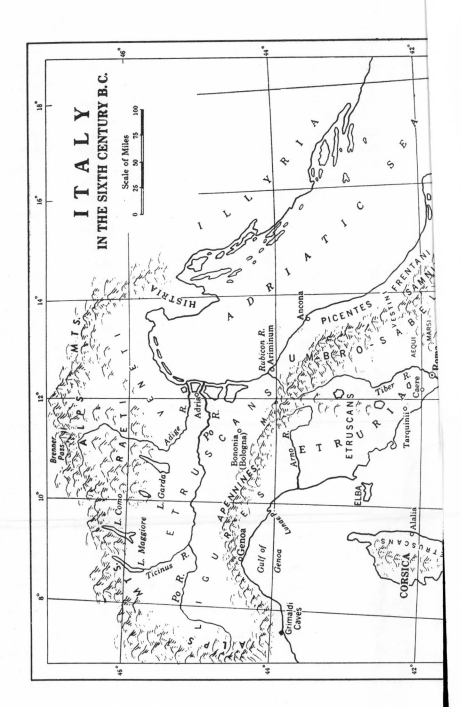

terremare), a name used to designate both these villages and the culture which they have revealed. Since the identity of the builders of the *terremare* villages is unknown, they have been called, for convenience, *terramaricoli*.

Early excavators believed that the *terremare* settlements were constructed on piles like the *palafitte* villages and, in fact, were an adaptation of the lake villages to dry or possibly marshy ground. They also held that all the settlements were laid out according to a uniform trapezoidal plan with streets intersecting at right angles and surrounded by an earthen wall and a ditch filled with water. These views were based upon inadequate evidence and must be discarded, along with the theory that this type of village was the antecedent of the later Roman military encampment. The *terremare* villages had no uniform plan. The houses were huts, at first round and later oblong, with walls of wickerwork and clay strengthened by wooden posts of which the lower portions are in many cases still in position. Only rarely is there any proof of pile foundations, and these are late and due, apparently, to protracted flooding of the sites in various localities. The villages were sometimes surrounded by crude earth walls, ditches, and palisades.

TERREMARE CULTURE.   The *terramaricoli* were much more advanced than the *palafitte* peoples, and had close affinities with the contemporary Bronze Age culture of the Hungarian plain. These northern invaders were primarily farmers and cattle raisers. They were also active as hunters, practised weaving, and were skilful workers in wood and bronze. Seeds of flax, beans, and two varieties of wheat found in remains of their villages indicate their crops. Their domestic animals were horses, oxen, sheep, swine, and dogs. Their coarse pottery, their bronze tools and weapons, and their ornaments had distinctive Central European forms. Besides axes, spearheads, and daggers of bronze, they used two-edged cutting swords, or rather long knives, of the same metal. They seem also to have used wheeled carts, and for musical instruments had horns or trumpets of bronze.

The inhabitants cremated their dead and buried the ashes in jars known as ossuaries or cinerary urns. At first these were deposited, closely packed in rows, in cemeteries adjacent to the villages. Later on, the individual urns were separated by stone slabs, and finally individual graves were constructed. For a time, the dead were burned in their clothing, but no equipment of any sort was buried with the ashes. With the use of separate pits for the urns, however, it became customary to deposit weapons, ornaments, and pottery vessels, along with the cinerary urn. Growth of wealth, greater consciousness of individuality, and influence of the older inhabitants, with whom peaceful relations began to develop as subjects or neighbors, modified the original simplicity and uniformity of their burial rites.

BRONZE AGE IN THE PENINSULA.   There is not as yet a clear picture of the origins of the Bronze Age cultures of peninsular Italy. This is the period during which there must have been an infiltration of new peoples in sufficient numbers to spread over the area the Italic dialects which almost everywhere had displaced the older language by the opening of the historic period. Italic dialects belonged to the family of Indo-European languages and show a close relationship with both Greek and Celtic. Accordingly their appearance in Italy must be explained by the general movement of Indo-European speakers whose southward pressure can be traced from Iran across upper Mesopotamia and Asia Minor to the Balkan peninsula in the period 2000 to 1000 B.C. Although the *palafitte* villagers and the *terramaricoli* may be regarded as belonging to this speech group, they were rather isolated from the main stream of peoples who made their way into the peninsula both around the head of the Adriatic Sea and across it from Illyria to the north of Greece. The view of a southward migration of *terremare* peoples is no longer acceptable. Much less can they be seen as the ancestors, however remote, of the Latins. It seems very probable that the occupation of most of the peninsula and of Sicily by the "Italians" took place in the late Italian Bronze Age and was completed by about 900 B.C.

BRONZE AGE IN SICILY AND SARDINIA. In Sicily and South Italy Bronze Age culture developed under influences from Crete and the Greek mainland and perhaps antedated its appearance in the north. From before 2000 B.C., trade relations were maintained with Minoan and Mycenaean centers of production as is shown by the contents of the Sicilian Bronze Age tombs. Among these may be mentioned long, narrow swords of the Cretan type, hatchets of bronze, leaf-shaped daggers, Mycenaean pottery, and ornaments of various sorts. In this period Sicily enjoyed greater prosperity and a higher cultural development than South Italy and exercised a strong cultural influence upon the mainland. It was also in the Bronze Age that the prehistoric culture of Sardinia reached its height. Great stone tombs were still built, but more unique and impressive were the massive stone towers called *nuraghi* which were probably fortresses.

V. Early Iron Age

TRANSITION FROM BRONZE AGE TO IRON AGE IN ITALY. The transition from the Bronze to the Iron Age was a slow development brought about by contacts with the Aegean and Danubian areas, which had anticipated Italy in the development of Iron Age cultures. Local mineral deposits of the peninsula and the Italian islands still remained unworked for some time. The transition was completed by about 900 B.C. in Sicily but not until a century later in some parts of the peninsula. There was no large-scale immigration into Italy early in the Iron Age, but instead a steady infiltration of small groups from the Danubian area which reinforced the already present speakers of Indo-European dialects both in the

Po valley and the Apennine regions. The early or prehistoric phase of Italian Iron Age lasted until about 600 B.C.

EARLY IRON AGE. The Early Iron Age in Italy was marked, l the Bronze Age, by the formation of many regional cultures. There w also a considerable distinction between the northern and southern zor that met and overlapped in central Italy. A major distinction between tl two was that cremation predominated in the northern zone, whereas i humation was the general practice in the southern. Cremation had bee introduced, as has been noted, by the Bronze and Early Iron Age immi grants from the north, but in the southern zone they had adopted th custom of inhumation from the older population, although they were able to impose on this element their Indo-European speech.

In the Po valley the chief cultures were the Comanine-Golaseccan in the central and the Atestine in the eastern sector. In the north of the peninsula there are distinguished the Villanovan south of the Po and east of the Apennines near modern Bologna, the Tuscan between the Arno and the Tiber, the Latian in the lower Tiber valley and Latin plain, and the Picene in the highlands of Picenum on the Adriatic coast. In the south, there have been identified archaeologically the Campanian, Apulian, Bruttian, and Sicilian cultures, each named for the region where it developed. Sardinia and Corsica lagged behind Italy and Sicily in passing from the Bronze to the Iron Age and, in fact, the Iron Age in Sardinia was marked by a cultural decline.

VILLANOVA CULTURE. The Villanova culture of the Bologna district may be regarded as typical of northern Italy in the Early Iron Age. Here the settlements were irregular villages of round huts. Earthenware and, later, bronze jars of a peculiar biconical shape were used to hold the ashes and bones of the dead. These jars were buried in pits covered with stone slabs (*tombe a pozzo*) or in rectangular stone-lined trenches (*tombe a fossa*). Swords, spears, and axes of iron served as weapons; rings and armlets of gold, pins with colored glass heads, amber beads, and disks were the chief ornaments. Garments were of wool fastened with elaborate bronze safety pins. A great improvement took place in bronze work, owing to the introduction of the process for making hammered bronze plates, a technique introduced from Asia Minor which the Villanovans learned from their Etruscan neighbors. This made possible the manufacture of bronze helmets, shields, and body armor, as well as vases, boxes, and other articles for domestic use.

ETRUSCAN AND GREEK MIGRATIONS. Migrations into Italy from east central Europe and Illyria which fell in the Late Bronze and Early Iron Ages ceased by 800 B.C. In the period that followed, two new peoples came by sea from the East and found homes for themselves on the shores of the peninsula and Sicily. These were the Etruscans and the Greeks. The former gained a foothold on the west coast north of the

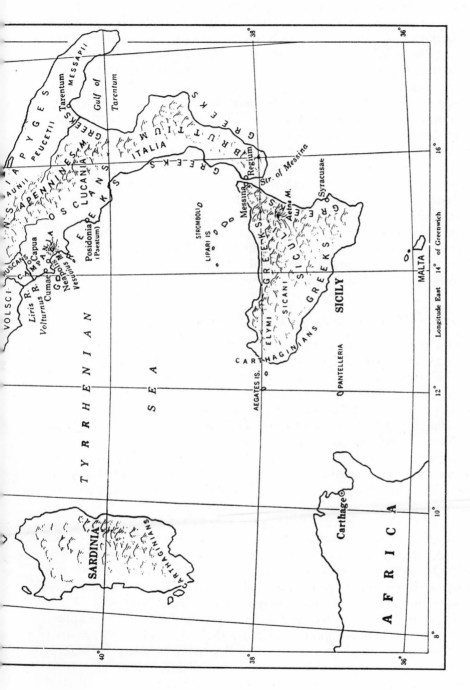

VOLSCI

A P Y G E S

AUNII

PEUCETII

MESSAPII

Tarentum

Gulf of

Tarentum

N S

APENNINES

GREEKS

M.

ITALIA

BRUTIUM

G R E E K S

TRUSCANS

O S C A N S

LUCANIA

E

CAMPANIA

Capua

Cumae

Neapolis

Vesuvius

Posidonia

(Paestum)

Liris R.

Volturnus

G R E E K S

STROMBOLI

LIPARI IS

Messina

Regium

Str. of Messina

Aetna M.

S

GREEKS

SICULI

Syracusae

T Y R R H E N I A N

S E A

ELYMI

SICANI

SICULI

GREEKS

CARTHAGINIANS

SICILY

PANTELLERIA

AEGATES IS.

MALTA

SARDINIA

CARTHAGINIANS

Carthage

A F R I C A

38°

36°

16°

14° of Greenwich

Longitude East

12°

10°

8°

40°

38°

36°

[19]

mouth of the Tiber; the latter planted their settlements on the southern coast from the heel of the Italian boot to the Bay of Naples. Etruscan immigration took place in the early eighth century, that of the Greeks between the middle of the eighth and the middle of the sixth century B.C. The settlements of the Etruscans and the Greeks were of great significance, for they brought Italy into much closer contact with the older cultures of the eastern Mediterranean. Through trade with Phoenician markets the Etruscans introduced Oriental products and influences and helped to diffuse the Hellenic culture of the Greek colonists. Under the influence of these contacts, the various peoples of Italy emerged from barbarism into conditions of civilized life and into the light of history, for it is to the Greeks that we owe the earliest surviving written records concerning Italy and its inhabitants. The relations of the Etruscans and Greeks to other peoples of Italy will be discussed in the following chapter.

The Early Iron Age in Italy witnessed the formation of the various peoples who were to play important historical roles. Beginning with the sixth century B.C., a connected historical outline of their political, cultural, and economic development may be presented.

VI. The Peoples of Italy in the Sixth Century B.C.

In the sixth century B.C., at the dawn of the historic period of the Italian Iron Age, as a result of the series of migrations described above, the distribution of peoples and languages in Italy was as follows.

THE LIGURES. The northwest corner of Italy, including the Po valley as far east as the Ticinus river and the coast as far south as the Arno, was occupied by the Ligures (Ligurians). They were the descendants of the Neolithic population with an admixture of the culturally superior northerners who settled in the central Po valley in the Chalcolithic and Bronze Ages. By the opening of historic times they spoke an Indo-European dialect. An important part of the population of Corsica was also of Ligurian stock.

PEOPLES OF THE CENTRAL AND EASTERN PO VALLEY. In the eastern part of continental Italy from the Po river northward to the Alps and from Lake Garda eastward to the peninsula of Histria (Istria) the chief people were the Veneti whose language was Indo-European and showed a remote affinity with Latin. They occupied the area in which the Atestine Iron Age culture had emerged. To the north and west of the Veneti, in the Alpine valleys and foothills, dwelt the Raeti, who apparently spoke an Indo-European dialect. By the sixth century the western Raeti, like the other peoples of the Po valley living between the Ligures and the Veneti, had come under the domination of Etruscan invaders from south of the Apennines. The Etruscans had also overrun the coastal strip to the north and east of the Apennines, the home of the creators of the Villanovan culture.

THE ETRUSCANS. In Etruria proper, the region on the west of the main Apennine chain between the Arno and the Tiber rivers, the bulk of the population probably was a mixture of the older Neolithic and Bronze Age stock and a numerous body of immigrants of Indo-European speech from the north in the Late Bronze Age. This basic element was dominated by the Etruscans, who differed from them in language and cultural tradition. By the close of the sixth century B.C. the Etruscans had extended their conquests into the central and eastern parts of the Po valley. At the same time they had sent out colonies to Corsica, Elba, and Campania, while Etruscan bands had established themselves at various points in Latium.

THE LATINS. South of the Tiber dwelt the Latins, who were destined to become the leading people in Italy and to make enduring contributions to world civilization. Like the basic element in the population of Etruria, the Latins probably had been formed by a union of invaders of Indo-European speech who cremated their dead, with the previous inhabitants who practiced inhumation. To these two elements there was added, about the beginning of the sixth century, a small percentage of Etruscans. Several small tribes bordering on Latium, such as the Falisci and the Hernici, were substantially the same as the Latins in race and language.

NORTH CENTRAL PEOPLES. In the valleys of the central and southern Apennines lived a large group of tribes often called the Umbro-Sabellians. They were not confined to the mountain area, for in the sixth century they extended down to the west coast south of Latium and to the middle Adriatic shore on the east. The Umbri, Sabini, Aequi, Marsi, Volsci, Vestini, Frentani, and the Samnites or Sabellians were their chief tribes. Basically, they seem to represent a survival of the older population with a strong admixture of northern invaders, who introduced an Indo-European element into their speech. Later these tribes expanded toward the southwest and south. The Umbro-Sabellians, together with the Latins and their kinsmen, formed the block of peoples usually called Italic, in contrast to Etruscan, Greek, Ligurian, and Illyrian. Their chief dialects were Umbrian in the north and several variations of Oscan in the south. All these were closely related to each other, and more distantly to Latin.

CAMPANIA AND SOUTH ITALY. Until the coming of the Greeks by sea toward the close of the eighth century and the Etruscans over land early in the sixth, Campania was occupied by a people called the Oscans who, apparently, had been little affected by contacts with the north. In historic times, their dialect, Oscan, was Indo-European, but this was a late development due to Samnite migrations, for originally the Oscans spoke another tongue. Oscan is now applied, however, to the Indo-European dialects of the southern Apennines. In Apulia, along the lower Adriatic coast of Italy and around the Gulf of Tarentum, the population was known as Iapygians. They included several tribes of which the most important were the Daunii, Peucetii, and Messapians. They spoke a common Indo-European tongue usually called Messapian, but their origin and that of their language are obscure. Possibly the latter was the result of an Illyrian intrusion from across the Adriatic. To the southwest, in Lucania and Bruttium, the basic population seems to have been much the same as that found by the Greeks in Campania and called Oscan or Oppican and Oenotrian. Later they were overrun by the expanding Samnites who brought in their Italic dialect, but quite possibly they had earlier learned an Indo-European tongue in the same way as the Messapians. Along the southwestern and southern coasts the Greeks were dominant, but they did not penetrate far into the interior.

THE ISLANDS. The population of Sicily prior to the Greek occupation was closely affiliated with that of the adjacent regions of south Italy. The Greeks distinguished an earlier element they called Sicani, later known as Siculi (Sicels). The Sicels spoke an Indo-European dialect. How this came about is not known, although here, too, there is the possibility of an Illyrian intrusion. In western Sicily dwelt a people called the Elymi of whose origins nothing is known. By the sixth century the southern, eastern, and part of the northern coasts were in the hands of Greek colonists, who had pushed well into the heart of the island. A few Phoenician settlements had been established on the far western coast. Sardinia was largely occupied by the people who had established themselves there in the Neolithic and Bronze Ages, but the Carthaginians had obtained a foot-hold on the southern coast. Likewise on Corsica, the older population remained almost undisturbed, although the Etruscans had won control of a strip along the eastern shore of the island.

From the foregoing survey of the peoples of Italy at the close of the sixth century B.C., it can be seen that there was neither racial nor cultural unity among the various sections of the country. This condition added a still more serious difficulty to the topographical obstacles placed by nature in the path of political unification and the growth of an Italian nation.

CHAPTER 3

ETRUSCANS AND GREEKS
IN ITALY

I. The Etruscans

ETRURIA. In the sixth century B.C. the region between the Tiber and the Arno west and south of the Apennines was dominated by the Etruscans. These people were known to the Greeks as Tyrsenoi or Tyrrhenoi and to the Romans as Etrusci or Tusci. According to a Greek tradition, they called themselves Rasenna. The memory of the Etruscan occupation is preserved in the name *la Toscana*, derived from the Roman form *Tuscanus*, which is the modern designation of their Italian homeland, while their Greek name is perpetuated in that of the Tyrrhenian Sea, which lies between the west coast of Italy and Corsica, Sardinia, and Sicily.

ORIGIN OF THE ETRUSCANS. The Etruscans differed from all the other historic peoples of Italy in language and certain other aspects of their culture. Even in ancient times these divergencies provoked a discussion of the original home of this people about which contradictory opinions were expressed. The Greek historian Herodotus, writing in the fifth century, recorded the tradition that they were immigrants from the west coast of Asia Minor. A later Greek writer, Dionysius of Halicarnassus, believed that they were a native Italian people. A similar difference of opinion prevails among modern scholars. The theory that the Etruscans were invaders who entered Italy by way of the Alpine passes has been rejected, however, and likewise the much stronger claim that they arose from a fusion of racial and cultural elements on the north central coast of Italy. The weight of linguistic evidence and certain Eastern aspects of their cultural tradition give incontestable support to the opinion that they were immigrants from the eastern Mediterranean, most probably from some point on the shores of Asia Minor, and that is the view adopted here. It must be emphasized that historic Etruscan civilization evolved in Etruria proper and was not introduced from abroad.

There is also considerable disagreement as to the date of their settlement among those who believe that the Etruscans came to Italy by sea. It no longer seems possible to identify them with the Tursha, one of the sea peoples which raided Egypt about 1226 B.C., which was one of the main arguments for an early arrival in Italy. In the light of the available archaeological evidence it seems most reasonable to place their settlement in the early part of the eighth century B.C., not too long before the beginnings of Greek colonization in Italy and Sicily. In any case the Etruscan settlement must not be thought of as a large-scale invasion, but rather

Etruscan Horses from Tarquinii (Fourth–Third Century B.C.)

as a succession of small bands coming in the wake of early traders possibly seeking sources of iron and copper.

CONQUEST OF ETRURIA. The number of Etruscan invaders may have been small, but they possessed a higher culture than the native population. Their superiority in arms and organization enabled them to seize strategic points along the coast, where they founded the cities of Vetulonia, Populonia, Tarquinii, Caere, Rusellae, and Vulci. This building of cities is in itself evidence for the Etruscans coming from the eastern Mediterranean. Later arrivals pushed inland, establishing themselves as masters in the earlier settlements of the Iron Age. There they formed the cities of Orvieto, Volaterrae, Volsinii, Felsina, Cortona, Arretium, Clusium, Perusia, and Veii. There is a tradition that twelve of these Etruscan cities were united in a league primarily for joint celebration of religious festivals. All the cities were politically independent and were governed by kings assisted by the heads of noble families called *lucumones*. Later the kingships disappeared, and the governments became aristocracies.

The Etruscans proper never constituted more than a small minority of the population in the towns of Etruria. Like the Norman adventurers who conquered and ruled over Naples and Sicily in the eleventh and twelfth centuries A.D., they remained a dominant aristocracy. Although able to impose their language upon their Italian subjects, they did not merge with them as did the Normans with the English in England but kept them dependent and exploited their labor and their military strength for their own ends.

EXPANSION IN ITALY. Toward the close of the seventh century B.C. or early in the sixth, bands of Etruscans crossed the Tiber and conquered a large part of Latium. They occupied Rome and other important sites. Not much later they pushed on southward into the rich lowlands of Campania, where Capua became their chief center. Finding the coast already occupied by the Greeks, they tried in 524 to capture the Greek city of Cumae but were vigorously repulsed. A little earlier, however, they had been more successful in dealing with Greek colonists on the island of Corsica. With the help of the Carthaginians, they forced the Greeks to abandon their colony of Alalia (about 536) and retained for themselves sole access to the vast Corsican forests, although they never occupied more than a narrow strip along the eastern coast of the island.

Late in the sixth century the Etruscans crossed the Apennine barrier and descended into the Po valley. Here they conquered the central region between the Ligures and the Veneti from the Adriatic coast to the Alps. North of the Apennines, their chief city was Felsina near modern Bologna. Their seaport Adria, founded in the territory of the Veneti just north of the mouth of the Po, has given its name to the Adriatic Sea. Another flourishing part was Spina, south of the Po delta.

In the sixth century B.C. the Etruscans were the most powerful political group in Italy, although the opposition of the Greeks in Campania prevented the unification of the country under their authority. The position of the Etruscans, however, was insecure because of their failure to build up a stable political organization. Both within Etruria and without, their conquests had been effected by small bands of warriors acting in loose cooperation. These bands founded separate states which were not united by any firm alliance and did not recognize any central authority, although they regularly helped each other in time of war. At the same time, their oppressive treatment of their subjects caused these to be disloyal or indifferent to their overlords. Accordingly, the more they expanded the more precarious Etruscan rule became.

DECLINE OF ETRUSCAN POWER. The first losses were suffered in Latium. In 507 certain Latin cities, aided by Aristodemus, the Greek ruler of Cumae, defeated an Etruscan army at Aricia, and about the same time the Romans shook off Etruscan rule. Later, in an effort to strengthen their position, the Etruscans launched a great attack upon Cumae by sea and by land. Hieron, the ruler of Syracuse, came to the rescue and destroyed the Etruscan fleet (474). Etruscan sea power was broken, and ships of Syracuse raided Corsica, Elba, and the coast of Etruria. These attacks were repeated in the early fourth century by Dionysius I of Syracuse, who also seized the Etruscan ports on the Adriatic. In Campania the expansion of the Samnites from the central Apennines brought about the downfall of Etruscan rule, which ended with the fall of Capua in 438. About 400, Celtic tribes descended through the central Alpine passes into the Po valley and soon overran the territory which the Etruscans had held in continental Italy. Henceforth the Etruscans were confined within the limits of Etruria proper, and their later history will be treated in connection with the expansion of Rome and their absorption into the Roman state. The decline of Etruscan power did not result in destruction of Etruscan culture which continued to progress and to produce interesting work for several centuries. The economic decline of Etruria dates from the later stages of Roman conquest of the area in the third century B.C. and was gradually followed by cultural decay until the beginning of the Christian era.

ETRUSCAN CIVILIZATION. Etruscan civilization is a synthesis of that brought to Italy by the Etruscans themselves with that of the Italian peoples whom they conquered. It also contained a liberal admixture of Greek influences, largely the result of commercial contacts with the Greek colonies to the south. The Greeks themselves passed through a period in which their civilization, especially their art, was affected by Near Eastern techniques, and it is no wonder that early Etruscan civilization also reflects this orientalizing tendency. This civilization was based on agriculture, industry, and commerce, all of which experienced a great impetus under Etruscan direction.

The Etruscans planted vineyards and olive orchards, cultivated grain for export, and bred horses. In order to provide new land for cultivation and to prevent soil erosion they dug tunnels and built dams on an extensive scale. They fully exploited the mineral resources of the areas under their control, promoting ironworking in Etruria and opening up the iron mines of Elba. They also worked the copper deposits of Corsica and the copper and tin ores of Etruria. Their bronzes, especially their mirrors and candelabra, enjoyed high repute even in fifth-century Athens. Their goldsmiths and silversmiths, too, fashioned elaborate ornaments of great technical excellence. The native black pottery called *bucchero nero* improved greatly in quality after the Etruscan occupation, and the ceramic industry was expanded by the production of imitations of imported Greek wares.

The Etruscans were seamen before they settled on Italian soil and long continued to be a powerful maritime people. They established commercial relations with the Phoenicians and Carthaginians almost from the date of their settlement in Italy. By the early seventh century B.C. they had developed an active trade with Greece, as is evidenced by the contents of their tombs and the influence of Greece upon their civilization. In the sixth century they traded directly with Athens, and this trade seems to have been carried on largely in Etruscan vessels. There was also an extensive trade with the Greek cities of South Italy, and there were groups of Greek traders settled in Etruscan seaports both on the Tyrrhenian and Adriatic coasts. The growth of commerce ultimately led to the introduction of coinage. About the close of the sixth century the Etruscans gave up using rough lumps of copper as a medium of exchange and employed coins of the Greek cities of Ionia. After 500 B.C. Populonia and other Etruscan cities began to issue gold, silver, and copper coins, using at first a standard adopted from Lydia but later discarding this in favor of the Greek standard in vogue in Euboea and Campania. The Etruscans, as well as the Carthaginians, were jealous of Greek expansion in the western Mediterranean, and about 536 B.C. a combined effort of these two peoples drove the Greek colonists from Corsica. From this time Etruscan domination in the Tyrrhenian Sea was firmly established, and this may have been responsible for the reputation for piracy which they enjoyed among the Greeks.

CITIES AND CEMETERIES. Our knowledge of Etruscan civilization is derived mainly from the ruins of their cities and from their tombs.

In the course of their conquests, the Etruscans occupied the older local settlements which, for the most part, were situated on hilltops or in other easily defensible positions. Under Etruscan rule these communities grew into prosperous towns fortified with ramparts of earth sometimes partly faced with stone. The purely stone city walls of polygonal blocks or of regular ashlar masonry once regarded as Etruscan work of the sixth century B.C. must now be dated in the late fourth or subsequent centuries, and outside of Etruria proper they are post-Etruscan. The most important pub-

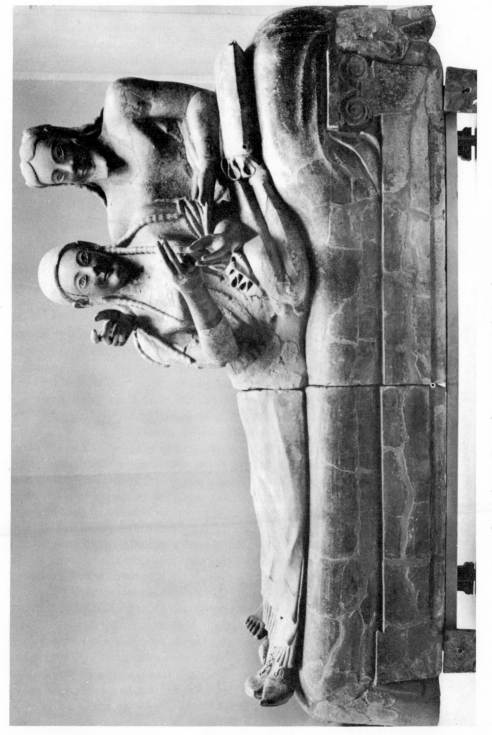

Tomb of the Reliefs at Caere (Fifth Century B.C.)

Sarcophagus from Caere Showing a Married Couple (ca. 550–500 B.C.)

lic buildings were the temples. The typical Etruscan temple was an almost square structure set on a high base and having a portico or pillared entrance porch almost as large as the interior chamber (*cella*). The *cella* itself was often divided into three parts to accommodate the cult of a triad of deities. Walls were of sun-dried brick resting on stone courses; columns and the beams of the steeply pitched roof were of wood. All wooden parts were faced with colored terra cottas, and the roof was ornamented with figures of the same material. Private houses were of wood or sun-dried brick and in some cases were built around a central, open court, in the so-called Greek peristyle fashion. The Romans credited the Etruscans with developing distinctive types of column and domestic hall (*atrium*), both later called Etruscan, and from the Etruscans they learned the use of the arch and vault.

In their burial rites the Etruscans practised both inhumation and cremation. The graves of the poorer classes were pits or trenches in which ash urns or sarcophagi were deposited. The tombs of the nobles, which constitute the most striking memorials of Etruscan civilization, were of various types: *tumuli* or artificial mounds of earth enclosing a burial chamber, *tholoi* or circular stone vaults built into hillsides, and corridor tombs with many chambers excavated in solid rock. The larger corridor tombs were evidently family burial vaults and were elaborately decorated with reliefs carved on their rock walls or with painted friezes, from which decorations we derive most of our information regarding the Etruscan appearance, dress, and customs. This use of mural paintings is another link between the Etruscans and the eastern Mediterranean area. Many gold ornaments and other costly articles found in Etruscan tombs of the seventh and sixth centuries B.C. attest the wealth of the ruling aristocracy.

ART. Etruscan art takes many forms: painting on vases and the walls of tombs, incised designs on bronze chests and mirrors, statues and statuettes of bronze and terra cotta, reliefs on grave steles, sarcophagi, and cinerary urns, terra cotta architectural ornaments, and gold and silver jewelry. The greatest impulse to artistic productivity came to the Etruscans from the Greeks in the sixth century, and thereafter they derived continuous inspiration from Greek art. Some Greek artists seem to have settled in Etruria and founded schools there, but Etruscan artists were by no means slavish imitators of Greek originals. While they copied the form, subjects, and technique of the latter, they always preserved their own basic conceptions and thus succeeded in creating a truly native art of their own. Although this art lacked the idealism, the sense of pure beauty, the rhythm, harmony, and restraint of the Greek, it excelled in naturalness, force, and vivacity, and is a true reflection of the Etruscan outlook on life in this world and in the hereafter. The most famous product of Etruscan sculpture is a terra cotta group of the late sixth century from Veii called the "Contest for the Sacred Hind." Although Greek influences are obvious in the subject and its treatment, the chief figure, that of the god Apollo, shows distinctive Etruscan characteristics. Perhaps some of these qualities may be due to the artistic traditions of the pre-Etruscan element in the population.

RELIGION. Religion played a very prominent part in Etruscan life. The Etruscans worshipped numerous gods and believed in powerful malicious spirits which controlled the afterworld. In their desire to interpret the will of the gods and to ward off impending evils, they developed an elaborate system for forecasting the future by examining the livers of sacrificed animals and by interpreting the significance of flashes of lightning and numerous other omens. The use of liver-divination is evidence which connects the Etruscans with peoples of western Asia. The Etruscans readily adopted both Italian and Greek gods, and with the Greek deities came a great deal of Greek mythology. Among the higher gods, they paid particular reverence to a triad composed of Tinia, Uni, and Menerva, corresponding to Jupiter, Juno, and Minerva in the Roman pantheon. In order to honor their dead and to ensure them immortality, the Etruscans believed that it was necessary to offer to the gods the lives of others. Here is the origin of gladiatorial combats at funerals and perhaps the explanation of the cruel massacres of prisoners of war which the Etruscans perpetrated.

LANGUAGE. The Etruscan language presents a peculiarly difficult problem. It is known chiefly from over 9,000 inscriptions, of which most are short dedications on funerary monuments. They are written in an early form of the Greek alphabet which the Etruscans probably brought with them to Italy. Etruscan survived as a spoken language in Italy until as late as the second century A.D. Written records in the language existed in sufficient abundance at the middle of the first century to aid the Roman Emperor Claudius in his composition of a lengthy history of the Etruscans, a work no longer extant. Although the value of the Etruscan letters is known, the meaning of a considerable number of words has been ascertained, and something has been learned about Etruscan grammar, all attempts to translate the language have thus far failed. Some evidence points to its affiliation with the pre-Indo-European languages of western Asia Minor.

THE ETRUSCANS AND ITALIAN CIVILIZATION. The general impression of the Etruscans is that they were a wealthy, luxury-loving people, but by no means the voluptuaries whom certain Greek writers represent.

In Etruscan society women occupied a prominent place. Not only did they have great freedom in social intercourse, but often descent was reckoned on the maternal rather than the paternal side.

Quick to appreciate and adopt the achievements of others, the Etruscans were rather unoriginal. A strain of cruelty is revealed in their religion, particularly in the rites celebrated in honor of the dead. Bold and energetic warriors, they nevertheless lacked a spirit of discipline and cooperation and were incapable of developing a stable political organization. Yet on the whole, they were most active in the promotion of civilization in early Italy. In town planning, road building, architecture, art, warfare, political organization, and religion, they profoundly influenced all the Italian peoples with whom they came into contact, particularly those of the central and northern part of the peninsula.

II. The Greeks

GREEK COLONIZATION. It has been pointed out that as early as the eighth century the Greeks had begun their colonizing activity in the western Mediterranean. In the next two centuries, they settled the eastern and southern shores of Sicily, stretched a chain of settlements on the Italian coast from Tarentum to the Bay of Naples, and established themselves at the mouth of the Rhone and on the Riviera. The opposition of Carthage shut them out from the western end of Sicily and from Spain; the Etruscans closed to them Italy north of the Tiber; while the joint action of these two peoples excluded them from Sardinia and Corsica.

In the fifth century the Greek cities in Sicily and Italy were at the height of their power and prosperity. In Sicily the Greeks penetrated from the coast far into the interior, where they brought the Sicels under their domination. Their position was challenged by the Carthaginians; but the victory in 480 B.C. of Gelon, ruler of Syracuse, at Himera secured the Sicilian Greeks in the possession of the greater part of the island and freed them from all danger of Carthaginian invasion for over seventy years. Six years later, his brother and successor, Hieron, by his naval victory off Cumae, crushed the Etruscan naval power and delivered the mainland Greeks from all fear of Etruscan aggression. The extreme southwestern projection of the Italian peninsula, known to the Greeks as Italia, was completely under their control from sea to sea; but northward as far as Posidonia on the west coast and eastward to Tarentum their territory did not extend far from the seaboard. Likewise in Campania, their cities Cumae and Naples were closely confined to the coast by the Etruscans. It was in this region, apparently, that the Romans came to call the Greeks "Graeci" instead of "Hellenes," the common name they had adopted for themselves. How firmly the Greeks were established in south Italy and how deeply it was permeated by their culture may be judged from the name *Great Hellas*[1] which they applied to this area.

The Greeks possessed even less political cohesion than did the Etruscans. Each colony was a city-state, a sovereign independent community, owing

[1] In Latin *Magna Graecia*.

no political allegiance even to its mother city. Thus colonial Greece reproduced all the political characteristics of the motherland. Only occasionally,
in times of extreme peril, did even some of the Greek cities lay aside their
mutual jealousies and unite in the common cause. Larger political structures, such as those that the tyrants of Syracuse built up by the subjugation
of other cities, were purely ephemeral, barely outliving their founders. Individual cities also were weakened by incessant factional strife within their
walls. The result of this disunion was to restrict Greek expansion and to
pave the way for the eventual conquest of the Western Greeks by the
Italian "barbarians."

DECLINE OF GREEK POWER IN ITALY AND SICILY.   Even
before the close of the fifth century the decline of the Western Greeks had
begun. In Italy their cities were subjected to repeated assaults from the
expanding Samnite peoples of the central Apennines. In 421 Cumae fell
into the hands of a Samnite band, and thenceforward the Greek cities
further south were engaged in a struggle for existence with the Lucanians
and the Bruttians, Samnite offshoots. In Sicily the Carthaginians renewed
their assault upon the Greeks in 408. For a time (405–367) the genius
and energy of Dionysius I, tyrant of Syracuse, welded the cities of the
island and the mainland into an empire which enabled them to withstand
their foes. His empire had only been created by breaking the power of the
free cities, and after his death they were left weaker and more disunited
than ever. After further warfare, by 339, Carthage remained in permanent
occupation of the western half of Sicily, while in Italy only a few Greek
towns, such as Tarentum, Thurii, and Rhegium, were able to maintain
themselves, and that with ever-increasing difficulty, against the Italians.
Even by the middle of the fourth century an observant Greek predicted the
speedy disappearance of the Greek language in the West before that of
the Carthaginians or Italians. Their final struggles, however, must be
postponed for later consideration.

THE GREEKS IN ITALIAN HISTORY.   The Greeks brought Italy
into the light of history and into contact with the more advanced civilization of the eastern Mediterranean. From Greek geographers and historians
we derive our earliest information regarding the Italian peoples, and they,
too, shaped the legends that long passed for early Italian history. The
presence of Greek towns in Italy gave a tremendous stimulus to the cultural
development of the Italians, both by direct intercourse and indirectly
through the Etruscans. In spreading Greek influence, Cumae, the most
northerly of the Greek colonies and one of the earliest, played a very
important part, as did the Greeks who, by about 500 B.C., had settled in
Latin towns at Rome's doorstep and probably in Rome itself. The more
highly developed Greek political and military institutions, Greek art,
Greek literature, and Greek mythology found a ready reception among

the Italian peoples and profoundly affected their political and intellectual progress. Traces of this Greek influence are nowhere more noticeable than in the case of Rome itself, and the cultural ascendency which Greece thus early established over Rome was destined to last until the breakup of the Roman Empire.

PRIMITIVE MONARCHY
AND REPUBLIC:
FROM PREHISTORIC
TIMES TO 27 B.C.

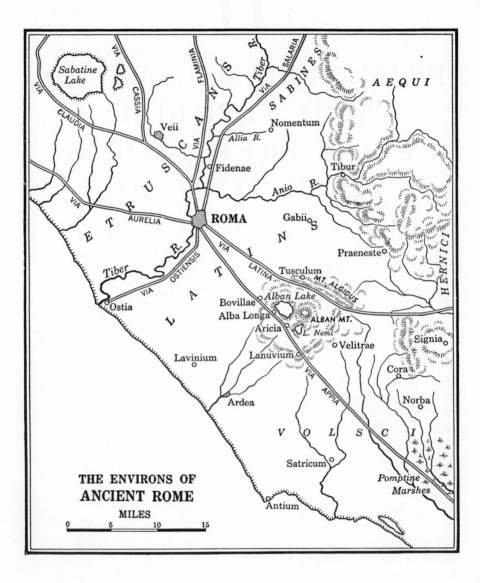

**THE ENVIRONS OF
ANCIENT ROME**

MILES

0   5   10   15

EARLY ROME TO THE FALL
OF THE MONARCHY

I. The Latins

LATIUM AND THE LATINS. The district south of the Tiber, extending along the coast to the promontory of Circeii and from the coast inland to the slopes of the Apennines, was called in antiquity Latium. The northern part of Latium, now known as the Roman Campagna, is an undulating plain intersected by watercourses and dominated by the isolated volcanic mass which culminates in the Alban Mount rising over 3,000 feet above sea level. At the opening of the historic period this region was occupied by an Italic people called the Latins (*Latini*). They were a mixed people in which the dominant element was formed by the descendants of northern invaders, a cremating folk who had found their way south of the Tiber about the close of the Bronze Age. These invaders had absorbed the previous occupants of the country, probably a sparsely settled pastoral folk, who had been there since Neolithic times. Later, in the Early Iron Age, there appears to have been an intrusion of an inhumating people, probably of Sabine stock, who descended the Tiber valley and ultimately amalgamated with the Latins. South of the Alban Mount, however, the land was held by Sabellian peoples, in particular the Volsci.

EARLY LATIN CULTURE. Until the close of the seventh century B.C., the inhabitants of Latium remained an agricultural and pastoral people little affected by the cultural developments taking place elsewhere in Italy. Their settlements were villages built upon defensible eminences, with cemeteries placed outside the inhabited area. In these cemeteries they deposited the ashes of their dead in clay urns made in the form of the huts in which they lived. These huts were round or elliptical structures with wattle and plaster walls supported by a wooden framework. The sloping thatched roof was held in place by exterior beams or poles which extended from the ridgepole part way down the sides. In the roof was a hole which served as a vent for the smoke from the hearth. The roof terminated in overhanging eaves, and the single doorway was flanked on either side by one or two wooden pillars. The doorway was large and served not only as an entrance and exit but also, since there were seldom windows, to admit light and air to the interior.

CULTURAL PROGRESS. From the end of the seventh century B.C. Latium enjoyed a much richer cultural life. The change was mainly due to Etruscan influence, which in many places was accompanied by Etruscan political domination, but also to Carthaginian, and more particularly Greek, traders who began to frequent the coast towns. The villages developed into towns with fortified citadels and protecting earthen walls and were adorned with temples built and decorated in Etruscan style. The grave deposits show the presence of a wealthy class easily distinguishable from the majority of the people. It seems also that the population had increased considerably and that arable land was in demand and had to be intensively cultivated, if to this age may be attributed the dams and drainage works, still visible today, that were constructed at various places to win new ground or protect fields from erosion.

POLITICAL CONDITIONS. There is no evidence for a union of all the Latins in a single state. On the contrary, they were divided into many independent units called *populi* (peoples). Each *populus* occupied a definite district (*pagus*) and had its central point in its fortified town (*oppidum*). There was, however, a marked tendency by the stronger of these petty states to absorb the weaker, and many of the sixty-five towns whose names have been preserved had merged with their neighbors before the close of the sixth century.

LATIN LEAGUES. The general feeling among the Latins that they were united by ties of common inheritance and common interests found expression in associations of towns for the joint worship of dieties widely recognized among all the Latins. Most important of these associations was the religious league which celebrated the annual festival of the Latin Jupiter (*Jupiter Latiaris*) on the Alban Mount. It is uncertain how many Latin towns participated in the Alban festival. Tradition has preserved the number forty-seven for the end of the sixth century, and this number is not improbable. Tradition also records that the town of Alba Longa on the west shore of the Alban Lake was the early head of the league, but this refers to religious and not political leadership. Each of the communities which joined in the celebration contributed its quota of the offerings and received a share of the sacrifices. In spite of the political fate of the Latin towns, this festival of prehistoric origin was maintained until well into the Christian era.

The Latins also had a military league for mutual defense. In this association leadership passed from one town to another as their respective military and political strength changed. This league had as its patron divinity the goddess Diana, whose cult was celebrated jointly by all of the allied cities in a sacred precinct consisting of a grove and an altar maintained by the *pro tempore* dominant city. There is archaeological evidence for such a precinct at Lavinium in the sixth century, and a literary tradition of another at Tusculum, probably later in date, indicating that both of these towns had for a time been predominant in the league. Toward the close of the sixth century the leadership had shifted to Aricia, which headed the opposition to the Etruscans and was the scene of their decisive defeat by the Greeks from Cumae with the support of the Latins themselves in 507 B.C. Aricia, too, had its precinct of Diana in which an inscription, read by the Roman writer Cato the Elder, recorded the names of eight Latin towns and mentioned a Latin dictator. These eight towns were probably free from Etruscan overlordship, and the dictator was the representative of the dominant state who directed the league's activities.

II. Origins of Rome

SITE OF ROME. Rome, the Latin *Roma,* is situated on the Tiber about fifteen miles from the sea, where the river makes its way through a cluster of low hills. There, on the left or eastern bank are the three isolated eminences called the Capitoline, Palatine, and Aventine. Stretching out toward them from the high ground farther east are the spurs known as the Quirinal, Viminal, Esquiline, and Caelian. All these formed part of Rome of the later Republic and the Empire, the City of the Seven Hills, which also extended across the Tiber to the west bank where it included both the low ground along the river and the height of Mount Janiculum. This extent was the result of a long period of growth; the beginnings of Rome were much more humble.

GROWTH OF THE CITY. The origins of Rome go back to prehistoric times. As Rome grew in importance, men's curiosity on this point was aroused, and speculation began to supply the want of historical evidence. Legends arose which ultimately came to form the traditional version of the founding of Rome. In this can be detected contributions from both the Romans and their Greek neighbors in Italy and Sicily. Before the close of the fourth century B.C., the Romans attributed the foundation of the city to a figure called *Romulus,* whose name is derived from that of Rome itself. Romulus, son of the god Mars and the daughter of a king of Alba Longa, was credited with the establishment of a city on the Palatine hill. Meanwhile the Greek desire to explain the origin of Rome by linking it with their own past had given rise to myths in which the founder of the city appears as the descendant of a Greek hero. The most significant of these Greek tales was the one whose roots go back to the sixth century and which eventually established a connection between Rome and the Trojan prince Aeneas, son of the goddess Aphrodite. In his wanderings after the destruction of Troy, Aeneas made his way to Italy, where either his son or his grandson founded Rome. Owing to the Greek cultural ascendency over the Romans, the latter partially accepted the Greek myth and by the end of the third century B.C. combined it with the native tradition. The resultant composite version was that Aeneas came to Latium and founded Lavinium, his son Ascanius founded Alba Longa, and Romulus, his descendant after many generations, was the founder of Rome. In this legend there is little of historical worth, except perhaps a faint reflection of the early importance of Alba Longa in Latium and the memory of a prehistoric settlement on the Palatine. Roman writers of the late third and the second centuries B.C. differed widely on the date of the founding of Rome, but in the first century the date 753 B.C. came to be accepted generally and to serve as the basis for reckoning events in terms of years "from the founding of the city." If by the "foundation" of Rome is meant the appearance of an Iron Age settlement on the Palatine, then this date may well be approximately correct; at the very least it is not contradicted by the surviving archaeological evidence. In default of written records we must rely mainly upon such evidence in any attempt to picture the early stages in the growth of the city.

The recent find of some Apennine Bronze Age pottery in a fill on the low ground near the Tiber indicates that there was a settlement on the site of Rome about 1500 B.C., but its location is unknown, and there seems to be no continuity between this settlement and those of the early Iron Age. Excavations have shown that in the latter period, from the ninth to the seventh century B.C., there were several distinct communities on the hills overlooking the marshy area which later became the site of the celebrated Forum of the city Rome. One of these, and at first probably two, occupied the Palatine Hill. Here the foundations of the dwellings show that they were rectangular huts with rounded corners and walls of interwoven branches plastered with mud and supported by upright posts, conforming in general to the type of hut revealed by the hut-shaped cinerary urns from Latium. The cemetery of the Palatine community lay on the northeast side of the Forum area. Here the earliest graves contained cremation burials, the ashes of the dead being deposited in the customary hut-shaped urns. Inhumation burials began later, but cremation continued along with the new rite.

Similar cemeteries on the Quirinal, Viminal, and Esquiline seem to indicate the presence of contemporary settlements on these hills also, although some authorities deny the existence of any on the Viminal and the Esquiline, considering the latter to be an extension of the Palatine settlement. The cemetery on the Esquiline contained inhumation burials almost exclusively, but in that on the Quirinal at first cremation alone was practiced. The use of these contrasting burial rites contemporaneously suggests that the early occupants of the Roman hills were of different cultural traditions, and supports the view of the Romans themselves, who believed they were a people of heterogeneous origins. The inhumers may possibly have been Sabine intruders in a region predominantly Latin.

These early communities were sprawling villages with no regular ground plan. It may be assumed that each was an independent political unit ranking as an *oppidum*.

About the middle of the seventh century B.C., the old Palatine cemetery ceased to be used and an extensive part of the Forum area was built over with huts of the Palatine type. This points to an expansion of the Palatine

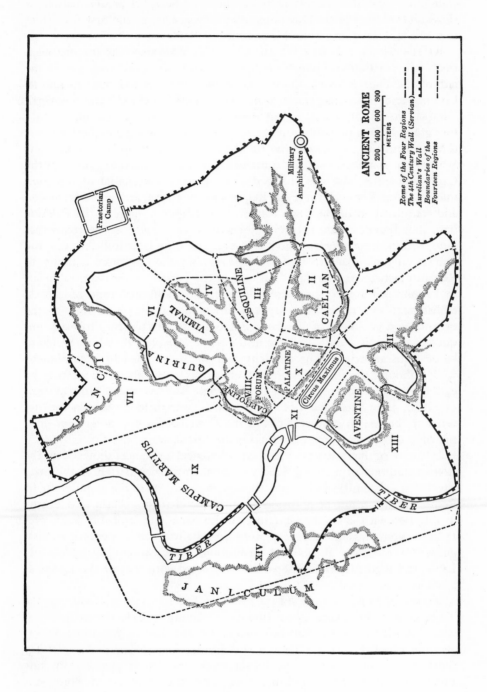

ANCIENT ROME

0 200 400 600 800
METERS

Rome of the Four Regions --·--·--
The 4th Century Wall (Servian) ————
Aurelian's Wall ━━━━━
Boundaries of the
Fourteen Regions --------

Praetorian Camp

Military Amphitheatre

V

IV

ESQUILINE

III

II

CAELIAN

I

VIII

VIMINAL

VI

QUIRINAL

PINCIO

VII

CAPITOLINE

FORUM

PALATINE

X

Circus Maximus

XII

XIII

XI

AVENTINE

XIII

CAMPUS MARTIUS

IX

TIBER

TIBER

XIV

TIBER

JANICULUM

community and its absorption by conquest or peaceful amalgamation of those on the other hills. This union may be regarded as the first important step in the formation of the historic city of Rome.

ROME OF THE FOUR REGIONS.   The next step was the organization of the earliest city which can with certainty be called Rome. It is the city of the Four Regions, known in historic times as Palatina, Esquilina, Collina, and Sucusana (later Suburana). These included the Quirinal, Viminal, Esquiline, Caelian, and Palatine hills, as well as the intervening low ground. This probably was the area included from the earliest historic times within the *pomerium*, the ritually consecrated boundary of the city. Within the *pomerium* but not embraced in any of the four regions was the Capitoline hill which was fortified and served as the citadel of the community. Thus Rome of the Four Regions may be regarded as an expansion and consolidation of the town formed earlier by the union of the Palatine with its adjacent communities. The cessation of burials in the cemeteries lying within the *pomerium* about 600 B.C. or a little later indicates that the unification took place then, for burials within the city were contrary to Roman practice. As this date falls within the period of Etruscan influence in Latium and agrees approximately with the traditional time of the establishment of an Etruscan dynasty in Rome, it is probable that the organization of Rome of the Four Regions was effected by Etruscan conquerors. This view finds support in the name *Roma* itself, which seems to be of Etruscan origin. The new city was not surrounded by a continuous wall, although the individual hills were protected by the sixth century by earthen embankments with ditches in front. The Aventine Hill, as well as part of the plateau back of the Esquiline, was included within the city walls of the fourth century B.C. but remained outside the *pomerium* until the time of the Emperor Claudius in the first century A.D.

HISTORIC ROMANS.   The archaeological evidence shows that the Roman tradition of a strong Sabine element in the population of the early city has a substantial basis. But though it is true that the population of Rome was the result of a fusion of different elements, Latin and Sabine mainly but with a slight admixture of Etruscan and probably even pre-Italic, nevertheless the Romans were essentially a Latin people. In language, in religion, in political institutions, they were characteristically Latin, and their history is inseparably connected with that of the Latins as a whole.

ROME'S STRATEGIC SITUATION.   The location of Rome, on the Tiber at a point where navigation for seagoing vessels terminated and where an island made transit easy, made it commercially important. It was also the gateway between Latium and Etruria and the natural outlet for the trade of the Tiber valley. Furthermore, its central position in Italy gave it a strategic advantage in its wars. But the greatness of Rome was not the result of its geographic advantages; it was the outgrowth of the energy and political capacity of its people, qualities which became a national heritage because of the character of the early struggles of the Roman state.

III. The Early Monarchy

TRADITION. "In the beginning," wrote the Roman historian Tacitus, "kings ruled the city Rome."[1] The accuracy of this statement is attested by the mention of the *rex* or king in an inscription of the sixth century B.C. and by the survival of this term in later times in the title *rex sacrorum* or "king of the sacrifices," which was borne by one of the higher priests, as well as by the strength of the Roman tradition regarding an early period of monarchical rule. It is quite impossible, however, to present any reliable history of Roman monarchy because, when Roman historians began to write they found scarcely any records of the regal age, and oral tradition had become confused. Consequently the Roman account of the reigns of the kings is a reconstruction by annalists and antiquarians who sought to attribute the origins of Roman political and religious institutions to these rulers.

According to the accepted Roman version, seven kings ruled Rome between the founding of the city and the establishment of the Republic about 509. The first of these, Romulus, and his alleged Sabine colleague Titus Tatius, may not have been historical personages. The six successors of Romulus—Numa Pompilius, Tullus Hostilius, Ancus Marcius, Lucius Tarquinius Priscus, Servius Tullius, and Lucius Tarquinius (Superbus) —probably were historical, although we can place little reliance upon the characteristics and exploits assigned to each. Apparently the first three were pre-Etruscan and may have ruled the Palatine community before and after the absorption of its neighbors; the last three date from the sixth century when Rome was under Etruscan domination. By name, as well as by tradition, the Tarquinii were Etruscan, and Servius Tullius may well have been an Etruscan whose name has survived in a Latin form.

In spite of the unreliability of the Roman account of the age of the kings, it is possible to draw a general picture of conditions in Rome under its kingly rulers, based on the survival in later times of religious, political, and social institutions that had their origin in the early stages of the Roman state, and on the results of archaeological studies that have revealed much of the character of early Roman civilization.

POLITICAL ORGANIZATION OF THE REGAL PERIOD. The political institutions of the early Roman state bore a strong resemblance to those of other city kingdoms built up by immigrants from the north in Greece and Italy. They comprised the kingship, a council, an assembly of

[1] *Annales* 1, 1.

the people, and the smaller units into which the citizens were grouped for the better performance of their obligations and the exercise of their rights.

The Roman monarchy apparently was not purely hereditary but elective within the royal family, like that of primitive Greek states, where the king was the head of one of a group of noble families, chosen by the nobles and approved by the people as a whole. The king was war-lord, chief priest, and judge in matters affecting the public peace. His authority, called the *imperium*, included the right of scourging and execution. Its symbols were the *fasces*, small bundles of rods enclosing an axe, carried by attendants called lictors. The royal power was not absolute, for its exercise was tempered by custom, by the lack of any elaborate machinery of government, and by the practical necessity for the king to avoid alienating the community.

The council was called the Senate (*senatus*), which, as its name indicates, was originally a council of elders but, following the pattern of similar councils in the city states of Greece, had become a council of nobles. The details of its organization are not known, but its functions were primarily advisory. From a very early date the Roman people were divided into thirty groups called *curiae*, which at one time may well have corresponded to territorial divisions. Membership in the *curiae* was probably hereditary, and each *curia* had its special cult, which was maintained long after the *curiae* had lost their political importance. Apparently the *curiae* were grouped into three larger units called tribes, ten *curiae* to each tribe. The names of these tribes, *Ramnes*, *Tities*, and *Luceres*, survived in later times as the names of cavalry corps in the army, which was recruited at first on a tribal basis.[2]

When the members of all the *curiae* met, they constituted the popular assembly known as the Curiate Assembly (*comitia curiata*). It was convoked at the pleasure of the king to hear matters of interest to the whole community such as adoptions, wills, and grants of citizenship. It did not have legislative power, but such important steps as the declaration of war or the appointment of a new *rex* required its formal sanction.

EXPANSION UNDER THE KINGS. According to later tradition, Rome grew to be the chief city in Latium under the kings, having absorbed several smaller Latin communities in the immediate neighborhood, extended her territory along the lower course of the Tiber to the seacoast, where later the port of Ostia was founded, and even conquered Alba Longa, the former religious center of the Latins. This tradition conflicts with archaeological evidence, which indicates that other towns were dominant in the Latin League during the sixth century and that Rome did not attain such dominance until after 500. The legend of Rome's greatness under the monarchy seems to have been the creation of the earliest Roman

---

[2] The view of Roman writers that these tribes corresponded respectively to the Latin, Sabine, and Etruscan elements in the Roman people is undoubtedly false.

historians, who sought to provide their city with a past worthy of its later greatness.

FALL OF THE MONARCHY.   According to Roman tradition, the monarchy came to an end in 509 B.C. with the abolition of the kingship, although it survived as a shadow of its former self in a lifelong priesthood. This date may be accepted as approximately correct even if no confidence can be placed in the dramatic Roman account of the misdeeds of the second Tarquin as the cause of a revolt that swept away the Etruscan dynasty. It is reasonable to think that there had been a gradual decline of royal power as a result of the growing strength of the nobles, similar to the case in many Greek city-states and probably paralleled in the other Latin towns. The actual expulsion of the last Tarquin may well have been carried out by force. The Romans later credited their own nobles with this *coup d'état*, but it has been suggested with great plausibility that it may have been carried out by a rival Etruscan Lord, Lars Porsenna. The Romans admitted that Porsenna captured Rome and imposed humiliating conditions upon its inhabitants to make it subject to himself, but they maintained that he did this in order to avenge the Tarquins. Since he restored neither the Tarquins nor the monarchy, however, it is probable that he was an enemy and not a friend of that dynasty. In any event his overlordship could not long have survived the Etruscan defeat at Aricia (507). The fall of the Etruscan dynasty did not mean the expulsion of all Etruscans from Rome, for some of the leading families of the Roman nobility were of Etruscan origin and a district in the city continued to be called the Etruscan quarter.

ETRUSCAN INFLUENCE IN EARLY ROME.   While Etruscan domination failed to alter the Latin character of the people, it left many traces in various aspects of Roman life, notably in official paraphernalia, military organization, and religious practices, such as the employment of *haruspices* or Etruscan diviners. The *Cloaca Maxima*, or great sewer, probably at first an open ditch, which drained the Forum, belonged to the Etruscan period. In early Roman art and architecture Etruscan influence is particularly noticeable. The earliest temple of Jupiter on the Capitoline was built in the sixth century in Etruscan style, and the statue of Jupiter it contained and its terra cotta roof decoration were ascribed to Etruscan artists. Indeed, the association of the three divinities—Jupiter, Juno, and Minerva—in a triad worshipped in this temple was an imitation of widespread Etruscan practice. Under the Etruscan kings there was some development of industry in Rome, particularly in pottery, bronzeworking, and ironworking. In this connection may be noted the introduction of the worship of Minerva, goddess of handicraft and patroness of trade guilds. It is possible that the organization of the eight early trade guilds of free craftsmen, the names of which reveal the scope of the industrial life of kingly Rome, fell within the period of Etruscan rule. These trade guilds were those of flute players, goldworkers, smiths, dyers, shoemakers, leather-workers, bronzeworkers, and potters. The use of music on state occasions and the celebration of public games and festivals were popular Etruscan practices that were early adopted by the Roman state.

IV. Early Roman Society

POPULUS ROMANUS. The oldest name of the Romans was *Quirites*, a name which long survived in official phraseology but which was superseded by the name *Romani*, derived from that of the city. The body of those eligible to be soldiers, to participate in the public religious rites, and to attend the meetings of the popular assembly, with their families, constituted the Roman state—the *populus Romanus*.

At the base of Roman society was the household (*familia*), a closely knit economic as well as social unit. Such households claiming descent from a common ancestor formed a clan or *gens*. These *gentes* were social rather than political groups, for they did not form political subdivisions, even though they might exercise a great deal of influence upon the public life of the community. Each clan was distinguished by its gentile name,[3] borne by all its members, and each celebrated its own religious rites (*sacra*), from which all outsiders were excluded.

PATRICIANS AND PLEBEIANS. At the close of the regal period the *populus Romanus* comprised two distinct social and political classes. These were the patricians and the plebeians. Many of the latter class were clients. These class distinctions had grown up gradually under economic and social influences and, in antiquity, were not confined to Rome but appeared in many Greek communities also at a similar stage of their development.

The patricians were the aristocracy. Their influence rested upon their wealth as great landholders, their superiority in military training and equipment, their clan organization, and the support of their clients. Their position assured to them political control, and they had early monopolized the right to sit in the Senate. The senators collectively were called *patres*, whence the name *patricii* (patricians) was given to all the members of their families and to their descendants.

The patrician aristocracy formed a social caste, the product of a long period of social development, and this caste was enlarged in early times by the recognition of new *gentes* as possessing the qualifications of the older clans (*patres maiorum* and *minorum gentium*). Like its Greek counterpart, the patrician order became a closed one and refused to intermarry with

---

[3] For example: all members of the Cornelian *gens* were called Cornelius, those of the Julian *gens*, Julius. In addition, each had a personal name (*praenomen*) used before the clan name (*nomen*), and in later times a family name (*cognomen*) regularly followed the *nomen*. These three elements appear in such names as Lucius Cornelius Scipio, Gaius Julius Caesar.

the nonpatrician element. The patricians were quarrelsome, their ideals warlike, and they occasionally used their power selfishly and even unscrupulously to maintain their economic and political preeminence, even if it meant injury to the weaker classes in the state.

The clients apparently were tenants who tilled the estates of the patricians, to whom they stood for a long time in a condition of economic and political dependence. Each head of a patrician household was the patron of the clients who resided on his lands. Clients were obliged to follow their patron to war and to the political arena, to render him respectful attention and, on occasion, pecuniary support. Such duties were called "offices" (*officia*). The patron, in his turn, was obliged to do anything of benefit (*beneficia*) to his client, such as protecting his life and interests, especially in courts of law. Legal protection was important to clients, since patricians controlled the judicial system. The ties that bound client and patron were based on mutual faith, and at least in the historical period were accordingly extralegal and moral in nature. For either patron or client to fail in his obligations was sacrilege. This relationship, called *patronatus* on the side of the patron, *clientela* on that of the client, was hereditary on both sides. The client-patron relationship was one of the most important, characteristic, and permanent features of Roman life, and, in one form or another, it was to determine the further development of society, politics, and even foreign policy.

The nonpatrician element were the plebeians or *plebs*. They were free citizens—the less wealthy landholders, tradesmen, craftsmen, and laborers —who could not sit in the Senate and so had no direct share in the administration. Beyond question, however, they were included in the *curiae* and could vote in the *comitia curiata*. Nor is there any proof of a racial difference between plebeians and patricians. It is not easy to determine to what degree clients participated in the political life of the community. In the general use of the term, the plebs included the clients, who later, under the Republic, shared in all the privileges won by the plebeians and who, consequently, must have had the status of plebeians.

The sharp social and political distinction between nobles and commons, between patricians and plebeians, is the outstanding feature of early Roman society and affords the clue to the political development of the early republican period.

CHAPTER 5

EXPANSION OF ROME TO
UNIFICATION OF THE
ITALIAN PENINSULA:
ca. 509–265 B.C.

The history of the two and a half centuries after the fall of the Roman monarchy rests upon a somewhat more secure foundation than that of the age of kings. Although there was no contemporary historical writing and no important literary productivity of any kind, documents and records of various sorts like the Law Code of the Twelve Tables, individual statutes, census records, lists of magistrates and official calendars were committed to writing in increasing numbers. No more than a skeleton narrative could be made from these written sources for the period before 300 B.C., however, and later Roman historians had to rely largely on folk tales and the oral traditions maintained by Rome's leading families. For several reasons these stories and traditions came to be padded heavily with fictitious details by the time Romans were first writing history about 200 B.C. History was written by members of the new senatorial oligarchy that developed in the course of the third century, and their reconstruction of past events had to satisfy the pride of its two elements, the old patrician families and their newer plebeian associates. Furthermore, national pride required them to present a narrative that would command respect by those masters of historical writing, the Greeks, with whom they were establishing ever closer cultural relations. Accordingly, much biased or fictitious information ultimately found its way into the extant canonical versions of early Roman history in the works of Livy and Dionysius of Halicarnassus, written towards the end of the first century B.C. In some cases archaeological data can be used as a check on literary tradition, but the interpretation of such data is often controversial. Accordingly, only the bare outline of the history of the early Republic can be reconstructed, and that outline must be based on an often unreliable source tradition.

I. The Young Republic and Its Neighbors:
509–392 B.C.

ROME AND THE LATIN LEAGUE.   According to the later Roman account, Rome at the close of the regal period was by far the strongest city in Latium. Actually, it seems to have had no greater power than some of its

Latin neighbors. Rome's territory probably did not exceed fifty square miles in area, was confined to the left bank of the Tiber, and did not even reach the sea at its mouth. It fell a prey to the Etruscan Lars Porsenna and does not seem to have liberated itself entirely by its own efforts.

Early in the fifth century Rome was at war with the Latin League, and was finally victorious in the battle of Lake Regillus near Tusculum. The

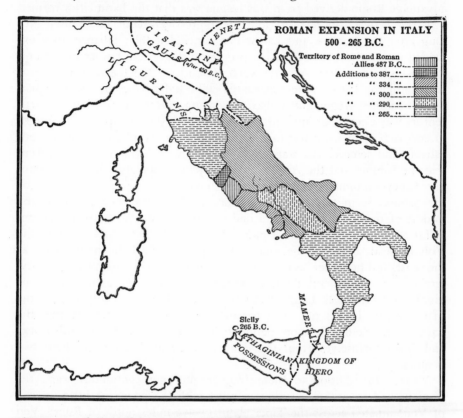

victory was followed by a treaty ascribed to a Roman, Spurius Cassius, and dated in 493 (486).[1] The terms ascribed to this treaty seem to have been drawn from a much later pact,[2] but one result was that Rome became for a time the dominant city in the League. This primacy was marked by the dedication of a grove and altar to Diana on the Aventine Hill.[3] This was

[1] There is considerable uncertainty in the chronology before 300 B.C. For this reason both traditional and corrected dates have been given, the latter in parentheses.

[2] These terms were agreed to when the alliance was renewed in the early part of the fourth century. A bronze copy of the treaty drawn up at that time, which may have been the treaty actually concluded by a Spurius Cassius, survived into the first century B.C. The terms are discussed later in the present chapter.

[3] According to another view, the foundation of the Roman sanctuary to Diana dates from the regal period and is to be ascribed to the wishes of Servius Tullius to cement relations with the Latin League.

a suitable site for a sanctuary common to the members of the League, since it was outside the *pomerium* and thus open to foreigners for purposes of worship. This alliance of Rome with the other Latin cities had a natural basis in their common ethnic and cultural traditions as well as in the common dangers which threatened all Latins from the Etruscans on the north and the highland Italian peoples to the east and south. One great advantage Rome derived from this league was that the Latin cities formed a barrier between its territory and the aggressive Aequi and Volsci. Not long after the Romans and Latins had concluded their alliance, they extended it to include the Hernici, a people on the eastern border of Latium.

WARS WITH THE AEQUI AND VOLSCI. On the northeast, east, and south the Latins were confronted with Italic tribes of the Sabellian group: Sabines, Aequi, and Volsci. According to Roman tradition, the fifth century was a period of intermittent warfare with these peoples, who sought to encroach upon Latin territory. Although accounts of these wars are unreliable and some of the wars themselves may be fictitious, it is apparent that the Sabines and the Aequi, pressed by overpopulation in their mountain valleys, sought to expand into the lowlands of Latium. The raids of the Sabines seem to have been unsuccessful border forays, but by the middle of the century the Aequi had penetrated into the heart of Latium, as far as Tusculum and Mt. Algidus. By the close of the sixth century the Volsci already occupied the southeastern part of the Latin plain as far as the coast, and here they seem to have met with a Latin attempt to win new territory for settlement. Evidence for this comes in the establishment of Signia and Norba as Latin foundations in Volscian territory during the fifth century. It was not until toward the close of the century that the Latins with Roman support definitely overcame both Aequi and Volsci and freed themselves from the danger of encroachments by these two peoples.

VEII. In addition to these frequent but not continuous wars, the Romans had to sustain a serious conflict with the powerful Etruscan city of Veii, situated across the Tiber about twelve miles north of Rome. Veii was a flourishing town, controlling a larger and richer territory than Rome. Excavations have shown that it was an important place from the tenth to the beginning of the fourth century B.C. It had come under Etruscan influence in the course of the eighth century and was now the bulwark of Etruscan power in southern Etruria. The contents of its tombs have revealed the wealth and the extensive foreign trade of the Veientes, while imposing sculptural remains from its temple show that they were in contact with the Greek cultural influences then so powerful throughout Italy. It is probable that the cause of the war with Rome was a conflict of commercial and political interests in northern Latium. War broke out in 407 (402), shortly after the Romans had taken Fidenae, a town which controlled a crossing of the Tiber above Rome. According to tradition the Romans blockaded Veii for eleven years before it fell, but this tale looks like an invention of Roman annalists in imitation of the legendary ten years' siege of Troy. In the course of this war the Romans introduced the custom of paying their troops, a practice which enabled them to keep citizen soldiers under arms throughout the year if necessary. Veii was destroyed, its population enslaved, and its territory incorporated in the public land of Rome. This annexation was the first great expansion of Roman territory.

II. The Gallic Invasion

GAULS IN THE PO VALLEY. The Romans had scarcely emerged victorious from the contest with Veii when a sudden disaster overtook them from an unexpected quarter. About 400 B.C., Celtic tribes crossed the Alpine barrier, probably by way of the Brenner Pass, and moved into the Po valley. This inroad was part of the expansion of the Celtic peoples from their homeland in the upper Danubian region of central Europe, from which they were slowly being forced to migrate by pressure of Germanic peoples to the north. The invaders belonged to that branch of the Celts known as Gauls. They conquered the Etruscans, who formed the ruling class in the central part of the valley, and well before the close of the fourth century had occupied all the land from the Ticinus river and Lake Maggiore southeastward to the Adriatic between the mouth of the Po and Ancona. This district came to be known as Cisalpine Gaul, i.e., Gaul on the near side of the Alps.

The Gauls formed eight tribes, which were often at enmity with one another. Each tribe was divided into many clans, and there was continual strife between the factions of the various chieftains. They were a barbarous people, living in rude villages and supporting themselves by cattle-raising and primitive agriculture. Their chief industry was metalworking, in which they displayed considerable skill and artistic ability. Drunkenness and love of strife were their characteristic vices, war and oratory their passions. Ancient writers describe them as a tall, blond, and blue-eyed race. Brave to the point of recklessness, they were formidable warriors, and the ferocity of their first assault inspired terror even in the ranks of veteran armies. Their chief weapons were long, two-edged swords of soft iron, which frequently bent and were easily blunted; for defence they carried small wicker shields. Their armies were undisciplined mobs, greedy for plunder, disinclined to prolonged, strenuous effort, and utterly unskilled in siege operations. These weaknesses nullified the effects of their victories and prevented their occupation of Italy south of the Apennines. During the fourth century, however, before they settled down to exploit the rich agricultural resources of the Po valley, the Gauls were very restive. Large bands made frequent incursions into the peninsula in search of adventure and plunder.

SACK OF ROME. In 390 (387) a band of these marauders crossed the Apennines and besieged Clusium in central Etruria. Thence, angered, as was said, by the hostile actions of Roman ambassadors who had been sent to persuade the Gauls to withdraw, they marched directly upon Rome. The Romans mobilized their forces and met the Gauls near the Allia, a small tributary of the Tiber above Fidenae. The fierce onset of the Gauls routed the Roman army. Many were slain, and most of the survivors were forced to take refuge within the ruined fortifications of Veii. Deprived of the protection of their army and having no city wall, the citizens in a body evacuated Rome and fled to neighboring towns. The Capitol, however, being adequately fortified, was left with a small garrison. The Gauls entered and sacked Rome but failed to storm the citadel. Apparently they had no intention of settling in Latium, and, after a delay of seven months, upon information that the Veneti were attacking their new settlements in the Po valley, they accepted a ransom of 1,000 pounds of gold[4] and marched home. Their decision may have been hastened by knowledge of the gathering of a Roman and allied force at Veii. The Romans at once reoccupied and rebuilt their city and soon after provided it with more adequate defences in the wall later miscalled Servian. This wall consisted of a thick earthen embankment faced with stone and protected by a ditch from which the earth for the wall had been thrown up.

LATER GALLIC INCURSIONS. For some time the Gauls continued their incursions into the peninsula, even penetrating as far south as Apulia. But not until 360 (357) did they appear again in Latium. On that occasion they raided as far as the Alban Hills, but the Romans feared to meet them and remained within their walls. When, however, a fresh band appeared in 349, the Romans were prepared. They and their allies blocked their path, and the Gauls retreated, unwilling to risk a battle. Rome thus became the successful champion of the Italian peoples, their bulwark against the barbarian invaders from the north. In 331 the Gallic tribe of the Senones and the Romans concluded peace and entered upon a period of friendly relations which lasted for the rest of the fourth century.

III. Conquest of the North and Center of the Peninsula,
Disruption of the Latin League, and the Samnite Wars:
390 (387)–280 B.C.

WARS WITH THE AEQUI, VOLSCI, AND ETRUSCANS. The disaster that had overtaken Rome impressed the civilized world profoundly and was noted by contemporary Greek writers. But the blow left no

---

[4] At the (1964) rate of $35 an ounce this would be $420,000. In view of the comparative poverty of early fourth-century Rome, it is likely that the ransom has been greatly exaggerated.

permanent traces, for only the city, not the state, had been destroyed. Encouraged by their enemy's defeat, the Aequi, Volsci, and the Etruscan cities previously conquered by Rome took up arms; but each met defeat in turn. Rome retained and consolidated her conquests in southern Etruria. Part of the land was allotted to Romans, and four tribal districts were organized there. On the remainder, two Latin colonies, Sutrium (383) and Nepete (372), were founded. It was not until 351 that the Etruscans were so badly beaten that they abandoned their attacks on Rome and sued for peace. The Aequi and Rome's former allies, the Hernici, who had seized the opportunity to assert their independence, were speedily subdued. Not so the Volsci, who fought long and bitterly to preserve their independence and regain control of Southern Latium. In 358 the Romans annexed most of their territory and settled it with Roman colonists organized in two tribal districts. But even this did not end the struggle. Only with the fall of their chief city, Antium, in 338 did the Volsci abandon their resistance and accept a Roman alliance.

EXPANSION OF THE SABELLIANS.[5] While the Romans were consolidating their power in southern Etruria, Latium, and northern Campania, the more southern regions were being overrun by peoples of Sabellian stock from the valleys of the central Apennines. While Roman expansion was that of a settled agricultural people whose conquests were motivated fully as much by the necessity of protecting themselves from foreign attacks as by the desire to find new lands for colonization, that of the Sabellians was caused almost entirely by overpopulation. About once in each generation bands of young men were forced to emigrate and descended upon the neighboring lowland areas to win homes for themselves.

From the middle of the fifth century the force of these migrations was felt all over the southern part of the Italian peninsula. Capua (438) and Cumae (421) fell into Sabellian hands. Farther south, Sabellian settlements gave rise to the people known as the Lucanians, before whose advance the Bruttians were driven into the southwestern extremity of Italy. During the fourth century both the Apulians and the Greek cities of the south were forced to defend themselves against repeated attacks from the expanding Sabellians. Unlike the Romans, who created a single, powerful state supported by military alliances, the Sabellians split up into several independent groups. Those who settled in the Campanian cities amalgamated with the older population and were repeatedly at war with fresh waves of invaders from Samnite territory. The Lucanians were united in a military federation free from the control of their kinsmen in their former homeland. The Samnites, as the latter were called, also formed a loose confederacy of kindred peoples whom poverty drove to plundering raids

---

[5] Sometimes called Oscans. But the term *Oscan* seems originally to have applied to part of the pre-Sabellian population in south central Italy (see p. 21).

or attempted conquests at the expense of the descendants of earlier emigrants from the same mountain hinterland.

END OF THE LATIN LEAGUE: 338 (336) B.C. An even greater menace than hostility of the Etruscans and Volsci and the potential hostility of southern mountaineers was the attempt of the Latins to break their alliance with Rome. Before Rome had recovered from the shock of the Gallic victory, several of the more important Latin cities deserted the Latin League and challenged Rome's predominance in Latium. Although they received support from the Hernici and Volsci, they were defeated and forced to join with the rest of the Latins in accepting a close alliance with Rome (358). It was probably at this time that most of the terms later ascribed to the accord between Rome and the Latins early in the fifth century were formally agreed to. It is noteworthy that in this new pact Rome does not appear as one of the cities of the Latin League, *primus inter pares*, but as an outside power confronting the cities of the League. The treaty provided for a close offensive and defensive military alliance with each party contributing equal forces for joint military enterprises and dividing the spoils of war. At the same time they exchanged private rights of citizenship. This meant that a Roman could transact business in a Latin city with the assurance that his contract would be protected by the law of the said city, and could also acquire and hold property there (right of *commercium*), while if he married a woman from a Latin city this would be a legitimate union and his children would inherit both his property and his citizenship (right of *conubium*). Conversely, a citizen of a Latin community would enjoy the same privileges in Rome.

In the conflict terminated in 358 B.C., the majority of the Latin towns had remained faithful to their alliance, but in 340 (338) the whole Latin League rose against the Romans. They had come to realize that alliance with Rome would inevitably lead to domination by Rome, and this they were unwilling to accept. Several acts by Rome were sufficient to justify their fears. In 358 the Romans had not allowed them any part of the land annexed from the Volsci. In 354 they had concluded an alliance with the Samnites of the mountain region to the southeast of Latium. The purpose of this was cooperation against Gallic invasions, but the Latins now felt hemmed in between Romans and Samnites. Then in 348 a treaty was concluded between Rome and Carthage, in which the Romans asserted their suzerainty over Latium.

What ultimately provoked revolt within the Latin League were the results of a Roman alliance with Capua (343), the second city of Italy, which requested Roman aid against the Samnites. The Romans, apparently assuming that a major war with the Samnites was only a matter of time, wished to fight before the League became too disunited. The result was the first Samnite War (343–341 B.C.), an inglorious episode in Roman military history marked by mutiny, reverses, and a peace treaty that callously

Temple of Poseidon at Paestum (ca. 450 B.C.)

abandoned to the Samnites some of Rome's recently acquired Campanian allies. It seemed to the Latins and Campanians that there was no longer any reason for acknowledging Roman hegemony and protection if their interests were to be treated so cavalierly, and they combined forces to continue the war against the Samnites and to attack their own erstwhile Roman leaders. The Latin War followed (340–338), and the Romans, materially aided by their former Samnite enemies, were completely victorious. The Latin League was dissolved, and the individual cities had to accept Rome's terms. Five of them were deprived of their independence and incorporated in the Roman state. The rest, including the Latin colonies, became Roman allies with the obligation of furnishing troops. They lost the rights of trade and intermarriage with each other but continued to enjoy them with Rome. They also lost the privilege of forming leagues or other associations.

ROME AND THE CAMPANIAN CITIES. In the first year of the Latin war the Romans succeeded in detaching the Campanians from their alliance with the Latins and induced them to make a separate peace. Three Campanian cities, including the important towns of Capua and Cumae, were granted Roman citizenship and thus became part of the Roman state. The same treatment was accorded to two other strategic cities between Latium and Campania. Thus Roman territory was extended to the Bay of Naples. The members of these communities did not receive full Roman citizenship, for they lacked the right to vote and to hold office in Rome, although, like full citizens, they had the obligation of military service. Nevertheless they had advantages. They were now assured of protection against foreign attack, in particular against their new enemies the Samnites, and in their private and business relations with Romans they had the full benefit of Roman laws. These cities also remained at least locally self-governing communities and retained their constitutions and laws, except where they voluntarily accepted those of the Romans. Apparently Romans who moved to Capua and the other towns enjoyed there the same privileges that the Campanians did when they took up residence in Rome.

Following the Latin War, the Romans strengthened their communications with Campania by occupying the Volscian hill-country. This territory was secured by alliances with some peoples, the annexation of others, and the planting of strategic Roman and Latin colonies.

CLASH OF ROMANS AND SAMNITES IN CAMPANIA. Fear of the Samnites had induced the cities of northern Campania to accept incorporation in the Roman state, and it was this resumed policy of supporting the more civilized and peaceful lowlanders against their aggressive highland neighbors that led to a prolonged and desperate struggle between Rome and the Samnites. In this conflict all the peoples of the central and northern parts of the peninsula became involved; its result was the establishment of Roman supremacy throughout the whole area. Having used the Samnites to help subdue the Latins in the recent war, the Romans thereafter ignored their alliance with the mountaineers. The latter, for a time at least, do not seem to have regarded Roman annexation of northern Campania as a hostile act. It may have been that this apparent indifference was due to the preoccupation of the Samnites with a war against the Tarentines, who were supported by an able ally, Alexander, king of the Molossians in northern Greece (334–331).

When the war with Tarentum ended, the Samnites, who still looked upon Campania as a legitimate field for expansion, intervened in the party struggles in the Greek city of Naples and garrisoned the town with the support of one faction. Cumae became involved in the struggle and sought Roman support. In 327 (325) the Romans besieged Naples and took it when the Samnite garrison was induced to evacuate the city by the pro-Roman party. Thereupon Naples became a Roman ally, and open warfare began again between the Romans and Samnites.

SAMNITE WARS: SECOND PHASE, 326 (324)–304 B.C. The Samnites were brave and warlike. They were not greatly inferior to the Romans in numbers, and their military organization was better adapted to mountain fighting. On the other hand, the Romans were superior in the open country and had the advantage of a greater centralization of authority, which insured unity and continuity of policy in a long conflict. The Roman plan was to encircle the Samnites by alliances with the peoples of central Italy to the north of Samnium and with the Apulians to the southeast.

Apparently the Romans won some successes in the opening years of the war, but these were more than counterbalanced by an overwhelming defeat in 321 (319). A Roman army attempting to march from Campania through Samnium into Apulia, was trapped in a valley called the Caudine Forks and compelled to surrender. The terms of surrender included the acceptance of a peace under which the Romans vacated some of the border territory claimed by the Samnites and agreed not to renew the war.

During the next few years the Romans strengthened their position in Apulia and increased and reorganized their army. They adopted a formation which was more suitable for maneuvering in rough country and perhaps rearmed some of their troops by providing them with javelins in place of spears. In 316 they reopened hostilities, and initial success lay with the Samnites, who won a great battle at Lautulae near Tarracina in southern Latium (315). For a moment Campania wavered in its loyalty, but a Roman victory recovered the lost ground and placed the Samnites on the defensive. In the upper valley of the Liris river, in Campania, and in Apulia, the Romans planted colonies that served as fortresses to block the exits from Samnium and as bases for Roman attacks. The Romans also constructed a paved highway, known as the Via Appia, from Rome to Capua, which assured them of uninterrupted communications with Campania even in the rainy season.

Seeing that the extension of Roman influence across central Italy would cut them off from the north, the Samnites persuaded the Etruscan cities, whose treaties with Rome were lapsing, to create a diversion by attacking Roman territory in southern Etruria. This attack obliged the Romans to divide their forces and momentarily relieved the pressure on the Samnites. In two swift campaigns, however, Roman armies penetrated north-central Etruria and forced the cities that had taken up arms to accept a new peace (309–308 B.C.).[6] The Samnites then succeeded in detaching the Hernici, Aequi, and Paeligni from their alliance with Rome and thus prolonged hostilities in the central Apennines. By 304, however, the Romans had reduced these tribes and also brought the Samnites to terms.

The Samnites retained their independence and their own territory, with the exception of certain frontier districts, but their position in regard to Rome had become much weaker. By virtue of alliances the Romans had acquired control of Apulia and southern Campania. Other alliances assured them of the military support of the warlike Marsi, Marrucini, Frentani, Paeligni, and some city-states among the Umbrians. The revolt of the Hernici had been punished by confiscation of territory and annexation of several of their towns as citizen communities. At the close of the war the Aequi met a similar fate, and part of the Sabine country was annexed with the grant of citizenship to its inhabitants. Colonies were planted on some of the confiscated land; the rest was divided up among individual Roman citizens. This expansion of Roman territory was marked by organization of new tribal districts.

THIRD PHASE: 298–290 B.C.   In 298 the Samnites resumed their war against Rome. During the second Samnite war the Romans had an alliance with the Lucanians, which had kept them friendly to Rome although militarily inactive. Still later, in 303, Rome cooperated with them in a war against Tarentum, which was aided by Cleonymus, king of Sparta. Afterwards, for some unknown reason, part of the Lucanians became hostile to Rome, and apparently the Samnites supported this anti-Roman faction, but in spite of Samnite intervention, the Romans were able to induce the Lucanians to resume their alliance.

A more serious threat arose from joint action by the Gauls, Samnites, and Etruscans. Stirred by the arrival of new transalpine migratory bands, the Gauls of the Po valley were once more restive and began to raid the peninsula. As Rome would inevitably oppose these inroads, it was easy for the Samnites to secure the cooperation of the Gauls against the common enemy, and some of the Etruscan cities were encouraged to rise again against Rome. The Sabines also joined Rome's enemies, whereas the Picentes, who had good reason to fear Gallic expansion, made an alliance

---

[6] So the later Roman version, but there are several improbabilities in the narrative, and these campaigns seem to have been invented from the later Roman invasion of Etruria of 295 B.C.

with Rome. In 295 the Samnites sent an army to meet the Gauls in Umbria, where the united forces fought the Romans at Sentinum. Here the Romans won a decisive victory, which proved to be the turning point. The Etruscans were defeated in their own country, and Samnium lay open to Roman attack. By systematically ravaging the country the Romans forced the Samnites to sue for peace. A portion of their land was confiscated, and they were obliged to accept the status of Roman allies (290). The Romans then turned their attention to the Sabines, who could offer little resistance. Their territory was annexed, and they were made Roman citizens without voting rights. Rome was now the dominant power in peninsular Italy.

WARS WITH THE GAULS AND ETRUSCANS. Although the Samnites had been conquered, the Gauls were still restive and for a time constituted a serious threat on Rome's northern frontier. In 284 the tribe of the Senones, who were settled on the Adriatic coast north of Picenum, attacked Arretium in Etruria. While attempting to relieve this allied city, the Romans suffered a costly defeat. Aroused by this disaster, Rome invaded the Senones' country, defeated them, and drove them out of the peninsula. Their former territory was added to the public land of Rome but continued to be known as the Ager Gallicus (The Gallic Land). Another tribe, the Boii from the Po valley, then marched into Etruria and joined forces with certain Etruscan towns that had broken their alliances with Rome after the battle of Arretium. The Romans crushed their united armies at the Vadimonian Lake near Volsinii (283 B.C.). When a second raid in the following year met a like fate, the Boii made peace and by 280 the warring Etruscan cities had again accepted an alliance with Rome.

IV. Roman Conquest of South Italy: 281–270 B.C.

ITALIANS AND GREEKS IN SOUTH ITALY. Peace in the north came none too soon for the Romans, who had become involved in the conflict between the Greeks of South Italy and their Italian neighbors. Ever since the collapse of the empire of Dionysius I of Syracuse, in the years following his death in 367, Greek cities in the far south of the peninsula had been exposed to constant attacks by the Lucanians, Bruttians, and Messapians, and only a few of them had succeeded in remaining free. Of these, Tarentum was by far the largest and most powerful. A manufacturing and trading city, it had the strongest navy in Italy and gradually assumed the role of protector of the Italian Greeks. The forces of the Tarentines were by no means a match for those of the Italians, however, and they were from time to time to enlist the services of military adventurers from the Greek world. The first of these was King Archidamus of Sparta, who fell fighting against the Lucanians in 338. Four years later Alexander, king of Epirus and uncle of Alexander the Great, succeeded in defeating the Lucanians and Bruttians. He made a treaty with Rome, in which the Tarentines were probably included, but when the latter realized that Alexander intended to create an empire of his own in South Italy, they deserted him, so that he was defeated and killed by the Italians (330). Still later, in 303, they called in another Spartan king, Cleonymus. More fortunate than his predecessors, Cleonymus forced the Lucanians to make peace. Since the Romans had supported their allies, the Lucanians, in this war, they must also have agreed to the peace.[7] A few years later Agathocles, king of Syracuse, assisted the Italian Greeks against the Bruttians (after 298). He also made an alliance with the Messapians and Peucetians of Apulia, perhaps directed against the Romans. When Agathocles died in 289 his kingdom disintegrated, and the western Greeks were left without a protector. When the Lucanians made an attack upon the Greek city of Thurii, the Thurians appealed to Rome for aid, since they regarded the Romans as more powerful than the Tarentines and more reliable than the Greek mercenary kings. As the Lucanians had broken their alliance with Rome after the Gallic victory at Sentinum, the Romans accepted Thurii as an ally and came to its rescue (282). A Roman army defeated the Lucanians, who were supported by the Bruttians, relieved Thurii, and left a Roman garrison there. Two other Greek cities, Locri and Regium, also became Roman allies and received Roman garrisons for their protection.

Roman intervention at Thurii confirmed the suspicions of the Tarentines which had been aroused by Rome's establishment of a Latin colony at Luceria (315) in Tarentum's Apulian sphere of interest. When a small Roman fleet appeared off the harbor of Tarentum contrary to the terms of a treaty (either that of 334 or that of 303), which excluded Roman warships from the Gulf of Tarentum, they attacked it without delay. Some Roman vessels were sunk, and the Tarentines ousted the Roman garrison from Thurii and occupied the town. A Roman demand for reparations was rejected, their ambassadors were publicly insulted, and a Roman army thereupon invaded Tarentine territory to enforce the demand.

In the meantime, the Tarentines had succeeded in enlisting the support of Pyrrhus, king of Epirus. They could also count upon cooperation from Messapians, Samnites, Lucanians, and Bruttians. With this backing they were prepared to defy Rome.

WAR WITH PYRRHUS AND TARENTUM. Pyrrhus was probably the most skilful Greek general of the time, and he brought with him into Italy an army organized and equipped according to the Macedonian system of Alexander the Great, which had become the standard in the Greek world. His force comprised 20,000 heavy-armed infantry forming the phalanx, 3,000 Thessalian cavalry, and 2,000 archers. He also had twenty war elephants—animals that had first appeared on Greek battlefields twenty years before but were as yet unknown to the Romans. The first

---

[7] Livy represents Cleonymus as having been defeated by the Lucanians and Romans, but this seems to be a falsification dictated by Roman pride.

engagement was fought near Heraclea (280), and the Romans were driven from the field after a severe struggle. The superior generalship of Pyrrhus and the consternation caused by his war elephants won the day, but his own losses were so heavy as to give rise to the expression "a Pyrrhic victory." As fighters the Romans had shown themselves the equal of the foe; and their tactical organization, perfected in the Samnite Wars, had proved its value in its first encounter with the military experts of Greece. In consequence of his victory at Heraclea, Pyrrhus was able to advance as far north as Latium, but he withdrew again without accomplishing anything. He also sent an embassy to Rome with proposals for peace, but his terms were rejected. The next year Pyrrhus won another hard-fought battle near Asculum in Apulia in which he was wounded. Although he was unable to exploit his victory, the Romans now opened negotiations that Pyrrhus welcomed. Before an agreement was reached, however, the Carthaginians, who feared the intervention of Pyrrhus in Sicily, offered the Romans money and ships. Their offer was accepted, the negotiations with Pyrrhus dropped, and Rome and Carthage agreed that if either of them should make a treaty with the common foe it would reserve the right to aid the other if the latter's country were invaded. In the meantime the Carthaginian fleet was to cooperate with the Romans.

PYRRHUS IN SICILY: 278–275 B.C. Pyrrhus determined to answer an appeal from the Sicilian Greeks and to leave Italy for Sicily. After the death of Agathocles in 289 the Greeks in Sicily fell upon evil days. The Carthaginians renewed their attacks, and a new foe appeared in the Mamertini—Campanian mercenary soldiers of Agathocles who seized Messana and made it their headquarters for raiding the Greek cities. Caught between these two enemies, the Greeks appealed to Pyrrhus, who came to their aid, possibly with the hope of uniting Sicily under his own control. His success was immediate. The Carthaginians were forced to give up all their possessions except Lilybaeum, and Pyrrhus stood ready to carry the war into Africa. At this juncture the exactions that he laid upon his Sicilian allies and their fear that his victory would make him their permanent master made them desert him and seek peace with their enemies. Deprived of their assistance and seeing that his allies in Italy were hard pressed by the Romans, he abandoned his Sicilian venture.

END OF THE WAR. Pyrrhus returned to Italy but lost part of his fleet in a naval battle with the Carthaginians. He reorganized his forces and advanced into Samnium to meet the Romans. Near Beneventum he attempted to surprise a Roman army, but he failed and suffered a repulse (275). He then abandoned the offensive and retired to Tarentum. Leaving a garrison in that city, he transported what remained of his forces to Greece, where conditions seemed favorable for him to conquer Macedonia. Three years later he was killed while fighting in southern Greece, and his garrison at Tarentum turned over the citadel to the Romans. Tarentum had to surrender to Rome and receive a permanent Roman garrison. Along with the other Greek cities of South Italy, it then became a Roman ally.

As a penalty for its continued hostility, the Samnite confederacy was broken up. Much land in Samnium was taken by the Romans and used for the founding of Latin colonies. The Lucanians received more generous treatment, having to surrender only the former Greek city of Paestum and its territory. The Bruttians became Roman allies but were forced to give up half of their forests on the Sila mountains.[8]

In the North, the Romans experienced further trouble with certain Etruscan towns and had to fight with their former allies, the Picentes. The latter were punished with loss of territory, but most of them, together with the Sabines, received full Roman citizenship in 268. By 265 all of peninsular Italy was united under Roman suzerainty.

V. Roman Confederation

ROMAN FOREIGN POLICY IN ITALY.   Rome united the Italian peninsula in the form of a confederation. In retrospect, the successive steps in this process appear so methodical and consequential as to create the impression of deliberate and relentless planning. The early Romans were no different, of course, from many other peoples of any age in their belief that an increase in their territory could be a desirable goal in itself, but it is not to be supposed that a conscious goal was consistently pursued through many generations by Roman statesmen. Probably it was not until nearly the end that the Romans realized where their policy was leading them. In any case, one cannot believe in the protestations of Romans writing at a much later date that the wars they waged were inevitably just and purely defensive. War was the normal state of affairs in primitive Italy, and the Romans as well as their fellow Italians lived in constant threat of attack by hostile neighbors. The early Romans were certainly not possessed of a political morality different from that of other peoples dwelling in the peninsula, and were undoubtedly guilty of their share of aggressive wars. Many early Italian peoples sought to rationalize their own warlike acts, and the Latins, Faliscans, and Umbro-Sabellians all had special ceremonies and priestly colleges to justify them. At Rome it was the business of the priestly Fetiales solemnly to proclaim that Rome resorted to war only in answer to aggression and when other means of redress had been exhausted. Such attempts to place the responsibility for a war upon the enemy are common to all ages and are not always convincing. If the Romans may not be convicted of consistent imperialism prior to 265, at any rate the methods they pursued in their relations with other peoples of Italy made their domination inevitable in view of the Roman national character and their

---

[8] Some scholars believe that the confiscation of this area occurred after the Hannibalic War, i.e., after 201 B.C.

political and military organization. These methods early became established maxims of Roman foreign policy. The Romans waged even their defensive wars offensively and rarely made peace save with a beaten foe. As a rule, the enemy was forced to conclude a treaty with Rome that assured Rome of his military support against other foes. Such a treaty was regarded as perpetually binding, and any attempt to break the relationship it established was regarded as a hostile act. Possibly the Romans regarded this as the only policy that would guarantee peace, but it inevitably led to further wars, for it resulted in the continuous extension of the frontiers defended by Rome and therefore continually brought Rome into contact and conflict with new peoples. The voluntary allies of Rome were not allowed to leave the Roman alliance; such action was treated as equivalent to a declaration of war and regularly punished with severity. This practice gradually transformed Rome's independent allies into dependents.

From the middle of the fourth century Rome seems deliberately to have sought to prevent the development of a strong state in the southern part of Italy and to this end gladly took under her protection weaker communities threatened by stronger neighbors, although such action inevitably led to war with the latter. Thereby she avoided the limitations of the fetial law, which sanctioned war only in response to direct aggression. Although Rome's protection of weaker powers in this period was typically expressed in formal alliances and treaties, at the same time her statesmen were coming to realize the possible advantages in regarding as clients those states seeking her help. Such client states could be bound to Rome not by formal treaty but by unwritten moral obligations that Rome could interpret to her own advantage. The realization of this idea was to have a profound effect on the development of a more sophisticated Roman foreign policy.

A conquered state frequently lost much of its territory. Portions of this land were set aside for the foundation of fortress colonies to protect the Roman conquests and overawe the conquered. The rest was incorporated in the public domain to the profit of rich proprietors and landless citizens. Usually Roman soldiers shared in the distribution of the movable spoils of war, sometimes a huge booty, as after the subjugation of the Sabines and Picentes in 290. Rome's long series of successful and profitable wars (for she was ultimately victorious in every struggle after 387) engendered in her people a self-confidence and a martial spirit that soon led them to conquests beyond Italy. During this period of expansion within Italy, Roman policy was guided by the Senate, a body of statesmen possessed of keen political insight and great determination, who not only made Rome mistress of the peninsula but laid enduring foundations for her power.

It is difficult to say how far the Romans were consciously influenced in their foreign policy by overpopulation, caused by the exhaustion of the soil of Latium after centuries of intensive cultivation. The ability to stand the losses of so many serious wars without apparent diminution of military strength and to found large numbers of colonies, particularly in the latter part of the fourth and the first half of the third centuries, points to a surplus population and unsatisfactory economic conditions among the rural classes. A demand for new land and the ambition of a new element in the ranks of the Roman governing circles may account for the more aggressive foreign policy pursued after the overthrow of the Latin League.

ROMAN CONFEDERATION. The Roman confederation was really an empire consisting of Rome as the dominant power and a number of allied states as dependents. Broadly speaking, there were two classes of allies: (1) the Latins and (2) the federated states.

THE ROMAN STATE.[9] As a result of confiscations of territory and the extension of Roman citizenship to various city and tribal communities, the area of the Roman state (the *ager Romanus*) had expanded from some 50 square miles in 509 to about 10,000 square miles in 265, and it comprised about one fifth of the Italian peninsula. Along the west coast it extended in a broad strip from near Tarquinii in Etruria southward to the Bay of Naples, and from the latitude of Rome it stretched northeastward across the Apennines to the Adriatic.

The Roman citizens who constituted the free population of this territory were of two classes: (1) full citizens and (2) citizens without the right to vote or hold office in Rome.[10] Full citizens resided in the city Rome, in municipal towns, and in small rural communities. For administrative purposes, the citizen body was organized into tribes on the basis of residence in districts into which Rome and Roman territory were divided. There were also a number of colonies of Roman citizens planted mainly in harbor towns of Italy that lay at one time beyond the Roman frontiers. These were really small garrisons of citizens, usually only three hundred in number, whose duty it was to protect the ports from sea raids and to insure the loyalty of their inhabitants to Rome. Twenty-seven of these citizen colonies came to be established altogether. Their military character is clearly expressed in the exemption of the colonists from active army service.

The second class of Romans, who had all the obligations but only the private rights of citizenship, comprised the inhabitants of towns in Etruria, Latium, and Campania that had received, in most cases voluntarily, this form of association with Rome. These towns were called municipalities (*municipia*), a term implying originally that their inhabitants had the full burdens but not the full rights of citizens. The *municipia* of citizens without the right of suffrage retained much local independence and their former officials. In their external relations, however, they were under the jurisdiction of the higher Roman magistrates. *Municipia* of full citizens also appear to have enjoyed some local autonomy under their former constitutions, although the functions and powers of their magistrates un-

---

[9] See map following.
[10] *Cives sine suffragio et iure honorum.*

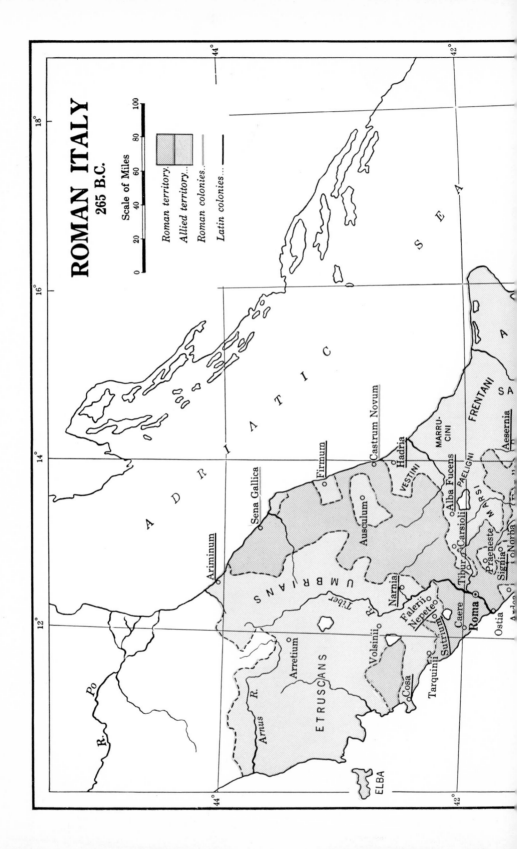

ROMAN ITALY
265 B.C.

Scale of Miles

0   20   40   60   80   100

Roman territory.
Allied territory....
Roman colonies....
Latin colonies....

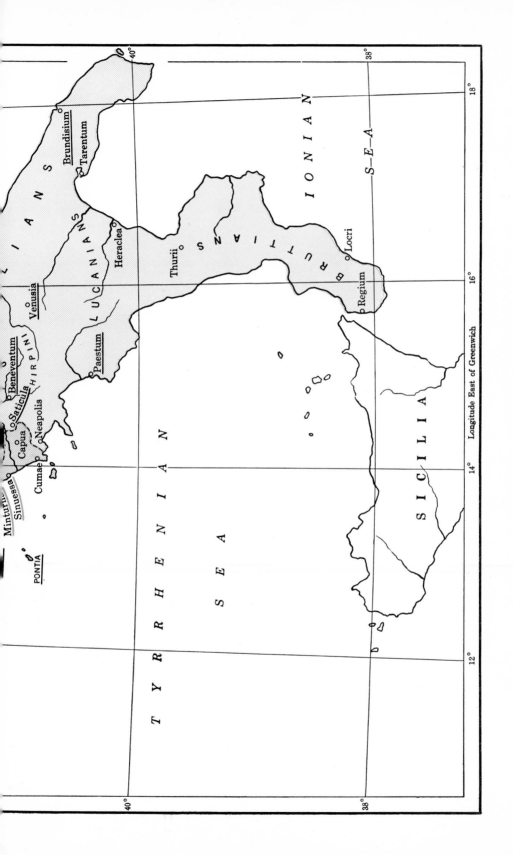

doubtedly suffered serious curtailment. The municipal system was a distinctly Roman contribution to solving the problem of local government in an enlarged city-state. Rome was not only the capital city; it was the *state*, for all Romans were citizens and could exercise their public rights of citizenship only in Rome itself. The municipalities were a means of incorporating other city-states into the Roman without the dissolution of their community life or a violent break with their previous traditions, customs, and culture. The status of municipalities without the right of suffrage was only a halfway stage in the complete amalgamation with Rome of previously independent communities, for they all ultimately attained full citizenship. For the new citizens it brought advantages as well as obligations, while preserving for them much local independence. For the Romans, it brought an increase of manpower, which helped to meet growing military burdens and also saved the older citizens from having to share their power and responsibilities with too many unassimilated foreigners.

LATIN ALLIES. Of the non-Romans in Italy, the people most closely bound to Rome by ties of blood and common interests were the Latin allies. They included: (1) the old Latin towns of Tibur, Praeneste, and one c: two others not absorbed by Rome in 338, (2) the nine Latin colon ːs founded by the Latin League prior to its political dissolution at that (ɑte, and (3) twenty-one new Latin colonies founded by Rome in Italy fter 338. Most of the colonists for these later colonies were poor Rom⍺ ɪ and Latin citizens, but in some cases citizens of other allied states werᵉ lso enrolled as settlers. Whatever their origin, members of a Latin col took the status of Latin allies, but if any one of them left a son of military age in his place, he had the privilege of moving to Rome and becoming a citizen. Each colony had full rights of local self-government, with its own laws, magistrates, and the right to issue coins and control its own census. Its constitution was modeled upon Rome's, and its citizens enjoyed rights of *commercium* and *conubium* with Rome and with the other Latin towns, except that the last twelve colonies founded between 268 and 181 had *commercium* only. The Latin colonies were large towns having citizen bodies comprising 2,500, 4,000, or 6,000 heads of households. As each colonist received enough land to support a family, large areas had to be assigned by the Roman state from confiscated territory for these settlements. Latin colonies were primarily military. Founded at strategic points on conquered territory, they formed one of the strongest supports of Roman power. Colonization of this character also served to relieve overpopulation and satisfy land hunger in Latium. Contrasted with the other allies of Rome, the citizens of Latin towns formed the *nomen Latinum* (people of the *Latin name*). If they happened to be in Rome they could vote in the Tribal Assembly in a tribe determined by lot. Unlike the Roman citizens without the suffrage, they did not serve in the Roman legions but formed separate detachments of horse and foot.

ITALIAN ALLIES.   The rest of the peoples of Italy—Italian, Greek, Illyrian, or Etruscan—were the federate allies of Rome, the *socii Italici*. These constituted some 150 separate communities, city or tribal, each bound to Rome by a special treaty (*foedus*), determining its specific relations to Rome. In all these treaties, however, there were two common features, namely, the obligations to lend military aid to Rome and to surrender to Rome control over their relations with other states. No taxes of any kind could be imposed by Rome upon an allied community. Allied troops were not incorporated in the legions but were organized as separate infantry and cavalry units (*cohortes* and *alae*), raised, equipped, and officered by the communities themselves. They were, however, commanded by Roman generals; and if several allied detachments were combined in one corps, by a Roman officer. The allied troops received their subsistence from Rome and shared equally with the Romans in the spoils of war. The Greek cities of South Italy were excused from service on land but were obliged to furnish warships with their crews to the Roman fleet, and for this reason they were called naval allies (*socii navales*). All the federate allies had *commercium*, and the majority *conubium* also, with Rome. Apart from their obligations toward Rome, each of the allied communities was autonomous, having its own language, laws, and political institutions.

In many cases, as for example in the Etruscan cities, the treaties of alliance with Rome were strengthened by the strong bond of sympathy that existed between the local aristocracies and the senatorial order at Rome. The foreign relations of Rome were directed by the Senate, which represented the views of the wealthier landed proprietors, and it was only natural that the senators should have sought to ally themselves with the corresponding social class in other states. This class represented the more conservative and, from the Roman point of view, more dependable element, while the support of Rome assured to the local aristocracies control within their own communities.

ROMAN IMPERIALISM IN ITALY.   Although peninsular Italy was united under the Roman *imperium*, it by no means formed a single state. Rather, it was an agglomerate of many states and many peoples whose sole point of contact was that each was allied with Rome. These alliances constituted a military confederation, but for all practical purposes they created a Roman empire in Italy. In the organization of the confederation, the Romans exhibited a high degree of statecraft. They did not seek rigid uniformity but adapted themselves readily to varied conditions in different parts of Italy. Where they found a high degree of urbanization, as in Latium, Campania, the Greek South, northern Apulia, and Umbria, they left the city-states as the existing political units. In less highly civilized areas, such as Bruttium, Lucania, southern Apulia, Samnium, and other regions of central Italy, they recognized the tribal states and accorded them a place in their system of alliances. Although they made extensive annexations at the expense of obstinate foes, under pressure of military necessity and need of room for colonization, this practice was not carried to an extreme. Relentless in the prosecution of war, the Romans showed themselves lenient in imposing peace. Most of their conquered opponents received moderate terms, and nowhere did the Romans interfere internally. The reward of this tolerant attitude came in the loyalty displayed by the allies during wars of the following century.

Although there was as yet no such thing as an Italian nation, still it was at this time that the name *Italia* was first applied to the whole of the peninsula and the term *Italici* (Italians) was employed, at first by foreigners but later by themselves, to designate its inhabitants.[11]

[11] The several elements in the Roman military confederation may be seen at a glance from the following scheme:
I. Roman citizens   (*a*) with full civic rights (*optimo iure*)
                     (*b*) with private rights only (*sine suffragio*)
II. Roman allies   (*a*) Latin allies
                     (*b*) Federate peoples of Italy

GROWTH OF THE COMMONWEALTH: 509–287 B.C.

While the Romans were expanding and building up their confederation in Italy, the Roman state experienced a profound internal evolution. This was brought about in part by the necessity of modifying the government to meet the needs of a rapidly growing community and in part by a successful struggle by the plebeians to secure political and other privileges monopolized at first by the patricians.

I. Early Republic

CONSTITUTION OF THE EARLY REPUBLIC: THE MAGIS-TRATES. Upon the overthrow of the Monarchy, the Romans set up a republican form of government, of which the chief executive office was filled by two annually elected magistrates, or presidents, called at first praetors but later consuls. Together they exercised the old kingly power known as *imperium*, symbolized by the rods and axes (*fasces*) carried by the lictors. The *imperium* also involved *auspicium*, the right to take the auspices or omens by which the gods were believed to declare their approval or disapproval of public acts. Both consuls enjoyed these powers equally and, by his veto, one could suspend the other's action. Thus from the beginning of the Republic annuality and collegiality (the division of authority among colleagues of equal rank) were characteristics of the Roman magistracy. As time went on, the Romans recognized the advantage of an occasional concentration of all state power in the hands of a single magistrate; and so, in times of emergency, the consuls, acting upon the advice of the Senate, nominated a dictator, who was senior to the consuls themselves for a maximum period of six months. The dictator, or *magister populi*, as he was called in early times, appointed as his assistant a master of the horse (*magister equitum*). The dictatorship was Latin, not Roman, in origin. It was the title given to the commander in chief of the forces of the Latin League, and when dominant in the League, Rome must have supplied such dictators. It was thus natural that Rome should later adopt the concept of dictatorship into her own constitution as well fitted to deal with external and internal emergencies, while it was given a specific Roman character. Most of the dictators whose names have been preserved with any degree of reliability belong to the late fifth and fourth centuries

B.C. Only patricians were eligible to hold the consulship, the dictatorship, and the mastership of the horse.

THE SENATE. At the side of the magistrates stood the Senate. By the third century B.C. this council had a fixed membership of three hundred but it is debatable whether it was so large at the beginning of the Republic. At that time appointments to the Senate were made by the consuls from members of the patrician clans. The senators held their seats for life unless guilty of grave public or private misconduct.

Disappearance of the monarchy greatly increased the importance of the Senate. Its primary duty was to act as an advisory council to the consuls, as it had to the kings. Since the consuls were annual officers who became private citizens when their terms ended, the Senate, as a permanent body, had much more influence over them than it had over the monarchs who had ruled for life. It can hardly be said that the consuls were subordinate to the Senate at this period, but they would be reluctant to act contrary to its advice. The Senate also acquired the right to sanction or to veto resolutions passed by the Assembly, which could not become laws without the Senate's approval. The composition of the Senate and the life tenure of its members made it a strongly conservative body devoted to maintaining the interests of the patrician aristocracy.

THE ASSEMBLY OF THE PEOPLE. During the early years of the Republic, the only Assembly of the People was the old Curiate Assembly of the regal period. The Assembly elected the annual consuls and approved or rejected such proposals as the latter placed before it. Its powers were limited to voting, for it did not have the right to initiate legislation or to discuss or amend measures that were presented to it. Its legislative power, furthermore, was limited by the Senate's right of veto.

In the Assembly the voting was open, either by show of hands or oral declaration. The members of each *curia* voted as a unit, the majority within the *curia* determining the vote. Under these conditions it is probable that the voting in the *curiae* was often controlled by the patricians, through their personal influence and the support of their clients who would fear to oppose their wishes.

THE PRIESTHOODS. In Rome a special branch of the administration was that of public religion, which dealt with the official relations of the community with its divine protectors. This sphere was under the direction of a college of priests, headed by the *pontifex maximus*. Special priestly brotherhoods or guilds cared for the performance of particular religious ceremonies, while divination in its political aspect was under the supervision of the college of augurs. With the exception of the *pontifex maximus*, who was elected by the people from an early date, the priesthoods were filled by nomination or cooptation, and their tenure was lifelong. The acts of worship previously performed by the king were carried out by a priest who preserved the memory of the kingship in his title King of the Sacrifices (*rex sacrorum*). In the order of the priesthoods the "king" ranked first, even though he was appointed by the *pontifex maximus*. The priesthood did not form a separate caste in the community, and, since the priestly offices were held by men who also acted as magistrates and senators, the official religion was subordinated to the interests of the state and tended to assume a purely formal character.

At the beginning of the Republic the priests exercised a very consider-able influence on public affairs. They were the custodians of religious law, which was enforced by punishing crimes looked upon as offenses against the gods; they alone knew the exact formulas which had to be employed in important legal transactions; the *pontifex maximus* had charge of the calendar, fixed the dates of public festivals, and announced each month what days were open and what closed to public business. The members of the college of augurs could cause the postponement of any public acts by proclaiming an unfavorable omen. For these reasons it was not merely a matter of prestige but also of practical advantage to the patricians that all priesthoods be filled by members of their class.

PATRICIAN DOMINATION. From the foregoing survey of the Roman constitution at the opening of the fifth century B.C., it is apparent that the patricians were in complete control of the government. They monopolized the magistracies, the Senate, and the priesthoods. Through these they controlled the Assembly and the administration of justice. A study of patrician clan names shows that at this time there were between 40 and 50 such clans. It has been estimated that these comprised about 1,000 families, or a total of 4,500 persons, who constituted between 7 and 8 percent of the total citizen population.[1] Although little accuracy can be claimed for these figures, they are at least a fair approximation; and it is not surprising that the domination of this aristocratic minority was soon challenged by the plebeian majority.

II. Tribes, Reorganization of the Army, and Establishment of the Centuriate Assembly

NEW TRIBAL SYSTEM. Under the Etruscan kings, the original division of the Roman citizens into three tribes was supplanted by the formation of four new tribes which took their names from regions of the city. These were territorial divisions within the *pomerium* and their mem-bers were the citizens residing in each. In the first half of the fifth century B.C. the new Roman government organized five rural tribes with topo-graphical names outside the *pomerium* between it and the boundary of

---

[1] Beloch, *Römische Geschichte*, pp. 220–223. The chief objection to these figures is that they imply too high a total number of citizens, in view of the size of the military levy. In a rural society the larger landholding families may have formed a much larger proportion of the population than in one with a more complex economy.

the Roman state, i.e., the territory known as the *ager Romanus*. Shortly after 450 the Romans seized a bridgehead on the right bank of the Tiber in the present Vatican area. There on land wrested from the Veientes, they marked out a new tribal district called Romilia after the like-named patrician clan whose members furnished the leadership and the military strength employed in the enterprise. After the Roman occupation of Fidenae in 426, nine more rural tribes were organized on the left bank of the Tiber forming a belt outside the original rural tribes and facing Rome's Latin allies. All these tribes were named after patrician clans. This is eloquent testimony to the contemporary influence of the patricians in the state and also to the military support they could find among their clients, who furnished the bulk of the settlers in the new districts. Shortly before 400, however, the Romans created two more rural tribes with topographical, not clan names. This held true of all other tribes organized in the course of expansion in Italy. The return to a topographical nomenclature bears witness to the waning of patrician domination of the Roman government due in large part to a decline in their military importance. The plebeians now supplied a large proportion of the Roman cavalry. Cavalry itself was being supplanted by heavy armed infantry as the decisive factor in Italian warfare, and it was the plebs who supplied the needed foot soldiers.

Altogether thirty-one rural tribes were created, the last two in 241. After that date colonists in new areas, or non-Romans who received grants of citizenship, were assigned to one or another of the existing rural tribes, a practice which had been in vogue from the middle of the fourth century. The thirty-five tribes served as administrative units for registration of citizens and their property and so became the basic divisions for raising military levies, for collecting property taxes, and for the classification of citizens into new voting groups.

MILITARY REFORMS. According to Roman tradition, which here seems factual, the army of the regal period was a levy of 3,000 infantry and 300 cavalry, recruited equally from each of the three early tribes. Thus each tribe supplied a regiment of 1,000 infantry commanded by a tribune of the soldiers (*tribunus militum*) and a troop of 100 cavalry. We know practically nothing, however, of the army of the early republic except that the number of centuries (i.e., units of 100 men) of cavalry at some time had been increased from three to six. These cavalry units were drawn originally from the patricians, for they alone had sufficient wealth to provide horses and armor. The chariots of earlier days had been discarded, and the horsemen, although few in numbers, were the decisive factor on the battlefield. They were not true cavalry but rather mounted infantry whose horses gave them great mobility. In battle they did not charge in solid ranks but engaged in duels with enemy leaders. If necessary, they dismounted and fought on foot, and if the enemy fled they remounted for pursuit. The infantry, inferior in training and equipment, was supplied wholly or mostly by the plebeians.

In the latter part of the fifth century the infantry levy was raised from thirty to forty centuries, a total of 4,000 men. Such an increase seems to indicate a corresponding increase in the number of citizens who could furnish the full equipment of an infantry soldier. This comprised a leather cap with bronze plates, bronze body armor and greaves, a leather shield, an iron sword, and a spear. Those who possessed this equipment were called the class (*classis* or "calling"); the rest of the citizens were rated as "below the class" (*infra classem*). The latter could be called upon for military service for which inferior equipment was adequate; but they were not included in the regular line of battle, which was that of the Greek *phalanx*, a solid formation of heavy-armed infantry all equipped alike. Shortly before 400 B.C., possibly on account of the war with Veii, the levy was increased from 4,000 to 6,000. This was accomplished by organizing new "classes" from poorer property holders, who furnished fewer centuries than the original "class," which now became the first class. In 366 (361) the levy was raised to 8,400 men, organized in two legions.

These military changes reflect an important development in the art of warfare and had far-reaching consequences in political life. In the first place, they show that among the Romans and their neighbors in Italy foot soldiers armed and drilled in the new fashion were proving more efficient than horsemen, a fact that the Greek world had learned about two centuries earlier. Secondly, the struggle for existence compelled the state to draw more and more heavily upon the less privileged plebeian class for military service, with consequent pressure for increasing the political rights of the plebs.

This is clearly seen in the establishment of a new assembly of the people, originally modeled upon the military system of the latter part of the fifth century B.C. In this assembly the citizens of military age voted by centuries in the order of the property classes in which they were enrolled for the performance of military duties, and the number of voting centuries assigned to each class was equal to the number furnished by that class for military service. Thus, at first, the *equites* or horsemen had six centuries or, we may say, six votes. In the first class, the juniors (*iuniores*) or men between seventeen and forty-six years of age who were liable to active service were given forty centuries, and the juniors in the second and third classes ten centuries each. These were the men who served as the heavy-armed infantry. The total number of their voting centuries was sixty, which corresponded to the infantry levy of 6,000 men. Since the assembly was a political and not a military body, provision had to be made for the senior men, those forty-six years of age and over only liable for garrison duty. This was done by assigning to the seniors of each class the same number of voting centuries as to the juniors, except in the case of the cavalry. The former *equites* apparently voted in the senior centuries of the first class. Because the assembly voted century by century it came to be called the Centuriate Assembly (*comitia centuriata*) to distinguish it from the older Assembly of the Curiae.[2]

The foregoing account of the early organization of the Centuriate Assembly is a reconstruction based upon the description of that body at the close of the fourth century made by Romans writing at a much later date. About 300 B.C. there were eighteen equestrian centuries and five property classes.[3] In the classes, the number of junior centuries was now eighty-four, corresponding to a levy of 8,400 men or two legions of 4,200 each. As before, the number of senior centuries in each class was equal to that of the juniors, so that the five classes comprised one hundred and sixty-eight centuries of juniors and seniors. The first class had eighty; the second, third, and fourth, twenty each; and the fifth, thirty. Besides these, there were five supernumerary centuries made up of two centuries of mechanics and two of musicians (both crafts originally detailed to special military duties), and one for those who lacked the property qualification for the fifth class and were called proletarians.[4] Altogether the one hundred and seventy centuries of the classes together with the eighteen equestrian and five supernumerary centuries totaled one hundred and ninety-three voting units.

In its completed form, the Centuriate Assembly was a political and not a military organization. It included many who were unfit for military duties, and the term *century* had lost its original meaning of a company of one hundred with the organization of the senior centuries, for the men of that age group were far less numerous than the juniors. By the close of the fourth century the equestrian centuries were also ceasing to function as a true cavalry corps and becoming merely a special class of well-to-do patrician and plebeian property holders. The bulk of the active cavalry in the Roman armies was now supplied by the Italian allies, although many young aristocrats continued to serve in this branch throughout the Republic. The old infantry phalanx made up of centuries had been superseded by the new legionary formation, in which the units were maniples of sixty and experience, not wealth, determined a man's position in the ranks. Nevertheless, the memory of the military origins of the assembly was perpetuated not only in the use of classes and centuries but also in certain

---

[2] An alternate theory, which has much to be said for it, ascribes the foundation of the Centuriate Assembly to the monarchic period and to King Servius Tullius. According to this view the Assembly and the timocratic military organization on which it was based fell into abeyance upon the establishment of the Republic and were reintroduced in the fifth century.

[3] The property ratings of each class were fixed in terms of bronze currency; the earlier method of assessment is unknown.

[4] That is, those who had no taxable property, only offspring (*proles*). They were called also *capite censi,* or those registered by name only.

practices. For a long time it continued to assemble in military formation with officers and corps standards; it regularly met on the parade ground, the Campus Martius, outside the *pomerium*, for an army could not be assembled within the city; it could be convened only by a magistrate with military authority; and when it was meeting a war flag was raised on the Janiculum Hill where a guard was stationed.

When the Centuriate Assembly was organized it took over the most important functions of the Curiate Assembly and became the chief popular assembly. It elected all the higher magistrates, acquired the sole right to declare war, voted upon legislative proposals submitted to it by the consuls or other magistrates with *imperium*, and acted as a court of appeal for citizens upon whom a magistrate had pronounced a capital penalty, scourging, loss of citizen rights, or a heavy fine. The legislative power of the Centuries was limited for a long time, however, by the veto power of the patrician senators (the *patrum auctoritas*), who had to ratify measures passed by the assembly before they became law. This restriction was practically removed by the Publilian Law (339), which required the *patres* to ratify in advance proposals that were to be presented to this assembly. In like manner, the elections of the Curiate Assembly were subject to the *patrum auctoritas*, and in the case of officials with *imperium* this authority had to be conferred upon the successful candidates by a law of the Curiate Assembly. This law of the Curiae soon became a mere convention, and by the Maenian Law passed about 287 candidates had to be approved by the *patrum auctoritas* before the elections were completed.

In the Centuriate Assembly many of the practices established in connection with the Assembly of the Curiae were maintained. There was no right of discussion or amendment, and business was restricted to matters presented by the presiding magistrate. The system of group voting was retained also, each century having a single vote, determined by the majority within the century. The centuries voted in a fixed order, and the vote of each was reported as soon as it had completed its polling. The eighteen equestrian centuries voted first; they were followed by the centuries of the first class; these by the centuries of the second class, and so on until a majority of the centuries had voted in favor of or against a measure or in favor of the number of candidates to be chosen at any election. Once a majority was reached, the voting ceased, and on many occasions the centuries of the lower classes were never called upon to express an opinion. This was true particularly whenever the equestrian centuries and those of the first class voted unanimously, for together they had ninety-eight votes, which was a majority of the total of one hundred and ninety-three. We have no means of ascertaining, however, how often these two groups voted in unison. Establishment of the Centuriate Assembly put the higher propertied classes in control of the voting in elections and legislation. This broke down the influence of the patrician clans exercised through the

Curiae and organized the citizen body strictly on the basis of property. In place of aristocratic control it set up a timocracy or rule of wealth in which the dominant part was played by that class which made the greatest contribution to the military in the latter part of the fifth and the first half of the fourth centuries B.C. The Curiate Assembly was not abolished. In addition to conferring the *imperium* on the consuls and praetors elect, it met under the presidency of the Pontifex Maximus to witness or confirm ceremonial acts that were mainly religious. By the close of the Republic, the function of this Assembly had become so purely formal that its meetings were attended only by thirty lictors who represented the Curiae.

III. Expansion of the Magistracy

CONSULAR TRIBUNATE.   The changes in the military system and the accompanying organization of the Centuriate Assembly reacted upon the magistracy. Shortly after the middle of the fifth century the two annual consuls were replaced with increasing regularity by boards of officials called military tribunes with consular power (*tribuni militum consulari potestate*). Between 444 and 427 (436–418) there were six boards of three tribunes; from 426 to 406 (417–402), three boards of three and seven of four; and from 405 to 367 (401–363) thirty-three boards which normally comprised six members, although the number in some is doubtful. The title *tribune* means tribal officer, and the military tribunes were the commanders of the levies from the respective tribes. Since these originally numbered 1,000 from each tribe, the title *military tribune* came to be used for the commanders of thousands even when the army was no longer organized on a tribal basis. It is in this sense that it appears to have been employed during the late fifth and early fourth centuries. Accordingly the military tribunes with consular power were simple magistrates who held the consular *imperium* and received a purely military title because at first the state needed more than two officials qualified for consular commands. Later, however, other reasons may have influenced the Senate in calling upon the Centuriate Assembly for so many years in succession to elect consular tribunes rather than a pair of consuls.[5]

CONSULSHIP RESTORED.   In 366 (362) the use of military tribunes with consular power was abandoned permanently. The dual consulship was restored, and for the future military tribunes appear only as

---

[5] One explanation of the origin of this tribunate offered in antiquity and still held in some quarters is that it was created to take the place of the consulship as an office to which plebeians might be admitted while they were still excluded from the regular presidency. Against this view, besides the existence of another explanation equally old which has been adopted above, it may be urged that although the military tribunate first appeared in 444 B.C. it was not until 40 years later that plebeians were elected to it. Further, plebeians appear in only six of the fifty-one colleges of military tribunes elected between 444 and 367.

legionary officers under the command of consuls or other magistrates. Six tribunes were assigned to each legion; and since the legion now numbered 4,200, the military tribune ceased to be a commander of 1,000 men.

PRAETORSHIP.   When the consulship was restored, the numerical weakness of this office was corrected by the establishment of a new magistracy, the praetorship. Its holder, the praetor, was elected annually by the Centuriate Assembly and took charge of civil jurisdiction, relieving the consuls of this responsibility. The praetor was regarded as a junior colleague of the consuls and exercised the *imperium*. Consequently he could take command of an army, convene the Senate or an assembly, and exercise the other consular functions.

CENSORSHIP.   An important step in the expansion of the magistracy was the creation of the censorship about 443 (435). This coincided closely with the beginnings of the use of property qualifications for military service and with the appearance of the consular tribunate. As their name indicates, the censors were originally officials for taking the census; and since in Rome the census was taken normally every five years, censors were elected only at the beginning of each new census period. The censors were two in number, and, unlike the other magistrates, they held office for eighteen months. They were chosen by the Centuriate Assembly but did not have the *imperium*. Their earliest duty was to register all citizens and their properties by tribes and to assign them to the appropriate classes and centuries as soldiers and as voters in the Centuriate Assembly. The development of this system of registration adequately explains the inauguration of the censorship, since neither consuls nor military tribunes could have performed the duties of censors in addition to their other obligations. At an early date, perhaps from the foundation of their office, the censors had charge of letting public contracts, and their assessments formed the basis for the collection of the property tax (*tributum*) in war time. By the end of the fourth century they had acquired the right to revise the list of the senators when they took the census. Since this involved an examination of the public and private conduct of senators, there arose that power which has survived in the modern conception of a censorship, namely, the supervision of morals. The loss of the right to enroll the Senate greatly diminished the influence of the consuls over that body.

QUAESTORSHIP.   In the early Republic the consuls appointed two officers called quaestors to act as their deputies in administering criminal justice. Not long after the middle of the fifth century the quaestors became magistrates and were elected by the people. In 421 their number was increased to four, of whom two served as public treasurers (*quaestores aerarii* or *urbani*). The other pair acted as assistants to the consuls; they accompanied the latter to war and performed the duties of quartermasters in charge of supplies and payment of troops.

AEDILESHIP.   Evidence for the growth of the city Rome and the increasing burden of municipal administration this entailed is found in the establishment of the aedileship, probably when the quaestorship became a magistracy.

Like the dictatorship, this office was of Latin origin, and its original function was the care of records and public money. It appears first as attached to the temple of Diana on the Aventine Hill, which once served as a shrine for the Latin League. By the middle of the fifth century this shrine had become the center of a plebeian movement against the patricians, and the aediles appear as assistants of the plebeian officials, the tribunes of the plebs. In the early fourth century they were associated with the temple of Ceres, the new center of plebeian activities. When they became state magistrates, they acted as superintendents of public works, as market commissioners, and as police magistrates. At first they were two in number and were elected from among the plebeians. In 366 (362), however, upon the restoration of the consulship, their number was increased to four by the addition of two "curule" aediles, so called because they could use the seat known as the curule chair, which had been a prerogative of the higher magistrates. For some time the curule aedileship was open only to patricians, but its duties were the same as those of the plebeian aediles.

PROMAGISTRACY. Roman magistrates were elected for one year only, and after 342 reelection to the same office could only be sought after ten years. This entailed some inconveniences, especially in the conduct of military operations, for when campaigns lasted longer than one year the consul in command had to give place to his successor when his own term of office expired. Thus the state was unable to use for a longer period men who had displayed special military capacity. The difficulty was eventually overcome by the prolongation, at the discretion of the Senate, of the command of a consul in the field for an indefinite period after the lapse of his consulship. The person whose office was thus extended was no longer a consul but acted "in the place of a consul" (*pro consule*). This was the origin of the promagistracy. It first appeared in the campaign at Naples in 327; and, although for a time rarely employed, its use eventually became very widespread and extended to other offices.

CHARACTERISTICS OF THE MAGISTRACY. By the close of the fourth century the Roman magistracy had attained the form it preserved until the end of the Republic. It consisted of a number of committees, each of which, with the exception of the quaestorship, had an independent sphere of action. They were the executive branch of the government, entrusted with enforcing the laws and carrying out the routine administration of the state in consultation with the Senate. Certain of them had military as well as civil authority. Among these committees there was a regularly established order of rank ascending as follows: quaestors, aediles, censors, praetors, consuls. Except for the censorship, which was regularly filled by ex-consuls, politicians usually advanced from one magistracy to another in this order. A distinctive feature of the committee system was the right of

any magistrate to veto the action of his colleague or colleagues. This applied
to the consulship as well as to the lower magistracies; but in order to avoid
too frequent use of veto, the consuls alternated each month in taking charge
of the administration when both were in the city, and when both were
with the army they held the chief command on alternate days. Magistrates
of higher rank enjoyed greater authority (*maior potestas*) than all those
who ranked below them and as a rule could forbid or annul the actions of
the latter. In this way the consuls, or the dictator, were able to exercise a
negative control over the activities of all other magistrates. The unity
which was given to the administration by this theory of *maior potestas*
was increased by the Senate, a council whose influence over the magistracy
grew as the consulate lost in power and independence through the creation
of new offices. All magistrates were said to have *potestas*, but only the
dictator, consuls, and praetor had *imperium*. Consequently, these latter
were the only ones who could exercise military command, summon the
people on their own authority to assemble for elective or legislative purposes, and try civil and criminal cases of more than trivial importance.
All magistrates, however, had the power to enforce their orders by the
arrest of disobedient persons. The great power and the relative freedom
of action enjoyed by the magistrates, who were immune to prosecution
while in office, are outstanding features of the constitution. The respect
for public authority which they implied is one of the characteristics of early
Roman society.

IV. Plebeian Struggle for Political Equality

CAUSES OF THE STRUGGLE.   The expansion of the magistracy and
the development of the Centuriate Assembly were accompanied by and
related to the persistent effort made by the plebeians to secure admission
to all the offices and privileges that originally were monopolized by the
patricians. Their demands were vigorously opposed by the latter, whose
position was sustained by tradition, by their control of the government,
by individual and class prestige, and by the support of their numerous
clients. Among the plebeians there was an ever-increasing number whose
fortunes ranked with those of the patricians and who refused to be excluded
from the government. They were enrolled in the equestrian centuries and
became plebeian leaders. A factor of greater importance, however, than
the presence of this element in determining the final outcome of the
struggle was the demand made upon the military resources of the state by
numerous foreign wars. Plebeian soldiers shared equally with patricians
in the dangers of war, and equality of political rights could not long be
withheld from them. As their services were essential, the patrician senators were farsighted enough to concede to their demands whenever a refusal would have led to civil war. It has been seen already how the

requirement of military service from the citizens on the basis of property qualifications led to the formation of an assembly in which voting power was distributed on the same principle. Though the formation of the Centuriate Assembly was regarded as a severe blow to the patrician aristocracy, however, it by no means gave adequate voice to the grievances of the poorer plebs. One of these was that the knowledge and custody of the customary civil and criminal law, of legal procedure, and also enforcement of the laws were all a monopoly of the patrician magistrates and priests, who naturally manipulated them to the advantage of their own class. In the later stages of the struggle, a great cause of discontent was the indebtedness of the poorer landholders, whose plots averaged only a few acres. This was caused in great part by their enforced absence from their lands upon military service, by the burden of the *tributum* or property tax levied for military purposes, and by their lack of capital with which to rent public land to make ends meet. Their condition was rendered the more intolerable because of the harsh laws of debt, which permitted the creditor to seize the debtor and to sell him into slavery.

Evidence that discontent was rife at Rome may be found in the tradition of three unsuccessful attempts to set up a tyranny, that is, to seize power by unconstitutional means, made by Spurius Cassius (478), Spurius Maelius (431), and Marcus Manlius (376), patricians who figure in later tradition as popular champions.

PLEBEIAN REVOLT. The first objectives of the plebs in their struggle to secure equality with the patricians were to provide themselves with officers to act as their spokesmen and to defend them against exploitation by the patricians; to organize a plebeian assembly for the regular election of such officers and for passing legislation in the interest of the plebs, and to force the patricians to make public the law in written form. This last goal was achieved first.

CODIFICATION OF THE LAW. In the middle of the fifth century B.C. the patricians, under pressure from the plebeians, and following the example set by the Greek city-states some two centuries earlier, drew up and published a code of law. There can be little doubt that this codification was influenced by the codes which had long been in use in the Greek cities of Italy with which the Romans had contact, and there is a not implausible tradition that a Roman commission was sent to Athens to study the laws of Solon.

The task of codifying the law was entrusted to ten magistrates called decemvirs who took the place of the consuls for the year 450 (443). According to later accounts, this commission had not completed its task at the end of a year and was succeeded by a second board of ten. Probably this second decemvirate is fictitious, and the work of the original commission seems to have been completed by the consuls of the following year. The code which was thus compiled was set up in public on twelve wooden tablets and for that reason was known as the Law of the Twelve Tables[6] Attempts have been made to attribute the code to much later dates, but even though its language may have been revised subsequently, there is no good reason to question the time of its original publication.

Only scattered quotations from the Twelve Tables have survived, but these, supplemented by references in later writers, suffice to give a general idea of the character and content of the code. It was in no sense a constitution but simply a compilation of the customary civil and criminal law, with rules for legal procedure and certain social regulations, as, for example, restrictions upon elaborate funeral rites. Though primitive in many respects, the code was simple and logically arranged, which qualified it to serve as the basis of a more highly developed legal system. It was held in great respect by Roman jurists of later centuries. The Twelve Tables sanctioned the arrest and imprisonment of insolvent debtors by their creditors and the right of the latter to sell them into slavery in default of other means of recovering the debt.[7] They also gave legal force to the patrician refusal to recognize intermarriage between the orders. In spite of these illiberal provisions, the publication of the code was advantageous to the plebeians, for the law was now known to all and not, as heretofore, only to patricians.

TRIBUNES OF THE PLEBS. The initial steps taken by the plebeians to provide themselves with spokesmen occurred in the first half of the fifth century, but they cannot be reconstructed with any degree of reliability owing to the meagre and contradictory character of the Roman tradition.[8] There is no doubt that a crisis developed about the middle of that century, which brought the state to the brink of civil war and resulted in an agreement between the two orders whereby the position of the plebeians within the state was improved notably. Important concessions were wrung from the patricians by the plebeian revolt, which, as the Romans believed, took the form of a secession of the plebs to their center on the Aventine Hill and a threat to form a new state for themselves. This may be substantially correct. Henceforth the plebeians elected annually ten officials of plebeian birth called Tribunes of the Plebs (*tribuni plebis*) in imitation of the military tribunes. The patricians recognized these tribunes as public officials but not as magistrates in the strict sense of the term, for they were elected by the plebeians alone. They also acknowledged the right of such a tribune to intervene on behalf of any person who sought his aid against unjust or oppressive acts of a patrician magistrate or private citizen, and

---

[6] This posting of the law implies some degree of literacy among the Romans.

[7] The Code specified that these debtors should be sold across the Tiber, i.e., not to a Roman or a Latin but in enemy territory. This implies that the whole of the right bank of the Tiber facing Roman territory was still in the hands of Rome's arch enemy, Veii.

[8] One Roman source placed the organization of the plebeian tribunate in 494 B.C. with two tribunes. Boards of four and five are reported also, but the names of these tribunes are suspect.

by uttering the word *veto* (I forbid) to stop such action. The tribune was able to make his veto effective since the plebs swore to treat as accursed and to execute without trial any person who disregarded the tribune's veto or violated the sanctity of his person. This is definite proof that in origin the tribunate was an unconstitutional, revolutionary office.

PLEBEIAN ASSEMBLY AND TRIBAL ASSEMBLY. Legal status was accorded also to the meeting of the plebeians under the presidency of their tribunes. This plebeian assembly met in the Roman Forum and comprised the citizens of the tribal districts, who recorded their votes tribe by tribe. The majority within each tribe determined how it should vote, and a simple majority of the tribes decided the action of the assembly as a whole. Although it cannot be said with certainty that the patricians were excluded from this assembly, constitutionally they regarded it as speaking for the plebs only and not for the whole state. Hence it was called the Council of Plebs (*concilium plebis*) and not the Tribal Assembly. Its resolutions, called plebiscites,[9] were binding on plebeians only; but, from the late fourth century at least, if the resolutions were approved by the Senate, they became valid for all Romans. In the course of the fourth century the consuls began to summon for legislative purposes an assembly that virtually duplicated the Council of the Plebs but was called the Tribal Assembly (*comitia tributa*) because it was presided over by a magistrate with *imperium* and was open to all citizens. It voted in the same way as the Council of the Plebs and its laws were subject to the veto power of the Senate. Although much more democratic than the Centuriate, the Tribal Assembly was by no means a radical body. Most of the citizens had the conservative outlook of a rural society, and in many of the tribes the patricians exercised great influence through the votes of their clients. Many modern students of Roman history maintain that from this time until the end of the Republic the distinction between Council of the Plebs and the Tribal Assembly was scrupulously preserved. The use of these terms by Roman historians, however, indicates that they came to be regarded as one institution whose functions depended upon whether the presiding officer was a tribune or a magistrate. The one or two passages which tend to support the view of two separate assemblies are late and appear to be the result of legalistic definition rather than actual custom. Naturally, the term Council of the Plebs continued in use for a long time, but that of Tribal Assembly seems to have replaced it in common parlance, and this usage will be followed here.

CANULEIAN MARRIAGE LAW. It will be recalled that the Law of the Twelve Tables affirmed the illegitimacy of marriages between patricians and plebeians. This was a mark of inferiority strongly resented by the plebs. At the same time it came to be a practical disadvantage

---

[9] From the opening formula *plebi scitum* (Resolved by the plebs).

to the patricians in view of their declining numbers, which made it desirable for them to contract marriages for their sons and daughters with the wealthier plebeian families. It is not surprising to find that this disability was removed by the Canuleian Marriage Law attributed to 445 (437).

PLEBS AND THE HIGHER MAGISTRACIES. The plebeians would not rest content with holding the quaestorship and aedileship, when the monopoly of the magistracies with *imperium* still gave the patricians control of army commands, of the administration of justice, and of public policy. Here the patricians tenaciously maintained their prerogatives throughout the whole of the fifth century. It was not until 400 (396) that plebeians were elected to the highest magistracy and then as military tribunes with consular power. In this and the following year, and again in 396 (392), if the traditional lists can be trusted, plebeians constituted a majority of the board of consular tribunes, then six in number. The explanation of this sudden but temporary domination of the military tribunate by plebeians is probably to be found in the contemporary military reforms, which gave greater voice to the plebeians in the Centuriate Assembly, and in the vicissitudes of the current war with Veii, which could have forced the patricians to acquiesce in the conferment of *imperium* upon plebeians of proven military capacity. After the conquest of Veii the patricians reasserted their control of the chief magistracy. On only three more occasions before 366 (362) were plebeians elected to the consular tribunate, and only once (379, when they had three out of six members) did they succeed in gaining more than one seat in the college.

The struggle for control of the chief magistracy is reflected in the tradition of a period of anarchy in Rome, that is, one for which no magistrates with *imperium* were recorded in the official list, presumably because those who held office did not obtain it constitutionally. How long this condition persisted is uncertain, although probably it did not exceed one year and the writers who made it of longer duration did so in order to fill in a gap in their chronology. At any rate, the anarchy must be placed between 375 and 370.

With the definitive restoration of the consulship in 366 (362) the right of the plebeians to hold that office was formally recognized, and one of the consuls of 366 was a plebeian. To the year 367 (363) tradition assigned several laws, called Licinian-Sextian from their authors, the plebeian tribunes Lucius Sextius (consul in 366) and Gaius Licinius. One of these is said to have prescribed that at least one consul in each year should be a plebeian. The rule was observed between 366 and 355, but between 355 and 342 there were seven occasions when both consuls were patricians. After 342, however, this does not seem to have occurred again, and some believed that a law passed at that date made it possible for both consuls to be plebeians but not patricians. Although this is possible, it was not until 172 that the consulship was held by two plebeians.

After their admission to the consulship the plebeians could not be barred from the other higher magistracies. They gained the dictatorship in 356, the censorship in 351, and the praetorship in 337. The curule aedileship was also opened to them and was held by patricians and plebeians in alternate years.

THE PLEBS AND THE SENATE.   Since the custom was early established that ex-consuls, and later ex-praetors, should be enrolled in the Senate, the opening of these offices to the plebs began to give the latter an ever-increasing representation in that body. As distinguished from the *patres* or patrician senators, the plebeians were called *conscripti,* "the enrolled," and this distinction was preserved in the official formula *patres conscripti* used in addressing the Senate. The fusion of leading plebeians with patricians in the Senate gave rise to a new oligarchy in the Roman state: the senatorial oligarchy or nobility (*nobilitas*) of officeholders. This consisted of a large group of influential patrician and plebeian families which, for some time at least, was continuously given new life by the accession of prominent plebeians who entered the Senate by way of the magistracies. From 366 to 265 about ninety consulships were held by members of thirty-six plebeian *gentes,* which may be considered in this way to have attained the rank of nobility. Thus the Senate, by opening its ranks to the leaders of the plebs, emerged from the struggle with prestige and influence increased rather than impaired.

CENSORSHIP OF APPIUS CLAUDIUS: 312 B.C.   One of the censors who entered office in 312 was the patrician Appius Claudius, who was responsible for the construction of the Via Appia and the Aqua Appia, Rome's first aqueduct. Apparently the program of Appius, who completely dominated his colleague, met with considerable opposition from the members of his own class on account of the expense involved, and he therefore sought to create a strong political clientele among the plebeians. Since the censors had recently received the authority to enroll the Senate, Appius took this opportunity of introducing many plebeians into that body, among them some sons of freedmen, that is, of emancipated slaves who had become Roman citizens. It was said that the consuls ignored the list prepared by Appius and summoned the Senate on the basis of the previous membership. Another measure attributed to Appius was the granting of permission to residents of the city to be enrolled in whatever tribe they might choose and to have their property registered wherever they might wish. This would enhance the voting power of the urban citizens, who would no longer be restricted to the four city tribes but could also be spread among the rural tribes. The censors of 304 are said to have restricted the city residents once more to the urban tribes. In spite of these rebuffs Appius continued for a long time as one of the most influential figures in public life, attaining the consulship twice and being also praetor and dictator.

A sequel to the censorship of Appius Claudius was the aedileship of

Gnaeus Flavius. Flavius was the son of a freedman and a clerk in the service of the curule aediles. Through the influence of Appius he was elected to the curule aedileship as the first Roman whose father had been a slave to obtain that office (304). To Flavius was attributed the publication of a handbook explaining procedure in the courts for the benefit of plaintiffs and defendants.

THE PLEBS AND THE PRIESTHOOD.   The last stronghold of patrician privilege was the priesthood. Until the close of the fourth century, the only religious office which had been opened to the plebeians was that of the board in charge of public sacred books, which also regulated the state religious ceremonies. In 368 (364) the membership of this board was increased from two to ten (called *decemviri sacris faciundis*), half of whom were plebeians. But in 300 the plebs gained access to the higher priesthoods by virtue of the Ogulnian Law, which increased the number of pontiffs by four and that of the augurs by five and required the new places in each college to be filled with plebeians. Henceforth it was impossible for the patricians to use religious law and practice to hamper plebeian political activity.

VALERIAN LAW ON APPEALS: 300 B.C.   One of the characteristic features of the early constitution was the power of magistrates with *imperium* to enforce their orders by various penalties, of which scourging and execution were the most severe. In the year 300 a Valerian Law restricted the magistrates' right of coercion by forbidding the execution or scourging of anyone who had appealed, presumably to an assembly as provided in the Law of the Twelve Tables. Similar Valerian Laws were assigned by Roman writers to the years 509 and 449, but if they are historic, it is difficult to see the necessity for the law of 300. In any case the right of appeal could only be exercised within the limits of the *pomerium* or possibly one mile beyond; it was not valid against the power of the magistrate outside these limits where military authority prevailed[10]

HORTENSIAN LAW: 287 B.C.   The end of the struggle between the orders came in 287 as the result of an economic crisis which had far-reaching political repercussions. Throughout the fourth century, the problem of debts owed by Roman peasants had become more and more acute, and tradition contains references to several attempts to alleviate their burdens. It is probable that overpopulation and soil deterioration in Latium had something to do with these conditions, but perhaps the chief cause of indebtedness at this time was the demand for military service made upon poorer landholders. The pay which these received was little more than enough to pay for their food, which they had to buy for themselves; and though they might share at times in the spoils of war, their frequent absence from their farms made it hard for them to raise crops to support

---

[10] The sphere in which the *imperium* was subject to appeal was called *domi* (at home), that in which it was unrestricted was known as *militiae* (on service).

their families or to supplement their harvests by wages earned as farm laborers. Tenant farmers were especially hard hit. Demands for relief followed the conclusion of the long Samnite Wars. The Senate, which represented the creditor class, repeatedly refused to approve remedial legislation proposed by the tribunes and passed in the Tribal Assembly. The obstinacy of the Senate forced the plebeians to take drastic action. The plebeian soldiers under arms marched off to the Janiculum Hill across the Tiber and threatened to secede from the Roman state.[11] In the face of this threat the Senate yielded and appointed Quintus Hortensius, a plebeian, as dictator to settle the controversy. He succeeded in alleviating the distress of the debtors, although exactly what his solution of the problem was is not known. He then passed the Hortensian Law, which provided that all future measures voted in the Tribal Assembly should become law without either previous or subsequent approval in the Senate.

THE CONSTITUTION AFTER 287 B.C. As a result of the Hortensian Law the Tribal Assembly acquired greater legislative independence than the Assembly of the Centuries. It tended to become the legislative assembly *par excellence*, while the Assembly of the Centuries remained the senior elective assembly. For legislative purposes the Tribal Assembly could be convened by a magistrate with *imperium* or by a tribune; for the election of the plebeian tribunes and aediles it had to be summoned by a tribune; while to elect the quaestors, curule aediles, and, eventually, twenty-four military tribunes for the annual levy, it must be called together by a magistrate. For all purposes the Assembly of the Centuries had to be convened and presided over by a magistrate. It elected the consuls, praetors, and censors. It must be remembered that these were both primary assemblies, that each comprised the whole body of Roman citizens, but that they differed in organization. As we have seen, centuries composed of the wealthy outnumbered those of the poor in the Centuriate Assembly. The Tribal Assembly was more democratic only insofar as each tribe contained citizens of every class, all of whose votes carried equal weight within the tribe.

INCREASED IMPORTANCE OF THE TRIBUNATE. The influence of the tribunes was greatly enhanced by the Hortensian Law, as well as by various privileges which they had already acquired by 287 or shortly thereafter. The more important were the right to sit in the Senate, to address and even to convene that body, and the right to prosecute any magistrate before the Tribal Assembly. The first was an extension of the tribunician right of veto, whereby this invalidated a proposal under discussion in the Senate to avoid waiting for a magistrate's attempt to execute it after it had become law or a senatorial decree. To permit the tribunes to veto at this stage, they had to be allowed to hear the debates in the Senate. At first they did so from their bench, which they set at the door of the meeting

---

[11] Roman tradition records five such secessions. Of these, the two that seem authentic are those of c. 450 and 287 B.C.

place, but finally they were permitted to enter the council hall itself. The power of prosecution made the tribunes the guardians of the state against any misconduct on the part of a magistrate. From this time on the tribunes had practically the status of magistrates.

The struggle of the orders left its mark on the Roman constitution in providing Rome with a double set of government organs. The tribunate and Assembly of the Tribes arose as purely plebeian institutions, but they came to be incorporated in the organization of the state along with the magistracies and the assemblies, which had always been institutions of the whole Roman people.

After 287 all political distinctions between patricians and plebeians disappeared. Although social prestige still clung to the old patrician families, intermarriage with plebeians weakened even this distinction, and the sole remnants of the former patrician prerogatives were exclusive rights to certain of the older priesthoods of no political significance and to the curule aedileship in alternate years. In form, at least, the constitution was a democracy with sovereign power vested in the popular assemblies. In practice the coalition of leading plebeian families with patricians largely nullified the power of the assemblies and gave to the government a decidedly oligarchic character. This oligarchy was itself split up into factions based on various *gentes* that competed for the important magistracies and for the conduct of public policy. Details of the operation and significance of factional politics will be reserved for a later chapter.

V. Roman Military System

Upon the history of no people has the character of its military institutions exercised a more profound effect than that of Rome. The Roman military system rested upon the universal obligation of citizens to render military service, but the degree to which this obligation was enforced varied greatly at different periods. For the mobilization of manpower was dependent upon the type of equipment, methods of fighting, and organization of tactical units in vogue at various times, as well as upon the ability of the state to equip its troops and the strength of the martial spirit of the people.

ARMY OF THE MONARCHY AND EARLY REPUBLIC.   There has been occasion already to refer to various stages in the development of the Roman military system and their relation to contemporary political conditions. On the basis of archaeological evidence supported by tradition, the army of the regal period has been described as similar to that of the neighboring Etruscan cities and resembling in general the early Greek armies depicted in the Homeric poems. It was the levy (*legio*) called out by tribes and curies, but the leading role was played by the nobility, who were superior in equipment and training to the poorer citizens. The nobles rode to battle in chariots or on horseback and hence were known as *celeres* (mobile troops) or *equites* (horsemen), although they usually fought on foot. The rest of the citizens served as ordinary infantry and were called *pedites* (foot-soldiers). The armies of the early Republic were of the same type, except that the use of chariots had been given up.

ORGANIZATION OF THE PHALANX.   Under Greek influence in the latter part of the fifth century the Romans adopted the system of recruitment on the basis of property and remodeled their tactical organization so as to make better use of their infantry. At first one and eventually three higher property classes supplied heavy-armed infantry; two lower property classes furnished light troops. On the battlefield the centuries or companies of heavy infantry were united in the phalanx.[12] From this time the strength of the Roman army rested in its infantry, and cavalry became less important. The relation of this new system of recruitment and tactical organization to the creation of the censorship and the formation of the Centuriate Assembly has been discussed.

The introduction of pay for troops in the field at the time of the siege of Veii both lessened to same degree the economic burden of service upon the poorer soldiers and enabled the Romans to undertake campaigns of longer duration, even such as involved winter operations.

MANIPULAR LEGION.   How long the phalanx organization was maintained is not known, except that it did not survive the Samnite wars. In its place appeared the legionary formation, in which the largest units were the legions of about 4,200 infantry, divided into maniples of 120 (or 60) men, each capable of maneuvering independently.[13] This arrangement allowed increased flexibility of movement in broken country and the adoption of the *pilum*, or javelin, as a missile weapon. Both the javelin and the *scutum*, or oblong shield, were typical Samnite weapons, and the Romans had a tradition that they had adopted them in imitation of the Samnites. While reorganizing their infantry, the Romans strengthened the *equites* and developed them into a more efficient cavalry force, although they came to rely more and more upon the mounted troops of their federate allies.

Apparently property qualifications no longer counted for much in the army organization, as the men now were assigned to their places in the ranks on the basis of age and experience, and the state furnished the necessary weapons to those who did not provide their own. By the third century all able-bodied men holding property valued at 4,000 asses[14] were regularly called upon for military service. The others were liable to naval service, but only in emergencies were they enrolled in the legions. Ordi-

[12] I.e., an unbroken line of infantry several ranks deep.

[13] For battle, the legion was drawn up in three separate lines with intervals between the maniples in each.

[14] At this time the *as* was probably reckoned as a pound of bronze (see below, p. 94).

narily the service amounted to sixteen campaigns in the infantry and ten in the cavalry. The field army was raised from those between seventeen and forty-six years of age; those forty-six and over were liable only for garrison duty in the city. The regular annual levy consisted of four legions, besides 1,800 cavalry. This number could be increased, and the Roman forces in the field were supplemented by at least an equal number in the contingents from the Italian allies.

ROMAN DISCIPLINE.   The Roman army was thus a national levy, a militia. It was commanded by the consuls, the annually elected presidents of the state. Yet it avoided the characteristic weakness of militia troops, for the frequency of wars and the length of the period of liability for service assured the presence of many veterans in each levy and maintained a high standard of military efficiency. The consuls, if not always good generals, were generally experienced soldiers, for a record of ten campaigns was required of the candidate for public office. Their subordinates, the military tribunes, were also veterans, some having seen five and others ten years of service. The factor that contributed above all else to the success of the Roman armies was their iron discipline. The consular *imperium* gave its holder absolute power over the lives of soldiers in the field, and death was the penalty for neglect of duty, disobedience, or cowardice. The most striking proof of the discipline of the Roman armies is that after every march they were required to construct a fortified camp, laid out according to fixed rules and protected by a ditch, a wall of earth, and a palisade for which they carried the stakes. No matter how strenuous their labors had been, they never neglected this task, in striking contrast to the Greek citizen armies, which could not be induced to construct such works. The fortified camp rendered the Romans safe from surprise attacks, allowed them to choose their own time for joining battle, and gave them a secure refuge after a defeat. It played a very large part in the operations of their armies, especially such as were conducted in hostile territory. Characterized as it was by the same subordination of the individual to the common interest and respect for public authority that were often marked features of Rome's political life, her military system proved definitely superior to that of the other peoples of Italy and was the chief single factor in her conquest of the peninsula.

CHAPTER 7

SOCIETY AND RELIGION
IN THE EARLY REPUBLIC

I. Social and Economic Life

THE HOUSEHOLD. The cornerstone of the Roman social structure was the household (*familia*). The state was an association of households, and it was the individual's position in a household that determined his status in the community. The Roman household was a larger unit than our family. It comprised the father (*pater familias*), his wife, his sons with their wives and children, if they had such, his unmarried daughters, and the household slaves.

PATRIA POTESTAS. The *pater familias* possessed authority over all other members of the household. His power over the free members was called *patria potestas* (paternal authority), over the slaves it was *dominium* (lordship). This paternal authority was in theory unrestricted and gave the father the right to inflict the death penalty upon those under his power. In practice, however, the exercise of the *patria potestas* was limited by custom and by the habit of consulting the older male members of the household before any important action. There is a strong parallel between the power of the *pater familias* over his dependents and that of the kings, and the later magistrates, over the citizens.

The household estate (*res familiaris*) was administered by the head of the household. At the death of a *pater familias* his sons in turn became the head of *familiae*, dividing the estate. The mother and unmarried daughters, if surviving, now passed into the power of a son or the next nearest male relative of the deceased. Although the Roman women were thus continually in the position of wards, they nevertheless took a prominent part in the life of the household and were not restricted and secluded like the women of Athens and the Greek cities of Asia. Membership in the household was reckoned only through male descent, for daughters when they married passed out of their own *familia* into that to which their husbands belonged.

In spite of the apparent severity of family discipline, there is ample evidence that Roman domestic life not only permitted but fostered the development of genuinely affectionate relations between parents and children.

EDUCATION. There was no system of public education, and such instruction as was given to the Roman youth was regularly imparted by fathers to their sons. It consisted of training in sports, such as running, swimming, boxing, wrestling, and the use of arms; of instruction in habits of cleanliness and good conduct; of practical training in farming; in a knowledge of the traditions of the state and the legends of the Roman heroes; and in an acquaintance with the conduct of public business through attendance at places where this was transacted. Naturally, the quality and scope of such training varied according to the social and economic status of each household.

At the age of eighteen the young Roman entered upon a new relation to the state. He was now liable to military service and qualified to attend the public assemblies. In these respects he was emancipated from the paternal authority. If he subsequently was elected to a magistracy, his father obeyed him like any other citizen, although he might make use of his *patria potestas* to influence his son's action in political matters.

The discipline and respect for authority acquired in the family were carried by the Roman into his public relations, and aroused in him a sense of obligation to the interests of the state that was perhaps the strongest quality in the Roman character. It was supplemented by the characteristic Roman seriousness (*gravitas*), developed under the stress of the long struggle for existence waged by the early Roman state. For the Romans the highest virtue was piety (*pietas*), which meant the dutiful performance of all one's obligations, to the gods, to one's kinsmen, and to the state. It was toward the state in particular that a Roman was expected to exhibit loyalty and devotion. Friends, relatives, life itself, must all be sacrificed for the good of the state. There can be no doubt about the importance of such values to Roman life. Later generations of Romans looked back to the lives of statesmen and generals of this period to find examples of patriotism worthy of imitation. These included Brutus the Elder, traditionally one of the first consuls, who had his own sons executed for treason; the Decii, who in three successive generations were said to have deliberately sacrificed their lives to save Roman armies; Manlius Torquatus, the consul who executed his son for a breach of military discipline; Manius Curius, who preferred poverty to wealth won by betraying his country. Even if such stories preserve kernels of historic truth, they represented a highly idealized and romanticized notion of the "good old days" thought up by Romans of the third and second centuries B.C. to furnish a contrast with the alleged moral decline of their own epoch. One may justly doubt whether early Roman aristocrats lived up very frequently to such self-effacing patriotic standards, despite their respect for authority.

Although the Romans were a serious, hardheaded, practical people, it must not be thought that Roman life was lacking in opportunities for relaxation and enjoyment. The festivals, public and private, were occasions of entertainment and merrymaking. This is true in particular of the "Great Games" celebrated after the harvest and of the Saturnalia at the end of the winter sowing in December.

RESPECT FOR TRADITION. Reference has already been made to the conservatism of the Romans and to how this characteristic was affected by their religious beliefs. It was further strengthened by the respect paid to parental authority and by the absence of intellectual training. In public affairs this conservatism was shown by the influence of ancestral custom—the *mos maiorum*. In the Roman government this became a very potent factor, since the Roman constitution was not a single comprehensive document but consisted of a number of separate enactments supplemented by custom and precedent and so interpreted. The importance of Roman conservatism and respect for the *mos maiorum* may be seen especially in several important concepts loaded with a meaning only palely reflected in their obvious English cognates and basic to Roman values for centuries. These included *dignitas*, that quality uniquely distinguishing great men who had served the state well, a prestige whose attainment gave meaning to the lives of senatorial statesmen; *auctoritas*, the main corollary to *dignitas*, a quasi-legal quality which demanded that the Romans follow the advice of elder statesmen by virtue of their character, station, and acknowledged superiority in public life; and *libertas*, freedom not to challenge or change the established order, but rather to do what laws and the *mos maiorum* allowed. These attitudes go a long way toward explaining why democratic development at Rome was to be abortive. The Roman public tended not to question leadership and to be content with a society which gave and demanded unequal privileges and responsibilities, so long as *libertas* guaranteed at least a minimum of personal rights.

HOUSEHOLD LIFE. In this period Roman household architecture shows but a slight advance from prehistoric times. The main part of each house was a large hall or room with an open hearth. This room, from its smoke-blackened appearance, was called the *atrium*. The *atrium* was the center of domestic life and served as a common work, reception, and dining room for the master and his servants. Food was simple, the main item in the daily menu being cakes or porridge of wheat or oatmeal. This was supplemented by beans and other vegetables. Bread was a later addition. Meat was not a staple article of diet but was enjoyed upon occasions of festival and sacrifice. For fruits there were pears, apples, grapes, and figs, while olive oil took the place of butter. Wine, usually mixed with water, was the regular beverage. As far as possible each household was self-sufficient. The farm and pastures provided food and drink, and clothing was largely homemade. Extras could be secured by barter in the markets which were held every ninth day. In Rome, where there was a large landless population which could not furnish its own necessities, the cattle and vegetable markets were of great importance. Here also flourished the craftsmen and shopkeepers who provided manufactured articles of necessity or luxury.

ECONOMIC CONDITIONS. Until the second half of the third century B.C. the Romans were, apart from the city plebs, almost exclusively a stock-raising and agricultural people. Until the fourth century they were

cut off from access to the mouth of the Tiber by the territories of Veii
north of the river and of Lavinium to the south, so that their contacts with
Carthaginian or Greek traders previous to that time were necessarily indirect, coming through Etruscan and other Latin cities. The one large
scale commercial enterprise in which they participated from the fifth century was the salt trade. Salt was brought from the salt pans north of the
lower Tiber by Veientine traders up the right bank as far as Rome. There
it was brought across to the left bank and transported by Roman merchants
across Roman territory and up the Tiber valley by way of the Via Salaria,
"Salt Road" (see map, p. 36), into the Sabine hill country. After the
fall of Veii the Romans took over the production as well as the distribution
of the salt.

The indifference of the Roman government to overseas commerce is well
illustrated by the texts of two treaties with Carthage which have come
down to us. The earlier of these was attributed to 509, but both probably
belong to the late fourth century when Rome controlled access to the towns
of Latium. By these treaties Carthaginians enjoyed free access to Latium,
whereas Romans and their allies were restricted to a limited number of
Carthaginian ports.

The Law of the Twelve Tables presents a picture of a society primarily
agrarian in character. Not only was there private ownership of land, but
the rights and obligations of landholders were clearly understood and
enforced. By contrast, the law of contract was in a very undeveloped state.
The laws regulating the rates of interest also reflected the view of an
agrarian people. By the Twelve Tables the annual rate was fixed at $8\frac{1}{3}$
percent, and a usurer who exceeded this limit was liable to fourfold
damages, whereas a thief was obliged to restore only twice the value of
the stolen property. The same rate was said to have been re-established in
357, apparently owing to neglect of the older law, and ten years later it
was reduced to $4\frac{1}{6}$ percent. In 342, apparently, all loans at interest were
forbidden, but this restriction did not long remain in force. Enslavement
for debt and imprisonment of a debtor by his creditor, which had been
permitted by the Twelve Tables, were abolished in 326. This measure was
a great relief to the poorer citizens but must have been regarded as a severe
blow by the creditor class.

Still another proof of Roman indifference to commercial activities is
found in the slowness which the government showed in developing a
system of coinage. With the expansion of Roman territory, the internal
market inevitably took on considerable importance, and it can hardly be
doubted that the greater portion of the city plebs were merchants, shopkeepers, and artisans. The external trade of Rome was carried on by
foreigners. It was the agrarian and not the commercial and industrial
class that profited most from the Roman conquests in Italy. With the
founding of colonies and the opening up of large sections of public land
for individual settlement, the number of landholders increased greatly,

and the oligarchy, which held aloof from mercantile pursuits, leased large sections of the public land for purposes of cultivation or stock raising. As a result of this practice the senatorial order gradually developed into a class of agricultural capitalists. If the Licinian-Sextian law, placing a limit on the size of holdings of public land, really was passed in 367 (363), as some Roman writers believed, it would seem that agricultural capitalism had become a menace before the middle of the fourth century. The size of the holdings permitted by this law (500 *iugera* or about 310 acres) seem wholly out of proportion to the limited extent of the Roman public land at that time, and this and other reasons make it extremely doubtful that it should be assigned to so early a date.

Slavery was a well-established institution but does not yet seem to have been economically important. Most of the slaves were prisoners of war who had not been exchanged for Roman captives or ransomed by their own state. As the early wars were waged chiefly with neighboring Italian peoples, these slaves were of the same general stock as the Romans. It is not surprising, then, that when a slave was set free with proper formalities he was admitted to Roman citizenship. These *liberti*, as they were called, became clients of their former masters, although the old hereditary client-age had disappeared by the third century and a much looser relationship had taken its place, one in which most of the client's obligations to his patron were based on some form of contract. Freedmen citizens were not eligible for public office, but this restriction did not apply to their descendants.[1]

DEVELOPMENT OF A SYSTEM OF COINAGE.   The lack of interest in commercial activities displayed by the governing class in the early Republic was the chief reason the Romans were so slow in issuing a coinage of their own, although they were in contact directly or indirectly with Etruscans, Greeks, and Carthaginians, all of whom had their own systems of coinage. The Romans made use of more primitive standards of value in public and private business transactions. Their word for money, *pecunia*,[2] derives from a time when they reckoned values in cattle or sheep, a practice common to other pastoral and agricultural peoples on a similar cultural level. During the fifth century this practice was still in use but was giving way to the use of bronze as a common standard of value. This bronze was current in lumps or bars which could be broken into pieces of varying weight (*aes rude*). Since the bronze lacked any mark that would guarantee its weight and purity, it had to be weighed at each transaction. The standard unit of weight was the Roman pound of twelve ounces. In the latter part of the fifth century a law fixed the value of one ox or ten sheep as 100 pounds of bronze in payment of fines. This must have corresponded closely to the current market price.

Until the close of the Samnite Wars (290) the Romans got along

---

[1] See p. 84. In public law *liberti* were called *libertini*.
[2] From the Latin *pecus*, a flock or herd.

without any coinage of their own, although their ally, the Greek city of Naples, seems to have issued bronze coins with a Greek inscription indicating affiliation with Rome (ca. 327). Early in the third century, however, Rome put into circulation bronze bars weighing about six pounds and marked with designs on two sides that indicated a Roman origin and probably served as marks of weight and purity. Possibly their appearance should be connected with the appointment of Rome's first mint masters, traditionally ascribed to 289. These bars called *aes signatum* continued in use until they yielded to the competition of true coins. Most contemporary students of Roman numismatics are now agreed that the earliest Roman coins were issued in 269 in both silver and bronze. The standard silver coin was a two-drachm[3] piece worth ten pounds of bronze. The standard bronze coin was an *as* weighing one pound (*aes libralis* or *grave*). There were also smaller bronze coins worth fractions of the *as*. This system of coinage lasted without modification until ca. 235.

BACKGROUND OF ROMAN LITERATURE.   Although the art of writing was introduced into Rome through Etruria as early as the sixth century B.C., it can hardly be said that the Romans had developed a literature even by the time of the unification of Italy under their domination. In this they resembled their closest neighbors, the Etruscans and Oscan-speaking Sabellians. Even at this early period, however, one can detect certain features of Roman writing which were to remain basic throughout its development and which differentiated it from its Greek counterpart. Unlike prose, the writing of poetry in early Rome never really attained the high degree of respectability it enjoyed among the Hellenes, and there was not even a word for "poet" native to the Roman vocabulary. Poetry, although recognized as decorative, was not central to public life, and the broadly based support of and interest in poetic literature, apparent in the best periods of Greek history, were almost totally absent. The Romans were always conscious of their literary inferiority to the Greeks and borrowed or adapted Hellenic forms and themes to serve their own artistic purposes, which tended to be practical and nationalistic rather than disinterestedly aesthetic.

It is characteristic that, although many things were committed to writing at Rome at an early date, they were technical or professional rather than artistic in character. Among them were public documents and records of various sorts, such as laws, treaties, lists of magistrates, commentaries of the consuls, census lists, and the annual notices of important events compiled by the pontiffs. There were also religious works, including ritual ordinances, the books of the pontiffs and augurs, and religious hymns. Of a different character were the inscriptions placed below the wax masks of family ancestors in the houses of the nobles, the funeral orations held

---

[3] Two drachms or drams = ¼ ounce.

in their honor, and songs sung to celebrate their exploits. Drama was foreshadowed by the presentation of Etruscan stage performances and Oscan farces (*fabulae Atellanae*) in Rome in the fourth century B.C. on the occasion of public festivals. But the former were limited to dancing and music, and the latter consisted chiefly of coarsely humorous improvisations. There were also crude forms of popular versification, the so-called Fescennine and Saturnian verses, of a mocking and joking character, composed to be sung at weddings and in triumphal processions. About the beginning of the third century Greek influences began to affect the development of literary forms. Greek meters were adopted in popular verse, and the first Roman book of a literary character, the *Sententiae* (*Proverbs*) of Appius Claudius the Censor, was composed in verse on a Greek model. The same writer published a speech he had delivered before the Senate in 279, opposing the conclusion of a peace treaty with King Pyrrhus.

LEGAL PROGRESS. For the period under consideration the Law of the Twelve Tables remained the law of the state, with only slight modifications introduced by statutes or interpretations. Primitive though it was, this code shows that the Romans had already made considerable progress in the development of private law. The separation between law and religion was almost complete, and the right of a person who had been wronged to take private vengeance upon the wrongdoer had been superseded by the state regulation of the penalties to be paid by the guilty party. Self-help had not entirely disappeared, however, and in private suits the plaintiff was authorized personally to bring the defendant before the magistrate or to arrest him if he was a defaulting debtor. As might be expected in a community where many citizens were illiterate the spoken words of a contract attested by witnesses (and not a written copy) were given legal validity. One great weakness in the code was the limited means provided for defence of rights and enforcement of obligations. A remedy was found in the development of additional forms of prosecution or "actions at law" (*legis actiones*), published, as has been noted, by Gnaeus Flavius about 304. In these actions both parties had to use set phrases, and the slightest verbal error caused the one who made the mistake to lose his suit.

II. Religious Beliefs and Practices

ROMAN CONCEPTIONS OF DEITY. By the opening of the republican period Roman religion was a composite of beliefs and ceremonies reflecting past political and cultural experience. The basic stratum was what we may call the Roman element—that is, religious ideas which the Romans held in common with the Latins and other closely related Italic peoples. As early as the sixth century this element was overlaid and permeated with influences derived from Etruscans and Greeks.

Although traces of a belief in magic and of the worship of natural objects and animals or of gods conceived in animal form survived from earlier stages in Roman religious experience, the basis of specifically Roman religious ideas is found in "animism." Animism is the belief in a large number of spiritual beings more powerful than man who reveal themselves in the phenomena and processes of the natural world. These spirits were thought of as incalculable, impersonal forces, and the power exhibited by any of them was called *numen* (plural *numina*). In time, such *numina* came to be thought of as emanating from divinities who were regarded as personalities with definite characteristics and names. These were the "gods," *dei*, who belong to the more advanced stage of religious development called "deism."

Since the primitive Roman gods developed from the spirits of an earlier age, we can understand why for a long time the Romans worshipped them without images or temples. Each god, however, was regarded usually as residing in a certain locality, and there only could his worship be carried on. These early gods lacked human attributes, their power was admitted, but they inspired no personal devotion. Until influenced by religious ideas originating among peoples at a higher culture level, the Romans did not develop any unified and coordinated view of the divine powers or their relation to man and the universe, nor created a body of religious myths. Roman theology consisted almost entirely of ideas about individual gods and their special powers and ceremonial acts to avert their ill will or obtain their favor.

IMPORTANCE OF RITUAL. While recognizing their dependence upon divine powers, the Romans considered their interrelationship in the nature of a contract. If man observed the proper ritual in his worship, the god was bound to act propitiously; if the god granted man's desire, he must be rewarded with an offering. If man failed in his duty, the god punished him; if the god refused to listen, man was not bound to continue his worship. Thus Roman religion consisted essentially in the performance of ritual, wherein the correctness of the performance was the chief factor. This is illustrated by the use of the Latin word *religio* (religion). At first the term seems to have meant the general feeling of fear experienced by men in the presence of natural phenomena they did not understand. Then it came to mean the obligation to perform certain acts suggested by this feeling of awe, that is, religious duties.

Since the power of the gods could affect the community as well as the individual, it was necessary for the state to observe its obligations toward them with the same scrupulous care as did individual citizens. Knowledge of these obligations and their performance constituted the sacred law of Rome, which became a very important part of public law. This sacred law was guarded by the priesthood, and here we have the source of the power of the pontiffs. The pontiffs not only preserved the sacred traditions and customs, but they also added to them by interpretation and the establishment of new precedents. The pontiffs themselves performed or supervised the performance of all public acts of a purely religious nature and likewise prescribed the ritual to be observed by the magistrate in initiating public political acts.

The power of the augurs rested upon the belief that the gods issued their warnings to men through natural signs and that it was possible to discover the attitude of the gods towards any contemplated human action by observing natural phenomena. Insofar as the state was concerned, the augurs were the guardians of the science of the interpretation of such signs or auspices. The magistrate initiating any important public act had to take the auspices, and if the augurs declared any flaw therein or held that any unfavorable omen had occurred during the performance of the said act, they could suspend the magistrate's action or render it invalid.

Roman priests were not intermediaries between the individual Roman and his gods but rather officers in charge of one branch of the public administration. They were responsible for the due observance of the public religious acts, just as the head of the household supervised the performance of the family cult. Thus Roman religion was essentially social in character and marked by an absence of individualism. Prophecy and private divination were discouraged.

CULT OF THE HOUSEHOLD. It is in the cult of the household that the true Roman religious ideas are best seen. The chief divinities of the household were Janus, the spirit of the doorway; Vesta, the spirit of the hearth; the Penates, the guardian spirits of the store-chamber; the Lar Familiaris, which may be regarded as the spirit of the cultivated land transplanted within the house to guard the family fortune; and the Genius, originally conceived as the male procreative force, especially that of the head of the household, which only at a later date was regarded as his spiritual double. The corresponding female quality, the Juno, was quickly anthropomorphized and, as the like-named goddess, became part of the Capitoline triad.[4] Besides these powers there were many others which were considered to be in control of the manifold aspects of the life of the household and its individual members, including birth, marriage, and death. Although the *pater familias* may be regarded as its priest, the worship of certain powers revered within the house was carried out by his wife and daughters.

The historic Romans maintained the two burial rites of inhumation and cremation. Under Greek and Etruscan influences, they came to believe that the spirits of the deceased went down to the underworld, to the realm of the gods below (*di inferi*). Thence, at certain times of the year, they returned to visit the earth, and upon these occasions there were celebrated the festivals of commemoration and propitiation, which served to keep

---

[4] See below, p. 98.

alive the memory of the ancestors and to ward off any baneful influences these might otherwise exercise upon the fortunes of their descendants.

CULT OF THE FARM. As early Rome was essentially a farming community, most of its divinities and festivals had to do with the various phases of agricultural life. Festivals of the sowing, the harvest, the vineyard, and the like, were annually celebrated in common, at fixed seasons, by the households of the various *pagi*.

STATE CULT. Our earliest knowledge of the public or state cult of Rome is derived from the calendar of the annually recurring public festivals, which in its earliest form dates from about 500 B.C. At this stage the state religion was that of an essentially agricultural community and consisted mainly in the performance of certain rites of the household and of the farm by or for the people as a whole. The state cults of Vesta and the Penates, as well as the festival of the Ambarvalia, the annual solemn purification of the fields, were of this nature. The state religion also included the worship of divinities whose personalities and powers were conceived more distinctly than those venerated in the house and in the fields. Some of these had originally been the gods of certain clans (*gentes*) whose cults had been taken over by the state. Chief among the state gods originally were the triad, Mars, Jupiter, and Quirinus. By the time of the dedication of the temple of Jupiter on the Capitoline Hill (509) these had given way to a new triad—Jupiter, Juno, and Minerva. Jupiter Optimus Maximus, called also Capitolinus from his place of worship, was originally a sky god but, acquiring other attributes, was finally revered as the chief protecting divinity of the state. Juno was the female counterpart of Jupiter and was the great patron goddess of women. Minerva, as we have seen, was the patroness of craftsmen. Mars, originally a god of agriculture as well as of war, became in the state cult of the Republic essentially the patron deity of warlike, "martial," activities and gave his name to the military training ground of Rome, the *Campus Martius* or Field of Mars.

FOREIGN INFLUENCES. The earliest calendar of state festivals included the worship of foreign gods whose cult had been adopted officially by the community. Some of these are obviously Etruscan; others, though partly disguised by Etruscan and Latin names, belong to the earliest circle of the gods of Greece. Such were Ceres, the Greek Demeter, and Liber, the Greek Dionysos, both earth deities closely connected with agriculture. In the latter part of the sixth century, under the influence of the Etruscan kings, there was a fresh influx of Greek divinities drawn from the ranks of the Homeric gods. Among these were Apollo, Minerva = Athena, and Diana = Artemis. Greek religious influence was fostered greatly by the acquisition of the Sibylline Books, a collection of oracles brought from Cumae to Rome toward the close of the regal period, placed under the care of a priestly commission, and consulted by the pontiffs in times of public emergency. To the Etruscans the Romans owed the introduction of temples and statues in divine worship, although here the Etruscans themselves were probably indebted to the Greeks. Since association of the cults of Juno and Minerva with that of Jupiter originated in Etruria, it was natural that the temple of these gods, begun by the last of the Roman kings but dedicated at the beginning of the Republic, should have been built in Etruscan style and decorated with the work of Etruscan artists. Greek artists, however, were called in to adorn the temple on the Aventine, erected in 493 in accordance with a Sibylline oracle, for the cult of Ceres, Liber, and Libera, that is, the Greek Demeter, Dionysos, and Kore. This marks the beginning of the predominance of Greek influences in religious art and architecture. Also built in the fifth century were temples for the worship of other Greek gods established at an earlier date; for Mercury (= Hermes) in 495, for Castor in 484, and somewhat belatedly for Apollo in 431 B.C. Thus, from the beginning of the fifth century and at least in its external aspects, Roman religious life presented a synthesis of Greek, Etruscan, and native elements. With the adoption of Greek sculptural forms for Roman gods came the acceptance of Greek mythology, which served to enrich the growing body of Roman religious ideas. Roman deities came to be identified with their closest Greek equivalents and to acquire the corresponding myths and forms of artistic representation.

Even later Etruscan and Greek rites continued to be introduced. After the capture of Veii the cult of Juno Regina practiced in that city was brought to Rome in 392 and worshipped with a Greek ritual. In 291 a new Greek cult was established officially at Rome with the erection of a temple to Aesculapius (Asklepios), the god of healing, whose worship was introduced directly from Epidaurus in Greece. Here again was the influence of the Sibylline books, which were said to have recommended this step as the means of checking a pestilence then raging in Rome.

RELIGION AND MORALITY. From the foregoing sketch it will be seen that Roman religion did not exert profound moral or inspirational influences. The early Romans asked their gods to grant them material rather than spiritual, blessings, to grant them health and wealth rather than virtue. Its hold upon the people was chiefly due to the fact that it symbolized the unity of the groups whose members participated in the same worship, i.e., the unity of the family and the unity of the state. Nevertheless, the idea of obligation inherent in the Roman conception of the relation between gods and men and the stress laid upon the exact performance of ritual inevitably developed among the Romans a strong sense of duty, a moral factor of considerable value; and the power of precedent and tradition in their religion helped to develop and strengthen the conservatism so characteristic of the Roman people.

CHAPTER 8

CONQUEST OF THE MEDITERRANEAN. FIRST PHASE—THE STRUGGLE WITH CARTHAGE: 264–201 B.C.

For the history of Roman expansion in the Mediterranean World during the period from 264 to 133 B.C. there is a sound chronology and an historical tradition which is both detailed and, in the main, dependable. Roman historical writing began about the close of the third century and from that time steadily increased in volume along with the development of literary taste and historical interest among educated classes in Rome. Not content with presenting annalistic narratives of the more remote past from the scanty materials at their disposal, Roman writers composed histories of their own times, for which they had more abundant and reliable information. Contemporary Greek historians also devoted considerable attention to Rome, particularly in its relation to the Greek world. Unfortunately for us, the works of most of the writers of this period have been lost, but the substance of their contributions has been preserved by historians of later date. The only one of the earlier writers whose work has survived to any considerable degree in its original form is the Greek Polybius, who was the foremost historian of his age. Brought to Rome as a political exile from Achaea in 167, he enjoyed the close friendship of leading Romans of his day and gained a keen insight into Roman political life. He wrote an account of the establishment of Roman supremacy throughout the Mediterranean between 220 and 145, prefaced by a brief survey of the period 264 to 220. But only his first five books reaching to 216 have come down to us intact; of the rest nothing remains but excerpts. For other substantial accounts of the period we have to turn to writers of much later date. The most important of these is the Roman historian Livy (59 B.C.–A.D. 17), whose narrative of the years 218 to 167 B.C., contained in books 21 to 45 of his great history of Rome, has been preserved. In the biographies written by Cornelius Nepos and Plutarch and in the historical works of the Greeks, Diodorus the Sicilian and Appian, there is much valuable information derived from the missing portions of Polybius and the lost works of other early writers.

I. Carthage and Her Empire

ROME A WORLD POWER. With the unification of Italy Rome entered upon a new era in her foreign relations. She was now one of the great Mediterranean powers and was inevitably drawn into the vortex of world politics. She could no longer rest indifferent to events beyond the confines of Italy. She assumed new responsibilities, opened up new diplomatic relations, developed a new outlook and new ambitions. At this time the other first-class powers were, in the East, the three Hellenistic monarchies—Egypt, Syria, and Macedon—which had emerged from the ruins of the empire of Alexander the Great, and, in the West, the city-state of Carthage. It was the position of this latter state as the dominant power in the western Mediterranean world from Sicily to the Strait of Gibraltar that made it the determining factor in Rome's foreign policy throughout the remainder of the third century B.C.

The city of Carthage had been founded on the northern coast of Africa near modern Tunis, opposite the western end of Sicily, as a colony of the Phoenician city of Tyre, toward the end of the eighth century B.C.[1] In the sixth century, when the cities of Phoenicia passed first under Babylonian domination and later were incorporated in the Persian Empire, their colonies, among them Carthage, severed political ties with the homeland and were left to defend themselves against surrounding natives.

The weakness of the other Phoenician settlements was the opportunity of Carthage. In the sixth and following centuries she brought them under her control and in addition founded new colonies of her own. She also extended her sway over the native Libyan population nearby. These Libyans were henceforth tributary under the obligation of rendering military service to the Carthaginians. The dependent Phoenician allies were similarly obligated. In the third century the Carthaginian empire included the northern coast of Africa from the Gulf of Syrtis westward beyond the Strait of Gibraltar; the southern and eastern coasts of Spain as far north as Cape Nao; Corsica; Sardinia; and Sicily, with the exception of Messana in the extreme northeast, the Kingdom of Syracuse in the southeastern part of the island, and a few smaller Greek states that still maintained their independence. The smaller islands of the western Mediterranean were likewise under Carthaginian control.

At this time the government of Carthage itself was republican in form and strongly aristocratic in tone. There was a primary Assembly for all Carthaginian citizens who could satisfy certain age and property requirements. This body annually elected the two chief magistrates, called suffetes, and the generals. For the former, qualifications of wealth and merit were prescribed. There was also a Senate and a Council, whose organization and powers are uncertain. The Council, the smaller body, prepared matters to be discussed in the Senate. The Senate was consulted by the suffetes on all matters and usually gave the final decision, although the Assembly was supposed to be consulted in case the Senate and suffetes disagreed. The

[1] The ancients believed that Carthage was founded in either 825 or 814, but modern archeological research makes the period 725–700 more likely.

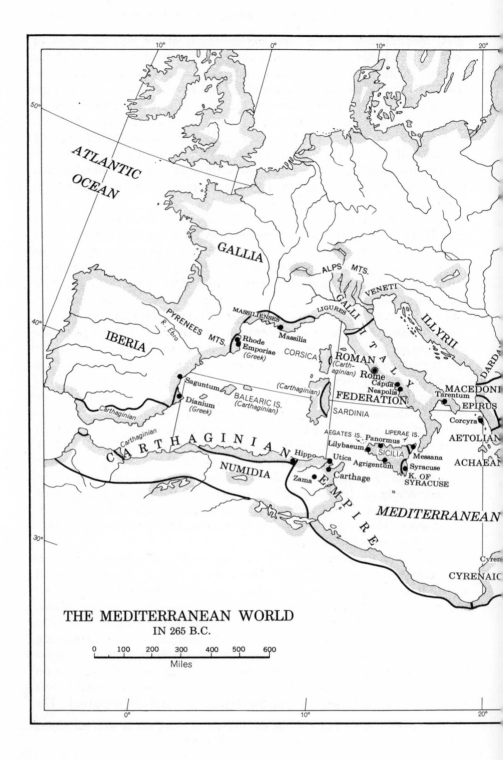

THE MEDITERRANEAN WORLD
IN 265 B.C.

0 100 200 300 400 500 600
Miles

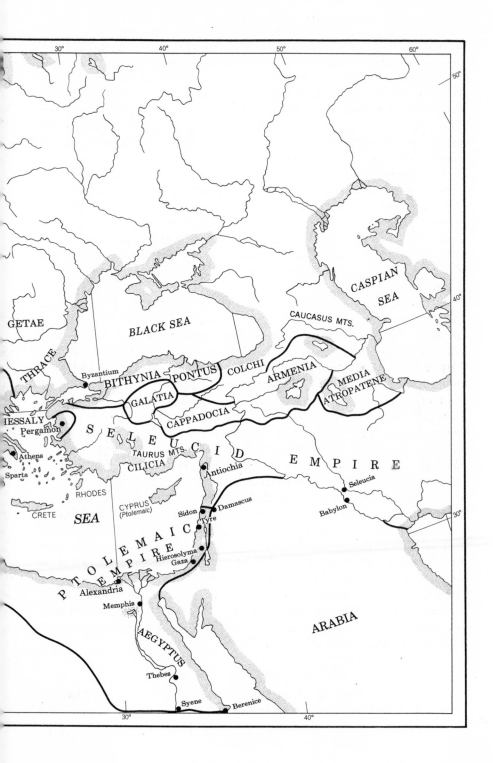

suffetes exercised judicial, financial, and religious functions and presided over the Council and Senate. The Carthaginian aristocracy was a group of wealthy families whose fortunes, made in commercial ventures and invested in estates, were handed down for generations in the same houses. From this circle came the Council and Senate, which directed state policy. The aristocracy itself was split into factions, struggling to control the offices and through them public policy, which they frequently subordinated to their own particular interests.

The prosperity of Carthage depended on her empire and the maintenance of a commercial monopoly in the western Mediterranean and the Atlantic north and south of the Strait of Gibraltar. This policy of commercial exclusiveness had caused Carthage to oppose Greek colonial expansion in Spain, Sardinia, and Sicily and had led to treaties which placed definite limits upon the trading ventures of the Romans and their allies and of the Greeks from Massilia and her colonies in Gaul and northern Spain.

Such a policy could only be maintained by a strong naval power, and Carthage was the undisputed mistress of the seas west of the Straits of Messana. The Carthaginians were expert shipbuilders, and their powerful fleet was manned by highly trained crews of citizen rowers and sailors. Unlike Rome, Carthage had no organized national army but relied upon mercenaries recruited from all quarters of the Mediterranean, among such warlike peoples as the Gauls, Spaniards, Libyans, Greeks and Italians. Generally speaking these mercenary armies served Carthage well throughout its history. They made up in experience what they occasionally lacked in discipline. When properly led and promptly paid, they were equal in fighting capacity to the armies fielded by the enemies of Carthage.[2]

This was the state Rome now faced, having conquered South Italy, and it was the first power she was to challenge in a war for dominion beyond the peninsula. The agrarian and uncommercial Romans had probably not maintained formal commercial relations with Carthage until the second half of the fourth century. The two treaties they made at that time show that Rome was uninterested in expanding her trade and suggest that there were no economic reasons to disturb the peaceful relations they enjoyed. A third treaty, concluded in 279, provided for military cooperation against Pyrrhus, but this alliance ended after the defeat of the latter; and with the removal of the common enemy a feeling of mutual suspicion seems to have arisen between the erstwhile allies.

II. The First Punic War: 264–241 B.C.

ORIGINS OF THE WAR. The first war between Rome and Carthage arose out of the political situation in Sicily. There the town of Messana was

---

[2] The Carthaginians were known to the Romans as *Poeni,* i.e., Phoenicians, whence comes the adjective "Punic," used in such phrases as the "Punic Wars."

occupied by the Mamertini, a band of Campanian mercenaries, who had been in the service of Syracuse but who had deserted and seized this town about 284. Because of their perpetual acts of brigandage, they were a menace to their neighbors, the Syracusans. Now under an energetic ruler, Hiero, who had assumed the title of king, the Syracusans succeeded in blockading Messana in 265, and its ultimate capture seemed certain. The Mamertini, without realizing the possible consequences of their action, appealed for help both to Rome and Carthage, since both powers might well be interested in humbling a city recently allied with Pyrrhus. A Carthaginian naval commander who happened to be near Messana with his squadron accepted their request and introduced a garrison into the town. The appeal to Rome arrived after this development and placed the Senate in a quandary. Even though the Mamertini were not exactly the kinds of friends Rome might wish to have, it was traditional Roman policy to accept as allies any weaker power that appealed for her protection.

The Senate realized that to grant this request might well lead to war with Carthage, but it also recognized that the Carthaginian occupation of Messana would give Carthage control of the Strait of Messana and constitute a perpetual threat against southern Italy. The more conservative members of the Senate may well have feared that a war would aid the careers of new men of talent from the plebeian class who would attain the higher magistracies and make their way into the Senate, thus enlarging the plebeian senatorial aristocracy. But this very prospect may have appealed to those who advocated interference in Sicily regardless of the consequences. The strength of these conflicting considerations made the Senate unwilling to assume responsibility for a decision, and the matter was referred to an assembly, probably that of the Centuries. Although the people, allegedly, were war-weary and had no enthusiasm for another conflict, they were persuaded by their leaders to approve the alliance with the Mamertini because of its advantages, which may have been represented as constituting a guarantee against any attack upon South Italy. It may also be that the people, less farsighted than the Senate and overconfident because of their victorious wars in Italy, did not appreciate the danger or difficulties of a possible conflict with the Carthaginians.

A consular army of two legions was levied to relieve Messana, and an advance force made its way into the harbor in spite of the presence of the Carthaginian fleet in the strait. Thereupon the Mamertini, apparently having reconsidered their position, decided that Roman protection was preferable to Carthaginian and compelled the Punic garrison to withdraw from the town. At Carthage, the government decided to recover Messana. An army was sent for that purpose into Sicily, Hiero of Syracuse was won over to a Carthaginian alliance, and both parties joined in blockading the city. But the main force of the Romans contrived to cross over from Regium to Messana, and its commander, after some futile negotiations, attacked and defeated Hiero and the Carthaginians in turn. Messana was saved, but Rome was now at war with both Carthage and Syracuse.

On the basis of surviving evidence it is difficult to decide the question of "war guilt" in this important conflict. Against the Romans it may be said that their fears of Carthaginian occupation of Messana as a threat to Italy were at the very least exaggerated. Carthage apparently regarded Roman occupation of the city as interference in her sphere of influence. On the analogy of recent developments in Italy, Carthage could expect that Roman "protection" of Messana would lead to eventual incorporation in the Roman confederation. This she was determined to prevent.

WAR IN SICILY: FIRST PHASE, 263–256 B.C. The next year the Romans sent a large army, possibly 40,000 citizen and allied troops, into Sicily to press the war against Hiero. Their initial attacks were so successful that the king became alarmed. Given the opportunity of making peace upon paying an indemnity of 100 talents in silver, he abandoned the Carthaginians and concluded an alliance for fifteen years with Rome.[3] Aided by Hiero, the Romans now besieged the strongly fortified city of Agrigentum, a Greek town on the south coast of the island, which sided with Carthage and had received a Carthaginian garrison. When Agrigentum fell in 262, the Romans determined to drive the Carthaginians out of Sicily.

Roman operations in Sicily, however, could be conducted only at con-siderable risk, and the coasts of Italy remained exposed to continued raids as long as Carthage had undisputed control of the sea. This resulted from the Romans' traditional aversion to the sea and their consequent lack of interest in naval affairs. They had apparently felt no need for any naval organization at all until 311 B.C., when they built twenty triremes, manned by allies. Even this modest navy was maintained only intermittently and was allowed to fall into complete decay after the Pyrrhic War, when the Romans relied on a squadron of triremes supplied by Italiot allies. By 261 they realized the absolute necessity of building a large fleet on modern lines that could challenge Carthaginian naval supremacy. This was a turning point in the war. According to tradition, they took as their model a stranded Carthaginian warship and constructed 120 vessels, of which 100 were quinqueremes,[4] the regular first-class battleship of the day. The complement of each quinquereme was 300 rowers and 120 fighting men. With this armament, and some vessels provided by Roman allies, the consul, Gaius Duilius, put to sea in 260 and engaged the superior Cartha-ginian fleet off Mylae on the north coast of Sicily. Although the Carthagin-ian seamen were superior to the Roman and could maneuver their ships

---

[3] The talent was worth about $1,200 (1964) but had a much greater purchasing power. This alliance was renewed on a permanent basis in 248 B.C.

[4] The trireme was rowed by 150 oarsmen; the oars were grouped in threes and each man manipulated one oar. The quinquereme was propelled by large oars each manned by five rowers with a single bank of oars on each side.

Frieze Showing a Roman Warship

more speedily and skilfully, the Romans offset this advantage by employing a device at one time in use among the Greeks. Whenever a hostile ship came close enough to ram or board a Roman, the latter dropped a crane armed with long spikes upon the opponent's deck. By thus grappling the enemy, they enabled the legionaries, who were serving as marines, to board the Carthaginian ships and capture them in hand-to-hand fighting. The Romans thus neutralized superior Carthaginian seamanship by converting sea battles into land warfare. The Roman victory was as decisive as it was unexpected. As a result they were able to occupy Corsica and make an assault upon Sardinia in the next year; and, since they found it impossible to force a decision in Sicily, they were in a favorable position for attacking Carthage in its own African territory.

ROMAN INVASION OF AFRICA: 256–255 B.C.   Another naval victory, off Ecnomus, on the south coast of Sicily, in 256 cleared the way for the successful landing in Africa of an army under the consul Marcus Atilius Regulus. He defeated the Carthaginians and reduced them to such extremities that they sought to make peace. A peace honorable to both sides might have been made then and there, but Regulus, who was as overconfident as he was unimaginative, imposed such impossibly harsh terms that the Carthaginians decided to resume hostilities. At this juncture there arrived at Carthage, with other mercenaries, a Spartan soldier of fortune, Xanthippus, who reorganized the Carthaginian army. Early in the next year he offered battle, and by skilful use of cavalry and war elephants he inflicted a crushing defeat upon the Romans and took Regulus prisoner. A Roman fleet rescued the remnants of the expedition but was almost totally lost in a storm off the southern Sicilian coast.

WAR IN SICILY: SECOND PHASE, 254–241 B.C.   The Romans again concentrated their efforts against the Carthaginian strongholds in Sicily, which they attacked by land and sea. In 254 they took the important city of Panormus, and the Carthaginians were soon confined to the western extremity of the island. There they successfully maintained themselves in Drepana and Lilybaeum. Meanwhile the Romans encountered a series of disasters on the sea. In 253 they lost 150 ships on the voyage from Lilybaeum to Rome, in 250 the consul Publius Clodius suffered a severe defeat in a naval battle at Drepana, and in the next year a third fleet was destroyed by a storm off Phintias in Sicily.

In 247 a new Carthaginian general, Hamilcar Barca, took command in Sicily and infused fresh life into the Carthaginian forces. From the citadel of Hercte first, and later from Eryx, he continually harassed the Romans not only in Sicily but even on the coast of Italy. Finally in 242, when their public treasury was too exhausted to build another fleet, the Romans by private subscription equipped 200 vessels, which blockaded Lilybaeum and Drepana. A Carthaginian relief expedition was destroyed off the Aegates Islands, and it was impossible for their forces, now completely cut off in

Sicily, to prolong the struggle. Carthage was compelled to conclude peace in 241.

PEACE AND ITS CONSEQUENCES.   Carthage surrendered to Rome her remaining possessions in Sicily, with the islands between Sicily and Italy, besides agreeing to pay an indemnity of 3,200 talents (about $3,840,000) in twenty years. For the Romans the long struggle had been very costly. At sea alone they and their allies had lost some 500 ships and 200,000 men. Rome won the war not merely because of her characteristic tenacity and her superior generalship, but largely because she could tap in Italy manpower reserves far more numerous than those available to Carthage. Furthermore, the Carthaginian fleets never found a satisfactory defense against Roman boarding tactics. The Romans themselves preferred to believe that their victory was due to the superior bravery and discipline of Roman and allied troops, but in reality the war had shown that Roman legionaries were not noticeably better disciplined than properly led Punic mercenaries. As a result of the conflict Carthage had been bled white, she had lost the cornerstone of her empire in Sicily, and she had been replaced by Rome as the dominant power in the western Mediterranean basin.

Weakened as she was, Carthage immediately became involved in a life-and-death struggle with her mercenary troops. Upon their return from Sicily, these troops made demands upon the state for payment of rewards promised them by their general, Hamilcar. When these were refused, they mutinied and, joining with the native Libyans and the inhabitants of the subject Phoenician cities (Libyphoenicians), began a war for the destruction of Carthage. After a struggle of more than three years, in which the most shocking barbarities were practised on both sides and in which they were brought face to face with utter ruin, the Carthaginians, under the leadership of Hamilcar Barca, finally stamped out the revolt (238).

During the war, the Romans showed open sympathy with Carthage. They furnished the city with supplies, which they prevented their allies from selling to the rebels, and even permitted the Carthaginians to recruit troops in Italy. When the Carthaginian garrison in Sardinia revolted and asked the Romans to take over the island, they refused to do so, but after the struggle in Africa came to an end the Roman attitude changed. A Carthaginian force sent to recover Sardinia in 239 mutinied and joined the rebellious garrison. Hard-pressed by the native population, the mutineers sent another appeal for Roman intervention. The Roman Senate reversed its former attitude and made preparations to occupy the island. Carthage protested and proceeded to fit out a new expedition against the mutineers. The Romans chose to interpret this as a hostile act and declared war. It is difficult to account for the Roman change of policy. In the early stages of the revolt the Romans may have helped Carthage because they mistrusted anarchic or revolutionary movements wherever they occurred. Later, they perhaps did not wish the Carthaginian recovery to proceed too far and mistrusted the ambitions and influence of their old enemy Hamil-car. Perhaps also the Roman Senate had come to feel the natural unity of Italy and the adjacent islands and was determined to prevent the occupation of the latter by any foreign power. Carthage could not think of accepting the challenge and bought peace at the price of Sardinia, Corsica, and a penalty of 1,200 talents ($1,500,000), but this unjustifiable act of the Romans caused much bitterness. As a result of the acquisition of Sicily, Sardinia, and Corsica, the Tyrrhenian Sea became a Roman lake.

III. The Illyrian and Gallic Wars: 229–219 B.C.

THE FIRST ILLYRIAN WAR: 229–228 B.C. In assuming con-trol of relations between her allies and foreign states, Rome had assumed responsibility for protecting their interests; and it was the somewhat re-luctant fulfillment of this obligation that brought Roman arms to the eastern shores of the Adriatic. Rome's involvement in this area was an important step in the development of her foreign policy. It was here that she extended the principle she had already established in dealing with cer-tain Sicilian cities during the first Punic War—that of association without formal treaty. Rome thus assumed the status of patron and protector of weaker client states. As a patron her obligations were moral rather than legal and could therefore be interpreted flexibly. Although the client states were technically free to pursue policies of their own choosing, in fact their capacity for independent action depended on Rome's sufferance. In the absence of any written treaties, Rome could judge their actions in the light of her own interest and reward or punish client states accordingly.

Under a king named Agron an extensive but loosely organized state had been formed among the Illyrians, a semibarbarous people inhabiting the Adriatic coast north of Epirus. These Illyrians were allied with the king-dom of Macedonia and sided with the latter in its wars with Epirus and the Aetolian and Achaean Confederacies. In 231 Agron died and was suc-ceeded by his queen Tueta, who continued his policy of attacking cities on the west coast of Greece and practicing large scale piracy in the Adriatic and Ionian seas. Among those who suffered thereby were the south Italian cities. In 230, as the result of fresh and more serious outrages, they ap-pealed to Rome for redress. The Romans demanded satisfaction from Teuta; and, having their demands contemptuously rejected and one of their ambassadors killed, they declared war.

In the summer of 229 the Romans attacked the Illyrians with a fleet and an army so strong that the enemy could offer little resistance and in the next year was forced to sue for peace. Queen Teuta had to give up her recent conquests in Epirus (Albania) as well as the Greek cities which she had seized on the coast of the Adriatic and Ionian Seas, to promise not to send any armed vessels south of her own territory in Illyria, and to pay a war indemnity to Rome. The territory surrendered by Teuta became client states of the type described above. The island of Pharos and some adjacent territory in Illyria were given to a Greek adventurer, Demetrius of Pharos, as a reward for having aided Rome in the war. The cities of Corcyra, Epidamnus, and Apollonia also became clients and were neither subject to tribute nor formally accepted by treaty as Roman allies.

The fact that Rome first crossed the Adriatic to fight against the Illyrians aroused the hostility of their ally, Macedonia, the greatest of the Greek states. And although Macedonia had been unable to aid the Illyrians because of dynastic troubles that followed the death of King Demetrius II[5] (229), it regarded with jealous suspicion Rome's success and the establishment of a Roman sphere of influence east of the Adriatic. Conversely, the war established friendly relations between Rome and the enemies of Macedonia, the Aetolian and Achaean Confederacies, which rejoiced in the suppression of Illyrian piracy. The way was thus paved for the participation of Rome, as a partisan of the anti-Macedonian faction, in the struggles which had so long divided the Greek world.

SECOND ILLYRIAN WAR: 220–219 B.C.   The revival of Macedonian influence led indirectly to Rome's second Illyrian war. The alliance of Antigonus Doson, the new king of Macedonia, with the Achaean Confederacy and his conquest of Sparta (222) united almost the whole of Greece under Macedonian suzerainty. Thereupon Demetrius, the client prince whom Rome had established as ruler in his native Pharos but who had gone over to Macedonia, attacked some of the other Illyrian peoples and cities under Roman protection and led a piratical squadron into Greek waters (220). Rome, now threatened with a second Carthaginian War, acted with energy to crush a client, who, by believing in his absolute freedom of action, had dared to pursue a foreign policy hostile to that of his patron state. Macedonia, under Philip V, the successor of Antigonus Doson, was involved in a war with the Aetolians and their allies. Deprived of support from this quarter, Demetrius was driven to take refuge in Macedonia. His subjects surrendered, and Rome took possession of his chief fortresses, Pharos and Dimillos. Having thus taught her Illyrian clients the real meaning of patronage, Rome preferred to maintain her protectorate rather than annex the area directly opposite the heel of the Italian peninsula on the eastern shore of the Adriatic. Thereby she retained command of the Strait of Otranto. Although the Romans made no effort to exploit their victory at the expense of Macedonia, Philip regarded their Illyrian protectorate as a menace and made preparations for ousting them from what he considered to be the natural outlet of his country upon the Adriatic Sea.

WAR WITH THE GAULS IN NORTH ITALY: 225–222 B.C. In the interval between the two Illyrian wars Rome became involved in a

---

[5] Not to be confused with Demetrius of Pharos.

serious conflict with the Gallic tribes settled in the Po valley. For about half a century the Gauls had lived at peace with Rome, ceasing their raids into the peninsula and becoming a prosperous agricultural and pastoral people. It is claimed that they became alarmed at the Roman assignment of public land on their southern borders, called the Ager Gallicus, to individual colonists in 233 and that this caused them to take up arms. This territory had been Roman since 283, however, and its settlement could hardly have been interpreted as hostile. It is more probable that the new Gallic invasion was caused by fresh swarms from across the Alps, which some of the Cisalpine Gauls, who had forgotten the defeats of half a century earlier, perhaps invited, and certainly joined, for the sake of plunder. As early as 236 such a band of Transalpines had been brought in by the chieftains of the Boii to aid them in an attack upon Ariminum. But owing to dissensions among the Boii themselves this project came to nothing, and no further inroad into Roman territory was attempted until 225.

In that year a coalition of four Cisalpine tribes, reinforced by large numbers of Transalpine adventurers called Gaesati (spearmen), prepared to invade the peninsula. Both the Romans and their allies were seriously alarmed, for the memory of the Roman defeat at the Allia (387) had not been forgotten. Rome called for a special military census of the whole federation. The returns, according to Polybius, showed over 700,000 infantry and 70,000 cavalry, of whom the Romans accounted for 250,000 foot and 23,000 horse, while the rest belonged to the Latin and federate allies. Two consular armies, each over 50,000 strong, took the field. In addition the Cenomani, one of the Gallic tribes north of the Po, and the Veneti, joined the Romans and supplied 20,000 more troops. Expecting the Gauls to advance southward through Umbria, the Romans stationed one consul with his army near Ariminum to block their path. The defense of Etruria was entrusted to a smaller force, and the other consul was sent to Sardinia, possibly in fear of a Carthaginian descent upon that island.

Avoiding the army at Ariminum, the Gauls crossed the Apennines into Etruria, plundered the country, and defeated the army that had been left to guard this region. But the consul from Ariminum hastened to the rescue, the army in Sardinia was recalled, and the Gauls began to withdraw northward to place their spoils in safety. The Romans followed, and as the army from Sardinia landed north of the foe and cut off their retreat, the latter were surrounded and confronted at Telamon. They were annihilated in a desperate struggle won by Roman tactics and generalship. One of the Roman consuls fell on the field of battle.

Italy was saved, but the Romans decided to follow up their victory by a conquest of the lands of the Boii and the Insubres, both as a penalty for their conduct and as a guarantee against future invasions. In three hard-fought campaigns the Romans, although they failed to exterminate or dispossess these peoples, subjected them, forcing them to surrender part of their territory and to pay tribute. The Romans did not conquer without suffering heavy losses, and their ultimate success was to a considerable degree due to the cooperation of the Cenomani.

Between 221 and 219 the Romans extended their area of domination around the head of the Adriatic as far as the peninsula of Histria by the conquest of peoples who dwelt to the east of the Veneti. Thus, with the exception of Liguria and the upper valley of the Po, all Italy south of the Alps was brought within the sphere of Roman influence. The Latin colonies Placentia and Cremona were founded in the territory taken from the Insubres to secure the Roman authority in this region, but Hannibal's invasion of 218 found most of the Cisalpine Gauls ready to revolt against the Romans.

IV. The Second Punic War: 218–201 B.C.

CARTHAGINIAN EXPANSION IN SPAIN.   Almost immediately after the loss of Sardinia and Corsica a new field for Carthaginian expansion was opened in Spain. The initiative was taken by Hamilcar Barca, the victor in the mercenary war, who saw in this quarter an opportunity for repairing the fortunes of his state and compensating her for the loss of her insular possessions. Carthaginian interest in Spain dated from the latter part of the sixth century B.C., when Carthage conquered the native realm of Tartessus on the southern coast and closed the Strait of Gibraltar to the ships of other peoples. The older Phoenician settlements in this region, such as Gades, became subject to Carthage, as did some of the neighboring Iberian tribes. From her Spanish territory, Carthage obtained great quantities of silver, copper, and iron, besides agricultural products and fish. Tin from England and gold and ivory from the west coast of Africa were brought to the Mediterranean by the sailors of Gades, who made regular voyages in Atlantic waters. This early Carthaginian empire was overthrown by the ancient rivals of Carthage, the Greeks of Massilia, together with some of the Iberians. Gades, however, and the control of the strait remained in Carthaginian hands.

In 237, Hamilcar, then commander of Libya, crossed over into Spain, where he found the Phoenician subjects of Carthage hard pressed by attacks from native Iberian peoples. By skilful generalship and able diplomacy he extended Carthaginian dominion over many of the Spanish tribes and built up a strong army, devoted to himself and his family. Roman tradition accused Hamilcar of nursing an undying hatred towards Rome and interpreted his Spanish conquests as part of a carefully laid plan to develop the military strength of Carthage to a point where she could avenge her defeats of the First Punic War. His actions, however, do not seem to indicate that he planned any resumption of the conflict with the victorious enemy. A Roman mission sent in 231 to investigate his actions returned satisfied that he was merely seeking new resources with which Carthage could pay off her indemnity to Rome.

When Hamilcar was drowned during the siege of a Spanish town in 229, he was succeeded in command by his son-in-law Hasdrubal, who carried on his predecessor's program. It was Hasdrubal who founded New Carthage (Carthagena) to serve as the center of Carthaginian influence in Spain. Although Hamilcar may have begun his Spanish campaigns without express authorization from the Carthaginian Senate, his policy there, and that of Hasdrubal as well, had the continuous support of a substantial faction in that body. The annual revenue of from 2,000 to 3,000 talents ($2,400,000 to $3,600,000) derived from the Spanish silver mines may have been a potent factor in inducing the Carthaginians to acquiesce in the almost regal position that the Barcidae enjoyed in Spain.

But the Carthaginian advance in Spain alarmed the Greeks of Massilia, and of their colonies in Spain, Emporiae and Rhode, whose commercial interests and independence were thereby endangered. Friendship with the Massiliots had been the cornerstone of Rome's western policy, since they had traditionally been her eyes and ears in Gaul and Spain. They are said to have contributed to the ransom which the Romans paid to the Gauls in 387, and there seems little doubt that they secured the intervention of Rome at this time on their own behalf. In 226 the Romans sent an embassy to Hasdrubal and concluded a treaty which prohibited him from waging war to the north of the river Ebro but allowed him a free hand to the south even at the expense of the interests of Massilia. The terms of the treaty do not indicate that Rome was at all disquieted over the consolidation of Carthaginian power in Spain, and Hasdrubal on his part did nothing to provoke hostilities. At this time the Romans were too much alarmed by the gathering storm of the Gallic invasion to be concerned very seriously with the remote Iberian peninsula.

ROMAN ALLEGIANCE WITH SAGUNTUM.   A possible cause of future friction lay in Rome's relations with the Spanish port of Saguntum, a town which lay to the south of the Ebro. At some uncertain date, probably after the treaty with Hasdrubal, the Saguntines requested the protection of Rome. The Senate granted an alliance without a formal treaty, an act which meant the potential extension of Roman influence into Spain and which probably violated the spirit, if not the letter of the Ebro River treaty. This was but another instance of the increasingly frequent Roman practice of using client states as levers against other, larger states.

HANNIBAL AND ROME.   Upon the assassination of Hasdrubal in 221, Hannibal, son of Hamilcar, then in his twenty-sixth year, was appointed to the command in Spain. Soon afterward hostilities broke out between Saguntum and a Spanish people in the Carthaginian alliance who aided Saguntine political exiles. The Romans had recently interfered in the internal politics of Saguntum and helped to bring an anti-Carthaginian faction into power there, and now, fearing Carthaginian interference, the Saguntines appealed to Rome for protection. A Roman commission appeared before Hannibal in 219 and reminded him of the existence of the alliance. Hannibal avoided an immediate conflict by referring the commission to Carthage. By this time, however, it seemed to Hannibal that Sagntum was about to become another Messana, a Roman bridgehead in a properly Carthaginian sphere of interest. Relying on his devoted army and believing in his own military genius, he resolved to consolidate once and for all the Punic position in Spain and, calling Rome's bluff, to attack Saguntum.

Having obtained the backing of his government, Hannibal laid siege to Saguntum in 219 and captured it after a blockade of eight months. The Romans did nothing to aid the Saguntines, and the Senate obviously was not willing to fulfill its role as patron and go to war in defense of a client state in Spain. Roman inactivity seems to have encouraged Hannibal to embark on a second and even more daring campaign to strengthen his position in the peninsula: the conquest of Spain as far north as the Pyrenees, a clear violation of the Ebro River treaty. He was mistaken in believing that Rome would tolerate this menacing advance to the north as she had tolerated the conquest of Saguntum. In 218 a second Roman embassy appeared at Carthage to demand the surrender of Hannibal and his staff as the price of averting war with Rome. The pro-Barcid faction prevailed, and the Carthaginian Senate accepted the responsibility for the act of their general, whatever its consequences. The Roman ambassador replied with the declaration of war.

The great result of the First Punic War had been the destruction of the maritime supremacy of Carthage. Carthage never subsequently thought of contesting Rome's dominion on the sea, and consequently, while extending her empire in Spain and Africa, she had neglected to rebuild her navy. This fact was to be of decisive importance in the coming struggle. The dominant faction in the Roman Senate, led by the Aemilian and Scipionic clans[6] and responsible for the declaration of war and the conduct of the opening campaigns until 216, relied on Carthaginian naval weakness and planned an offensive war. One army, under the consul Publius Cornelius Scipio, was to proceed to Spain, supported by the fleet of Massilia, and detain Hannibal there, while a second army, under the other consul, Tiberius Sempronius Longus, assembled in Sicily to embark for Africa.

The Romans, however, had not taken into account the military genius of Hannibal, who realized that the best defense of Carthage and his Spanish base of operations was a direct attack on Italy. He knew that he could not transport his army to Italy by sea; and since he was already in

---

[6] On factional politics within the senatorial oligarchy, see below, pp. 145f.

northern Spain when Rome had declared war (May–June, 218), it seemed best to cross the Pyrenees, traverse southern Gaul, and to descend on Italy via the Alps. Among the Gauls of the Po valley he hoped to find recruits for his army, and he expected that, once he was in Italy, Roman allies would seize this opportunity of recovering their independence. Strategic and military problems preoccupied Hannibal early in the war, and at first he seems to have paid little attention to ultimate war aims other than defeating Rome and/or concluding a quick peace. Eventually he seems to have planned to break up the Roman federation in Italy and to reduce the Roman state to the limits attained in 340. In the long run this would have been the same as destroying Rome, since it would have relegated her to political insignificance and would have made her prey to the ambitions of other Italian states.

INVASION OF ITALY.   Late in the spring of 218 Hannibal forced a passage of the Pyrenees, leaving the passes under guard and resuming his march with a picked army of Spaniards and Numidians. His brother Hasdrubal[7] was left in Spain to collect reinforcements and follow with them. Hannibal arrived at the Rhone and crossed it by the time that Scipio reached Massilia on his way to Spain. The latter, failing to force Hannibal to fight on the banks of the Rhone, returned in person to Italy but sent his army, under the command of his brother, to Spain, a decision which had the most serious consequences for Carthage. Meanwhile Hannibal continued his march and, overcoming the intransigent opposition of the Alpine peoples whose territory he traversed, as well as the obstacles of bad roads, dangerous passes, cold, and hunger, crossed the Alps and descended into the plain of North Italy in the autumn of 218, after a march of five months.[8] His army, perhaps originally 40,000 strong, was reduced to 20,000 infantry and 6,000 cavalry. Two thirds of his elephants had perished.

Hannibal at once found support and an opportunity to rest his weary troops among the Insubres and the Boii, the latter having already taken up arms against the Romans. At the news of his arrival in Italy, Sempronius was at once recalled from Sicily; but Scipio, who had anticipated him, ventured to attack Hannibal with the forces under his command. He was beaten in a skirmish at the river Ticinus, and Hannibal was able to cross the Po. Upon the arrival of Sempronius, both consuls attacked the Carthaginians at the Trebia, only to receive a crushing defeat (December, 218). Hannibal then began his attempt to detach the Italians from the Roman alliance by releasing his Italian prisoners to carry word to their cities that he had come to set them free.

---

[7] Not to be confused with his namesake, Hamilcar's son-in-law.

[8] Authorities differ as to the pass which Hannibal used in crossing the Alps, arguing variously for the Little St. Bernard, Mont Genèvre, or Mont Cenis. Polybius, the best authority, seems to indicate Mont Cenis.

Hannibal wintered in north Italy and in the spring, with an army raised to 50,000 by the addition of Celtic recruits, prepared to invade the peninsula. The Romans divided their forces, stationing one consul at Ariminum and the other at Arretium in Etruria. Hannibal chose to cross the Apennines and the marshes of Etruria, where he surprised and annihilated the army of the consul Flaminius at the Trasimene Lake (217). Flaminius himself was among the slain. This victory was soon followed by another, in which the cavalry of the army of the second consul was cut to pieces. Hannibal then marched into Samnium, ravaging the country as he went.

These defeats caused a temporary eclipse in the influence of the Aemilian-Scipionic faction, and leadership of the war effort now swung over to that more cautious group of senators led by the Fabian clan. The Centuriate Assembly elected as dictator in this emergency the leader of this faction, Quintus Fabius Maximus. Fabius recognized the superiority of Hannibal's generalship and of the Carthaginian cavalry and consequently refused to be drawn into a general engagement. He followed the enemy closely and continually threatened an attack, so that Hannibal could not divide his forces for the purpose of raiding and foraging. Hannibal was able to penetrate into Campania, however, and thence to recross the mountains into Apulia, where he decided to establish winter quarters. The strategy of Fabius, who received the nickname of Cunctator (the Delayer) had not prevented the enemy from securing supplies, and devastating wide areas. It grew so irksome that the Centuriate Assembly violated all precedent in appointing Marcus Minucius, the master of the horse and an advocate of aggressive tactics, as a second dictator. But when Marcus risked an engagement, he was badly beaten, and only prompt assistance from Fabius saved his army from destruction.

CANNAE: 216 B.C.   Next spring found the Romans and Carthaginians facing each other in Apulia. The Romans were led by new consuls, Lucius Aemilius Paullus and Gaius Terentius Varro, who were authorized to risk a decisive battle to protect the territory of Rome's allies. This change of strategy brought on the battle of Cannae, one of the greatest battles of antiquity and the bloodiest of all Roman defeats. Here the Roman forces, numbering by tradition close to 80,000 men but probably nearer 50,000, were almost annihilated by the numerically inferior Carthaginians. At Cannae the consummate military genius of Hannibal was displayed, and his masterly tactics on this occasion have found admirers and imitators among the great commanders of all subsequent ages. Knowing that the Romans would try to crush his troops by a frontal attack, he drew up his infantry with their center of Gauls and Spaniards thrown well forward. Under pressure of the Roman assault, these troops gave ground while the wings, where the Libyan infantry were posted, held firm until the line was like a crescent with the Romans crowded between its encircling horns. In the meantime the Carthaginian cavalry had routed the Roman horsemen on both flanks and, turning back from pursuit, attacked the legions from the rear. Surrounded on all sides and thrown into confusion, the Romans were cut down where they stood. Only some 10,000 succeeded in forcing their way out of the trap. The consequences of the battle were serious. For the first time Rome's allies showed grave signs of disloyalty. In Apulia and in Bruttium Hannibal found many adherents. Ambassadors from Philip of Macedon appeared at his headquarters, the prelude to an alliance in the next year. Syracuse also wavered after the death of Hiero, the friend of Rome, and finally went over to Carthage. Most serious of all, Capua, the second city of Italy, opened its gates to Hannibal.

Still the courage of the Romans never wavered. In what was perhaps the most important decision of the war, they decided to persevere in their Spanish campaign when the temptation was strong to withdraw all available forces into Italy. They at once levied a new force to replace the army destroyed at Cannae. All in all about half of Rome's allies in Italy either defected to or were conquered by Hannibal. Under the circumstances this was surprisingly few, but it was sufficient to frighten the Romans and to induce them on occasion to institute a reign of terror when they recaptured disloyal cities. Hannibal, owing to the smallness of his army and the necessity of maintaining it in a hostile country, had to be on the march continually and could not undertake siege operations, for which he also lacked engines of war. Thus the Romans, avoiding pitched battles, were able to reduce systematically the towns which had yielded to Hannibal and to hamper seriously the provisioning of his forces. At the same time they still held command of the sea, kept up their offensive in Spain, and held their ground against Carthaginian attacks in Sicily and Sardinia.

ROMAN RECOVERY. In 213 the Romans invested Syracuse. The Syracusans, with the aid of engines of war designed by the physicist Archimedes, resisted desperately, but the Roman general Marcellus pressed the siege vigorously, and treachery caused the city to fall (211). Syracuse was sacked, its art treasures carried off to Rome, and for the future it was subject and tributary to Rome. In Italy, although the consul Tiberius Sempronius Gracchus was surprised and killed and Hannibal was able to occupy the cities of Tarentum (without its citadel), Heraclea, and Thurii, he could not prevent the Romans from laying siege to Capua. The next year he tried to force them to raise the blockade by a sudden incursion into Latium, where he appeared before the walls of Rome. But Rome was garrisoned, the army besieging Capua was not recalled, and Hannibal's march was in vain. Capua was starved into submission, its nobility put to the sword, its territory confiscated, and its municipal organization dissolved (211).

Upon concluding his alliance with Hannibal, Philip of Macedon hastened to attack the Roman possessions in Illyria. Here he met with some successes but failed to take Corcyra or Apollonia, which were saved by the Roman fleet. Rome's command of the sea prevented his lending any effective aid to his ally in Italy. Before long the Romans were able to induce the Aetolians to make an alliance with them and attack Macedonia. Thereupon other enemies of Philip, among them Sparta and King Attalus of Pergamon, joined the war on the side of Rome. Although the Achaean Confederacy supported Philip, the coalition against him was so strong that he had to cease his attacks on Roman territory, and Rome could be content with supporting her Greek allies with a small fleet, while she devoted her energies to the other theaters of war.

THE SCIPIOS IN SPAIN: 218–209 B.C.   The fall of Capua came at a moment most opportune for the Romans, since there was immediate need to send reinforcements to Spain. The army sent there in 218 under Gnaeus Scipio, who obtained a foothold north of the Ebro, was joined the next year by another under his brother Publius Cornelius. Thereupon the Romans crossed the Ebro and invaded the Carthaginian dominions to the south. A revolt of the Numidian prince Syphax caused the recall of Hasdrubal to Africa, and the Romans were able to capture Saguntum and induce many Spanish tribes to desert the Carthaginian cause, but upon the return of Hasdrubal and the arrival of reinforcements from Carthage, the Carthaginian commanders united their forces and were able to crush the two Roman armies one after the other (211). Both the Scipios fell in battle, and the Carthaginians recovered all their territory south of the Ebro. They were unable to capitalize on their Spanish success, however, because their generals failed to cooperate after the victory.

Undismayed by these disasters, the Romans determined to continue their efforts to conquer Spain because it was a recruiting ground for the Carthaginian armies and because continuance of the war there prevented reinforcements being sent to Hannibal in Italy. The fall of Capua and the fortunate turn of events in Sicily enabled them to release fresh troops for service in Spain. In 210, being dissatisfied with the cautious strategy of the propraetor Nero, then commanding north of the Ebro, the Senate determined to send out a commander from the Scipionic group who would continue to pursue its traditionally aggressive tactics. As the most suitable person they fixed on Publius Cornelius Scipio, son of the like-named ex-consul who had fallen in 211. Although he had won fame already as a military tribune, he was only in his twenty-fifth year and, having filled no magistracy except the aedileship, was technically disqualified from exercising the *imperium*. His appointment was therefore made the subject of a special law in the Centuriate Assembly, which nominated him to the command in Spain with the rank of a proconsul. This is the first authentic instance of the conferment of *imperium* upon a private citizen.

Since the armies of his opponents were divided in widely separated winter quarters, Scipio took the offensive, crossed the Ebro, and by a daring stroke seized the chief Carthaginian base, New Carthage (209). Here he found vast stores of supplies and, more important, the hostages from the Spanish peoples subject to Carthage. His liberation of them and his generous treatment of the Spaniards in general was in such striking contrast with the oppressive measures of the Carthaginians that he rapidly won over both the enemies and the adherents of the latter. In preparation for future campaigns he drilled his troops in intricate maneuvers and rearmed them with the finely tempered Spanish sword, adapted to cutting as well as thrusting, in place of the shorter Roman sword used solely for thrusting.

HASDRUBAL'S MARCH TO ITALY: 208–207 B.C.   Meanwhile in Italy the Romans proceeded steadily with the reduction of the strongholds in the hands of Hannibal. Tarentum was recovered in 210, and although Hannibal defeated and slew the consuls Gnaeus Fulvius (210) and Marcus Marcellus (208), his forces were so diminished that his campaign in Italy depended upon the arrival of strong reinforcements. Since his arrival he had received but insignificant additions to his army from Carthage, whose energies had been directed to the other theaters of war. Up to this time also Roman activities in Spain had prevented any Carthaginian troops leaving that country. After the fall of New Carthage and the subsequent successes of Scipio, Hasdrubal had to decide whether to face the Romans in Spain or to leave at once for Italy to support his brother. He courageously chose the former course, and, although he was defeated by Scipio in battle, he was able to save the bulk of his forces, elude pursuit, and cross the Pyrenees (208).

The next spring he arrived among the Gauls south of the Alps. Reinforced by them, he marched into the peninsula to join forces with Hannibal. It was essential for the Romans to prevent this. They therefore divided their forces. The consul Gaius Claudius faced Hannibal in Apulia, while Marcus Livius went to intercept Hasdrubal. Through the capture of messengers from the latter, Claudius learned of his position. Leaving part of his army to detain Hannibal, he withdrew the rest without the enemy's knowledge and joined his colleague Livius. Together they attacked Hasdrubal at the Metaurus; his army was cut to pieces and he himself slain. With this battle the doom of Hannibal's plans was sealed and with them the doom of Carthage. Hannibal himself recognized that all was lost and withdrew into the mountains of Bruttium. Although in 205 Hannibal's other brother Mago succeeded in landing another army in Liguria, he failed to accomplish anything of importance and was recalled in 203.

END OF THE WAR IN SPAIN AND GREECE.   For the first time during the war the Romans could look forward with confidence to the issue. In the two years (207–206) following the departure of Hasdrubal, Scipio completed the conquest of what remained to Carthage in Spain. In 205 B.C. he assumed the consulship in Rome and then went to Sicily to make preparations for the invasion of Africa, since the Romans were now able to carry out their plan of 218, which Hannibal had interrupted.

At the same time the Romans found themselves free from any embarrassment from Macedonia. In Greece the war had dragged on without any decided advantage for either side until 207, when the temporary withdrawal of the Roman fleet enabled Philip and the Achaean Confederacy to win such successes that their opponents listened to the intervention of the neutral states and made peace (206 B.C.). The next year the Romans also came to terms with Philip.

THE CAMPAIGN IN AFRICA: 204–202 B.C.   In 204 Scipio transported his army to Africa. At first he was able to do nothing before the combined forces of the Carthaginians and the Numidian chief, Syphax, who had renewed his alliance with them. In the following year, however, he routed both armies so decisively that he was able to capture and depose Syphax and to set up in his place a rival chieftain, Masinissa, whose adherence to the Romans brought them a welcome superiority in cavalry. The Carthaginians now asked for peace. An armistice was granted them. Hannibal and all Carthaginian forces were recalled from Italy, and the preliminary terms of peace were drawn up (203). Hannibal left Italy with the remnant of his veterans after campaigns that established his reputation as one of the world's greatest masters of war. For nearly fifteen years he had maintained himself in enemy country with greatly inferior forces. Now, after inflicting many severe defeats and never losing a major battle, he was forced to withdraw because he lacked resources, not because of the superior generalship of his foes. Before leaving Italy he set up a record of his exploits in the temple of Hera Lacinia in Bruttium, which survived to be read by the historian Polybius.

Hannibal's arrival in Carthage meant the return to power of the more intransigent and aggressive faction in the government bent on continuing the war. Consequently, the Carthaginians broke the armistice by attacking some Roman transports and refused to meet Scipio's demand for an explanation. Thereupon hostilities were resumed. At Zama (202) the two greatest generals the war had developed met in its final battle. Scipio applied the tactics of encirclement which he had learned from Hannibal but adapted to Roman military formations. Hannibal had anticipated such a maneuver and checkmated it by a proper disposition of his own forces. In spite of this, the retreat of the Carthaginian mercenaries at a critical moment and the timely return of the Roman and Numidian cavalry from pursuit of the routed Carthaginian horse resulted in a complete victory for Scipio.

PEACE: 201 B.C.   Zama did not decide the outcome of the war, which Carthage had already lost, but it did determine the kind of peace terms that Rome would impose on her defeated enemy. These were: the surrender of all territory except the city of Carthage and the surrounding country in Africa, an indemnity of 10,000 talents ($12,000,000), the surrender of all vessels of war except ten triremes, and of all war elephants, and the obligation not to make war anywhere without Rome's consent. The Numidians were united in a strong state on the Carthaginian borders, under the Roman ally Masinissa. Scipio returned to Rome to triumph "over the Carthaginians and Hannibal" and to receive, from the scene of his victory, the name of Africanus.

V. Effect of the Second Punic War Upon Italy

The destruction of the Carthaginian empire left Rome mistress of the western Mediterranean and by far the greatest power of the time. This victory had been attained, however, only after a tremendous struggle, probably the greatest that the ancient world ever witnessed, a struggle which called forth in Rome the patriotic virtues of courage, devotion, and self-sacrifice to a degree that drained her resources of men and treasure, leaving ineffaceable scars upon the soil of Italy, but arousing the admiration of subsequent generations.

One of the main factors in deciding the issue was Roman command of the sea, which Carthage never challenged seriously. Another was the larger citizen body of Rome and the basic friendliness between herself and her federate allies. This, with the system of universal military service, gave her a citizen soldiery superior in morale and numbers to the armies of Carthage. As long as Hannibal was in Italy, Rome kept upwards of 100,000 men in the field. Once only, after the battle of Cannae when she had to arm 8,000 slaves who were promised freedom as a reward for faithful service, was she unable to replace her losses by the regular system of recruiting. On the other hand, Carthage had to raise her forces from mercenaries or from subject allies. As her resources dwindled, the former became even more difficult to obtain, while the demands made upon the latter caused revolts difficult to subdue. It required the personality of a Hannibal to develop an *esprit de corps* and discipline such as characterized his army in Italy. A third factor was the absence in the Roman commanders of the personal rivalries and lack of cooperation which so greatly hampered the Carthaginians in Spain and in Sicily. Still one must not suppose that the Carthaginians did not display extreme tenacity and patriotism. The senatorial class especially distinguished itself by courage and ability, and there is no evidence of factional strife hampering the war effort. The Romans overcame the disadvantage of the annual change of commanders-in-chief by the use of the proconsulship and propraetorship often long prorogued, whereby officers of ability year after year retained the command of the same armies. This system enabled them to develop such able generals as Marcellus and the Scipios.

The cost of maintaining her fleet and her armies taxed the financial resources of Rome to the utmost, and at times the government had to resort to extraordinary measures to prosecute the war. In 216 a loan of money and supplies for the army in Sicily was sought and obtained from Hiero of Syracuse. The next year, in order to maintain the armies in Spain, it was necessary to appeal to the patriotism and generosity of several companies of contractors, who agreed to furnish supplies at their own expense upon promise of repayment as soon as the treasury was again in funds. In 214, when there was pressing need to fit out a naval force to meet the rebellion in Sicily, a special "liturgy" or public obligation was laid on the higher propertied classes, who had to furnish the cost of rowers out of their private resources. Four years later senators made a voluntary contribution of gold and silver for a similar purpose. In 209 the government had to make use of the reserve fund accumulating in the treasury for thirty years from the returns of the 5 percent tax on the value of manumitted slaves. This fund, known as the "sacred treasury," then amounted to 4,000 pounds of gold. When Scipio was making his preparations for his African campaign, the state was unable to furnish him with the necessary levies and ships, and with official approval, he had to appeal for volunteers and for donations of money and material.

An additional burden was inflation and the danger of a grain famine, caused by the disturbed conditions in Italy and Sicily and the withdrawal of so many men from agricultural occupations. In 210 the situation was relieved only by an urgent appeal to Ptolemy Philopator of Egypt, from whom grain had to be purchased at three times the usual price. This crisis passed, however, with the pacification of Sicily in the next year.

A heavy tribute had been levied upon the manpower of the Roman state. The wastage of blood in the struggle was undoubtedly reflected in a sharp decline in the number of men eligible for military service,[9] and the federate allies must have suffered at last as heavily. In 210, twelve of the Latin colonies refused to supply their quotas of troops, giving as an excuse the exhaustion of their manpower. The greatest losses fell upon southern Italy. Year after year the fields there had been laid waste and villages devastated by the opposing armies, until the rural population had almost entirely disappeared, the land had become a wilderness, and the more prosperous cities had fallen into decay.

---

[9] According to the census lists, Rome's manpower potential fell from about 280,000 at the beginning of the war to 237,000 in 209 B.C. But these figures, like almost all ancient statistics, are suspect.

CHAPTER 9

CONQUEST OF THE MEDITERRANEAN. SECOND PHASE—ROME AND THE GREEK EAST: 200–167 B.C.

I. Political Situation in the Near East in 200 B.C.

During the thirty-five years which followed the battle of Zama, Rome attained the same dominant position in the eastern Mediterranean that she had won in the West as a result of the First and Second Punic Wars. The explanation of Roman interference in the East and the rapid extension of her authority there lies in the political situation of the Hellenistic world at the close of the third century, one which Rome exploited by virtue of her increasingly important role as patron to states east of the Adriatic. To understand this situation it is necessary to survey briefly the character and policy of the more important Hellenistic states: Egypt, the Seleucid Empire, and Macedonia.

EGYPT. In the third century B.C. the kingdom of Egypt, ruled by the Macedonian dynasty of the Ptolemies, comprised the ancient kingdom of Egypt in the Nile valley, Cyrene, Palestine and the coast of southern Syria, Cyprus, and a number of cities on the shores and islands of the Aegean Sea. In Egypt the Ptolemies ruled as foreigners over a subject native population. They maintained their authority by a small mercenary army recruited chiefly from Macedonians and Greeks and by a strongly centralized administration staffed by Greeks. Since the ruler owned all the land, the native Egyptians—a majority of whom were peasants who gained their livelihood by tilling the rich soil of the Nile valley—were for the most part tenants of the crown and the restrictions and obligations to which they were subject made them, in effect, serfs. A highly developed but oppressive system of taxation and government monopolies, largely an inheritance from previous dynasties, enabled the Ptolemies to wring from their subjects the revenues to support a brilliant court life at their capital, Alexandria, and finance their imperial policy.

After 276 the aim of this policy was to secure Egyptian domination in the Aegean, among the states of Southern Greece, and in Phoenicia, whose value lay in the forests of the Lebanon mountains. Occupation of the outlying possessions brought Egypt into perpetual conflict with Macedonia and the Seleucid Empire, whose rulers made continual efforts to oust the

Ptolemies from the Aegean and from the Syrian coast. As a consequence, the Ptolemies were obliged to support a navy to give them the command of the sea in the eastern Mediterranean.

Destruction of the Egyptian fleet by the Macedonians in 242 ended the naval supremacy of the Ptolemies but did not force them to relinquish their territory in Syria and the Aegean. In 217, under pressure of an invasion by a Seleucid army, the Egyptian government was forced to arm a portion of the native population. With this aid the enemy was defeated and the immediate danger averted, but realization of their military importance led to demands by the native Egyptians for greater privileges and so to racial difficulties which permanently weakened the dynasty. This internal strife made the Ptolemies helpless to protect their foreign possessions or even to defend Egypt itself against future attacks.

THE SELEUCID EMPIRE. The empire of the Seleucids, known to the Romans as Syria and with its capital at Antioch on the Orontes, was by far the largest of the Hellenistic monarchies in extent and population, and in wealth it ranked next to Egypt. It stretched from the Aegean to the borders of India and included the southern part of Asia Minor, Mesopotamia, Persia, and northern Syria. The very size of this kingdom was a source of weakness because of the distances which separated its various provinces and the heterogeneous ethnic elements it embraced. As in Egypt, the power of the dynasty was upheld by a mercenary army and by the loyalty of Greek cities founded in large numbers by Alexander the Great and his successors. These islands of Greek culture did not succeed to any great extent in Hellenizing the native populations, however, which remained in a state of subjection, indifferent or hostile to their conquerors. The strength of the empire was sapped by repeated revolts in its eastern provinces and dissensions between the members of the dynasty.

These disintegrating forces temporarily disrupted the empire about 220, but the situation was retrieved by an able and energetic ruler, Antiochus III. After crushing the revolting governors of Media, Persia, and Asia Minor in a series of successful campaigns (212–204) Antiochus established his authority as far as the borders of India, gaining for himself the surname of "the Great," and recovered the eastern districts lost by his predecessors.

MACEDONIA. The kingdom of Macedonia, ruled by the house of the Antigonids, was the smallest of the three Hellenistic states in extent, population, and resources, but it possessed an internal strength and solidarity lacking in the others. In Macedonia the Antigonids, by preserving the traditional character of the patriarchal monarchy, kept alive the national spirit of the Macedonians, which made them loyal to the dynasty. They also retained a military system that fostered the traditions of the times of Philip II and Alexander and, since the Macedonian people had not lost its martial character, furnished a small but efficient national army. Outside of Macedonia the Antigonids controlled Thessaly and the eastern part of Greece as far south as the Isthmus of Corinth. Their attempts to dominate the whole of southern Greece were thwarted by the opposition of the Aetolian and Achaean Confederacies, which received considerable support from the Ptolemies. Rivalries among the Greek states eventually brought the Achaeans over to the Macedonian side, and in 222 Macedonia united most of central Greece and the Peloponnesus in a league under her suzerainty. This position was maintained by Philip V in spite of attacks by the Aetolians, Pergamon, and Rhodes during Rome's First Macedonian War (215–206).

In addition to these three great monarchies, there should be noted as powers of some importance the Confederacies, of which that of the Aetolians was on the northern side of the Gulf of Corinth and that of the Achaeans south of the same gulf; the kingdom of Pergamon; and the island republic of Rhodes. Pergamon on the northwestern coast of Asia Minor, lying between Macedonia and the Seleucid Empire, felt apprehensive of any increase in strength by its more powerful neighbors, while Rhodes, at that time the commercial center of the Aegean and possessed of a considerable navy, was inclined to share the fears of Pergamon.

CRISIS OF 202 B.C.   The death of Ptolemy IV in 203 placed upon the throne of Egypt an infant who was under the control of corrupt and incapable advisers. Antiochus III, encouraged by his recent triumphs, judged it a favorable moment to renew his attempt to take from Egypt its Syrian provinces. At the same time Philip V of Macedonia, actuated by a desire to balance the successes of Antiochus by conquests of his own, unexpectedly attacked and occupied several cities under Aetolian protection on the coast of Thrace and certain islands in the Aegean (202). Later writers claimed that Antiochus and Philip had allied to partition the Ptolemaic empire or at least the territories of the Ptolemies outside of Africa, but it is very doubtful if such an agreement really existed. Philip received an Egyptian embassy requesting his aid against Antiochus and seeking his daughter in marriage for the young king of Egypt. Philip seems to have abstained from attacking Ptolemaic possessions in the Aegean before 200. In 201 Philip's activities in the Aegean brought him into conflict with Attalus I of Pergamon and the Rhodians, who, being unable to check his operations and fearing a possible alliance between Macedonia and the Seleucid Empire, appealed to Rome for support. Although the action of Philip's allies in Greece had involved him in hostilities with Athens, it does not seem that the Athenians joined in the appeal to the Roman Senate. It was this step taken by Pergamon and Rhodes that brought about Roman intervention in the Greek East and led to Rome's Second Macedonian War.

II. The Second Macedonian War: 200–196 B.C.

ROME'S EASTERN POLICY TO 201 B.C.   Down to the year 201 Rome can hardly be said to have had any definite eastern policy. Diplomatic intercourse with Egypt had followed the visit of an Egyptian embassy to Rome as early as 273, but this had had no political consequences. Since that date she had come into conflict with the Illyrians and with Macedonia and had established a small protectorate across the Adriatic, but in so doing her actions had been spasmodic and had been brought about by the attacks of the Illyrians and Macedonians upon her allies or herself and were not the result of any aggressive policy of her own. The interest and outlook of Rome's agrarian oligarchy did not include Hellas as a whole or the Greek East. This may be seen in the favorable peace terms granted Philip V of Macedonia in 205, by which Rome abandoned her formal alliances with Philip's enemies, especially the Aetolians. This is the first known instance in which Rome failed to fulfill to the letter her written agreements with her friends, and marks an important stage in the growing sophistication of her foreign policy. These actions made her very unpopular in most of Greece. Her erstwhile allies, especially the Aetolians, protested that they had been left in the lurch, while other Greek states felt antagonistic because Rome had permitted the Aetolians to treat them brutally during the recent war. Rome still found it possible to maintain friendly relations, albeit without formal and possibly entangling treaties, with Pergamon, the Illyrians, some city-states of the Peloponnesus, and possibly Athens. Rome's general attitude toward the Greek world in the period 205–201 was watchful rather than disinterested; she had no vital or definite commitments in the area except the defense of her Illyrian clients.

ROMAN INTERVENTION: 200 B.C.   A combination of circumstances involving Illyria brought about the Second Macedonian War. After the peace of 205 Philip apparently misread the Roman attitude toward Greece as one of total disinterest and attempted by diplomacy to seduce the Illyrians from their connection with Rome. Just as Rome was observing the Illyrian situation with increasing disquiet in 202, the envoys of Rhodes and of Attalus I, King of Pergamon, arrived to inform the Senate of Philip's aggressions in the East and of his alleged pact with Antiochus to partition the Egyptian Empire. They requested Roman help. The Senate, basically unconcerned with what was going on in the Aegean and undisturbed by the unlikely prospect of the "alliance" between Philip and Antiochus being directed against Italy at some future date, was interested, however, in humbling the king who had stabbed her in the back during the recent war with Hannibal and who was now tampering with her Illyrian clients. It seized upon Philip's aggressions against Attalus as a possible *casus belli*. Roman ambassadors were sent to Greece in

201/200 to proclaim a basic change in Roman policy—protection of all Greeks against future Macedonian aggression—and to mobilize Greece under the Roman aegis against Philip. They also carried an ultimatum for Philip which they delivered to one of his generals, a demand that he refrain from war with any Greek state and that he submit his differences with Attalus to arbitration. The ultimatum revealed Rome's new aims: the reduction of Philip to the status of a client prince and the consequent conversion of Greece into a Roman protectorate. Although the Senate was apparently committed to war when these demands were not met, the Roman people as a whole shrank from embarking upon another war so soon after the close of the desperate conflict with Carthage. At first the Centuriate Assembly voted against the proposal, and at a second meeting was induced to sanction it only when the people were told they would have to face another invasion of Italy if they did not anticipate Philip's action. When the Assembly finally gave its approval, one of the Roman ambassadors whom the Senate had already sent to Greece to threaten Philip and encourage his opponents presented the formal declaration of war to the king, who was at that time engaged in the siege of Abydos on the Hellespont, whereupon the conflict began. In accordance with their instructions the ambassadors then visited Antiochus in Syria, perhaps to intercede on behalf of Egypt or to assure him of the good will of Rome so that he might not abandon his Syrian campaign and unite his forces with those of Philip in Macedonia. Roman diplomacy leading up to the war shows that at this stage of her history Rome took states unilaterally under her protection without the formality of a treaty and tended to regard her friends not as equals but as clients.

DEFEAT OF PHILIP.   Late in 200 a Roman army under the consul Sulpicius Galba crossed into Illyricum and tried to penetrate into Macedonia. Both in this and in the succeeding year, however, the Romans, although aided by the Aetolian Confederacy, Pergamon, Rhodes, and Athens, were unable to inflict any decisive defeat upon Philip or to invade his kingdom.

With the arrival of one of the consuls of 198, Titus Flamininus, the situation speedily changed. The Achaean Confederacy was won over to the side of Rome, and Flamininus succeeded in forcing Philip to evacuate Epirus and to withdraw into Thessaly. In the following winter negotiations for peace were opened. At the insistence of her Greek allies, Rome now demanded not merely a guarantee that Philip would refrain from attacking the Hellenes but also the evacuation of Corinth, Chalcis, and Demetrias, three fortresses known as "the fetters of Greece." Philip refused to make this concession.

The next year military operations were resumed with both armies in Thessaly. Early in the summer a battle was fought on a ridge of hills called Cynoscephalae (the Dogs' Heads), where the Romans won a complete victory. Although the Aetolians rendered valuable assistance in this engagement, the Macedonian defeat was due primarily to the superior flexibility of the Roman legionary formation over the phalanx. Philip fled to Macedonia and sued for peace. The Aetolians and his enemies in Greece sought his destruction, but Flamininus realized the importance of Macedonia to the Greek world as a bulwark against the Celtic peoples of the lower Danube and would not support their demands. The terms fixed by the Roman Senate were: autonomy of the Hellenes, in Greece and Asia; evacuation of the Macedonian possessions in Greece, in the Aegean, and in Illyricum; an indemnity of 1,000 talents ($1,200,000); and the surrender of nearly all his warships. These conditions Philip was obliged to accept (196). Soon afterwards he became a Roman ally.

PROCLAMATION OF FLAMININUS: 196 B.C.   At the Isthmian games of the same year Flamininus proclaimed the complete autonomy of the peoples who had been subject to Macedonia. The announcement provoked a tremendous outburst of enthusiasm among most of the Greek states. After spending some time in effecting this policy and in settling the claims of various states, Flamininus returned to Italy in 194, leaving the Greeks to make what use they would of their freedom. The dramatic proclamation of Flamininus is often attributed to the cultural philhellenism increasingly noticeable at this time among the Roman ruling class. Rome's interest in Greek freedom was not sentimental, but was rather the natural result of political and strategic considerations growing out of the recent war. Rome was now merely applying throughout Greece a policy that she had previously used in Messana, Saguntum and Illyria. If the Greeks were free, from the Roman point of view they enjoyed the freedom of client states, which, as a matter of course, would pursue a foreign policy compatible with Roman interests and which would form a bulwark against any hostile action on the part of Philip or Antiochus.

III. War with Antiochus the Great and the Aetolians: 192–189 B.C.

CAUSES OF FRICTION.   Even before Flamininus and his army had withdrawn from Greece, the activities of Antiochus had awakened the mistrust of the Roman Senate and threatened hostilities. The Syrian king had completed the conquest of Lower Syria in 198. Profiting by the difficulties in which Philip of Macedon was involved, he had then turned his attention toward Asia Minor and Thrace with the hope of recovering the possessions once held by his ancestor, Seleucus I. The Romans were at the time too much occupied to oppose him. Outwardly he professed to be a friend of Rome and to be limiting his activities to the reestablishment of his empire's former extent. Eventually, in 196 he crossed over into Europe and took Thrace. The Romans tried to induce him to withdraw but were unsuccessful. Two years later Antiochus himself opened negotiations with the Senate to secure Roman recognition of his claims to Thrace and to certain cities in Asia Minor which, relying upon Roman support, refused to acknowledge his overlordship. The Roman government, cynically enough, was willing to abandon its self-proclaimed status as protector of the Greeks in Asia if Antiochus would evacuate Thrace. Since Antiochus, although harboring no designs against Rome, refused to be forced out of his European possessions, he decided to support the anti-Roman elements in Greece to force Rome to yield the points at issue. Accordingly, he willingly received deputations from the Aetolians, who were the leading opponents of Rome among the Greeks

The Aetolians, Rome's allies in the war just concluded and greatly exaggerating the importance of their services, were disgruntled because Macedonia had not been entirely dismembered and they had been restrained from enlarging the territory of the Confederacy at the expense of their neighbors. In short, they wished to replace Macedonia as the leading Greek state. Accustomed to regard war as a legitimate source of revenue, they did not easily reconcile themselves to Rome's imposition of peace in Hellas. Ever since the battle of Cynoscephalae they had striven to undermine Roman influence among the Greeks, and now they sought to draw Antiochus into conflict with Rome.

WAR IN GREECE AND ASIA MINOR. In 192 they brought matters to a head by unexpectedly attacking some of Rome's supporters in Greece and seizing the fortress of Demetrias, which they offered to the king, to whom they also made an unauthorized promise of aid from Macedonia. Trusting in the support promised by the Aetolians, Antiochus sailed to Greece with an advance force of 10,000 men. Upon his arrival the Aetolians elected him their commander in chief. It so happened that Hannibal, forced to flee his native city in 196 owing to machinations of his enemies and the Romans, was then at the court of Antiochus, where he had taken refuge. Although it is sometimes alleged that he advised his protector to invade Italy, it seems likely that he was rather concerned with intrigues that might result in his reinstatement at Carthage. He may even have counseled moderation and tact in Syrian dealings with the Romans. He had little influence over Antiochus after 193, and the Syrian king made no serious use of his talents in the ensuing war.

In 191 a Roman army under the consul Acilius Glabrio appeared in Greece and defeated the forces of Antiochus at Thermopylae. The king fled to Asia. Contrary to his hopes he had found little support in Greece. Philip of Macedon and the Achaean Confederacy adhered to the Romans, and the Aetolians were made helpless by an invasion of their own country. The Rhodians and Eumenes, the new king of Pergamon, joined their navies to the Roman fleet.

As Antiochus would not listen to the peace terms laid down by the

Romans, the latter resolved to invade Asia Minor. Two naval victories, won with the aid of Rhodes and Pergamon, secured control of the Aegean, and in 190 a Roman force crossed the Hellespont. For commander the Senate had wished to designate Scipio Africanus, the greatest Roman general. As he had recently been consul he was now ineligible for that office. The law was circumvented by election of his brother Lucius to the consulate and his assignment to the command, and by the appointment of Publius to accompany him, apparently as a legate. This arrangement permitted Publius to assume practical direction of the campaign.

One decisive victory over Antiochus at Magnesia in the autumn of 190 brought him to terms. He agreed to surrender all territory north of the Taurus mountains and west of Pamphylia, to give up his war elephants, to surrender all but ten of his ships of war, to pay an indemnity of 15,000 talents ($18,000,000) in twelve annual instalments, and to abstain from attacking the allies of Rome. Unlike Carthage, he was still at liberty to defend himself if attacked. Peace upon these conditions was formally ratified in 188. This time Rome did not "free" all the Greeks as she had done in 196, since such an action would have produced too many petty states and future imbroglios. Some of the Greek city-states did receive their freedom, but Rhodes and Pergamon were the principal beneficiaries of the peace, which brought them an accession of territory at the expense of neighboring Greeks and non-Greeks alike.

The Romans had demanded from Antiochus the surrender of Hannibal, but Antiochus connived at his escape. Hannibal took refuge with Prusias, the king of Bithynia. In 186 Prusias made war upon Rome's ally, Eumenes of Pergamon, and appointed Hannibal as one of his commanders. Hannibal won a naval victory, but Rome intervened on behalf of Eumenes, and Prusias was forced to make peace. Again the Romans insisted upon the surrender of Hannibal, and Prusias was not in a position to refuse. Rather than be captured, Hannibal took poison. He died in 182, about a year later than Scipio Africanus, his conqueror at Zama.

THE SUBJUGATION OF THE AETOLIANS: 189 B.C. The Roman campaign of 191 against the Aetolians had caused the latter, who were also attacked by Philip of Macedon, to seek terms. The Romans demanded unconditional surrender, and the Aetolians decided to continue the struggle. No energetic measures were taken against them at once, but in 189 the consul Fulvius Nobilior pressed the war vigorously and besieged their chief stronghold, Ambracia. Since the obstinate resistance of its defenders defied all his efforts and since the Athenians were trying to act as mediators in ending the war, the Romans abandoned their demand for unconditional surrender. The Aetolians proved that they had not understood the meaning of clientship, and the Romans were determined that any peace treaty with them should express their dependent status. Peace was finally made on the following conditions: the Aetolian Confederacy was granted a permanent alliance with Rome on an unequal footing, with the obligation to support Rome against all her enemies; the Confederacy gave up all territory captured by its enemies during the war; Ambracia was surrendered and sacked; and the Romans occupied the pirate nest of Cephallenia.

IV. Third Macedonian War: 171–167 B.C.

ROME AND THE GREEK STATES.   Although by her alliance with the Aetolians Rome had planted herself permanently on Greek soil and in the war with Antiochus had claimed to exercise a protectorate over the Greek world, the Senate as yet gave no indication of reversing the policy of Flamininus, and the Greek states remained friends of Rome in the enjoyment of political "independence." It was not long, however, before these friendly relations became seriously strained and Rome was induced to embark upon a policy of political and then military interference in Greek affairs, which ultimately put an end to the apparent freedom of Hellas. The fundamental cause of the change was that, while Rome interpreted Greek freedom to mean liberty of action provided that the wishes and arrangements of Rome were respected, the Greeks understood it to mean the perfect freedom of sovereign communities and resented bitterly any infringement of their supposed rights. Keeping in mind these conflicting points of view, it is easy to see how difficulties were bound to arise, inevitably to be settled according to the wishes of the stronger power.

The chief specific causes for the change in Roman policy are to be found in the troubles of the Achaean Confederacy and the reviving ambitions of Macedonia. The Confederacy included many city-states which had been compelled to join it and which sought to regain their independence. This the Confederacy was determined to prevent. One such community was Sparta, and the policy of the Achaeans towards it in the matter of the restoration of Spartan exiles led the Spartans to appeal to Rome. The Roman reaction wounded the susceptibilities of the Confederacy without settling the problem, and the tendency of the Achaeans to stand upon their rights provoked Roman anger. Within the Confederacy there developed a pro-Roman party, ready to submit to Roman domination, and a national party determined to assert their right to freedom of action. After 180 the Romans deliberately fostered the aristocratic factions throughout the cities of Greece, feeling that they were the more stable element and more in harmony with the policy of the Senate. The democratic factions then began to look for outside support in Macedonia.

Philip V of Macedon considered that the assistance he had furnished to Rome in the Syrian War was proof of his loyalty and warranted the annexation of the territory he had overrun in that conflict. The Senate was not inclined to allow the power of Macedonia to attain dangerous proportions, and he was forced to forego his claims. Henceforth he was bitter toward Rome. He devoted himself to the development of the military resources of his kingdom with the ultimate view of challenging once again Rome's authority. At his death in 179 he left an army of from 30,000 to 40,000 men and a treasure of 6,000 talents ($7,200,000). His son and successor Perseus inherited his father's anti-Roman policy and entered into relations with the enemies of Rome everywhere in Greece.

ROMAN ATTACK ON PERSEUS.   The Senate was kept well aware of his schemes by his enemies in Greece, especially Eumenes II, King of Pergamon, the successor of Attalus I. Therefore it determined to forestall his plans and force him into war. In 172 a Roman commission visited Perseus and required of him concessions which meant loss of liberty. Upon his refusal to comply with their demands the commissioners returned home, and Rome declared war. When success depended upon energetic action, Perseus sought to avoid the issue and tried vainly to placate the Romans. In 171 a Roman force landed in Greece and made its way to Thessaly. In the campaigns of this and the following year the Roman commanders were too incapable and their troops too undisciplined to make any headway, but Perseus showed no ability to take advantage of his opportunities. Furthermore, by his parsimony he lost the chance to win valuable aid from the Dardanians, Gesatae, and Celts on his borders. Finally, in 168, the Romans found an able general in the consul Aemilius Paullus, who restored the morale of the Roman soldiers and won a complete victory over Perseus in the battle of Pydna. Perseus took flight but soon was obliged to give himself up. He was taken to Rome, where he was treated with ignominy and died in captivity. The Macedonian kingdom was at an end. Its territory was divided into four autonomous republics, which were forbidden mutual privileges of *commercium* and *conubium*. A yearly tribute of 100 talents was imposed upon them; the royal mines and domains became the property of Rome, and for a time the gold and silver mines were shut down.

ROMAN SETTLEMENT IN THE EAST.   Having disposed of Macedonia, the Romans turned their attention to the other Greek states with the intention of rewarding their friends and punishing their enemies. During the recent war the Greeks had realized that Perseus' defeat would make Roman power unchallengeable, and consequently anti-Roman parties had arisen in many parts of Greece. The situation was worsened, especially in the Peloponnese, by social disorder which added to the strife from political causes. Death or exile awaited the leaders of the anti-Roman parties, many of whose names became known from the papers of Perseus. Although the Achaeans had given no positive proof of disloyalty, 1,000 of their leading men, among them the historian Polybius, were carried off to Italy, nominally to be given the chance of clearing themselves before the Senate but really to be kept as hostages in Italy for the future conduct of the Confederacy.

The Rhodians, because they had endeavored to secure a peaceful settle-

ment between Rome and Perseus, were forced to surrender their possessions in Asia Minor in spite of a speech to the Senate by Cato the Elder,
who counseled moderation and common sense. Their commercial prosperity was crippled by the establishment of a free port at the island of Delos.
Eumenes of Pergamon, whose actions had made him suspect to Rome,
was subjected to humiliating treatment, although he kept his kingdom.
Far worse was the fate of Epirus, seventy of whose towns were sacked
and 150,000 of the inhabitants carried off into slavery.

Henceforth it was clear that Rome was sovereign in the eastern Mediterranean and that her friends and allies enjoyed only local autonomy,
while expected to be obedient to the orders of Rome. This is well illustrated by the anecdote of the circle of Popilius. During the Third Macedonian War, Antiochus IV, Epiphanes, King of Syria and former Roman
hostage, invaded Egypt. After the battle of Pydna a Roman ambassador,
Gaius Popilius, was sent to request his withdrawal. Popilius met Antiochus before Alexandria and delivered the Senate's message. The king
asked for time to consider, but the Roman, drawing a circle around him
in the sand, bade him answer before he left the spot. Antiochus yielded
and evacuated Egypt.

The spoils of this war with Macedonia brought such an enormous
booty into the Roman treasury that after 167 the war tax on property—
the *tributum civium Romanorum*—ceased to be levied. The income of the
empire enabled the government to relieve Roman citizens of all direct taxation.

V. Campaigns in Italy and Spain

During the Macedonian and Syrian Wars the Romans were busy
strengthening and extending their hold upon northern Italy and Spain.

PACIFICATION OF NORTHERN ITALY. Cisalpine Gaul, which
had been largely lost to the Romans since Hannibal's invasion, was recovered by wars with the Insubres and Boii between 198 and 191. The
great military highway, the *via Flaminia*, built from Rome to Ariminum
in 220, was extended under the name of the *via Aemilia* to Placentia by
way of Bononia in 187. Another, the *via Cassia* (171), linked Rome and
the Po valley by way of Etruria. New fortresses were established: Bononia
(189) and Aquileia (181) as Latin colonies; Parma and Mutina (183)
as colonies of Roman citizens. In this way Roman authority was firmly established and the way prepared for the rapid Latinization of the land between the Apennines and the Alps.

In the same period falls the subjugation of the Ligurians, whose border
raids had proved annoying. In successive campaigns, lasting until 172,
the Romans gradually extended their sway over the various Ligurian tribes
until they reached the territory of Massilia in southern Gaul. In the proc-

ess of pacification, 40,000 Ligurians were transplanted from their homes to vacant public lands in South Italy. A Latin colony was founded at Luca (180) and one of Roman citizens at Luna (177). Between 181 and 176 the Sardinian tribes rebelled, and this led to thorough subjugation of that island.

SPAIN.   The territory acquired from Carthage in Spain was organized in 197 into two provinces, called Hither and Farther Spain. The allied and subject Spanish tribes were not yet reconciled to the presence of the Romans, however, and serious revolts broke out. One of these was subdued by Marcus Porcius Cato in 196, another by Lucius Aemilius Paullus between 191 and 189, and a third by Tiberius Sempronius Gracchus in 179 and 178. The settlement effected by Gracchus secured peace for many years. In Spain were founded Rome's first colonies beyond the borders of Italy. Italica, near Seville, was settled in 206, and Carteia in 171, the former as a town (*oppidum*) of Roman citizens, the latter a Latin colony.

CHAPTER 10

THE CRISIS OF IMPERIALISM: 167–133 B.C.

CLIENT STATES AND PROVINCES. In the Greek East the battle of Pydna marked a decisive turning point in Roman foreign policy. After 168 the entire Hellenistic world was effectively reduced to the status of Roman clients. In the West, Carthage had been reduced to the same status since the Second Punic War, while Spain, where the Senate had attempted direct provincial administration, was restive. Throughout the period 167–133 control of foreign powers through the organization of client states remained the preferred policy of the Senate. This avoided annexation of territory as provinces, which would have meant too great a drain upon the resources of the state and created administrative problems. Only when the client-state system failed to produce the peace and subservience that Rome demanded were provinces formed. Such a failure was evident by mid-century in a crisis originating in wars in Rome's Spanish provinces and spreading to the dependent states when the latter revolted. The Spanish wars were to have important internal repercussions on the state, and the revolts elsewhere forced the Senate to abandon the client system in strategic areas, to annex Carthage and Macedonia, to establish direct control over Greece, and eventually to acquire territory in Asia Minor.

I. The Spanish Wars: 154–133 B.C.

REVOLTS OF CELTIBERIANS AND LUSITANIANS: 154–139 B.C. In 154 revolts broke out in both Hither and Farther Spain. The series of long and bloody campaigns that ensued were prolonged by the incapacity, cruelty, and faithlessness of the Roman commanders and caused a heavy drain upon the military resources of Italy. The chief opponents of the Romans were the Celtiberians of Hither, and the Lusitanians of Farther Spain. The desperate character of these wars and the progressive lowering of the property qualifications for military service in order to find the necessary levies made service in Spain very unpopular and occasioned a revival of the initiative of some tribunes in protecting the interests of hard-pressed peasants. In 151 and 138 tribunes actually imprisoned consuls enforcing the draft for the Spanish campaign. In 150 the proconsul Galba treacherously massacred thousands of Lusitanians with whom he had made a treaty. For this he was brought to trial by Cato but was acquitted.

The massacre led to a renewed outbreak under Viriathus, an able guerrilla leader who defied the power of Rome for about eight years (147–139). Forced eventually to yield, he was assassinated during an armistice by traitors suborned by the Roman commander. The complete subjugation of the Lusitanians soon followed.

WAR WITH NUMANTIA: 143–133 B.C.   Meantime in 143, war had broken out afresh in the nearer province, where the struggle centered about the town of Numantia. In 140 the Roman general Pompeius made peace upon easy terms with the Numantines but later repudiated it, and the Senate ignored his arrangements. A disgraceful surrender of the consul Mancinus and his army of 20,000 Romans to the Numantines took place in 137. By concluding a treaty the consul saved the lives of his men, but the Roman Senate perfidiously rejected his sworn agreement, made him the scapegoat, and delivered him to the Numantines, who would have none of him.

At length, weary of defeats, the Romans re-elected to the consulship for 134 their tried general Scipio Aemilianus, the conqueror of Carthage (146),[1] and appointed him commander in Spain. His first task was to restore the discipline in his army. Then he began a blockade of Numantia. After a siege of fifteen months the city was starved into submission and razed. A commission of ten senators reorganized the country, and Spain began a long era of peace.

II. Destruction of Carthage: 149–146 B.C.

THE THIRD PUNIC WAR: 149–146 B.C.—ITS CAUSES. The treaty which ended the Second Punic War had forbidden the Carthaginians to make war anywhere without the consent of Rome, which thus reduced Carthage to client status. At the same time their enemy Masinissa had been established as a powerful client prince on their borders. In such a situation future Roman intervention was inevitable, but Carthage was left in peace for a generation. After the exile of Hannibal in 196 the Carthaginians realistically accepted their dependent status and devoted their energies to the peaceful revival of their commerce and to the payment of reparations. The Romans would have been undisturbed by a remarkable economic revival if this had not suggested a possible resurgence of Punic political power as well. The Romans continued, perhaps exaggeratedly, to fear and suspect their former enemy and were therefore prepared to seize on any sign of political independence at Carthage as an excuse for her destruction.

The opportunity came through the action of Masinissa. This chieftain,

[1] See p. 138.

knowing the restrictions imposed on Carthage by her treaty with Rome and understanding the Roman attitude toward the city, frequently attacked Punic territory. Carthage could only appeal to Rome for protection, but Roman commissions repeatedly sent to adjust the disputes decided in favor of Masinissa. One member of a commission investigating Carthaginian complaints of frontier violations was old Marcus Porcius Cato, who was still obsessed with the fear Carthage had inspired in his youth and who returned from his mission filled with alarm at the wealth of the city. Henceforth he devoted all his energies to accomplish its overthrow. In the following years he concluded all his speeches in the Senate with the words, "Carthage must be destroyed."

Further friction with Masinissa occurred in 151 and resulted in hostilities in which Carthage suffered a disastrous defeat. The Romans at once prepared for war. Conscious of having overstepped their rights as clients, and fearful of Roman vengeance, the Carthaginians offered unconditional submission in the hope of obtaining pardon. The Senate assured them of their lives, property, and constitution, but required hostages and told them to follow the commands of the consuls, who crossed over to Africa with an army and ordered the Carthaginians to surrender their arms and engines of war. The Carthaginians, desirous of appeasing the Romans at all costs, complied. Then came the ultimatum. They must abandon their city and settle at least ten miles from the seacoast. This was practically a death sentence to the ancient mercantile city. The faction in the Carthaginian government that had advocated cooperation with the Romans was overturned by one advocating a last-ditch defense of Punic interests. The Carthaginians improvised weapons and, manning their walls, defied the Romans.

THE SIEGE OF CARTHAGE: 149–146 B.C.   For two years the Romans, owing to the incapacity of their commanders, accomplished little. Then disappointment and apprehension led the electorate to demand as consul Scipio Aemilianus, talented officer and adopted grandson of Scipio Africanus. He was only a candidate for the aedileship and legally ineligible for the consulate. But the restrictions upon his candidature were suspended by a law passed in the Tribal Assembly, and he was elected consul for 147. Another special law entrusted him with the conduct of the war in Africa. Scipio restored discipline in the Roman army, defeated the Carthaginians in the field, and energetically besieged the city. The Carthaginians suffered frightfully from hunger, and their forces were greatly reduced. In the spring of 146 the Romans forced their way into the city and captured it after desperate fighting in the streets and houses. The survivors, about 50,000, were sold into slavery, their city leveled to the ground, and its site declared accursed. Out of the Carthaginian territory the Romans created a new province, called Africa. The last act in the dramatic struggle between the two cities was ended.

III. Annexation of Macedonia and Dissolution of the Achaean Confederacy: 149–146 B.C.

THE FOURTH MACEDONIAN WAR: 149–148 B.C.   The mutual rivalries among the Greek states, which frequently evoked senatorial intervention, and the ill will occasioned by the harshness of the Romans toward the anti-Roman party everywhere caused a large faction among the Hellenes to look for the first favorable opportunity for freeing Greece from Roman suzerainty.

Relying on this antagonism to Rome, a certain Andriscus, who claimed to be a son of Perseus, appeared in Macedonia in 149 and claimed the throne. He made himself master of the country and defeated the first Roman forces sent against him. He was crushed the following year at Pydna by the praetor Metellus, however, and Macedonia was annexed as a Roman province (148).

WAR WITH THE ACHAEANS.   The Achaean Confederacy was one especially anti-Roman state. There the irksomeness of the Roman protectorate was heightened by the return of the 300 survivors of the political exiles of 167. The anti-Roman party, supported by the extreme democratic elements in the cities, was in control of the Confederacy when border difficulties with Sparta broke out afresh in 149. The matter was referred to the Senate for settlement, but the Achaeans did not await its decision. They attacked and defeated Sparta, confident that the Romans were preoccupied by the wars in Spain, Africa, and Macedonia.

The Senate determined to punish the Confederacy by detaching certain important cities from its membership. In 147 the Achaean assembly tempestuously refused to carry out the orders of the Roman ambassadors, although the Macedonian revolt had been crushed. Their leaders, expecting no mercy from Rome, prepared for war, and they were joined by the Boeotians and other peoples of central Greece. Everywhere they were supported by the poorer classes in the cities, who saw hope for economic betterment in a social revolution. The next year the Achaeans again refused to comply with Roman advice, whereupon the Romans sent a fleet and an army against them under the consul Lucius Mummius. Metellus, the conqueror of Macedonia, subdued central Greece, and Mummius routed the forces of the Confederacy at Leucopetra on the Isthmus (146). Corinth was sacked and burnt, its treasures were carried off to Rome, and its inhabitants sold into slavery. Its land, like that of Carthage, was added to the Roman public domain. Like Alexander's destruction of Thebes, this was a warning which the other cities of Greece could not misinterpret. A senatorial commission dissolved the Achaean Confederacy as well as the similar political combinations of the Boeotians and Phocians. The cities of Greece entered into individual relations with Rome. Those which had stood on the side of Rome, as Athens and Sparta, retained their previous status as Roman allies; the rest were made subject and tributary. Greece was not organized as a province but was put under the supervision of the governor of Macedonia.

IV. Acquisition of the Kingdom of Pergamon

PROVINCE OF ASIA. In 133 died Attalus III, King of Pergamon, the last of his line. In his will he made the Roman people the heir to his kingdom, probably with the feeling that otherwise disputes over the succession would end in Roman interference and conquest. The Romans accepted the inheritance, but before they took possession a claimant appeared in the person of an illegitimate son of Eumenes II, one Aristonicus. He occupied part of the kingdom, defeated and killed the consul Crassus in 130, but was himself beaten and captured by the latter's successor Perperna.

Out of the kingdom of Pergamon the Roman province of Asia was then formed (129). Occupation of this country made Rome mistress of both shores of the Aegean and gave her a convenient bridgehead for an advance farther eastward. For the unfortunate subjects of Attalus, incorporation in the Roman Empire proved the reverse of the blessing he had anticipated. The struggles of rival political factions in Rome made them victims of a long period of maladministration and fiscal oppression.

ROME, ITALY, AND THE EMPIRE: 264–133 B.C.

The winning of hegemony in the Mediterranean world entailed the most serious consequences for the Roman state. The wars described in the preceding chapters were, in fact, the ultimate cause of the crisis that led to the fall of the Roman Republic. The present chapter will trace the changes and indicate the problems that had their origin in these wars and the ensuing conquests. Such a survey may well begin by consideration of the character of Roman government during the epoch in question.

I. Rule of the Senatorial Oligarchy

CONSTITUTION FROM 265 TO 133 B.C.   During this period of expansion there were few changes of importance in the political organization of the state. The dictatorship had been discarded, although not abolished, before the close of the Hannibalic War, a step in harmony with the policy of the Senate, which sought to prevent any official from attaining too independent a position. In 242 a second praetorship, the office of the *praetor peregrinus* or alien praetor, was established. The duty of this officer was to preside over the trial of disputes arising between foreigners or between Roman citizens and foreigners. Two additional praetorships were added in 227 and two more in 197, in order to provide provincial governors of praetorian rank. Further increase in the number of these magistrates was avoided by the use of proconsuls and propraetors as provincial governors after 148. In 241 the last two rural tribal districts were created, making thirty-five tribes in all. Hereafter when new settlements of Roman colonists were undertaken or new peoples admitted to citizenship, they were assigned to one or another of the old tribes.

An important change was made in the organization of the Centuriate Assembly, very probably in the censorship of 241–240, when the last two tribes were created. Some of the details of the reform are debatable. It seems, however, that the centuries of the first classes were distributed on a tribal basis, an equal number of centuries of juniors and seniors of these classes being assigned to each tribe. Thus the first class was reduced from 80 to 70 centuries, 35 of juniors and 35 of seniors, while the total number of centuries was maintained at 193. The equestrian centuries were deprived of the right of taking the lead in proceedings by casting the first vote—a right henceforth exercised by a first-class century chosen by lot for each meeting. The equestrian centuries then voted with the rest of the first class, followed by the votes of the second class. Superficially, it might seem that this reform democratized the assembly with control being placed in the hands of a less wealthy group of rural landholders than before, since the equestrian centuries and those of the first class no longer constituted a majority. In reality, however, this reform only put the ruling oligarchy more firmly in control of the assembly. Granted the increasingly proletariat nature of the capital's population and the growth of large estates in its immediate vicinity, tribes in and near Rome had few citizens possessed of the property qualification to vote in the first classes. Centuries based on such tribes would be like rotten boroughs, easily manipulated by senatorial patrons. Furthermore, as a result of this reform the value of the individual vote was grossly unequal in the first classes, since centuries based on more populous tribes in the hinterland of Italy had no more influence than those less populous ones in and near the capital.

As early as the third century B.C. the Roman primary assemblies were thus becoming antiquated as vehicles for the expression of the wishes of a majority of Roman citizens. This was partly because of social and political developments consequent to the spread of the citizen body throughout Italy, the maintenance of Roman garrisons in the provinces, and the settlement of many Romans there and elsewhere outside the peninsula. All of these developments made it difficult for more than a minority of the electorate to attend the meetings of either assembly.

GOVERNING OLIGARCHY. The victory of the commons in the patricio-plebeian struggle had broken the patrician monopoly of political power and provided the state with institutions that gave it the appearance of a democracy. It never became such in fact. In spite of recognition of the sovereign power of the people, the government continued after 287 to rest, as before, in the hands of an oligarchy. This oligarchy itself was far different from the old patrician aristocracy. The patrician *gentes* formed an important element of the government and for a long time continued to supply a large proportion of the political leaders of Rome, besides enjoying great social prestige, but in addition to the patricians, the new oligarchy included a large group of plebeian families, some of which had taken the lead in the struggle for political equality, while others were immigrants to Rome from municipalities that had received the franchise and where they had belonged to the local aristocracies. By attaining public offices and subsequent enrollment in the Senate, this plebeian element had come to join the ranks of the older aristocracy. Community of interest, cemented by frequent intermarriage and adoptions, tended to promote solidarity among all elements of the ruling class. As the patrician *gentes* were gradually dying out, however, the oligarchy as a whole came to assume an increasingly plebeian character. While all families which had at any time had an ancestor in the Senate belonged to the Roman oligarchy, there were within this group distinctions based upon the rank of the offices which these ancestors had held. The highest distinction was reserved for the narrow circle of those to whom the Romans applied the term nobles or nobility (*nobiles, nobilitas*). Strictly speaking, this mark of respect was applied only to the descendants of those who had once held the highest *imperium*, as consuls, dictators, or military tribunes with consular power.

The new oligarchy was one both of wealth and of office. In the course of the third century the enlarged group of senatorial families succeeded in creating for themselves a real, if not legal, monopoly of the magistracies and thus of the regular gateway to the Senate and so tended to become a closed caste. They were able to maintain this monopoly and prevent a further enlargement of their charmed circle partly because of the expense involved in holding public offices, which were unsalaried, and partly because of the cost of conducting the election campaigns, which became increasingly great as time went on. The demands made upon the time of magistrates and senators also deterred all but persons of considerable fortune from seeking office. The candidate whose name was that of one of the families that had guided the fortunes of Rome for generations had an enormous advantage over one of unknown ancestry. The great development of voluntary clientage owing to changing economic conditions, the formation of far-reaching political alliances, and the personal canvassing of influential supporters were all on the side of a son of a wealthy and prominent house. Finally, the magistrate in charge of an assembly on election day had the right to reject the candidature of a person whom he disapproved. In the face of such obstacles it was rare that anyone not *persona grata* to the majority of the senators attained the quaestorship and so made his way into the Senate. Access to the consulship, the hallmark of nobility, was even more jealously guarded. The number of consuls from families that had only recently attained senatorial status declined steadily during the third century B.C. and of the 108 consuls elected from 200 to 146, only some eight belonged to families that had not held this office previously. By the second century B.C., control of Roman policies rested with less than twenty senatorial families, which, by virtue of their position, held an inordinate number of consulships. It was only individuals of exceptional force and ability, like Cato the Elder and later Marius and Cicero, who could penetrate these barriers and reach the highest office in the state. Such a one was styled a "new man" or "parvenu" (*novus homo*). This, then, was the oligarchy from which the Senate was recruited and which, through the Senate, ruled the Roman world.

SENATE'S CONTROL OF LEGISLATION AND ADMINISTRATION. Even though the will of the people was theoretically sovereign after the passing of the Hortensian Law in 287, in fact from that date to the tribunate of Tiberius Gracchus in 133 the Senate exercised a practically unchallenged control over the government of the Roman state. The

Senate was able to guide or nullify the actions of the magistrates, the tribunate, and the assemblies—a condition made possible by the composition
of the Senate, which, in addition to the ex-magistrates, normally included
all those above the rank of quaestor actually in office, and by the peculiar
organization and limitations of the Roman popular assemblies.

The higher magistrates were simply committees of senators elected by
the assemblies. Their interests were those of the Senate as a whole, and
constitutional practice required them to seek its advice on all important
matters. The Senate assigned to the consuls and praetors their spheres of
duty and appointed promagistrates and allotted them their commands, and
no contracts let by the censors were valid unless approved by the Senate.
Except when the consuls were in the city, the Senate controlled all expenditures from the public treasury.

The chief weapon of the tribunes, their right of veto, which had been
instituted as a check upon the power of the Senate and the magistrates, became an instrument whereby the Senate bridled the tribunate itself. After
287 the plebeians came to constitute a large proportion of those in the
Senate chamber, and it was not difficult for this body to get some tribune
to veto any measures of which it disapproved, whether they originated
with a consul or another tribune. The popular character of the tribunate
was merely lying dormant during most of the period. During the Spanish
wars at the middle of the second century B.C. tribunes had interceded to
protect the peasant yeomanry and even proposed legislation to that end at
variance with the wishes of the senatorial oligarchy. Such action por-
tended the eventual reactivation of the tribunate as a revolutionary instrument challenging senatorial control of government.

Because the popular assemblies could vote only on such measures or for
such candidates as were submitted to them by the presiding magistrates,
the Senate through its influence over magistrates and tribunes controlled
both the legislative and elective activities of the Comitia.

SENATE AND PUBLIC POLICY.   Since the Senate was a permanent body, easily assembled and regularly summoned by the consuls to discuss all matters of public concern, it was natural that the foreign policy of
the state should be entirely in its hands—subject, of course, to the right
of the Centuriate Assembly to sanction the making of war or peace—and
hence the organization and government of Rome's foreign possessions became a senatorial prerogative. It fell to the Senate to deal with all sudden
crises that constituted a menace to the state, such as the spread of the
Bacchanalian associations, which were ended by a senatorial decree of 186.

Even though the Greek historian and statesman, Polybius, an intimate
of governing circles in Rome about 150 B.C., viewing the Roman constitution, could call it a nice balance between monarchy as represented by the
consuls, aristocracy as represented by the Senate, and democracy as represented by the tribunate and assemblies, in actual practice the state was

governed by the Senate. From what has been said, however, it will readily be seen that the Senate's power rested mainly on custom and precedent and on the prestige and influence of itself as a whole and its individual members, not on powers guaranteed by law.

FACTIONAL POLITICS AND THE SCIPIOS.   From earliest times the Senate had been divided into a number of rival groups of allied families which sought to monopolize as far as possible the highest offices and honors in the gift of the state. Such political cliques were known as *factiones* or *partes*. They were not parties in the modern sense with doctrinaire political programs but were rather fluid groupings within the oligarchy aimed mainly at furthering the political ambitions of their members. The composition of these factions changed through the years as now one, now another of the great *gentes* on which they were based gained or lost in prominence. A constant factor in these political constellations was patronage exercised over lesser senatorial families by those already well established or on the ascendant. Thus an aspiring candidate for senatorial office had not only to solicit his own clients for their votes in assembly, but also to make firm connections by marriage or by political deals with established *gentes* that would guarantee him the votes of their clients as well.

Some factions occasionally sought to attain leadership in the state by espousing causes of reform or change in the existing order that actually might run counter to interests of the senatorial class as a whole. The leader of one such group in the Senate was Gaius Flaminius, who was allied politically with the Aemilian and Scipionic *gentes*. Between 233 and 217, with the backing of his party, the popular Flaminius, as tribune, consul, and censor, sought to build up a political following among the nonsenatorial gentry by encouraging, under his own patronage, the election of new men to high senatorial office. Through a statesmanlike act strengthening the state and improving his control over the elective assemblies, he reinvigorated the class of yeoman voters and soldiers by bringing about the subdivision of the Gallic Land among poorer Roman citizens in spite of the opposition of many senators. Flaminius has sometimes been described as a democrat. There seems no doubt that he and his political allies held more liberal views than many of his fellow senators, but it is doubtful that he or any other senator of his time, no matter how "liberal," ever seriously considered the championing of real political initiative on the part of Roman citizenry outside the senatorial oligarchy.

When Flaminius died at Lake Trasimene early in the Second Punic War, leadership in the Senate passed from the Aemilian and Scipionic factions supporting him to the more cautious and conservative Fabians and their party. After the military successes of Publius Cornelius Scipio Africanus in the closing phases of the war (206–201), the more "liberal" wing of the Senate, with Scipio the conqueror of Hannibal as its leader, returned to dominance. The further career of Scipio is illustrative of an important fact of political life within the senatorial oligarchy. Although split into factions, it was generally united in its desire to prevent any one man from achieving an absolutely preëminent political status.

Scipio reached the height of his influence at the close of the Second Punic War (201), after which, like any good senatorial oligarch, he devoted much attention to the strengthening of his faction and to the election of his political adherents to high office. His own position and that of his friends were by no means assured as a matter of course, and he had to campaign strenuously against other, rival factions, which were determined to reduce him to size. Although he was elected to his second consulship in 194 and although he was able to engineer the election of many of his friends to the highest offices, he also received rebuffs, as when Hannibal, toward whom he felt lenient, was driven from Carthage by a senatorial commission. Both Africanus and his brother Lucius were recalled from the East at the termination of the latter's consulship (end of 190), although normally a successful general was continued in his command until his campaign was concluded.

One of the chief spokesmen of the anti-Scipionic factions was Marcus Porcius Cato, a prosperous farmer who had entered politics as a new man under the patronage of Scipio's foes and who compensated for a total lack of ancestry by great oratorical ability and a display of sincere puritanical virtue. His intransigent hostility to Scipio may be explained in large measure by his complete acceptance of oligarchic political ideals, and he instinctively distrusted excessively brilliant careerists, like Scipio. In 190 there began a series of political prosecutions through which Cato and others sought to undermine the influence of the Scipionic faction by convicting some of its members of misconduct in public affairs, and the latter tried in turn to discredit their opponents. Finally, in 187 Cato sponsored a demand that Lucius Scipio account to the Senate for a sum of 500 talents, which King Antiochus III had paid to him as the first installment of the indemnity imposed upon him after his defeat at Magnesia. Africanus, who refused to admit that a commander was obliged to account for his disposal of the booty won by his army, promptly tore up his brother's account books in the presence of the Senate. His enemies claimed that the money in question could not be regarded as spoils of war. In 184 a tribune called upon Lucius to render an account to the Tribal Assembly, and only a personal appeal by Africanus to the people stifled the prosecution for the moment. At a later meeting of the Assembly, a heavy fine was imposed upon Lucius for peculation. When he refused to give security for payment, he was saved from imprisonment only by the intervention of a friendly tribune. Although the case was not pressed further, the influence of the Scipios was broken, and Africanus retired from public life until his death in 183.

RACE FOR OFFICE. It is frequently alleged that, following the Second Punic War, the Senate gradually abandoned the virtues of self-sacrifice, steadfastness, and patriotism, which had contributed so largely to Rome's triumph, and that it deteriorated in both capacity and morale. Such a view demands serious qualification. Even before 200 the oligarchy had resisted changes that might threaten its economic and social predominance; in times of crisis, like the Second Punic War, bitter political rivalries within the Senate were common. In much earlier times, despite later Roman attempts to idealize them, senators had not shown ethical qualms about treating weaker peoples brutally when it seemed advantageous for Rome to do so. In the course of the second century B.C. the prizes of officeholding in an expanding empire became evermore tempting, however, and opportunities for corruption and illicit gain thereby multiplied. Personal ambition and class interest, always characteristics of the senatorial order, were then merely operative in a larger political arena and for greater stakes than before. Officeholding, with the opportunities it offered for ruling subject peoples and of commanding in profitable wars, became a ready means for securing for oneself and one's friends the wealth needed to maintain the new standard of luxurious living now affected by the ruling class of the imperial city. The higher magistracies seemed especially valuable to the senators, since they were excluded by custom from banking and undertaking public contracts and were prohibited by a Claudian Law, passed in 218, from owning ships of sufficient carrying capacity to engage in overseas commerce. As a consequence, rivalry for office became intense, and customary canvassing for votes tended to degenerate into bribery both of individuals and of the masses. In the latter case it took the form of entertaining the public by lavish spectacles in the theater and the arena.

ATTEMPTS TO RESTRAIN ABUSES. There are indications that the Senate realized the greater temptations of the age and that it attempted to check political abuses. This may be seen in legislation regulating the senatorial *cursus honorum*. In 197, or shortly thereafter, tenure of the praetorship became a necessary qualification for the consulship. In 180 the Villian Law (*lex Villia annalis*) established minimum ages for holding the various curule magistracies: thirty-six for the curule aedileship, thirty-nine for the praetorship, and forty-two for the consulship. It is not certain whether this law made previous tenure of the quaestorship a necessary qualification for higher office or whether it provided for a fixed minimum age at which the quaestorship could be held. An interval of two years was required between successive magistracies. Normally a man would hold the quaestorship, and then the aedileship, which, although not imperative, involved the supervision of public games and festivals and in this way gave a good opportunity for ingratiating oneself with the populace. The praetorship and the consulship completed the *cursus honorum* in that order.[1] Somewhat later, about 151, reelections to the same office were forbidden. In the years 181 and 159 laws were passed establishing severe penalties for bribery of electors. Another attempt to check the same abuse was the introduction of the secret ballot for voting in the assemblies. The Gabinian Law of 139 provided for the use of the secret ballot in elections, two years later the Cassian Law extended its use to trials in the Comitia, and in 131 it was finally employed in the legislative assemblies.

These laws accomplished little, as they dealt merely with the symptoms, and not with the cause, of the problem. Granted its traditionally conservative outlook, the Senate was facing administrative, military, and social problems beyond its power to solve. The Senate's prestige rested largely upon its successful foreign policy; but its initial failures in the last wars with Macedonia and Carthage and the long and bloody struggles in Spain had weakened its reputation. It was also ignoring a fundamental social change within Italy that threatened to undermine Roman military power: the decline of the yeomanry.

ROME AND HER ALLIES IN ITALY.   On the whole the Roman state respected the treaty rights of the allies, both Latin and federate; and we hear of but few occasions when any infringement of their local independence occurred as the result of action by Rome. Such trespasses as occurred were isolated acts of Roman magistrates who exceeded their authority in making demands upon officials of allied communities, particularly in the matter of supplies and entertainment when passing through allied territory, and in punishing them for failure to obey or for showing lack of respect. There is no question that the allies made greater military contributions than the Romans themselves to the conquest of the Empire, but this was in proportion to their population. The allies suffered like the Romans during the Second Punic War, and the devastation and depopulation of their lands is reflected in a decline of one third in the levy made upon their manpower in the second century.

As for spoils of war—which, as a rule, were divided among the troops by their generals—the allied troops received the same share as their Roman comrades in arms except on one particular occasion. In the assignment of public lands for colonization, it appears that they received a share, but perhaps not always the share they were entitled to. It was inevitable that the growth of the Roman imperial power should react adversely upon the status of the allies. For example, Roman citizens probably received better treatment than they in Roman law courts. In fact, the Italians tended to sink into a position of greater and greater inferiority and to assume the status of clients at the disposal of their Roman patrons. Although they had no share in the government of the Empire, at least some of them were in a position to derive the same financial advantages as the Romans, as

---

[1] The tribunate was not considered as one of the regular magistracies, and the censorship, according to the custom previously established, followed the consulship.

traders and bankers, from the exploitation of the subject territories outside Italy. The generally disadvantageous position of the Italians was felt the more keenly as the cultural Romanization of Italy steadily if slowly progressed and ultimate absorption of the whole population of the peninsula into the Roman citizen body was inevitable.

Before 133 there was, however, no open demand for Roman citizenship by the allied communities. On the contrary, down to the middle of the second century, they were more anxious to maintain their independence than to be merged into the ranks of the ruling people. In 216 the Latin town of Praeneste refused an offer of Roman citizenship. On several occasions in the period 187—168 Latins and other allies who had migrated to Rome and been enrolled there as Roman citizens in accordance with a long-established privilege were removed from the rolls and forced to return to their former communities. In particular, a Claudian Law of 177 ejected those who had fraudulently attained citizen status. This must be interpreted as revealing not a jealous exclusiveness on the part of the Roman government but rather a compliance with the express desires of the allied states themselves. The attractions of life as artisans and laborers in the capital, which was booming in the first half of the second century, caused many small farmers throughout Italy to leave their homes and seek their fortunes in Rome. As a result, many of the allied states suffered a decrease in population, particularly in the elements upon which they relied for their military strength. They protested to the Senate against the Roman absorption of their citizens and secured their restoration to their own census lists. Conversely, the Romans were not so conscious of their own superior position as to pursue a narrow policy of exclusiveness towards their allies. The Campanians, who had been deprived of their partial citizenship in 210, were restored to their former position in 189, and in the next year full citizenship was extended to the three communities on the southern frontiers of Latium—Fundi, Formiae, and Arpinum—which formerly had only limited rights. The censors of 169 were extremely negligent in enforcing the law against fraudulent usurpation of citizenship by the allies, and there was no diminution of the right of Latins to receive Roman status after having held a magistracy in their respective towns. No matter how enlightened the Romans claimed to be in treating the Italians, the fact remained that the legal differences between the two groups were increasingly unrealistic and galling to people who realized that they were not masters in their own house.

II. Imperial Administration

SUBJECTS OR ALLIES?   The annexation of Sicily in 241 and of Sardinia and Corsica in 238 raised the question whether or not Rome should extend to her non-Italian conquests the same treatment accorded to the Italian peoples and include them within her military federation. The question was answered in the negative, and the status of federate allies was accorded only to communities that had previously attained this relationship or merited it by zeal in the cause of Rome and whose territory did not form a part of the Roman dominions. All the rest were treated as subjects, not as allies, even though they might be so called, and enjoyed only such rights as the conquerors chose to leave them. The distinguishing mark of their condition was their obligation to pay a tax or tribute to Rome. Except on special occasions, they were not called upon to render military service. This practice, once established, was extended to all other regions subsequently incorporated in the Roman empire.

PROVINCES.   At first the Romans tried to conduct the administration of Sicily, Sardinia, and Corsica through the regular city magistrates. Finding this unsatisfactory, they created in 227 two separate administrative districts—Sicily forming one, and the two adjoining islands the other—called "provinces" from the word *provincia*, which usually meant the sphere of duty assigned to a magistrate. Special magistrates were in fact assigned to them, two additional praetors being annually elected for this purpose. In like manner the Romans in 197 organized the provinces of Hither and Farther Spain, in 148 the province of Macedonia, in 146 that of Africa, and in 129 Asia. Subsequent conquests were treated in the same way. For the Spanish provinces two more praetorships were created, "with consular authority" because of the military importance of their posts. For those organized afterwards, no new magistrates were added, and the practice was established of appointing as governor an ex-consul or ex-praetor with the title of proconsul or propraetor. This change of policy is explained by the opposition of the nobility to creating new praetorships, which would increase the number of candidates annually available for the consulship, and to making a corresponding increase in the quaestorships, which would enlarge the opportunities for "new men" to enter the Senate. And it must not be forgotten that those who held magistracies in the city would welcome the innovation because it increased their chances of obtaining a provincial command with all its opportunities for acquiring wealth. The new method of appointing provincial governors subsequently became the rule for all provinces under the republican regime. As a rule the Senate decided what provinces should be "consular" and what "praetorian," but the actual allocation among eligible candidates of each rank was determined by lot subject to the possibility of rearrangement among the appointees. Occasionally, one of the regular provinces was entrusted to a consul in office. This was usually done by the Senate, although technically either of the Assemblies could do so by enacting a law.

PROVINCIAL GOVERNMENT.   Although each province had its own peculiar features, in general all were organized and administered in the following way. A provincial charter (*lex provinciae*), drawn up on the spot by a commission of ten senators and ratified by the Senate, fixed the rights and obligations of the provincials. Each province was an aggregate of communities (*civitates*) enjoying city or tribal organization, but having no political bond of unity except in the representative of Roman authority. There were three classes of these communities: the free and federate, the free and nontributary, and the tributary (*civitates liberae et foederatae, liberae et immunes, stipendiariae*). The first were few in number and, although within the borders of a province, did not really belong to it, since they were free allies whose status was assured by a permanent treaty with the Roman state. The second class derived ultimately from those states over which Rome had assumed a protectorate without a formal treaty and, not very numerous either, enjoyed exemption from taxation by virtue of the provincial charter, a privilege the Senate could revoke at will. The third group was by far the most numerous and furnished the taxes laid upon the province. As a rule each of the communities enjoyed its former constitution and laws, subject to the supervision of the Roman authorities.

Over this aggregate of communities stood the Roman governor and his staff. His term of office was annual but might be extended for several years by prorogation or simple failure to appoint a successor. His duties were threefold: military, administrative, and judicial. He commanded the Roman troops stationed in the province for maintenance of order and protection of the frontiers; he supervised relations between the communities of his province and their internal administration, as well as collection of tribute; he presided as judge over the more serious cases arising among provincials, over all cases between provincials and Romans or between Roman citizens. Upon entering his province, the governor published an edict, usually modeled upon that of his predecessors or the praetor's edict at Rome, stating what legal principles he would enforce during his term of office. The province was divided into judicial circuits (*conventus*), and cases arising in each of these were tried in designated places at fixed times.

The governor was accompanied by a quaestor, who acted as his treasurer and received the provincial revenue from tax collectors. His staff also comprised three *legati* or lieutenants, senators appointed by the Senate but usually nominated by himself, who were to assist him with their counsel and act as his deputies when necessary. He also took with him a number of companions (*comites*), usually young men from the families of his friends, who were given this opportunity of gaining a knowledge of provincial government and who could be used in any official capacity. In addition, the governor brought his own retinue, comprising clerks and household servants. Although he received no salary, the governor was allowed a very handsome sum for the expenses of himself and his staff.

PROVINCIAL TAXATION. The taxes levied upon the provinces were at first designed to pay the expenses of occupation and defence. Hence they bore the name *stipendium*, or soldiers' pay. The term *tributum* (tribute), used of the property tax imposed on Roman citizens, did not come into general use for the provincial revenues until later. As a rule the Romans accepted the tax system already in vogue in each district before their occupancy and exacted either a fixed annual sum from the province, as in Spain, Africa, and Macedonia, or one tenth (*decuma*) of the annual produce of the soil, as in Sicily and Asia. The tribute imposed by the Romans was not higher and usually lower than that exacted by previous rulers. The public or royal lands, mines, and forests of the conquered state were incorporated in the Roman public domain, and the right to occupy or exploit them was leased to individuals or companies of contractors. Customs dues (*portoria*) were also collected in the harbors and on the frontiers of the provinces.

The methods of tax collection varied from province to province and also with the different types of taxation. Normally, where the direct tax took the form of a fixed levy (the *stipendium* in a strict sense) as in Spain, the total sum was apportioned among the tributary communities, which raised their respective quotas by their own methods and turned them over to the provincial quaestor. Where this tax was a percentage of the annual crops, however, the Romans followed the custom they had employed in Italy and which was common throughout the Mediterranean world—that is, they leased the right to collect the tax within specific areas to private corporations of professional tax farmers (*publicani*) that made the highest bid for the privilege. These corporations made their profits from the excess of the amount they collected over the amount they had contracted to turn over to the state. The same method was employed in collecting indirect taxes such as customs dues, rentals, and pasturage taxes for the use of public lands in the provinces. In Sicily the *decuma* was farmed out to local *publicani*; only some years after the annexation of Asia (122) was the collection of a provincial tithe for the first time assigned to a company of Romans. Earlier in the century, however, Roman companies probably already had a monopoly over the collection of indirect taxes and rentals in all the provinces. The Roman corporations of *publicani* were joint-stock companies, with central offices in Rome and agencies in the provinces in which they were interested. A general manager (*magister*) with a board of associates directed the offices in Rome, and provincial agencies were entrusted to the care of district managers. The company officials were all members of what was called the equestrian order; their employees might be Romans of lower standing, Italians, provincials, freedmen, or slaves.

OPPRESSION IN THE PROVINCES. Under the systems of tax collection that obtained during most of the second century B.C. there was ample room for misgovernment on the part of greedy governors and their staffs. The temptations of unrestricted power proved too great for many senators, especially in provinces where they supervised local tax farming and where it was easy for them to divert revenue into their own pockets and cause hardship. It is true that there were Roman governors who maintained the highest traditions of integrity in public office, but there were also many who abused their power to enrich themselves. While the shortness of his term of office prevented a good governor from thoroughly understanding the conditions of his province, it served to augment the criminal zeal with which an avaricious magistrate, often heavily indebted from the expenses of his election campaigns, sought to wring a fortune from the hapless provincials. Bribes, presents, illegal exactions, and open confiscations were the usual means of amassing wealth. The almost sovereign position of the governor, with his military command and absolute power of life and death over all persons in the province and his freedom from immediate senatorial control, guaranteed him a free hand.

Another cause of oppression was to be found in the activities of the Roman bankers and moneylenders (*negotiatores*) who swarmed all over the provinces and even in adjacent districts where they might still have some protection from Roman authority. They were particularly numerous in the Greek East, where the cities were in a state of chronic bankruptcy and where they could place loans at exorbitant rates of interest. The bankers were drawn from the same class of Roman society as the *publicani*, although in many cases they were agents of senators, who were prohibited from engaging directly in such financial transactions. Consequently, when the *negotiatores* called upon the governors to help them collect outstanding debts, the latter frequently complied out of regard for their own political future. By placing soldiers at the disposal of the creditors or quartering troops upon delinquent communities, they forced the debtors to meet their obligations even if this meant their utter ruin.

Commands and governorships were most desirable, and not merely because they gave senators power and wealth during their tenure of office in the provinces. Rome's subjects were quick to realize the almost absolute power of their governors, and senators were just as quick to take advantage of the situation by assuming the familiar role of patrons toward provinces they ruled, and their patronage continued after they had laid down their offices and returned to Rome. As patrons they might arbitrate differences among the provincials, and, more importantly, facilitate their diplomatic relations with the Senate. In return, provincial clients might be called upon to further a patron's political career at the capital by attesting (not always sincerely or voluntarily) to his justice or clemency or by contributing to his campaign fund. Provincial clienteles thus established very often passed to the descendants of the original commander who had conquered a province or of some outstanding or beneficent governor. Such ties accounted in large measure for the unity and even the survival of the Empire in times of gross mismanagement or crisis.

ATTEMPTS TO REPRESS EXTORTION. Since control of provincial administration was vested by custom in the Senate, that body exercised a general supervision over the governor's conduct. Upon his return to Rome, it examined his accounts, his arrangements, and his claims to the honor of a triumph for his military exploits. Deputations from provincial communities approached the Senate to complain of a governor's action or, often under pressure, to commend his conduct. At first complaints might be taken before the tribunals which tried damage suits or might be made the basis of prosecutions before the Tribal Assembly. None of these methods proved effective in putting an end to the abuses. The mischief finally became so serious that in 149 the public conscience awoke to the ruin inflicted upon the provinces, and, by a Calpurnian Law, a standing court was instituted for the trial of suits for the recovery of damages from officials accused of extortion in the provinces (*quaestio rerum repetundarum*). This court was composed of fifty jurors drawn from the Senate and was presided over by a praetor. From its judgment there was no appeal. Its establishment marks an important innovation in Roman legal procedure in criminal cases, for hitherto all persons accused of serious crimes had to be tried either before an assembly of the people or before a magistrate, from whom they could appeal to the former. It is possible also that the Senate was encouraged to organize new provinces shortly after 149 because it believed that this court would be adequate to control provincial governors. It was useless, however, to expect very much from such a tribunal. The cost of a long trial at Rome, the difficulty of securing testimony, the inadequacy of the penalty, which was limited to restitution of damages, as well as the fear of vengeance from future governors, would deter the majority of sufferers from seeking reparation. Nor could an impartial verdict be expected from a jury of senators trying one of their own number for an offense which many of them regarded as their prerogative. So till the end of the Republic many provincials suffered from the oppression of their governors, as well as from that of the tax collectors.

III. Economic and Social Development

Roman expansion between 264 and 133 was marked by important and almost revolutionary changes in the economic and social life of Rome and Italy. An inevitable result of the extension of Rome's control over the Mediterranean world was that the population of Italy was brought into closer contact with lands of older culture and more advanced economic development in the Greek East. The Romans and their Italian allies thus felt the impact of Hellenistic civilization in all its aspects and hastened to appropriate for good or ill whatever of its features appealed to them. Italian agriculture, in particular, benefited by the introduction of new varieties of fruit trees and garden crops, of improved farm implements and superior agricultural techniques. To meet the needs of empire, the Romans abandoned their coinage based on a bronze standard for one based on a silver standard such as was common among the Hellenistic states. The new Roman coinage not only speedily supplanted the products of other Italian mints but gradually won for itself a dominant position throughout the Mediterranean. The most important developments of the period in Italy were the rise of large estates operated by slave labor, the decline of the free Italian peasantry, the growth of a numerous urban proletariat in Rome, the formation of a distinct Roman business and commercial class, and the introduction of a new scale of living among the well-to-do.

THE GREAT ESTATES.   Several causes contributed to the rapid growth of great estates (called by the Romans *latifundia*) as the dominant factor in Italian agriculture. Among them were the Roman system of administering the public domain, the inability of small proprietors to maintain themselves in the face of the demands of military service, their increasing preference to find a livelihood in one of the booming cities of Italy, the abundant supply of cheap slave labor provided by the numerous prisoners of war, and to some extent the devastation of the rural districts of South Italy in the Hannibalic War.

For centuries it had been established practice that those portions of public land not reserved for colonization should be open to occupation by citizens of Rome or allied communities for farming or pasturage. In return for this privilege the occupants were expected to pay rent to the Roman treasury, which amounted to one tenth of the produce in the case of field crops, one fifth in the case of fruits, and in that of pasture lands took the form of a tax based on the number of cattle or other animals. The amount of land available for occupation by private individuals was increased greatly as a result of Hannibal's campaign in Italy. In the southern part of the peninsula he had destroyed some four hundred communities, and the lands left depopulated and ownerless were taken over by Rome. In addition, the Romans punished the states that had gone over to Hannibal by confiscating a large portion of their territory, as a rule one third. The transplanting of 40,000 Ligurians from their native country to Samnium in 180 indicates how much waste land was at the disposal of the Roman government and may possibly be interpreted as an attempt to repeople this region. If so, except for attempts to colonize some of the coastal towns, it remained an isolated effort, and the bulk of the public land in the south continued to be free for individual exploitation.

Here, as elsewhere in Italy, those who profited most from this opportunity were the wealthier landholders who could command the labor necessary to bring considerable areas under cultivation and who possessed sufficient capital to stock the new farms. The advantages the landed aristocracy derived from the public land policy explains, in part at least, the opposition of the Senate to the division of the *ager Gallicus* for colonization in 233. After the lapse of several generations, the occupants of public lands regarded them as family property. In many cases all records of the original conditions of tenure and of the boundaries of the plots had disappeared, and the rents had ceased to be paid to the state.

By the second century B.C. new conditions had arisen which favored still further the rise of the *latifundia*. Ever since 218, members of the senatorial order had been prohibited by law from engaging directly in commercial enterprises outside of Italy. Banking and contracting were considered beneath the dignity of a senator, while agriculture ranked as the most honorable gainful occupation, so the governing class was practically compelled to invest in Italian land the new capital it acquired from the conquest and administration of the Empire. Not only did it seek to increase its holdings of public land but also to buy up farms of smaller proprietors wherever possible. At the same time the new trends in Italian agriculture developing under the influence of Hellenistic practices favored the capitalist farmer at the expense of his peasant neighbor.

Cereal agriculture declined because of soil erosion, too prolonged cultivation of a single staple, and the introduction of new and more profitable crops. Competition of grain imports from overseas provinces for consumption in the capital probably also depressed cereal agriculture in the immediate vicinity of Rome. Grain fields gave way to vineyards, olive orchards, market gardens, and, particularly in South Italy, to extensive grazing ranches. Farming became much more businesslike than heretofore. It was carried on by improved methods, and both expenses and profits were calculated with great care. Production was no longer chiefly for domestic needs but definitely directed toward a market. This type of agriculture was already highly developed in the Near East, in Carthaginian Africa, and in Sicily, and it was from these regions that the Romans learned about the new farm economy. About 150, Cato the Censor wrote his book *On Agriculture*, a practical manual for the owner of a large estate. Some four years later the Senate had translated into Latin the much more elaborate work of the Carthaginian Mago, much of which must have been applicable to Italy, although much probably had to do with conditions peculiar to Africa. The typical Italian *latifundia* were not very large when judged by American standards. Holdings of 100 and 240 *iugera* (66 and 158 acres) fall into this class. In ancient Italy where, owing to the absence of agricultural machinery, the normal size of a farm tilled by a single family was from four to eight acres, they constituted substantial domains. Many of the great proprietors owned a number of such farms scattered in various parts of the peninsula. According to Cato, an orchard of 100 *iugera* required the labor of 16 slaves, in addition to workers hired for specific tasks like harvesting an olive crop.

For the development of the *latifundia*, an abundant supply of cheap labor was essential. Throughout the second century this was furnished by the great numbers of captives taken in the course of Rome's victorious wars who flooded the slave markets of the Mediterranean. When these failed to meet the demand, the deficit was made good by the piratical slave-raiders of the Greek East. It has been estimated that some 250,000 prisoners of war were brought to Italy as slaves between 200 and 150 B.C. In addition to imported slaves, many were bred on the estates to be a source of profit to their masters. So long as slaves could be procured cheaply, they were preferred to hired free labor because they were not liable to be drafted for military service and could be exploited ruthlessly without fear of consequences. Cato's directions for handling slaves show that they were treated like cattle, and he callously recommended that they be turned out to starve when they were no longer fit for profitable work. On the plantations (*latifundia*) the slaves often worked in irons and at night were housed in underground prisons. The potential danger of the presence of large masses of slaves so brutally treated came to light in the First Sicilian Slave War, which broke out in 135. In this struggle some 70,000 slaves revolted and defied the Roman arms for three years. At the same time there occurred minor revolts in Italy, which were suppressed with great severity.

DECLINE OF SMALL FARMERS.   The spread of the *latifundia* was accompanied by a corresponding decline in the numbers of the peasant farmers throughout Italy. This was due in part to the fact that in certain areas the great proprietors resorted to illegal means to oust the peasants from their holdings on the public land and seized every opportunity to buy up their private allotments. A still more serious cause was the burden imposed upon the peasantry by the foreign wars of Rome. Since only citizens who had a property assessment of 4,000 asses were eligible to military service and since the great majority of them were farmers, Roman armies were recruited mainly from the rural population. When wars were no longer fought on Italian soil but all over the Mediterranean area and when it became necessary to maintain garrisons in some of the provinces, the armies could no longer be disbanded in the autumn and reassembled for the summer campaigns, so that the peasant soldiers could return to their farms to attend to at least part of the necessary agricultural tasks. Once in the ranks the Roman soldier was kept away from his home for several years in succession, to the inevitable detriment of his fields and his finances. These prolonged periods of military service, with the chance of temporary profits from the spoils of war, often unfitted men for the steady, laborious life of the farm. Many discharged soldiers, returning to farms which had been mortgaged for the support of their families and being unable or unwilling to gain a livelihood on their small holdings, were only too glad to sell out to their richer neighbors. There was no room for them as tenants on private land, and work as farm laborers was seasonal and very uncertain. Many of them migrated to Rome and to other expanding cities where life was exciting and where, until after the middle of the second century, there were plenty of jobs. Others migrated to Cisalpine Gaul, where new lands were still available for small farmers. Losses in war also made a heavy drain upon the Italian peasantry. As a result of these conditions, the number of men available for army service declined as the second century progressed and many yeomen lost their property,[2] so that it became increasingly difficult to raise the necessary levies. The tribunes intervened on several occasions to spare peasants from the draft, while the property qualification for service was progressively lowered in order to find the manpower to fight wars in Greece, Africa, and Spain. The rural population among the Roman allies suffered in the same way as the Romans themselves, as is indicated by their migration to Rome on such a large scale that their native cities had to ask the Senate to force them to return home. A very serious problem began to confront the Senate. Unless it was willing to adopt a nonaggressive foreign policy and give up its distant foreign possessions, it must continue to raise armies to prosecute wars of conquest and to garrison and defend the provinces, and these increasing military obligations had to be met by a population declining in eligible manpower.

The Romans were not altogether blind to the consequences of the expansion of the great estates. As early as 367 (362), if we may believe the tradition recorded by Livy, they had placed a limit of 500 *iugera* (310 acres) upon the size of individual holdings and also restricted the number of animals which any one person might run on the public pastures. The former restriction had soon become a dead letter, however, and the public pastures had been taken up by private occupants. Much later, at some date in the period 201–167 B.C., another law was passed which forbade anyone to hold more than 500 *iugera* of crop-producing public land or to maintain more than a cumulative total of 100 head of cattle and 500 head of smaller stock on additional tracts of public pasture. Although this was evidently an attempt to check the spread of *latifundia* and to limit the encroachment of grazing lands upon areas under cultivation, its provisions actually favored the landed oligarchy and did little to preserve the small farmer. Even the restrictions of this new law were openly disregarded, and the Senate felt both unwilling and unable to bring transgressors to account. Once occupied, public land was looked upon as an hereditary possession. In 173, the Senate authorized one of the consuls to fix the boundaries of public and private lands in Campania in order to check the encroachment of the latter upon the former, but eleven years later it found the whole region in the hands of private possessors and succeeded in recovering only 50,000 *iugera* by actually buying it back from the occupants. Victory rested with the great proprietors. The whole of Italy was not affected equally by the growth of the *latifundia*, however. In South Italy, Campania, Latium,

---

[2] Census records of the years 164 and 136 B.C., whose accuracy and meaning are doubtful, record a decline in numbers from 337,000 to 317,000.

and Etruria they dominated the scene, but in the highlands of Central Italy and Umbria the sturdy Italian peasants still held their own.

GROWTH OF THE CITY MOB. Rome itself, as well as the Italian peninsula, underwent a profound transformation during the period of conquest that began with the First Punic War. As a result of this process the City of the Seven Hills had become the political and the economic center of the Mediterranean world. By 133 it had a population of perhaps half a million, rivalling Alexandria and Antioch, the great Hellenistic capitals. Although not a great manufacturing center, Rome had always been an important market, and now her streets were thronged with traders from all lands and with persons who could cater in any way to the wants and the appetites of an imperial city. There was a large proportion of slaves belonging to the mansions of the wealthy and of freedmen engaged in business for themselves or for their patrons. Hither flocked also the peasants who for various reasons had abandoned their farms to depend upon the bounty of patrons to whom they might attach themselves in voluntary clientage or to pick up a living otherwise. Many of these former peasants found employment in the urban building boom financed by the influx of booty and tribute. But about 138 this ended, and staple grain prices rose simultaneously because of a slave war in Sicily. These events combined to produce a serious economic crisis among the urban proletariat.

The entertainments and largesses of food characteristic of the public festivals and election campaigns both attracted this element and helped to support it. Owing to slow transportation by land and its uncertainties by sea, the congestion of population in Rome made the problem of supplying the city very difficult, since a rise in the price of grain or a delay in the arrival of the Sicilian wheat convoy would bring the proletariat to the verge of starvation. Upon the popular assemblies the presence of this unstable element had an unwholesome effect. The Tribal Assembly in particular was now dominated by residents of the city and could always attend the meetings, and its actions were bound to be determined by the particular interests and passions of this portion of the citizen body. Furthermore, noncitizens as well as citizens could frequent *contiones* or mass meetings called to hear political addresses, and this afforded a ready means for evoking the mob spirit in the hope of overawing the Comitia, which was only too ready to favor proposals that promised the people some pecuniary advantage. This danger would not have existed if the constitution had provided adequate means for policing Rome. As it was, however, except for the magistrates and their personal attendants, there was no police force in the city, and, since the consuls lacked military authority within the *pomerium*, there were no armed forces at their disposal.

RISE OF THE BUSINESS CLASS. The restrictions placed by law and custom upon the business activities of the senatorial order naturally led to the appearance of a prosperous business class outside of the governing oligarchy. Its rise was stimulated by the practice of depending largely upon individual initiative for the conduct of public business. This opened up a wide field of state contracts to persons who had free capital and the necessary enterprise. By about 150, contracts were let for the construction of various public works, the operation of the Spanish and the reopened Macedonian mines, the collection of rentals from public lands in Italy and of harbor dues in Italy, Sicily, and Spain. Persons who undertook such contracts were called publicans *(publicani)*. They did not have to be men of very great means because they were permitted to form joint-stock companies with limited liability, although this was not legal in private business enterprises, and so could obtain the necessary capital from small as well as large shareholders. Banking, which included moneylending, was another profitable activity both in Italy and in the provinces. Since bankers paid interest on deposits, they must have found ample opportunities to make successful investments. Although Roman businessmen did not as yet engage actively in foreign enterprises, they doubtless controlled much local trade in Rome. They must have been active in shipping, particularly in the transportation of the grain collected as taxes in Sicily, Sardinia, and Africa and transported to Rome. If there had been no profits for Romans in owning ships of seagoing capacity, senators would not have been forbidden to own them. The inference is that the business class was interested in freeing itself from the competition of the senatorial element. Industry did not as yet offer many opportunities for Roman businessmen. There was little manufacturing for export from Italy, and most necessary articles were produced locally.

EQUESTRIANS.   The more prosperous businessmen and public contractors in the latter third and second centuries came to form a definite social class ranking behind the senatorial oligarchy and ahead of the populace. Since they were sufficiently wealthy to outfit themselves with horses, the censors regularly assigned them to cavalry service to supplement the equestrian centuries, hitherto recruited from the senatorial class. The businessmen were a distinctive group, and since they eventually formed a majority of the cavalry service, their class came to be called the equestrian order in a pregnant sense. The equestrians, no matter what the source of their wealth, resembled the senators in so far as they reinvested their capital in land. As a class they were basically apolitical, except when their commercial interests were threatened. Although many of them were wealthier than some senators, they lacked the prestige and influence that could only be obtained at Rome through senatorial offices, from which they were effectively excluded and for which, in fact, many were uninterested in competing.

NEW SCALE OF LIVING.   In the course of campaigns in Sicily, Africa, Greece, and Asia Minor, the Romans came into close contact with a civilization older and more sophisticated than their own, where the art of living was practised with a refinement and elegance unknown in Latium. In this respect the conquerors showed themselves ready to learn from the conquered, and all the luxurious externals of culture were gradually transplanted to Rome. The simple Roman house with its one large *atrium,* serving at once as kitchen, living room, and bedchamber, was slowly transformed. The *atrium* became a pillared reception hall, special rooms were added for the various phases of domestic life, in the rear of the *atrium* arose a Greek peristyle courtyard, and the house was filled with sculpture and other works of art, plundered or purchased in the cities of Hellas. The standards of living of the upper classes were rising, and an increasingly wide gulf yawned between the life of the rich and that of the poor. Nevertheless, the upper classes did not yet enjoy the luxuries typical of the late Republic and Empire, and later generations of Romans looked back on the second century B.C. as a period of relatively simple habits and customs.

TAXES ON LUXURIES. The gradual change in living standards did not come about without vigorous opposition from the champions of the old Roman simplicity, who saw in the new refinement and luxury a danger to Roman vigor and morality. The spokesman of the conservatives was Cato the Elder. In his censorship in 184 he assessed articles of luxury and expensive slaves at ten times their market value and made them liable to taxation at an exceptionally high rate, in case the property tax should be levied. Although the next censors let these regulations fall into abeyance, Cato's censorship was by no means the only strict one in the second century B.C., and other senators were no less disturbed by the growing sophistication of Roman life. Attempts to check the growth of luxury by legislation were futile, however. The Oppian Law restricting female extravagance in dress and ornaments, passed under stress of the need for conservation in 215, was repealed in 195, and subsequent sumptuary legislation in 182, 161, and 143 was largely ignored.

RECAPITULATION. In 133 the Roman state faced a series of problems that, taken together, formed an extremely critical situation. The economic basis of Roman society was unhealthy. Rome was now living largely from the exploitation of the provinces. The income derived from this source passed mainly to the officeholding oligarchy and, to a lesser degree, the business class. The lower classes profited little therefrom, and their condition deteriorated steadily as the Empire expanded. The same was true of most of the Roman allies in Italy. Far-reaching economic reforms were needed, reforms that would diminish the idle masses by providing them with profitable occupations in industrial or commercial pursuits or by rendering agriculture again attractive to the small farmer. At the same time political reforms were urgently required. The popular assemblies and the magistrates, organs of government adapted to a city-state, were proving incompetent to grapple with the problems of imperial administration. Signs of dissatisfaction were appearing among the Latin and Italian allies. The military resources of the state were declining, while its military burdens were growing greater than ever. The threat of mob violence and famine hung over Rome. This crisis had to be met at a time when the ruling class was unwilling to change its social, economic, and political attitudes and was therefore unable to find solutions to problems confronting the state.

IV. Cultural Progress

GREEK INFLUENCES. In addition to creating new administrative problems and transforming the economic life of Italy, the expansion of Rome gave a tremendous impulse to its cultural development. The chief stimulus was close contact with Hellenic civilization. Rome had been subject to Greek influences both indirectly through Etruria and directly from the Greek cities of South Italy, but with the conquest of the latter and the occupation of Sicily, Greece, and part of Asia Minor these influences became much more immediate and powerful. They were intensified by Greeks who flocked to Rome as ambassadors, teachers, physicians, merchants, and artists, and by the multitude of educated Greek slaves employed in Roman households. Since Hellenic civilization was more ancient and more sophisticated than the Latin, it was inevitable that the latter should borrow largely from the former and consciously or unconsciously imitate it. The intellectual life of Rome never attained the freedom and richness of that of Greece, upon which it was always dependent. In this domain, as Horace later phrased it, "Captive Greece took captive her rude conqueror."

NEW TENDENCIES IN ROMAN EDUCATION. One very important consequence of the contact with Hellenism was that Roman education developed new forms and ideals. The upper classes were no longer content with the traditional limited training based on familiarity with ancestral customs. In the course of the third and second centuries they demanded an acquaintance with Greek literature, rhetoric, and philosophy. Appreciation of these studies was stimulated by the visits to Rome of some of the most famous intellectual figures of the Hellenistic World, such as the Stoic philosopher Panaetius of Rhodes and Carneades, the founder of the New Academy at Athens, both of whom came to Rome on diplomatic missions. The Hellenistic point of view that training in rhetoric and philosophy should equip a man to attain success in public and private life through the practice of virtue accorded well with the practical tendencies of Roman character and helped to develop a broader Roman conception of cultured citizenship expressed in the word humanity (*humanitas*). Among the chief patrons of Hellenism were men of the type of Scipio Africanus the Elder; notably Titus Flamininus, Aemilius Paullus, and Scipio Aemilianus, at whose house gathered the leading intellectuals of the day, including the Achaean historian Polybius. In spite of the genuine admiration for Greek achievement aroused by the study of the masterpieces of Greek literature, the political ineptitude of their Greek contemporaries caused the Romans to regard them with some contempt.

A knowledge of Greek now became an essential part of the equipment of every educated man, and the demand for instruction in that language and in the other elementary subjects requisite for advanced cultural studies led to the appearance of schools conducted by professional teachers, although Roman practice remained hostile to any obligatory system of public education, and each parent directed his children's training as he saw fit. Schools remained privately conducted, for the most part under the patronage or even in the houses of men of prominence. Teachers were mainly educated slaves or freedmen, usually of Greek origin, and accordingly enjoyed little public esteem. To a certain degree those who conducted schools of rhetoric and philosophy shared in this lack of respect, for they too were Greeks, although freemen and of a higher social standing. In a certain sense Cato and other like-minded conservatives opposed these new cultural tendencies. It would be a mistake to regard Cato as a blind opponent of Hellenism on either political or cultural grounds. He learned to speak Greek at the age of thirty and the buildings erected during his censorship were based on Greek models. He was acquainted with Greek philosophy, literature, and educational theory, and his own written works owe much in organization and even content to the Greeks. He introduced Ennius to Roman society and quite probably knew Polybius. What Cato counseled was the acceptance of Hellenism after due consideration of what the Greeks had to offer that would suit the more staid and "puritanical" Roman ethic. The attitude of men like him in the Senate, which decreed the banishment of Greek philosophers and rhetoricians in 161, was probably due to fear that the latter were sophists and skeptics and therefore morally and politically undesirable.

PERSISTENCE OF OLDER CUSTOMS AND IDEALS. In many respects the Romans remained faithful to their traditional ideals. They continued to stress the educative value of practical experience and home environment rather than literary studies and kept up the practices that had their origins in an earlier period. Among these was the custom of entrusting a young man to an older person of reputation, whom he should attend constantly and who should be his model in both public and private life. Another custom peculiar to Rome was that of a funeral procession and panegyric oration accorded to distinguished members of aristocratic families. In the funeral cortège death masks of the deceased's ancestors were worn by mourners clad in the robes of office they had filled and bearing inscriptions recording their titles and honors. At the grave or before the funeral pyre an oration was delivered setting forth the glory of the dead and the services he and his house had rendered to the state. By this reminder of the greatness of their ancestors noble Roman youths were inspired to emulate their character and achievements.

THE RISE OF ROMAN LITERATURE. It has been pointed out already how little literature the native Roman genius produced before the Punic Wars. Close contact with Hellenistic civilization thereafter created both a taste and a demand for literary works. At first these developed in close imitation of Greek models, and as usual in the history of literature, poetry preceded prose.

A pioneer in the new movement was Livius Andronicus (ca. 284–204), a Greek freedman from Tarentum, who translated Homer's *Odyssey* into Latin Saturnian verse as a literary text for school use. In 240, at the request of the aediles, he translated a Greek tragedy and comedy for production at the public games in Rome. These were followed by numerous other translations and adaptations, as well as a hymn to the gods which he composed on the occasion of the invasion of Hasdrubal in 207. A contemporary of Andronicus, the Italian Gnaeus Naevius (ca. 270–199), showed greater independence and versatility. Not only did he create new plays by combining plots taken from more than one Greek original, he also wrote plays with purely Roman subjects. Perhaps his most notable achievement was an epic poem on the First Punic War, written in the native Saturnian meter. This probably gave inspiration to another literary pioneer, Quintus Ennius (239–169), a literary giant who, perhaps even more than Livius Andronicus, deserves to be called the father of Latin literature. A native of Calabria and educated in the Greek manner, he served as a soldier in Sardinia, was brought to Rome by Cato, became a Roman citizen and a protégé of the Scipios. His great work, a landmark in Latin literature, was the *Annals*, an epic poem in which he recounted the history of Rome from her legendary beginnings to 172. The *Annals* pointed the way for future generations of Latin epic poets by having as its central theme Rome's destiny as a world power and the glorification of her patriotic ideals. It eventually ranked with Vergil's *Aeneid* in popularity, but of its eighteen books only six hundred lines have survived. For his epic Ennius replaced the old Saturnian verse with the Latin hexameter, which he developed in imitation of the Greek. Ennius was a pioneer in the development of native Italian satire (*satura*), originally a medley of prose and verse, narrative and drama. In so doing he contributed to the most original and Roman of poetic genres. He was also a comic and tragic playwright; his tragedies, which were especially regarded, followed the models of Aeschylus and Euripides.

If Ennius pioneered in the development of the satire, Gaius Lucilius (ca. 180–ca. 103) in his "talks" (*sermones*) perfected it as a branch of literature devoted to informal criticism of one or more subjects of human interest. A native of southern Latium, of equestrian rank and therefore one of the few outstanding poets of the period not of lowly birth, he was patronized by Scipio Aemilianus. An outspoken critic of a wide range of human foibles and vices, he was a model and inspiration to many later poets of note, especially Horace and Juvenal. The disappearance of his poetry, except for fragments, is a very serious loss to our appreciation of Latin literature.

Dramatic literature developed rapidly under the demand for plays to be presented at the public festivals. The first poet to devote himself entirely to the comic stage was the Umbrian, T. Maccius Plautus (ca. 254–184), who learned his Latin at Rome, where he allegedly eked out a living, at first, as a laborer in a flour mill and as an actor and stagehand. Twenty-one plays survive from his pen. They follow closely the Attic New Comedy, essentially a comedy of manners, whose atmosphere and characters were as predictable as they were un-Roman: the misadventures of the lovesick swain, the braggart soldier, the woman of easy virtue, the misanthrope, and the social parasite. Plautus infused his works with a language and meter that were genuinely Italian. There can be no mistaking the earthy Latin quality of his ebullient wit, which, at least in his early plays, is characterized by a sheer love of slapstick farce and general buffoonery, later to be reflected in Shakespearean comedy. Another interesting figure among the comic playwrights of the second century was Caecilius Statius, a captive from the Gallic tribe of the Insubres in north Italy. A friend of Ennius, Statius copied Greek models closely but was noted for the ingenuity of his plots. Much better known, however, and ranking with Plautus as a playwright of distinction is Terence (P. Terentius Afer, ca. 195–159), who came as a slave from Africa to Rome, where he received his education and his freedom. All of Terence's six plays, produced in the period 166–160, have survived. Like Plautus, Terence was dependent on New Comedy, but his works are much less broadly humorous than his predecessor's. He was not so interested in the rowdy and boisterous, devoting much more attention than Plautus to subtle interplays of characterization and to a refined and elegant Latin style. For this reason he tended to appeal to a select and cultivated audience rather than to the public at large.

Tragedies continued to be written after Ennius, although our knowledge of notable figures and of works in this field is meager. One may mention Ennius' nephew Pacuvius (ca. 220–ca. 130) and L. Accius (ca. 170–ca. 85), who based their works on the Athenian dramatists Sophocles and Euripides. Accius' melodramatic works were extremely popular among his contemporaries and were highly regarded by sensitive Romans of later generations like Cicero, Horace, and Quintilian. By the last generation of the second century B.C., however, the most important period in Roman dramatic literature was drawing to a close. In both comedy and tragedy

Greek plots and characters were abandoned gradually for those of Roman origin. Tragedy in particular rapidly declined in popularity, since the Roman public was in general too uneducated to appreciate its worth and preferred pageants, comedies, mimes, and gladiatorial combats.

Latin prose developed more slowly, and the first prose literary works of the period were written in Greek. At the very beginning of the development of prose writing in either language at Rome, certain basic characteristics are evident. Unlike poetry, writing prose was an eminently gentlemanly occupation, especially befitting the attention of Rome's governing elite. The favorite prose genres, as might be expected, were history, in which Rome's ideals and traditions were no less emphasized than they were in epic poetry, and oratory, one of the chief by-products of statecraft. Roman senators deemed it worthy to write in prose on a variety of other subjects, provided they had practical value.

Earliest among prose works was a history of Rome from its origins to the end of the Second Punic War compiled about 200 by Fabius Pictor, a member of the Roman Senate who had fought in that war. His work was annalistic in form and was based on the annals of the pontiffs and such other documentary records as were available, but it depended also on oral tradition. Pictor chose to write in Greek, both because the only available historical models were in that language and because he wished to justify and explain the growth of Roman power to a Greek audience. Cincius Alimentus, a contemporary of Pictor, wrote another history of the same sort beginning with 729, also in Greek, and other annalists continued to use Greek during the first half of the second century B.C. But in the meantime, the first historical work in Latin prose, albeit on a Greek rather than an annalistic model, was produced by Cato the Elder. His *Origines*, an account of the beginnings of Rome and other Italian states and of the wars of Rome from 264 to 150, was a rambling, disconnected narrative interrupted by lengthy discussions of various sorts. Although the *Origines* has perished, Cato's earlier work on agriculture (*De agri cultura*) has survived and is the oldest work in Latin prose to be preserved intact. This type of technical handbook also had Hellenistic precedents. Cato wrote on a variety of other practical subjects, such as medicine, rhetoric, and probably law, and was therefore a pioneer on a wide range.

After Cato, Latin became the language of Roman historical writers, and many annalistic works were written by members of the oligarchy. A beginning was also made in historical studies of a higher type, not merely chronological narratives but analysis and interpretation as well. Such was the history of the Second Punic War by Coelius Antipater. Closely related to history was the publication of personal memoirs and collections of letters, which had its beginning in this period. There was also a small amount of more specialized and scientific writing, including works on constitutional law, astronomy, and natural history.

JURISPRUDENCE. In the field of legal writing we find a specific achievement of the Roman genius, affected little by Greek influences. Roman legal literature was an outgrowth of the need for interpretation by competent persons of the law as laid down in the code of the Twelve Tables and other enactments. At first this interpretation took the form of advice given by the pontiffs to magistrates or private individuals seeking their aid in determining the law as applied to definite cases. Tiberius Coruncanius, who became the first plebeian *pontifex maximus* in 253, apparently began the practice of admitting to his discussions of legal problems any persons who were interested in improving their knowledge of the law. His example was followed by others who did not belong to the pontifical college. In this way there grew up among the governing class a group of legal specialists called *iuris prudentes* or *iuris consulti*, "men learned in the law." They did not limit themselves to giving oral discussions and advice but soon began to write books on various aspects of the law. One of the earliest of these legal writers, who may be regarded as the founder of Roman juristic literature, was Sextus Aelius Paetus, consul in 198, whose ability won him the nickname of Catus, "the shrewd." He published a work which later generations regarded as "the cradle of the law." It contained three parts: one devoted to an exposition of the law of the Twelve Tables, the second to its interpretation, and the third to the methods of legal procedure. Paetus was followed by a long line of juristic writers, among whom were Cato the Censor and his son, whose fame as a lawyer excelled that of his father. It must be remembered that the jurisconsults were not professional lawyers in the modern sense. In the third and second centuries B.C. they formed a small circle of leading members of the senatorial order who from time to time held various public offices. They did not practice law as a business and took no fees for their services but pursued the study of the law because of its importance in the conduct of their official tasks and because, by interpreting the law for their friends, they increased their prestige and influence and thus indirectly furthered their own political careers. Through their interpretations, which shaped the decisions of magistrates and judges, the jurisconsults exercised a great influence upon the way in which Roman law was understood and enforced.

PRAETOR'S EDICT. The most important line of development in Roman law was through the edicts issued by the annual magistrates, especially those whose duties were largely of a judicial character, such as the city praetor and the praetor for the aliens in Rome and the provincial governors. Of these the most important was the edict of the city praetor who administered the law for Roman citizens throughout Italy. At the beginning of his term of office the praetor stated in his edict the principles which he would observe in enforcing the laws and the conditions under which he would admit prosecutions for redress of grievances. In this way both new legal principles and new remedies were introduced into the law by virtue of the praetor's magisterial authority without resort to legislation. As a later Roman jurist expressed it, the purpose of the edict was "to aid, supplement, and correct" the civil law. A noticeable improvement was made in procedure. Partly in addition to, and partly in place of, the old actions at law which were limited in number and unalterable in language, the praetor issued formulas suited to individual cases brought before him. That is to say, he formally laid the claim of the plaintiff before the judge and instructed the judge to render his decision according to whether the evidence supported or contradicted the condition so set forth. The formulary procedure proved so flexible and efficient that the Aebutian Law, passed some time in the latter half of the second century B.C., formally approved it and paved the way for the disappearance of the old actions at law. In general, the praetor's edict served the interests of equity in contrast to a strict interpretation of the law. Each praetor's edict was valid only for his own term of office, but it became the custom for a new praetor to incorporate into his own edict most or all of that of his predecessor. So reforms once introduced were perpetuated, and the edict grew to be a document of considerable length and came to need interpretation itself by jurists, just as the Twelve Tables did.

RELIGION.   During the period of imperial expansion penetration of Roman religion by Greek influences was even more marked than before. This penetration followed the already established identification of Greek and Roman divinities of similar attributes and the wholesale adoption of Greek mythological lore. By the close of the third century B.C. there was formally recognized in Rome a group of twelve greater divinities identical with the twelve Olympic gods of Greece. The minor Latin divinities fell rapidly into neglect, while their place was taken by others of Greek origin. The transformation of the old impersonal Roman deities into anthropomorphic Hellenic gods is reflected in the acceptance of Greek types for their representation in sculptured form, a strong demand for which arose following acquaintance with the works of art carried off from Syracuse and other Greek cities.

In the addition of Greek gods to the list of deities officially worshipped in Rome and in the acceptance of Greek ritualistic practices, the Sibylline oracles played a large part. At critical moments during the First and Second Punic Wars, when the state was in danger and appeals to the older gods were ineffectual, these oracles were consulted and frequently interpreted as authorizing a new cult or a new ceremony. A good example of this comes from the year 205, when the oracles were said to have recommended the institution of the cult of the Great Mother of Pessinus in Asia Minor and of her consort, Attis. This cult was formally established in the next year, with the transfer of the cult image, a black stone, from Pessinus to Rome. The Great Mother was not a Greek divinity but a nature goddess whose worship was native to Asia Minor, although somewhat rationalized by Hellenic influences. Shocked by the wildly emotional character of this worship conducted by a professional priesthood of multilated devotees, the Senate forbade Roman citizens to participate in it.

Generally speaking, the third century B.C. marked the end of the introduction of Greek deities under official auspices. After 200 the Senate tried to discourage innovations and would permit only the grafting of new cults on to traditional ones. This conservative religious attitude is shown in the suppression of the Bacchanalian societies in 186. Throughout South Italy the worship of Dionysus or Bacchus had flourished from an early date among the Greek population. Captives carried northward as slaves from this area following the war with Hannibal spread its rites throughout Campania and Etruria and introduced them to Rome itself. The adherents of the cult formed religious associations and practised its mystical ceremonies in secret. Rightly or wrongly, some of the members of these associations were accused and convicted of crimes of violence and immoral practices. The Senate concluded after investigation that the societies were engaged in a conspiracy against the state and ordered the consuls to disband them on both Roman and allied territory. It is probable that the criminal charges were greatly exaggerated and that the real grounds for action were the illegality of secret associations and a genuine Roman aversion to orgiastic religious rites. In spite of the suppression of the associations, the Senate did not forbid individuals to worship Dionysus under official supervision. This was an expression of a definite religious policy. The Roman state did not inquire into matters of belief, but neither did it tolerate the performance of ceremonies which appeared contrary to Roman standards of propriety and morality. This mistrust of foreign cults and their ritual observances also explains the banishment of Chaldean astrologers from Italy in 139.

SKEPTICISM AND STOICISM. Although the formalities of religion insofar as they concerned public life were still scrupulously observed, there was an ever-increasing skepticism with regard to the existence and power of the gods of the Graeco-Roman mythology and the efficacy of augury and divination. After about 200 there was a corresponding decline in the status of priesthoods. This was because the educated classes were influenced to a certain extent by the rationalism of Euhemerus, whose work on the origin of the gods had been translated by Ennius, and even more by the pantheism of Stoic philosophy. The Stoic doctrines, with their practical ethical prescriptions, made a strong appeal to the Roman character and found an able expositor in Panaetius of Rhodes, who taught under the patronage of Scipio Aemilianus.

PUBLIC FESTIVALS. Of great importance in the city were the annual public festivals or games, of which six came to be celebrated regularly by the middle of the second century, each lasting for several days. Five of these were celebrated by the aediles, one by the city praetor. A fixed sum was allotted by the state to defray the expenses of these exhibits, but custom required that this be largely supplemented from the private purse of the person in charge. In this way the aedileship afforded an excellent opportunity to win public favor by an exhibition of generosity. To the original horse and chariot races there came to be added scenic productions, wild-beast hunts, and gladiatorial combats, in imitation of those exhibited by private persons. The first private exhibition of gladiators was given at a funeral in 264, and the first wild-beast hunt in 186. These exhibitions soon became the most popular of all and exercised a brutalizing effect upon the spectators.

ROME THE CITY. The growth of Rome in population and wealth brought about a corresponding change in the appearance of the city, and in the third and second centuries B.C. it increasingly assumed the aspect of a Hellenized Italian town. The erection of tenement houses of several stories and a rise in rentals reflected the influx into the capital. Public buildings began to be erected on a large scale. The Circus Flaminius, which was used for horse races, wild-beast hunts, and gladiatorial combats, dates from the end of the third century. No less than fifteen temples and shrines, most of them rather small, were dedicated between 200 and 133. Two large basilicas or public halls, taking their name from similar structures built by Hellenistic rulers in the cities of the Greek East, were built for the use of magistrates and businessmen. Additional facilities for trade were provided by a new fish and meat market, new blocks of shops, and a dock on the Tiber to facilitate the unloading of ships. There were also a considerable number of porticos to provide shelter for merchants and idlers alike. Two new aqueducts were constructed to meet the needs of the growing urban population. The streets were paved with stone blocks and the sewage system repaired and extended. Ornamental arches adorned with statues were set up to commemorate Roman victories. Many other statues, the work of the great Greek sculptors, were carried off as spoils of war and placed as votive offerings in the new temples. Improvements were made in the quality of building materials. Public buildings were generally constructed of stone, sometimes coated with stucco; harder travertine blocks were used in place of the less durable tufa. As early as the third century Romans were using concrete; its use, perfected in the course of the second century, was to have a long history in the development at Rome of Hellenistic architectural ideas on a monumental scale. For the two temples of Jupiter and Juno dedicated in 146, marble was imported from Greece. Private buildings, however, continued for the most part to be built of crude brick and wood.

ROMAN ART. In the third and second centuries B.C. the Hellenistic style of art became general throughout Italy where, however, local variations in its interpretation had already appeared among the Etruscans and Italians. Greek influences therefore continued to have a direct effect upon

artistic tastes and techniques in Rome itself. Few artists of note seem to
have appeared among the Romans, who depended upon other Italians or
Greeks for the execution of the works which they planned. The Latin
genius was revealed more fully in the creation of practical rather than
ornamental works. Such were the paved highways, bridges and aqueducts, in which the arch was often used. In temple architecture the Romans blended with the Greek architectural orders traditional Italic and
Etruscan elements like the emphasis on axiality and the use of high
podiums and frontal entrances. Although a Greek architect was imported
for the temples of Jupiter and Juno built in 146, architecture, because of
its practical character, was highly esteemed in Rome, and Roman architects were beginning to win recognition abroad. As early as 170 the Syrian
King Antiochus IV Epiphanes hired a Roman architect to complete the
famous temple of Olympian Zeus begun in the sixth century B.C. in
Athens. The frequent use of round buildings, especially in the case of
smaller temples, shows an independent Roman tradition going back to
the round huts of prehistoric times.

Through familiarity with masterpieces of Greek sculpture carried off in
war or acquired by provincial governors, there slowly developed a taste
for fine statuary and an appreciation of Greek ideals in this field of art.
Although earlier such acquisitions were used to decorate public buildings,
there soon arose a demand for a similar adornment of private homes. This
demand led to a regular business of copying the works of Greek masters
for the Roman market.

It was in painting and secular sculpture that Roman taste asserted itself
most clearly. In painting there appeared the naturalness and the feeling
for depth and movement that characterized the tomb paintings of Etruria
and Campania, as well as the decorative designs on Etruscan bronzes. The
Romans also made extensive use of tomb paintings, but developed the
practice of exhibiting for popular edification large-scale pictures illustrat-
ing battles and other episodes of victorious foreign campaigns. Although
fragments of Roman tomb paintings have survived from as early as the
third century B.C., the triumphal paintings, which were housed in temples
and other private buildings, have all completely disappeared. Characteristically Roman was the fondness for portrait busts and statues. Their an-
tecedents may be found in the busts and figures which adorned the
Etruscan ash urns and sarcophagi, as well as in Etruscan bronze and terra
cotta statuary. The Roman love of portraiture found its expression in the
preservation of the wax death masks of the ancestors in the houses of the
Roman aristocracy and the carrying of lifelike statues of members of preceding generations in funeral processions. In addition, from an early date,
the Roman government had bronze statues erected to commemorate the
kings and the legendary heroes of the early Republic. Later it so honored
famous generals of the historic period and others who had rendered dis-

tinguished service to their country. By the end of the second century it had become a well-established custom for magistrates to set up statues in their own honor in public places. The outstanding feature of Roman portrait sculpture is its intense realism, which went far beyond the naturalness of Etruscan art (which in turn had often been reinforced by Hellenistic art) and insisted upon the representation of even unpleasing physical details.

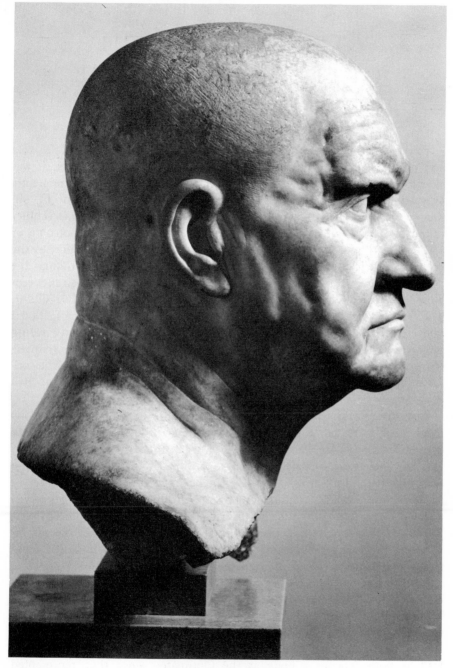

Roman portrait head

CHAPTER 12

STRUGGLE OF THE OPTIMATES AND THE POPULARES: 133–78 B.C.

ROMAN REVOLUTION. The century which began with the year 133 B.C. is commonly called the period of the Roman Revolution. It was an era of frequent and increasingly bitter civil strife, strife that frequently erupted into civil wars, which ultimately destroyed government by oligarchy and replaced it with a disguised kind of monarchy. This century of profound crisis was long in the making. It was the final outcome of the failure of the senatorial class to achieve a satisfactory solution to the economic, social, and political problems confronting Rome. Although the reasons for the Roman Revolution were in large measure social and economic, the course it took and its ultimate resolution were mainly political. The crisis was manifested by an intensification and broadening of factional political strife, traditional for centuries in a milder form, within the ruling oligarchy. Unlike most modern revolutions, it ended not with a dramatic change in the existing social and economic order, but rather with a conservative reorganization of the governing elite in the service of one-man rule.

The struggle saw the emergence of two political factions. On the one hand, there were the "Optimates" or "best men." These included the bulk of the senatorial politicians, who were devoted to the perpetuation of oligarchy. They were bitterly opposed to any modification of the existing situation that might affect adversely their prestige, political influence, or economic interests. The Optimates possessed formidable advantages which enabled them time after time to thwart all assaults on their prerogatives. These advantages were their control of the Senate and hence of the administration, their general unity of purpose, their wealth and inherited reputation, and their well-organized clientele at home and abroad.

Ranged against the Optimates were the "Populares," who led the elements more or less discontented with the existing order and demanding varying sorts of reform. These latter included the rapidly developing urban and rural proletariat in Italy, Rome's Italian allies, the equestrian class, and to a certain extent Rome's exploited subjects. The Populares did not lead as homogeneous a body as the Optimates, since they represented different classes and interests that did not always present a united front in the several crises of the prolonged conflict. At one time the equestrians, at another the city plebs, appear as the allies of the Optimates against the proponents of reform.

The Populares are sometimes called "the people's party," but this translation is rather misleading in its implications, since the Populares were only the leaders of the discontented and were drawn almost exclusively from a minority faction of the Senate. Some of these champions of reform were statesmen sincerely interested in righting wrongs and correcting abuses. Most of them, however, used reform programs as a means to an end, which, more often than not, meant the advancement of their own political careers and acknowledgment, by the very oligarchs they were ostensibly fighting, of their own preeminence and *dignitas*. Indeed, it was not uncommon for leaders of one faction to switch sides during their careers, if it appeared that pursuit of their *dignitas* would be facilitated thereby.

One commonly speaks of "ambition" as motivating the great figures of the Roman Revolution. This term must include a sense of how intensely political Roman society was, how the highly competitive energies of the ruling class, prevented by custom from finding outlets in arenas other than the political, were inevitably channeled into the race for office. In the days of Scipio Africanus brilliant and ambitious senators playing oligarchic politics according to the rules of the game were usually held in check by the Senate. Several generations later, however, the problems of governing the Empire had changed the game, and the stakes and rewards of officeholding had become much greater. The attainment of *dignitas* in this period meant the attainment of power undreamed of in any earlier era. In the first phases of the Roman Revolution, popular party leaders seem not to have realized the possible consequences of their wish to obtain preeminence among oligarchs by attacking the power of oligarchy. Even Optimate champions, who shared the political drive of their opponents, failed to understand that the new dimensions of power they wielded in defense of the Senate pointed toward the political dominance not of a class or even a faction, but of one man. By the last phase of the Revolution, however, it became increasingly evident that unbridled ambition in the service of either faction was incompatible with senatorial rule. Ultimately the conflict widened to include the whole Roman world and even some of the peoples beyond the frontiers of the empire, for the path to prestige and power lay in successful military operations, and hence the party chiefs sought a military force adequate to carry them to victory in the struggle for control of the government.

For this reason, in spite of unceasing internal disorders, the century marked an imperial expansion rivaling that of the Punic and Macedonian Wars. In Gaul Roman domination was extended to the Rhine and the Ocean; in the East practically the whole peninsula of Asia Minor, as well as Syria and Egypt, was incorporated in the Empire. With the exception of the region of Mauretania (i.e., modern Morocco, really a Roman dependency), Roman provinces completely encircled the Mediterranean. Another important result of the struggle was the creation of a new Italian nation by the admission to Roman citizenship of practically all the peoples dwelling in Italy up to the Alps. For subjects of Rome the era of civil wars was one of oppression and misery, since the needs of the rival factions and leaders caused shameless exploitation of the wealth and manpower of the provinces.

The period 133 to 78 covers the first stage in the struggle that ended the Republic and closes with the Senate in full possession of its old prerogatives, while the powers of the tribunate and Tribal Assembly have been seriously curtailed.

Although the events of the period were recorded in detail by contemporary Roman historians, the works of these men have not survived, and knowledge of the period today depends chiefly upon much later writers. From them a fairly clear idea of the main course of events is derived, but frequently their exact sequence and the motives and influences resulting in various courses of action or legislative enactments are very uncertain. The chief sources are Plutarch's *Lives* of Tiberius and Gaius Gracchus, Marius, and Sulla, and Appian's *Civil and Mithradatic Wars*, supplemented by the *Epitome* of Livy, and Sallust's *Jugurthine War*. To these must be added the short histories of Velleius Paterculus and the epitomists of the imperial period, as well as fragments from the more extensive histories of Diodorus and Cassius Dio. There are isolated but important references in Cicero's speeches and other writings and in some of the Roman antiquarians. Inscriptions are few but include considerable portions of some important laws.

I. Agrarian Reform of Tiberius Gracchus: 133 B.C.

LAND LAW OF 133 B.C.   The opening of the struggle was brought on by the agrarian legislation proposed by Tiberius Sempronius Gracchus, a tribune for the year 133. Gracchus, then thirty years of age, was one of the most prominent young Romans of his time, being the son of the like-named consul and of Cornelia, daughter of the great Scipio Africanus. Under his mother's supervision he had received a careful education, which included rhetoric and Greek Stoic philosophy. As quaestor in Spain in 137, he distinguished himself for courage and honesty in dealing with the native population and acquainted himself with the military needs of Rome.

The motives for the reform program he embarked upon as leader of a senatorial faction are complex and obscure. In part they may have been political. His *dignitas* had recently been wounded and his patronage with his Spanish clients undermined when the Senate rejected a treaty he had made with them. His espousal of reform would restore his *dignitas* and damage that of his opponents, especially the then dominant faction led by Scipio Aemilianus. Some have seen at work the liberal influences of the Greek education to which he had been exposed. Basically his motives were probably statesmanlike. He was aware of the economic crisis in Rome recently brought about by high prices and underemployment, and he saw in the decline of the free peasantry of Italy another menace to the state. When elected to the tribunate he drafted a law aimed at solving the problem of urban unemployment and reestablishing the class of free Italian peasants to provide new strength for the armies of Rome.

The bill was essentially conservative. Some years before, a certain Laelius (consul, 140), who belonged to the party of Scipio Aemilianus and who could hardly be accused of radical tendencies, had broached the question of land reform but had withdrawn his proposals because of the protests they aroused. Tiberius' proposed law was primarily designed to call into effect existing legislation which restricted the amount of public land that might be occupied by a single tenant but which had largely been disregarded. In a conciliatory spirit Tiberius Gracchus suggested that senatorial squatters should henceforth enjoy in full security possession of 500 Roman acres of public land.[1] Occupied land not in excess of the legal limit was to be granted to the holders in perpetuity without liability to tax or rent. In addition, the state was to compensate former holders for improvements they had made on those holdings surrendered according to law. The land recovered for public use was to be assigned to landless Romans and Italians in small plots, which they could not transfer to others and for which they were to pay a nominal rent to the state. A commission of three men (*III viri agris iudicandis assignandis*) was to be elected to take over the land claimed by the state and reapportion it to the new colonists.

In spite of the rather generous treatment accorded to the great proprietors by this Sempronian Law, it was stubbornly opposed by the senatorial aristocracy. This was not because the Senate did not recognize that the land question constituted a serious problem but because a majority of its members had already decided against any alteration in the status quo. Some of the landed aristocracy saw that a considerable portion of their holdings was threatened. In many cases it must have become impossible to distinguish between their private property and public lands in the possession of their families for several generations, and they did not know how much they stood to lose. Furthermore, ever since the tribunate of Gaius Flaminius in the third century, the conservative element had looked upon a division of public land as associated with the creation of a clientele by unorthodox means, and now they began to suspect Tiberius of ulterior political ambitions.

Angered by senatorial opposition, Tiberius withdrew from his measure

---

[1] Tiberius' law dealt only with occupied public land and did not include *ager publicus* that had been used as pasturage. There is a doubtful tradition that he also permitted an additional 250 Roman acres for each son with a maximum of 1,000 *iugera* for any household.

the proposals for compensation for improvements and the granting of ownership rights to public landholdings of less than the maximum legal size and sought to present his amended law to the Tribal Assembly. The Senate then resorted to the means by which it had long held forceful tribunes in check and induced one of the other tribunes, Marcus Octavius, to veto the law. Tiberius did not intend to be thwarted and, after all attempts at compromise had failed, he reluctantly but determinedly took the unprecedented step of appealing to the Tribal Assembly to depose Octavius on the ground that he was thwarting popular will. The Assembly responded by ousting Octavius, and the land law was passed without further opposition. Tiberius himself, his younger brother Gaius, and his father-in-law, Appius Claudius, were elected as the three commissioners to enforce the law. They received judicial authority to enable them to render judgment in cases where disputes arose regarding the ownership of land claimed by the state. It has frequently been held that the election of Tiberius to this office was illegal, but this is extremely doubtful, since the laws which forbade the appointment of the author of a law to a position created by it are of uncertain date and may have been later than 133.

FALL OF TIBERIUS GRACCHUS.   Once the land law was passed, its legality was recognized, even by the opposing faction. Nevertheless, the Senate tried to hamper the land commissioners by refusing to provide adequate funds for their expenses, which included the stocking of the allotments assigned to poor settlers. Tiberius proposed that money for this purpose be provided from the treasure of his father's client, King Attalus III of Pergamon, who had just died after bequeathing his kingdom to Rome.[2] This is a notable instance in which a provincial clientele affected factional politics at the capital. Tiberius' proposal was nothing less than a revolutionary challenge, in a constitutional sense, to traditional control by the Senate of finances and foreign affairs. Senatorial animosity was further aroused by the declaration of Tiberius that he would seek reelection to the tribunate for 132. Strictly speaking this was neither unconstitutional nor unprecedented, but it was certainly very unusual and contrary to the established practice of the third and second centuries. Tiberius felt that only as tribune could he assure the effective enforcement of the land law and refused to be dissuaded from his course. He was also credited with raising the question of giving citizenship to the Italian allies to compensate for the losses they might suffer from the operation of his land law. It seems unlikely, however, that he was greatly concerned with the allies, the basis of his power resting solely on the urban plebs and the rural proletariat. However this may be, senatorial extremists determined to prevent at all costs the reelection of Tiberius. The consul, Scaevola, related by marriage, like the Gracchi, to the Claudian faction, refused their appeal to take action against him. They organized their clients and slaves and

2 See p. 140.

attacked Tiberius and his followers in a public meeting in the Forum. Tiberius and three hundred of his adherents were massacred and their bodies thrown into the Tiber. A judicial commission, authorized by the Senate and presided over by the consuls of 132, sought out and punished with death or exile many of his prominent supporters.

FATE OF THE LAND COMMISSION.   For the moment the Senate had triumphed, although only by resorting to a means that in the long run was to prove its own undoing. The land law remained in force, and one of the consuls of 132, Popillius Laenas, although bitterly hostile to the Gracchan party, helped to carry out its provisions, perhaps in an attempt to detract from the achievements of the land commissioners. On the commission, Tiberius Gracchus was replaced by the father-in-law of Gaius, and subsequent vacancies were filled by active advocates of reform. Apparently in 130–129 the commission, then presided over by Fulvius Flaccus, caused great consternation among the Italian allies by questioning their right to plots bordering on public land and by the way in which they selected the portions of occupied public land to be reclaimed by the state. The allies claimed that their treaty rights were being disregarded and appealed to the famous Scipio Aemilianus, under whom their troops had served against Carthage and against Numantia, to represent their claims before the Senate. Scipio seems to have induced the Senate to exempt land claimed by the allies on the basis of grants or treaties from the jurisdiction of the commissioners. Their right to examine the title of properties occupied by Roman citizens seems not to have been withdrawn. How far Scipio would have gone in securing concessions for the allies is unknown, for he died unexpectedly in April or May of 129. He had become very unpopular with the Gracchan party, and some even accused his wife, Sempronia, the sister of the Gracchi, as well as their adherents, of being responsible for his sudden death.

When the question of the rights of the allies was raised again, it was upon the initiative of Flaccus, the land commissioner, who had been elected to the consulship for 125. He sponsored a law to grant citizenship to the Latin and Italian allies with an alternative of the right of appeal from the judgments of Roman courts and magistrates for the citizens of such communities as did not wish to be incorporated in the Roman state. This won the allegiance of the allies to the Gracchan party, and his proposal was energetically opposed by the Optimates, who correctly saw in the temporary alliance of the bulk of the Roman electorate and Italians a threat to oligarchic authority. The question of citizenship for the allies was to become a matter of party politics and could not be judged upon its merits. A political maneuver by the Senate succeeded in removing Flaccus to a military command in Gaul, and he had to abandon his proposal. The allies were doubly dissatisfied, since they had also been angered by a law concerning the consular elections of 126 that excluded them from Rome and so prevented the Latins in particular from voting by right of being domiciled in Rome or even of influencing the other voters. Of the Latin allies, the important town of Fregellae in Latium near the Samnite border had been most active in demanding Roman citizenship, and, when this was rejected, it revolted. The situation was serious, for the rebellion might have spread among the other Latin communities and from them to the Italian allies. The Romans acted energetically and at once besieged the rebellious city. As a result of treachery it soon fell, and they razed it to the ground as a warning to states that might be tempted to follow its example. None did so, and the revolt ended.

The census taken in 125 showed an increase of about 75,000 Roman citizens over that of 130: a total of 394,736 as against 318,828. No far-reaching conclusions can be drawn from these figures, which may well be inaccurate. In any case, the gain cannot all be ascribed to the land commission, although it had continued to function interruptedly since 133, for the census lists included all Roman citizens of eighteen years and over, and not merely those who had property sufficient to qualify them for military service. Undoubtedly many who failed to register after they lost their properties reported themselves when they received new allotments, but doubtless many others who hoped to share in the division of land enrolled. At the same time in the struggle for the control of the Assemblies, the leading men of both factions saw to it that their clients, in particular their freedmen, and other dependents were properly enrolled in the tribes and centuries.

II. Gaius Gracchus and the Senate: 124–121 B.C.

GAIUS GRACCHUS, TRIBUNE: 124–122 B.C. In 124 Gaius, the younger brother of Tiberius Gracchus and a former member of the land commission of 133, returned to Rome from a term as quaestor in the province of Sardinia and sought election to the tribunate. He was successful, and he entered upon office on December 10, 124. Gaius was a passionate orator, one of the most moving political speakers in Roman history. He was also a man of greater energy and more statesmanlike capacity than his brother. Traditions of Roman politics as well as ties of blood called him to support his brother's agrarian policy, but his aims were much more far-reaching and ultimately brought him into conflict with the Senate over other questions of public policy. For a time, however, he avoided any direct clash with his opponents while managing to retain the enthusiastic support of the poorer citizens. His popularity and influence were proved by his reelection to the tribunate in the summer of 123. In this the Senate seems to have acquiesced, although it is doubtful if any special legislation had been passed since the death of Tiberius sanctioning successive terms, for it was custom and not law which had forbidden the practice. Among the colleagues of Gaius in his second tribunate were his fiery ally Fulvius Flaccus, the consul of 125, and Marcus Livius Drusus, an active supporter of the Optimates.

LEGISLATION OF GAIUS GRACCHUS. Because the order in which Gaius Gracchus brought forward the numerous proposals that made up his extensive legislative program is not clearly known, it is hazardous to assign them to one or other of his two terms of office. It seems, however, that the bulk of his legislation fell between his reelection in 123 and the close of his official career in December 122. For convenience his measures may be grouped under three heads: judicial, economic and social, and imperial.

(a) Judicial. His first judiciary law condemned retroactively the sentences pronounced without privilege of appeal to the Assembly by the senatorial court that had punished the followers of Tiberius in 133. As a result the ex-consul Popillius, who had presided over this tribunal, was tried and sentenced to exile. His attention was then directed to the jurors in the civil courts, who hitherto had been drawn wholly from the Senate. In order to provide less partisan jurors, Gaius proposed that the Senate be increased by the enrollment of six hundred new members selected from the class with a property rating just below the senatorial. This suggestion met with considerable opposition, and Gaius dropped it. He did, however, secure the approval of a law which provided penalties for jurors found guilty of taking bribes. Lastly, at his instigation a colleague named Acilius introduced a law sometime in 123 or 122, which was enacted, drastically reorganizing the court for the recovery of damages from officials guilty of extortion from Roman subjects or allies. According to the mutilated text that has survived, the Acilian Law excluded magistrates in office, senators, and fathers, brothers, and sons of senators from the panel from which the fifty judges hearing each case were selected. Although the statement of specific qualifications of the new jurors has been lost, it is almost certain that it included the class of wealthy businessmen and landholders who henceforward were spoken of collectively as the equestrian order and had a property assessment of 400,000 sesterces.[3] This is apparently the earliest definition of the equestrian order in its widest extent. As a result of being given specific public duties, the equestrians became more conscious of their power and their special interests and entered upon a period of rivalry with the Senate. That Gaius fully realized the significance of this law is shown by his remark that, even if he should die, he would leave it as a sword thrust into the side of the Senate. In fact, the control of the court became a standing bone of contention between the two orders. Gaius undoubtedly had the welfare of provincials at heart when he transferred control over the tribunal from the senatorial order,

[3] About $20,000, at the 1964 value of silver.

which had rendered unjust or corrupt decisions. But subjects of Rome could hope for little improvement in its standards when they were placed in the hands of men who were interested in the financial exploitation of the provinces and could now intimidate honest governors when they endeavored to restrain the rapacity of tax collectors and moneylenders. The antibribery law had been passed when the judges came only from the senatorial order, and equestrians were not mentioned in it, so they were exempt from its provisions. Another result of Gaius' reform was that the equestrians for the first time became actively embroiled in factional politics.

(b) Economic and Social. One of the first steps taken by Gaius Gracchus to deal with the problem of the impoverished Roman citizens was the enactment of a grain law (lex frumentaria), which provided that the state should sell a fixed quantity of grain each month to citizens residing in Rome at a price which has been estimated as being considerably less than the current market rate. There can be little doubt that this law was supposed to stabilize prices for the benefit of the poor, who lived in perpetual danger of famine. Even before this, in emergencies, the Roman government had occasionally restored to such an expedient, but now it became a permanent obligation and constituted a regular charge upon the treasury. In the larger cities of the Greek East it had become a generally accepted doctrine that the state was responsible for the welfare of the poor, and it is probable that Gaius was both familiar with this doctrine and inspired by it. He also cannot have failed to see that this law would greatly increase his popularity with the city mob and might weaken to his advantage the ties between the Optimates and their clients, who would be less dependent upon patronage for their daily bread. The expense involved in offering grain at such a low price he may have justified on the ground that the people were entitled to some such share in the income derived from the Empire. The recipients of cheap grain did not receive it gratis but had to pay for it, and Gaius cannot strictly be accused of having instituted a grain dole. A step had been taken in that direction, however, and a way pointed out to those ready to court the good will of the people at the cost of the state. In order to store the necessary supplies of wheat, Gaius directed the construction of large granaries, and this work doubtless provided temporary employment for many free laborers.

Another project Gaius pushed vigorously was the construction or improvement of rural roads throughout Italy. These were probably intended to facilitate the transport of grain and other agricultural produce to the nearest local markets, for the city depended mainly upon supplies drawn from Sicily, Africa, and other countries by sea. Here was also a policy of providing work for the unemployed, as well as of agrarian colonization, for the lands abutting on the roads were assigned to farmers who undertook the responsibility of keeping the roads in repair in place of paying rental to the state.

Gaius was also the author of a special agrarian law, but little is known about its scope. A chance notice records that he restricted the amount of land which anyone might hold in Italy to 200 *iugera* (132 acres), which might be interpreted to mean that, in his desire to obtain more land for settlement, he greatly reduced the maximum set by Tiberius for occupants of public lands. If this were correct it would hardly have been passed over by all the more important writers. Perhaps this law authorized the founding of a number of colonies in Italy, although that may have been the subject of special legislation. At any rate Gaius resorted to such a plan to provide further opportunities for relieving overpopulation in Rome. Of the several colonial foundations attributed to him, two at least—Neptunia, adjacent to Tarentum, and Scolacium—were seaports. For these the colonists seem to have been persons of some means willing to engage in commerce rather than farming. By far the most important of his colonial projects was an attempt to found a new settlement at or near the site of Carthage, which had been uninhabited since its destruction in 146. This colony, called Junonia, was authorized by a law sponsored by the tribune Rubrius. In the spring of 122 Gaius and Fulvius Flaccus, two of the commission appointed to supervise the enterprise, went to Africa and organized the colony. The colonists, who numbered about six thousand, were enrolled from the whole of Italy and received unusually large allotments, 200 *iugera* each, which they held as personal property not subject to rental. Unquestionably this was an agrarian rather than a commercial foundation.

A minor piece of legislation carried by Gaius in the interests of the poorer citizens required that the state should furnish soldiers with clothing free of charge and make no deductions for this from their pay. This law also prohibited enlisting recruits under seventeen years of age.

(*c*) Imperial: Although the direction of imperial administration rested with the Roman Senate by long established custom, Gaius Gracchus did not hesitate to intervene in this sphere. One of his laws changed the system of allocating the consular provinces—that is, the spheres of duty, in particular foreign commands, assigned to the incoming consuls each year. The Senate had regularly designated these provinces after the elections, when they knew who the consuls-elect were. This made it possible for the senators, if so inclined, to assign provinces according to the proven capacities of persons concerned. But it also allowed them to use their power as a means of rewarding their friends and punishing their political opponents, as had been the case with Flaccus in 125. This power was lost when the law of Gaius compelled the Senate to designate the two consular provinces in advance of the election.[4]

Another law dealt with taxes in the recently organized province of

---

[4] This rule applied also to proconsular provinces, that is, those to which the consuls were to go as proconsular governors at the end of their year of office.

Asia. It provided that the contract for collecting the tax of 10 percent on the produce of all agricultural land in the province should be let by the censors in Rome to a single company of *publicani*. The result was that the provincial tax collectors were practically excluded from bidding for the contract, since the sum involved was beyond their resources and they would be at a great disadvantage in meeting the terms of the Roman censors. Since Asia was by far the richest Roman province, an opportunity was thus created for Roman businessmen to make huge profits. By this act, as well as by the Acilian Law, Gracchus won for himself the support of the equestrian order. Gracchus undoubtedly believed that the change in tax collection would aid the provincials of Asia, who were numbered among his family's clientele, since corrupt senatorial governors conniving with native tax farmers had extorted more than the legal amount from the population; but the result was unfortunate for the people of Asia, who were exposed to merciless exploitation by a largely irresponsible tax-collecting agency operating from the capital of the Empire.

The agrarian reforms of Tiberius Gracchus had brought up the question of the status of the allies of Rome in Italy, and events had made the Gracchan leaders champions of allied rights. Early in his second tribunate Gaius proposed to grant Roman citizenship to the Latin allies. This was countered by Livius Drusus, who suggested that the Latins be given complete immunity from scourging when serving under Roman officers.

The Optimates thus succeeded in dividing the non-Romans on the question of citizenship. The Latins already had voting rights under certain circumstances, even though they were not citizens. What they wanted was not so much citizenship as protection against arbitrary treatment by Roman magistrates. They apparently supported Drusus' measure at the price of abandoning the cause of the federate allies. Gaius apparently dropped his agitation for the moment but later drafted a more comprehensive measure in which he again proposed Roman citizenship for the Latins and at the same time Latin rights for the federate allies in Italy. This met with even stronger opposition than the earlier proposal. Italians flocked to Rome to support the law and influence the plebs on its behalf, but the Senate ordered the consuls to exclude from the city and its immediate vicinity all those not entitled to vote. Whether the law was vetoed by Drusus or was defeated in the Tribal Assembly, it failed to obtain the approval of the Roman electorate, which considered that its own interests would be endangered by the addition of many new voters. Thus the question of the allies was shelved for the time, and Gaius suffered a major political defeat which revealed that his influence with the Assembly had been seriously undermined.

FALL OF GAIUS GRACCHUS: 121 B.C.   The decline of influence with the Tribal Assembly, which meant the end of Gaius' political power, was brought about largely through maneuvers of the Optimates. Becoming alarmed at his success in being reelected tribune and at the dominant part which he exercised in forming and executing public policy, his enemies in the Senate planned his overthrow. They found a dedicated agent in his colleague, Livius Drusus, who devoted himself to the task of weaning the city electorate from Gaius by outbidding his proposed laws with others that appealed even more to the interests and prejudices of the voters. When Gaius proceeded slowly with the organization of his colonies in Italy, Drusus introduced a law authorizing the foundation of twelve colonies immediately. Each of these was to consist of three thousand colonists to be selected from the very poorest citizens, and there was to be no rental paid to the government for the individual allotments, as was the case in the Gracchan colonies. The Livian colonies were actually never founded. After the fall of Gaius Gracchus, when it was no longer necessary to play up to the city proletariat, the matter was dropped. It may be, however, that the provision affecting the rentals on allotments was enforced and extended to the Gracchan colonists. When Gaius renewed his attempt to extend the franchise to the Latins, while granting Latin status to the other Italian allies, his opponents openly appealed to the jealousy and exclusiveness of the mob. The campaign against Gaius culminated in an attempt to discredit his colony of Junonia during the period of seventy days he spent in Africa early in 122. He was accused of having exceeded the authorized number of colonists and of illegally admitting non-Roman settlers. False rumors of unfavorable omens said to have greeted the attempts to inaugurate the colony were circulated. The Optimates obviously feared that Gaius might become the patron of flourishing and far-flung colonies. The effect of these various efforts was seen when Gaius sought the tribunate for a third time in the summer of 122. He failed to secure reelection, and in the following December his tribunate ended.

In 121 the Senate sponsored an attempt to annul the Rubrian Law that had ordered the founding of Junonia. Gaius, who seems to have feared assassination, allowed his friends to provide a bodyguard. An unimportant member of the staff of the consul Opimius was killed in a brawl between adherents of both factions. The Senate seized upon this pretext to authorize the consul to take necessary measures to safeguard the state. Opimius promptly organized an armed force of senators, equestrians, and their slaves. He then summoned Gaius and his former colleague Flaccus before the Senate. Since it was clear that they would not be treated fairly, they determined to resist arrest and occupied the Aventine hill with their supporters. There they were attacked by Opimius at the head of his levies and a force of Cretan archers in Roman service who happened to be in the city. The Gracchans were routed, Flaccus was killed, Gaius had himself stabbed by a faithful slave to avoid capture, and many of their followers were arrested and executed. About three thousand allegedly perished.

THE GRACCHI AND THE CONSTITUTION.   The failure of the

Gracchi was regarded a great political tragedy by their political adherents, who held their memory in high esteem. It was equally execrated by their opponents, who had a greater influence upon Roman historical literature. Both men were earnest patriots, sincerely convinced of the necessity of solving the problems they attacked and equally sure of the rightness of the plans they proposed, but, in attempting to overcome the opposition to their measures, they followed a course that shook the foundations of the constitution and presented a direct challenge to the Senate's control of the government. They can hardly be credited with the deliberate intention of sidetracking the Senate in favor of the Tribal Assembly led by a popular tribune continuously reelected to that office, but at least that was the temporary effect of their actions, and here they are open to serious criticism. An attempt to make the fickle Assembly direct the government was not statesmanlike, for the Assembly was both more incompetent than the Senate and more open to wholesale corruption, nor could it any longer pretend to speak for the Roman citizen body. As it turned out, the Senate regained its position but lost greatly in prestige and authority. It owed its victory to violence and not to constitutional practice, and this afforded a precedent that might be turned against itself. As long as it lasted, the alliance of the equestrians and the urban proletariat proved stronger than the Senate, and this lesson, too, was not lost upon later statesmen. In addition to the loss of some of its prerogatives, the Senate was weakened by the consolidation of the businessmen into a vigorous political party that usually opposed it. The greatest future danger lay in the bitter resentment among those who had suffered from the Senate's ruthlessness and in the division of political leadership into two hostile political factions, the Populares and the Optimates. For the provincials, the legislation of Gaius opened the way to further oppression; the question of allied citizenship was shelved for the moment but was destined to be raised again and more violently.

In 120 the strength of the Senate's position was tested by the trial of the ex-consul Opimius for his actions under the decree of the Senate for the safeguarding of the state. His acquittal not only gave legal sanction to the slaughter of the Gracchans but justified passing the decree itself. For the future, this so-called "last decree" (*senatus consultum ultimum*) gave the Senate a new and powerful constitutional weapon for crushing its opponents. But the victory of the Senate was by no means absolute. With the exception of the Rubrian Law, which was repealed, the statutes of the Gracchi remained in force, and even the colonists in Africa were allowed to remain in occupancy of their land. Three laws finally settled the vexed question of public lands. The first, possibly passed in 121 or 120 but more probably a provision of Livius Drusus' colonial law of 122, permitted the Gracchan colonists to sell their allotments. Thereupon rich proprietors began once more to buy them out or to force them to evacuate their holdings. Somewhat later (111) the land commission was abolished as a result of a law of the tribune Spurius Thorius, of which the text is partly preserved. It forbade further distributions of public land in Italy and guaranteed present possessors of public land in their tenure if they paid rent, the income from which was to be used for disbursements to the poor. The third law, passed in 109/8, declared private property free from any form of rental all lands assigned by the Gracchan commissioners and all former holdings of public land up to the limit of 500 *iugera* set by the Gracchan legislation. Further encroachment upon public pasture lands was forbidden, and the use of these was strictly regulated. It is difficult to estimate the net results of this period of agrarian legislation, but it has been estimated that altogether the large landlords lost about 1,000,000 acres of farm lands and that this, plus the limitation on the size of the flocks and herds they could run on the pasture lands, struck a severe blow at the power of the senatorial class. There is no way of knowing how many new settlers (perhaps 50,000 in all) remained on their farms after they were allowed to sell them, nor how far the potential military strength of the state was increased.

III. Rise of Gaius Marius

FRONTIER WARS.   While at Rome interest centered in the struggle between the Gracchans and the Senate, on the frontiers of the empire Roman armies were engaged in a continuous series of wars for the defense of Roman territory. On the borders of Macedonia and Illyricum there were struggles with Celtic tribes south of the Danube, in northern Italy raids of Alpine peoples had to be repressed, and in the western Mediterranean the depredations of pirates compelled the Romans to occupy the Balearic Islands. The seizure of these islands in 123–121 secured to Rome full command of the sea route to Spain. On Majorca, the largest of the group, two colonies of Roman citizens were founded with settlers recruited among the Italians resident in Spain. More important was the Roman advance after 125 in Transalpine Gaul. Here the Romans, in answer to an appeal from their ally Massilia, fought against the Gallic Saluvii, a people whose territory lay north of that city. The subjugation of the Saluvii and of neighboring Ligurian peoples in 123 gave the Romans control of a route across the Maritime Alps from Italy to the valley of the Rhone, secured by permanent occupation of a fortified post at Aquae Sextiae.

This Roman success alarmed more powerful Gallic tribes, particularly the Allobroges east of the Rhone and the Arverni to the west. These two peoples formed a coalition to oppose further Roman advance, while a rival people, the Aedui, to the north of the Arverni, took the side of Rome. Hostilities began when the Romans demanded the surrender of fugitives from the Saluvii. In 121 the Allobroges and the Arverni were defeated in a great battle fought near the junction of the Rhone and the Isère by the consul Fabius Maximus and the proconsul Gnaeus Domitius Ahenobarbus. This victory made the Romans masters of southern Gaul from the Alps to the Pyrenees, except for the territory of Massilia. In spite of senatorial opposition, a colony of Roman citizens from Italy was founded at Narbo, perhaps under the influence of the business interests at Rome. Apart from the abortive attempt of Gaius Gracchus at Junonia, this was the first colony of its type to be founded beyond Italy.

JUGURTHINE WAR. Shortly after the occupation of southern Gaul, the Romans became involved in a much more serious conflict, which revealed to the world the corruption of members of its ruling class and rekindled the smoldering fires of internal political strife. The scene of the new struggle was North Africa, and its occasion was the death in 118 of Micipsa, successor to Masinissa as king of Numidia and a loyal ally of Rome. He bequeathed his kingdom jointly to his two sons, Adherbal and Hiempsal, and a nephew, Jugurtha, whom he had adopted some years before. Jugurtha was able and energetic but also ambitious and unscrupulous. As commander of the Numidian contingent in the Roman army under the orders of Scipio Aemilianus at the siege of Numantia, he had gained military experience and an insight into the weaknesses of the Roman oligarchy. While preparations were being made to divide the kingdom among the three heirs, Jugurtha had Hiempsal assassinated and expelled Adherbal. The latter fled to Rome and appealed for aid on the basis of the alliance with Rome which he had inherited from his ancestors. It is difficult to understand the motivation of the Roman Senate in the imbroglio that followed. Rome had no obligation to interfere in North Africa, and she was distracted by movements of German tribes to the north. The Senate may have preferred to curb Jugurtha diplomatically rather than through war, and the tales of his corrupting the Senate may well be exaggerated. In any case, so successful were his agents that a Roman commission, sent in 116 to partition Numidia between the rivals, gave Jugurtha the western and richer part of the kingdom, leaving the eastern half to Adherbal. Jugurtha, however, aimed at ruling all of Numidia and so provoked Adherbal to war. In 113 he defeated him and blockaded him in his capital, Cirta, which was defended with the aid of the local Italian business community. Adherbal again appealed to the Senate for aid. Two Roman commissions sent to investigate the situation succumbed to Jugurtha's diplomacy, and Cirta was forced to surrender. Adherbal and all its defenders were executed.

The slaughter of so many Italians raised a storm in Rome, where the business elements and populace forced the Senate, inclined to wink at Jugurtha's disregard of its African settlement, to declare war. In 111 a Roman army under the consul Bestia invaded Numidia. Again Jugurtha resorted to bribes and secured terms of peace from the consul after a sham submission. Opponents of the Senate saw through the trick, however, and forced an investigation. Jugurtha was summoned to Rome under safe conduct to give evidence as to his relations with the Roman officials in Numidia. He came and bought the intervention of two tribunes who prevented his testimony from being taken. Relying too much upon his ability to purchase immunity for any action, he ventured to procure the assassination in Rome itself of a rival claimant to the Numidian throne (110). His friends in the Senate dared protect him no longer and he had to leave Italy.

The war reopened, and the first operations ended late in 110 or early 109 with the defeat and capitulation of a Roman army, which was forced to pass under the yoke, to be released only when its commander consented to recognition of Jugurtha's position and an alliance between him and Rome. In this shameful episode bribery and treachery had played their part. The terms were rejected at Rome, and a tribunician proposal to try those guilty of misconduct with Jugurtha was ratified by the Assembly. In the same year the consul Quintus Caecilius Metellus took command in Africa. One of his officers was Gaius Marius. Marius was born of an equestrian family of Arpinum and was therefore a new man, but his political ambition equalled that of any senatorial noble. Like any other parvenu, he had to build up a faction with the help and patronage of established and influential senators. He was first a protégé of Scipio Aemilianus, whom he served in the Numantine War. He had then successfully managed state contracts and, with the patronage of the Metelli, had been elected tribune in 119, praetor in 115, and propraetor in Spain in 114. Marius was not content merely to be a senator but had his eye on becoming one of the leading statesmen. His further career, in which he turned against the very oligarchs who had launched him, is explained in part by the failure of the latter to encourage his claims to preeminence.

In contrast to former commanders against Jugurtha, Metellus was both energetic and honorable. He began a methodical devastation of Numidia and forced Jugurtha to abandon the field and resort to guerrilla warfare. He also tried to stir up disloyalty among the king's followers. But he failed to terminate the war by killing or capturing Jugurtha. When Metellus scornfully refused Marius' request to be allowed to return to Rome and stand for the consulship in 108, Marius intrigued to get the command transferred to himself, alleging that Metellus was purposely prolonging the campaign. Finally Metellus let him go, and he was elected consul for the following year (107). The Senate, wishing to keep Metellus in command, had not designated Numidia as a consular province, and so the popular party passed a law in the Tribal Assembly conferring the command against Jugurtha upon Marius. This intervention by the Assembly in the traditional right of the Senate to distribute provincial commands boded ill for the oligarchy. Nevertheless, the Senate yielded to this encroachment upon its acknowledged rights, and Marius superseded Metellus in 107.

His quaestor was Lucius Cornelius Sulla, scion of a decayed patrician family, who was destined to become the bitter rival of his chief.

In the meantime, although the position of Jugurtha had been strengthened by an alliance with his father-in-law Bocchus, king of Mauretania, Marius was able to continue the strategy of Metellus, seizing towns and fortresses that might serve as enemy bases. Ultimately he won two hard-fought victories over the united forces of the two kings, and Bocchus, fearing an inevitable Roman victory, opened negotiations. At length, pressed by Sulla, who had risked a journey to the camp of the Mauretanian, Bocchus connived at placing Jugurtha in the hands of the Romans as a captive. This ended the war, and Marius returned in triumph to Rome in 105. There he found that, in defiance of precedent, he had been elected consul for the ensuing year, owing to the fear of a barbarian invasion of Italy from the north and to popular confidence in him as a result of his success in Africa. Jugurtha, after gracing his victor's triumph, was executed in the public prison at Rome.

Apart from adding a small section of Numidia to the Roman province of Africa, the Senate did not seize upon the opportunity presented by the defeat of Jugurtha to annex more territory. The part of Numidia which bordered on Mauretania was united to the kingdom of Bocchus as a reward for his services; the rest was made into a client kingdom under the rule of a native prince. The restoration of peace opened this country once more to the Italian business interests. Upon Rome itself the repercussions of the Jugurthine War were of great significance. The prestige of the Senate, already weakened by the assaults of the Gracchi, was diminished still further by its apparent corruptibility and bungling and by the intervention of the Populares and the equestrians in foreign policy. The elevation of Marius, the man of the hour, tended to overshadow the solid achievements of nobles like Metellus and Sulla. Once again it had been shown that a coalition of the equestrian order and the city mob could control public policy, and in the person of Marius the war had produced a leader under whom these elements could unite.

IV. Invasion of the Cimbri and the Teutons

GERMANIC MIGRATION. The barbarian menace that led to the election of Marius to his second consulship was the effect of the wanderings of Germanic and Celtic peoples, chief of whom were the Cimbri and the Teutons. These two tribes, suffering from overpopulation and perhaps from the pressure of warlike neighbors in their homeland in south Jutland, undertook a mass migration in search of a new and richer home. After making their way into the middle Danube valley, they turned westward and in 113 invaded the lands of the Taurisci, allies of Rome, who lived north of the Alps between the upper Drave and the Danube. A Roman army sent to help the Taurisci suffered a disgraceful defeat. The migratory horde then turned west toward the Rhine, being joined by the Tigurini, a branch of the Celtic Helvetians, and by the Ambrones, a tribe of uncertain origin. In 111, these united peoples crossed the Rhine into Gaul, where they came into conflict with the Roman armies defending this area. Upon the refusal of their demand for lands within the Roman frontiers, the Cimbri inflicted a severe defeat upon the consul Marcus Julius Silanus in 109, although they failed to follow up their success. The Tigurini, however, kept threatening South Gaul and caused a revolt of Roman allies in the vicinity of Tolosa. In 107 another consular army was almost annihilated by the Tigurini, and its commander Lucius Cassius Longinus was killed. A year later the consul Quintus Servilius Caepio recovered Tolosa without opposition from the invaders, who had withdrawn from allied territory, and punished it by carrying off its immense temple treasures. Three years afterward he was tried and condemned for defrauding the state of this booty, which disappeared mysteriously on its way to the coast. Danger threatened again when the Cimbri and Teutons marched down the Rhone Valley. Two Roman armies, one under Caepio as proconsul and the other under the consul Gnaeus Mallius Maximus, moved to meet them. The jealousy and incompetence of the Roman commanders led to the destruction of both of their armies in a great battle near Arausio (Orange), in which 60,000 allegedly fell on the Roman side. This was the greatest disaster suffered by Roman arms since the fateful day of Cannae. The way to Italy lay open, but once more the Germans failed to take advantage of their opportunity. The Cimbri crossed the Pyrenees into Spain, while their allies withdrew beyond the Roman sphere in Gaul. It was probably at this time that Transalpine Gaul (Gallia Narbonensis) was organized as a province.

MILITARY REFORMS OF MARIUS. At this juncture (105) the people voted Marius his second consulship for 104 and gave him the command against the barbarians, thereby disregarding the legal interval of ten years between holding the office. He set to work at once to create an army for the defence of Italy. He made use of his experience in raising troops for the Jugurthine War and, as before, accepted as recruits citizens whose lack of property had previously disqualified them for service in the legions. He also depended more upon voluntary enlistments than upon the enforcement of the universal obligation to military service for a certain number of campaigns. It had been very difficult to raise enough troops by the old system, due largely to a decrease in the number of those possessing adequate property qualification, partly to a decline of military spirit among the well-to-do, and partly to the residence of many citizens outside of Italy. The Roman government had been forced gradually to lower the property qualification for military service. Marius went one step further, and, without realizing the revolutionary importance of his action, he accepted men without any property at all—the proletariat—in his legions. This transformed military service from an obligation towards the state into a career that could provide employment for numbers of landless and unemployed Romans. It is sometimes contended that soldiers recruited on this basis were no longer anxious to return to civilian occupations but were willing to serve for many years under the command of a successful general. In reality, however, they regarded military service rather as a means to an end—a plot of land or a bonus provided by their commanders—and they were by no means anxious to serve long terms under arms. Thus to some degree military service and its ultimate rewards seemed to present a solution of the problems of poverty and unemployment among the lower classes of citizens. Marius' innovation also relieved the state of pressing manpower problems and made easy the creation of standing armies in certain provinces, like Spain, that required the continuous presence of troops.

More significant was the fact that loyalty to the state came to be supplanted by devotion to a successful general and that the latter could rely upon his soldiers to support him against the civil authority, or upon his veterans, who became his clients, to back him in his subsequent political career. It was armies of this new type that made possible the political careers of the great generals of the next century.

Marius also made important changes in legionary equipment, tactics, and organization. In part he generalized developments in the military establishment that preceded him, in part the reforms were his own innovations. He instituted weapons training based on that used in the gladiatorial schools and introduced an improved type of *pilum* or throwing spear, whose metal head broke away from the wooden shaft on impact and thus prevented its being thrown back by the enemy. To increase mobility he had his troops carry their entrenching tools, which were quickly dubbed "Marius' mules" (*muli Mariani*). He generalized the practice of combining maniples into larger units known as cohorts, which then became the standard tactical unit in the legion. Thereafter the paper strength of the legion was 6,000 men, grouped into 10 cohorts of 600 each, consisting of 6 centuries of 100 troops. Legions no longer fought in three separate lines, and all the infantry received the same arms. In the Marian legion the officer cadre subordinate to the legionary commander, normally a consul, consisted of six military tribunes and sixty centurions, six in each cohort. The centurions, superbly disciplined and experienced veterans, were the real backbone of the military establishment. There was no noncommissioned officer cadre. Beneath the centurionate the Roman army officially recognized only the existence of private soldiers (*milites*), who could perform tactical and administrative functions, however, sometimes highly specialized. The military reforms of Marius were thus important not only because of their social and political consequences but also because they notably increased the fighting strength of the army.

DEFEAT OF THE BARBARIANS.   During the years 104 and 103
Marius kept his army in Gaul, guarding the passage to Italy, while he completed the training of his troops and dug a new channel at the mouth of
the Rhone to facilitate the passage of his transports into the river. He was
reelected to the consulship for 103 and again for 102, since the barbarian
danger continued. In 102 the Cimbri returned from Spain and, joining the
other tribes, prepared to invade Italy. The Teutons and Ambrones followed
the direct route from southern Gaul, while the Cimbri and Tigurini moved
north of the Alps to enter Italy by the eastern Alpine passes. Marius permitted the Teutons and Ambrones to march by him; then he overtook and
annihilated them at Aquae Sextiae. In the meantime the Cimbri forced the
other consul, Quintus Lutatius Catulus, to abandon the Brenner Pass and
withdraw south of the Po, allowing them to winter north of that river.
Marius returned to Italy to join his colleague and face the new danger. The
next year, consul for the fifth time, he met and destroyed the Cimbri on
the Raudine plains near Vercellae. The Tigurini then gave up their attempt
to penetrate Venetia and returned to their former home in Switzerland.
Italy was saved from a repetition of the Gallic invasion of the fourth
century.

The Roman victories, won over greatly superior numbers, were due
largely to the superior equipment and discipline of the Roman troops but
also in part to the total lack of strategic planning or organization by the
barbarians. The defeat of the barbarians also showed that the vitality of
the Roman state was by no means exhausted and that men of energy and
ability were not lacking, although under the existing régime it required a
crisis to bring them to the front. Such a man was Marius, now the dominant figure in politics.

SECOND SICILIAN SLAVE WAR: 104–101 B.C.   While the
barbarians were threatening Italy, Rome was called upon to suppress disorders in other parts of her Empire, some of which were put down only
after considerable effort. In 104 occurred a serious rebellion of the slaves in
Sicily, headed by two leaders, Salvius and Anthenion, the former of whom
took the title of King Tryphon. The rebels became masters of the open
country, defeated the first forces sent against them, reduced the Sicilian
cities to the verge of starvation, and were only subdued by a consular army
under Manius Aquilius in 101.

ROME AND THE CILICIAN PIRATES.   Before the slave war in
Sicily was ended, the Romans were forced to try to suppress piracy in the
Mediterranean. Piracy had been on the increase ever since the decline of
Rhodian sea power following the Second Macedonian War. Rome had
neglected to maintain a navy adequate even for policing the seas, since
there was no longer any rival maritime power. The pirates were at the
same time slave traders, making a business of kidnapping all over the Mediterranean, particularly in the East, to supply the slave mart at Delos. In 104

the king of Bithynia complained to the Senate that one half of his able-bodied men had been carried off into slavery. This traffic was winked at by the Romans, since they needed many slaves for their plantations and their business interests profited by the trade. The depredations of the pirates at length became too serious to be ignored, and in 102 the praetor Marcus Antonius was given a special command against them. They had their chief strongholds on the Cilician coast and the island of Crete, and Antonius proceeded to Cilicia, where he destroyed several of their towns and annexed some territory, which became the province of Cilicia. The trouble was not over, however, and probably in December of 101 a law was passed in Rome closing the harbors under Roman control to pirate vessels.

The Romans at this time had also to face revolts in Spain, which broke out spasmodically down to 95, as well as continual inroads of barbarians from Thrace into the provinces of Macedonia and Illyricum.

V. Populares and the Senate

ATTACKS UPON THE SENATE IN ROME. The prestige of the Optimates' party, rudely shattered in the Jugurthine War, suffered still further blows from incompetence and disregard of the public interest by its members who held commands in the war with the Cimbri and Teutons. This situation encouraged spokesmen of the popular party, who counted heavily upon the support and the popularity of Marius, to attack both individual senators and the body as a whole. One of the leaders in this movement was Gaius Servilius Glaucia, who, probably as tribune in 104, sponsored the passage of a law abrogating one passed two years before by senatorial influence changing the composition of juries for trial of cases of extortion from exclusively equestrian membership to one of both senators and equestrians. By the Servilian Law this court was made up once more of equestrians only, as under the Acilian Law of 123. In the same year a second tribune, Gnaeus Domitius Ahenobarbus, put through a law lessening the control of the nobles over appointments to the official priestly colleges. The Domitian Law limited cooptations to vacancies in these colleges to persons previously elected in an assembly of seventeen tribes chosen by lot, as was the practice in the election of the Pontifex Maximus. A year later another tribune, Lucius Appuleius Saturninus, engineered the condemnation of Caepio and Mallius, who were responsible for the disaster at Arausio, by a tribunal set up by one of his own laws for the trial of persons accused of treason.

COALITION OF SATURNINUS, GLAUCIA, AND MARIUS. During his tribunate in 103 Saturninus had sponsored some important legislation. One law established a special court to try cases of treason, which was conceived of as an offense against the majesty (maiestas) of the Roman people. Thereby he wished to protect popular party leaders against oligarchical violence. He tried to win further support from the city electorate by a law renewing the regular sale of grain at rates below the market price, a procedure suspended after the death of Gaius Gracchus. He also courted the good will of Marius by another law, which provided land grants of 100 *iugera* (62 acres) each in Africa for Marian veterans. A coalition among Saturninus, Glaucia, and Marius came about to secure a sixth consulship for Marius, for 100, and at the same time the praetorship for Glaucia and a second tribunate for Saturninus. They were successful, but the three entered upon office without any definite political program. Saturninus proposed laws providing lands for veterans in Gallia Narbonensis and authorizing the founding of colonies of Latin status in Sicily, Achaea, and Macedonia. Special clauses required all senators to swear they would recognize the provisions of the laws as valid once they had been passed. The Senate tried to block these measures by inducing certain tribunes to veto them, and the city voters opposed the colonial law because allies were to be admitted to the new settlements and Marius was empowered to grant Roman citizenship to select persons in each of these communities. Marius wished to legalize grants of citizenship he had previously made to individual allied auxiliary troops in the field as a reward for bravery. During his previous tribunate and his recent election campaign Saturninus had not hesitated to appeal to violence, and on this occasion he made use of Marius' veterans to rout the opposition. The laws were enacted, but the proposed settlement in Gaul was never carried out, and very little was done about the colonies in other provinces. Marius was already alarmed at the violent conduct of his associates, and its continuance led to a complete break with them. He had never been a social revolutionary, and now that he had what he wanted, prestige and dignity second to no other senator, he became estranged from his violent associates and gradually sought a *rapprochement* with the oligarchy.

Seeking to perpetuate their position, Saturninus and Glaucia became candidates for public offices for 99. Saturninus was reelected tribune for a third time, but Glaucia, illegally a candidate for the consulship while still a praetor, played into the hands of his enemies by having his chief rival murdered. This so offended public opinion that the Senate passed the last decree and called upon Marius to restore order. He forced the surrender of Saturninus, Glaucia, and their followers, who had taken up a position on the Capitoline Hill, and placed them for safekeeping in a public building. There they were killed by their enemies, who tore off the roof and stoned them to death with tiles. Marius suffered a political eclipse; he had been unable to control his own partisans or to protect them from mob violence when he had taken them into custody. His political faction evaporated. The Senate was once more triumphant and the Populares were divided and discredited. By organizing a professional army, Marius had created a new basis of power for ambitious men to exploit: a military clientele. Marius had not exploited that clientele and become a revolutionary, but it would not be long before such armies were used as instruments of despotic power.

VI. Attempted Reforms of Livius Drusus 91 B.C.

SENATORIAL POLICY. The Optimates celebrated their triumph by initiating a number of political trials, which resulted in the condemnation of a few minor supporters of Saturninus and Glaucia. They also sought to check demagogic legislation by a law declaring the inclusion of unrelated topics in any single legislative enactment illegal and requiring that the customary interval of three market days between the formal publication of an impending measure and the actual voting on it should be strictly observed. Equally significant of the Optimates' attitude was the passage of a law in 95 that banished Latin and Italian allies from Rome and instituted a search to find those illegally posing as Roman citizens. Although this action corresponded to previous senatorial policy, it was not provoked by any special danger and was a gratuitous insult to the allies, whose loyalty in the Jugurthine and Cimbric wars had been crucial.

TRIAL OF RUTILIUS RUFUS: 92 B.C. Although the senators and the equestrians combined against the terrorism instituted by the popular demagogues, the coalition was not lasting. As Gaius Gracchus foresaw, the control of the law courts proved a standing bone of contention between the two orders. Especially aggravating to the senators was the use of the court established to try cases of extortion to force the provincial governors to administer the provinces in the interest of financiers. A scandalous instance of this abuse was the case of Rutilius Rufus in 92. He had been legate under Mucius Scaevola, governor of Asia, in 98, and both had sternly checked any unjust exactions there by agents of the *publicani*. A trumped-up charge of extortion was now brought against Rutilius, who was tried and found guilty. His fate was to serve as a warning to officers who took their provincial obligations seriously.

LEGISLATIVE PROGRAM OF MARCUS LIVIUS DRUSUS. One of the tribunes in 91 was Marcus Livius Drusus, son of the like-named opponent of Gaius Gracchus. An Optimate by inheritance and disposition, the younger Drusus had come to realize the serious situation threatening the Senate, and accordingly had embarked on a program of legislative reform. This program revived memories of the Gracchi, but it was intended to bolster senatorial control by weaning away the traditional supporters of popular party leaders and increasing the Optimates' clientele. At first Drusus sought to win over the poorer voters by laws authorizing the founding of new colonies and fresh distributions of public land to individuals and the revival of public distributions of cheap grain. Next he brought forward a proposal for correcting the abuses of the court for the trial of cases of extortion. This was to be accomplished by having the jurors chosen half from the Senate and half from the members of the equestrian order, and he may also have proposed to increase the Senate to 600 by admitting 300 equestrians. Equestrian jurors were to be made retro-actively liable to prosecution for accepting bribes—a project that espe-cially interested him, since he wished to punish the jurors who had condemned his uncle, Rutilius Rufus. Although these were sound meas-ures, they were too moderate to secure warm support from the bulk of the Senate and evoked vigorous protests from the equestrians. Nevertheless they all apparently became law. Finally, Drusus raised again the question of enfranchising both Latin and Italian allies. Here he met with strong opposition from the Roman populace as well as from a senatorial faction that feared the personal power he might wield as the successful patron of the newly enfranchised. Although some leading Optimates like the Dean of the Senate, M. Aemilius Scaurus, stood by him, that body decreed that the Livian laws already passed were unconstitutional, since they violated the law against "omnibus" bills. Before the end of the year Drusus was assassinated, and thus ended the last attempt of a civilian to reform the government by peaceful means.

VII. Italic or Marsic War:[5] 90–88 B.C.

The death of Drusus triggered a revolt of the Italian allies. They had been in close contact with him and had taken steps to revolt if his bill should fail to pass. After the Senate had refused to entertain a renewed demand for their admission to citizenship, they took up arms. Led by the Marsi and the Samnites, a group of the peoples in the central highland region organized a confederacy with its capital at Corfinium in the terri-tory of the Paeligni, which was renamed Italia. Military necessity de-manded some organization to manage the war effort. The confederacy established a council of war, while the actual conduct of operations was entrusted to two generals in chief and twelve subordinate commanders chosen from the peoples participating in the struggle. A federal coinage was issued, specimens of which have survived, many bearing a figure of the goddess Italia, the guardian deity of the union.

Practically all of the warlike peoples of central and southern Italy either were included in the confederacy or fought with it. The rebels were a match for the Romans in numbers; through long service in the Roman armies they had become thoroughly versed in Roman military organiza-tion, tactics, and discipline, and they could count upon leaders of proved ability. The Latin colonies remained true to their allegiance, as did the Greek cities of south Italy, whose action virtually cut off the Italians from

---

[5] Later called the Social War, i.e. the War with the Allies.

the coast. Umbria and Etruria, although disaffected, did not take up arms at once. Rome possessed a great advantage in her control of the sea, which enabled her to draw upon the resources of the provinces in men, money, and materials, and thus was in a much better position to sustain a prolonged struggle.

ITALIC VICTORIES AND ROMAN CONCESSIONS. Hostilities opened in 90, the allied forces attempting to reach Etruria in the north and occupy Campania in the south, the Romans seeking to forestall them by vigorous thrusts into the heart of allied territory. In the south the Italians, in spite of one defeat, achieved great success. They overran a large part of Campania and broke through to the coast. Further victories gave them control of Apulia and Lucania. In the north the struggle was more even, and the Romans balanced several disasters by equally significant successes. In this sphere Marius, who served as a *legatus* or deputy commander, rendered valuable service. On the whole the balance of success favored the allies, and the Romans began to have doubts about the future. The allied cities in Etruria had been prevented from joining the rebels only by a timely promise of citizenship, and both Senate and people were ready to make further concessions. Early in the year the consul Lucius Julius Caesar put through the Julian Law, which granted Roman citizenship to all Latin colonies and to all allied communities that had not taken up arms. Another provision of the law empowered commanders to grant citizenship to non-Roman soldiers in the field. By these measures the Romans assured themselves of the support of the Etrurians and Umbrians and rewarded the loyal Latins and Greek federate allies. Shortly afterward, two tribunes of the year 89 carried the Plautian-Papirian Law, which offered Roman citizenship to all members of Italian communities who would claim it within sixty days. This offer applied to individuals, both citizens of allied communities under arms and those who had not accepted citizenship under the Julian Law. A third law, the work of Gnaeus Pompeius Strabo, consul in 89, gave Roman citizenship to all communities in Cisalpine Gaul south of the Po, and Latin rights to those north of that river.

THE COLLAPSE OF THE REVOLT. These concessions not only checked the spread of the rebellion, but, by giving to the allied peoples the rights for which they were fighting, they caused serious desertions from the ranks of those in the field, and the movement was doomed to rapid failure. The effect was seen in the change in the fortunes of war in 89. In spite of desperate resistance on the part of those who refused to accept anything short of independence, the Romans were everywhere successful. The consul Pompeius practically ended hostilities in the north and Sulla, in his capacity as *legatus*, broke the power of the allies in south Italy. Organized resistance among the rebels died out in the course of the year 88.

By taking up arms, the Italians had won for themselves and the Latins the rights reason had long conceded as their due but withheld from them through national and factional jealousy. This jealousy continued to show itself in the enrollment of the new citizens among the old. In order to limit their influence in the Assemblies, they were registered in only eight or ten of the thirty-five tribes. Naturally they were dissatisfied with this arrangement, and the question of their distribution became a prominent political issue. Virtually all Italians were now Romans, however, and in the course of the next few generations the various ethnic elements in Italy were welded into a single nation. It was impossible for the magistrates of Rome to oversee local administration throughout an area as wide as all Italy, and the Italian communities were organized as municipalities with limited rights of self-government, regularly administered by boards of four magistrates (*quattuorviri*) elected by the municipal citizens. With the adoption of Roman public and private law came the spread of the Latin language. Local dialects gradually disappeared, and a uniform culture developed on the basis of a common citizenship.

VIII. First Mithradatic War: 89–85 B.C.

MITHRADATES VI, EUPATOR, KING OF PONTUS.   In 89 the attention of the Senate was drawn to a threat to its suzerainty over the client kingdoms in Asia Minor. This threat resulted from the establishment of the kingdom of Pontus under an able and ambitious ruler, Mithradates Eupator, and the Senate was anxious to settle the Italic question as quickly as possible. Mithradates had succeeded in 121 to the throne of northern Cappadocia, a small kingdom on the south shore of the Black Sea, whose Asiatic population was Hellenized and whose rulers claimed descent from the ancient royal house of Persia and, with more justice, from Seleucus, the founder of the Greek kingdom of Syria. Mithradates shared the throne with his brother for over six years, under his mother's regency, but when he became eighteen years of age in 115 he seized the government for himself. Subsequently he extended his power over the eastern and northern shores of the Black Sea, as far west as the Danube. Thus he built up the kingdom of Pontus (the coastland of the Black Sea), a name later applied to his native state of North Cappadocia.

Mithradates also sought to extend his sway in Asia Minor, especially in Greater Cappadocia. This brought him into conflict with Rome, whose policy was to prevent the rise of any dangerous neighbor in the East and which refused to allow its settlement of Asia Minor to be disturbed. Mithradates attempted no less than five times between 112 and 92 to bring this district under his control, but each time he was forced by Roman interference to forego the fruits of his victories, since he was not yet prepared for war. In 91 he occupied the kingdom of Bithynia, which lay between Pontus and the Roman province of Asia, but again he yielded to Rome's demands and withdrew. When Roman commissioners encouraged the king of Bithynia to raid his territory and refused him satisfaction, he decided to challenge Roman arms, seeing that Rome was now involved in the war with her Italian allies. Hostilities began late in 89.

MITHRADATES IN ASIA AND GREECE. Mithradates was well prepared. He had a trained army and a fleet of three hundred ships. He experienced no difficulty in defeating the forces raised by the Roman authorities and speedily overran Bithynia and most of the Roman province of Asia. Meanwhile his fleet swept the Aegean Sea. The Roman provincials, who had been unmercifully exploited by taxgatherers and moneylenders, greeted Mithradates as a deliverer in many cases. At his order on a set date in 88 they massacred the Romans and Italians resident in Asia, allegedly 80,000, a step which was meant to bind them firmly to the king.

In the same year the populace of Athens, in the hope of overthrowing their oligarchic government set up with the support of Rome, seized control of the state and joined Mithradates. One of the king's generals, Archelaus, while on his way to Athens, exterminated the Italian colony at Delos, the center of Roman commercial and banking interests in the East. From this blow the island port never fully recovered. Archelaus soon won over most of southern Greece to his master's cause, while Mithradates sent a large army to enter Hellas by the northerly route through Thrace and Macedonia.

SULLA AND THE POPULARES IN ROME. This situation produced a crisis in Rome. Sulla, who was elected consul for 88, was allotted the command in the East upon the outbreak of hostilities but was unable to leave Italy, since he was besieging Nola in Campania. Marius, although in his sixty-eighth year, was as ambitious as ever and schemed to secure the command against Mithradates for himself. In this he was supported by many equestrians, who knew Sulla to be a supporter of the Optimates. The Marians supported the tribune Publius Sulpicius Rufus, who had brought forward a bill to enroll new citizens and freedmen equally in each of the thirty-five tribes. Sulpicius organized a bodyguard of equestrians and instituted a reign of terror. He pushed his law through by force in spite of consular opposition. When Sulla left the city to join his army, a law was passed in the Assembly transferring his command in the East to Marius. Sulla refused to admit the legality of the act and, relying on his troops, marched on Rome. Having taken the city by surprise, he had Sulpicius, Marius, and others of their party outlawed. Sulpicius was killed, but Marius was able to escape to Mauretania. The Sulpician Laws were abrogated, and Sulla introduced a number of reforms to strengthen the position of the Senate. The most significant of these were the ones that made senatorial consent necessary before any measures could be submitted to one of the Assemblies and a law which restricted the type of legislation that

could be brought by tribunes before the Tribal Assembly. Upon the conclusion of his consulate, Sulla embarked with his army for Greece early
in 87.

SULLA IN THE EAST.   After driving the forces of Archelaus and
the Athenians from the open country, Sulla began the siege of Athens
and its port Piraeus in the autumn of 87. Athens was completely invested, but in spite of hunger the resistance was prolonged until March
86, when Sulla's troops penetrated the walls and the city was sacked.
Many of the inhabitants were massacred, but the public buildings were
spared. Piraeus was taken by storm soon after at terrific cost to the victors,
but its citadel Munychia held out until evacuated by Archelaus.

From Athens Sulla hastened to meet the army of Mithradates, which
had penetrated as far as Boeotia. At Chaeronea the numerically inferior
but better disciplined Romans won a complete victory. At this juncture the
consul Lucius Valerius Flaccus arrived in Greece at the head of another
army, with orders to supersede Sulla. The latter was not disposed to give
up his command, and Flaccus, fearing to force the issue, set out for Asia
by way of Macedonia and Thrace. This left Sulla free to meet a new
Mithradatic army that had crossed the Aegean. At Orchomenus he attacked and annihilated it. Mithradates still controlled the Aegean, and
Sulla, unable to cross into Asia, was forced to winter in Greece.

Lucius Lucullus, Sulla's quaestor, appeared in the Aegean in 85 with a
fleet he had gathered among Rome's allies in the East. He defeated the
fleet of Mithradates and secured Sulla's passage to Asia. The king's position was now precarious. His exactions had alienated the Greek cities,
which now began to desert him. Flaccus, after recovering Macedonia and
Thrace, crossed the Bosphorus into Bithynia, where he was killed in a
mutiny of his soldiers and was succeeded by his legate Fimbria, who was
popular with the troops because he let them plunder. Fimbria proved
energetic. He defeated Mithradates and recovered the coast as far south
as Pergamon (86). Mithradates was ready for peace, and Sulla was anxious to have his hands free to return to Italy, where the Marians were
again in power. The king opened negotiations soon after the battle of
Orchomenus, but it was not until 85 that peace was concluded on the following terms: the king was to surrender Greater Cappadocia, Bithynia,
the Roman province of Asia and his other conquests in Asia Minor, to
pay an indemnity of 2,000 talents, and to give up part of his fleet. His
kingdom of Pontus remained intact.

Sulla spent the following winter in Asia, readjusting affairs in that
province. The rebellious communities were punished by the quartering of
troops upon them and by being forced to contribute to Sulla the huge
sum of 20,000 talents, or $24,000,000. To raise this amount they were
forced to borrow from Roman bankers and incur a crushing burden of
debt. In 84 Sulla crossed to Greece, there to complete his preparations to

return to Italy. The Greek states had suffered heavily in the recent campaigns. Sulla had carried off the temple treasures of Olympia, Delphi, and Epidaurus. Attica and Boeotia had been ravaged and depopulated, and the coasts had been raided by the Mithradatic fleet.

IX. Sulla's Dictatorship

POPULARES IN ROME: 87–84 B.C. While Sulla was conducting his successful campaign in Greece, the Marian party had again won the upper hand in Italy. Scarcely had Sulla left Italy with his army when the consul Lucius Cornelius Cinna re-enacted the Sulpician Laws. Although his colleague Gnaeus Octavius and the senatorial faction drove him from the city and had him deposed from office, he received the support of the army in Campania and of the Samnites, who were still under arms, although the Senate tried to win their support by a promise of citizenship. Meanwhile Marius had returned to Italy and raised an army in Etruria. Both he and Cinna advanced on Rome. They forced their opponents to capitulate, had Cinna reinstated as consul, and the banishment of Marius revoked. Sulla's laws were repealed and his property confiscated. Of particular importance was the final distribution of the Italian allies throughout all the tribes, which was begun at Cinna's behest during the censorship of 86–85. The upper income groups were redistributed first, while the poorer Italians were not included in the reform until a senatorial decree to that effect in 84. Since the latter had not been enrolled in a census, they could not vote in the Centuriate Assembly, which continued to reflect the interests of the more conservative and well-to-do.

Upon his return to Rome Marius massacred his leading opponents among the Optimates, including the consul Octavius, until he was stopped by Cinna. On January 1, 86 Marius entered upon his seventh consulship and died a few days later. His successor, Lucius Valerius Flaccus, was sent to supersede Sulla, a mission which cost him his life, as related above. In 85 the war with Mithradates was ended, and the Marians had to face the prospect of Sulla's return at the head of a victorious army. Cinna, now in his third consulship, and his colleague Gnaeus Carbo proceeded to raise an opposing army. They illegally prolonged their office for the next year (84) and made preparations to cross the Adriatic and meet Sulla in Macedonia. But the army gathered for this purpose at Brundisium mutinied and murdered Cinna. Carbo prevented the election of a successor and held office as sole consul. The Senate had previously begun negotiations with Sulla to prevent further civil war. He now demanded the restitution of property and honors both for himself and all those who had taken refuge with him. The Senate was inclined to yield but was prevented by Carbo.

RETURN OF SULLA. In the spring of 83 Sulla landed at Brundisium at the head of an army of 40,000 veterans who had sworn to remain under his orders. To prevent the Italians from joining his enemies, he declared his intention to respect all privileges that had been granted to them, but the bulk of the new citizens, particularly in Samnium and Etruria, supported the cause of the Populares. On the other hand, Sulla was joined at once by the young Gnaeus Pompeius, son of the consul of 89, who had raised an army on his own authority in Picenum, and by other men of influence. In the operations which followed the Marian leaders showed themselves lacking in cooperation and military skill. Sulla penetrated into Campania, where he defeated one consul, Norbanus, at Mount Tifata. The other consul, Scipio Asiaticus, began negotiations with him and was deserted by his army, which went over to Sulla.

In the following year Sulla advanced into Latium and won a hard-fought victory over the younger Marius, now consul, at Sacriportus. Rome fell into his hands, and Marius took refuge in Praeneste. Sulla then turned against the second consul, Carbo, in Etruria and, after several victories, forced him to flee to Africa. In a final effort the Marians, united with the Samnites, tried to relieve Praeneste. Failing to accomplish this, they made a dash upon Rome. But Sulla appeared in time to save the city and utterly defeat his enemies in a bloody contest at the Colline Gate. Praeneste fell soon after; Marius committed suicide, and, except at a few isolated points, all resistance in Italy was over.

SULLA'S VENGEANCE.   Sulla was absolute master of the situation and at once proceeded to punish his enemies and reward his friends. Cold-bloodedly, without any legal condemnation, his leading opponents were marked out for vengeance. Their names were posted in lists in the Forum to indicate that they might be slain with impunity and that their goods were confiscated. Rewards were offered to informers who effected the death of such victims, and many were included in the lists to gratify the personal enmities of Sulla's friends. The goods of the proscribed were auctioned off publicly under Sulla's direction, and their children and grandchildren were declared ineligible for public office. From these proscriptions the equestrians suffered particularly; 2,600 of them are said to have perished, together with ninety senators. The Italian municipalities also felt Sulla's vengeance. Widespread confiscations of land, especially in Samnium and Etruria, enabled him to provide for 150,000 of his veterans, whose settlement did much to hasten the Latinization of these districts. Ten thousand slaves of the proscribed were set free by Sulla and took the name of Cornelii from their patron. Apparently these arrangements were given the sanction of legality by action of the Senate and subsequent legislation. After this initial period of violence and bloodshed, Sulla seems to have been very careful to respect legal precedent and there were no further acts of outright lawlessness.

SULLA'S LEGISLATION.   Sulla's aims went further than the destruction of the Marian party. He sought to recreate a stable government in the state and, like Augustus fifty years later, paid great attention to constitutional forms. Both consuls being dead, he caused the appointment of an *interrex* who, by virtue of a special law, could appoint a dictator for an unlimited term to enact legislation and reorganize the commonwealth (*dictator legibus scribundis et rei publicae constituendae*). Sulla's appointment to that office occurred late in 82. The scope of his powers and their unlimited duration gave him unprecedented autocratic authority.

The general aim of Sulla's legislation was to restore the Senate to the position it had held prior to 133 and to guarantee the perpetuation of this condition. He institutionalized those recent tendencies in government that seemed compatible with senatorial domination and attempted to check those that did not. His reforms fall into two classes: some, not long-lived, were directed at securing the rule of the Optimates; the rest, of a nonpartisan character and so of greater permanency, sought to increase administrative efficiency. Those of the first group were a renewal and extension of his reforms of 88. The tribunes lost the right to initiate legislation in the Tribal Assembly, and their intercession was restricted to interference with the exercise of the magistrate's *imperium*. To deter able and ambitious men from seeking the tribunate, it was made a bar to further office. Senators were once more made eligible for all juries, while equestrians were disqualified. The Domitian Law of 104 was abrogated, and the practice of coopting the members of the priestly colleges was revived. Most important of Sulla's administrative reforms was that which concerned the magistracy. The order of offices in the *cursus honorum* established by the *lex Villia Annalis* of 180 was redrafted. An age limit was set for eligibility to each office, and an interval of ten years was required between successive tenures of the same post.[6] The number of quaestors was increased to twenty, that of the praetors raised from six to eight. In connection therewith the method of appointing provincial governors was regulated. Sulla realized the danger to senatorial power inherent in prolonged provincial commands and therefore sought to circumscribe the powers of promagistrates and to limit their tenure of office. By the organization of the province of Cisalpine Gaul, the number of provinces was raised to ten. Each year the eight praetors and probably the two consuls, upon the completion of their year of office in Rome, were normally to be appointed in the provinces as propraetors and proconsuls for one year only. This system was artificial and inflexible and did not take into account the possible desirability, in times of crisis, of proroguing provincial commands beyond the annual term.

As before, the Senate designated the consular provinces prior to the

---

[6] The minimum age for the quaestorship was fixed at thirty years, for the praetorship at thirty-nine, and for the consulship at forty-two. Under Sulla at the latest, the minimum age requirement for tenure by patricians of the senior magistrates was two years below that of plebeian senators.

election of the consuls who would be their proconsular governors. The consuls were not deprived of the right of military command, and as before, regularly assumed control of military operations in Italy. The consular *imperium* remained senior to that of the provincial governors and might be exercised beyond the frontiers of Italy. In practice, however, the consuls were not regularly employed for overseas campaigns, since the Senate now arrogated to itself what had previously been a prerogative of the Assembly, namely, the right of selecting any person whatever to exercise military *imperium* in any sphere. A new field for the activity of the praetors arose from the establishment of special jury courts for the trial of cases of bribery, treason, fraud, peculation, assassination, and assault with violence. These were modeled on the court for damage suits brought against provincial officers and superseded the old procedure with its appeal from the verdict of the magistrate to the Comitia. Some of these courts antedated Sulla's legislation, and the dictator simply extended to all fields the preexisting court system. For the future the administration of criminal justice in Rome was based on his reforms. To provide a sufficient number of jurors for these tribunals, Sulla, possibly by virtue of the censorial powers he enjoyed as dictator, increased the membership of the Senate from three hundred to five or six hundred by enrolling equestrians who had supported him. He thus put into effect a similar measure attributed to Livius Drusus and extended his clientele to embrace many equestrians throughout Italy. The increased number was maintained by the annual admission of the twenty ex-quaestors, whereby censors were rendered unnecessary for enrolling the senators. No censorship was held during the decade following Sulla's dictatorship, since the Senate did not wish to increase the number of voters in the first classes of the Centuriate Assembly and thereby decrease their own ability to manipulate that organization through patronage. The administration, especially in its imperial aspects, was more than ever concentrated in the Senate's hands.

While Sulla was settling affairs in Rome and Italy, the Marians in Sicily and Africa were crushed by his lieutenant Gnaeus Pompeius, better known as Pompey, their leader Carbo being taken and executed. In 82 Sulla had the Senate confer upon Pompey the command in this campaign with the *imperium* of a propraetor, although he had not yet held office. The campaign ended, Pompey demanded a triumph, an honor previously granted only to regular magistrates. Sulla at first opposed his wishes, but, as Pompey was insistent and defiant, he yielded to avoid a mutiny that might have led to civil war, and he even accorded him the honor of the name Magnus or "the Great." Pompey returned to Italy and celebrated his triumph the 12th of March, 79.

SULLA'S RETIREMENT AND DEATH: 78 B.C.   Sulla undoubtedly did not aim at a dictatorship for life or at the introduction at Rome of a kind of Hellenistic kingship. Having "restored" republican government under senatorial control in the year 81, he apparently abdicated his power in stages, resigning his dictatorship at the end of that year, being consul with a colleague in 80, and becoming a private citizen without office in 79. He retired to enjoy a life of pleasure on his Campanian estate, relying for his personal security and that of his measures upon his clientele, made up of his veterans and the Cornelian freedmen. In the following year he died at the age of sixty.

SIGNIFICANCE OF SULLA.   Sulla's genius was both military and political. He added new dimensions to the role played by the military in affairs of state, and he was the first to realize the use of client professional armies as a means of guaranteeing political predominance, through civil war if need be. It was after Sulla that the great *ad hoc* provincial commands, created in emergencies to handle military situations beyond the ability of the normal standing armies to control, became the prize of politicians whose striving after *dignitas* exceeded Sulla's own. Sulla's career thus foreshadows those of Pompey, Caesar, and Augustus. Like other politicians of his age, Sulla was not doctrinaire, nor was he committed wholly as a matter of principle to any one faction or program. Rather, like Marius and other statesmen, his political outlook and affiliation were determined largely by those factors that might gratify his ambition. Early in his career he was by no means a convinced Optimate, and it was probably as a result of his marriage connection with that faction and the opposition of the Populares to his Mithradatic command that brought him firmly into the senatorial camp. The longing for *dignitas* then led him into civil war. Eventually he came to identify political stability with continued oligarchic control of government. Unfortunately, although he cannot be dismissed as a reactionary, his reforms displayed little vision or understanding of social and economic problems eroding the basis of senatorial power and, in particular, they did nothing to relieve the menace of professional armies led by generals impatient of civil control.

CHAPTER 13

RISE OF POMPEY
THE GREAT: 78–60 B.C.

EXTRAORDINARY COMMANDS. After the death of Sulla in 78, Roman history centered around the lives of a small group of eminent men whose ambitions and rivalries were the determining factors in politics. This was because neither the Senate nor the Assembly had the power to control the men whom the needs of the Empire thrust into military auhority. The generation of Marius and Sulla had seen the rise of the client army, which was revealed as the true power in the state, and the disturbances of the Italic and Civil Wars supplied many needy recruits who sought service with a popular and successful general for the rewards it lay in his power to bestow. As military achievements were the sole sure foundation for political success, able men made it their ambition to be entrusted with an important military command. The dangers of civil and foreign wars compelled the Senate at first to confer military power upon the few available men of recognized ability, even when it distrusted their ulterior motives, and later such appointments were made by the Assembly through a coalition of the general and the tribunate. In this way arose the so-called extraordinary commands, those that involved a military *imperium* in some way exceeding that of regular constitutional officers and requiring creation or definition by a special enactment of the Senate or Comitia. The man who first combined extraordinary commands with patronage over armies and provinces in order to gain power was Pompey the Great.

Knowledge of the events of the years 78 to 60 depends mainly upon the same authorities as for the period immediately preceding. Of particular value are Plutarch's *Lives* of Pompey, Crassus, and Sertorius, and the contemporary speeches of Cicero. Sallust's *Histories*, which covered in detail the years 78 to 67, are represented only by fragments, but his monograph on the *War with Catiline* is preserved intact. Another important source, beginning with 68, is the fully extant portion of the *Roman History* of Cassius Dio who, for his account of the last century B.C., relied largely upon Livy.

I. Pompey's Command Against Sertorius in Spain: 77–71 B.C.

THE REVOLT OF LEPIDUS. It was not to be expected that Sulla's measures would long remain unchallenged. Those dispossessed of their property, those disqualified for office, and the equestrians who sought to regain control of the courts were all anxious to undo part of his work.

They found a leader in Marcus Lepidus, who, as consul in 78, the very year of Sulla's death, sought to renew the distribution of cheap grain to the masses in Rome, which Sulla had suppressed, to restore the Marian exiles, and to reinstate the dispossessed. Failing to carry his proposals, he took advantage of the excuse afforded by disorders in Etruria between the former landholders and the Sullan colonists to raise an army in North Italy, where he had been assigned the province of Cisalpine Gaul for the coming year. He rallied to his support the discontented elements from Etruria and marched on Rome, demanding reelection to the consulship for 77. Near Rome he was defeated by his colleague Quintus Lutatius Catulus but managed to escape and to cross over to Sardinia with many soldiers. There he died shortly after, but the bulk of his forces, under Marcus Perperna, withdrew to Spain to join Sertorius, who was also leading a rebellion against the senatorial faction. In the meantime the supporters of Lepidus in North Italy were crushed by Pompey, to whom the Senate had given a subordinate command in view of his military experience, a mistake which they were soon to regret very bitterly.

SERTORIUS IN SPAIN.   Quintus Sertorius was by far the ablest of the Populares who had been associated with Cinna and Marius. As early as 88 his military talents had earned him the jealousy of Sulla, who prevented his election to the tribunate at that time. During the following years he showed his statesmanlike qualities by opposing excesses of his political partners. In 83, he was appointed propraetor for Hither Spain, but two years later, after the defeat of the Populares in Italy, he was driven out of his province by Sulla's nominee and forced to flee to Africa. Thence, after various adventures, he returned to Spain in 80 to lead a revolt of the Lusitanians. His ability as a guerrilla leader, the confidence he aroused among the Spaniards, and his initial successes produced considerable alarm in Rome. To crush the revolt Sulla dispatched Quintus Caecilius Metellus, one of the consuls of 80, as governor of Farther Spain, but he failed to make any headway. In 79, the propraetor in command of Hither Spain was defeated and killed by the forces of Sertorius, and a like fate befell the proconsul of Gallia Narbonensis, who came to the aid of Metellus (78). By the close of 77 Sertorius had won control of almost all of Hither Spain and much of the farther province. He regarded himself as the legitimate governor of Hither Spain and professed to have taken up arms not against Rome but against the Sullan faction then dominant in the Senate. He employed Populares as his civil and military subordinates and organized a Senate from among them.

POMPEY'S EXTRAORDINARY COMMAND: 77 B.C.   The Senate being unwilling to come to terms with Sertorius, it was imperative to send a new commander and a new army to Spain. As neither consul was willing to face Sertorius, Pompey, who had refused to disband his troops at the orders of Catulus, sought the command. Although he was ineligible because of his youth and lack of a previous official career, such was the dearth of able men at the disposal of the Optimates that, in spite of considerable opposition, they passed a decree conferring upon him proconsular *imperium* and entrusting him with the war in Hither Spain. Even after the arrival of Pompey with an army of 40,000 men, Sertorius was more than able to hold his own throughout the campaign of 76. At the close of the year, through the agency of the pirates, he allied with Mithradates, King of Pontus, who was again on the point of war with Rome. In 75 Pompey and Metellus were more successful since their superior numbers and resources were beginning to tell. Sertorius was still able to keep the field, however, and Pompey felt obliged to call upon the Senate for reinforcements.

Arrival of reinforcements enabled Pompey to gain the upper hand in 74 and 73 and made victory a certainty. In order to prevent desertions, Sertorius resorted to severe punishments, which alienated the Spaniards, who were already estranged by acts of his subordinates. He was further hampered by dissensions in the ranks of his Roman supporters. The center of disaffection was Perperna, who treacherously assassinated Sertorius in 72 and assumed command of his forces. Soon afterwards Perperna himself was defeated by Pompey, taken captive, and executed. The revolt was broken and pacification of Spain speedily followed. Pompey was able to return to Italy in 71.

II. Command of Lucullus Against Mithradates: 74–66 B.C.

ASIA MINOR AFTER SULLA'S SETTLEMENT. After concluding peace with Sulla in 85, Mithradates consolidated his kingdom and reorganized his forces in expectation of a renewal of the struggle with Rome. He recognized that Sulla had been ready to make peace only because of the situation in Italy, and his inability to secure written confirmation of the terms of the treaty warned him that the Romans still contemplated his complete overthrow. He was attacked in the years 83 and 82 by Lucius Murena, proconsul of Asia, but was able to defend himself, and Sulla once more brought about a cessation of these hostilities, generally called the Second Mithradatic War. During the years 78–75, the Romans proceeded systematically with the conquest of the mountainous districts in southern Asia Minor, including Lycia and Pamphylia. Tigranes of Armenia, son-in-law of Mithradates, had meantime enlarged his dominions by the annexation of Greater Cappadocia and Syria (83), where he terminated the rule of the house of Seleucus.

THIRD MITHRADATIC WAR. In 75 Nicomedes III, King of Bithynia, died and bequeathed his kingdom to the Roman people. The Senate accepted the inheritance and made Bithynia a province, but Mithradates championed the claims of a son of Nicomedes and determined to dispute the possession of Bithynia. He raised an efficient army and navy, was in league with the pirates, and made an alliance with Sertorius, who supplied him with officers and recognized his claims to Bithynia and parts of Asia Minor. Rome was threatened with another serious war. One of the senatorial faction, the consul Lucius Lucullus, had himself assigned by senatorial decree to the provinces of Cilicia and Asia with command of the main operations against Mithradates, while his colleague Cotta received Bithynia and a fleet to guard the Hellespont. Simultaneously a praetor, Marcus Antonius, was given an extraordinary command against the pirates with an unlimited *imperium* over the Mediterranean Sea and its coast. He proved utterly incompetent, however, was defeated in an attack upon Crete, and died there.

Early in 74, Mithradates invaded Bithynia. There he was confronted by Cotta, whom he defeated and blockaded in Chalcedon. Thereupon he invaded Asia and laid siege to Cyzicus. Lucullus cut his communications, and in the ensuing winter he was forced to raise the siege and retire with heavy losses into Bithynia. The following year a fleet Lucullus had raised defeated that of Mithradates in the Aegean Sea. This enabled the Romans to recover Bithynia and invade Pontus. In 72 Lucullus routed Mithradates and forced him to take refuge in Armenia. In the course of this and the two following years, Lucullus completed the subjugation of Pontus by systematic reduction of its fortified cities. Cotta undertook the siege of Heraclea in Bithynia and on its fall in 71 returned to Rome. Lucullus spent the winter of 71–70 in Asia reorganizing the financial situation. The cities there were laboring under a frightful burden of indebtedness to Roman bankers and taxgatherers, as a result of the exactions of Sulla. Lucullus interceded on behalf of the provincials and, by achieving a reduction of the accumulated interest on their debts, enabled them to pay off their obligations in annual instalments. This care for the provincials won him the enmity of Roman financial interests, which sought to deprive him of his command.

As the war could not be ended so long as Mithradates was at large, Lucullus demanded his surrender from Tigranes. When the latter refused, Lucullus invaded Armenia, defeated the king, and took his capital, Tigranocerta, in 69. The following year Lucullus tried to subjugate Armenia completely but was prevented by the mutinous conduct of his troops. He was unpopular with his men because he maintained discipline and protected the subject peoples from the excesses of the soldiers. Some of his legions had come to the East with Fimbria in 86 and clamored for the discharges to which they were entitled. In 68 Mithradates reappeared in Pontus, and the next spring Lucullus had to return from Armenia to face him, whereupon Tigranes began to recover lost ground. Because of mutiny in his army Lucullus was forced to remain inactive. He had already been superseded in the command of Asia, Cilicia, and Bithynia, which had come under his control with the return of Cotta, and his enemies in Rome deprived him of all authority in 66.

III. Revolt of the Gladiators: 73–71 B.C.

SPARTACUS. While Pompey was fighting Sertorius in Spain and Lucullus was pursuing Mithradates in Bithynia, a serious slave war arose in Italy. It began in 73 with the revolt of gladiators from a training school in Capua under the leadership of the Thracian Spartacus and the Gauls, Crixus and Oenomaus. Taking refuge on the slopes of Vesuvius, they rapidly recruited large numbers of runaway slaves. They defeated the armies of two Roman praetors and overran Campania, Lucania, and all southern Italy. By the end of the year 73 their number had grown to 70,000.

The next year they divided their forces; the Gauls and Germans followed Crixus, the Thracians Spartacus. The two consuls took the field against them, and Crixus and his horde were defeated in Apulia. Spartacus then marched north, intending to make his way through the Alps to Thrace. The consuls pursued him, but he defeated them, one after the other. He likewise cleared the road to the north by defeating the proconsul of Cisalpine Gaul, but his followers refused to leave Italy and turned southward, plundering as they went. Not venturing to attack Rome, Spartacus retired to south Italy.

COMMAND OF CRASSUS: 72–71 B.C. In view of the lack of success of the consuls of 72, the Senate appointed as extraordinary commander the praetor Marcus Licinius Crassus, one of Sulla's veteran officers, who volunteered his services. After restoring discipline among his troops, Crassus succeeded in penning up Spartacus in the peninsula of Bruttium. Spartacus hired some Cilician pirates to transport him to Sicily, but after receiving their price they sailed off, abandoning him to his fate. He then forced his way through Crassus' lines, but his followers split into two detachments, each of which was overtaken and defeated. Spartacus fell in battle, and six thousand of his following were crucified. Crassus had striven to bring the revolt to a close before Pompey might arrive in Italy on his way from Spain and only too gladly obey a summons to crush the rebels. This Crassus could fairly claim to have accomplished, even though a body of five thousand slaves escaped to North Italy, where they were met by Pompey and annihilated.

The Sparticist revolt highlights the ghastly conditions obtaining among slaves on the great plantations. Spartacus was not, however, the social revolutionary sometimes described. His support was scattered among rural slaves, and he made no attempt at enlisting the urban servile classes among his followers. His revolt, while possibly causing some improvement in working conditions, is important chiefly for its political repercussions, in particular for the confrontation between Pompey and Crassus that it brought about.

IV. Consulship of Pompey and Crassus: 70 B.C.

END OF THE SULLAN CONSTITUTION. Both Pompey and Crassus, flushed by their respective victories in Spain and in Italy, now demanded the right to stand for the consulship for 70. Crassus was eligible to seek this office, for he had held his praetorship probably in 73, and two years would have elapsed before he entered upon the consulship. Pompey's candidature was clearly unconstitutional, however, for he was still below the required age and had not qualified by holding the quaestorship and praetorship. Under these conditions, the Senate was bound to resist his request to become a candidate. It also opposed the candidacy of Crassus, distrusting him almost as much as Pompey. In the end the Senate had to yield. Since both commanders were also seeking permission to celebrate triumphs and used this pretext to keep their troops under arms, they cowed the opposition. The first breach in the Sullan constitution was made when Pompey was granted a dispensation from the provisions of the *lex Villia annalis*.

Pompey and Crassus bid for support of the Populares by promising to restore to the tribunate all its former privileges and for that of the equestrians by proposing to reinstate them as judges in the courts. Overawed by the forces arrayed against it, the Senate granted the generals their triumphs and permitted the passage of a law exempting Pompey from the legal requirements of his candidacy. Burying their personal rivalry, Pompey and Crassus supported each other to the full, with the result that both were elected to the consulship for the coming year. In office, they completed the overthrow of the Sullan constitution. By the Aurelian Law of 75, the tribunes had been permitted once more to seek other offices; now they regained in full their previous rights in legislation and the exercise of the veto power. Another Aurelian Law in 70 revised the composition of the juries in the public courts. For the future each jury was to be drawn in equal numbers from the three orders of the senators, the equestrians, and the tribunes of the treasury (*tribuni aerarii*). There is much uncertainty as to the exact status of these tribunes, but it seems clear that they were a class of persons of considerable property, whose assessment was equal to that of the equestrians. At any rate both classes could be said to represent the business interests in Roman society. At Pompey's insistence censors were elected for the first time since Sulla's dictatorship. They revised the senatorial lists and enrolled citizens in the various military classes. Pompey sought thereby to build up a strong faction, not merely among the new senators who would be indebted to him for their status, but also among those well-to-do citizens who had previously been excluded from the

Centuriate Assembly during the period of the suspension of the censorship. These latter Pompey could use to break senatorial monopoly over the Assembly that had been traditional since the creation of the "rotten boroughs" in 241.

TRIAL OF VERRES. In the year 70, prior to the passing of the Aurelian Law reforming the juries, there occurred the trial of Gaius Verres, ex-propraetor of Sicily, a case notable because the prosecution was conducted by the young Marcus Tullius Cicero, whose accusation, contained in his published *Orations against Gaius Verres*, is illuminating commentary upon an unusual instance of provincial misgovernment under the Sullan regime. The senatorial juries had protected the interests of the provinces no better after 82 than had the equestrian juries established by Gaius Gracchus. They had shown themselves venal, and a provincial governor who made judicious disbursements could be confident that he would be acquitted of any charges of extortion brought against him. Relying on this, Verres, propraetor of Sicily in 73–71, had carried off from that province money and valuables estimated at 40,000,000 sesterces ($2,000,000). He had openly boasted that he intended the profits of one year for himself, those of the second for his friends and patrons, and those of the third for his jurors. At the beginning of 70 the Sicilian cities sued Verres for restitution of damages and chose Cicero as their advocate. The trial was to have important political repercussions. Verres had abused Pompey's Sicilian clients and was closely connected with the Optimates, with whom Pompey was then embroiled. The trial thus became a test of strength between the two factions.

The advocate Cicero, a native of Arpinum, the birthplace of Marius, was then in his thirty-sixth year, a *novus homo* who had chosen the bar rather than a military career to break into the senatorial charmed circle. He, too, had Sicilian clients, since his upright conduct as quaestor in western Sicily in 75 had earned their confidence and since his successful conduct of the defence in several previous trials had marked him as a pleader of exceptional ability. Verres had entrusted his case to Quintus Hortensius Hortalus, an Optimate regarded at the time as the foremost Roman orator, and every conceivable device was used to prevent the case from coming to trial. Another prosecutor appeared, claiming a better right than Cicero to sue Verres. This necessitated a trial to decide which could better claim to represent the Sicilians. Cicero was able to expose the falsity of the claims of his rival, who was acting in collusion with Verres. He then proceeded to Sicily, where he gathered his evidence in fifty of the 110 days allowed him. Before the hearing, elections for the next year were held and Hortensius elected consul, but Cicero was returned as aedile in spite of all efforts of his opponents to weaken his prestige by electoral defeat.

The trial was set for the fifth of August, and, as there were fifty holidays for various festivals between that date and the end of the year, the defense hoped to drag out the trial until after January first, when a praetor friendly to Verres might preside over the court. Cicero thwarted them by abstaining from any long formal speech of accusation, contenting himself with a brief statement of the obstacles the defense had placed in his way, a threat to punish in his capacity of aedile any attempts at corruption, and a short statement of the charge against Verres. He then called his witnesses. Hortensius found himself without any arguments to combat and could not refute the evidence. Before the hearing of witnesses was concluded, Verres went into exile. He was condemned in his absence, and Cicero became the leading advocate of the day. It must be admitted that condemnation of Verres by a jury of senators was partly due to the danger of the loss of their privileges which threatened them under the reform being discussed.

PROVINCIAL MISGOVERNMENT. The evidence brought out against Verres was afterwards used by Cicero in composing his *Second Pleading against Verres* (*actio secunda in Verrem*), which was never delivered, of course, but was a political pamphlet in the form of a fictitious oration. It explains the devices the governor used in amassing a fortune at the expense of his province. By initiating false accusations, by rendering, or intimidating other judges to render, unjust decisions, Verres confiscated property whose sale value went into his own pockets. He sold justice to the highest bidder. He saved himself expense by defrauding the collectors of port dues of the tax on the valuables he shipped out of Sicily, and he added to his profits by the sale of municipal offices and priesthoods. He entered into partnership with the *decumani*, collectors of the 10 percent produce tax, and ordered the cultivators to pay whatever the collectors demanded and then, if dissatisfied, seek redress in his court, a redress which, needless to say, was never gained. He loaned public funds at usurious rates of interest and either did not pay in full or paid nothing for wheat purchased from Sicilian communities for the Roman government, while charging the state the market price. At the same time he insisted upon the cities commuting into money payments, at rates far above current prices, the grain allotment due for the upkeep of the governor's establishment. At times the demands made upon cultivators exceeded the total of their annual crop, and in despair they fled from their holdings. To the money gained by such methods Verres added a costly treasure of works of art, which he collected from individuals and cities by theft, seizure, and intimidation. Even the sacred ornaments of temples were not spared. All who resisted or denounced him, even Roman citizens, were subjected to imprisonment, torture, or execution. These iniquities were carried out in defiance of the provincial charter; but there was no power in his province to restrain him, and the Senate, which should have done so, remained indifferent to the complaints that were carried to Rome. The sad truth was that, after all, Verres was only more shameless and unscrupulous than many a provincial governor, and consequently the sympathies of the Senate were with him rather than with his victims, the provincials.

V. Commands of Pompey Against the Pirates and in the East: 67–62 B.C.

THE PIRATE SCOURGE.   Both Pompey and Crassus had declined proconsular appointments to follow their consulship because there were no provinces available promising an opportunity to augment their influence or military reputation. They remained in Rome watching for some more favorable chance to employ their talents. Pompey found such an opportunity in the ravages of the Cilician pirates. After the failure of Marcus Antonius (74–72), Caecilius Metellus had been sent to Crete in 69. In the next two years he reduced the island to subjection and made it a province. His operations there did little to check the pirate plague. So bold had these robbers become that they did not hesitate to raid the coasts of Italy and even to plunder Ostia. When their depredations finally interrupted the importation of grain for the city, a famine threatened, and decisive measures had to be taken.

THE GABINIAN LAW: 67 B.C.   The only way to deal with the problem was to appoint a commander with power to operate anywhere against the pirates, and the obvious man for the position was Pompey. The Senate mistrusted him, however, and also feared the consequences of creating such an extensive extraordinary command. Pompey had stood on the side of the Populares since 71, and now, like Marius, he found the tribunate an aid in attaining his goal. In 67 the tribune Aulus Gabinius proposed a law appointing a single commander of consular rank with command over the whole sea within the pillars of Hercules and all Roman territory to a distance of fifty miles inland. His appointment was to be for three years, and he was to have the power to nominate senatorial *legati*, to raise money in addition to what he received from the quaestors, and to recruit soldiers and sailors for his fleet. This command was modeled upon that of Antonius the praetor in 74, but it conferred even higher authority and greater resources. The Senate bitterly resisted passage of the bill; but it passed with the support of Cicero and a rising young noble seeking political connections, Gaius Julius Caesar, and the Senate was forced to relinquish its prerogative of creating extraordinary commands. Although no person had been nominated in the law of Gabinius, the opinion of the voters had been so clearly expressed in a *contio* that the Senate had to appoint Pompey. He received twenty-four *legati* and a fleet of five hundred vessels.

FATE OF THE PIRATES.   Pompey set to work energetically and systematically. In forty days he swept the pirates from the western Mediterranean. In forty-nine more he cornered them in Cilicia—where he forced the surrender of their strongholds. His victory was hastened by the mildness shown to those who submitted. They were granted their lives and freedom and in many cases were used as colonists to revive depopulated Mediterranean towns. Within three months he had brought the pirate war to a triumphant conclusion, but his *imperium* had three years still to run and he was anxious to gather fresh laurels.

THE MANILIAN LAW: 66 B.C.   Opportunity was not wanting. The conclusion of the pirate war coincided with the temporary check to Roman arms in Pontus, due to the disaffection of Lucullus' troops and the machinations of his enemies in Rome. Pompey now sought to have Lucullus' command added to his own, and in this he had the support of the equestrian order. Early in 66 one of the tribunes, Gaius Manilius, proposed a law transferring to Pompey the provinces of Bithynia and Cilicia and conduct of the war against Mithradates and Tigranes. Cicero, then a praetor, supported the measure in his speech, *For the Manilian Law*. His support was probably due to the fact that he wished to gain political support from the equestrians by taking a stand against Lucullus. The Senate strongly opposed any extension of Pompey's military authority, but the bill was passed, and he took over the command of Lucullus. He was given unlimited power to make peace or war and enjoyed a concentration of military power hitherto unexampled in Roman history. His eastern command made a striking impression on his contemporaries and forms a prominent landmark on the road from the Republic to the Principate.

POMPEY IN THE EAST.   After making an alliance with the king of Parthia, who diverted the attention of Tigranes by an invasion of Armenia, Pompey advanced into Pontus to attack Mithradates. The latter was soon forced to withdraw into Lesser Armenia, where Pompey overtook him and dispersed his army. Failing to find a refuge with Tigranes, who distrusted him, Mithradates made his way to the Greek cities of the Crimea, which were under his overlordship. Tigranes came to terms with Pompey and was permitted to retain his kingdom as a Roman ally who might check undue ambitions on the part of Parthia. The following year (65) Pompey conquered the inhabitants of the hill country south of the Caucasus between the Black and the Caspian Seas. They became dependent allies of Rome. The district of Pontus on the north coast of Asia Minor was broken up. The western part was joined to the province of Bithynia, which was known henceforth as Bithynia and Pontus; the rest was assigned to allied states.

In 64 Pompey turned his attention to Syria, where chaos had reigned since Lucullus took it from Tigranes and left it a prey to rival local dynasts. Pompey decided to treat it as conquered territory and annexed it as a province. He then intervened in a struggle between rival claimants to the throne of the kingdom of Judaea. After a brief conflict, in which the temple of Jerusalem was stormed by Roman troops, he installed his nominee as High Priest at the head of the government but without the title of king. A large part of Judaea was annexed to Syria, that portion left under the rule of the High Priest became a Roman dependency closely supervised by the governor of the Syrian province.

The career of Mithradates came to an end while Pompey was in Judaea. With tireless energy he had recruited new forces among his subjects on the north shore of the Black Sea and proposed to join the Celtic peoples of the Danube valley in an invasion of Italy, but his soldiers and subjects alike were hostile to this undertaking. A revolt against him was vigorously suppressed, but a mutiny of the soldiers headed by his son, Pharnaces, trapped him in his citadel at Pantacapaeum, and he had himself put to death (63). Thus the Mithradatic War finally came to an end. As a leader of the Greek East against Rome, Mithradates had displayed undeniable talent and perseverance. In the long run, however, he was unable to convert his war into a crusade that might have unified the various peoples he sought to lead, peoples bound to him only by their common dislike of Roman rule. The Mithradatic wars were, nevertheless, very important in the history of the Roman Republic, since they forced the state to create extraordinary commands for their resolution and since they compelled the Romans to control more closely an East that had given them so much trouble.

POMPEY'S EASTERN SETTLEMENT. Pompey displayed a high degree of political and even statesmanlike acumen in his eastern territorial arrangements during and after the Mithradatic War. In essence he created a continuous belt of Roman provinces along the coasts of the Black and Mediterranean Seas from northern Asia Minor to Syria. Behind these provinces to the east he extended Rome's sphere of interest through a band of client states, which, although not administered by Rome, followed her lead in foreign affairs. These client states formed a buffer against the powerful Parthian Empire. In his provincial arrangements Pompey fostered the development of urbanism wherever possible. He did so partly because Hellenism, the most important unifying cultural force in the Near East, had been based traditionally on city life. He was no less interested in using cities as a rational basis of local government and taxation, and, through his political reorganization, he would become the patron of many communities that would swell his foreign clientele. As a result of his eminently rational system of organization, tribute to Rome increased by 70 percent, and, in the eventual civil war with Caesar, Pompey would be able to find support in the East where he was regarded by many as a benefactor.

After regulating the political situation in Asia Minor, Syria, and the adjacent countries, Pompey started on a triumphal return to Italy with his victorious army and rich spoils of war.

VI. Conspiracy of Catiline: 63 B.C.

ROME IN THE ABSENCE OF POMPEY. While Pompey was adding to his military reputation in the East, his activities were watched with jealous and anxious eyes not only by Optimates but also by his rivals for leadership among the Populares. The attitude of the Optimates is clearly revealed in the prosecution of two tribunes who had been among his active supporters in 67 and 66. Gaius Cornelius, tribune in 67, responsible for a law obliging the praetors to render decisions according to the terms of their own edicts and largely responsible for the Calpurnian law on bribery —which prescribed the double penalty of a fine and future exclusion from public life for persons guilty of bribery at elections—was brought to trial on a general charge of treasonable conduct. His colleague, Gabinius, who, besides proposing the law creating Pompey's command against the pirates, was author of two other useful measures (one forbidding the lending of money to provincials in Rome, the other forcing the Senate to make the reception of embassies the first item of business in February instead of delaying until senators had been bribed), escaped a similar fate only by joining Pompey. Manilius, whose law had transferred the command of Lucullus to Pompey in 66, was the object of two indictments.

The departure of Pompey left Crassus as the outstanding champion of the Populares in Rome. Crassus found that his wealth was no adequate counterpoise to Pompey's military achievements and therefore sought by devious means to build up a political clientele and to secure for himself the military backing which he so obviously lacked. In 65 he induced a tribune to propose a measure authorizing the annexation of Egypt on the pretext that the previous king had willed it to the Romans. In spite of the riches of that country and the prospect of an easy conquest, the proposal was rejected by the bulk of the Senate, which had adopted a hands-off policy towards Egypt, and by Cicero, who championed Pompey's interests.

A potential although not yet actual rival to both Pompey and Crassus was Gaius Julius Caesar, who was rapidly becoming one of the leading figures in Roman public life. Caesar was born in 100, of the patrician *gens* of the Julii, but, since his aunt was Marius' wife and he himself had married Cinna's daughter, his lot was cast with the Populares. As a young man he had distinguished himself by refusing to divorce his wife at Sulla's behest, and Sulla had been with difficulty induced to spare his life, saying that he saw in him many a Marius. For the time being Caesar judged it prudent to withdraw from Rome to Rhodes. While in the East he was captured by pirates and, after being ransomed, fulfilled his threat to avenge himself by executing his captors. After the death of Sulla, Caesar returned to Rome and devoted his more than average oratorical abilities to the Marian cause. In 69 or 68 he was quaestor in Farther Spain, and, after his return to Rome, he became closely associated with Crassus in the attempt to develop a counterpoise to Pompey's influence. While aedile in 65 he won a reputation by the extraordinary lavishness with which he celebrated the public festivals, by the restoration of the public monuments of the campaign of Marius, and by supporting the prosecution of agents in the Sullian proscriptions. The splendor of his shows had obliged Caesar to contract heavy debts, and Crassus was in all probability his chief creditor. Both were therefore interested in procuring for Caesar a position in which he could find money to pay his debts.

Unrest in Rome was heightened by the presence there of a number of ruined men, both Marians dispossessed by Sulla and Optimates who had squandered their resources or been excluded from the Senate by the censors of 70.

Foremost among them was Catiline (Lucius Sergius Catilina), a patrician with little family influence but possessed, like many of his contemporaries, of great daring and an even greater ambition and sense of his own *dignitas*. He was one of a group of politicians, like Crassus and Pompey, who had launched their careers during the Sullan revolution. He had risen to the praetorship and served as propraetor in Africa without, however, having gained the backing of the Optimates or of the factions following Crassus and Pompey. He had presented himself as a candidate for the consulship for 65 but had been rejected by the consul in charge of the elections, probably because he was under indictment for misgovernment in his province. His *dignitas* wounded, he sought revenge, along with two other candidates who, indeed, had been elected but then convicted of bribery, disqualified, and dropped from the Senate. They enlisted others in a conspiracy and laid plans to murder the consuls, who were finally chosen as they entered upon office on January 1, 65, and seize control of the government. Their actions aroused suspicions that mischief was afoot, and the incoming consuls were provided with a bodyguard, whose presence caused the plot to fall through. No action was taken against the plotters, but their position was uncomfortable, and Crassus took advantage of this to offer some of them protection in order to absorb them into his clientele and thus to have their services at his disposal in the future. One of these was Catiline.

CICERO CONSUL.   In the year 64 three candidates presented themselves for the consulship, Catiline, Gaius Antonius, a noble of the same type as Catiline, and Cicero. The first two were supported by Caesar and Crassus, who hoped to use them. Cicero, as a *novus homo*, was distasteful to the Optimates, but they felt that Catiline must be defeated at all costs, and so they supported the orator, who was elected with Antonius as his colleague. From that time Cicero ranged himself with the Optimates, and his political watchword was the "concord of the orders" (*concordia ordinum*), that is, an alliance of the propertied classes, both senatorial and equestrian, to stabilize the constitution and to prevent future *coups d'état* like Catiline's. Of the consular provinces for 62 Cicero received by lot Macedonia, and Antonius, Cisalpine Gaul. As the latter was dissatisfied, Cicero resigned Macedonia to him, in return for his public assurance of abstaining from opposing Cicero's acts during their year of office.

On the first day of his consulate in 63, Cicero delivered a speech in which he scathingly criticized a land bill proposed by the tribune Servilius Rullus. This bill aimed to create a commission of ten members of praetorian rank, elected in a special Comitia of seventeen tribes chosen by lot by Rullus. These commissioners were to be vested with extraordinary powers for five years, including the right to sell public land in Italy and in Pompey's recent conquests, to exercise judicial authority, to confiscate lands, to found colonies, and to enroll and maintain troops. The bill would have given the commissioners extraordinary military authority both in Italy and in the provinces, guaranteed by the income derived from the sale of land. Pompey was excluded from the commission by a clause requiring the personal appearance of candidates. Everyone was aware that the measure was devised by Caesar and Crassus and that they would dominate the commission. The attack upon the Senate's control of public land and general mistrust of the purposes of a bill of this sort caused such strong opposition, however, that its sponsors did not bring it to a vote.

Caesar could console himself with victory in another sphere. The position of Pontifex Maximus had become vacant. By a tribunician bill the *lex Domitia*, revoked by Sulla, was again brought into effect and election to the priesthood entrusted to an Assembly of seventeen tribes. In the ensuing election Caesar, supported by Crassus' money, was victorious.

CONSPIRACY OF 63 B.C.   In July of 63, the consular elections for the next year were held. Catiline was once more a competitor, but now he lacked Crassus' support. By proposing a general cancellation of debts, he sought to rally around him both nobles of broken fortunes like himself and all needy and desperate characters throughout Italy, such as, for example, dispossessed Sullan veterans. He was bitterly opposed by Cicero, who capitalized on the public apprehension that Catiline would resort to violence. Cicero had the backing of the business interests and most senators, who looked upon Catiline as a menace. The result was that Catiline was defeated. In desperation he conspired to overthrow the government by armed force. While one of his associates began to raise an army among the Sullan veterans in Etruria, Catiline made preparations to seize control of the city and open the gates to these troops, who were to be concentrated secretly near Rome. Cicero, on the alert, got news of the conspiracy and produced enough evidence to induce the Senate to pass the "last decree" and empower him to take all necessary measures to save the state. For want of adequate proof of his complicity, Catiline was not arrested in Rome and soon left the city to join his supporters in Etruria. The Senate now declared him a public enemy and ordered Cicero's colleague Antonius to take the field against him. In the meantime the conspirators who remained in Rome set December 17, the opening day of the festival of the Saturnalia, as the date for a rising in Rome, when the city was to be fired, the consuls and other prominent men killed, and a reign of terror instituted. This plan was betrayed to Cicero by a delegation of Allobroges from Gallia Narbonensis who happened to be in Rome and whom the plotters had endeavored to enlist on their side. Cicero arrested five of the leading Catilinarians and took timely precautions to prevent an outbreak. Catiline now realized the futility of a march on Rome and tried to escape with his army into Cisalpine Gaul, but he was overtaken by Antonius and forced to give battle near Pistoria. There he and most of his followers fell. Instead of leaving the matter to the regular courts, Cicero convened the Senate to decide the fate of the prisoners in Rome. He favored their immediate execution and found strong support among the more prominent senators. Caesar proposed that they be confined to certain Italian municipalities for the rest of their lives. When a majority seemed likely to approve this sentence, a strong speech by Cato the Younger, a man of uncompromising loyalty to the constitution, won them back to Cicero's point of view. At the latter's orders the conspirators were executed. The suppression of the conspiracy added considerably to Cicero's reputation, but his execution of the plotters without trial left him open to future attack, since it was not at all certain that the actions of the Catilinarians had been so treasonous as to warrant suspension of their right to protection under the law or that the situation had been sufficiently grave to permit a consul to ignore normal legal procedure. On the other hand, Caesar gained credit for moderation and respect for citizens' rights, and Cato for great vigor and force of character. The whole Catilinarian episode seems more important than it really was because of Cicero's involvement and because it is so well documented in the surviving sources. The conspiracy was actually little different from *coups d'état* of the Marians in the decade of the 80s. It was significant at least in that it was the first time since Marcus Lepidus in 78 that anyone had attempted to start a civil war, and the course of the uprising indicated that the propertied establishment were basically interested in preserving the status quo.

VII. The Coalition of Pompey, Crassus, and Caesar: 60 B.C.

POMPEY'S RETURN. Toward the close of the year 62 Pompey arrived in Italy from the East and, contrary to the expectations of those who feared that he would prove a second Sulla, immediately disbanded his army. Pompey wanted enhancement of his *dignitas* no less then any man of his age, but he was at heart a constitutionalist, and, rather naïvely, he thought that the oligarchy would give him his due. The following September he celebrated a memorable triumph. From the spoils of his wars, he deposited 50,000,000 denarii in the treasury, gave half as much to his higher officers, and distributed 71,000,000 denarii ($14,200,000) as a bonus among the lower officers and soldiers. In addition, the taxes from his annexations increased the revenues of the Empire by 35,000,000 denarii ($7,000,000) annually.[1] To bring his achievements to a fitting con-

---

[1] The denarius, worth twenty cents, had a much greater purchasing power and was the average daily wage of a Roman laborer.

clusion, Pompey now pressed the Senate to ratify the arrangements made in the East and to provide land grants for about 40,000 veterans discharged from his legions. Without an army at his back, he was no longer feared by the senators, who had many scores to settle with him. Led by Lucullus and others whom Pompey had humiliated, the Senate insisted upon examining his acts in detail and refused to ratify them *en bloc* as he demanded. When in 60 one of the tribunes proposed a land bill for his veterans, the opposition of the Optimates was so effective that the plebiscite was abandoned. While in this way the Optimates lost the opportunity of winning Pompey over to their side, they also offended Crassus and the equestrians. The *publicani* who had contracted to collect the taxes of the province of Asia found that owing to poor harvests there they would be unable to raise as much revenue as they had agreed to pay the treasury. They therefore sought to have the terms of their contract modified. Although Crassus supported this request, it was refused by the Senate, largely through the opposition of Cato. These events rudely dashed Cicero's hopes for a concord of the orders.

No settlement had been reached when Caesar returned to Rome in 60. He had held a praetorship in 62 and for the following year had been governor of Farther Spain, where he performed the rather astonishing feat of waging successful border wars, conciliating the provincials, and at the same time finding the means to pay off his debts, which were estimated at 25,000,000 sesterces ($1,250,000). He now requested a triumph and permission to stand for the consulship while waiting outside the city for the right to make a triumphal entry. Owing to Cato's intervention, the Senate failed to act on his petition, and he at once decided to forego the triumph and press his candidacy at the coming elections. Supported by Crassus and some leading Pompeians, he was elected consul; his colleague was Calpurnius Bibulus, the nominee of the Optimates. Although involved in some of Crassus' schemes, Caesar had never been an enemy of Pompey and in fact had at times cooperated with his agents in Rome. He found no great difficulty, then, in reconciling these two leaders and in forming with them a secret coalition to attain their particular aims in his coming consulship. In the light of subsequent events, this unofficial coalition has come to be known as the First Triumvirate. It was an important turning point on the road to one-man rule in Rome and was brought about by unrealistic and intransigent senatorial policy which threw these three men together.

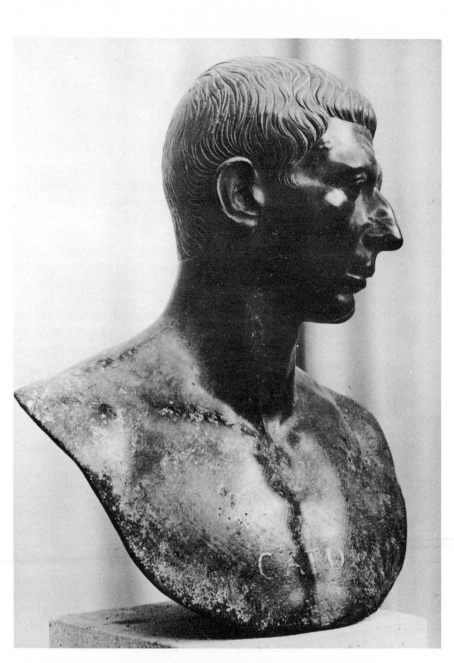

Portrait head of Cato the Younger

C H A P T E R   I 4

RIVALRY OF POMPEY AND
CAESAR AND CAESAR'S
DICTATORSHIP: 59-44 B.C.

For the history of the thirty years between the First Triumvirate and the close of the civil wars in 30 B.C., our literary sources are in large measure the same as for the years following the death of Sulla: Appian, Cassius Dio, Velleius Paterculus, the *Epitome* of Livy, Plutarch, and Cicero. To the *Lives* of Plutarch already mentioned must be added those of Caesar, Mark Antony, and the younger Cato; and Cicero's speeches and other works are supplemented for the years 60 to 43 by his invaluable collection of *Letters*, which at times give an almost day-by-day account of important happenings in Rome. Of great importance also are Caesar's own *Commentaries* on the Gallic War and on the Civil War, the first of which was completed by his friend Hirtius, who also wrote an account of the Alexandrine War. These are supplemented by similar narratives of the African and Spanish Wars written by anonymous officers of Caesar's staff. A Roman account of Caesar's career is found in the biography called *Divus Julius* by Suetonius Tranquillus early in the second century A.D. There remain also in inscriptional form considerable fragments of important legislative enactments that throw light upon Caesar's administrative reforms.

I. Triumvirate in Action

CAESAR'S CONSULSHIP: 59 B.C.   Once in office, Caesar began to fulfill his engagements to his partners in the Triumvirate. Exact dating of his measures is difficult, but it seems that the early spring of 59 was a crucial period for the Triumvirate, since Pompey then revealed the extent of his commitment to Caesar's designs by marrying Caesar's daughter Julia. Early that year he laid before the Senate a law to provide lands for Pompey's veterans and needy citizens in Rome through the distribution of arable public land outside Campania and other properties to be purchased. But when this proposal met with strong opposition, largely instigated by his bitter critic, Cato, he brought his bill directly before the Tribal Assembly. There it was vetoed by tribunes of the Optimates' faction and by obstructive use of the *auspicium* on the part of Bibulus. Caesar then called upon Pompey and Crassus for support. With the aid of Pompey's veterans he chased his opponents from the Forum. The bill became law, and Bibulus shut himself up in his house in protest and refused to participate in the conduct of public business. Since the land to be used in carrying out this measure proved inadequate, Caesar introduced in late April a second law, opening for colonization public land in Campania then under lease to tenants of the state. This law also passed over the vigorous opposition of Cato. Caesar made use of his henchman, the tribune Vatinius, to carry through a law ratifying all Pompey's dispositions in the East and a second granting to delinquent tax-farmers of Asia a remission of one third of their contract price. Although much of Caesar's legislation was determined by the blatantly personal interests of the triumvirs and was passed by means of violence and terrorism, he was also the author of several constructive and even statesmanlike measures. These included a *lex Iulia de repetundis* that remained on Rome's statute books for six hundred years as a measure to control extortion of provincial populations by their governors. Another law decreed the publication of senatorial resolutions in a kind of "Congressional Record," (*acta diurna*) which prevented the garbling of official documents by interested magistrates and, incidentally, publicized Caesar's own legislation.

CAESAR'S PROCONSULAR COMMAND.   Caesar laid the foundations for his future career by securing for himself an extraordinary military command, probably in the very early spring of 59. For 58 the Senate apparently had designated the forests and cattle roads of Italy as the province for both the consuls of the preceding year. The Senate tried thereby to fob off a harmless *provincia* on Caesar rather than provide him with an opportunity to win glory and power through military command. The last thing Caesar wished to be was a kind of Secretary of the Interior, and he seized upon the first excuse to set aside this arrangement. He seems at first to have been interested in campaigning to the northeast of Italy, along the Danube, against the Dacians who were threatening Macedonia. His henchman Vatinius proposed a law, passed by the Tribal Assembly, conferring on him the combined provinces of Cisalpine Gaul and Illyricum, with a garrison of three legions, for a term of five years (ending on March 1, 54). Cisalpine Gaul was to be an important source of strength for him. He had won clients there in 65 by championing a proposal to extend full Roman citizenship to all those of Latin status, and the Po valley was an excellent recruiting area. Somewhat later in 59 the governor of Transalpine Gaul suddenly died, and the Senate, at Pompey's instigation, added this province to his command on a yearly basis and gave him another legion. Caesar's primary interest promptly shifted to this area. Disturbances among the Gauls, due to a Germanic invasion from across the Rhine and a threatened migration of the Celtic Helvetii from their home in Switzerland, held out hopes for winning military laurels.

For the rest of the year Caesar's proconsular command ran concurrently with his consulship, and he was able to raise and maintain troops in Italy and by virtue of this to exert tremendous pressure upon the political situation in Rome. The length of his proconsular command also assured him immunity for a considerable period from any attempt to hold him responsible for unconstitutional acts perpetrated during his consulship.

COALITION CONTINUES. Caesar's consulship was an open defiance of constitutional checks on consular authority and revealed that the triumvirate was stronger than the established organs of government and that the Roman Empire was now really controlled by three men. Well might Cato say that the coalition was the beginning of the end of the Republic. Within the triumvirate Pompey was the dominant figure, owing to his military renown and the influence of his veterans. Caesar appeared as his agent yet displayed far greater political insight and succeeded in creating for himself a position that would enable him to play a more independent future role. The coalition did not break up at the end of Caesar's consulship; its members were determined to retain their control of state policy. Although public opinion in Rome became hostile to them in the latter part of 59, they secured the election of two of their supporters as consuls for the ensuing year and Caesar married the daughter of Piso, one of the consuls-elect.

To secure themselves from attack, the triumvirs felt it necessary to remove from the city their two ablest opponents, Cato and Cicero. The latter had refused all proposals to join them and had sharply criticized them on several public occasions. His banishment was secured through the agency of the tribune Clodius, whose transfer from patrician to plebeian status Caesar had facilitated. Clodius was a demagogue who proposed legislation, such as the conversion of grain distributions into an outright dole, that would make him popular and consolidate the position of the triumvirs. He hated Cicero because the latter had testified against him when he was on trial for sacrilege. Early in 58 Clodius carried a bill outlawing any person who had Roman citizens put to death without regular judicial proceedings. This law was aimed at Cicero for his share in the execution of the Catalinarian conspirators. Finding that he could not rely upon support of his friends, Cicero went into exile without awaiting trial. He was formally banished, his property was confiscated, and he himself sought refuge in Thessalonica, where the governor of Macedonia offered him protection. Cato was entrusted with a special mission to accomplish the incorporation of Cyprus, then ruled by one of the Egyptian Ptolemies who had lost favor with the triumvirs, into the Roman Empire, and his Stoic conception of duty prevented him from refusing the appointment. Caesar remained with his army in the vicinity of Rome until after Cicero's banishment and then set out for his province.

II. Caesar's Conquest of Gaul: 58–51 B.C.

DEFEAT OF THE HELVETII AND GERMANS: 58 B.C. In 58, Caesar, relatively untried as a commander, entered his Gallic province. Transalpine Gaul (Gallia Narbonensis) embraced the coast districts from the Alps to the borders of Spain and the land between the Alps and the Rhone as far north as Lake Geneva. The country stretching from the Pyrenees to the Rhine and from the Rhone to the ocean was called *Gallia comata* or "long-haired Gaul" and was occupied by a large number of peoples of varying character. These were regarded as falling into three groups, (1) those of Aquitania, between the Pyrenees and the Loire, where there was a large Iberian element, (2) those called Celts, in a narrow sense of the word, stretching from the Loire to the Seine and the Marne, and (3) the Belgian Gauls, dwelling between these rivers and the Rhine. Among the latter were peoples of Germanic origin.

The culture of the Gauls showed marked contrasts. Living in an area particularly blessed by nature, they had developed agriculture, animal husbandry, and mining. In part as a result of their proximity to the Greek trading city of Massilia, they had learned the arts of commerce and used both Greek coinage and their own. In some areas they had developed small towns. They were illiterate, except for their priestly class, the Druids. The latter were important as judges and because they controlled religious observances and beliefs. Although obscure, these included belief in immortality of the soul, worship of gods in sacred groves, and human sacrifice. Although conscious of a general unity of language, race, and customs, the Gauls had not developed a national state, owing to the mutual jealousy of the individual peoples. Tribal chiefs ruled the Belgian Gauls. Elsewhere aristocracies, who feuded among themselves and with the Druids, were in control. The bulk of the population was in a semiservile condition.

Rome had sought to protect the Narbonese province by establishing friendly relations with some of these Gallic peoples and had long before (ca. 121) made an alliance with the Aedui. Conditions in *Gallia comata* had been disturbed about 70 by an invasion of Germanic Suevi from across the Rhine, under their king, Ariovistus. They had been invited by the Sequani to help them fight their rivals, the Aedui, and had been promised lands in return for their services. In 61, the Aedui suffered a crushing defeat, which forced them to come to terms with the Sequani. The Aedui appealed to Rome for aid on the basis of their alliance, but the Romans were engaged in putting down a serious revolt in Gallia Narbonensis, occasioned by the exactions of officials and greed of Roman moneylenders, and did not respond. Two years later, Ariovistus, whose people had settled in the region now known as Alsace, sent an embassy to the Senate, which recognized him as a "friend of the Roman People," which was equivalent to approving his present status in Gaul. The next threat to the peace of Gaul came from the Helvetii, who had planned to migrate from Switzerland as early as 61 but set out only in March of 58 on a search for new homes in western Gaul. They planned to traverse part of Gallia Narbonensis, but Caesar arrived in time to prevent their crossing the upper Rhone into the province. In provoking a war he was certainly motivated by the desire to enhance his *dignitas* as well as by the wish to safeguard the Roman province to the south. As they turned westwards into the territory of the Sequani and Aedui, he followed, overtook, and defeated them in two battles. He then forced them to return to their former home and accept an alliance with Rome. Caesar then learned that Ariovistus had taken advantage of Roman indifference to strengthen his position in Gaul. He had reduced the Sequani to subjection and was threatening the Aedui, and a fresh band of Suevi was about to cross the Rhine to support him. It now became Caesar's aim to prevent the development of a strong Germanic state in Gaul. Since Ariovistus refused to limit his freedom of action, Caesar marched against him, defeated him near Strassburg, and drove him and his people across the Rhine. His victories made Caesar the dominant power in Gaul outside the Roman province, and this caused many of the leading Gallic tribes to ally themselves with Rome. Of the warlike Belgae, however, only one people, the Remi, came over to Rome's side.

SUBJUGATION OF THE BELGAE, VENETI, AND AQUITANIANS: 57–56 B.C. The next year (57) Caesar marched against the united forces of the Belgae, defeated them, and subdued many tribes, especially the Nervii. Simultaneously his legates received the submission of the peoples of Normandy and Brittany. During the following winter some of them, led by the Veneti, broke their alliance and attacked Caesar's garrisons. Thereupon he built a fleet, which in the course of the next summer destroyed that of the Veneti and captured their coastal strongholds (56). Henceforth, the Romans possessed naval supremacy on the Atlantic coast of Gaul. The same year witnessed the submission of the Aquitani, which brought practically the whole of Gaul under Roman sway.

THE CONFERENCE OF LUCA: 56 B.C. Meanwhile important changes had taken place in the situation at Rome. Pompey had broken with Clodius and supported the tribune Titus Annius Milo, who pressed for Cicero's recall. A law of the Assembly withdrew his sentence of outlawry, his property was restored, and the orator returned in September, 57, to enjoy a warm reception in the municipal towns and at the capital. For the moment Pompey and the Optimates were on friendly terms, and he used a grain famine in the city to secure his own appointment as curator of the grain supply (*curator annonae*) for a period of five years. This appointment carried with it proconsular *imperium* in Italy and abroad and the control of the ports, markets, and traffic in grain within Roman dominions. It was really an extraordinary military command. Pompey relieved the situation but could not suppress the disorders in Rome, where Clodius and Milo defied law and order with their armed gangs.

The news of Caesar's victories and the influence he was acquiring in the city by a judicious distribution of the spoils of war provoked the ambitions of Pompey and Crassus, whose political friendship had waned. Consequently Caesar felt it necessary for the coalition to reach a new agreement. Accordingly, while wintering in Cisalpine Gaul, he arranged a conference at Luca in April, 56, where the three settled their differences and laid future plans. They agreed that Pompey and Crassus should be consuls in 55, that the former should be given the Spanish provinces and Libya for five years, that Crassus should have Syria for an equal period, and that Caesar's command in Gaul should be prolonged for an approximately equal period, with the proviso that the question of appointing his successor should not be raised before March 1, 50.

These arrangements were duly executed. Since it was too late for Pompey and Crassus to be candidates at the regular elections in 56, they forcibly prevented any elections being held that year. The following January, after compelling the other candidates to withdraw, they were elected. Thereupon a law of the tribune Gaius Trebonius made effective the assignment of the provinces agreed to at Luca. Once more it was made plain that the coalition actually ruled the Empire. Cicero, indebted to Pompey for his recall, was forced to support the triumvirate; the Optimates found their boldest leader in Cato, who had returned to Rome early in 56.

CAESAR'S CROSSING OF THE RHINE AND INVASIONS OF BRITAIN: 55–54 B.C. During the winter of 56–55 two Germanic tribes, the Usipetes and the Tencteri, crossed the lower Rhine into Gaul. The next summer (55) Caesar attacked and annihilated their forces, only a few escaping across the river. As a warning against future invasion, Caesar bridged the Rhine and made a demonstration on the right bank, destroying his bridge when he withdrew. Toward the close of the summer he crossed the Straits of Dover to Britain, nominally to punish the Britons for aiding his enemies in Gaul. Owing to the lateness of the season, however, and the smallness of his force, he returned to Gaul after a brief reconnaissance campaign on the Kentish coast.

The following year, after gathering a larger fleet, he again landed on the island with a force of almost 30,000 men. This time he forced his way across the Thames and received the submission of Cassivellaunus, the chief who led the British tribes against the invaders. After taking hostages and receiving promises of tribute, Caesar returned to Gaul. Although southeast Britain was not subdued, Caesar could claim to have rendered its inhabitants subject and, besides enlarging the geographical knowledge of the time, he brought back numbers of captives. In Rome the exploit produced great excitement and enthusiasm.

REVOLTS IN GAUL: 54–53 B.C.   Although the Gauls had submitted to Caesar, they were not yet reconciled to Roman rule, which put an end to their intertribal wars and to the feuds among the nobility. Many of the tribes were restive and not inclined to surrender all hopes of freedom without another struggle. In the course of the winter 54–53 the Nervii, Treveri, and Eburones in Belgian Gaul attacked the Roman detachments stationed in their territories. One of these was cut to pieces, but the rest held out until relieved by Caesar, who stamped out the rebellion.

REBELLION OF VERCINGETORIX: 52 B.C.   A more serious movement started in 52 among the peoples of central Gaul, who found a national leader in Vercingetorix, a young noble of the Arverni. The revolt took Caesar by surprise when he was in Cisalpine Gaul and his troops still scattered in winter quarters. He recrossed the Alps hastily, secured the Narbonese province, and succeeded in uniting his forces. These he strengthened with German cavalry from across the Rhine. A temporary check in his attack on Vercingetorix at Gergovia caused the Aedui to desert the Romans, and the revolt spread to practically all of Gaul. Caesar was on the point of retiring to the Narbonese province, but after repulsing an attack, he penned up Vercingetorix in the fortress of Alesia. A great effort made by the Gauls to relieve the siege failed to break Caesar's lines, and the defenders were starved into submission. The crisis was over, although another year was to pass before the revolting tribes were all reduced and Roman authority reestablished (51). Caesar used all possible mildness in his treatment of the conquered, and the Gauls were not only pacified but won over. In the future they were among his most loyal supporters. The conquest of Gaul was an event of supreme importance for the future of the Roman Empire and for the development of European civilization. For the time *Gallia comata* was not formed into a province. Its peoples were made allies of Rome, under the supervision of the governor of Narbonese Gaul, were obliged to furnish auxiliary troops, and for the most part were liable to a fixed annual tribute. Caesar's campaign in Gaul had given him the opportunity to develop his unusual military talents and to create a devoted veteran army. His power had become so great that both Pompey and the Optimates desired his destruction, but he was in a position to fight, if necessary, to avoid being eliminated. The plots laid in Rome to deprive him of his power had made him hasten to quell the revolt of the Gauls with all speed. When this was accomplished, he was free to turn his attention to Roman affairs.

III. Dissolution of the Triumvirate

PARTHIA.   The Parthians had originally been a seminomadic people speaking a kind of Persian who had settled to the southeast of the Caspian Sea about 250 and who had gradually extended their control over the

Mesopotamian and eastern satrapies of the declining Seleucid Empire. They remained a landholding minority ruling various subject peoples. Their kingdom, even though covering an area that had been permeated by Greek culture following the conquest of Alexander the Great, was only superficially Hellenized. They were important particularly for their contributions to the arts of war, since they excelled in the use of both heavily mailed cavalrymen, known as cataphracts, and swift mounted bowmen whose tactics at first baffled the Romans. Relations between Parthia and Rome dated from a mission of Sulla (92) and had been friendly until 65, when Pompey refused the claim of the Parthian king to lands in northern Mesopotamia. Ten years later Aulus Gabinius, as proconsul of Syria, had contributed to a further worsening of relations by supporting a rebel claimant to the Parthian throne. It was under such circumstances, and with the design of winning military prestige in a war against the Parthians to balance that of the other triumvirs, that Crassus set out for Syria in the autumn of 55.

DEATH OF CRASSUS: 53 B.C.   Crassus had no real excuse for opening hostilities, but the Parthians were potentially dangerous neighbors, and a campaign against them promised profit and glory. In 54, Crassus made a short incursion into Mesopotamia and then withdrew to Syria. The next year he again crossed the Euphrates, intending to penetrate deeply into the enemy's country, but he had underestimated the strength of the Parthians and the difficulties of desert warfare. Surenas, the Parthian commander, had organized a force of 10,000 mounted archers, supported by a supply train of a thousand camels carrying a reserve supply of arrows, which enabled the bowmen to maintain their fire for long periods. The archers were backed by a thousand mail-clad lancers mounted on heavy war horses also partially protected by armor. In the Mesopotamian desert near Carrhae the Romans were surrounded and cut to pieces by the Parthian horsemen. While endeavoring to lead the survivors to safety, Crassus was enticed into a conference and treacherously slain, and only a small remnant of his force of 40,000 men escaped (53). The Parthians were slow to follow up their advantage, and Crassus' quaestor, Gaius Cassius Longinus, was able to hold Syria. Roman prestige in the East had received a severe blow, however, and for the next three centuries the Romans found the Parthians dangerous neighbors. The death of Crassus tended to hasten a crisis in Rome, for it brought into sharp conflict the incompatible ambitions of Pompey and Caesar, whose estrangement had already begun with the death of Pompey's wife Julia in 54.

PRINCIPATE OF POMPEY: 52 B.C.   At the end of his consulship Pompey left Rome but remained in Italy, on the pretext of his curatorship of the grain supply, and governed his province through legates. In Rome disorder reigned. No consuls were elected in 54, nor before July of the following year. The partisans of Clodius and Milo kept everything in confusion. Pompey could have restored order but preferred to let events take their course and thereby to create a situation that would force the Senate to grant him new powers. Owing to conflicts between the supporters of the candidates, no consuls or praetors could be elected for 52. In January of that year Clodius was slain by Milo's bodyguard on the Appian Way, and the ensuing outburst of mob violence in the city forced the Senate to appeal to Pompey. He was made sole consul, until he should choose a colleague, and entrusted with the task of restoring order. His troops pacified the city. Milo was tried on a charge of public violence, convicted, and banished. Pompey had attained the height of his official career. He was sole consul, he had provinces embracing the Spains, Libya, and the sphere assigned to him with the grain curatorship, he could govern his provinces through *legati*, and his armies were maintained by the treasury. He was the chief power in the state, for the Senate was helpless without him, and he was justly regarded by contemporaries as the First Citizen or Princeps. In many ways his position foreshadowed the Principate of Augustus. Nevertheless, Pompey did not wish to overthrow the republican regime; his ambition was to be regarded as the indispensable and permanent mainstay of the government and to enjoy corresponding power and honor. In such a scheme there was no room for a rival, and therefore he was no longer willing to promote Caesar's interests at the almost certain expense of his own. This gradually won him over to the Optimates, who were alarmed by Caesar's wealth, influence, and growing reputation and feared him as a dangerous enemy.

Caesar's immediate aim was to step directly from his provincial command into a second consulship. He knew that he had reached a position that caused many to desire his destruction and that when he surrendered his *imperium*, he would be prosecuted on various charges by his enemies. He had no intention of placing himself in their power, however, and so he influenced the tribunes of the year 52 to carry a law permitting him to be a candidate for the consulship in absentia. He could not legally hold a second consulship before 48, but Pompey's consulship of 52 was a violation of this constitutional provision, and Caesar may have hoped to secure permission to seek the office for 49. At any rate until sometime in 52 he could look forward to holding the consulship in 48, under the terms of the Sempronian Law on the consular provinces. Since this law required that consular provinces be designated in advance of the election of possible appointees and since no question of Caesar's successor could legally be raised before March 1, 50, the magistrates of that year would have already received their provincial appointments, and those of 49 would be the first ones eligible to take over the Gallic provinces in 48. If Caesar counted on this automatic prolongation of his command, his calculations were disturbed by two laws Pompey carried through in 52. One of these contained a clause forbidding candidates to seek magistracies when absent from Rome. This would deprive Caesar of the privilege so recently conferred upon him, and his friends raised vigorous protests against it. Pompey excused himself on the ground that it was due to an oversight that Caesar's rights had not been confirmed and added to the law after it had passed a clause which exempted Caesar from its effects. It is doubtful how sincere Pompey was, although he had as yet made no open break with Caesar. It is also doubtful that his alteration of the law was valid. Pompey's other law provided that in future provincial governors should not be the outgoing consuls and praetors of each year but nominees of the Senate selected from ex-magistrates whose terms had expired at least five years before their appointment.[1] Although Pompey may be credited with a sincere desire to improve the quality of imperial administration by discouraging candidates for high offices from incurring heavy debts they would seek to repay from the profits of a certain and immediate provincial governorship, the fact remains that under the new law a successor to Caesar could now be appointed immediately after March 1, 50. He would now have to return to Rome and seek the consulship as a private citizen without immunity from prosecution. To prevent this, Caesar had to rely upon the tribunes' veto. While Caesar's position was threatened, Pompey secured his own future by having his command in Spain extended for another five-year term.

POMPEY'S BREAK WITH CAESAR. The question of Caesar's recall from Gaul became the focal point of politics in Rome for the next two years, and the failure to reach a mutually satisfactory agreement on this issue was the cause of a new civil war. One of Caesar's enemies, the consul Marcellus, agitated for Caesar's recall as early as 51, on the ground that the war in Gaul was over, but his proposal was defeated in the Senate. Pompey, who stuck to the letter of the law, was willing to press for Caesar's return right after March 1, 50 and began negotiations with Caesar, who at this time seems to have been anxious to secure the consulship for 49. These negotiations came to nothing, and when March 1, 50 arrived all efforts to assign consular provinces were blocked by Caesar's agent, the tribune Curio. Various proposals put forth by Pompey and the Optimates were aimed at bringing about the termination of Caesar's command before his election to the consulship. Caesar was not willing to risk cessation of his *imperium* while Pompey remained in Italy at the head of an army. He offered, through Curio, to disband his army and return to Rome if Pompey would likewise disband his troops. This was approved by a large majority in the Senate on December 1, 50, but the resolution met with a consular veto. At the request of Marcellus, the consul, Pompey then assumed command of the government forces in the peninsula. On January 1, 49, the Senate, under pressure of the Optimates and Pompey's

---

[1] It was under this law that Cicero, who had been consul in 63 B.C. and had not had a provincial command, was appointed proconsul of Cilicia for 51 B.C.

supporters, voted that Caesar should surrender his command by a fixed date or be declared a public enemy. The resolution was promptly vetoed, however, by Marcus Antonius (Mark Antony) and Quintus Cassius, two of the new board of tribunes. Angry at being thwarted in this way, the Optimates drove Antony and Cassius from the Senate by threats of death. Then on January 7 the Senate passed the "last" decree, calling upon the consuls and other magistrates, including Pompey as proconsul, to protect the state and at the same time pronouncing Caesar a public enemy. Caesar's friends fled the city and hurried to meet him in Cisalpine Gaul, where he and a small part of his army were waiting, ready for this emergency. The fugitive tribunes appealed to him for protection, and he could claim that, in addition to maintaining his own interests, he was defending the sanctity of the people's chosen representatives.

IV. Civil War Between Caesar and the Senate: 49–46 B.C.

CAESAR'S CONQUEST OF ITALY AND SPAIN: 49 B.C. The senatorial conservatives had forced the issue, and for Caesar there remained the alternative of victory or destruction. He possessed the advantages of a loyal army ready for immediate action and the undisputed control over his own troops. His land laws had given him large numbers of clients in Campania, the city populace was now well disposed towards him, and his generous treatment of the towns of Cisalpine Gaul in the matter of Roman citizenship had made them his backers. His opponents had no veteran troops in Italy, and although Pompey acted as commander in chief of the senatorial forces, he was greatly hampered by having to defer to the judgment of the consuls and senators who were in his camp. It was obviously to Caesar's advantage to take the offensive and to force a decision before his enemies could concentrate against him the resources of the provinces. Hence he determined to act without delay, and, upon receiving news of the Senate's action on January 7, he crossed the Rubicon, which divided Cisalpine Gaul and Italy, with a small force, ordering the legions beyond the Alps to join him at once. The Italian municipalities opened their gates at his approach, and the newly raised levies went over to his side. In vain the Senate sought to slow his advance by opening negotiations. Caesar, although he renewed his offer to disband his troops if Pompey did so, an offer which his opponents would not accept, maintained the tempo of his southward march. Everywhere his mildness to his opponents won him new adherents. Pompey had originally planned to make a stand in Italy and had gone to Apulia to raise troops, but his plan was thwarted by the stubbornness of the governor designate of Transalpine Gaul, L. Domitius Ahenobarbus. Against Pompey's advice, Ahenobarbus insisted on making a stand with his army against Caesar at Corfinium in central Italy. Ahenobarbus was defeated, his troops went over to Caesar, and Pompey's cause in Italy became hopeless. Pompey was thus forced to abandon Italy and withdraw to the East, intending later to concentrate upon the peninsula from all sides—a plan made feasible by his control of the sea. Caesar divined his intention and tried to cut off his retreat at Brundisium but he could not prevent his embarkation. With his army and a majority of the Senate, Pompey crossed to Epirus. Owing to lack of a fleet, Caesar could not follow, and he returned to Rome. There some of the magistrates were still functioning, in conjunction with a rump Senate. Being in dire need of money, he wished to obtain funds from the treasury. When he was opposed in this by a tribune, Caesar ignored the latter's veto and forcibly seized the reserve treasure the Pompeians had left behind in their hasty flight. Meantime Caesar's lieutenants had seized Sardinia and Sicily and crossed over into Africa to secure the sources of the grain supply of Rome. He himself determined to attack the well-organized Pompeian forces in Spain and destroy them before Pompey was ready to attack from the East. On his way to Spain Caesar began the siege of Massilia, which resisted him. Leaving the city under blockade, he hastened to Spain where, after an initial defeat, he forced the surrender of the Pompeian armies. Some of the defeated joined his forces; the rest were dismissed to their homes. Caesar hastened back to Massilia. The city capitulated on his arrival and was punished by requisitions, the loss of its territory, and the temporary loss of its autonomy. Caesar then pressed on to Rome, where he had been appointed dictator by virtue of a special law. After holding elections in which he and an approved colleague were returned as consuls for 48, he resigned his dictatorship and set out for Brundisium. There he had assembled his army and transports for the passage to Epirus.

BATTLE OF PHARSALUS: 48 B.C. During Caesar's Spanish campaign Pompey had gathered a large force in Macedonia—nine Roman legions reinforced by contingents from the Roman allies. His fleet, recruited largely from the maritime cities in the East, commanded the Adriatic. Nevertheless, at the beginning of winter (November, 49), Caesar effected a landing on the coast of Epirus with part of his army and seized Apollonia. Pompey arrived from Macedonia in time to save Dyrrhachium. Throughout the winter the two armies remained inactive, but Pompey's fleet prevented Caesar from receiving reinforcements until the spring of 48, when Marcus Antonius landed with another detachment. As Caesar's troops began to suffer from shortage of supplies, he was forced to take the offensive and tried to blockade Pompey's larger force in Dyrrhachium. The attempt failed, Caesar's lines of investment were broken, and he withdrew to Thessaly where he was followed by Pompey. Relying on superior numbers and, in particular, his preponderance in cavalry, Pompey decided the time had come to yield to the demands of the senators in his camp and risk a battle. Near the town of Old Pharsalus he attacked Caesar, but was defeated and his army dispersed. Pompey himself sought refuge in Egypt. There he was killed by order of the king, whose father he had protected in the days of his power. Pompey's great weakness was that his resolution did not match his ambition. His ambition led him to seek a position incompatible with the constitution, while his lack of resolution prevented his overthrowing the constitution. The Optimates had sided with him only because they held him less dangerous than Caesar. Had he been victorious they would have sought to bring about his downfall.

CAESAR IN THE EAST: 48–47 B.C. After Pharsalus Caesar pursued Pompey but arrived in Egypt after the latter's murder. His ever-pressing need for money probably induced him to intervene as arbiter in the name of Rome, in the dynastic struggle then raging in Egypt between the twenty-year-old Cleopatra and her thirteen-year-old brother, Ptolemy XIV Dionysus, who, following the Egyptian custom, was also her husband. Caesar, having seized the young king, brought back Cleopatra, whom the people of Alexandria had driven out. Angered at this and resenting his exactions, the Alexandrians revolted and from October, 48 to March, 47, besieged Caesar in the royal quarter of the city. Having few troops with him, Caesar was in danger and able to maintain himself only through his control of the sea, which enabled him eventually to receive reinforcements. He released the young king, who promptly joined the besiegers. Caesar's relief was effected by a force raised by Mithradates of Pergamon, who invaded Egypt through Syria. In cooperation with him Caesar defeated the Egyptians in battle, Ptolemy Dionysus perished in flight, and Alexandria submitted. Cleopatra was married to a still younger brother and given the kingdom of Egypt. Caesar had succumbed to the charms of the Egyptian queen and spent the rest of the winter in her company. He was finally called away to face a new danger in Pharnaces, son of Mithradates Eupator, who had taken advantage of the civil war to emerge from the Crimea and overrun Pontus, Lesser Armenia, and Cappadocia. Hastening through Syria, Caesar entered Pontus and defeated Pharnaces at Zela. After settling affairs in Asia Minor, Caesar hurried to the West, where his presence was urgently needed.

CAESAR'S CAMPAIGN IN AFRICA: 46 B.C. Both the fleet and the army of Pompey had been dispersed after Pharsalus, but Caesar's delay in the East had given the Optimates an opportunity to regroup. They gathered in Africa, where Caesar's lieutenant Curio, who invaded the province in 49, was defeated and killed by the Pompeians through the aid of King Juba of Numidia. From Africa they were now preparing to attack Italy. In Rome Caesar was appointed dictator for 47 with Antony as his master of the horse. Here disorder reigned as a result of financial distress caused by the war. Antony, who was in Rome, proved unable to deal with the situation. Caesar reached Italy in September (47), and soon restored order in the city. He was then called upon to face a serious mutiny of his troops, who demanded money and land and their release from service. By boldness and presence of mind Caesar won them back to their allegiance and set out for Africa in December 47. He landed with only a portion of his troops and was held in check at first by the senatorial forces under Scipio and Juba. He was supported by King Bogud of Mauretania and a Catilinarian soldier of fortune, Publius Sittius. After receiving reinforcements from Italy Caesar besieged the seaport Thapsus. Scipio came to the rescue but was completely defeated in a bloody battle near the town. The whole of the province fell into Caesar's hands. Cato, who was in command of Utica, did not force the citizens to resist but committed suicide. Other senatorial leaders, including Juba, either followed his example or were taken and executed by the Caesarians. Caesar returned to Rome, where he celebrated a lavish triumph over Gaul, Egypt, Pharnaces, and Juba. He was now undisputed master of the state and proceeded to settle the problem of governing the Roman world according to his own judgment.

V. Dictatorship of Julius Caesar: 46–44 B.C.

CAESAR'S PROBLEM. From July 28, 46 to March 15, 44, Caesar ruled the Roman Empire with dictatorial powers, his position unchallenged except for a revolt of the Pompeian party in Spain, which required his attention from the autumn of 46 to the spring of 45. His victory over Pompey and the Optimates obliged him to provide the Empire with a stable form of government, and this responsibility he accepted. Sulla, when faced with the same problem, had been content to place the Senate once more at the head of the state. From his own experience Caesar knew how futile this policy would be. Neither could the ideal of Pompey commend itself as a means of ending civil war and rebellion. Caesar was prepared to deal much more radically with the old regime, although death overtook him before he could complete his reorganization. The goal of his policy will be understood best from a consideration of his official position during the year and a half following the battle of Thapsus.

HIS OFFICES, POWERS, AND HONORS. Caesar's autocratic position rested ultimately upon the support of his veterans, of the associates who owed their advancement to him, and of such small forces as he kept under arms; it was legalized by his tenure of various offices, special powers, and unusual honors. Foremost among his offices was the dictatorship. He had already held this for a short time in 49 and again in 47. In 46 he was appointed dictator for ten years, in the following year for life. Simultaneously he was consul, an office which he held continuously from 48, usually with a colleague but as sole consul in 45. In addition to these offices he enjoyed the personal inviolability of the tribunes of the plebs and the right to sit with them on certain public occasions. It is unlikely that he received the full powers of the tribunician authority (*tribunicia potestas*) as the historian Cassius Dio suggests. He had been Pontifex Maximus, the head of the state religious organization, since 63 and in 48 was admitted to all the patrician priestly corporations. In 46 he was given the powers of the censorship under the title of "prefect of morals" (*praefectus morum*), at first for three years and later for life. In addition to these official positions of more or less established scope, Caesar received other powers not dependent upon any office. He was granted the right to appoint to both Roman and provincial magistracies, until in 44 he had the authority to nominate half the officials annually, and in reality appointed all. In 48 he received power to make war and peace without consulting the Senate, in 46 the right of expressing his opinion first in the Senate (*ius primae sententiae*), and in 45 the sole right to command troops and to control the public moneys. The next year advance ratification was given to all his future arrangements, and magistrates entering upon office were required to swear to uphold his acts. Concentration of these powers in his person placed Caesar above the law and reduced the holders of public offices to the position of his servants. Honors to match his extraordinary powers were heaped upon him, partly by his own desire, partly by the servility and fulsome flattery of the Senate. He was granted a seat with the consuls in the Senate, when not consul himself; he received the title of parent or father of his country (*parens* or *pater patriae*); his statue was placed among those of the kings of Rome, his image was placed in the temple of Quirinus; the month Quintilis, in which he was born, was renamed Julius (July) in his honor; a new college of priests, the Julian Luperci, was created; a temple was erected to Caesar's Clemency and a priest (flamen) appointed for the worship there; and he was authorized to build a house on the Palatine with a pediment like a temple. Most of these honors he received after his victory over the Pompeians in Spain in 45. The title *imperator* (Emperor), however, which was regularly the prerogative of a general entitled to a triumph and was surrendered along with his military *imperium*, was employed by Caesar continuously from 49 until after the battle of Thapsus in 46, when he celebrated his triumph over the Gauls and other non-Roman enemies. He assumed it again after Munda the following year.

CAESAR'S AIM: MONARCHY. Taking into account the powers Caesar wielded and his lifelong tenure of certain offices, there can be no doubt that he intended to establish autocratic government of some kind at Rome. It has been alleged that Caesar wished to transplant to Rome a Hellenistic type of kingship, in which the monarch sought justification for his autocracy through deification. There is, however, no convincing evidence that this was so, and the exalted honors he received, although unprecedented, are explicable within the Roman tradition. That ultimately he would have dared to assume the title "rex," which was anathema to the Roman upper class, is more doubtful. At the time of the Latin festival in January, 44, some of the mob actually hailed Caesar as "rex," and at the feast of the Lupercalia in February, Antony publicly offered him a diadem, which he ostentatiously refused. Monarchy, of whatever form, implies succession, but Caesar had made no plans along such lines before his sudden death.

CAESAR'S REFORMS. Upon his return to Rome after the battle of Thapsus, Caesar began a series of reforms that affected practically every side of Roman life and reveal an astonishing versatility and competence on the part of their author. One of the most useful of these was the reform of the calendar, which he carried out in his capacity of Pontifex Maximus. Hitherto the Romans had used a lunar year of 355 days, with its New Year's Day originally on March 1, after 153, for civil purposes at least, on January 1.[2] It had been customary to correct this lunar year approximately to the solar year by adding an intercalary month of 22 days in the second, and one of 23 days in the fourth year of each successive four-year period. For personal or political reasons the pontiffs in recent years had neglected to make the necessary intercalations, so that in 46 the Roman year was over two months ahead of the solar year. By adding the requisite number of days to the year 46, Caesar brought the Roman calendar back into harmony with solar time. He then introduced a new calendar, worked out by the Greek astronomer Sosigenes of Alexandria, and this went into effect on January 1, 45. It was based on the Egyptian solar year of $365\frac{1}{4}$ days and provided for cycles of four years of which the first three had 365 days each, and the fourth or "leap" year 366 days with an extra day added in February after the 24th of the month.[3]

Abuse of the grain dole was partially rectified by the reduction of the number of recipients from about 320,000 to 150,000. This decrease was made possible in part by establishing many poor persons in colonial settlements, in part by excluding those not really dependent upon the dole for their livelihood. In the interests of public order, Caesar dissolved the plebeian colleges and guilds, with the exception of the ancient associations of craftsmen. Many of them had become political clubs and contributed to the recent disturbances in the city. The composition of the juries was changed by the removal of the tribunes of the treasury, but the reason for this is not clear. The penalties for criminal offences were increased. Caesar also laid plans for a much-needed codification of the Roman law, but these were not carried into effect. To meet administrative needs and to have more positions at his disposal to reward his supporters, he increased the number of quaestorships from twenty to forty and the praetorships from eight to sixteen. There was a corresponding increase in the number of the public

---

[2] The religious year which regulated festivals and the like had also come to be reckoned from January 1 at some date prior to Caesar's reform.

[3] This Julian calendar, as it came to be called, survived the Roman Empire and remained the calendar of the Christian world until it was corrected, at the orders of Pope Gregory XIII, in 1582 by the omission of ten days then and of three intercalary days in every 400-year period since, as the Julian year was about eleven minutes longer than the true solar year.

priesthoods. Pompey's law requiring provincial governors to be selected from ex-magistrates who had been five years out of office was disregarded, and a new law restricted proconsular governors to terms of two years and propraetorian governors to terms of one year. A number of plebeian families was elevated to patrician status to take the place of patrician clans that had died out and to furnish holders of patrician priesthoods. The number of senators was raised from five or six hundred to nine hundred, the new members being recruited from Caesar's partisans, including Italian equestrians, his veteran officers, and adherents from the western provinces upon whom he had bestowed the franchise. Thereby he sought to strengthen his political faction in the way traditional to Roman politicians. As early as 48 and again in 46 he relieved a financial crisis by measures that alleviated debtors' burdens, but he also protected creditors from incurring too heavy losses. With the object of obtaining more land for agricultural purposes, he planned to drain the Pomptine marshes in Latium and the Fucine lake in the Marsic country. To minimize the danger from rural slaves, he required at least one third of shepherds and herdsmen to be persons of free birth. Other projects he did not live to carry out were the construction of a new highway across the Apennines to the Adriatic coast and the improvement of the harbor at Ostia, both of primary commercial importance.

Caesar's reorganization of local government throughout Italy was a reform of fundamental importance. This was accomplished by a series of laws, some of which did not come into effect until after his death. As the result of the creation of new municipal centers in rural districts, all of Italy was divided into municipal areas, each consisting of a town and the territory dependent upon it for local administration. Local autonomy of a uniform type was conferred upon these communities, irrespective of their origin as colonies or as *municipia*. Each was governed by a board of locally elected magistrates, whose functions were the same everywhere although their titles might differ, and by a council recruited primarily from ex-magistrates. The development of municipal autonomy in Italy removed a heavy burden from the Roman magistrates, in particular the praetors, and laid the basis for the later extension of the municipal system throughout the provinces.

COLONIZATION. Caesar carried out a broad program of colonization that revealed a keen appreciation of economic needs and was also significant for the future relationship between Italy and the provinces. He provided for many of his veterans by settling them in Italy on properties he had confiscated from enemies who had fallen in battle or refused to be reconciled to him. In so doing he did not found any new colonies or upset any existing municipal organizations, so that there was no serious disturbance of the agricultural population as a result of these land grants. Many others received lands in the provinces, particularly in Narbonese Gaul and Africa, where they either formed the nuclei of new colonies or augmented the population of earlier foundations. Colonial settlements were also founded in the provinces with colonists drawn from the urban proletariat of Rome, who were more fitted for commercial and industrial occupations than for farming. It is reported that some 80,000 of the city populace were cared for in this way. Many of these colonies were seaports, like Sinope and Heraclea on the Black Sea, Corinth, where Caesar proposed to dig a canal through the Isthmus, and Carthage, where he successfully revived the project of Gaius Gracchus. Many colonies arose in Spain, partly through conferment of colonial rights upon communities that had supported Caesar loyally and partly through actual colonization. Among communities of the latter sort was the colony at Urso, made up of freedmen from Rome who settled on a site confiscated from its Pompeian inhabitants. A large part of the charter of this colony is extant[4] and corresponds closely to the municipal government Caesar had organized in Italy. The widespread establishment of Roman colonies, the generous conferment of Roman citizenship upon individual provincials, and the liberal granting of Latin rights in Narbonese Gaul as a preliminary step to Roman status—all indicate that Caesar envisaged the possibility of a future Roman Empire based on uniform Roman citizenship.

MUNDA: 45 B.C. Caesar was a magnanimous conqueror. No Sullan proscriptions disgraced his victory. After Pharsalus he permitted all the republican leaders who submitted (among them Cicero) to return to Rome. Even after Thapsus, at the intercession of his friends he pardoned bitter foes like Marcus Marcellus, one of the consuls of 51. There remained some irreconcilables, led by his old lieutenant Labienus, Varus, and Gnaeus and Sextus Pompey, sons of Pompey the Great, who fled after Pharsalus with a small naval force to the western Mediterranean. In 46 they were joined by Labienus and Varus and landed in Spain, where they rallied to their cause the old Pompeian soldiers who had entered Caesar's service but who had been alienated by his *legatus*, Quintus Cassius. The Caesarian commanders could make no headway against them, and it became necessary for the dictator to campaign in person. In December, 46, he set out for Spain. Throughout the winter he tried vainly to force the enemy to battle. In March, 45 the two armies met at Munda, where Caesar's eight defeated thirteen Pompeian legions. The Caesarians gave no quarter, and the Pompeian forces were annihilated. Labienus and Varus fell on the field, Gnaeus Pompey was later taken and executed, but his brother Sextus escaped. Caesar returned to Italy in September 45, and celebrated a triumph.

ASSASSINATION OF JULIUS CAESAR: MARCH 15, 44 B.C. His victory at Munda had strengthened Caesar's autocratic position and was responsible for the granting of most of the exceptional honors that have been noted. It was now clear at Rome that Caesar did not intend to restore the Republic which he made no bones about calling a sham. In the conduct of government he allowed no freedom to either Senate or Assembly, and,

---

[4] The *Lex Coloniae Genetivae Iuliae*.

although in general mild and forgiving, he was quick to resent any attempt to slight him or question his authority. The realization that Caesar contemplated establishing an autocracy aroused bitter animosity among many of the old governing oligarchy, who chafed under the restraints imposed upon them by his autocratic power and resented degradation of the Senate to the position of a mere advisory council. It could hardly be expected that the Roman aristocracy, with all their traditions of imperial government, would tamely submit to being excluded from political life except as ministers of an autocrat who was until lately one of themselves. This attitude was shared by many who had hitherto been active in Caesar's cause, as well as by republicans who had been reconciled to him. Among these disgruntled elements a conspiracy was formed against the dictator's life. The originator of the plot was the ex-Pompeian Gaius Cassius, whom Caesar had made praetor for 44, and who won over Marcus Junius Brutus, a member of the house descended from that Brutus reputed to have delivered Rome from the Tarquins. Brutus had gone over to Caesar after the battle of Pharsalus and was highly esteemed by him, but Brutus was persuaded that it was his duty to imitate his ancestor's conduct. Other conspirators of note were the Caesarians Gaius Trebonius and Decimus Junius Brutus. In all some sixty senators shared in the conspiracy. They set the Ides of March, 44, as the date for execution of the plot. Caesar was now busily preparing a campaign against the Dacians north of the lower Danube, to be followed by a war against the Parthians, who had been a menace to Syria ever since the defeat of Crassus. This defeat Caesar aimed to avenge and, in addition, definitely to secure the eastern frontier of the Empire. An army of sixteen legions and ten thousand cavalry was being assembled in Greece for this campaign, and Caesar was about to leave Rome to assume command. He is said to have been informed that a conspiracy against his life was under way but to have disregarded the warning. He had dismissed his bodyguard of soldiers and refused one of senators and equestrians. On the fatal day he entered the Senate chamber, where the question of granting him the title of king in the provinces was to be discussed. A group of the conspirators surrounded him and, drawing concealed daggers, stabbed him to death. He fell at the foot of Pompey's statue.

ESTIMATE OF CAESAR'S CAREER. Roman writers who preserved the republican tradition honored Brutus, Cassius, and their associates as tyrannicides who tried to save the Republic in the name of liberty. Cato, who died rather than witness the triumph of Caesar, became their hero. This is an extremely narrow and partisan view. The Republic Caesar had overthrown was no popular government but one of a small group of Roman nobles and capitalists who exploited for their own personal ends and for an idle city mob millions of subjects in the provinces. The republican organs of government had ceased to voice the opinion even of the whole Roman citizenry. Governing circles had proven incapable of improving the situation and had completely lost the power of preserving peace. Radical reforms were imperative and could be effected only with superior force. In his resort to corruption and violence in furthering his own career and in his appeal to arms to decide the issue between himself and the Senate, Caesar must be judged according to the practices of his time. Except in degree, his ambition and drive for prestige and *dignitas* was typical of the senatorial class in that intensely political age, and he advanced himself, of necessity, by the means his predecessors and contemporaries employed. Although, strangely enough, he did not appear so to contemporaries, Caesar deserves to rank as one of the most fascinating and genial personalities in Roman history and, indeed, in the whole course of Western civilization. He was at once in the front rank among Roman writers, statesmen, and generals. In war he was equally remarkable as a tactician and a strategist, and in political life he displayed a similar capacity to develop a general plan of action and to manage the details of party conflicts. He was by no means an opportunist but formulated his comprehensive policies long in advance and worked consistently towards their realization. Better than any others of his time he appreciated the general political tendencies of the age, and more than any of his rivals he contributed towards shaping and guiding these tendencies. Although he was ruthless and cold-blooded in pursuing his ends and maintained an aristocratic aloofness in all his relations, his personal charm enabled him to create a remarkable *esprit de corps* among his troops and evoked a corresponding loyalty and solidarity among his political adherents. His family connections and the character of his genius led him to seek *dignitas* with the popular party; but this did not involve his adherence to democratic principles of government, and the autocratic ideal he strove to realize toward the close of his life was the logical outgrowth of the power and independence he enjoyed in his proconsular command. His supreme courage and self-confidence are revealed in his acceptance of the responsibility for guiding the destinies of the civilized world and in his attempt to do away with the old order and to set up a new regime that promised to give peace and security both to Roman citizens and provincials. Caesar fell because he was too open and direct in assuming autocratic powers. In spite of his great capacities as statesman and politician, he had been unable to build up a faction that would embrace all the influential elements in the state, especially the senatorial oligarchy, without which Rome could not be governed. After Caesar some form of monarchical government was inevitable, but a successful successor to Caesar would have to be more devious and gradual in establishing one-man rule. Above all, he would have to reconcile the oligarchy to such rule, as Caesar had failed to do, by proclaiming, not that the Republic was a sham, but rather that it was being restored.

GROWTH OF THE ROMAN EMPIRE

265 B.C. — 44 B.C.

Allied States indicated thus: **EGYPT**

0	100	200	300	400	500	600

Miles

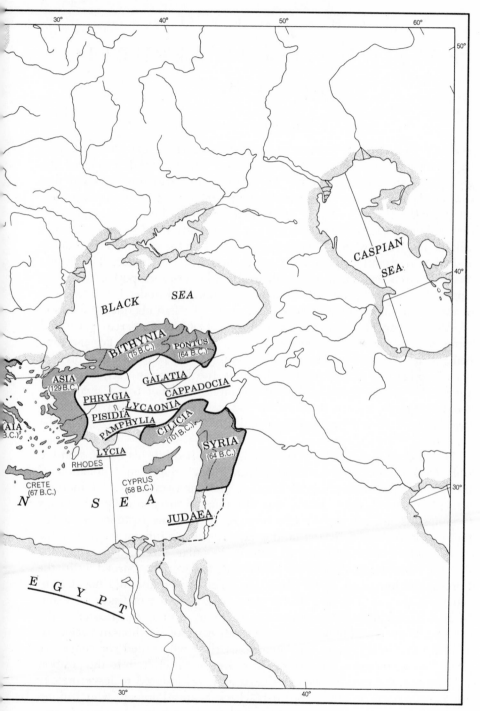

CASPIAN
SEA

BLACK   SEA

BITHYNIA
(75 B.C.)   PONTUS
(64 B.C.)

ASIA   GALATIA
(129 B.C.)   CAPPADOCIA

PHRYGIA
LYCAONIA
PISIDIA
PAMPHYLIA   CILICIA
(101 B.C.)

LYCIA   SYRIA
(64 B.C.)

RHODES

CRETE   CYPRUS
(67 B.C.)   (58 B.C.)

JUDAEA

N   S E A

E   G   Y   P   T

CHAPTER 15

PASSING OF THE REPUBLIC: 44–27 B.C.

I. Rise of Octavian

POLITICAL SITUATION AFTER CAESAR'S DEATH. Caesar had made no arrangements for a successor, and his death produced the greatest consternation in Rome. The conspirators evidently expected that control of affairs would revert back to the Senate. Instead of finding their act greeted with an outburst of popular approval, however, they found that, although Caesar was dead, the Caesarian party lived on in his former officers, his veterans, and the city populace, led by the consul Mark Antony and Marcus Aemilius Lepidus, Caesar's master of the horse. The Senate met on March 17, and it was evident that a majority supported the assassins, but they were afraid of the legion Lepidus had under his orders and of the Caesarian veterans in the city. Antony, who had obtained possession of Caesar's papers and money, took the lead of the Caesarian party and came to terms with its opponents. His actions are revealing. For the time being at least he had no quarrel with them, provided they did not prevent his consolidating his position as head of the Caesarian faction. It was agreed that the conspirators should go unpunished but that Caesar's acts should be ratified, even those which had not yet been carried into effect, that his will should be approved, and that he should receive a public funeral.

The reading of Caesar's will revealed that he had left his gardens on the right bank of the Tiber as a public park, had bequeathed a donation of three hundred sesterces (about fifteen dollars or two and a half months' wages) to each Roman citizen, and had adopted his grandnephew, Gaius Octavius, as his son and heir to three-fourths of his fortune. Although the oration Antony delivered on the day of Caesar's funeral seems to have been mild, it was sufficient to inflame popular sentiment against the dictator's murderers. The mob seized Caesar's corpse, burned it in the Forum, and buried the ashes there. The chief conspirators did not dare to remain in the city. Decimus Brutus went to his province of Cisalpine Gaul, Marcus Brutus and Cassius lingered near Rome. Antony was master of the capital and overawed opposition by his bodyguard of six thousand veterans. He held in check Lepidus and other Caesarians who called for vengeance upon the conspirators. Lepidus was won over by his election to the position of Pontifex Maximus to succeed Caesar and was induced to leave the city for his province of Hither Spain to check Sextus Pompey, who had reappeared in Farther Spain and defeated the Caesarian governor. It was hoped that Sextus would be satisfied with permission to return to Rome and compensation for his father's property. Caesar's arrangements for the provincial governorships had assigned Macedonia to Antony and Syria to Dolabella, who became Antony's colleague in the consulate at Caesar's death. This assignment Antony altered by a law granting him Cisalpine Gaul and the Transalpine district outside Gallia Narbonensis for a term of six years, in violation of a law of Caesar's, which limited proconsular commands to two years. Dolabella was to have Syria for a like period, and Decimus Brutus was given Macedonia in exchange for Cisalpine Gaul. The consuls were to occupy their provinces at once. To Brutus and Cassius for the next year were assigned the provinces of Crete and Cyrene; for the present they were given a special commission to collect grain in Sicily and Asia. The two left Italy for the East, however, with the intention of seizing Macedonia and Syria. Although Antony showed no signs as yet of following Caesar's path to absolute power, for their own protection they needed force to balance his.

OCTAVIAN. Antony found an unexpected rival in Caesar's adopted son, Gaius Octavius, a sickly but able youth of eighteen years. At the time of Caesar's death he was at Apollonia in Illyricum with an army being assembled for the Parthian war. From the very beginning Octavius showed determination, ruthlessness, and ambition equal to that of his adoptive father. He aimed at one goal: leadership of the Caesarian faction, and he coolly contemplated the struggle with Antony that would result. Against his family's advice, he returned to Rome and claimed his inheritance. Antony, who was not about to help a rival, had spent Caesar's money and refused to refund it. Octavius began the creation of a Caesarian party of his own. Lacking influential family connections, he made good Caesarian legacies to citizens and veterans by selling property, by borrowing, and by dispersing the Caesarian war chest he had commandeered upon landing at Brundisium. Gradually he acquired a following, especially among equestrian financial interests. In spite of delays caused by Antony, his adoption was legalized the next year, and he assumed the magic name of Caesar.[1]

Antony clearly underestimated the cunning ambition of this youth, although he soon became aware of his mistake. He himself was anxious to occupy his province of Cisalpine Gaul. When Decimus Brutus refused to evacuate it, Antony determined to drive him out, and he obtained permission to recall the four legions from Macedonia for that purpose. Before their arrival Octavian, acting without any authority, raised a force among Caesar's veterans in Campania, and two of the four Macedonian legions deserted to him on the march from Brundisium to Rome. The Caesarians

---

[1] After the adoption his full name was Gaius Julius Caesar Octavianus. Although he was known as Caesar by his contemporaries, it is more convenient to refer to him henceforth as Octavian, to distinguish him from his adoptive father.

were now divided into two parties, and Octavian began to cooperate with
the republicans in the Senate, since the backing of senior statesmen would
increase his own authority. The latter were thus encouraged to oppose
Antony, with whom reconciliation was impossible for them in any case.
Cicero, who was not among the conspirators but who had subsequently
approved Caesar's murder, was on his way to join Brutus when he heard
of the changed situation in Rome, and he returned to assume the leadership
of the republican party. Antony left Rome for the Cisalpine province early
in December, 44, and Cicero induced the Senate to ally with Octavian
against him. In his *Philippic Orations* he gave full vent to his bitter hatred
of Antony and aroused the latter's undying enmity.

WAR AT MUTINA: DECEMBER, 44–APRIL, 43 B.C. In
Cisalpine Gaul Decimus Brutus, relying upon the support of the Senate,
refused to yield to Antony. He was blockaded in Mutina, and the Senate
made preparations for his relief. Antony was ordered to leave the province,
and Hirtius and Pansa, who became consuls in January, 43, took the field
against him. The aid of Octavian was indispensable, and the Senate conferred upon him the propraetorian *imperium* with consular rank in the
Senate. The combined armies defeated Antony in two battles in the vicinity
of Mutina, forcing him to give up the siege and flee toward Transalpine
Gaul. Pansa died of wounds received in the first engagement, and Hirtius
fell in the course of the second. Ignoring Octavian, the Senate entrusted
Brutus with the command and the task of pursuing Antony. The power of
the Senate seemed reestablished, for Marcus Brutus and Cassius had succeeded in their design of gaining control of the eastern provinces, Dolabella
having perished in the conflict, and they were at the head of a considerable
military and naval force. The Senate conferred upon them supreme military
authority (*maius imperium*) in the East and gave to Sextus Pompey, then
at Massilia, a naval command. At last Cicero could induce the senators to
declare Antony a public enemy. He no longer felt the support of Octavian
a necessity and expressed the attitude of the Optimates toward him in
saying "the young man is to be praised, to be honored, to be set aside."[2]
It was soon evident that the experienced orator had entirely misjudged this
young man who, so far from being a tool of the Senate, had used that body
for his own ends. Octavian refused to aid Decimus Brutus and demanded
from the Senate his own appointment as consul, a triumph, and rewards
for his troops. His demands were rejected, whereupon he marched upon
Rome and occupied the city. On August 19 he had himself elected consul
with Quintus Pedius as colleague. The latter carried a bill establishing a
special court for the trial of Caesar's murderers, who were condemned and
banished. The same penalty was pronounced upon Sextus Pompey. The
Senate's decree against Antony was revoked and the way was open for a

---

[2] *Laudandum adulescentem, ornandum, tollendum,* Cicero, Fam., xi, 20, 1.

possible reconciliation between Octavian and Antony, whose ambitions could only be furthered by an antisenatorial coalition.

II. Triumvirate of 43 B.C.

ANTONY, OCTAVIAN, AND LEPIDUS. On his way to Trans-alpine Gaul Antony met Lepidus, whom the Senate had summoned from Spain to assist Decimus Brutus. Lepidus was a Caesarian and, alarmed by the success of Marcus Brutus and Cassius, allowed his troops to go over to Antony. Decimus Brutus, in pursuit of Antony, joined forces with Plancus, governor of Narbonese Gaul. Upon news of the events in Rome, Plancus abandoned Brutus and joined Antony. Brutus was deserted by his troops and killed while fleeing in Gaul. Antony and Lepidus now marched upon Italy.

Octavian had taken care to have the defense of Italy entrusted to himself and hastened north to meet their advance. Both sides were ready to come to terms and unite their forces to crush their common enemies, Brutus and Cassius. At a conference of the three leaders on an island in the river Renus near Bononia, a reconciliation between Antony and Octavian was effected and plans laid for their cooperation in the immediate future. The three decided to have themselves appointed triumvirs for the settlement of the commonwealth (*triumviri reipublicae constituendae*) for a term of five years. They were to have consular *imperium* with the right to appoint magistrates, and their acts were to be valid without the approval of the Senate. They divided among themselves the western provinces: Antony received those previously assigned to him; Lepidus took the Spains and Narbonese Gaul, while to Octavian fell Sardinia, Sicily, and Africa. Octavian was to resign his consulship but in the next year was to be joint commander with Antony in a campaign against the republican armies in the East while Lepidus protected Rome. The triumvirate was legalized by a tribunician law (*the lex Titia*) of November 27, 43, and they entered office formally the first of January following. Unlike the secret coalition of Pompey, Crassus, and Caesar, the present one constituted a commission clothed with almost supreme public powers.

THE TRIUMVIRS IN ITALY. Formation of the coalition was followed by proscription of the enemies of the triumvirs, partly for the sake of vengeance but largely to secure money for their troops from the confiscation of the properties of the proscribed. Among the chief victims was Cicero, whose death Antony demanded. He died with courage for the republican ideal to which he was devoted, but it must be recognized that this devotion was to the cause of a corrupt oligarchy, whose crimes he refused to share, although he forced himself to condone and justify them. The exactions of the triumvirs did not end with the confiscation of the goods of the proscribed. Special taxes were laid upon the propertied classes in Italy, and eighteen of the most flourishing Italian municipalities were marked out as sites for veterans' colonies.

In 42 Octavian dedicated a temple to Julius Caesar in the forum where his body had been burned. Later by a special law Caesar was elevated among the gods of the state with the name of Divus Julius. Meanwhile Octavian found difficulty in occupying his allotted provinces. Africa was eventually conquered by one of his lieutenants, but Sextus Pompey, who controlled the sea, had occupied Sardinia and Sicily. His forces were augmented by many of the proscribed and by adventurers, and Octavian could not dislodge him before setting out against Brutus and Cassius.

PHILIPPI: 42 B.C.   These republican generals had raised an army of 80,000 Romans, in addition to allied contingents, and taken up a position in Thrace to await the triumvirs. In the summer of 42 the latter transported their troops across the Adriatic, in spite of their enemies' fleet, and the two armies faced each other near Philippi on the borders of Macedonia and Thrace. An indecisive battle was fought. Antony defeated Cassius, who committed suicide, but the troops of Brutus routed those of Octavian, who was incapacitated by illness. Shortly afterwards Brutus was forced by his soldiers to risk another battle. This time they were completely defeated, and Brutus took his own life.

DIVISION OF THE EMPIRE.   The two victorious triumvirs now redistributed the western provinces. Lepidus, whom they suspected of intrigues with Sextus Pompey and whose hostility they could now risk, was for the time left out of consideration. Cisalpine Gaul, because of its strategic situation, was not assigned to anyone but ceased to be a province and was annexed to Italy, whose political boundaries at length coincided with its geographical frontiers. The whole of Transalpine Gaul was given to Antony; Octavian received the two Spains, Sardinia, and Africa on the understanding that he would turn over Africa to Lepidus if his conduct warranted it. From the time of the meeting near Bononia Antony had been the chief of the coalition, and his prestige was enhanced by his success at Philippi. It was now agreed that he should settle conditions in the eastern provinces and raise funds there, while Octavian should return to Italy and assign the promised lands to their troops. This decision was of momentous consequence for the future. In the summer of 41 Antony officially summoned Cleopatra to Tarsus in Cilicia to demand money of her. He had probably known her when she had been Caesar's mistress. She now became his, but there is no indication that Antony was madly in love with her. He followed her to Egypt that winter, but he left soon thereafter, and the two did not meet again for four years.

OCTAVIAN IN ITALY: 42–40 B.C.   In Italy Octavian was confronted with the task of providing lands for some 170,000 veterans. The eighteen municipalities previously selected for this purpose proved insufficient, and a general confiscation of small holdings took place, whereby many persons were rendered homeless and destitute. A few, like the poet

Virgil, found compensation through the influence of a powerful patron. Confiscations, following close on the heels of the proscription, only further embittered Octavian's relations with the propertied classes, especially the senatorial oligarchy, which regarded him as a pitiless and opportunistic revolutionary. His administration was also greatly hampered by opposition from the friends of Antony, led by the latter's wife Fulvia and his brother Lucius Antonius. Hostilities broke out in which Lucius was besieged in Perusia and starved into submission (40). Fulvia went to join Antony, while others of their faction fled to Sextus Pompey, who still held Sicily. Of great importance to Octavian was his acquisition of Gaul, which came into his hands through the death of Antony's legate, Calenus. He could now safely turn over Africa with a considerable garrison to his colleague Lepidus. An indication of an approaching break between Octavian and Antony was the former's divorce of his wife Clodia, a step-daughter of Antony and his marriage with Scribonia, a relative of Sextus Pompey, whom he hoped to win over.

TREATY OF BRUNDISIUM: 40 B.C. While Octavian was involved in the Perusian war, the Parthians had overrun the province of Syria, and, in conjunction with them, Quintus Labienus, a follower of Brutus and Cassius, penetrated Asia Minor as far as the Aegean coast. Antony thereupon returned in haste to Italy to restore his waning influence there and to gather troops to reestablish Roman authority in the East. Both he and Octavian were prepared for war, and hostilities began around Brundisium, which refused to admit Antony. At the insistence of the soldiers in both armies, however, a reconciliation was effected, and an agreement known as the Treaty of Brundisium was made. It provided that Octavian should have Spain, Gaul, Sardinia, Sicily, and Dalmatia, while Antony should hold the Roman possessions east of the Ionian Sea. Lepidus retained Africa, and Italy was held in common. To cement the alliance Antony, whose wife Fulvia had died, married Octavia, sister of Octavian.

TREATY OF MISENUM: 39 B.C. The following year Antony and Octavian were forced to come to terms with Sextus Pompey. He still defiantly held Sicily and had wrested Sardinia from Octavian. His command of these islands and of the seas about Italy enabled him to cut off the grain supply of Rome, where famine broke out. This brought about a meeting of the three at Misenum, in which it was agreed that Sextus should govern Sardinia, Sicily, and Achaea for five years, should be consul and augur, and receive a monetary compensation for his father's property in Rome. In return he engaged to secure peace at sea and convoy the grain supply for the city. The terms of the treaty were never fully carried out, however, and in the next year Octavian and Sextus were again at war. The former regained possession of Sardinia but failed signally in an attack upon Sicily (38).

TREATY OF TARENTUM: 37 B.C. In 39 Antony returned to the East, where the Illyrians were threatening the Macedonian frontier and the Parthians still occupied Asia Minor and Syria. One of his generals won a decisive victory over the Illyrians; another drove Labienus out of Asia Minor, recovered Syria, and repelled a second Parthian inroad. In 38 Antony returned to Italy at the request of Octavian, who was alarmed at the activities of Sextus Pompey. Octavian did not arrive in time for the meeting, and Antony did not wait for him. The next year the two triumvirs conferred at Tarentum, since Octavian needed Antony's support after his defeat by Sextus and Antony wanted more Italian troops for his projected invasion of Parthia. Neither trusted the other, but in spite of their mutual suspicions they were formally reconciled by Octavia. They agreed that Antony should supply Octavian with 120 warships for his operations against Sextus, in return for which Octavian should give him four of the legions in Africa. Antony fulfilled his share of the bargain, but not Octavian. Since the power of the triumvirs had legally terminated on December 31, 38, they decided to be reappointed for another five years, until the close of 33. This appointment was perhaps carried into effect by a special law, like the first.

DEFEAT OF SEXTUS POMPEY: 36 B.C. Octavian now energetically attacked Sicily, while Lepidus cooperated by besieging Lilybaeum. At length, in September, 36, Marcus Vipsanius Agrippa, Octavian's ablest general, destroyed the bulk of Sextus' fleet in a battle off Naulochus. Pompey fled to Asia, where two years later he was captured by Antony's forces and executed. After the flight of Sextus, Lepidus challenged Octavian's claim to Sicily, but his troops deserted him for Octavian, and he was forced to throw himself upon the latter's mercy. Stripped of power and retaining only his office of Pontifex Maximus, he lived under guard in an Italian municipality until his death in 12 B.C. His provinces were taken by Octavian. The defeat of Sextus Pompey and the deposition of Lepidus gave Octavian sole power over the western half of the Empire and inevitably tended to sharpen the rivalry and antagonism that had long existed between him and Antony. In the same year Octavian was granted the tribunician sacrosanctity and the right to sit on the tribune's bench in the Senate. Of even greater significance in the long run was his assiduous building up of a political clientele, especially in the years after the Treaty of Brundisium. Not only was he patronizing equestrians and new men, he also openly sought the support of republican oligarchs by furthering their careers. The young revolutionary was clearly trying to reconcile himself to the classes that mattered and was extending his political nexus throughout Italy against the day of possible conflict with Antony.

III. Victory of Octavian

ANTONY'S FAILURE AGAINST PARTHIA. After the treaty of Tarentum, Antony proceeded to Syria to prepare the invasion of Parthia which he began in 36. Avoiding the Mesopotamian desert with its fateful memories of Crassus, he took a more northerly route through Armenia into Media Atropatene, relying upon the support of the Armenian king, Artavasdes. The latter proved false, however, and the Parthians were able to destroy the Roman train of siege engines and their reserve supplies of food. After a vain attempt to reduce the fortress of Praaspa, Antony was obliged to abandon his expedition and save his army by retreating. Although vigorously pursued by the Parthian horsemen, he managed by skilful and courageous generalship to lead most of his troops back to Armenia. His losses amounted to over 20,000 men, and his reputation suffered severely from his complete failure. Without reinforcements from the West it was hopeless for him to think of any further moves against the Parthian Empire. When Octavian returned those of his ships that had survived the naval battles around Sicily without the promised legions, he realized that Octavian planned to cut him off from Italy and that he must reestablish himself in the West or resign himself to a position of inferiority. All that he could do for the moment was to conclude an alliance with a rebellious Parthian vassal, the king of Media Atropatene, and to occupy Armenia, whose king was carried off as a prisoner in punishment for his disloyalty.

ANTONY AND CLEOPATRA. The breach between Antony and Octavian was widened by Antony's connection with Cleopatra. Antony publicly married the Egyptian Queen in Antioch in 37, and after his Parthian defeat he refused Octavia, his legal Roman wife, permission to join him. This was equivalent to an open renunciation of his friendship with Octavian. Although he was certainly emotionally involved with Cleopatra, his marriage may be attributed more to the financial support she brought him from Egypt for his Parthian war than to any blind infatuation. It is not so clear what tangible benefits Cleopatra expected from the connection. Her immediate aim seems to have been the extension of Ptolemaic influence and the revival of her empire. This was the apparent point of a pageant staged at Alexandria in 34. Antony and Cleopatra, the latter in the guise of the goddess Isis,[3] appeared seated high on golden thrones. In an address to the assembled public, Antony proclaimed Cleopatra "Queen of Kings" and ruler of Egypt, Cyprus, Crete, and Coele-Syria. Joint ruler with her as "King of Kings" was her son Ptolemy Caesarion, whom Antony formally recognized as the child of Julius Caesar. The two young sons of Antony and Cleopatra also received royal titles: the elder as King of Armenia, Media, and Parthia; the younger as King of Syria, Phoenicia, and Cilicia. Their daughter, Cleopatra, received Cyrene as her portion. Antony claimed no royal title for himself, but Cleopatra had prompted him to make territorial arrangements that Octavian could repre-

---

[3] As early as 38, while in Athens, Antony had taken the title of New Dionysus, anticipating that he, like the Dionysus of Greek legend, would be a conqueror of Asia. He did not, however, make regular use of this title, nor did he consider that it deified him in the eyes of Romans.

sent as an unpatriotic partition of Rome's eastern provinces made at the behest of a foreign queen.

FINAL BREAK: 32 B.C.   During the years 35 to 33 Octavian carried on a series of victorious campaigns against Illyrian tribes east of the Adriatic Sea, thus keeping his forces in fighting trim and adding to his reputation for courage if not for brilliant leadership. In 33, the news of Antony's acknowledgment of Caesarion as Caesar's son reached Octavian and provoked him to protest against this as he had against Antony's treatment of Octavia. At the same time he gave no satisfactory answer to Antony's request for more troops from Italy and land grants for his veterans. Both principals indulged in a campaign of mutual vilification, in which they were actively supported by their followers. The effect of this propaganda is seen in the confused and contradictory accounts of these years in later historical works. It is extremely difficult, if not impossible, for us to recover an accurate picture of many aspects of the situation. In particular it is impossible to estimate the real worth of Antony, who apparently was both able and worthy of respect, and not the indolent drunkard portrayed in Octavian's propaganda.

The Triumvirate terminated legally at the close of 33. For the next year the two consuls were Antony's nominees. To win support in Rome, Antony had written a letter to the Senate in which he asked approval for all actions and arrangements he had made in the East and offered to surrender his powers as triumvir and restore the old constitution. The consuls were unwilling to divulge the contents of the letter because they feared the effect on public opinion of the request for approval of Antony's grants of kingdoms to Cleopatra and her children. One of them attacked Octavian, however, and only by a tribune's veto was he prevented from introducing a motion that Octavian should surrender his *imperium* at once. Octavian then overawed the Senate by appearing with an armed bodyguard, with interesting results. Both consuls and perhaps a third of the Senate, including numerous and prominent statesmen of republican and Caesarian background, fled to Antony. Antony was clearly no mere adventurer if he could attract such a following, and just as clearly Octavian, in spite of his efforts, had failed to win over many members of the governing establishment. Antony's reply was to divorce Octavia publicly, which would only be interpreted as a declaration of war on her brother. Octavian then produced what he claimed to be Antony's will. There is no way of telling whether it was authentic or not. In any case, the parts that were published were intended to inflame public opinion against Antony and Cleopatra, in particular the ones confirming the dispositions he had made in favor of the Ptolemaic dynasty. Having prepared the way through clever propaganda, Octavian was ready in 32 to take a momentous step to unite the citizenry behind him in the coming conflict and to broaden by extraconstitutional means his political clientele and to transcend all factions. He requested all classes of the Roman citizenry in Italy and the western provinces to give him a personal oath of allegiance in order to become the leader of all factions, *dux partium*. This was done in many places without coercion by his agents. It was this oath of allegiance that provided him with a basis of authority, for the powers of the Triumvirate had lapsed. Fortified by this expression of public confidence, Octavian caused Antony's *imperium* to be abrogated and his designation as consul for 31 to be canceled. Not wishing to appear the instigator of civil strife, Octavian finally proclaimed a *bellum iustum* against Cleopatra.

ACTIUM AND AFTER. In the fall of 33 Antony and Cleopatra began to mobilize their forces at Ephesus. Many of the prominent Romans in Antony's suite objected to Cleopatra, realizing that her presence was adding grist to Octavian's propaganda mill, but she stayed. It was her money that was financing the war. The next year an army of almost 90,000 men and a fleet of five hundred warships were assembled and led across the Aegean to Greece. Since a landing in Italy could not yet be effected, Antony's forces went into winter quarters in the Gulf of Ambracia (32–31). In the spring of 31 Octavian and his general Agrippa crossed the Adriatic with an approximately equal force and confronted their enemies outside the Ambracian Gulf at Actium. Agrippa successfully blockaded Antony's fleet, while Octavian's army was able to cut off Antony's supplies by occupying strategic points on the mainland. Antony's position rapidly worsened. Cleopatra's presence depressed morale, and desertions to Octavian increased. What happened next is uncertain. Antony decided either to fight a decisive battle at Actium or to break the blockade. A naval battle followed, a minor engagement magnified later by Augustan propaganda. For unknown reasons Cleopatra fled the fighting with her treasure ship, and Antony followed her to Egypt. Resistance on land and sea against Octavian promptly collapsed.

The victor advanced slowly eastward and in the summer of 30 began his invasion of Egypt. Antony's attempts at defense were unavailing; his troops deserted to Octavian, who occupied Alexandria. Hearing a rumor that Cleopatra had taken her life, Antony committed suicide. Cleopatra was taken prisoner. Finding that her conqueror was inexorable and that it was impossible for her to save her kingdom for herself or for her children, she followed Antony's example rather than grace Octavian's triumph in Rome. This was probably what the latter had hoped for. He had magnified her part in the struggle in order to solidify Italian opinion behind him, but he had no wish to be held responsible for her execution. Ptolemy Caesarion, however, and Antony's elder son were executed because their lineage made them potential rivals of the victor. The kingdom of Egypt became a province of the Empire. Its treasures reimbursed Octavian for the expenses of his late campaigns and enabled him to distribute the promised bonuses to his veterans. After reestablishing the old provinces and client kingdoms in the East, but on territorial principles already established by Antony, Octavian returned to Rome in 29 and celebrated a three-day triumph over the non-Roman peoples of Europe, Asia, and Africa, whom he or his generals had subjugated during his Triumvirate.

At the age of thirty-three Octavian had made good his claim to the political inheritance of Julius Caesar. His victory over Antony closed the century of civil strife that had begun with the tribunate of Tiberius Gracchus. War and proscriptions had exacted a heavy toll from Romans and Italians; Greece, Macedonia, and Asia had been brought to the verge of ruin; the whole Empire longed for peace. Everywhere Octavian was hailed as savior of the world. The founder of a new golden age, men were ready to worship him as a god.

IV. Society and Intellectual Life in the Last Century of the Republic

UPPER CLASSES. The characteristics of Roman society in the last century of the Republic resulted from trends that were developing earlier as a result of Rome's imperial expansion. The upper classes comprised the senatorial nobility and the equestrians, the former finding their goal in public office, the latter in banking and financial ventures, and both often callously exploiting the subjects of Rome. Provincial investments were the most lucrative forms of business enterprise. Rome had become the financial as well as the political capital of the Mediterranean world, and Roman businessmen flocked to the provinces with ready money to invest for themselves or as agents for others. Many Romans acquired large provincial estates; others exploited mines and forests, undertook public contracts, or acted as bankers. The most profitable of all types of business was moneylending, in particular to client princes and cities where the transactions were large-scale. Senators and magistrates did not hesitate to make such loans personally or through trusted agents, even if in so doing they competed with the equestrians. The provincial rate of interest was 12 percent per year as a rule, although Marcus Brutus made a loan to Salamis in Cyprus at 48 percent and later sought military authority for his agent to enable him to collect the debt.

Generally speaking, luxury and extravagance were noteworthy features of upper-class life during the period. The palaces of the wealthy in Rome were supplemented by villas in the Sabine hills, at watering places on the Campanian coast, and at other attractive points. The word *villa*, originally designating a farmhouse, now meant a country seat equipped with all the conveniences of city life. A large share of the commerce of Italy consisted in the importation of articles of luxury to adorn the town and country houses of the well-to-do. These included statuary, paintings, silverware, tapestries, furniture of rare woods, antiques from Greece, marble columns, and goods dyed with costly Tyrian purple.[4]

Solidarity of family life, which had been the foundation of Roman morality was fast disappearing. In general, wives no longer came under the authority (*manus*) of their husbands upon marriage and so retained control of their properties acquired by inheritance or dowry through guardians appointed from their own families. Consequently women played an increasingly independent and important part in society. In Rome at least, the age was one of changing morals, and divorces were common. At the same time social intercourse was characterized by a high degree of urbanity and the good manners that mark cultured society.

WORKING CLASSES. (*a*) *In Rome.* Of the life of the people who thronged the high tenement houses and narrow streets of Rome we know very little. Until the Assembly was overawed or superseded by armed forces, however, the city populace could not be ignored by the upper classes. Their votes had to be courted by magnificent displays at the public games, by entertainments and largesses, and care had to be taken to provide them with food to prevent their becoming a menace to the peace. Political rivalries led to repeated attempts to bribe the proletariat by increasing and cheapening the monthly grain dole initiated by Gaius Gracchus until, by the time of Caesar's dictatorship, some 320,000 male citizens were receiving public relief entirely at the state's expense. Caesar's colonization projects enabled him to reduce the number on the dole by more than half, but he could only lessen and not abolish this burden on the treasury. During the last century of the Republic this class of citizen pensioners changed in character. A large element therein was no longer of Roman or Italian stock but was composed of the descendants of emancipated slaves or emancipated slaves themselves who, as freedmen (*liberti*), had become Roman citizens. Sulla's 10,000 Cornelii swelled the ranks of this new citizenry, which was a cosmopolitan group representing all the races of the Mediterranean world, in particular those of the East. It is impossible, however, to determine the percentage of freedmen in the population. Still another element came to increase the size of the city: throngs of free aliens who frequented the world's capital to practice their multifarious trades and professions. Among the working classes the scale of living was very low. Unskilled labor possibly received a wage of from 17 to 20 cents per day at the end of the Republic, and the cost of food and lodging consumed about four fifths of a man's earnings. The mild Italian climate made the problem of clothing relatively simple, while the state provided entertainment in connection with the public festivals and games, so that even for the very poor conditions were by no means intolerable.

(*b*) *Throughout Italy.* In spite of the upheavals of civil war, proscriptions, and land confiscations, Italy remained surprisingly prosperous

---

[4] Actually a shade of red.

during the last century of the Republic. This is explained, at least in part, by the fact that Italy throughout the period continued to import wealth and tribute from the provinces. The status of Italian rural labor is rather obscure. It is sometimes alleged that the Gracchan land reforms and successive redistributions of land in favor of the veterans of revolutionary armies redressed partially the previous buildup of *latifundia*. It seems more likely, however, that the yeomanry was still declining throughout the period. The Gracchan settlement had proved abortive, since economic conditions were working against the small farmer. Veterans' resettlement probably replaced other proprietors of middling substance, while *latifundia* were actually formed in some cases to reward leaders of dominant factions during periods of proscription. Free labor existed on Italian farms and ranches, certainly, since the legislation of Julius Caesar required that one third of ranch labor be free. Some free labor was contracted for use at harvest time as a supplement to servile hands. The use of free labor as *coloni* or tenant farmers was probably more widespread than it appears in surviving sources. These tenants lived on small leaseholds into which the great estates were divided. For obvious reasons they became clients of their landlords.

ROME THE CITY. The age of the civil wars saw many changes and developments in the appearance of Rome. Two new aqueducts, the Tepula in 125 and the Julia in 33, supplied the needs of the still-growing population. New and superior building materials came into extensive use. In place of the old soft volcanic *tufa*, the creamy white limestone called *travertine* was largely employed from the second century in the construction of public buildings. The Romans had been developing the use of concrete since the third century; now they applied its use to ever more grandiose interpretations of Hellenistic styles. The exterior surfaces of concrete structures were regularly faced with stone, at first with small irregular fragments (*opus incertum*) and later with carefully cut square or lozenge-shaped pieces arranged to form a network pattern (*opus reticulatum*). Toward the close of the period it had become the fashion to veneer the faces of buildings with slabs of travertine or marble. Sulla, Pompey, and Julius Caesar were among those who improved the appearance of Rome by erecting new and imposing public edifices. Caesar also planned to rebuild the city extensively but had to leave these plans to be carried out in part by Augustus. Sulla commenced the reconstruction of the Capitolium or temple of Jupiter Capitolinus, which had been burned in 83, and Pompey erected on the Campus Martius Rome's first permanent theater (55). Another important building was the Tabularium or Public Record Office completed on the west side of the Forum by Quintus Catulus, the consul of 78. Its ruins are the most striking example of republican architecture found in Rome today. Rome suffered heavily from great fires, of which seven are recorded for this period. In spite of the addition

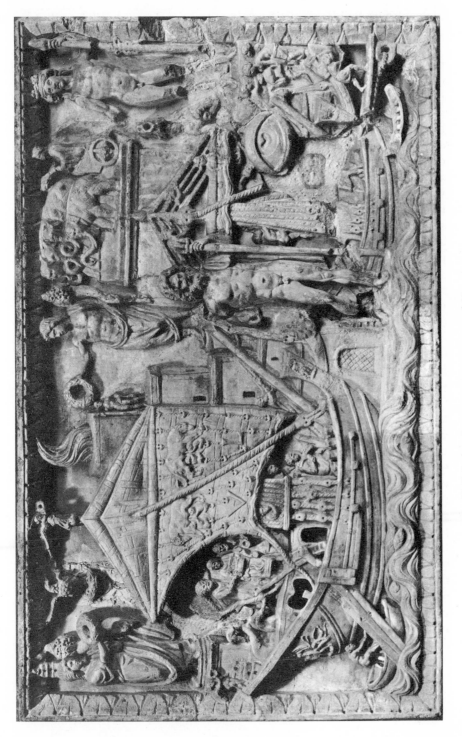

Relief showing commerce at port of Rome

of many fine buildings it still presented a comparatively drab and unimpressive appearance compared to the larger cities of the Greek East.

ART.   The interest of Romans in works of art, evidenced as early as the third and second centuries B.C., increased in the first. Greek influence continued paramount, as the Romans demanded copies of Greek masterpieces of painting and sculpture. The artists who executed such works were almost all Greek, and the mechanical copying of sculpture was facilitated by the use of pointing machines. Greek influence was no less noticeable in the minor arts like pottery, glassware, and jewelry. The last century of the Republic also saw an increase in the plastic decoration of tombs and especially in the production of portrait sculpture. The latter betrays what is generally described as a typical Roman desire for photographic realism, which may have its roots in native Etruscan or Italic art. The sculptors who made these portraits were Greek, however, and Hellenistic canons were also realistic, if more idealized, so that this portrait style was probably an adaptation of Greek canons to Roman taste.

RELIGION.   This period witnessed a striking decline of interest in religion and of faith in the public or official cults of the state. This was in part due to Greek mythology, which changed the current conceptions of Roman divinities, and to Greek philosophy, with its varying doctrines on the nature and powers of the gods. The latter especially affected the upper classes of society, upon whom fell the duty of maintaining the public cults. Throughout the period many priesthoods declined in importance; those that kept their prestige did so only because they could be used for political purposes. An increase in the numbers of priestly colleges and the substitution of election for cooptation brought in many members unversed in the ancient traditions, and the holders of the priesthoods in general showed great ignorance of their duties, especially with regard to the state calendar. Some religious associations, like the Arval Brotherhood, ceased to exist, and knowledge of some of the minor deities was completely lost. Some patrician priesthoods, involving serious duties and restricting the freedom of their incumbents, were avoided as much as possible. At the same time the private religious rites, hereditary within family groups, decayed. While the attitude of educated circles toward the state cults was thus indifferent or skeptical, it is hard to tell about that of the common people. They probably cared little about the religious content of the state cults. It is to this period that may be attributed the first gravestone inscriptions indicating Roman belief in an afterlife. Orgiastic and emotional religions from the East appealed to all classes and took root in spite of general hostility to them on the part of the authorities.

STOICISM AND EPICUREANISM.   The philosophic systems making most converts among educated Romans were Stoicism and Epicureanism. The former had been introduced to Rome by Panaetius, whose teaching was continued by Posidonius. It appealed to the Romans as a practical rule of life for men in public affairs. On the other hand, the doctrine of Epicurus that men should withdraw from the annoyances of political life and seek happiness in pleasure, that is, intellectual pleasure, was interpreted by Romans as sanctioning sensual indulgence and became the creed of those who adopted a life of ease and indolence.

EDUCATION. Education from the time of the Gracchi to the age of Cicero and Caesar continued to be dominated by Greek influences. After receiving his primary instruction at the hands of an elementary teacher (*ludi magister*), the pupil went to the school of a *grammaticus*. Here he followed a standard curriculum, which included literature, dialectic, arithmetic, geometry, astronomy, and music. These subjects were the liberal arts (*artes liberales*). Greek literature was the main curriculum and the mathematical and scientific subject matter was also Greek. The Romans obviously failed to develop the same interest in mathematics and music that was characteristic of the Greek mind. They were content to study the former as far as practical and preferred to leave the latter subject to professionals. Higher education was received in special schools of oratory and philosophy or was gained by private study and intercourse with distinguished men. The teaching of philosophy and oratory was conducted mainly by Greek professors, and in oratory Greek was the regular language of instruction. A reaction against these Greek rhetorical schools, perhaps because they were expensive and popular among the aristocracy, caused the establishment of a rival Latin school by Plotius Gallus, who followed Roman models and trained his pupils in Latin. His school was suppressed for political reasons by the censors of 92, but it seems to have been later revived. In addition to pursuing these advanced studies at Rome, it had become the fashion for well-to-do young Romans to complete their education in the schools of Greece itself, which might be called the universities of the day. Cicero, whose career illustrates very well the contemporary system of higher education, was such a student. After finishing his preliminary studies, he remained in Rome, where he regularly attended the speeches of well-known orators; received an introduction into Roman jurisprudence under Q. Mucius Scaevola, a leading jurisconsult; studied Greek literature and the art of poetry, Roman history, Greek philosophy, and rhetoric with representatives of the Stoic school and the Academy; and consistently practiced declamation, largely in Greek. Later he visited Greece, spending six months at Athens, where he pursued his philosophic and rhetorical studies. From Athens he went to Asia Minor, where he visited several cities and ended his period of foreign study at Rhodes. Later he was proud to acknowledge the educational debt owed to the teachers and schools of Greece. Cicero expressed the finest conception of education known from ancient Rome. He emphasized the need of higher cultural studies, selecting history, jurisprudence, and philosophy as those which, supplementing literature and rhetoric, comprise the fields of learning necessary for the attainment of the cultural ideal—*humanitas*.

LITERATURE. The last century of the Republic saw the completion of the amalgamation of Greek and Roman culture. The resulting Graeco-Roman civilization was bilingual and was based on Greek intellectual and Roman political achievement. It was the mission of the Empire to spread this civilization among the barbarians of the West. The age was marked by many-sided, keen, intellectual activity, which brought Rome's cultural development to its height. This Greco-Roman culture was almost exclusively, however, a possession of the upper classes.

DRAMA. The field of drama was an exception to the generally high level of literary productivity during the last century of the Republic. The writing of tragedy for public performance had practically ceased by the end of the second century, as had the creative adaptation of Greek comedy. Comedies in Roman dress and with Italian settings, *fabulae togatae*, were in vogue for a time, and older dramatic works were revived. Of greater popularity in the long run, however, were farces and mimes. The former were derived from Oscan prototypes. With few exceptions they had no claim to being literature, since they scarcely ever rose above the level of ribaldry, as highly improvised as it was crude. The mimes, which ultimately derived from Greek prototypes well known in south Italy, were especially notorious for their indecent language and plots. Theatrical exhibitions were produced on an increasingly lavish scale and were often given in conjunction with public games.

POETRY. A significant circle of poets, many of them coming from north Italy, turned away from the epic themes that had traditionally appealed to the Roman temperament and produced poetry of a much more personal, subjective, and even romantic nature. These "modernists" often took as technical inspiration for their epigrams and elegies the works of the Hellenistic school of Greek poets writing at Alexandria. The new poetry appealed to a highly educated class, conversant alike with the literature of the Greek classic and Hellenistic periods, as well as with modern production, and able to appreciate the most elaborate and diversified meters. The best exponent of this movement at Rome was Gaius Valerius Catullus (ca. 84–ca. 54), a native of Verona, who was drawn into the vortex of fashionable society at the capital as a young man. There he became infatuated with the profligate Clodia, the Lesbia of his poems, sister of P. Clodius, tribune of 58. Catullus was the best lyric poet Rome produced; indeed, he is one of the foremost lyric poets of all time. Passionate, volatile, and utterly frank in expressing his often tortured emotions, he was rather unique in articulately defying traditional puritanical ideals and *gravitas*. He and others of his circle also produced political epigrams lampooning a wide range of personalities, including Julius Caesar.

Unique among Roman poets in a very different way was Titus Lucretius Carus (ca. 98–55), an obscure personality who was either a client or member of the aristocratic clan of Lucretii. Lucretius combined rare poetic and intellectual gifts with a very Roman sense of mission. His didactic masterpiece, *On the Nature of the Universe (De rerum natura),* was a sublime attempt to free the minds of men from fear of the power of the gods and of death by propagating the philosophical beliefs of the Hellenistic Greek philosopher Epicurus. The essence of the Epicurean doctrine, which derived ultimately from the atomic theory of Democritus, held that the world and all living creatures were produced by an accidental combination of atoms falling through space. The creation and operation of the world accordingly took place without divine intervention. Furthermore, the soul, like the body, was material and mortal; since death merely meant the decay of the body into its component atoms, there was no future existence to anticipate. A doctrine so closely related to the science of physics might scarcely seem a subject for esthetic development in the grand manner, but Lucretius was able to transform it into an always eloquent and often majestic poem designed to liberate man from unhappiness and superstition. Reception of his work varied. In general the senatorial intelligentsia tried to ignore it, since Epicureanism was widely regarded as subversive, undermining as it did the state religion on whose manipulation their political control depended in part. Some poets, however, like Virgil and Horace were deeply influenced by it.

ORATORY. It was through the study and practice of oratory, one of the most typically Roman interests, that Latin prose attained its perfection between the time of the Gracchi and Julius Caesar. Political and legal orations were weapons of party strife and were frequently polished and edited as political pamphlets. Along with political documents of this type, appeared orations that were not written to be delivered in the Forum or Senate but were addressed solely to a reading public. Two oratorical styles competed for primacy: the Asian, which was showy and ornamental, and the Attic, which was simpler and more direct. Among the great forensic orators of the age were the two Gracchi, of whom the younger, Gaius, was reputed to be the most effective speaker that Rome ever knew. Others of note were Marcus Antonius, grandfather of the triumvir, Lucius Licinius Crassus, and Quintus Hortensius Hortalus. But it was Cicero who brought to its perfection the Roman oration in its literary form.

Cicero (106–43) epitomized the intellectual and literary interests of the senatorial intelligentsia of the late Republic. He was above all things an orator. Until past the age of fifty his literary productivity was almost entirely in this field, and he made significant contributions to the theoretical study of the forensic art. Steering a middle course between the Asian and Attic styles, he produced a style peculiarly his own—sonorous, rhythmical, and shot through when needed with brilliant irony and invective. In his hands Latin prose attained its highest development as a vehicle for the expression of human thought. In his later years, when the opportunity for free forensic oratory was being limited by political developments, he turned increasingly to Greek philosophy and undertook the great task of making it accessible to the Roman world. Acquainted with the leading philosophies of classical Greek and Hellenistic civilizations, he was an eclectic, a popularizer and transmitter rather than an original thinker. All of Western civilization is deeply indebted to him, however, since he embodied Rome's cultural mission in the world: the transmission of the values of classical antiquity. In a series of brilliant essays he expressed his views on political theory and ethics. Platonic inspiration is evident in his *De Republica*, in which he set forth the actual constitution of an ideal state. The Stoic substratum to much of his ethical thinking, stressing as it did an active life in improving mankind, is revealed in works like *De Officiis* and *De Senectute*. In addition to his speeches and oratorical and philosophical treaties, Cicero left to posterity a great collection of letters, which were collected and published by his freedman secretary, Tiro. His correspondence with his friends is a mine of information for the student of society and politics in the last century of the Republic, especially because it is so candid. Cicero has been criticized occasionally by posterity for his vanity, his opportunism, and his attachment to a form of government that was not worth saving. In his defense it may be said that in many ways he was a child of his age. At crucial moments he was courageous in upholding his political beliefs, no matter how unrealistic. In any case, his possibly real personal weaknesses cannot obscure the fact that he holds a preeminent place among men of letters in Western civilization.

HISTORICAL WRITING.   History, along with oratory, continued to command a great deal of attention among Rome's educated elite. Indeed, political events following the Gracchi further stimulated interest in the subject, and a flood of historical literature resulted. Two developments are noteworthy in this connection: the continued influence on Roman letters of universal history in the tradition of Polybius, whose exponents were almost all Greek, and, more importantly, the emergence of annalistic history.

The annalistic approach to history, characteristically Roman, was stimulated about 123 by publication by the Pontifex Maximus of the *Annales Maximi*, lists of magistrates and important events that had been kept for several centuries. The works of annalists of the latter second and early first centuries have not survived, but two of them writing during the Sullan period—Q. Claudius Quadrigarius and Valerius Antias—deserve mention because they were later used by Livy. The reliability of the Sullan historians was not great, since they consciously embroidered their narrative for rhetorical effect and since family and political considerations often compelled them to convert history into heroic legend.

More significant was Gaius Sallustius Crispus (86–ca. 34), whom subsequent generations ranked as the foremost Roman historian. Sallust served with Caesar in the Civil War, governed Africa, was indicted for extortion but escaped conviction, and occupied the remainder of his life with writing. His reputation rested primarily upon his *Histories*, a detailed treatment of the period 78–67, which unfortunately is almost entirely lost. His shorter works, the *War with Jugurtha* and the *War with Catiline*, have been preserved. These are political pamphlets biased in favor of the Populares and Caesar and bitterly hostile to the Optimates, whom he rather inconsistently denounced for their unscrupulous venality. Although not incapable of portraying fairly his political enemies and the faults of his own party, he did not attain a high level of objectivity. He owed his reputation more to his stylistic ability than to the historical significance of his writings. His spare, epigrammatic style, modeled on Thucydides, served as an inspiration to Tacitus.

The biographer Cornelius Nepos also may be classed among the historians. Only parts of one of his works survive, a collection of biographies of eminent Romans and foreigners. The lives are both uncritical and lacking in redeeming literary qualities.

The *Commentaries* of Julius Caesar on the Gallic and Civil Wars deserve high praise both as history and as lucid expression. Directed to members of his own class, they were designed to make it impossible for the oligarchy to refuse his claims to greatness and *dignitas* and to his just rewards. In that sense the *Commentaries* are partisan, but they are in no way tendentious propaganda. Considering the motivation behind their publication, they bespeak an astonishing degree of fairness, objectivity, and honesty on the part of their author. Caesar was also an effective orator in the Attic tradition, but his speeches were never published.

Of great interest to later ages were the works of the antiquarian and philologist, Marcus Terentius Varro, (116–27), the most learned Roman of his time. His great work on Roman religious and political antiquities is lost, but a part of his study *On the Latin Language* is still extant, as well as his three books *On Rural Conditions*. The latter give a good picture of farming on the plantations of the larger landholders during the period 67 to 54.

JURISPRUDENCE. Roman law continued its development both in substance and in theory. Contacts with foreign legal systems and philosophies proved a fruitful stimulus. In Italy the praetor for aliens (*praetor peregrinus*), and in the provinces Roman governors, had to administer law to foreigners. They had to face the problem of providing a law that would give substantial justice to litigants. Since the Roman Civil Law applied only to Roman citizens, it could not serve their purpose. They solved the problem by publishing in their edicts legal rules which could be enforced between Romans and aliens, as well as between aliens of different citizenships, when these sued in courts presided over by Roman magistrates. Thus a body of law applicable to free persons irrespective of citizenship was formed. This law possessed advantages in its liberality, i.e., freedom from technicalities, and in its fairness (*aequitas*); thus much of it was taken over in the Civil Law by the adoption of its rules in the edict of the urban praetor, particularly after the extension of Roman citizenship to all of Italy. From the Roman point of view this new element in the law was called the *ius gentium*, or Law of Nations, which was defined as "that part of the law which we apply both to ourselves and to foreigners." Through this channel the Civil Law accepted principles and usages developed by Greeks and other foreign peoples, but only when they had become thoroughly assimilated and adapted to Roman conditions. From Greek philosophy, Roman juristic writers derived another concept of the Law of Nations as a law "common to all mankind." From the same source they also received the idea of a Law of Nature (*ius naturae* or *naturale*)— that is, a universal divine law emanating from right reason, the power that governs the universe. This Law of Nature was looked upon as the source of the Law of Nations or as being identical with it. These philosophic concepts did not contribute anything to the substance of Civil Law, but they provided Roman jurists with a philosophic justification of law and encouraged them to attempt to systematize Roman law according to fundamental legal principles.

The most influential legal writers were Quintus Mucius Scaevola, who compiled a systematic treatment of the Civil Law in eighteen books, Servius Sulpicius Rufus, a contemporary of Cicero, and his pupil Aulus Ofilius, a friend of Caesar. Sulpicius was a most productive author, whose works included *Commentaries* on the Twelve Tables and on the Praetor's Edict, as well as studies on special aspects of Roman law. Ofilius was also a voluminous writer, notable as the first to arrange the Praetor's Edict systematically. During the last century of the Republic interpretation of the law was no longer the prerogative of a few oligarchs who had held priesthoods. The circle of *jurisprudentes* broadened considerably to include lower classes, and equestrians and even freedmen set themselves up as legal authorities. Since these latter often had only a superficial acquaintance with Roman legal tradition, and since the state exercised no control over them, it is no wonder that their interpretations of law tended to confuse rather than to enlighten. The plans of Pompey and Caesar to codify the law were in part prompted by the desire to end this confusion.

PART

III

PRINCIPATE
OR EARLY EMPIRE:
27 B.C.–A.D. 285

ESTABLISHMENT OF THE PRINCIPATE:[1] 27 B.C.–A.D. 14

Only a small part of the extensive Roman and Greek literature dealing with the history of the Roman Empire from 27 B.C. to A.D. 235 has survived. For the early part of this period until A.D. 96, the basic works are: Cassius Dio's *History*, of which the extant portion runs to A.D. 46; the *Annals* of Tacitus, which, with some notable gaps, cover the years A.D. 14 to 66; and the remains of his *Histories*, which deal with the events of the year A.D. 69 and part of 70. These are supplemented chiefly by Suetonius' *Lives* of the emperors from Augustus to Domitian, the appropriate portion of Velleius Paterculus, whose history stopped with A.D. 30, and several brief historical surveys and biographical collections compiled in the fourth and fifth centuries A.D. Much historical information is also contained in the *Geography* of the Greek Strabo, written in A.D. 17–18. The inadequacies of the literary record are partially made good by thousands of Latin and Greek inscriptions from Italy and the provinces, and of Greek papyri from Egypt, which illustrate in detail administrative, economic, and social life. An inscription that is also a notable historical document is the record of his career composed by the Emperor Augustus and set up after his death in Rome and in the provinces under the title of the *Deeds of Augustus* (*Res Gestae Divi Augusti*).

I. The Princeps

SETTLEMENT OF 27 B.C.   Octavian, the young revolutionary, pitiless proscriber, and clever propagandist had developed into a statesman of the highest order during the fifteen years following Caesar's death. During his sixth and seventh consulships, in the years 28 and 27, Octavian surrendered the extraordinary powers he had exercised during the war against Antony and Cleopatra and, as he later expressed it, he placed the commonwealth at the disposal of the Senate and the Roman people. This step did not imply that the old machinery of government was restored without modifications and restrictions or that Octavian intended to abdicate his position as arbiter of the Roman world. He would hardly have been justified in so doing, for such action would have led to a repetition of the anarchy that followed the retirement and death of Sulla. In disposing

---

[1] The spelling Principate (with a capital *P*) is used to distinguish the form of government prevailing between 27 B.C. and A.D. 284 from the principate as the office of the *princeps*.

of his rivals, Octavian had assumed the obligation of giving the Roman Empire stable government. He might truly claim to have been called by consent of the Roman world to reorganize the government, and public sentiment was prepared to allow him great latitude in this task. It demanded strong administration, even if this could be attained only at the expense of republican institutions.

While ambition and duty alike forbade him to relinquish his hold on the state, Octavian shrank from realizing the ideal of Julius Caesar and establishing autocracy. From this he was deterred by the fate of his adoptive father and by his own devious conservatism, which gave him such shrewd understanding of Roman temperament. His solution of the problem was to retain the old Roman constitution as far as was practicable, while securing such powers as would enable him to uphold the constitution and prevent a renewal of civil war. What powers and honors were necessary to this end, Octavian determined on the basis of practical experience and not a little experimentation between 27 and 2 B.C. His restoration of the commonwealth thus signified the end of a regime of force and paved the way for new authority legally conferred upon him.

THE IMPERIUM. Nothing had contributed more directly to the failure of the Republic than the growth of the client army and the inability of the Senate to control its commanders. It was therefore absolutely necessary for the guardian of peace and of the constitution to command supreme military authority. On January 13, 27—the birthday of the new order—Octavian, by vote of the Assembly and Senate, received for ten years the command and administration of the provinces of Spain, Gaul, and Syria, the chief provinces where peace was not yet firmly established and which consequently required the presence of most of the Roman armies. Egypt, which he had annexed to the Empire in 30 B.C., was also subject to his *imperium*. It is uncertain, however, whether the *imperium* granted him over those provinces in 27 was proconsular or whether he controlled them in his capacity as consul. Provinces controlled by the Senate did not come under his *imperium*, although he could guide their administration by virtue of his *auctoritas*. His solution of the military problem was an extraordinary command that found its precedents in those of Lucullus, Pompey, and Caesar but was of such scope and duration that it made him, in effect, commander in chief of the imperial army.

TITLES AUGUSTUS AND IMPERATOR. On January 16, 27 B.C. the Senate conferred upon Octavian the title of Augustus (Greek, *Sebastos*), by which he was henceforth known. It was a term implying no definite powers but, being an epithet equally applicable to gods or men, was well adapted to express his exalted position. A second title was that of Imperator. Following republican custom, this had been conferred upon Augustus by his army and the Senate after his victory at Mutina in 43, and in imitation of Julius Caesar he converted this temporary title of honor into a permanent one. Finally in 38, he placed it first among his personal names (as a *praenomen*). After 27 Augustus made twofold use of the term: as a permanent *praenomen*, and as a title of honor assumed upon victories won by his officers. From this time the *praenomen* Imperator was a prerogative of the Roman commander in chief. In the Greek-speaking provinces, where his power rested exclusively upon his military authority, the title Imperator was understood as the expression of his unlimited *imperium* and was translated in that sense by *autocrator*. From the *praenomen* Imperator is derived the term emperor, commonly used today to designate Augustus and his successors.

TRIBUNICIAN AUTHORITY: 23 B.C.   From 27 to 23 the authority of Augustus rested upon his annual tenure of the consulship and his provincial command. In the latter year Augustus faced crises in his regime which included an important conspiracy, an almost fatal illness, and quite possibly, a temporary split in his own faction regarding the *de facto* designation of his own nephew as his successor, and he was forced to modify the powers of the principate. He resigned the consulship, since its perpetual tenure violated republican precedent and since by holding it, he reduced the opportunity of senators to obtain much coveted nobility. In its stead he received for life, in the summer of 23, the tribunician authority (*tribunicia potestas*) from the Senate and people. As early as 36 he had been granted the personal inviolability of tribunes, and in 30 their right of giving aid (*auxilium*). To these privileges must now be added the right of intercession and of summoning the Assembly (*jus agendi cum populo*). In this way Augustus acquired control over comitial and senatorial legislation and openly assumed the position of protector of the city plebs. He was amply compensated for the loss of civil power, which his resignation of the consulship involved, and he also got rid of an office which must be shared with a colleague of equal rank and the perpetual tenure of which was a violation of tradition. The tribunician authority was regarded as being held for annual periods, which Augustus reckoned from 23.

SUPPLEMENTARY POWERS AND HONORS.   When he received tribunician authority, a series of senatorial decrees added or gave greater precision to his powers. The most important of these concerned his *imperium*. Since he had resigned the consulship, he no longer had *imperium* within the *pomerium* of Rome or even, perhaps, in the provinces assigned to him in 27 B.C. To remedy this situation he was definitely granted proconsular *imperium* in his provinces in 23 and the right to enter Rome without surrendering it. This proconsular *imperium* was defined as *maius*, which made it higher than that of other proconsuls, who, consequently, would be subject to his orders. This *imperium* Augustus never surrendered. When its first term was about to lapse in 18 B.C., he had it renewed for five years and subsequently for another term of five and then three of ten years, thus preserving the continuity of his proconsular command until his death. Among his new prerogatives was the right to introduce the first topic for consideration in the Senate. It was probably in 27 that Augustus received the unrestricted right of making war or peace. In 22 B.C. he was granted the right to call meetings of the Senate. Three years later he was accorded the consular insignia, with twelve lictors, and the privilege of taking his seat on a curule chair between the consuls in office. These marks of honor gave him precedence among the magistrates that his authority warranted. On the other hand, in 22 Augustus refused the dictatorship and the perpetual consulship, which were voted him at the insistence of the city populace, although he may well have accepted censorial powers in 29, 19, and 12 B.C. on the occasion of forthcoming *lectiones senatus*.

THE PRINCIPATE. It was by the gradual acquisition of all these powers that the position Augustus was to hold was finally determined. This position may be defined as that of a magistrate whose province was a combination of various powers conferred upon him by the Senate and the Roman people and who differed from the other magistrates in the immensely wider scope of his functions and the greater length of his term. These powers were separately conferred upon him and for each he could urge constitutional precedents. His dominant position, if it rested in the last analysis on control of armed force and support of the governing establishment, was derived no less from that general *auctoritas* that senior statesmen had always possessed. It cannot be said that his word was law, but it would have been inconceivable and un-Roman to question the judgment of a man whose prestige obviously outclassed that of any senator. As he held no definite office, he had no definite official title, but in receiving such wide powers he came to surpass all other Romans in authority, in the influence he was able to exercise on account of his political position, and so he came to be designated as *princeps*, i.e., the first of the Roman citizens (*princeps civium Romanorum*). This was in accordance with good republican usage, for Pompey and other leading men had previously been called *principes* by their contemporaries. Beginning with Augustus there was a difference, however. If previously there had been many *principes*, i.e., many senior statesmen heading factions and possessed of approximately equal prestige, henceforward there was room for only one such statesman. The *princeps* in this latter sense was the ultimate source of all patronage, and other statesmen could only bask in his reflected glory. From the word *princeps* arose the term principate to designate the tenure of office of the *princeps*, a term which we now apply also to the system of government that Augustus established for the Empire. The culmination in the evolution of his principate and the crowning honor of his career was received by Augustus in 2 B.C., when the Senate, on the motion of one who had fought under Brutus at Philippi, conferred on him the title of "Father of His Country" (*pater patriae*), thus marking the reconcilation between the bulk of the old aristocracy and the new regime.

II. Senate, Equestrians, and Lower Classes

THREE ORDERS. The social classification of the Romans into the senatorial, equestrian, and lower classes passed, with sharper definitions, from the Republic into the Principate. For each class a distinct field of opportunity and public service was provided, conforming as far as possible to previous traditions: for senators, the magistracies and the chief military posts; for the *equites*, a new career in the civil and military service of the *princeps*; and for the lower classes, service as privates and subaltern officers in the professional army. These orders were by no means closed castes, however. The way lay open to able and successful men for advancement from the lower to the higher grades and for the consequent infusion of fresh vitality into the ranks of the latter.

THE SENATE AND THE SENATORIAL ORDER. The senatorial order was composed of members of the Senate and their families. Its distinctive emblem was the broad purple stripe on the toga. Sons of senators assumed this badge by right of birth; equestrians, by grant of the *princeps*. Of the former, however, those who failed to qualify for the Senate were reduced to the rank of equestrians. The possession of property valued at 1,000,000 sesterces ($50,000) was made a requirement for admission to the Senate.

The prospective senator, after completing a term of military service as tribune in a Roman legion or a prefect of a detachment of auxiliary cavalry, was obliged to fill one of the minor city magistracies known as the board of twenty (*viginti-virate*), and then, at the age of twenty-five, to become a candidate for the quaestorship, which admitted one to the Senate. From the quaestorship the senatorial career led through the regular magistracies, the aedileship or tribunate and the praetorship, to the consulship. As an ex-praetor and ex-consul, a senator might be appointed a promagistrate to govern a senatorial province, a legate to command a legion or administer an imperial province, or a curator in charge of some administrative commission in Rome or Italy.

During the Republic the Senate had been the center of administration, and Augustus intended that it should continue to be so for most of the Empire. Through the ordinary magistrates it governed Rome and Italy, and through the promagistrates the senatorial provinces. To render it capable of fulfilling its task and to reestablish its prestige, the Senate, which now numbered over one thousand, had to be purged of many undesirable members admitted during the recent civil wars. In 28 B.C., Augustus supervised a revision of the senatorial list, and two hundred unworthy persons were excluded. On that occasion his name was placed at the head of the new roll as the *princeps senatus*. A second recension ten years later reduced the total membership to six hundred. A third in 11 B.C. conducted by Augustus, and a fourth in A.D. 4 carried out through a specially chosen committee of three, left the number unchanged. The Senate was recruited automatically by the annual admission of the twenty retiring quaestors,[2] but since tenure of the higher magistracies carried with it senatorial rank, the *princeps* could use recommendations to the praetorship and consulship to appoint men who had not met normal requirements for enrollment. Thus many prominent equestrians became senators.

In the latter part of his principate, the prestige of the Senate was enhanced by its employment as a court of justice, sitting under the presidency of the consuls for the trial of serious charges brought against senators. Its resolutions also gained added importance because they tended to acquire the force of law and because the Senate thereby was gradually becoming a legislative body at the expense of the popular assemblies. An important new procedure was introduced in drafting senatorial decrees. Early in his reign (probably between 27 and 18 B.C.) Augustus established a standing committee (*consilium*) composed of prominent magistrates and fifteen senators chosen by lot. This committee advised the *princeps* and, with him, prepared the agenda for plenary sessions of the Senate. This probouleutic cabinet was replaced by another advisory committee in A.D. 13, which was designed to facilitate the coming transition of power from Augustus to his successor Tiberius. Apart from these two formal councils, there were also informal advisory committees made up of political friends of the emperor, whom he would consult from time to time on various administrative and judicial matters. Augustus succeeded where Julius Caesar had failed in successfully reconciling the Senate to the idea of one-man rule. He did so by accommodating his regime to the traditional senatorial desire for the attainment of prestige and *dignitas* through office-holding, which once again became respectable and safe. Now, however, political advancement was a function of imperial patronage, and in dispensing it to the senatorial order, Augustus was characteristically cautious. This may be seen in the elections to the consulship, still the highest republican office in the state, and the one that conferred much coveted nobility on its holders. At first Augustus tended to patronize new men to strengthen his faction. During the middle part of his reign (18 B.C.–A.D. 4) he often encouraged election of members of ancient noble houses, an index of his growing reconciliation with the republican nobility and his need of their support of his dynastic policy.

EQUESTRIAN ORDER. For the conduct of public administration, the *princeps* required a great number of assistants in his personal employ.

---

[2] The number of quaestors had been reduced from 40 to 20 in 27 B.C.

For his legates to command the legions or his provinces with delegated military authority, Augustus could draw upon senators, but both custom and senatorial prestige forbade their entering his service in other capacities. Yet, freedmen and slaves, who might well be employed in a clerical position, obviously could not be made the sole civil servants of the *princeps*. Augustus therefore drew into his service equestrians, whose business interests and traditional connection with finances seemed to make them peculiarly fitted as his agents in the financial administration of the provinces. This was perhaps the most revolutionary reform of his regime, and the equestrians for the first time became upwardly mobile and an essential part of the governing establishment.

The equestrian order was open to all Roman citizens who were eighteen years of age, of free birth and good character, and possessed a census rating of 400,000 sesterces ($20,000). Admission to the order was controlled by the *princeps* and carried the right to wear a narrow purple stripe on the tunic and to receive a public horse, the possession of which qualified an equestrian for civil and military service. With bestowal of the public horse, Augustus revived the long-neglected annual parade and inspection of the *equites* in Rome, a ceremony that those who lived far away could not, of course, attend.

Like the career of the senators, that of the equestrians included both military and civil appointments. At the outset of his public career the equestrian held several military appointments, which later came regularly to include a prefecture in an auxiliary infantry or cavalry corps, a tribunate of a cohort of troops stationed in Rome, and a regular legionary tribunate. He was then eligible for a procuratorship, that is, a post in the civil service, usually the administration of the finances. After filling several of these many procuratorships, an equestrian might finally attain one of the great prefectures, as commander of the city watch, administrator of the grain supply of Rome, commander of the imperial guards, or governor of Egypt. At the end of his equestrian career he might be enrolled in the senatorial order. Thus through the imperial service the equestrian order was bound closely to the *princeps*, and from its ranks there gradually developed a nobility thoroughly loyal to the new regime. The equestrian class itself was continually enlarged and rejuvenated by the admission of select members of the lower classes, in special cases even freedmen.

THE ASSEMBLIES AND THE LOWER CLASSES. The Assemblies, which had supposedly voiced the will of the Roman people, were not abolished, although they could no longer claim to speak for the Roman citizenry. They still were elective and legislative bodies, but their freedom in the choice of candidates for offices was restricted by Augustus' practice of recommending and actually canvassing for candidates for the several magistracies, and his tribunician authority effectively controlled the laws submitted for their approval. An essentially minor change was

Portrait head of Augustus

introduced in the Centuriate Assembly, probably in A.D. 5, when, pursuant to a *lex Valeria Cornelia,* the prerogative vote was entrusted to ten centuries of senators and equestrians. These centuries, created in honor of the emperor's dead grandsons, were merely decorative and intended to enhance the dignity of the upper classes; in no way did their existence modify Augustus' control over the Assembly.

While the city mob, accustomed to receive free distributions of grain and to be entertained at costly public spectacles, was a heavy drain on the state, the vigorous third estate in the Italian municipalities supplied the lower officers of the legions. These were the centurions, mainstay of discipline and efficiency of the troops, who sometimes advanced to an equestrian career.

III. Military Establishment

REORGANIZATION OF THE ARMY. Upon his return to Italy in 30 B.C., Augustus found himself at the head of an army of about 500,000 men. Of these he released more than 300,000 and settled them in colonies or in their native municipalities on lands it was his boast to have purchased and not confiscated. Partly to meet military and strategic needs, he established a state posting service (*cursus publicus*) along the highways and rivers of the Empire to transmit dispatches and to move troops and supplies. He then proceeded to reorganize the military establishment by gradually rationalizing the precedents of the century of civil war. Whereas before there had been many standing armies, Augustus now created one force equal to all emergencies. Voluntary enlistment supplied most of the recruits, as before, although conscription was sometimes necessary. He made an important change in the officer cadres. During the civil wars such posts had been held with increasing frequency by men of low social background who had risen from the ranks, and a professional officer class tended to develop. By restoring such posts—in particular the legionary tribunate—to equestrians and fledgling senators and by reintegrating thereby officers' military and civilian careers, he restored the prestige of the office and prevented the development of a possibly dangerous military vested interest. The army continued to comprise the two traditional categories of troops, legionaries and auxiliaries. At first the legionaries served for sixteen years, which had been the legal limit for military service during the Republic.

LEGIONS AND AUXILIARIES. As during the civil wars, legionaries were recruited from Roman citizens living in Italy or the provinces or from provincials who now received Roman citizenship upon their enlistment. The legions each comprised nominally 6,000 men, of whom 120 were cavalry and the rest infantry, but often they were not maintained at full strength. By 13 B.C., apparently, there were 28 legions under arms; but when 3 were lost in Germany in A.D. 9 they were not replaced, so that the number remained at 25, giving a total of about 150,000. The auxiliaries, who took the place of contingents regularly raised from Roman allies during the Republic, were recruited from among the most warlike subject peoples of the Empire, and their numbers were approximately equal to the legionaries. Augustus began to systematize their organization into small infantry and cavalry corps (cohorts and *alae*), each 480 or 960 men strong, to enlist them under Roman direction for definite terms of service, and to give them Roman officers. It was not until much later that this regime was imposed on all auxiliary units, and many of them continued to be raised and led by native chieftains and for varying periods of service. At the expiration of their term, the auxiliaries were granted Roman citizenship both for themselves and their families.

PRAETORIANS.   A third category of troops, which, although greatly inferior in number and military value to the legions and auxiliaries, played a very influential role in the Principate, was the praetorian guard. This was the imperial force which attended Augustus in his capacity of commander in chief of the armies. Its organization was thoroughly precedented and corresponded to the headquarters guard of commanders of the Republic. It was influential because it was kept in Italy, at first partly and later entirely at Rome, while the other troops were stationed in the provinces. Under Augustus the praetorian guard comprised nine cohorts, each 1,000 strong, the whole commanded by two praetorian prefects of equestrian rank. The praetorians were recruited exclusively from Italy and enjoyed shorter service and higher pay than the other corps. As part of the armed forces of the Empire should also be reckoned the police and fire brigade of Rome, since these had a military organization and were under the command of the *princeps*. Together they numbered 10,000 men.

CONDITIONS OF SERVICE.   It was not until A.D. 6 that the term of enlistment and the conditions of discharge were fixed for the several classes of troops. From that date service in the praetorian guard was for sixteen years, in the legions for twenty, and in the *auxilia* for twenty-five. On discharge the praetorians received a bonus of 5,000 denarii ($1,000), while the legionaries were given 3,000 denarii ($600) in addition to land. The discharged legionaries were regularly settled in colonies throughout the provinces. What provision was made for veterans of the auxiliary forces is unknown. To meet this increased expense Augustus was obliged to establish a military treasury (the *aerarium militare*), endowed out of his private patrimony and supported by revenue derived from two newly imposed taxes, a 5 percent inheritance tax (*vicesima hereditatium*), which affected all Roman citizens, and a 1 percent tax on all goods publicly sold (*centesima rerum venalium*).

NAVY.   For policing the coast of Italy and the adjacent seas, Augustus created a permanent fleet with stations at Ravenna and Misenum. Conforming to the relative unimportance of the Roman navy, in contrast to its military, establishment; the personnel of this fleet was recruited largely from provincials, although for some time imperial freedmen were admitted to naval service. As occasion demanded special fleets were organized to cooperate in military expeditions.

The military system of Augustus strongly emphasized and guaranteed the supremacy of Italy and the Italians over the provincials. Both the officers and the *élite* troops were drawn almost exclusively from Italy or the latinized parts of the western provinces. In like manner reservation of the higher grades of civil administration, the second prop of Roman rule, to Roman senators and equestrians, as well as exclusion of the provincial imperial cult from Italy, marked clearly the distinction between the conquering and the subject races At the same time it was Augustus himself who pointed the way to the ultimate Romanization of the provincials by the bestowal of citizenship as one of the rewards for military service and by the settlement of colonies of veterans in the provinces.

IV. Revival of Religion and Morality

IDEALS OF AUGUSTUS.   A counterpart to the governmental reorganization effected by Augustus was his attempt to revive the old-time Roman virtues, which had been increasingly disregarded during the last centuries of the Republic. This moral regeneration of the Roman people he conceived as the essential basis for a new era of peace and prosperity. The reawakening of morality was necessarily preceded by a revival of religious rites and ceremonies, which recently had passed into desuetude through the attraction of new cults, the growth of skepticism, and the general disorder into which the administration had fallen as a result of civil strife. His religious policy was not directed merely towards a revival of neglected cults and customs. It also aimed to foster and guide new religious impulses that were stirring in his world and to make use of these tendencies to strengthen his hold on the beliefs and loyalty of both Romans and provincials.

REVIVAL OF PUBLIC RELIGION.   One step in restoring the public state cults was the reestablishment of the ancient priestly colleges devoted to the performance of particular rites or the cult of particular deities. To provide these colleges with the required number of patrician members, Augustus created new patrician families. He himself was enrolled in each of these colleges and, at the death of Lepidus in 12 B.C., was elected chief pontiff, (*pontifex maximus*) head of the state religion. A second measure was the repair of temples and shrines that had fallen into decay. The temple of Jupiter Capitolinus, those of Quirinus and Magna Mater, besides eighty-two other shrines of lesser fame, were repaired or restored by him. One of his generals, Munatius Plancus, renewed the temple of Saturn in the Forum.

Realizing that the confusion and uncertainty of the Civil Wars had greatly stimulated the worship of such deities as Fortune, Peace, Mercury the god of wealth, and Hercules the bestower of earthly goods, Augustus fostered the cults of these gods, building new shrines in their honor and linking himself with them publicly by giving them, in such forms as Fortuna Augusta, Pax Augusta, and Mercurius Augustus, his own surname of Augustus. He also sought to impress the people with the religious affiliations of his Julian gens, and, consequently, with the divine atmosphere that surrounded him. With this in mind he erected a new temple to Mars the Avenger in his new Forum and another to the deified Julius on the old Forum, at the spot where Caesar's body had been burned. On the Palatine Hill, adjacent to Augustus' residence, arose the magnificent temple of Apollo, also a protector of the Julian house, whom Augustus honored as the giver of victory over his rivals and the savior of the state from the turmoil of the Civil Wars.

THE LARES AND THE GENIUS AUGUSTI. Among the divinities whose cult had been revived were the Lares, the guardian deities of the crossways and protectors of household peace and prosperity, whose worship was especially practised by the common folk. Between the years 12 and 7 B.C., each of the 265 precincts or *vici* into which the city of Rome was then divided was provided with a shrine dedicated to the Lares and the Genius of Augustus, that is, the divine spirit that watched over his fortunes. Worship was conducted by a committee of masters, annually elected by the inhabitants of each precinct. In this way the city mob, while not worshipping the *princeps* himself, were yet encouraged to look upon him as their protector and guardian.

IMPERIAL CULT. A new religion that was to be symbolic of the unity of the Empire and the loyalty of the provincials appeared in the cult of Roma and Augustus, commonly known as the imperial cult. The worship of the goddess Roma, the personification of the state, had sprung up voluntarily in the cities of Greece and Asia after 197 B.C., when the power of Rome began to supplant the authority of the Hellenistic monarchs, whose deification by their subjects was the theoretical basis of their autocratic power. Such voluntary worship had been accorded to individual Romans, as Flamininus, Sulla, Caesar, and Mark Antony. As early as 29 B.C. the cities of Pergamon in Asia and Nicomedia in Bithynia erected temples dedicated to Roma and Augustus and established quinquennial religious festivals called *Romaia Sebasta*. Other cities followed their example, and before the death of Augustus each province in the Orient had at least one altar dedicated to Roma and the *princeps*. Far from suppressing this spontaneous veneration, Augustus accepted it and fostered and directed its development, because he realized the political value of such an expression of reverence and devotion.

From the East the imperial cult was officially transplanted to the West.

In the year 12 B.C. an altar of Roma and Augustus was established at the junction of the rivers Rhone and Sâone, opposite the town of Lugdunum (modern Lyons), the administrative center of Transalpine Gaul apart from the Narbonese province. Here the peoples of Gaul were to unite in the outward manifestation of their loyalty to Roman rule. A similar altar was erected at what is now Cologne, in the land of the Ubii, between 9 B.C. and A.D. 9. Both in the East and in the West the maintenance of the imperial cult was imposed upon provincial councils, composed of representatives of the municipal or tribal units.

MUNICIPAL CULT OF AUGUSTUS IN ITALY. The imperial cult in the provinces was an expression of the absolute authority of Rome and Augustus over their subjects. For that very reason Augustus could not admit its development on Italian soil, for to do so would be to deny his claim to be a Roman magistrate, deriving his authority from the Roman people, among whom he was the chief citizen, and would stamp his government as monarchical and autocratic. In Italy there was a strong tendency, however, to see in Augustus a divine deliverer from war and strife and a guardian deity of peace and security. To many men he seemed the one destined to usher in a new world era. In 27 B.C. the poet Horace acclaimed him as Mercury incarnate, and municipalities and individuals in southern Italy spontaneously established his worship. There is no evidence that this direct cult of Augustus was encouraged or even persisted in any official form, although after the year 12 B.C., in many Italian municipalities there were created religious colleges of *Augustales* or priestly officers called *Seviri Augustales*, whose name indicates that they were concerned with some phase of the cult of the *princeps*. In all probability they served to maintain a cult of the Genius of Augustus, either alone or in conjunction with some other divinity, such as Mercury or Hercules. As the Augustales were drawn largely from the class of freedmen who were no longer admitted wholesale to full Roman citizenship, Augustus both assured himself of the loyalty of these *libertini* and gratified their pride by encouraging their municipal office. Other municipal institutions that served to reawaken an interest in religion, to maintain a martial spirit and military exercises, and to enhance the atmosphere of religious sanctity surrounding the personality of Augustus were the associations or clubs of young men (*iuvenes*) that underwent a widespread revival and reorganization under his patronage. These clubs were not restricted to the municipalities but also flourished in Rome.

SOCIAL LEGISLATION. Augustus was not content to trust solely to the moral effects of religious exercise. He also resorted to legislative action to check the unpuritanical tendencies of his age. The Julian Laws of 19 and 18 B.C. aimed at the restoration of family life, the encouragement of marriage, and the discouragement of childlessness by placing disabilities upon unmarried and childless persons. These measures provoked great opposition, but Augustus was in earnest and supplemented his earlier laws by the Papian Poppaean Law of A.D. 9 which gave precedence to fathers over less fortunate persons among the candidates for public office. A commentary on the effectiveness of his earlier laws was the fact that both the consuls sponsoring this one were bachelors. By example as well as by precept, Augustus sought to check the luxurious tendencies of the age, and in his own household he furnished a model of ancient Roman simplicity.

To prevent the Italian element in the Roman citizen body from being swamped by the influx of masses of liberated slaves drawn largely from the Near East, Augustus sponsored two laws, the Fufian Caninian of 2 B.C. and the Aelian Sentian of A.D.4 the first limiting the number of slaves a master could liberate by his will, and the second placing severe restrictions on a slaveholder's right to free his slaves during his lifetime. A Junian Law, passed probably in 17 B.C., granted a new kind of Latin citizenship to the considerable number of former slaves who had been emancipated by their owners without the formalties necessary to secure citizenship for them or, indeed, public recognition of their freedom. For the future, slaves thus informally liberated joined this class of Julian Latins. Freedmen even if legally emancipated, could no longer exercise the public rights of Roman citizens, although their sons enjoyed this privilege.

NEW ERA.   By 17 B.C. Augustus felt that the foundations for a new era in the state had been securely laid. In that year he celebrated the festival known as the Secular Games.[3] The inaugural choral ode (the *Carmen Saeculare* or Secular Hymn) was written by the poet Horace.

V. The Golden Age of Augustus

The epochal nature of the changes wrought by Augustus in the political life of his world were reflected in literary production, and it is no accident that his age marks the culmination in the development of Roman poetry. Through certain poetic genres and personalities, the literary history of the Augustan Age was linked to the last decades of the Republic. Some of the great talents were maturing artistically during the final phases of the civil wars. Some had even been republican in their political outlook and had suffered because of it. Augustus early realized the propaganda value inherent in poetry as a means of advertising the ideals of his regime, and even during his career as a revolutionary he sought to attract the loyalty of the rising generation of artistic talent. In so doing he was acting within Roman tradition, since it had long been usual for prominent aristocrats to display their munificence and increase their fame by drawing poets and artists into their clientele. If Augustus was not the sole patron

---

[3] From the Latin *Saeculum*, a period now thought of as a century in duration.

of Roman letters, even during his principate, he was by far the most important. He was aided in this role by the equestrian Maecenas, who identified and encouraged artistic endeavor at the emperor's behest. Only a brief outline of the literary creativity guided by these men can be attempted here.

Although many of the Augustan poets owed their financial security to the not disinterested motives of the regime, they were by no means time-servers. The greatest of them believed sincerely in the ideals of a government that had put an end to civil wars and had ushered in an era of peace. They found it easy to sing of the old-fashioned Roman virtues of sobriety and duty to the gods and to the fatherland and to celebrate the rustic virtues of a regenerated Italy, virtues that Augustus himself was stressing in his program of social and moral reform.

VIRGIL. Foremost among the poets of the new era was Virgil (Publius Virgilius Maro, 70–19 B.C.). The son of a small landholder of Mantua, Virgil had lost his farm in the confiscations of 42. Eventually he received compensation through the intercession of Maecenas. His first poems, begun in the time of his adversity, were the *Eclogues*, pastoral works inspired by Hellenistic models. These were followed by the *Georgics*, a farmer's handbook whose composition was suggested by Maecenas. The *Georgics* display Virgil's increasing maturity as a poet, his ability not merely to follow Greek models, but also to master them and infuse them with a genuinely Latin spirit. They bespeak his intuitive identification with his beloved Italy and are an eternal commentary on the old-fashioned joys of rustic labor. These early works were but a prelude to his epic masterpiece, the *Aeneid*, whose composition was suggested to him by Octavian in 29. Virgil spent the remaining years of his life working on it, and it was all but complete when he died. In many ways the *Aeneid* is the artistic quintescence of all that the Romans demanded from poetry. A work written in the service of a national ideal, it was designed to demonstrate Rome's divine mission as ruler of the world. In Aeneas, Virgil portrayed the ideal Roman, one who subordinated personal feelings and emotions to a sense of duty, *fides*, and *pietas*, in accomplishing his ordained mission, the establishment in Italy of the Roman race. Virgil's allusions to the Julian house suggested to contemporaries that they were to find in the emperor the same virtues and a similar mission, the refounding of Rome. The *Aeneid* stands as an artistic monument to Roman belief that individuals are instruments of destiny, and at the same time it is filled with a haunting tenderness and sympathy for human suffering unique in Latin literature.

HORACE. A very different kind of artistic genius was Virgil's friend, Horace (Quintus Horatius Flaccus 65–8 B.C.), son of a freedman from south Italy. Horace had served with Brutus at Philippi, and, like Virgil, had lost his land. Virgil introduced him later to Maecenas, and by 33

Horace had gained financial independence through the gift of a farm in the Sabine Hills near Rome. Where Virgil was shy and introverted, Horace was genial and sophisticated. Beginning with *Epodes* and *Satires*, written in the decade following 41, he revealed himself as an urbane and detached observer of human foibles. Although an Epicurean, he admired the Augustan virtues of rustic simplicity, which he celebrated in his lyrical *Odes*. His *Epistles*, written toward the end of his life, were comments on human nature and literature, rather mellower than his earlier works. Horace ranks with Catullus as one of the best Latin lyric poets, and his mastery over meter combined with his remarkable happiness of phrase have made him the delight of cultivated society in both antiquity and modern times.

ELEGAIC POETS. There were other poets who, although capable of first-rate work, did not rise to the literary heights of Virgil or Horace. These include the two elegaic poets Tibullus (ca. 48–19 B.C.) and Sextus Propertius (fl. 28–16 B.C.). Tibullus escaped Maecenas' orbit and apparently remained to the end an unreconstructed republican. At his best he wrote sensitively of his loves and of the Italian countryside. Propertius was more robust and passionate. Although encouraged by Maecenas to write patriotic verse, he was more at home with love poetry.

OVID. One brilliant poet, Ovid (P. Ovidius Naso, 43 B.C.–A.D. 17), was regarded as a disgrace to the New Era and paid the penalty for it. His *Metamorphoses*, in which he playfully integrated stories from classical mythology, and his *Fasti*, a metrical calendar filled with religious and historical lore, were innocent enough; but his frivolous and extremely popular love poems, like the early *Amores*, and then the *Ars Amatoria* (ca. A.D. 1), a rollicking, amoral masterpiece on relations between the sexes, seemed to approve of licentiousness in the Roman upper classes, just at a time when Augustus was struggling to make life more puritanical. In A.D. 8 Ovid was implicated in a scandal involving the imperial house (possibly the disgrace of the emperor's granddaughter, Julia), and Augustus seized the opportunity to have him banished to Tomi on the Black Sea coast. Ovid then sent back to the capital a series of appeals filled with self-pity and begging for reinstatement, but he was never allowed to return.

LIVY. The Augustan era also saw the production of outstanding prose, and ranking with Virgil and Horace as one of the literary giants of the age was the historian Livy of Padua (Titus Livius, 59 B.C.–A.D. 17). Twitted by Augustus for being an admirer of Pompey, Livy nevertheless was deeply affected by Augustan ideals, especially the romantic glorification of Roman ancestral ways (*mos maiorum*) that gave direction to his work. His annalistic history of Rome from its foundation to his own day (*ab urbe condita libri*) was a great work of art, an *Aeneid* in prose, celebrating the past greatness of Rome and the virtues by which this had been attained. Livy did not approach his sources scientifically or with a sufficiently critical sense, but it seems unfair to criticize on such grounds a work that was not intended to be a scholarly handbook. The Romans quickly realized that his was the "classic" and canonical version of their past, but since the work was very long, they preferred to read it in abridged versions. Consequently, three quarters of the original 142 books have perished, although summaries of those parts dealing with the period 167–9 B.C. survive.

VI. Provinces and Frontiers

IMPERIAL ADMINISTRATION. Although conferment of his great provincial command upon Augustus in 27 B.C. had the effect of dividing the Roman provinces into two classes, senatorial and imperial, and thus creating an administrative dyarchy, this division did not extend to general imperial policy. Unity was preserved by definition of the proconsular *imperium* of the *princeps* as higher than that of the proconsuls and by the close cooperation existing between Augustus and the Senate. This is brought out very clearly in the fact that in 7–6 B.C. Augustus issued two edicts, correcting abuses in the judicial administration of Crete and Cyrenaica, which together formed a senatorial province, and, in 4 B.C. he published in Cyrenaica a decree passed by the Senate in the recommendation of which he had concurred. This decree greatly simplified and reduced the cost of the process of bringing to trial a Roman official accused of having practiced extortion in any province. It also established the Senate, instead of the former jury court, as the judicial body having cognizance of such cases. In announcing the decree to the provincials, Augustus wrote that it ought to "show to all the inhabitants of the provinces the pains taken by the Senate and himself to prevent any of their subjects being made the victim of unjust treatment or extortion." In these words can be seen the formulation of a policy at the center of government of enlightened imperialism directed toward the welfare and not the spoliation of the subjects of Rome. In conformity with this new policy provincial taxation was revised and put upon a sounder basis. This was important, since the main expense of the military and civil establishment was defrayed by provincial revenues. As a basis for accurate estimate of their resources for purposes of taxation and recruitment, Augustus ordered a comprehensive census of the population and an evaluation of property in each newly organized district and provided for a systematic revision of the census in all the imperial provinces. A general chart of the Empire was compiled on the basis of an extended survey conducted under the direction of Agrippa.

SENATORIAL AND IMPERIAL PROVINCES. Although, in general, it might be said that the imperial provinces were those with garrisons of legionary troops and the senatorial those without such garrisons, this distinction did not hold good in all cases. For periods of varying lengths, the proconsuls of Macedonia, Illyricum, and Africa had legionary forces at their disposal and surrendered these only when the frontiers passed beyond their provinces. Nor was the original allotment of the provinces permanent. In 22 B.C. Augustus gave Gallia Narbonensis back to the Senate because the rapid progress of Roman colonization there had made it "more a part of Italy than a province." In the same way and for the same general reason, the district of Baetica, comprising a large part of Farther Spain, was made a senatorial province. Southern Greece, previously under the control of the governors of Macedonia, was also made a separate province (Achaia) and placed under the Senate. On the other hand, Augustus in 11 B.C. took over Illyricum, where the progress of Roman arms had been interrupted by the war with Antony and Cleopatra and where Rome was confronted by warlike and restless peoples in the hinterland. Somewhat later Cilicia and in A.D. 6 Sardinia became imperial provinces because of conditions necessitating military action. Finally, the new provinces organized by Augustus in territories conquered by his generals remained under his control.

Outside of the two classes of provinces but really within the bounds of the Roman Empire, Augustus permitted the existence of some client kingdoms. They enjoyed internal autonomy and were not subject to taxation by Rome, but their foreign relations were controlled by the *princeps*, and they were bound to render military aid on demand. Their rulers acknowledged Roman overlordship and in some cases were dependent on Roman support for their authority. Such kingdoms were Mauretania, Thrace, Judaea, Galatia, Cappadocia, and Lesser Armenia, of which Galatia and Judaea were transformed into provinces by Augustus.

PROVINCIAL OFFICIALS. Representation of Rome in the senatorial provinces continued very much as it had been under the Republic. Governors for these provinces were selected by lot from eligible ex-consuls and ex-praetors, of whom the former must have been ten, the latter five years out of office. All alike were now called proconsuls, although only Asia and Africa were reserved for those who were actually ex-consuls. The term of office was still normally one year. Each proconsul had as his assistants a quaestor and three propraetorian legates whose appointment was approved by the *princeps*. In the imperial provinces the Roman officials were deputies of the *princeps*, and this fact is reflected both in their titles and in their conditions of service. As governors of the more important provinces with legionary garrisons, Augustus appointed legates of propraetorian rank (*legati Augusti pro praetore*) from senators who had held the consulship or praetorship, without reference to the period which had elapsed since their magistracies. An exception was the governor of Egypt, who was an equestrian with the title of prefect, although he had three legions under his orders. In the imperial provinces of lesser military importance garrisoned only by auxiliary troops, the governors were not senators but equestrians, whose title was, as a rule, prefect, later procurator. Other officials in the larger provinces were the legates in command of the legions (*legati legionis*), in Egypt prefects, who were subordinates of the legate of Augustus, and the imperial procurators who had charge of provincial finances and, being appointed directly by the *princeps*, were practically independent of the governors. There was no limit upon the term of service of imperial officials, who were kept at their posts as long as they were efficient or until Augustus had need of them elsewhere. Since they were appointed by him, they could also be dismissed at his pleasure. Both imperial and senatorial officials now received regular salaries, which removed one of the earlier causes of extortion by provincial governors.

FOREIGN POLICY OF AUGUSTUS.   Augustus, since he was commander in chief of the armies and in charge of the administration of the most important border provinces, was entrusted by the Senate with the direction of the foreign relations of the state. It is widely accepted that Augustus expanded Roman territory only to secure defensive frontiers behind which the Empire might develop peacefully, but such a view must be strictly qualified. Although personally not an outstanding general, Augustus was as mindful of the lures of military glory as the great *principes* of the Republic. No Roman added more territory to the Empire than he. This expansion did not seem defensive to Augustan poets, who presumably were propagandizing the emperor's aims. There seems good reason to believe that Augustus was an aggressive imperialist, forced to be content with the attainment of defensive frontiers by events that occurred toward the end of his reign.

SETTLEMENT IN SPAIN.   The northwestern corner of the Spanish peninsula was still occupied by independent peoples, the Cantabri, Astures, and the Callaeci, who harassed with their forays the pacified inhabitants of the provinces. To secure peace in this quarter, Augustus determined upon the complete subjugation of these peoples. In 26 B.C. he himself, and next year his lieutenants, Antistius and Carisius, conducted campaigns against them in their mountain fastnesses and, overcoming their desperate resistance, settled them in the valleys and secured Roman territory by founding colonies of veterans not only there but also elsewhere in the peninsula, as at Emerita (Merida) and Caesaraugusta (Saragossa). A subsequent revolt in 20–19 B.C. was crushed by Agrippa. It was after the pacification of Spain that Augustus surrendered Baetica to the Senate, while he created a new imperial province called Lusitania in the western part of the peninsula.

PACIFICATION OF THE ALPINE DISTRICTS: 25–8 B.C.   A similar problem was presented by the Alpine peoples, who not only made devastating raids into northern Italy but also occupied passes in the west offering the most direct routes between Italy and Transalpine Gaul. In 26 B.C. in the neighborhood of the Little St. Bernard, there occurred a revolt of the Salassi, who had been subdued eight years before. In the following year they were completely subjugated, and those who escaped slaughter were sold into slavery. A highway was built across the pass and was guarded by a military colony at Augusta Praetoria (Aosta). In 16 B.C. the district of Noricum (modern Tyrol and Salzburg) was occupied by Publius Silius Nerva, after a raid of the Noricans into the Istrian peninsula. In 15 B.C. the stepson of Augustus, Nero Claudius Drusus, crossed the Brenner Pass and forced his way over the Vorarlberg range to Lake Constance, subduing the Raeti on his way. On the shores of Lake Constance he met his elder brother, Tiberius Claudius Nero, who had marched eastward from Gaul. Together they defeated and subjugated the Vindelici. The Danube was now the Roman frontier on the north, and the way was open for the greatest military project of his reign, expansion beyond that river into Germany. A number of isolated campaigns completed subjugation of the remaining Alpine peoples by 8 B.C.

GAUL AND GERMANY. Caesar had left Gallia Comata crushed but still unsettled and not fully incorporated in the Empire. It fell to Augustus to complete its organization, a task accomplished between 27 and 13 B.C. Subsequent to the transfer of Gallia Narbonensis to the Senate, Gallia Comata was divided into three districts: Aquitania, Lugdunensis, and Belgica. During the lifetime of Augustus, however, these formed an administrative unit under one governor, with subordinate legates in each district. The colony of Lugdunum was the seat of administration and of the imperial cult. No attempt was made to latinize the three Gauls by founding other Roman colonies; they remained divided into sixty-four separate peoples, called *civitates*, with tribal organization under the native nobility. As early as 27 B.C. Augustus had taken a census of Gaul and fixed its tax obligations on this basis. The rich lands of Gaul were important as a source of imperial revenue, as a recruiting area for the auxiliary forces, and as a western base for his projected expansion against Germany.

Such expansion was prompted only in part by a desire to keep Gaul, restive under its new burdens, from being stirred up by Germanic invasions from beyond the Rhine like those of the Sugambri in 17 and 12 B.C. For some years Augustus seems to have been preparing for a grandiose German war, a project that was to occupy him almost to the end of his reign. He aimed first at subduing the area between the Rhine and Elbe. Initially at least he may not have excluded the notion of expansion beyond the latter river. The Germans, like the Gauls at the time of the Roman conquest, were divided into a number of independent tribes usually fighting among themselves and hence incapable of forming a lasting combination against a common foe. Individually they were powerful and courageous, but their military efficiency was impaired by their lack of unity and discipline.

Drusus, conqueror of the Raeti, was appointed to command the Roman army. He first secured the Rhine frontier by construction of a line of fortresses stretching from Vindonissa (near Basle) to Castra Vetera (near Xanten). The latter and Mogontiacum (Mainz) were his chief bases.

Crossing the river, he overran and subjugated the territory between the Rhine and the Elbe in four campaigns (12–9 B.C.). His operations were greatly aided by his fleet, for whose use he constructed a canal from the Rhine to the Zuider Zee, in order to provide a shorter and safer route to the mouth of the Elbe. Cooperation of the fleet also facilitated the conquest of the coast peoples, among them the Batavi, who became firm Roman allies. On the return march from the Elbe in 9 B.C., Drusus was fatally injured by a fall from his horse. His brother Tiberius succeeded him and strengthened the Roman hold on the transrhenane conquests. Drusus was buried in Rome, whither Tiberius escorted his corpse on foot, and was honored with the name Germanicus.

MIDDLE AND LOWER DANUBE.   To the east of the Adriatic the provinces of Illyricum and Macedonia were subject to constant incursions by the Pannonians, Getae (or Dacians), and Bastarnae, peoples settled in the middle and lower Danube valley. Marcus Licinius Crassus, governor of Macedonia, defeated the Getae and Bastarnae in 30 and 29 B.C., crossed the Balkans, carried the Roman arms to the Danube, and subdued the Moesi south of that river. It was some time, however, before the various Thracian tribes were finally pacified, and a client kingdom under the Thracian prince Cotys interposed between Macedonia and the lower Danube. Meantime, to secure the southern flank of the German front, the Pannonians were conquered in a number of hard-fought campaigns, which were brought to a successful conclusion by Tiberius (12–9 B.C.), who made the Danube the boundary. The contemporaneous and related conquest of Pannonia and of Germany between the Rhine and the Elbe was one of the greatest feats of Roman arms and reveals the army at the height of its discipline and organization. In 13 B.C., during a lull in these frontier struggles, the Senate voted the erection of an altar to the peace of Augustus (the *ara pacis Augustae*), in grateful recognition of his maintenance of peace within the Empire and pacification of foreign enemies.

REVOLTS IN ILLYRICUM AND GERMANY.   For several years following the death of Drusus no further conquests were attempted until A.D. 4, when Tiberius was again appointed to command the army of the Rhine. After assuring himself of the allegiance of the Germans by a demonstration as far as the Elbe and by establishing fortified posts, he prepared to complete the Roman conquest west of that river by attacking the kingdom of the Marcomanni, in modern Bohemia, between the Elbe and the Danube. In A.D. 6 Tiberius was about to advance northward from the Danube, in cooperation with Gaius Saturninus, who was to move eastward from the Rhine, when a revolt broke out in Illyricum, which forced abandonment of the undertaking and the conclusion of peace with Maroboduus, the king of the Marcomanni. This revolt, in which both Pannonians and Dalmatians joined, was due largely to the fact that these tribes had not been thoroughly subjugated, but also to some degree to the severity of the

Roman exactions, especially levies for the army. For a moment Italy was threatened with invasion. In the raising of new legions even freedmen were conscripted. But the arrival of reinforcements from other provinces enabled Tiberius after three years of ruthless warfare utterly to crush the desperate resistance of the rebels (A.D. 9). The organization of Pannonia and Moesia as separate provinces followed the re-establishment of peace.

Until the last year of the war in Illyricum the Germanic tribes had remained quiet under Roman overlordship. In A.D. 9, provoked by the attempt of the new Roman commander, Publius Quinctilius Varus, to subject them to stricter control, they united to free themselves from foreign rule. The Cherusci and Chatti were the chief peoples in the coalition, and Arminius, a young chieftain of the Cherusci who had served in the Roman *auxilia* and received citizenship and equestrian rank, was its leading spirit. Varus and his army of three legions were surprised on the march in the Teutoburg Forest and completely annihilated. Rome was in panic over the news, but the Germans did not follow up their success. Tiberius was again sent to the point of danger and vindicated the honor of Rome by two successful expeditions across the Rhine. No attempt was made to recover permanently the lost ground. The idea of possibly limitless expansion in central Europe was given up, and the Rhine became the frontier, with momentous consequences for the future of the Empire and of Europe. The coast peoples remained Roman allies, however, and a narrow strip of territory was held on the right bank of the Rhine. The reason for this retreat to the Rhine lay in the weakness of the Roman military organization, already strained to the utmost by the Illyrian revolt and the difficulty of finding recruits for the Roman legions among the Italians. The cry of Augustus, "Quinctilius Varus, give back the legions!" gives the clue to his abandonment of Germany.

EASTERN FRONTIER.   Between the Roman provinces in Asia Minor and the upper Euphrates lay a number of client kingdoms—Galatia, Pontus, Cappadocia and Lesser Armenia, and Commagene. At the death of Amyntas, king of Galatia, (25 B.C.), his kingdom was made into a province, but the others were left under their native dynasts. Across the Euphrates lay Armenia, a buffer state between the Roman possessions and Parthia, and strategically important because it commanded the military routes between Asia Minor and the heart of Parthia. To establish a protectorate over Armenia was therefore one of Augustus' great ambitions. Defeat or even conquest of Parthia, cornerstone of his eastern policy during much of his reign, would reassert the glory of Roman arms, wipe out the shame of the defeats of Crassus and Antony, and guarantee Roman territory from Parthian attack. During the presence of Augustus in the East (22–19 B.C.), Tiberius placed a Roman nominee on the Armenian throne and received by diplomatic means from the Parthian king, Phraates IV, the Roman standards and captives in Parthian hands, a success that earned

Augustus the salutation of Imperator from his troops. Later Phraates sent four of his sons to Rome as hostages. Parthia was therefore regarded as a client kingdom. With Armenia also dependent on Rome, it seemed only a question of time before Roman armies would cross the Euphrates and force the annexation of Parthia as a province. But unforeseen events in Armenia diverted Augustus' attention, and the final confrontation with Parthia never took place. The Roman protectorate over Armenia was by no means permanent. By about 6 B.C. the national, pro-Parthian faction had gained the upper hand. Between 1 B.C. and A.D. 2 Gaius Caesar, grandson of Augustus, restored Roman influence, but none of the several Roman appointees to the Armenian throne was able to retain his position. At the death of Augustus, the kingdom, then without a ruler, had escaped from Roman control. The northern flank of Asia Minor had meantime been made secure through the organization of the Bosporan Kingdom as a client state by Agrippa in 14 B.C.

To the south of the Roman province of Syria lay the kingdom of Judaea, ruled by Herod the Great from about 37 B.C. to his death in 4 B.C. His kingdom was divided among his three sons, Philip, Herod Antipas, and Archelaus. Archelaus inherited Judaea but proved to be an unpopular ruler. At the request of both Jews and Samaritans, he was deposed and exiled by the Romans in A.D. 6. Judaea then became a Roman province, ruled by a prefect residing at Caesarea. Augustus was aware of Jewish religious sensibilities, and Roman rule in the province was tactful.

In Arabia, Augustus sought to bring under Roman control the rich spice land of Arabia Felix, the southwestern coast of the peninsula. The invasion of Arabia Felix in pursuit of revenue clearly shows that Augustus' foreign policy was not solely defensive and aimed at attaining greater security. Success would have given the Romans control of trade between the Mediterranean and India by way of the Red Sea, for this was the point of transshipment of goods from India and Somaliland, on their way to the markets of Syria and Egypt. Relying upon the support of the Nabataean Arabs, who controlled the region to the south and east of the Dead Sea, Aelius Gallus, the Roman commander, assembled a large force in Egypt in 25 B.C. and transported it across the Red Sea to the Arabian shore. The following year he marched south through a desert where his troops suffered severely from lack of food and water. Shortage of these necessities at length forced him to abandon the expedition and return ingloriously to Egypt. This expedition was not a complete failure, however, since the Arabs, impressed by Rome's show of strength, accepted friendship with Rome and abandoned their monopoly of the straits at the south end of the Red Sea.

EGYPT AND NORTH AFRICA. In 25 B.C. Egypt had been invaded by the Ethiopians, who ravaged the upper part of the country. They were defeated and driven out by the prefect Gaius Petronius. Petronius pursued them far into the Sudan and took their capital, Napata. He then secured the southern frontier of Egypt by annexing and garrisoning a border district south of the First Cataract. Although the attempt to occupy Arabia Felix had failed, Rome came to control through Egypt a very large share of the trade with India since, owing to the recent discovery of the monsoon winds in the Indian Ocean, many merchant ships began to make annual voyages from the Red Sea ports of Egypt directly to India and Ceylon.

Further west on the North African coast, Augustus enlarged the old province of Africa by adding to it the kingdom of Numidia. He then appointed the former Numidian king, Juba II, whose wife was Cleopatra, the daughter of Mark Antony, to be king of Mauretania (25 B.C.), which he reestablished as a client kingdom. This placed the restless tribes of Algeria and Morocco under a dependable ally of Rome.

Augustus was a realist. Teutoburg and his difficulties with Armenia taught him that the Empire could not sustain the imperialistic aims he had so long pursued. At his death he left it as a maxim of state for his successors to abstain from future expansion, which meant that the conquests he had been able to realize were to establish in their essential features the future boundaries of the Roman Empire.

VII. Administration of Rome

POLICE AND FIRE PROTECTION. It had been Augustus' intention that the administration of the city of Rome, like that of Italy, should be conducted by the Senate through the magistrates. Because some very important branches of city government were either neglected or mismanaged, he felt compelled, however, partly in response to popular appeals, to organize them efficiently and to assume continuous responsibility for them. Of prime importance since the days of the Gracchi was the problem of policing Rome and the suppression of mob violence, which had threatened orderly government. To a certain extent the formation of the praetorian guard served to overawe the city mob and to prevent any revolutionary movement, even though at first only three of the praetorian cohorts were stationed in the city. In order to check nonpolitical disorders, suppress crime, and carry on other police functions, Augustus found it necessary to organize three urban cohorts, each originally of 1,500 men, who were regarded as soldiers and ranked above the legionaries but below the praetorians. At the death of Augustus the command of these cohorts was held by the City Prefect (*praefectus urbi*), whose office had been made permanent and who was appointed from among the senators of consular rank.

Between 12 and 7 B.C., for other administrative purposes, Augustus had Rome divided into fourteen regions subdivided into 265 precincts (*vici*). Each region was put in charge of one of the tribunes or aediles. Almost as important as the problem of police was that of protection against fire,

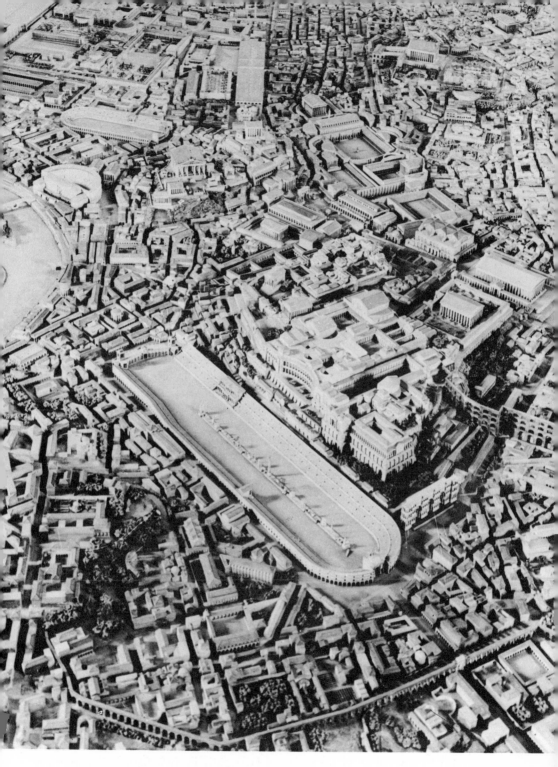

Model of Imperial Rome

which had been neglected almost completely under the Republic. As early as 21 B.C. Augustus tried to improve the situation by supplying the aediles responsible for this sphere of city government with a force of 600 slaves. This arrangement proved ineffective, and in A.D. 6 he created a special corps of 7,000 men to serve both as a fire brigade and as night police. This corps was organized in seven cohorts, one for every two of the fourteen regions, and was commanded by an equestrian appointee of the *princeps* whose title was prefect of the watch (*praefectus vigilum*).

GRAIN SUPPLY. Another vital problem was maintaining an adequate supply of grain for the city. On several occasions under the Republic this had presented such difficulties that extraordinary measures had been necessary to save the citizens from starvation, but no permanent solution had been reached. A famine in 22 B.C. was so serious that the Senate was forced to call upon Augustus to cope with it. He did so by assuming a temporary curatorship of the grain supply, and thereafter he may have exercised general supervision of it. Actual administration, however, seems to have remained for some time in the hands of two special aediles whose office Caesar had created for this purpose. At the next crisis, in A.D. 6, they were replaced temporarily by two senatorial curators, they in turn by an equestrian prefect of the grain supply (*praefectus annonae*). His duty was to see that there was always enough grain imported into Rome to supply the market at a reasonable price. It is doubtful that he was in charge of the regular monthly distribution of free grain to the city mob, a task carried out by other equestrian prefects of lower rank. By 2 B.C. the number on relief had been fixed at 200,000 properly registered citizens. With the creation of the prefecture of the grain supply, Augustus definitely assumed responsibility for the whole problem of the city's provisioning.

Other aspects of the government of Rome taken away from the annual magistrates were turned over to permanent commissions composed of senatorial curators of consular or praetorian rank. Such were the commissions in charge of aqueducts, temples and other public buildings, and that which was established in the year after the death of Augustus to supervise the banks and channel of the Tiber to prevent floods in the city.

A parallel encroachment upon the Senate's administrative control of Italy, also in the interests of efficiency, was made when Augustus was entrusted in 20 B.C. with the administration of Italian highways. This he also carried on through a commission of senatorial curators.

VIII. Problem of Succession

POLICY OF AUGUSTUS. In theory the position of the *princeps* was that of an officer who derived his powers from the Senate and the Roman people, and choice of his successor lay legally in their hands. Theoretically, this meant that the principate was a political prize to which any distinguished scion of an ancient republican family might lay claim, and there were those who thought they were worthy of the office. Augustus realized that to leave the field open to rival candidates would inevitably lead to a renewal of civil war. Therefore he determined to designate his own successor and make the latter's appointment undisputable. His own early career as son and heir of Julius Caesar warned him that his heir to the principate must be found in his own household, and his precarious health was a constant reminder that he could not wait to settle this problem. From the early years of his reign he arranged matrimonial alliances of relatives to other important families without regard to their personal preferences, to the end that in the event of his death there would be a member of the Julian house prepared to assume his office. He was merely adapting traditional republican practice to his own special purpose of assuring the continued dominance of his family and its faction in the state. The unexpected length of his life, however, meant that Augustus outlived many of those whom he looked upon as the heirs to his position in the state.

MARCUS MARCELLUS AND AGRIPPA. Augustus had no sons and only one daughter, Julia, by his second wife Scribonia. But Livia Drusilla, whom he took as his third wife in 38 B.C., brought him two stepsons, Tiberius and Drusus. Yet not one of these but his nephew, Marcus Marcellus, was his first choice as successor. Marcellus married Julia in 25 B.C. The next year, at the age of nineteen, he was admitted to the Senate, and in 23 B.C., as aedile, he won the favor of the populace by his magnificent public shows. When Marcellus died that year, Augustus turned to his loyal adherent Agrippa, to whom Julia was now wedded. In 18 B.C. Agrippa received proconsular *imperium* and the *tribunicia potestas* for five years, powers that were reconferred with those of Augustus in 13 B.C.

TIBERIUS. Agrippa died the next year, and Augustus, believing his eldest stepson Tiberius, conquerer of Noricum, to be the one best qualified to succeed himself, forced him to divorce the wife to whom he was devoted and to marry Julia. At that time he was given the important Illyrian command, and in 6 B.C. the tribunician authority was granted him for a five-year term. Tiberius, recognizing that he was merely to be the eventual guardian of the two elder sons of Agrippa and Julia, Gaius and Lucius Caesar, whom Augustus had adopted and taken into his own house, and being disgusted with the flagrant unfaithfulness of Julia, retired into private life at Rhodes, thereby incurring his stepfather's displeasure.

GAIUS AND LUCIUS CAESAR. Gaius and Lucius Caesar assumed the garb of manhood (*toga virilis*) at the age of fifteen in 5 and 2 B.C., respectively. On these occasions Augustus held the consulship and gave each son in turn the title *princeps inventutis*, thus designating them as new heads of cadets of the equestrian order. They were exempted from the limitations of the *cursus honorum* so that each might hold the consulate in his twentieth year. In A.D. 1 Gaius was sent to the East with proconsular *imperium* to settle fresh troubles in Armenia. There in the siege of a petty fortress he received a wound from which he died in A.D. 4. Two years previously Lucius had fallen a victim to fever while on his way to Spain. In the meantime Augustus had experienced another blow in his discovery of the scandalous conduct of Julia. Her guilt was the more unpardonable in view of the efforts of her father to reform the moral tone of society. She was banished to the island rock of Pandataria, and her companions in crime were punished, most with banishment, one with death on a charge of treason (1 B.C.). Her elder daughter, also called Julia, later met the same fate for a similar offence.

TIBERIUS AGAIN.   On the death of Gaius Caesar, Augustus turned once more to Tiberius, who had been permitted to leave Rhodes at the intercession of Livia. In A.D. 4 he was adopted by Augustus and received the *tribunicia potestas* for ten years. In A.D. 13 his tribunician power was renewed, and he was made the colleague of Augustus in the *imperium*. Tiberius was, in effect, coregent, differing from Augustus only insofar as his personal *auctoritas* was not so great. Tiberius himself had been obliged to adopt his nephew Germanicus, the son of Drusus, who married Agrippina, the younger daughter of Agrippa and Julia. Before his own death Augustus had thus set the precedent of designating the successor in the principate by association in authority, and adoption where necessary.

IX. Achievement of Augustus

DEATH OF AUGUSTUS.   In A.D. 14 Augustus held a census of Roman citizens. They numbered 4,937,000, an increase of 826,000 since 28 B.C. In the same year he set up in Rome an inscription recording his exploits and the sums he had expended on the state. One copy of this was found inscribed on the walls of the temple of Roma and Augustus at Ancyra (modern Ankara) in Asia Minor and hence is known as the Monument of Ancyra. Another, less complete, has been discovered at Antioch in Pisidia. On August 19, A.D. 14 Augustus died at Nola in Campania, at the age of seventy-six.

AUGUSTUS AS POLITICIAN AND STATESMAN.   Augustus was successful because he was able to extend his political faction, step by step, in the period 44–27 B.C. until it embraced the whole state. Realizing the paramount importance of patronage in Roman life, he saw to it that every important class, vested interest, and pressure group looked ultimately to him alone for rewards and advancement. A ruthless revolutionary in his early career, he nevertheless developed into a statesman of the highest order. What he established was a stable regime that, in fact, was a disguised kind of monarchy cleverly hidden behind a constitutional, republican facade. What followed him—a new era of peace and consolidation of

Roman civilization—was the greatest justification of his work, to which both Rome and Western civilization are deeply indebted.

WEAKNESSES OF HIS SYSTEM.   Certain grave weaknesses were present in his reorganization of the state, however. The disguised monarchy he established could easily develop into autocracy, since emperors were immeasurably more powerful than the second partner in administration, the Senate. Initiative in government had passed from an oligarchy to one man, and the inevitable result was the gradual abdication by the Senate of whatever residual responsibilities the emperors chose to leave it and the increasingly obvious concentration of power in imperial hands. Of even greater importance was Augustus' ultimate reliance on the control of military force as the single most important prop to imperial authority, from which followed the eventual realization by the military that it could make or unmake emperors. Furthermore, although he basically reformed the political structure of the Roman state, he did not touch its social and economic organization, except to expand the governing elite to include the equestrian order. The Augustan system of government rested primarily on the support of the upper classes, who as a matter of course were left to enjoy their traditional privileges. In effect, Augustus sanctioned and petrified the top-heavy class structure of the Greco-Roman world. The economic expansion that followed in the wake of the peace he created thus primarily benefited only a small minority of the population. The producing lower classes continued to live near subsistence level and were the first in the Empire to feel the effects of economic recession, when the Augustan system became increasingly expensive to operate.

CHAPTER 17

THE PRINCIPATE UNDER THE JULIO-CLAUDIANS[1] AND FLAVIANS: A.D. 14-96

Establishment of the Principate profoundly changed the character of Roman political history. Politics as practised during the Republic was no longer possible. The *princeps* might permit critics but dared not suffer opponents. The political history of Rome narrowed to matters of foreign relations and events at the capital, where associates and officers of the *princeps* strove for a dominant voice in his councils. Although the importance of imperial personalities in determining policy and law should not be underestimated, it must be remembered that administration at all times depended as much on imperial advisers and on factions in the governing establishment supporting the emperors as it did on the emperors themselves. The government of the Empire was always evolutionary, and rulers making seemingly basic reforms often merely coordinated or rationalized *ad hoc* changes in government made by their subordinates or predecessors. It is not surprising then to find that historians of the Principate focused their attention largely on the personal relations of the emperors with their households, their officers, and the Senate, and on the wars of the time, neglecting some less spectacular but highly significant developments in administration, law, religion, society, and economic life.

I. Tiberius: A.D. 14-37

TIBERIUS PRINCEPS.   At the death of Augustus, Tiberius Caesar assumed command of the army by right of his *imperium* and, through his tribunician authority, convoked the Senate to pay the last honors to Augustus and decide on his successor. Like Julius Caesar, Augustus was deified, and a priestly college of Augustales, chosen from the senatorial order, was founded to maintain his worship in Rome. In accordance with a wish expressed in his will, his widow Livia was honored with the name Augusta. The title of Augustus was bequeathed to Tiberius, who now received from the Senate and Assembly the other honors and powers his predecessor had made prerogatives of the *princeps*. His *imperium* was conferred for life, however, not for a limited period. The ease of his succession shows how solidly the Principate was established at the death of its founder.

---

[1] Note genealogical table, p. 537.

In the person of Tiberius, a member of the Claudian *gens* by birth, of the Julian by adoption, these two noble houses were united, and from this Julio-Claudian line came the first four successors of Augustus in the principate.

CHARACTER AND POLICY. Tiberius was now fifty-five years of age. He had spent most of his life in public service and had a full appreciation of the responsibility the *princeps* must assume. He was the incarnation of the old Roman sense of duty and at the same time exhibited the proud reserve of a Roman patrician. Stern in his maintenance of law and order, he made an excellent subordinate; when called upon to guide state policy, he displayed hesitation and lack of decision. The incidents of his marriage with Julia and his retirement at Rhodes, which practically amounted to exile, had rendered him bitter and suspicious, and he utterly lacked the personal charm and adaptability of his predecessor. Although he continued the policy of consulting groups of his political friends on matters of public policy, he did not revive Augustus' standing committee of senators, which perhaps accounts in part for his frequent misunderstandings with the Senate. Such an incident occurred during meetings of the Senate after the death of Augustus. Tiberius, conscious of his unpopularity, sought to have the Senate press upon him the appointment as successor to Augustus and feigned reluctance to accept, a course that made the senators suspect he was laying a trap for possible rivals. No *princeps*, however, tried more conscientiously to govern in the spirit of Augustus or upheld more rigidly the rights and dignity of the Senate. Even his severest critics admitted that, until his removal to Capri in A.D. 26, Tiberius governed with moderation and tact. At the beginning of his principate he transferred from the Assembly to the Senate the right of election to the magistracies, thus relieving the senators from the expense and annoyance of canvassing the populace.[2]

MUTINIES IN ILLYRICUM AND ON THE RHINE. Two serious mutinies followed the accession of Tiberius, one in the army stationed in Illyricum, the other among the legions on the Rhine. Failure to discharge those who had completed their terms of service and the severity of service itself were the grounds of dissatisfaction. The Illyrian mutiny was quelled by Tiberius' own son Drusus, and the army of the Rhine was brought back to its allegiance by his nephew Germanicus, the son of his brother, the elder Drusus, whom Tiberius had adopted at the command of Augustus in A.D. 4. Germanicus had married Agrippina, daughter of Agrippa and Julia, and was regarded as the heir of Tiberius, in preference to the latter's younger and less popular son, Drusus.

CAMPAIGNS OF GERMANICUS: A.D. 14–17. To restore discipline among his troops and relieve them from the monotony of camp

---

[2] The honorary prerogative centuries mentioned above, p. 277, persisted in the Centuriate Assembly until at least A.D. 23.

life, as well as to emulate his father, Germanicus, without the authorization of Tiberius, led his army across the Rhine. Although the German tribes were still united in the coalition formed in the time of Varus and, under their leaders Arminius and Inguiomerus, offered vigorous opposition to the Roman invasion, Germanicus was able to ravage the territory between the Rhine and the Weser in three successive campaigns (14–16) and inflicted several defeats upon the Germans. Arminius and his allies were by no means subdued, however, and the Romans sustained heavy losses. One army narrowly escaped the fate of the legions of Varus, and twice transports of Germanicus were struck by storms in the North Sea. For these reasons Tiberius forbade prolongation of the war and recalled Germanicus, trusting for the future to diplomacy rather than force of arms. On his departure each of the three Gauls (Aquitania, Belgica, and Lugdunensis) was made an independent province, and two new administrative districts, called Upper and Lower Germany, under legates of consular rank, were created on the left bank of the Rhine. Financial administration of the two Germanies, remained united with that of *Gallia Belgica*. Freed from the danger of a Roman invasion, the Germanic tribes led by Arminius now engaged in a bitter struggle with Maroboduus, king of the Marcomani, which led ultimately to the latter's overthrow. Not long afterward Arminius himself fell victim to the jealousy of his fellow tribesmen (19).

EASTERN MISSION AND DEATH OF GERMANICUS: A.D. 17–19. After his return from Gaul, Germanicus was sent by Tiberius on a special mission, with an *imperium* outranking that of the provincial governors, to settle affairs in the East, where the Armenian question had again become acute. Once again an Armenian king, this time the choice of his own people, received his diadem from the representative of Rome. In the East, Germanicus displayed the same indifference to the policy of the *princeps* as he had done in the West. He violated the rule established by Augustus that no senator should visit Egypt without special permission. During his stay in Egypt he alleviated a famine in Alexandria by distributing grain stored in public granaries. This visit earned him a severe rebuke from Tiberius, who was alarmed by his conduct. A bitter quarrel developed in Syria between Germanicus and Piso, the legate of the province. When Germanicus fell ill and died there, many accused Piso of having poisoned him. Piso was called to Rome to stand trial on that charge, as well as the better founded ones of insubordination and violence. Finding that the popularity of Germanicus had biased popular opinion against him and that Tiberius refused him protection because he had attempted to assert his rights by armed force, he committed suicide. Agrippina, the ambitious wife of Germanicus, believed that Tiberius had been responsible for her husband's death from motives of jealousy. She openly displayed her hostility to the *princeps* and by plotting to secure the succession for her own children helped to bring about their ruin and her own.

PLOT OF SEJANUS. Tiberius no less than Augustus intended that one of his family should succeed to the principate, but the question of succession was exacerbated by the hostility between Tiberius, Agrippina, and their respective factions, as well as by the ambitions of the praetorian prefect, Sejanus. In 23 Drusus died. Since the death of Germanicus he had been looked upon as the logical heir to the principate. It was later alleged that Sejanus had poisoned Drusus. Grieving over the loss of his son and possibly disturbed by the conduct of Agrippina, whose elder sons Nero and Drusus were now next in line for the principate, Tiberius withdrew from Rome in 26 and took up residence on the island of Capri off the Bay of Naples. His removal gave rise to further misunderstandings between himself and the Senate, but of much greater importance was the opportunity it furnished the able and ambitious Sejanus to create a position of strength that would ensure his own regency over an imperial prince upon Tiberius' eventual death. Sejanus seems to have had in mind the young and presumably pliable Gaius, Agrippina's youngest son, and he therefore played on Tiberius' suspicions to remove the other members of the house of Germanicus. On charges of treason, Nero and Agrippina were deported from Italy, and the former was forced to commit suicide. The young Drusus was imprisoned in Rome. Sejanus shared the consulship with Tiberius and received from the Senate proconsular *imperium* in the provinces. He had also persuaded the *princeps* to sanction his betrothal to Julia, Tiberius' granddaughter. In the end he overplayed his hand. An influential faction of senators, although tolerant of an equestrian *novus homo* in the governing oligarchy, refused absolutely to accept him as a possible regent with powers and pretensions far greater than their own. What happened next is obscure. This faction apparently threatened to withdraw support from Tiberius' government if Sejanus were not dropped. Sejanus, probably aware that his position was precarious, prepared a *coup d'état*. Of this Tiberius was informed. The emperor acted secretly and energetically. In 31 Sejanus and many of his supporters were arrested and executed. Agrippina was left to die in exile, and her son Drusus perished in his prison.

LAST YEARS OF TIBERIUS. The emperor became increasingly morose as the years passed and his fears of treachery increased. The law of treason (*lex de maiestate*) was rigorously enforced, often with good reason. The emperor's estrangement from the Senate was almost complete, and the senators lived in terror of being accused by informers (*delatores*). In their anxiety to conciliate the *princeps* they were only too ready to condemn colleagues. It was with undisguised relief that they heard the news of his death on March 16, A.D. 37, in his seventy-eighth year.

The memory of his later years caused Tiberius to pass down in the traditions of the senatorial order, represented by Tacitus and Suetonius, as a ruthless tyrant and obscured his real services as a conscientious and economical administrator. His parsimony made him unpopular with the city mob but was a blessing to the provincials, to whose welfare Tiberius directed particular attention, while he tried to protect them against the oppression of imperial officials. During most of his reign the peace of the Empire was disturbed only by a brief rising in Gaul (21) and a rather prolonged struggle with Tacfarinas, a rebellious Berber chieftain, in Numidia (17–24).

II. Gaius Caligula: A.D. 37–41

ACCESSION. Tiberius left as heirs his adoptive grandson Gaius, the sole surviving son of Germanicus, better known by his childhood nickname of Caligula ("Bootsie") acquired in the camps on the Rhine, and his grandson by birth, Tiberius Gemellus, the son of Drusus. Prompted by a powerful faction, the Senate immediately conferred the powers of the principate upon Gaius, the elder of the two, then twenty-five years of age. The resentment of the senators toward Tiberius found expression in their refusing him the posthumous honor of deification. Gaius adopted his cousin but within a year had him executed.

EARLY POPULARITY. The early months of Gaius' rule seemed the dawn of a new era. Pardoning of political offenders, banishment of informers, reduction of taxes, coupled with lavishness in public entertainments and donations, all made Gaius popular with the Senate, the army, and the city populace. He was a weakling in body and in mind, however, and a serious illness, brought on by excesses, may have left him mentally deranged. In any event, his undisciplined character succumbed completely to the temptations of power.

ABSOLUTISM HIS IDEAL. Reared in the house of his grandmother Antonia, daughter of Antony and Octavia, in company with eastern princes like Herod Agrippa, he possibly came to look upon the principate as an autocracy of the Hellenistic type. He certainly went to ridiculous extremes in realizing his conception of his position. He was the first emperor in Rome to insist on being a god in life, claiming deification for his sisters, and building a lofty bridge connecting the Palatine Hill with the Capitoline, so that he might communicate with Jupiter, his brother god. He prescribed the sacrifices to be offered to himself and was accused of seeking to imitate the Ptolemaic custom of sister marriage. Thoroughly consistent with absolutism was his scorn of republican magistracies, his disregard of the rights of the Senate, and his attempt to have himself called *dominus* or "lord."

CONFLICT WITH THE JEWS. His demand for the acknowledgment of his deification by all inhabitants of the Empire brought Gaius into conflict with the Jews, who had been exempted from this formal expression of loyalty. In Alexandria there was a large Jewish colony, hated by the Alexandrians for claiming citizenship in the city and enjoying exceptional privileges. These seized the opportunity of a visit of Herod Agrippa, king of a petty Jewish principality, to insult the Jewish community by burlesquing him and his followers. Then, in order to avoid the consequences of this mockery of Gaius' friend, they tried to show their loyalty by forcing the Jews to worship images of the *princeps*. Refusal of this demand furnished the mob with a pretext for sacking the Jewish quarters and forcibly installing the statues in some synagogues. The Jews sent a delegation to plead their case before Gaius but could obtain no redress. In the meantime Gaius ordered Petronius, the legate of Syria, to set up his statue in the temple at Jerusalem, by force, if necessary. The prudent Petronius, seeing that this would bring about a Jewish revolt, delayed obeying the order, and then the death of Gaius relieved him of the necessity of executing it at all.

TYRANNY AND ITS END. In less than a year the reckless extravagance of Gaius had exhausted the immense surplus Tiberius had left in the treasury. To secure new funds he resorted to tyrannical measures, extraordinary taxes, judicial murders, confiscations, and forced legacies. By these means money was extorted not only from Romans of all classes but from provincials as well. Ptolemy, king of Mauretania, was executed for the sake of his treasure and his kingdom claimed as a province. With the annexation of Mauretania, the Roman encirclement of the Mediterranean was at last complete.

Gaius contemplated invasions of Germany and of Britain, but the former ended with a military parade across the Rhine and the latter with a march to the Strait of Dover. The fear awakened by his capricious violence soon resulted in a conspiracy against his life. In January, 41 he was assassinated by a tribune of the praetorian guards whom he had grossly insulted and by others who feared that they might fall victims to his caprice. His wife and infant daughter shared his fate.

III. Claudius: A.D. 41–54

NOMINATION AND APPOINTMENT. In their enthusiasm at the death of Gaius, the Senators debated the possibility of restoring the Republic. They soon realized they were not in control of the situation. The praetorian guard, some of whom had discovered and dragged from his hiding-place the uncle of the murdered *princeps*, Tiberius Claudius Caesar Germanicus, saluted this younger brother of Germanicus as Imperator. The reluctant Senate was obliged to acquiesce in his nomination and to grant him the title Augustus together with the powers and honors of the principate. Although Claudius was not the first to buy military loyalty, his rewarding of the praetorians with a donative set a regrettable precedent for future emperors. The new *princeps* was already over fifty years old, without any real experience in public life. Because of his ungainly appearance and a general impression of ineffectiveness, Claudius had never been considered seriously as a potential candidate for the principate. Fussy and pedantic, often influenced unduly by his wives and freedmen, Claudius was nevertheless a more able and independent-minded emperor than the surviving hostile historical tradition indicates.

GOVERNMENT POLICY. As a thoughtful student of Roman history, Claudius was rather conservative in his general policy and endeavored to govern in the spirit of Augustus and Tiberius. Toward the Senate he showed the greatest respect and did all within his power to force it to take an active part in government. He assumed the censorship in 47 for the traditional term of eighteen months, an office Augustus had avoided because its tenure might have seemed too autocratic. In this office he followed the Republican practice and took a colleague. Claudius attempted to check abuses in the application of the law of treason and to restrain professional informers. In spite of such gestures of good will, many senators and equestrians conspired against Claudius and were executed on charges of treason. Others fell as a result of cabals concocted by the emperor's freedmen and by his last two wives, Messalina and Agrippina, all of whom sought to destroy possible enemies. In the administration of the treasury and of roads and public works in Rome and Italy, the *princeps* encroached still further upon the Senate's sphere of action. Of particular importance was the building of a new harbor with docks and warehouses at Ostia, in order to improve the facilities for handling the grain supply of Rome. The most significant innovation was his conversion of a number of secretaryships held since Augustus by freedmen in the household of the emperors into influential ministries of state. This was done to increase administrative efficiency in coping with the emperor's expanding executive responsibilities. Claudius' freedmen functioning in these ministerial posts were able and ambitious men. Pallas, as *a rationibus*, was minister of finance; his rival Narcissus was made minister of correspondence (*ab epistulis*). Other ministers were those in charge of petitions addressed to the *princeps* (*a libellis*), of judicial investigations or trials he conducted (*a cognitionibus*), and of the imperial library (*a studiis*). Through the first four of these positions, freedmen supervised practically all branches of government directed by the *princeps* and so came to have a great influence upon his decisions and policies. They lacked the traditional ideals and restraints of the nobility. Often they abused their power to amass riches by the sale of favors, and some of them accumulated great fortunes in this way. It was due to their influence that many freedmen were given appointments as imperial procurators and that the latter officials in the provinces were granted judicial authority in matters affecting the claims of the financial branch of administration.

THE PROVINCES. Following the precedent of Julius Caesar rather than that of Augustus, Claudius decided upon the annexation of Britain. In this he was motivated apparently by an exaggerated estimate of the resources of the island and the advisability of popularizing himself with the legions by a successful campaign conducted under his auspices. There was also some justification for the expedition in the fact that the free Belgian tribes of Britain were a potential menace to the peace of the Gallic shore. Conditions in Britain had changed in some ways since the days of Julius Caesar. In the southeast of the island a kingdom of some consequence had been established by Cunobelinus (Cymbeline, died A.D. 40) with its capital at Camulodunum (Colchester). Although primarily agricultural, this kingdom also had developed a lively commerce with the continent, and this trade was steadily improving the standard of living of the British nobility and drawing them toward the orbit of Roman civilization. To the west of this kingdom were tribes composed of descendants of refugees from Caesar's invasion of Gaul. The king of one such tribe, dispossessed by Cymbeline, appealed in Rome to Claudius for reinstatement. This appeal was the immediate justification for the Roman invasion. In 43 the emperor's legates Aulus Plautius, Flavius Vespasianus, and Ostorius Scapula overran Britain as far as the Thames. Claudius himself was in nominal command at the crossing of the Thames and the occupation of the Belgian royal town of Camulodunum (Colchester), which was made a Roman colony and capital of the province of Britain, formed out of the conquered territory. With the erection of a temple to Rome and Augustus at Camulodunum, the imperial cult was set up in the new province. After the return of Claudius to Rome, Roman authority was extended steadily over wider areas on the island. A frontier line was established along the Trent and Severn Rivers, north of which Roman legions occasionally ventured on punitive missions. In North Africa, Claudius found himself faced by a revolt that broke out in Mauretania as the result of the attempt of Gaius to convert that kingdom into a province. After two years of hard fighting, native resistance was crushed, and Mauretania was divided into two imperial provinces, Mauretania Caesariensis in the east and Mauretania Tingitana (Tangier) in the west (42). Another new province was formed in 46 by the annexation of the client kingdom of Thrace upon the death of the native ruler. This policy was also carried out in Judaea, which Claudius had placed in 41 under Herod Agrippa, as a gesture of reconciliation toward the Jews following the excesses of Caligula and as a reward to a personal friend who had been instrumental in securing Claudius' own throne. Upon the death of King Herod in 44, however, the greater part of the country reverted to provincial status and was governed by an imperial procurator.

Throughout the provinces, Claudius was active in founding colonies and in promoting the organization of towns as Roman or Latin municipalities. While censor he defended before the Senate, in a speech that has been preserved in part, his liberality in the extension of Roman citizenship, and apparently he enrolled some Gallic notables among the senators. He did open the public magistracies to all Roman citizens in Gaul, which meant that henceforth they were on the same footing as Romans in Italy with respect to admission to the senatorial order. The census taken in 47–48 showed 5,944,000 Roman citizens, nearly a million more than in the time of Augustus. Claudius personally paid much attention to provincial administration. Here he showed himself to be a well-meaning ruler, who tried to make his subordinates efficient and honest. His reply—recently found on a papyrus from Egypt—to the petition of the Alexandrians for permission to form a city council throws a favorable light on his statesmanship.

AGRIPINA THE YOUNGER AND THE DEATH OF CLAUDIUS. In 48 a crisis occurred in the household of the *princeps*. His wife Messalina became infatuated with a young noble named Gaius Silius, and their relations gave rise to a belief that they were conspiring to have Silius seize the principate. The freedmen of Claudius felt endangered and decided that Messalina must be removed. Their spokesman Narcissus induced Claudius to order her execution and saw that it was carried out. It was Pallas who induced the *princeps* to take as his fourth wife his own niece Agrippina, daughter of Germanicus, whose ambitions were fatal to her husband. By Messalina, Claudius had a son, Britannicus, and a daughter, Octavia. The former was regarded as the future successor of Claudius, but Agrippina determined to secure the principate for her own son Domitius, whose father was her first husband Gnaeus Domitius Ahenobarbus. In 50 she succeeded in having Claudius adopt Domitius with the name of Nero Claudius Caesar. A year later, when he was only thirteen years old, Nero was given the title *princeps juventutis* and granted proconsular *imperium* outside of Rome. Thus he was openly designated as the future emperor. In 53 he married Octavia, his sister by adoption. Narcissus still championed the cause of Britannicus, however, and Agrippina, who feared that further delay would endanger her plans, had Claudius poisoned.

IV. Nero: A.D. 54–68

FIRST FIVE YEARS. The accession of Nero was expected, and his appointment to the principate was carried through without opposition or delay, since Agrippina had secured the support of the praetorians by the promise of a handsome donative. Nero was only sixteen years old when he succeeded Claudius, and for five years the government was actually carried on by his most influential advisers, the praetorian prefect Afranius Burrus from Gallia Narbonensis and Lucius Annaeus Seneca, the famous philosopher from Spain, whom Agrippina had appointed as his tutor in 49. Under their direction the administration, while strongly autocratic in tone, was highly efficient and conducted with proper consideration of the best interests of the Empire. Agrippina did not mean to be deprived of participation in the councils of state, however, and attempted to act as regent for her son and to retain the influence she had acquired toward the end of Claudius' reign. She was opposed both by Nero and by his able advisers, who catered to his baser instincts to keep him under their control. In 55 Nero had his adoptive brother Britannicus poisoned, through fear of his rivalry. Finally, influenced by his mistress, Poppaea Sabina, the wife of Titus Salvius Otho, he had Agrippina murdered (59). Thereupon he divorced Octavia (later banished and executed) and married Poppaea.

NERO AT THE HELM. Freed from any rival influence, Nero, now twenty-two years of age, began to run the government. After the death of Burrus in 62, Seneca lost his influence over the *princeps*, who took as his chief adviser the worthless praetorian prefect, Tigellinus. The Senate, whose support had been courted by Burrus and Seneca, was now without any influence, and, since his wanton extravagances emptied the treasury, Nero was forced to resort to oppressive measures to satisfy his needs. The sole object of his policy was gratification of his whims. An ardent phil-Hellene, he sought to introduce into Rome Greek gymnastic and artistic competitions of the Hellenistic type. Believing that he was an artist of extraordinary genius, he desired the applause of the successful performer, and in 65 he appeared publicly in the theatre as singer and musician. Nothing could have more deeply alienated the upper classes of Roman society. Eager to duplicate his theatrical successes in the home of the muses, Nero visited Greece in 66 and exhibited his talent at the Olympian and Delphic games.

FIRE IN ROME AND FIRST PERSECUTION OF THE CHRIS-TIANS: A.D. 64. In 64 a tremendous fire, which lasted for six continuous days and then broke out a second time, devastated most of the city of Rome. Nero was accused of having caused the fire, but there is absolutely no proof of his guilt. He did seize the opportunity to rebuild the damaged quarter on a new plan that did away with offensive slum districts and to erect his famous "Golden House," a magnificent palace and park on the Esquiline. Popular opinion demanded a scapegoat for the disaster, and Nero's advisers blamed the Christians in Rome, probably because they were known to be unpopular with the masses. Many Christians were tried and condemned on charges of anarchistic tendencies and suffered terrible deaths. This was the first persecution of the Christians conducted by the Roman government.

ARMENIAN PROBLEM: A.D. 51–67. In 51 an able and ambitious ruler, Vologases, came to the Parthian throne. When the Roman client king of Armenia was captured and killed by the neighboring Iberians, Vologases seized the opportunity to make his brother Tiridates the Armenian king. When the news reached Rome after the accession of Nero, Gnaeus Domitius Corbulo was sent to Asia Minor to reassert Roman suzerainty over Armenia. It was not until late in 57 that he was able to mobilize his forces. In two campaigns he overran Armenia and set up a Roman puppet as king (60). Vologases had been unable to oppose Corbulo because of a serious rebellion in his own empire. In 61, however, he set out to reestablish his brother in his lost kingdom. Upon failure of negotiations with Rome, he invaded Armenia, blockaded the Roman governor of Cappadocia, Caesennius Paetus, who had tried to anticipate the Parthian attack, and forced him to purchase his safety and that of his troops by agreeing to the Roman evacuation of Armenian territory (62). The situation was saved by Corbulo, then legate of Syria, who was finally entrusted with the sole command of operations and forced Vologases to meet Roman terms (63). Tiridates retained the Armenian throne but acknowledged Roman overlordship by coming to Rome to receive his crown from Nero.

REVOLT IN BRITAIN: A.D. 60.   Under Claudius the Romans had extended their dominion in Britain northward as far as the Humber and westward to Cornwall and Wales. In 59 Suetonius Paulinus occupied the island of Mona (Anglesea), chief seat of the Druids. While he was so engaged, a serious revolt broke out among the Iceni and Trinovantes, who lived between The Wash and the Thames River. It was caused by the severity of the Roman administration and in particular by the Roman procurators' ill-treatment of Boadicea, queen of the Iceni, who headed the insurrection. The Roman towns of Camulodunum (Colchester), Verulamium (St. Alban's), and Londinium (London) were destroyed, and 70,000 Romans were allegedly killed. A Roman legion was defeated, and it was not until Paulinus returned and united the scattered Roman forces that the insurgents were checked. The Britons were decisively defeated, and Boadicea committed suicide.

CONSPIRACY OF PISO: A.D. 65.   About 62 a series of treason trials began in Rome, occasioned partly by the desire to confiscate the property of the accused and partly by the suspicion that inevitably accompanies tyranny. The resulting insecurity among the senatorial order naturally produced a real attempt to overthrow the *princeps*. A wide-reaching conspiracy led by the senator Gaius Calpurnius Piso and involving one of the praetorian prefects, was discovered in 65. Among those executed for complicity were the poet Lucan and his uncle Seneca. Later notable victims of Nero's vengeance were Thrasea Paetus and Barea Soranus, Stoic senators, whose guilt was their silent but unmistakable disapproval of his tyranny. No man of prominence was safe; even the famous general Corbulo was forced to commit suicide in 67. Nero sought to strengthen his position by appointing reliable men to strategic commands, but the loyalty of these very appointees was undermined, since they could easily be persuaded that the erratic emperor might soon threaten their lives. Their insecurity was to be the cause of Nero's downfall.

REBELLION OF VINDEX: A.D. 68.   On Nero's return from Greece, upon which he had bestowed the gift of "freedom," a more serious movement began in Gaul, where Gaius Julius Vindex, legate of the province of Lugdunensis, revolted with support of the provincials, who were suffering under the pressure of taxation. Vindex was joined by Sulpicius Galba, governor of Hither Spain, who assumed leadership of the revolutionary movement and who quickly built up a faction among other disaffected legates. The commander of Upper Germany, Verginius Rufus, disapproved of the revolutionary turn of events, since he believed that only an uncoerced Senate should name a *princeps*. After a conference with Vindex, his troops got out of hand and slaughtered the Gauls in the former's army. Vindex committed suicide, and Verginius, true to his ideals, declined the principate when it was offered him by his officers and troops. Surprisingly enough, Nero found some support among the officers of other provincial field armies, but his fate was sealed by his own cowardice and by the treachery of the prefect Nymphidius Sabinus, who bought the support of the praetorian guards for Galba. The Senate followed their lead, and Nero fled from Rome and killed himself with the help of a faithful freedman. With Nero's death the Julio-Claudian dynasty came to an end.

V. Year of the Four Emperors: A.D. 68–69

POWER OF THE ARMY. The year 68–69 witnessed the accession of four emperors, each the nominee of powerful factions in the officer cadres of their respective field armies. Up to this time the praetorian guard had already acclaimed emperors. Now, as Tacitus expressed it, the fatal secret of the Empire was discovered, namely, that the *princeps* could be nominated elsewhere than in Rome. Although the principate theoretically was founded by the universal consent of the Roman world, from its inception the power of the *princeps* had rested directly upon his military command, and the civil war of 68–69 showed how completely the officers of the professional field army could become masters of the situation. It was they who manipulated *esprit de corps* of their men, and the impetus to revolution came from the ambitions of those above and not from the legionaries themselves, who were the tools of their commanders.

GALBA: A.D. 68. Galba, who succeeded Nero, was a man of good family but moderate attainments and soon showed himself unable to maintain his authority. That he would have been held "fit to rule, had he not ruled," was the judgment of Tacitus. He had never been enthusiastically supported by the Rhine legions or the praetorians. His severity in maintaining discipline, added to his failure to pay the promised donative, completely alienated the guards. At the news that the troops in Upper and Lower Germany had declared for Aulus Vitellius, legate of the latter province (January 1, 69), Galba sought to strengthen his position by adopting as his son and destined successor, Lucius Calpurnius Piso, a young man of high birth but no experience. By this step he offended

Marcus Salvius Otho, the one-time husband of Nero's wife Poppaea Sabina and one of Galba's staunch adherents, who hoped to succeed him. Otho now won over the disgruntled praetorian guards, who slew Galba and Piso and proclaimed Otho Imperator.

OTHO: JANUARY–APRIL, A.D. 69. The Senate acquiesced in this decision, but not the legions of Vitellius, already on the march to Italy. They crossed the Alps unopposed but were checked by the forces of Otho at Bedriacum, north of the Po. Without waiting for the arrival of reinforcements from the Danubian army, Otho ordered an attack upon the Vitellians at Cremona. His army was defeated, and he took his own life.

VITELLIUS: APRIL–DECEMBER, A.D. 69. Vitellius was then recognized as *princeps* by the Senate, and his forces occupied Rome. Vitellius owed his nomination to the energy of the legates Valens and Caecina but, although well-meaning and by no means tyrannical, he lacked energy and force of character. He was unable to control his soldiery, who plundered the Italian towns, or his officers, who enriched themselves at the public expense, while he devoted himself to gastronomical pleasures.

Meanwhile the army of the East, which had recognized Galba, Otho, and, at first, Vitellius, set up its own Imperator, Titus Flavius Vespasianus, who, as legate of Judaea, was conducting a war against the Jews. Vespasian proceeded to occupy Egypt thus cutting off the grain supply of Rome, while his ablest lieutenant, Mucianus, set out for Italy. The Danubian legions, who had supported Otho, now declared themselves for Vespasian and, led by Antonius Primus, marched at once upon Italy. The fleet at Ravenna espoused Vespasian's cause, and Caecina, who led the Vitellians against Primus, contemplated treachery. His troops remained loyal, but they were defeated in a bloody night battle at Cremona. The way lay open to Rome. Vitellius then opened negotiations and offered to abdicate, but his soldiers would not let him and suppressed a rising in Rome led by Vespasian's brother. The city was then stormed and sacked by the army of Primus, and Vitellius was slain.

VESPASIAN: DECEMBER, A.D. 69. Vespasian obtained his recognition as *princeps* from the Senate and the troops in the West and entered Rome early in 70.

VI. Vespasian and Titus: A.D. 69–81

REBELLION IN GAUL AND GERMANY: A.D. 69. The new *princeps* inherited two serious wars, both national revolts against Roman rule, one in Gaul and Lower Germany, the other in Judaea. The movement in Lower Germany was headed by Julius Civilis, a Batavian chieftain, formerly a Roman officer, who won over the eight Batavian cohorts attached to the Rhine army. The Batavians were disaffected because the Roman authorities had recently attempted to reorganize on stricter lines[3]

---

[3] The reorganization of auxiliary forces, begun by Augustus, was not yet complete.

the auxiliary cohorts they had traditionally provided the Roman army. At first Civilis posed as a supporter of Vespasian against Vitellius and besieged the Vitellian garrison at Vetera in the lower Rhineland, but at the news of the former's victory he renounced his allegiance to Rome and called to his aid Germanic tribes from across the Rhine. Simultaneously the Gallic Treveri and Lingones, the former led by Julius Classicus and Julius Tutor, the latter by Julius Sabinus—both nobles who had served as Roman officers and enjoyed Roman citizenship—rose in rebellion and sought to establish an empire of the Gauls with its capital at Trèves (Augusta Treverorum). They were joined by the Roman legions stationed on the Rhine. The remaining peoples of Gaul, however, refused to join the revolt, preferring the Roman peace to a renewal of the old intertribal struggles.

Upon the arrival of an adequate Roman force despatched by Mucianus, Vespasian's representative in Rome, the mutinous legions returned to their duty, the Treveri and Lingones were subdued, and Civilis was forced to flee into Germany. The Batavi returned to their former status of Roman allies (70), and the auxiliary forces they furnished the Roman army were henceforth led and organized along the lines originally established for *auxilia* by Augustus.

FRICTION IN JUDAEA. From the year A.D. 6 Judaea had been a Roman province, except for its brief incorporation in the principality of Herod Agrippa I (41–44). During this time the Jews had occupied a privileged position among Rome's subjects, being exempted from military service and the obligation of the imperial cult, notwithstanding the design of Caligula to set up his image in the temple at Jerusalem. These privileges were a constant source of friction between the Jews and the Greco-Syrian inhabitants of the cities of Palestine, frequently necessitating intercession by Roman officials. Another cause of unrest in Judaea was the pressure of taxation, which rendered agriculture unprofitable and drove many persons from the plains to the mountains where they became brigands. A more deep-seated cause of animosity to Roman rule was that the Jews were a religious community and that for them national loyalty was identical with an uncompromising devotion to their religion. They resented the rule of foreigners, not merely because it meant loss of political freedom but because it was an offence to their religion. The situation was not helped by the incompetence and tactlessness of Roman officials whose actions often needlessly wounded Jewish susceptibilities. The Jews themselves were not united. There were groups of various religious attitudes, like the Essenes, some of whose Dead Sea scrolls have survived. In addition, there was an upper class of wealthy landholders and also a lower class of less well-to-do persons that included many impoverished peasants. The former were the party of the Sadducees, who monopolized the higher religious offices, including that of the High Priest. Opposed to them were the Pharisees, who held most of the lower priesthoods and laid great stress upon the strict observance of Jewish law in all aspects of human relations. In general, the Sadducees were inclined to cooperate with the Romans and in turn were supported by Rome, whereas the Pharisees were strongly nationalistic and consequently anti-Roman. It is improbable that the Pharisees actually wished to bring about a revolt, but they set in motion events they could not control and strengthened the development of a party of direct action, the Zealots, who aimed to liberate Judaea from the Romans by force, trusting in the support of Jehovah. By 66 all Judaea was in a ferment, and it required little incitement to produce a national revolt.

THE JEWISH REBELLION: A.D. 66–70. Hostilities broke out in 66 in Jerusalem, where the Roman garrison was driven out by the rebels. At the same time a decision of the Roman government that Jews were not entitled to citizenship in Caesarea, the capital of the province, provoked a riot in which the Greek population massacred the Jews. Similar outbreaks occurred in other towns of Judaea, now one party now the other being the aggressor, and the disorders spread beyond the bounds of Judaea to Syria and Egypt. The Romans awoke to the seriousness of the situation when the legate of Syria, Cestius Gallus, who had marched on Jerusalem, was forced to beat an ignominious retreat.

Late in 67 Vespasian was appointed to command an army of 50,000 assembled for the reconquest of Judaea. In this and the following year he reduced the open country and isolated fortresses and was ready to blockade Jerusalem, where most Jews had fled for refuge. Upon hearing of Nero's death, he postponed his attack on the city and did not resume active operations until after the accession of Vitellius. Shortly afterward, however, his own elevation to the principate caused a further suspension of hostilities for ten months, during which factional strife raged fiercely within the city.

Vespasian entrusted the conclusion of the war to his eldest son Titus, who at once began the siege of Jerusalem (70). The city had a triple line of fortifications, and within the inner wall were two natural citadels, the temple and the old city of Mount Zion. The population, swollen by many refugees, suffered terribly from hunger but resisted with the fury of despair. Experience and numbers told; the walls were stormed, and the Romans forced their way into the temple, which was destroyed by fire. Mount Zion still held out but finally was taken by assault. Jerusalem was destroyed, and Judaea became a province under an imperial legate. The political community of the Jews was dissolved, and they were subjected to a yearly head tax of two denarii (40 cents) each, payable to the temple of Jupiter Capitolinus, in consideration of which they enjoyed their previous immunities. Titus commemorated his victory by the arch which still stands near the Roman Forum. One of its reliefs represents the spoils from the temple, carried in the triumphal procession at Rome.

VESPASIAN'S ADMINISTRATION. Vespasian was the first *princeps* not a patrician. He was a native of the Italian municipality of Reate, and his father had been of only equestrian rank. Both he and his brother, however, had won admission to the Senate. In order to establish a link between his family and the Julio-Claudian line, he followed the example of Galba, Otho, and Vitellius in assuming the name of Caesar, which was becoming a title rather than a family name. From this time its use became a prerogative of the family of the *princeps*. He also made regular use of the title Imperator at the beginning of the imperial name, a practice neglected under the successors of Augustus but revived in the later years of Nero.

The new *princeps* was not a brilliant man but possessed the humble virtues of tenacity, sobriety, and industry, together with a homely wit, which fitted him to deal with a situation requiring firmness, tact, and patience rather than bold innovations. He was a competent general respected by the soldiery, and he was an expert financier. Vespasian received the powers and titles of the principate by virtue of a senatorial decree, confirmed by a law of the Assembly, yet with characteristic realism he dated the beginning of his rule from his salutation as Imperator by the troops in the East. In 73 he assumed the censorship with Titus as his colleague and took a census of the Empire. Simultaneously he filled the ranks of the Senate, depleted by executions and the recent civil wars. He took this opportunity of introducing into the Senate many distinguished provincials, of making extensive grants of citizenship in the provinces, and of bestowing Latin status upon all non-Roman communities in Spain, as a step preliminary to their Romanization.

To the Senate, Vespasian accorded respect and recognition of its judicial authority, but he excluded it from any effective participation in government. Nor did he trouble to disguise the fact that he was the real master. At first some senators tried to assert for themselves and their colleagues some control over policy, but their efforts were cut short, as was an attempt to prosecute the informers who had flourished under Nero. Very soon most of the Senate was reconciled to the situation, and subsequent friction between Vespasian and certain small groups among the senators was entirely due to the intransigent attitude of the latter. One of these groups, led by Helvidius Priscus, son-in-law of the Paetus Thrasea whom Nero had executed and like him a Stoic, indulged in a futile advocacy of republicanism in a cult of Brutus and Cato the Younger. Priscus went so far as to abuse and insult the *princeps* publicly and was therefore exiled from Italy. Subsequently he was executed, probably for conspiracy, although the details are unknown. Another group of so-called philosophers, apparently Cynics rather than Stoics, was so violent in their attacks, not only upon the *princeps* and the principate but upon orderly government in general, that Vespasian banished professional astrologers and philosophers from the capital.

The most serious problem Vespasian had to face was that presented by the finances, for the extravagance of the preceding emperors had left the government bankrupt and the provinces financially exhausted. To reestablish solvency Vespasian was obliged to impose new taxes and avoid all needless expenditures. For more efficient management of revenues, he established, under imperial procurators at Rome, new treasuries to which flowed revenues from rich provinces like Asia and Egypt. He not only succeeded in making the state solvent but was able to carry out extensive building operations in Italy and in the provinces. In Rome the Capitoline Temple, burned in the fighting with the Vitellians, was rebuilt, a temple of Peace was erected on the Forum, and the Colosseum arose on the site of one of the lakes of Nero's Golden House. Vespasian also granted state support to the teachers of Greek and Roman oratory in Rome.

Another problem was the restoration of discipline in the army, which had broken down in the conflict of 69–70. It has been seen, in connection with the repression of the revolt in Germany, how the dangers of national loyalties among the auxiliaries were averted by tighter organization. It remained to deal with the citizen soldiery. Four of the mutinous legions from the Rhineland garrison were disbanded and replaced by new ones. The Praetorian Guard, dissolved by Vitellius and replaced by detachments drawn from his legionaries, was reconstituted with cohorts of Italians as before. In order to assure himself of its loyalty, Vespasian appointed his son Titus as commander.

PROVINCES AND FRONTIERS. The emperor's efficiency and honesty were reflected in many of the provincial officials he appointed and in the tone of provincial government. He deprived Greece of the freedom Nero had granted and made it once more a senatorial province, while Sardinia and Corsica were again placed under imperial control. Rhodes, Samos, and Byzantium lost their status of free and federate communities and were incorporated in adjacent provinces. A new province was formed in Lycia and Pamphylia in Asia Minor. Most of these changes probably were made to increase imperial revenues, but there were others that showed Vespasian's care for frontier defense. The Roman hold on Britain was strengthened by the conquest of the Brigantes north of the Humber River and the Silures in southern Wales. Roman influence was reasserted among the German tribes on the right bank of the lower Rhine. In upper Germany Vespasian annexed the territory between the Rhine and the upper Danube, including the Schwarzwald and Odenwald areas, thus obliterating a dangerous salient in the frontier and shortening communications between the armies in Germany and in the Danubian provinces. The exposed boundary between Rhine and Danube was soon fortified by Vespasian's successors.

Further east on the Danube two strong camps for legionary troops were constructed at Carnuntum and Vindobona (modern Vienna). The Euphrates frontier was strengthened by the creation of a single large province embracing Galatia, Cappadocia, and some adjacent districts, as well as by the establishment of Roman garrisons at the important points of Satala and Melitene, which controlled routes across the upper Euphrates into Armenia. To the south the client kingdom of Commagene, which Gaius had restored to its native dynasty, was added to Syria. The latter province was further enlarged by extension of its eastern frontier to include several minor principalities, probably including the caravan city of Palmyra. In Africa, a brief campaign sufficed to quiet the Garamantes, who had disturbed Roman territory to the south of the Gulf of Syrtis.

VESPASIAN'S ACHIEVEMENT.   When Vespasian died in 79, he had reestablished order throughout the empire, rehabilitated its finances, and replaced the government on a sound basis. He had also made certain that the succession should remain within his own family. For his achievements he well deserved the honor of being called the second founder of the Principate.

PRINCIPATE OF TITUS: A.D. 79–80.   On the death of Vespasian, Titus was not only praetorian prefect but also a colleague of his father in the *imperium* and tribunician authority. This made his succession a matter of course, and without delay he received the powers and honors of the principate from the Senate. During his rule of little over two years, he showed himself thoroughly worthy of his high office. He rigorously repressed professional informers, refused to punish those who conspired against him, and, in spite of his geniality and generosity, kept careful watch on finances.

Two great disasters marred his otherwise uneventful principate. In 79 an eruption of Vesuvius buried the cities of Pompeii, Herculaneum, and Stabii near the Bay of Naples beneath a thick deposit of ash and lava. Thus protected, the buildings of these towns have been preserved to a remarkable degree, and the excavation of Pompeii in particular has revealed with wonderful freshness an Italian municipality under the early Principate. In the following year Rome was once more devastated by fire, which raged for three days and destroyed Vespasian's new temple of Jupiter Capitolinus.

Titus died following an attack of fever in September, 81. He was deeply mourned by the Roman world, and his memory was treasured as that of an ideal *princeps*. Like Vespasian, he received posthumous deification from the Senate.

VII. Domitian: A.D. 81–96

AUTOCRATIC IDEALS.   Titus was succeeded by his younger brother, Domitian, who was saluted as Imperator by the praetorians and received from the Senate without opposition the powers and titles of the principate on September 14, 81. Owing to his ambition, Domitian had not been given any active share in government by either Vespasian or Titus. From the beginning of his principate he displayed increasingly strong autocratic tendencies. Significant of this were his numerous consulships and, in addition, his use of the censorship with the title of perpetual censor (*censor perpetuus*) from 85 onwards. Even more emphatically his outlook becomes clear in the title "Lord and God" (*dominus et deus*), which was used unofficially but publicly by officers of the imperial household, by contemporary writers, and even by the emperor himself. He seems also to have made an oath by the genius of the *princeps* obligatory in certain public documents. The same tendencies found expression in his establishment of the priestly college of the Flaviales, modelled on that of the Augustales in Rome, to perpetuate the worship of his deified father and brother. It was abundantly clear that he intended to place the Senate in a subservient position and to control the government completely. Such a course inevitably provoked hostility in the ranks of the Roman nobility, which also resented his philhellenic leanings, evidenced in the establishment of a festival in honor of Capitoline Jupiter in imitation of the Olympic Games and in other imitations of Greek practices.

In the winter of 88–89 Antonius Saturninus, the legate of Upper Germany, arranged his own salutation as Imperator by the two legions under his command at Mogontiacum (Mainz). He counted upon the adherence of other provincial commanders and upon aid from the German Chatti, who invaded Roman territory on the right bank of the Rhine. The Germans were unable to cross the river owing to the breakup of ice that had temporarily bridged it, and Saturninus was defeated and killed by the governor of Lower Germany, who remained loyal to the emperor. Alarmed at the outbreak, Domitian punished relentlessly all those suspected of complicity in the conspiracy. Fearful of other plots against him, he began to suspect leading senators and his most able officers and lent a ready ear to false accusations made by professional informers. Thus there began another reign of terror for the nobility, which not only made the governing establishment hate him and all his works but also strongly biased the attitude of the historian Tacitus toward the Principate and its founder. The so-called philosophers were banished again from Italy; many prominent persons were executed on trumped-up charges of treason, others on the ground of "atheism." Among the latter were some notable converts to Judaism or Christianity, whose beliefs ran counter to Domitian's leanings toward deification. His own cousin, Flavius Clemens, fell victim to this charge; and the latter's wife, Domitilla, a niece of Domitian, who, if not an active Christian, was at least a patron of the Christian community in Rome, was exiled.

Domitian cannot be dismissed as a mere tyrant. He was an energetic administrator who personally directed all branches of the government and required of his subordinates a high standard of public service. Of special interest was his probable reorganization of the military supply service in which a central headquarters, the *castra peregrinorum*, was set up at Rome for couriers and supply officials going to and from the capital and legionary headquarters. These couriers, the *frumentarii*, were shortly to take on subsidiary functions as secret service agents. Domitian also organized new mounted units at the capital, the *equites singulares*, recruited from noncitizens of the Rhine-Danube frontier areas and serving as a personal bodyguard. In Rome, he improved the water system, increased the facilities for storing grain and other provisions, and completed the restoration necessitated by the great fire of 80. This gave him the opportunity to rebuild the temple of Capitoline Jupiter on a magnificent scale and to restore the damaged public libraries, in which he was particularly interested. He also completed other unfinished structures and built new ones. Among them were the temple of Vespasian and Titus and another of the Flavian Gens. At the Alban Lake he built a splendid villa at great expense. The urban populace was kept content with shows of various sorts and distributions of money, while the pay of the soldiers was increased by one third, an increase that scarcely compensated the troops for a rise in prices. These expenditures, added to the costs of border wars, placed a severe strain on the treasury.

In contrast to Vespasian, Domitian, who took over a financially sound state, was liberal in money matters and at first remitted unpaid taxes of five years' standing. He was no careless spendthrift, however, and insisted upon strict collection of future public revenues. His persecution of the senators has been blamed upon his desire to increase his income by confiscating property of the condemned, but on the whole these judicial murders seem to have had political rather than economic causes. Domitian's legislation was tinged with severe, old-fashioned Roman morality. He restricted the performance of mimes and farces, tried to suppress vice, and made it more difficult for slaves to obtain their freedom. He enforced the death penalty for Vestal Virgins convicted of adultery and in one case revived the antiquated form of punishing by burying alive. Such cruelty shocked public opinion, all the more since the *princeps* himself had one of his nieces as his mistress. In spite of his personal use of informers, he punished many who brought unfounded accusations, along with the writers of defamatory or scurrilous attacks upon prominent persons. Owing to his influence, the administration of justice was largely freed from bribery and partiality. In the provinces Domitian pushed the work of Romanization his father had undertaken. As governors and other provincial officers, he tried to select able and honest men with the result that the provinces flourished under his rule. He favored small farmers by granting freehold possession to those established on odd lots of land not included in the regular surveys, but his attempt to check the spread of vineyards by forbidding the planting of new ones in Italy and the transformation of one half of those in the provinces into grain land was an unsound venture in agricultural legislation. It does not seem to have been enforced rigorously, although the newer winelands of Gaul and the Danubian provinces may have been affected by it.

DEFENSE OF THE EMPIRE.   Although he did not depart radically from the Augustan precepts of nonexpansion, Domitian realized the value of military successes as a support for autocracy, and he carried on a vigorous frontier policy. In Africa, a revolt of tribes of the Nasamones in eastern Tripoli ended with their annihilation (85–86), and energetic action was taken against other nomads in Mauretania who resented the Roman policy of fostering agriculture at the expense of pasturage. More important was the Roman expansion in Britain directed by the legate Julius Agricola, who commanded the province from 77 to 84.

After seizing the island of Mona (Anglesea), a stronghold of Druidism, and completing the subjugation of northern England, Agricola led his armies deep into Scotland. In the mountainous country beyond the Clyde and the Firth of Forth, he defeated the Caledonians under their chief Calgacus (84). His fleet, skirting the coast, sailed around the north of Scotland and reaffirmed the fact, discovered centuries before by a Greek navigator, that Britain was an island. With the northern frontier of Britain secured by his victory, Agricola was recalled before he could carry out a projected invasion of Ireland. The military situation on the Danubian frontier required concentrated effort in that quarter. In 83, Domitian himself led an army across the Rhine from Mogontiacum and carried out a successful campaign against the Chatti, who were stirring up trouble in the area. As a result the Romans occupied the region of the Wetterau between the Lahn and Main rivers as far as the crest of the Taunus mountains and protected by a chain of forts and watchtowers. During the revolt of Saturninus (89), the Chatti overran part of this area, but the Roman frontier was reestablished when the rebellion was put down. It was the experience with Saturninus that led Domitian to adopt the policy of not quartering more than one legion in any of the permanent frontier camps. At the same time he separated the financial administration of the two German provinces from that of Gallia Belgica, with which it had hitherto been united. Between the Upper Rhine and the Danube, Domitian advanced the line of fortified posts to shorten and strengthen the frontier and communications in the angle of the two rivers.

Powerful peoples faced the Romans across the middle and lower Danube, and in dealing with them Domitian was less successful than on the Rhine. These were the Germanic Marcomanni and Quadi in Bohemia, the Sarmatian Iazyges between the Danube and Theiss rivers, and the Dacians, who occupied the greater portion of modern Hungary and Rumania. Of all these, the Dacians were the most dangerous, for they had been welded together by an able king, Decebalus. In 85 a Dacian band crossed the Danube into Moesia, where they defeated and killed the Roman governor.

Domitian himself brought reinforcements and drove the invaders back across the river. In attempting to invade Dacia, however, the praetorian prefect Cornelius Fuscus suffered a disastrous defeat, in which he and most of his army perished. In 88 a new Roman general, Tattius Julianus, was more successful and won a signal victory. At this point the Marcomanni, Quadi, and Iazyges, who previously had been friendly to Rome, took up arms. Domitian hurriedly took the field, invaded their territory, and met with a reverse that forced him to resort to diplomacy as well as to arms. He came to terms with Decebalus, who gave up his prisoners of war and formally acknowledged the overlordship of Rome but received in return an annual subsidy and the services of a number of Roman military engineers (89). The conclusion of this treaty enabled Domitian to enjoy the honor of a double triumph, over the Dacians and Chatti, and to concentrate his attention on the Iazyges and their German neighbors. It was not until 93 that order was reestablished along the middle Danube. For the moment Domitian had succeeded in relieving the Danubian provinces of barbarian pressure, but, as events were to show, his settlement was only temporary. In the course of the Dacian war, the province of Moesia was divided in two, called, respectively, Upper and Lower Moesia.

DOMITIAN'S ASSASSINATION. The closing years of Domitian's rule were occupied largely with the trials of persons whom he suspected as enemies. No one, whatever his rank, seemed safe. In self-defense, some of those who feared his suspicions decided to anticipate their own execution by striking first. A plot was formed in which his wife Domitia and the two praetorian prefects were the leaders, and on September 18, 96 he fell victim to the dagger of an assassin. His memory was cursed by an exultant Senate, and his name was erased from public monuments.

VIII. The Principate in Theory and Practice

At the death of Domitian the Principate had been in existence for 123 years. During this period, with the exception of parts of the years 68 and 69, it was ruled by two dynasties: the Julio-Claudian, which included the descendants by blood and adoption of the founder, Augustus; and the Flavian, the family of its restorer, Vespasian. This reveals clearly the strength of dynastic loyalty and the desire of emperors to found or to perpetuate a dynasty, which was voiced by Vespasian when he declared that either his sons should succeed him or no one. In the face of these tendencies it was impossible for the Senate to exercise any freedom of choice in the selection of a new appointee. Its role was virtually limited to conferring the appropriate powers and honors upon a single candidate chosen by forces beyond its control. Application of the hereditary principle did not prove a thoroughly satisfactory basis for the selection of the holders of *imperium*, since it could put at the head of the state such unworthy and incompetent rulers as Gaius and Nero, as well as the oppressive autocrat Domitian.

Another grave weakness was the absence of any constitutional means of removing an unsatisfactory *princeps* from office. His powers were conferred upon him for life, and so long as he had the support of the praetorian guard and the rest of the military establishment, he could defy any attempt to depose him. The only recourse was conspiracy leading to assassination or open rebellion resulting in civil wars between troops stationed in different parts of the Empire. The experiences of the year 68–69, however, were so disastrous and so dangerous to the Empire as a whole that responsible officers long shrank from resorting again to this desperate expediency. A certain standard of efficiency, justice, and personal conduct came to be regarded as essential in a *princeps*, and failure to measure up to it endangered the life of the delinquent or, at least, led to withholding posthumous honors by the Senate. The judgment of the senators, who voiced the opinion of the governing classes, when not overridden by the succeeding *princeps*, may be taken as evidence of the degree to which each emperor met the exacting requirements of his office as set by Augustus and confirmed by public opinion. When Claudius, Vespasian, and Titus received deification after death, as had been accorded to Augustus, it meant that they had exercised their powers constitutionally. When, on the contrary, the Senate formally execrated the memory of Nero and Domitian,[4] it publicly expressed the view that their actions had been unconstitutional. It did not mean, however, a blanket invalidation of their acts, since this would have led to unnecessary confusion and uncertainty in law and administration. When Tiberius, Galba, Otho, and Vitellius received neither deification nor execration, the Senate was refusing to endorse but was not prepared openly to condemn them, an attitude easily understood in view of the short principates of the three last-mentioned emperors.

The attitude of the Senate was determined largely by the interpretation each *princeps* placed upon his own position. Here two conflicting views were evident. One was that the principate was a magistracy, that its holder was the first among his fellow citizens, that there was a legal limitation upon his authority, and that he must act within traditionally established precedents. This was the attitude of Augustus, Tiberius, Claudius, and also of Vespasian and Titus. The other view was that the principate was an autocracy, that the authority of the *princeps* was supreme in all spheres, that the Senate and all public officials were his subordinates, that he could disregard established rights and customs, and that he was not a magistrate in the Roman sense but rather a monarch. Such was the position taken by Gaius and Domitian, who also claimed recognition while still living as a deity by Roman citizens. Nero was also such a ruler, although he did not

---

[4] Caligula was never officially condemned.

press the question of deification. In the opinion of the senatorial order, the former was the "constitutional," the latter the "unconstitutional" interpretation, which the Senate felt bound to resent and which led inevitably to persecution by the emperors in question. It had become clear that even under a constitutional principate the *princeps* himself must be the ruler and that there was no room for independent action by the Senate and magistrates. This realization was responsible at times for resentment by some senators, who maintained a futile cult of the ideals of the oligarchic Republic and engaged in an entirely useless criticism of the Principate as a form of government and personal attacks upon certain emperors, thus provoking retaliation. The Principate could not be abolished, and more was to be gained by loyal support of a constitutional *princeps* than by hostile non-co-operation. For the Empire as a whole, the new form of government had so far proved to be generally beneficial.

CHAPTER 18

ROMAN PEACE AND THE MILITARIZATION OF THE GOVERNMENT: A.D. 96–235

The period between the death of Domitian in 96 and that of Severus Alexander in 235 falls into two parts. During the first of these, which closes with the death of Marcus Aurelius in 180, the Roman Empire reached its maximum territorial extent, population, and material prosperity. This was due to a happy combination of internal peace and well-intentioned government, which produced for the Mediterranean area such a degree of security and well-being, otherwise unexampled in its history, that this epoch has been looked upon as the golden age of Roman imperialism. In the latter part of the period, these enviable conditions were disturbed by oppression, by a renewal of civil war between the armies, and by economic difficulties, all of which produced a crisis that threatened the existence of the state. Unfortunately, no adequate literary narrative exists for either half of the period. Of Dio's great work, which ran to 222, all that survives are parts of the last two books, while for the rest we have to depend upon an epitome made in the eleventh century. The only even relatively contemporary history that has survived was written by another Greek, Herodian, who, shortly before 250, composed a narrative for the years 180 to 238. A series of imperial biographies, beginning with Hadrian's, is supplied by the fourth-century compilation known as the Augustan History (*Historia Augusta*). For the period in question the *Lives* in this collection, although containing much worthless material, are based upon generally reliable sources. Of considerable historical worth are the *Letters* of Pliny the Younger, which contain his correspondence during his governorship of Bithynia in 111–113. Finally there are late epitomes and brief biographical collections, also valuable for the earlier period of the Principate. Owing to the relative dearth of literary evidence, we must rely all the more on contemporary inscriptions, papyri, coins, and material remains in order to gain even a reasonably complete picture of the civilization of the Roman Empire at its height.

I. Nerva: A.D. 96–98

NERVA'S ACCESSION. Before assassinating Domitian, those involved in the conspiracy had selected a successor acceptable to the Senate. Their choice was Marcus Cocceius Nerva, a leading senator, distantly related on his mother's side to the Julio-Claudian line. Nerva was sixty years of age and had had a distinguished public career without, however, any experience in a military command that might have won him the support of the soldiery, among whom Domitian was very popular. Nevertheless, when the Senate appointed him *princeps*, the provincial officer cadres acquiesced in their action. The praetorians, whose commanders had taken an active part in Domitian's assassination, were quieted for the moment by a donative. The policy of the new *princeps* was in strong contrast to his predecessor's. He won the confidence of the nobility by taking an oath never to execute a senator and by suspending the operation of the laws against high treason. He recalled political exiles and philosophers and permitted those who had suffered because of informers to avenge their wrongs by prosecutions until these were carried to excess and had to be stopped.

NERVA AND ITALY. During his brief rule Nerva, as was natural in view of his previous experience and because he wished to consolidate support for his regime, displayed a much greater interest in Italy than in the provinces. Immunity from the 5 percent inheritance tax was extended more widely than heretofore, an improvement was made in the method of adjudicating controversies between the treasury and private individuals, and an agrarian law provided for a distribution of lands to needy citizens. Nerva also established a relief system for poor farmers and the children of paupers. This scheme was extended and perfected by succeeding emperors.

SELECTION OF A COLLEAGUE AND SUCCESSOR. In spite of its honesty and respect for constitutional practice, Nerva's government failed to win the prestige necessary to keep the praetorian guard under control. In 97 the guard mutinied and killed several of those who had taken a leading part in Domitian's assassination. After this it was clear that the old, ailing, and childless *princeps* could save his authority and his life only by adopting as successor a man who could discipline the praetorians and receive the unanimous support of the legions, whose loyalty to Nerva was more than suspect. Nerva formally adopted as his son Marcus Ulpius Traianus, a tried soldier in command of the troops in Upper Germany. From the Senate, Trajan received the title of Caesar marking him as Nerva's prospective successor, together with tribunician authority and proconsular *imperium*, which made him virtually a colleague of the *princeps*. Three months later, on January 25, 98, Nerva died peacefully in Rome, and a grateful Senate added his name to those of his deified predecessors. Nerva was well-intentioned but weak. The most important event of his reign was his adoption of Trajan. By designating such a successor, Nerva probably prevented the outbreak of a civil war on the part of field commanders, which could have rivalled in gravity the events of 68–69.

II. Trajan: A.D. 98–117

A PROVINCIAL AS PRINCEPS.   Upon the death of Nerva, Trajan automatically became emperor. A native of the Roman colony of Italica in Farther Spain, whose father nevertheless had had a distinguished career as senator, he was the first *princeps* of provincial origin. His appointment indicates the declining dominance of the strictly Italian element within the Empire and the emergence of a new imperial nobility of wealthy provincials who had won recognition in imperial service. Trajan himself possessed unusual qualifications for the high office to which he was called. His affability and modesty enabled him to work with the Senate and at the same time to enjoy the personal affection and respect of civilians and soldiers alike. His military training had been unusually thorough. He was a general of outstanding merit, and his main interest was military. He was also an energetic and conscientious administrator who kept himself well informed on all governmental problems and displayed sound judgment in dealing with them. From the outset he was a firm ruler. The praetorian guard was promptly brought under control, and senatorial governors who had taken advantage of Nerva's inertia to abuse their office were tried before the Senate. There was no suspicion of tyranny. Trajan repeated Nerva's oath not to pronounce the death sentence upon a senator and rejected all ceremonies and customs associated with deification.

BENEVOLENT PATERNALISM.   In Italy, Trajan extended the system of relief to children of the poor, a step first taken by private individuals in the case of municipalities in which they were interested and made a public policy by Nerva. The government made loans to landholders at low rates of interest, and income from this source was paid to municipal authorities, who used it for the support of needy boys and girls. At the same time in Rome many children were granted the right to share in the public distributions of grain. The primary purpose of this scheme seems to have been to check a decline in the population of Italy by encouraging parents to raise more children. The farm loans were also a stimulus to Italian agriculture, and in general the government may have been trying to combat a threatened economic decline in Italy occasioned by competition from the western provinces.

Another example of Trajan's benevolent paternalism is to be seen in his attempt to rehabilitate municipal finances. Some Italian municipalities became heavily indebted owing to mismanagement of public funds and an extravagant building program. In order to help them out of their financial difficulties, the *princeps* appointed commissioners called curators to direct or advise municipal authorities. This practice was not limited to Italy but extended to provincial towns as well. In special cases imperial officials were empowered to deal with municipal finances over wide areas, like the commissioner entrusted with the task of restoring order in the free cities of Achaea. The chief reason Trajan took over for a time the administration of Bithynia from the Senate was so that he could send out Pliny as his legate to end the confusion that reigned in the administration of the municipalities of that province.

Trajan also showed concern for provincial welfare by improving the means of communication throughout the Empire by extensive repairs to existing highways and the construction of many new ones. Some of the latter were designed primarily to serve military purposes, but they also proved advantageous to trade and travel. He reorganized the state postal system (*cursus publicus*) by placing at its head an equestrian *praefectus vehiculorum*. Use of the highways by state officials became much more frequent during his reign. In addition to roads, the *princeps* supported on a generous scale the building of other useful public works such as aqueducts, bridges, canals, and harbor facilities. Rome also was the scene of numerous and costly building operations, the most notable being the construction of the magnificent forum named after Trajan himself. The generosity of the *princeps* was revealed further in his liberal treatment of the citizens of the capital. He rebuilt the harbor works at Ostia, where the grain for the city was unloaded, and subsidized millers and bakers. His public distributions of money (*congiaria*) made on three successive occasions were on an unprecedented scale, and the entertainments he provided to celebrate his victories were also unprecedented in their duration and splendor. Those given in 107 to mark final victory over the Dacians lasted one hundred and twenty-six days, taken up largely with gladiatorial combats and wild-beast hunts.

AGGRESSIVE IMPERIALISM: DACIAN WARS. In his foreign policy Trajan broke with the precepts laid down by Augustus at the end of his reign, and, confident in his own leadership and the strength of the imperial armies, he reverted to the aggressive imperialism of the Republic. His first objective was the conquest of Dacia, for Domitian's agreement with Decebalus was regarded in Rome as both disgraceful and unsatisfactory, since the existence of a strong Dacian kingdom was a perpetual menace to the peace of the lower Danubian provinces. The immediate cause of hostilities is unknown, but in 101 Trajan personally led an invasion of Dacia. He was opposed vigorously by Decebalus, still king of the Dacians and a valiant opponent. In his first campaign Trajan failed to obtain a decisive result, but in 102 he penetrated into the heart of Dacia and forced Decebalus to sue for peace. The Dacian king was obliged to give up the Roman technicians he had received from Domitian, together with his military machines, to acknowledge Roman overlordship, and to render military service to the Empire. Trajan returned to Rome and celebrated his victory with a triumph. At his orders a permanent stone bridge was built across the Danube below the Iron Gates to secure communications with the northern bank. Decebalus was not content to remain a

Roman vassal and prepared to recover his people's independence. In 105 he provoked resumption of hostilities by attacking the Iazyges, who were Roman allies. This was followed by annihilation of the small Roman garrisons left in Dacia to secure Roman influence. Trajan hastily left Rome for the front, where he held the Dacians in check while he concentrated a force for a new offensive and won the allegiance of neighboring tribes who had joined Decebalus. The following year he invaded Dacia for the second time. His victory in 106 was complete. The Dacian capital was taken, and Decebalus committed suicide. Such of the Dacians as did not surrender or abandon their country were hunted down and exterminated. Dacia was made a Roman province and was peopled with settlers from different parts of the Empire, particularly from Asia Minor and Syria. From the Dacian gold mines, placed under imperial control, came a steady income that helped materially to meet the increased governmental expenditure occasioned by Trajan's internal policies. The occupation of Dacia was significant because the Romans now had a bulwark protecting the provinces south of the Danube and a vantage point for controlling the restless tribes both east and west of the new province. To commemorate his Dacian wars, Trajan erected a stone column over one hundred feet high in his new forum. The column, still in place, is decorated with a spiral band of sculptured reliefs that give a vivid pictorial narrative of the operations of the successive campaigns.

In North Africa, Trajan continued the policy of his predecessors. He advanced the southern frontier of Numidia to the Sahara and thus opened up much new land for agricultural settlement. The desert tribes were held in check by stationing the legionary garrison of the province at the strategic point of Lambaesis, not far from which the colony of Thamugadi (Timgad) was founded.

INVASION OF PARTHIA. Even during his preoccupation with the Dacian question, Trajan found time to devote to problems of the eastern frontier. In 105, he ordered the governor of Syria to annex the kingdom of the Nabataean Arabs, which lay to the east of southern Syria and Palestine. This task was carried out without serious opposition, and the occupied territory was organized as the province of Arabia (106). Possession of the region gave the Romans control of the caravan routes leading from the Arabian coast of the Red Sea northward to Damascus and the harbor towns of Syria.

A much more serious venture was Trajan's attempt to apply to the Armenian and Mesopotamian frontiers the methods that had proved successful on the Lower Danube. The opportunity came in about 110, when the Parthian king Osroes deposed the Armenian ruler, who was a Roman client, and appointed as king another member of the Parthian royal house without consulting the Roman emperor, thus breaking the arrangement that had preserved peace between Rome and Parthia since the time of Nero.

Ruins of Timgad

Trajan, knowing that the Parthians had negotiated with Decebalus, determined to take advantage of this infringement of Rome's treaty rights in Armenia in order to effect a settlement of the frontier difficulties in this quarter on a new basis. Leaving Rome in the autumn of 113, he proceeded to the East and invaded Armenia in the course of the following summer at the head of a large army. Little resistance was encountered, the Armenian king was removed, and his country was made an imperial province. From Armenia, Trajan led his forces into upper Mesopotamia, where the rulers of the several petty states either acknowledged his overlordship or fled. After the Roman occupation of Armenia, this region for strategic reasons could not be left in Parthian hands, and like Armenia it became a Roman province. Leaving garrisons in the newly won territories, Trajan withdrew to spend the winter of 115–116 in Antioch. After his conquest of Armenia he added the name Optimus to the list of his official titles. The lack of opposition he had thus far encountered decided Trajan to complete the conquest of Mesopotamia. In the spring of 116 he opened his offensive with an attack on Adiabene, a state on the left bank of the Tigris whose king remained loyal to his Parthian overlord. Adiabene fell easily, and from it was formed another province known as Assyria. The way was now open to the Parthian capital, Ctesiphon, which surrendered at the approach of the Roman Emperor. During the winter of 115–116, Trajan sailed down the Tigris from here to the head of the Persian Gulf, and then returned to Babylon. There he learned that Assyria and Mesopotamia were in revolt and that Parthian armies were advancing on Assyria and Armenia. The situation was dangerous for the Romans. They had overrun rather than conquered the lands they had annexed because Osroes was engaged in suppressing revolts among his own people and could not spare troops to oppose them. Now he was in a position to attempt recovery of his lost dominions. Trajan and his generals proved equal to the emergency. After some initial defeats, the Roman armies recovered control of both northern and southern Mesopotamia. Adiabene was lost, however, and the Parthian invasion of Armenia was checked only by the surrender of a part of the country. Trajan felt that it would be too difficult a task to retain control of southern Mesopotamia, so he turned it over to a Parthian noble who had deserted to the Romans and who was crowned at Ctesiphon as King of Parthia. Trajan himself withdrew to Antioch.

The partial surrender of the Roman conquests was largely due to a serious rebellion of the Jews in the eastern provinces. This began in Cyrenaica in 115 and spread rapidly to Cyprus, Egypt, Palestine, and Mesopotamia. The movement was caused by Messianic Jewish yearnings and was actually led by a Jewish "king." It was waged against their Hellenic or Hellenized neighbors and their gods, but developed also into a challenge to Roman authority, particularly after the Parthian successes of 116. Wherever the Jews got the upper hand, they perpetrated horrible massacres upon the Greeks, who retaliated in kind when they found opportunity. Trajan acted promptly, and the rebels were ruthlessly suppressed. Order was restored everywhere except in Egypt, where fighting went on under Trajan's successor and the scars of the conflict took long to obliterate.

DEATH OF TRAJAN.   In the early summer of 117 Trajan prepared for another campaign in Mesopotamia to support his appointee to the Parthian throne, who was unable to maintain his position. Worn out by his strenuous exertions of the preceding three years, however, he fell ill and left Antioch for Rome. On the way he grew worse and died at Selinus in Cilicia about August 9, 117. At the point of death he adopted as his son his younger relative and one-time ward, Publius Aelius Hadrianus, whom he had left in command in the East. Trajan's conduct and achievements in war and peace alike caught the imagination of the Romans and caused his memory to be treasured through the following centuries. For later generations, he was the Optimus Princeps, the model emperor.

III. Hadrian

HADRIAN'S ACCESSION.   When the report of Hadrian's adoption reached the army in Syria, the soldiers immediately saluted him as Imperator. He at once assumed the powers and titles of the principate, and when the news reached Rome the Senate could only accept the accomplished fact and confirm him in his authority. Hadrian, also a native of Italica, was a son of a cousin of Trajan's, had married Sabina, a granddaughter of Trajan's sister Marciana, and since early youth had been closely associated with his predecessor. Trajan had not marked him out as his successor by taking him as a partner in the *imperium* or the tribunician authority, however, and it may well be that the two men were not entirely in sympathy. There were those who believed that the story of his adoption was a fiction devised by Trajan's widow, Plotina, who wished to secure the succession for Hadrian. The new *princeps* had had a distinguished military career and enjoyed the loyal support and confidence of the army, so that he appears to have been the logical choice to follow his countryman in the principate. The only opposition seems to have come from a small faction of Trajan's generals who were his natural rivals and may have resented his abandonment of Trajan's policies. Four outstanding members of this group, among them the noted Moorish cavalry leader Lusius Quietus, were accused of conspiring against Hadrian in 118 and condemned to death by the Senate, even before the *princeps* returned to Italy. Hadrian made an unusually generous donation to the soldiers upon his accession. When he arrived in Rome he treated the city populace as liberally, and soon after he remitted to defaulting taxpayers in Italy and the provinces the arrears of the past fifteen years, amounting to some $45,000,000.

GOVERNMENTAL POLICY.   Hadrian's accession heralded a reign whose goals were consolidation, centralization, and unification of the government of the Empire. Far more than his predecessor the new *princeps* took a broad imperial, as contrasted with a more traditionally Roman, conception of the Empire and the objectives of imperial policy. His early education had been predominantly Greek, and from this he derived both a great admiration for Hellenism and a deep appreciation of its basic importance in contemporary Greco-Roman civilization. He had even been dubbed "Greekling," a nickname that perhaps still implied a degree of scorn in some circles at Rome.

Hadrian was a man of restless energy and extraordinary versatility. Taking as his motto the philosophic dictum that "the ruler exists for the state, not the state for the ruler," he exhibited the most unsparing devotion to duty in his endeavor to govern by this standard. There was no branch of administration in which he was not zealously interested and upon which he failed to leave a personal impression. In order to acquaint himself thoroughly with the needs of the various sections of the Empire and to take measures for their welfare, he made two extended tours through the provinces—one in 121–126, the other in 129–132, spending altogether more than half of his principate outside of Italy. Regarding the principate his view was similar to that of Trajan. He treated the Senate with respect and consideration. He took an oath, which he carefully observed until toward the close of his career, not to condemn its members to death, but he did not accord it any significant share in government. Deeply and continuously immersed though he was in affairs of state, Hadrian yet found time to foster cultural interests and showed a keen appreciation of literary studies and of art.

DEFENSIVE IMPERIALISM. Trajan's invasion of Parthia had depleted the Roman treasury and failed to accomplish his purpose of settling the problem of the eastern frontier. The Roman hold on Armenia and Mesopotamia was precarious, and the Roman nominee to the Parthian throne could not maintain his position. Trouble had broken out also on the lower Danube, in Mauretania, and in Britain, while the Jewish revolt had not yet been completely suppressed. Peace and recuperation were a necessity, and Hadrian immediately took steps to secure them. He concluded peace with the Parthians, surrendering all claims to Assyria and Mesopotamia, and reverted to the previous policy of treating Armenia as a client kingdom under a Parthian ruler who acknowledged Roman overlordship. In his frontier policy Hadrian went on the defensive. His ideal was a peaceful and prosperous state, adequately protected against attack from without, devoting its energies to development of economic and cultural resources. On all sides he strengthened the border defenses and their garrisons, particularly in Britain, where he ordered the construction of his famous Wall from the mouth of the Tyne to the Solway Firth, and along the frontier in Germany. Hadrian's defensive policy accentuated the already existing tendency for imperial armies to become garrison troops recruited locally from the border provinces where they were stationed. Under the Emperor's watchful eye standards of discipline and efficiency among the troops were maintained at the highest level. The only serious military operation Hadrian was called upon to undertake was the suppression of a new rebellion of the Jews in Palestine. This was occasioned by their resentment at the founding of a Roman colony at Jerusalem with an altar to Jupiter on the site of the former Temple of Jahweh, and Hadrian's prohibition of circumcision, which he regarded as inhumane. Under the leadership of Simon, called Bar Kochba (Son of the Star), the Jews seized Jerusalem and defied the Roman armies. Only after a struggle of two years (132–134), in which both parties fought with great ferocity and the Jewish population of Judaea was practically exterminated, could the revolt be put down.

ADMINISTRATIVE REFORMS. As a reformer Hadrian was a coordinator of tendencies already operating in government as well as an innovator. To aid him in administering justice and framing legislation, Hadrian used jurists more frequently in his *ad hoc* councils than his predecessors. Under his auspices Salvius Julianus, one of the most influential Roman legal writers, codified and edited the Praetor's Edict, which now embodied to a substantial degree the principles and procedures of Roman civil law. The Praetor's Edict was in effect "frozen," and an important avenue of adding to the law independent of the emperor was closed. Even before Hadrian, few magistrates would have dared to change the edict on their own initiative. In order to relieve the praetor's courts of excessively heavy dockets, Italy outside of Rome was divided into four districts, each under a judicial officer of consular rank appointed by the emperor. This was a further step in the gradual elimination of the Senate's administrative control of Italy and in the approximation of its status to that of a province. In general Hadrian enhanced the importance of the equestrian class and its influence in the government of the empire. He increased the number of procurators and generalized the tendency under previous emperors to appoint equestrians rather than freedmen to the great secretaryships of the treasury, of correspondence, etc., which had been established in the preceding century, although the freedman element at the highest echelons of administration did not disappear completely. Another change was creation of a class of officials called advocates of the fiscus (*advocati fisci*) as prosecutors for the treasury, whose office was regarded as an alternative to subordinate military commands in the equestrian public career. An important innovation in military administration was made when Hadrian gave an official table of strength and organization to the noncommissioned officer cadres in the army and defined their use in the headquarters clerical staffs of their commanders.

PUBLIC WORKS. Hadrian's expert handling of imperial finances enabled him to carry out a tremendous building program almost everywhere. He founded many cities, among them Antinoopolis in Egypt in honor of his favorite Antinous, who was drowned in the Nile, and Adrianople in European Turkey, which still preserves his name. He was particularly devoted to Athens, where he held the office of archon and where he completed the great temple of Olympian Zeus besides adding a new suburb known as "the city of Hadrian." In Rome, in addition to many lesser structures, Hadrian erected a magnificent double temple to Venus and Roma and his own mausoleum, the present Castel Sant' Angelo. At Tibur (Tivoli) he built a vast and splendid villa adorned with statues.

CHOICE OF A SUCCESSOR.   Hadrian had no children and no intimate and trusted friends with whom he shared his plans. His aloofness made the Senate at first suspicious, later hostile. In 136 he fell ill of a painful and incurable disease, which warned him that he must provide for a successor. His aged brother-in-law, who showed signs of aspiring to the principate, was executed together with his youthful grandson. The choice of the emperor fell upon a senator named Lucius Ceionius Commodus, whom he adopted as Lucius Aelius Caesar and who was given tribunician authority. When Aelius died early in 138, Hadrian adopted another senator Titus Aurelius Antoninus, a member of a Roman family from Narbonese Gaul. Since Antoninus was well advanced in age, Hadrian made him adopt in turn the son of the deceased Commodus, Lucius Verus, and also Marcus Aurelius Antoninus, a nephew of the emperor's wife and, like her, of Spanish descent. Titus Aurelius Antoninus received both the *imperium* and tribunician authority and became Hadrian's partner in the principate. When Hadrian died on July 10, 138, the energetic action of his successor prevented the Senate from execrating his memory and secured his deification.

IV. The Antonines: A.D. 138–192

ANTONINUS PIUS: A.D. 138–161.   The death of Hadrian left Titus Aurelius Antoninus in sole possession of the principate. His action in securing the deification of his adoptive father from the reluctant Senate won for him the title of Pius, as the personification of the Roman virtue of piety or sense of obligation in both divine and human affairs. His filial piety was shown still further in his completion of Hadrian's tomb and the erection of a temple for his worship as Divus Hadrianus. Just and mild in his public as well as his private life, Antoninus acted in perfect harmony with the senators, in accordance with whose wishes he removed the four judges whom Hadrian had appointed for the administration of justice in Italy.

The policies of Antoninus were generally a continuation of Hadrian's. Although called upon to repress serious frontier troubles in Britain and Mauretania, to check Parthian encroachments in Armenia by a vigorous remonstrance, and to put down some minor insurrections in the eastern provinces, he adhered strictly to a defensive frontier policy. He improved the border defenses, notably in Raetia and in Britain, where he had an earthen wall built from the Firth of Clyde to the Firth of Forth well to the north of Hadrian's Wall. Unlike Hadrian, however, Antoninus refrained from visiting the provinces in person, because of the expense imperial journeys caused the provincial communities. Owing to his careful handling of finances, he was able to give liberal entertainment to the populace, carry out numerous building projects, and yet remit delinquent taxes. Probably the greatest achievement of this principate was in the field of Roman law. Not only did Antoninus insist on the impartial administration of justice, but the law itself was greatly liberalized through the introduction of principles of equity and began to receive at the hands of juristic writers its characteristically systematic form.

In 139 Antoninus conferred the title of Caesar upon the elder of his adopted sons, Marcus Aurelius, to whom six years later he gave his daughter in marriage. Then in 146 he caused the Senate to confer upon Marcus the tribunician authority and the *imperium* outside of Rome, and Marcus became a junior partner in the principate. When Antoninus died in March, 161 Marcus at once became sole *princeps*.

DUAL PRINCIPATE: MARCUS AURELIUS (161–180) AND LUCIUS VERUS (161–169).   Marcus Aurelius took as his colleague his adoptive brother, Lucius Verus, and for the first time a principate was inaugurated under the joint rule of two Augusti. Real power rested in the hands of Marcus, for Verus was weak, indolent and sensual. His chief merit was that in matters of government, at least, he loyally deferred to his brother's judgment. Marcus Aurelius was by nature a student and philosopher and a devoted follower of Stoicism. His noble character is revealed in his communings with himself, his *Meditations*. Fired by no ambition and lacking any enthusiasm for his task, he nevertheless undertook the government of the Empire as a duty and devoted himself unsparingly to this service. It was a bitter irony that he, ideally fitted for peace, should have been called upon to spend his remaining years in an almost unceasing struggle to save the state from its external foes.

WAR WITH THE PARTHIANS: A.D. 161–165.   At the very beginning of the new regime, the Parthian king, Vologases III, invaded Armenia. The Roman legate of Cappadocia, who led an army to meet the attack, was defeated and killed. The Parthians broke into Syria, where they won a victory over the Roman garrison and ravaged the country. In view of the crisis, Marcus Aurelius sent Verus to the East, where, although he displayed neither energy nor capacity, his able generals restored the situation. In 163, Statius Priscus reestablished Roman authority over Armenia and installed a new Roman vassal. In 164–165 Avidius Cassius marched into Mesopotamia and captured both Seleucia and the Parthian capital, Ctesiphon. He was unable to follow up his victory, since an outbreak of disease among his troops forced him to retreat, the army suffering serious losses from sickness and hunger. The Parthians recovered for the moment their lost ground in Mesopotamia and even regained control of Armenia. In 166, the Romans resumed the offensive, drove the Parthians out of northern Mesopotamia and permanently occupied it as far east as the Khabur river. A few years later the Parthian governor of Armenia was removed, and it became once again a Roman client state. But these gains hardly compensated for the· havoc wrought by the plague, possibly small-pox, which soldiers returning from the East spread throughout the Empire and which claimed many victims.

WAR ON THE DANUBIAN FRONTIER: A.D. 167–175. Before the eastern situation had reached a satisfactory settlement, a much more serious condition had developed on the Danubian frontier. There the Marcomanni, Quadi, Iazyges, and some lesser tribes united in an attempt to force their way into the provinces. The army of the Danube, weakened by the withdrawal of strong detachments for service in the East, was unable to check their assaults; Noricum and Pannonia were overrun, and the barbarians reached Aquileia at the head of the Adriatic. Conditions were critical, owing to lack of adequate troops, disorganization caused in army camps by plague, and depletion of the treasury through the expenses involved in the Parthian War, and Marcus Aurelius was forced to adopt heroic measures to cope with them. He raised money by auctioning off treasures of the imperial household, drafted slaves and gladiators into the army, and even hired mercenaries among the Germans and Scythians. Marcus himself, accompanied by Verus, assumed command of operations against the invaders. Aquileia was relieved of its besiegers, and the struggle for the recovery of Noricum and Pannonia began. While this was still in progress, Lucius Verus died of apoplexy (169), leaving Marcus as sole Augustus. He continued to press the war with vigor, the barbarians being driven back across the Danube, and, in spite of a serious invasion of Dacia and a raid of a people called the Costoboci that penetrated the Balkan peninsula as far as Athens, the Romans gained the upper hand. In 172 the emperor crossed the Danube and defeated the Quadi in their own territory. A similar fate met the Marcomanni in the following year. Both peoples were forced to surrender their captives, together with large numbers of cattle and horses, and to render military service to Rome, while some thousands of them were settled on waste lands in the provinces under the obligation of tilling the soil and serving in Roman armies. It remained to deal with the Iazyges and the Costoboci of eastern Galicia. These also were attacked in their homelands with the aid of German allies of the Romans, while the Quadi were punished again for failure to observe their treaty. Marcus became convinced that the only way to obtain lasting peace was to follow Trajan's example in dealing with the Dacians, and he therefore planned to annex the lands of the Marcomanni and Sarmatians. News of the rise of a usurper in Syria compelled him to forego this project and be content with imposing the same terms on the Iazyges as he had upon the Marcomanni and Quadi (175). The victories of the campaigns of 172–175 were commemorated by a column erected in Rome by Marcus' son and successor with reliefs depicting scenes from military operations in imitation of Trajan's memorial of the Dacian Wars.

DUAL PRINCIPATE AGAIN: MARCUS AURELIUS AND COM-MODUS: A.D. 177–180. While he was combatting the barbarians of central Europe, the peace of the Empire was further disturbed by an out-break in Gaul, a rising of the Moorish tribes in Mauretania, and a serious rebellion of the herdsmen of the Nile Delta in Egypt. The last-mentioned revolt was put down by the great general of the Parthian War, Avidius Cassius, who had been legate in his native province of Syria since 167, and, since 169, had been entrusted with the general supervision of affairs in the East. Upon a false report of the death of Marcus, Cassius proclaimed himself emperor and won recognition in Syria, Judaea, Cilicia, and Egypt (175). News of this usurpation forced Marcus to bring the war with the Iazyges to a hurried conclusion so that he could proceed to the East as soon as possible. Upon his arrival there he found that news of his approach had caused Cassius to be deserted and executed by his own followers. The episode warned Marcus of the necessity of making proper provision for a successor. Upon his return to Rome he had his son Lucius Aelius Aurelius Commodus, then a mere youth of sixteen, proclaimed Augustus and made his partner in office.

DANUBIAN PROBLEM ONCE MORE: A.D. 178–180. It was not long until the restless tribes on the Danubian frontier caused fresh troubles, which forced Marcus Aurelius again to take command of forces in the field, where he was joined later by Commodus. Once more he subdued the Marcomanni and the Quadi and planned for the permanent Roman occupation of their territory, which included modern Bohemia and Moravia, in order to strengthen the defences of the Empire. For a second time he was robbed of the fruits of victory, on this occasion by his own death. Marcus Aurelius died at Vindobona (Vienna) on March 17, 180, and the principate passed to Commodus, whom he had enjoined to carry the war to a successful conclusion.

COMMODUS SOLE PRINCEPS: A.D. 180–192. Commodus, the ignoble son of a noble father, is one of the few Roman emperors of whom nothing good can be said. Although it may seem strange that Marcus Aurelius, who could not have been blind to his weaknesses, took him as a colleague and designated him as his successor, it must be remembered that, short of executing him, it was practically impossible to exclude him from the principate. One possibility remained untried: to have given him a senior colleague who might have stood to him in the same relation as Marcus himself had stood to Verus. It may have been that Marcus hoped that the responsibilities of office would sober the young man or that he would take the advice of his father's tried and trusted subordinates.

Disregarding parental injunctions, Commodus made peace with the

Marcomanni and Quadi upon the terms they had previously enjoyed, and even these he subsequently relaxed. As soon as possible he hastened back to Rome to enjoy the delights of the capital. Cowardly, cruel, and sensual, he pursued a life of pleasure and left the government in the hands of a succession of favorites who used their power to further their own interests. Proud of his physical strength, he sought to win the plaudits of the mob by appearing in the arena as a hunter of wild beasts or as a gladiator who incurred no risks in killing his opponents. His patron god was Hercules, whose emblems of club and lion's skin were depicted on his statues, and of whom he regarded himself the living manifestation.

Quite indifferent to any principles of government, Commodus scorned the Senate. When a conspiracy against his life was discovered, his vengeance fell heavily on the senatorial order. By largesses and favors, he maintained the support of the praetorians, who in return protected him from his enemies. In spite of his neglect of duty, the provincial commanders maintained the integrity of the Empire. Border wars with the Moors, with the Caledonians in Britain, and with other tribes in Dacia, were waged with success, but a mutiny of the troops in Britain was checked only by acquiescence to their demands. More alarming were serious outbreaks within the Empire, due apparently to economic distress. Gangs of robbers roamed throughout Italy, and in Gaul disorderly elements formed bands large enough to capture cities and wage open war with government forces.

The extravagance of the *princeps* and his associates emptied the treasury and created a financial crisis. Informers reappeared, through whose agency judicial murders were perpetrated with widespread confiscation of property. Commodus took the final step in a despot's career by seeking deification and actually issued coins on which he appeared as a god. In his infatuation with gladiatorial exploits he finally determined to assume the consulate on January 1, 193 in gladiator costume. On the preceding night, however, he was strangled by his wrestling companion, who had been bribed by the praetorian prefect, Quintus Aemilius Laetus, who feared for his own safety, with the collusion of the favorite mistress and the chamberlain of the despicable ruler.

V. Dynasty of the Severi: A.D. 193–235

SECOND WAR OF THE LEGIONS: A.D. 193. Events of the years following the death of Commodus resemble those of 68–69, when the praetorian guard mutinied and appointed a *princeps*, only to find that commanders of the frontier armies refused to acquiesce in its action and engaged in civil war to make themselves candidates. The praetorians accepted the nominee of their prefect Laetus, Publius Helvius Pertinax, a senator of humble birth but proved military and administrative capacity, who was then City Prefect. His nomination was approved by the Senate, which readily accorded him the honors and power of the principate. But Pertinax was no tool of those who raised him to power and he maintained firm discipline in the guard. This, coupled with economies necessitated by the exhausted condition of the treasury, cost him the support of both the praetorians and the subordinates of the imperial establishment. After a rule of less than three months, he was murdered by a mutinous detachment of praetorians (March 28, 193). The praetorians, whose support was courted by two rivals for the vacant office, then auctioned off the nomination to an elderly and wealthy senator, Marcus Didius Julianus, who promised them a donative of 25,000 sesterces ($1,250) apiece. The Senate could only confirm their choice.

News of the death of Pertinax and the succession of Julianus provoked revolts in two of the great army corps of the empire, those of the East and of the Danubian frontier. The speed with which they acted suggests that their commanders had already contemplated and prepared their *coups d'état*. Almost simultaneously Gaius Pescennius Niger, the legate of Syria, and Publius Septimius Severus, legate of Upper Pannonia, engineered their salutation as Imperator by the troops under their respective commands. The sympathies of both the people and the Senate in Rome seem to have been with Niger, but Severus was nearer to Rome and hastened to take advantage of his position to secure recognition of his claims. Assured of the support of the four legions on the Rhine, as well as of at least eleven of the twelve stationed along the Danube, he marched rapidly upon Rome, assuming the name Pertinax to indicate that he regarded himself both as avenger of the murdered *princeps* and adherent of his principles of government. Julianus at first prepared resistance, then tried vainly to make terms with Severus. When the praetorians tried to save themselves by deserting their appointee, the Senate, forced by Julianus to proclaim Severus a public enemy, now dared to deify the dead Pertinax, to condemn Julianus himself to death, and to ratify the nomination of Severus. A soldier murdered Julianus on June 1, and a few days later Severus entered Rome at the head of his troops. He distributed the customary donation to the soldiery and the populace, took an oath not to execute a senator without a trial before the Senate, and punished through its agency some of the supporters of Julianus. Besides executing those of the praetorians who had taken part in the murder of Pertinax, Severus disarmed and disbanded the whole guard, and replaced it with a new one of 15,000 veterans from the Danubian legions upon whose loyalty he could depend. His position was by no means secure, however, since Pescennius Niger had obtained recognition in the eastern provinces, was in a position to cut off the Egyptian supply of grain to Rome, and had already sent an advance guard to occupy Byzantium, which commanded the crossing of the Bosporus. Before leaving for the East, Severus felt it necessary to guard against a revolt by the legate in Britain, Clodius Albinus, who, like Niger, was popular in Rome and was suspected of aiming for the principate. He offered Albinus the position of Caesar, an indication that he was next in line for the succession and, when Albinus accepted, had this title conferred upon him by the Senate.

WAR WITH PESCENNIUS NIGER: A.D. 193–194. Severus then followed the troops he had already dispatched to check the advance of Niger's army. Before he arrived on the scene, however, his generals had blockaded Byzantium and crossed over into Asia Minor, where they had won two military victories over their opponents, one near Cyzicus and the other near Nicaea. When Severus brought up reinforcements, Niger withdrew into Syria south of the Taurus mountains. In the spring of 194 Severus descended into Cilicia and defeated Niger in a decisive battle at Issus. Niger tried to escape into Parthia but was overtaken and killed. Heavy penalties were meted out to individuals and communities that had supported him. Severus then determined to invade Mesopotamia, where the client state of Osrhoëne had revolted and Roman influence was endangered. Overrunning Osrhoëne and upper Mesopotamia as far as the Tigris, he sent an army across that river into Adiabene. From these exploits he was recalled to meet a new danger in the western part of the empire (December, 195). In the meantime, Byzantium, which held out against its besiegers for more than two years, was starved into surrender. Its fortifications were destroyed, its officials and garrison killed, the property of its citizens confiscated, and it was reduced to the status of a village dependent upon the neighboring city of Perinthus.

DEFEAT OF CLODIUS ALBINUS: A.D. 196–197. The situation demanding the presence of Severus and his army in the West was brought about by Albinus' claim to the principate. He had gradually come to realize that Severus and his ambitious Syrian wife, Julia Domna, had no intention of allowing the succession to pass to him instead of to their own sons and that unless he acted quickly he could not escape the fate prepared for him. Acting in collusion with a large number of senators in Rome, he had himself proclaimed Augustus by his soldiery and crossed over into Gaul, where he established his headquarters at Lugdunum. Severus replied by having Albinus declared a public enemy by the army in Mesopotamia and later by having his eldest son, Bassianus, better known as Caracalla, proclaimed Caesar, with the name of Marcus Aurelius Antoninus.

In February, 197, the armies of the rival emperors faced each other at Lyons. After a desperate struggle, the Danubian legions won, and Albinus took his own life. Lugdunum, the richest city in the western provinces, was sacked and burned and never recovered its prosperity in ancient times. Severus was now the unchallenged ruler of the Empire and could take full vengeance upon his enemies. Supporters of Albinus in Gaul, Germany, Britain, and Spain were relentlessly hunted down, and in Rome twenty-nine senators convicted of intriguing with him were summarily executed. At the demand of Severus, the Senate confirmed the army's nomination of Caracalla as Caesar, together with his use of the Antonine name, to which they added the title of Emperor Designate (*imperator destinatus*). After a short stay in Rome, Severus was called once more to the East because of the aggressive action of the Parthian ruler.

SECOND PARTHIAN WAR: A.D. 197–199. Taking advantage of Roman preoccupation with the struggle between the rival emperors, Vologases IV, King of Parthia, had invaded Armenia and northern Mesopotamia, where he laid siege to the Roman stronghold Nisibis. At the approach of Severus in the winter of 197/198, Vologases raised the siege of Nisibis and retreated before the Romans, who pressed on into Parthian territory. Seleucia on the Tigris was occupied without opposition, and Ctesiphon, although vigorously defended, was taken and sacked. On his return march up the Tigris valley, Severus attempted, without success, to capture the strong rock fortress of Hatra, which had defied the efforts of Trajan to storm it. A second attempt in 199 was equally unsuccessful. Northern Mesopotamia remained firmly in Roman hands, however, and was organized as a province with Nisibis as its capital. Failure of the Parthians to check the Roman invasion and prevent destruction of their capital hastened the internal decay of their empire. After spending two more years in the East visiting Egypt and other provinces, Severus and his family returned to Rome in 202 to celebrate the tenth anniversary of his salutation as Imperator.

GOVERNMENT OF SEPTIMIUS SEVERUS. Severus was a native of Leptis Magna in Tripoli, which formed part of the Roman province of Africa. Although his family was of Punic stock and retained Punic cultural traditions, they were thoroughly Romanized in their political outlook. Born to equestrian rank, he had begun his public life as an advocate of the *fiscus* but was admitted to senatorial status by Marcus Aurelius and thereafter followed the career of a senator. He had the interests of a bureaucrat and soldier and was a realistic politician, well aware of the problems of his day. He exhibited to a greater degree than any of his predecessors a provincial point of view on problems of imperial government, but he was not doctrinaire or anti-Italian in his administration. Possessed of wide administrative and military experience, endowed with considerable intellectual ability, determined, even ruthless in attaining his ends, Severus profoundly modified the structure of the principate. From the first he aimed to found a new dynasty, and as a necessary step toward this, he proclaimed himself in 194 son by adoption of Marcus Aurelius and so made himself the descendant and heir of the deified emperors since Nerva. To vindicate the honor of his family, he made the Senate annul their condemnation of Commodus and deify him, as the army had already done at his instigation. The ruling family then became a deified household (*domus divina*) in large degree basing its claim to rule on its divine ancestry. No wonder the term *dominus* came into regular use for a *princeps* with this background and Rome, as the imperial residence, was called the "sacred" city.

If by Romanization is meant a sincere desire to solve the problems of Empire as he understood them, then Septimius Severus was Roman to the core. Although the net result of the changes he introduced was a radical modification of the basis of imperial power in the direction of increased autocracy and militarization, Severus cannot be accused of intentionally riding roughshod over the conventions observed by the ablest of his predecessors. He merely read the signs of his age, and, like any able Roman, reacted to them realistically. If he excluded the Senate from any real share in government, he merely furthered a tendency operative long before him under good and bad emperors alike. Like his immediate predecessors, he tended to admit to the Senate more Easterners and Africans than Westerners, an indication that he acknowledged the Romanization of the former areas. He made noncommissioned officer cadres of the army more mobile by nominating the sons of the highest legionary centurions to equestrian posts and encouraged equestrians to specialize in military careers. Since such specialists were increasingly in demand, he named acting governors of equestrian rank in place of senatorial legates, substituted equestrians for senators in other administrative positions, and placed the three legions he raised for his second Parthian War under the command of equestrian prefects. The exceptional status of Italy, already modified by Hadrian, was further changed by Severus. The praetorian guard was henceforward recruited from the legions and thereby reflected their general provincialization. He cannot be accused of excluding Italians from the guard, however, and some Italians continued to serve in it until it was disbanded early in the fourth century. He did break precedent by stationing one of the newly raised legions on Italian soil in the vicinity of Rome. The old standing courts presided over by the praetors were abolished, and jurisdiction in the cases they had tried was transferred to the city prefect in Rome and within a circuit of one hundred miles of the city, and to the praetorian prefect beyond that limit.

As the importance of the senatorial order declined, that of the equestrians in the imperial service rose correspondingly as Septimius increased the number of procuratorial posts. In particular, the praetorian prefecture gained greatly in power and prestige. Not only did the prefect judge cases arising in Italy beyond the hundredth milestone from Rome, he also, as the deputy of the *princeps*, heard appeals from provincial tribunals. The supervision of the transportation of grain to Rome was taken from the prefect of the grain supply and given to the praetorian prefecture. In the absence of the *princeps*, the praetorian prefect presided over his judicial councils, and he was the commander in chief of all the armed forces in Italy. From 193 to 205, this office was held by Gaius Fulvius Plautianus (who, like Severus, was born in Africa) at first with a colleague but alone after 200. Owing to the concentration of authority in his hands and the degree to which he enjoyed the confidence of Severus, he was even more powerful than Seianus under Tiberius. In spite of his unpopularity with Julia Domna, Plautianus induced Severus to marry his daughter, Plautilla, to Caracalla, then co-Augustus with his father (202). Later Caracalla, influenced by his mother and personally resenting the influence of Plautianus, caused his downfall. He instigated a false charge of treason against his father-in-law and, when the latter denied the accusation, had him killed by a lictor in the presence of the *princeps* himself. Thereafter Severus revived the practice of having two praetorian prefects in office at the same time, and his choice of the jurist Papinianus as one of his new appointees testifies to the increased importance of the judicial duties of the prefecture.

Severus was legally minded. This, added to the presence of several distinguished lawyers in his councils, accounts for the numerous and important changes in law that date from his principate. In general these follow the humanitarian tendencies shown in the legislation of Hadrian, Antoninus Pius, and Marcus Aurelius, liberalizing the provisions of law by introducing principles and practices drawn from legal systems of non-Roman origin in vogue in the Hellenistic East and by developing legal concepts based on Stoic philosophy. Characteristic also was the effort to protect weaker members of society against oppression or exploitation by the stronger, and those of inferior political status (the *humiliores*) against the pressure of the official classes (the *honestiores*).

In his conception of the principate Severus regarded the army as the prime source of the imperial authority and accorded the soldiery preferential treatment. He owed his own nomination and his victory over his rivals to the legions under his command, and the importance he attached to their role in the choice of a *princeps* is shown by his having them declare Albinus a public enemy, Caracalla a Caesar, and Commodus a *divus*, all before he brought these actions before the Senate for confirmation. The recruitment of the praetorian guard from selected legionaries and especially the garrisoning of a legion at the Alban Lake may be regarded as measures to eliminate all opposition to the ruler in Rome and Italy. They also served to create the nucleus of a mobile field force ready to operate where needed under the emperor's command. Although Severus increased the pay of the legionaries by one third, this probably did no more than compensate them for inflation. The greater prestige of the military is also shown by the widespread admission of discharged centurions to the equestrian order and to the civil service and the emergence of veterans as an important element in the governing class of provincial municipalities. Severus granted the troops permission to contract legal marriages while in service and to live with their families in settlements adjacent to the army camps. This is certainly an indication of his favor to the military, although he was merely giving official sanction to the type of common-law connections that had existed long before his reign. In spite of these and other concessions, there is no evidence that Severus relaxed the training and discipline of the soldiers or that he deliberately fostered the provincialization of the legions by excluding Italians from the centurionate. Provincialization was the inevitable result of Romanization of the provinces and recruitment of the legions from the areas in which they had their permanent quarters. There can be little doubt that the policy of Severus made the army more conscious of its superiority to the civilian elements in the Empire.

Severus paid great attention to the welfare of the provincials. He endeavored to protect them from outside attack as well as from internal disorders. Border defences were repaired or improved, and much was done to stimulate municipal prosperity as well as to repair losses caused by civil wars and the brigandage that followed. Antioch, once punished for its support of Niger, recovered its autonomy, as did Byzantium, which was rebuilt on a generous scale. Syria and Britain were each divided into two provinces, and Numidia was separated from Africa, probably to weaken the influence of the governors concerned. Governors, now generally called *praesides*, were strictly supervised in an attempt to prevent them from exploiting the provincials. Great attention was paid to municipal organization, including the rights and duties of the different classes of the population. For fiscal reasons Alexandria and the native towns of Egypt were granted municipal councils, which now became responsible, as elsewhere, for the collection of local taxes and the performance of other obligations imposed on the local administrative centers. Although associations of businessmen and craftsmen obliged to undertake certain public services were exempt from other duties, their own responsibilities were more clearly defined and sharply enforced. In Syria, the Danubian provinces, and particularly in Africa the imperial policy bore fruit. These regions also profited greatly from imperial generosity in the construction of public works.

Severus inherited an empty treasury and had to undertake two costly wars at the outset of his principate. His building program, his generosity to the city populace and the soldiers, and an increase in the military and civil services added to normal expenses of government. The need of more money was met in part by depreciating the silver coinage by about one third and, at least early in his reign, by many issues of it. The result was inflationary. To a far greater extent additional revenue was provided from the wholesale confiscation of property of those who had supported his rival, Albinus. The extent of these properties was so great that for their administration it was necessary to create a separate treasury department called the *Res* or *Ratio Privata* (the Private Purse). Although, as the name indicates, the estates of the *Res Privata* were regarded as the personal property of the *princeps*, the officials in charge of this department were regular members of the imperial service, and the revenues they administered were used largely to meet costs of government.

WAR IN BRITAIN AND DEATH OF SEVERUS: A.D. 208–211.
Withdrawal of the troops of Albinus from Britain in 196 so weakened its
garrison that the province suffered repeated raids of Caledonians from the
north. The Romans had been forced to give up the land between the Walls
of Hadrian and Antoninus Pius, and even Hadrian's Wall had been
breached. Between 204 and 207 Roman commanders gradually restored
the situation and rebuilt the Wall, as well as fortifications farther south.
In 208 Severus himself took the field, accompanied by both his sons, very
probably to give the latter a chance to share in a victorious war. Caracalla,
the elder, had been saluted as Augustus by the army as early as 198, while
his younger brother Geta had been made Caesar at the same time. After a
successful campaign in which he penetrated far into Scotland, Severus conferred the title of Augustus upon Geta also (209). Fighting was resumed
in 210 and 211. In the course of his preparations for the campaign in 211,
Severus died at Eburacum (York) in February, at the age of sixty-five.
Caracalla thereupon made peace with the Caledonians and, accompanied
by Geta, returned to Rome, where they completed the funeral rites for
their father and secured him the honor of deification.

CARACALLA:[1] A.D. 211–217, AND GETA: A.D. 211–212.
The bitter enmity that had long smoldered between the two brothers broke
into the open with the removal of their father's restraining influence. Each
sought to build up a strong faction among officials and soldiers. Their
mother made every effort to reconcile them, in vain. After little more than
a year of joint rule, Caracalla found the opportunity to have Geta murdered. Alleging that he had acted in self-defense because of a conspiracy
directed against him, he won over the praetorians by bribes and executed
many suspected of belonging to Geta's faction. Among them was the
prefect Papinian.

INTERNAL POLICY.   Caracalla was weak, cruel and cunning, superstitious and given to debauchery. He deserves to rank with Caligula, Nero,
and Commodus as a thoroughly unworthy holder of the principate. His
early elevation to the rank of Augustus without the chastening influence
of a career of public service had strengthened his natural tendency to
despotic conduct and created in him a complete scorn of constitutional
practices. The advice attributed, perhaps wrongly, to his father, to enrich
the soldiery and neglect all else, may well be taken as the most consistent
trait in his policy. He courted their good will by a general increase of their
pay by one half and by frequent and lavish donations. Soon after the
assassination of Geta, in 212, Caracalla issued the famous *Constitutio
Antoniniana* (Antoninian Constitution), by which he conferred Roman
citizenship upon all free residents of the Empire who had not yet received
it. Those affected were primarily the provincials who, according to Roman

---

[1] So-called because of his custom of wearing a modified form of the *Caracalla,* a close-
fitting Gallic coat. Note genealogical table, p. 537.

law, had the status of aliens or Latins, and this grant was the logical culmination of the policy of his predecessors in bestowing citizenship upon provincial communities and upon veterans of the auxiliary corps. It seems that practical considerations of a financial nature led Caracalla to take this step, since he would thereby increase the collection of the 5 percent inheritance tax on estates, even those of middling substance, paid only by Roman citizens. At all events, the constitution excited little comment among contemporaries, and it was not until later times that it came to be looked upon as a most significant event in the Romanization of the provinces. On the whole, Caracalla took little interest in matters of internal administration, leaving them to the care of his mother, the imperial councils, and the higher officials, who carried on the government in the spirit of Severus.

GERMANIC AND PARTHIAN WARS. Caracalla devoted a great deal of attention to military matters and personally assumed command of his field armies. In 213 he campaigned successfully against the Alamanni, a newly formed group of Germanic peoples who threatened the province of Raetia. He then proceeded against some of the tribes on the upper Rhine, whose attack he bought off and whom he subsidized as Roman allies. Under his direction the frontier fortifications in Raetia and Upper Germany were greatly strengthened.

After settling affairs on the northern frontier, Caracalla in 214 proceeded to the East, where he sought to imitate the feats of his hero, Alexander the Great, whose reincarnation he believed himself to be. Before his departure, Caracalla strengthened his hand by treacherously seizing the kings of Osrhoëne and Armenia. Owing to the struggle between two brothers, Vologases V and Artabanus, for the Parthian throne, conditions seemed favorable for an attack upon Rome's eastern rival. The opening of hostilities was deferred by the desire of Vologases to avoid war and his yielding to Caracalla's demands. Caracalla then visited Egypt, where for uncertain reasons he massacred large numbers of the people of Alexandria. Upon his return to Syria, he demanded that Artabanus, who meantime had gotten control of Parthia, give him his daughter in marriage. When Artabanus refused, Caracalla invaded and ravaged Media unopposed (216). He made preparations to renew his attack in the following spring, but he was assassinated near Carrhae on April 8, 217 by orders of the praetorian prefect, Marcus Opellius Macrinus.

MACRINUS AND DIADUMENIANUS: A.D. 217–218. Macrinus was saluted Imperator by Caracalla's army and was recognized without opposition as the new *princeps* by the Senate. He at once bestowed the title of Caesar upon his young son Diadumenianus, whom he later proclaimed Augustus. Macrinus was a native of Mauretania and the first equestrian to attain the principate without having entered the senatorial order. He owed his advancement to his administrative and legal talents and displayed both moderation and good sense in his conduct of government. He lacked the prestige of a successful general and sought to win support for himself by generous donations to the soldiery and citizens of Rome, by deference toward the Senate, and by securing the deification of Caracalla, to placate the Severan faction. Defeated by Artabanus in Mesopotamia, he purchased an expensive peace from the Parthians and also made considerable concessions to the Armenian king. Such conduct alienated what little good will he had managed to develop among the troops.

RESTORATION OF THE SEVERAN DYNASTY; THE ROLE OF JULIA MAESA. Taking advantage of this situation, the members and followers of the house of Severus in Syria attempted to regain the principate for their dynasty. The leading spirit in the movement was Julia Maesa, sister of Julia Domna, who died soon after the murder of her son Caracalla. As claimant to the imperial power, Maesa presented the fourteen-year-old Varius Avitus Bassianus, son of her daughter Julia Soemias and a Syrian notable of senatorial rank. Bassianus was a grandnephew of Julia Domna and hence, by marriage, of Septimius Severus also. Much of the Syrian army was won over and saluted Bassianus as Imperator under the name of Marcus Aurelianus Antoninus. The forces remaining loyal to Macrinus were defeated (June 218), and both he and his son were subsequently captured and killed. Bassianus assumed the imperial titles and was accepted as *princeps* by the Senate. A few governors and legates who opposed his claims were executed.

ELAGABALUS: A.D. 218–222. Bassianus by hereditary right was priest of the Sun God worshipped under the name of Elagabal at Emesa, and hence he was himself generally known as Elagabalus. Of all the holders of the principate, none was so unworthy as this Syrian youth. Devoted as he was to the sensuous ritual of his oriental divinity, he transferred its cult image, a conical black stone, to Rome and endeavored to establish its worship as that of the supreme deity. To the imperial titles he formally added that of "most exalted priest of the Unconquered Sun God Elagabalus." Almost entirely immersed in ritual ceremonies and debauchery, he appointed worthless favorites to the highest offices. His grandmother, Julia Maesa, really directed the government. Realizing the hostility that was developing against Elagabalus and conscious of his complete ineptitude, she prevailed upon him to adopt his cousin Alexianus, son of Julia Mamea, as Marcus Aurelius Alexander and to appoint him Caesar (221). Elagabalus repented of his decision and tried to rid himself of Alexander. Thereupon the praetorians, instigated probably by Maesa and Mamea, murdered Elagabalus and his mother, along with many of his despised associates (222). The memory of the late *princeps* was condemned and the god Elagabalus sent back to his Syrian home.

SEVERUS ALEXANDER: A.D. 222–235. The principate passed without incident to Alexander, who took the cognomen Severus to emphasize his affiliation with the dynasty the latter had established. Like his cousin, the new Augustus was a mere boy of fourteen and at the time of his accession, quite incompetent to rule alone. He was dominated by powerful personalities like Ulpianus, praetorian prefect and famous jurist, who was *de facto* head of state in the early years of the reign, and by his own grandmother and mother. In what was apparently a genuine gesture to win the good will of the governing establishment, a council of senators was formed to confirm matters of policy decided on by the emperor and his ministers of state. At least in appearances senatorial interests were thus protected. When Alexander's grandmother died in 226 his mother acquired additional influence. Already enjoying the rank of Augusta, she soon acquired the high-sounding title "Mother of Augustus and the camps and the Senate and the fatherland" (*mater Augusti et castrorum et senatus et patriae*), which indicated her dominant position. Her jealousy of a rival caused her to drive even her son's wife into exile. The general government policy continued the traditions established by Septimius Severus. Attempts were made to strengthen the finances and to improve the efficiency of administration. The spread of elementary education seems to have been encouraged, and abuses in the application of the law of treason were corrected. The prestige of the praetorian prefecture was enhanced by the admission of some, although not all, of the prefects to senatorial rank while still in office. Control of the soldiery continued to be a crucial problem.

Mamea's training had made her son both studious and virtuous, but as he grew up Alexander showed himself lacking in courage and self-reliance and never emancipated himself from his mother. He was utterly unfitted for military command and failed to win the respect of the armies. In 228 the praetorians mutinied and murdered their prefect, Domitius Ulpianus, in the imperial palace without the *princeps* being able to protect him or at the time to punish those responsible. Alexander's incompetence as a general was all the more disastrous since new and aggressive foes began to threaten the Empire. In 226 or 227 the Parthian Empire of the Arsacids was overthrown by a rebellious vassal Ardaschir (Artaxerxes), king of Persia, who founded a new Persian Empire under his own dynasty, the Sassanids. This revival of the Persian Empire was accompanied by one of the national Mazdean or Zoroastrian religion. The nationalistic character of the new state was also reflected in its foreign policy, for it claimed all the territories once a part of the old Persian Empire, including the Asiatic provinces of Rome and Egypt. After an unsuccessful attack on Armenia, Ardaschir invaded Roman Mesopotamia in 230, and again in 231. He won no great successes, but the situation in the Near East had become serious for Rome, and all attempts at negotiation failing, Alexander was compelled to take the field against him. In the spring of 232, the Romans tried to invade Persia by three separate routes. Nowhere were they successful, and one division suffered a severe defeat. The Persians' losses were so heavy that they could not exploit their victory, however. Although no formal peace was made, the Roman frontier was restored, and Alexander returned to Rome to celebrate an unmerited triumph (233).

Alexander's return to the West was hastened by news that Germanic tribes were threatening the frontiers of the Rhine and the Danube. Preparations were made to attack the Alamanni, and the *princeps*, accompanied by his mother, took command of the army with headquarters at Mainz. Influenced by Mamea, he preferred to negotiate rather than fight, and bought peace from the barbarians. This cost him the respect of his troops, who were ready to fight, and who were also disgruntled at his subservience to his mother, whom they accused of parsimony. A mutiny broke out, led by Gaius Julius Verus Maximinus, a Thracian peasant who had risen from the ranks to high command. Alexander and Mamea were executed, and Maximinus was proclaimed Augustus (235). With this rebellion the Empire entered upon a half century of internal confusion and civil war.

VI. Development of the Principate to Severus Alexander

The five emperors from Nerva to Marcus Aurelius inclusive are often called the "good emperors," as if they alone had been worthy rulers. While inaccurate, the suggestion does point up the contrast between the legal character of their reigns and the insecurity felt under their predecessor Domitian as well as the lack of any principles of their immediate successor Commodus. It also reflects the favorable opinion of the senatorial class upon their constitutionality when compared with the autocratic tendencies of Domitian and the military monarchy of the Severi. The high level of capacity displayed by Trajan, Hadrian, Antoninus, and Marcus Aurelius also showed the advantages of selection by adoption over selection on the dynastic principle, which brought Commodus, Caracalla, and Elagabalus to the principate.

The former four emperors had kept the army under strict control, so that it had not interfered with imperial nominations. With the death of Commodus first the praetorians and then the legionary corps again assumed the right to select their imperator, and the soldiery exhibited a strong feeling of dynastic loyalty, which accounts for the Severan restoration in the person of Elagabalus. Under the later Severi, however, even this sense of loyalty dwindled under weak rulers and as the troops realized that the fate of the Empire rested in their hands, even though formal action by the Senate remained necessary to confer the appropriate authority on the new *princeps*. With Marcus Aurelius, Verus, and Commodus, and later with Septimius Severus and his sons, the principate was held in partnership by two or more Augusti, a situation that foreshadowed the regular practice of the later Empire. The only attempt really to share the office with a colleague was made by Aurelius in the case of Verus, primarily out of respect for the intentions of their adoptive father. His conferment of the rank of Augustus upon Commodus, like the action of Severus with Caracalla and Geta, was motivated primarily by concern for the succession. Significant was the attempt of Septimius Severus to establish the legitimacy of his dynasty by claiming descent from Marcus Aurelius, thus gaining as ancestors deified emperors. His example was followed by Elagabalus and Severus Alexander, both of whom fictitiously claimed Caracalla as a parent. Notable also was the role played by the Syrian princesses of the Severan house, who followed, but with greater success, the example set by Agrippina, the mother of Nero.

This period saw the Senate surrender to the *princeps* and his officers all active participation in the government. The process went on just as steadily under the constitutional as under the autocratic emperors. Extension of the functions of the prefects of the watch and grain supply, and of the commissions Augustus and his successors had set up to superintend construction and maintenance of public works in Rome and Italy, deprived most of the regular city magistrates of any real responsibility. When, under Severus Alexander, the tribunate and the aedileship ceased to be required steps in the senatorial career, these offices became nominal. From the time of Augustus, senatorial curators had presided over the public works commissions, but Claudius had added equestrian procurators who took over the real direction of their activities. Severus dispensed with the curators and placed procurators in charge. As early as Nero, control of the old treasury (the *aerarium Saturni*) had virtually been removed from senatorial jurisdiction by the appointment of two prefects of praetorian rank designated by the *princeps* as its directors. The diversion of its revenues to ministers of the *princeps* caused it to diminish steadily in importance, until after Severus it gradually sank to the condition of a municipal treasury for the city of Rome. By the time of Nero the Senate had lost any real freedom in the elections to the various magistracies, and between his principate and the death of Severus, it had also been deprived of any effective share in legislation. The Assembly had rapidly declined in importance during the first century A.D., and no trace of its activity as a formal organization can be found later than the time of Nerva. For a time this resulted in enhancing the legislative importance of the Senate, whose decrees acquired the validity of law, but by the time of Hadrian, if not earlier, the influence of the *princeps* had seriously encroached on its freedom of action and discussion. In effect, the Senate was rapidly abdicating its roll as the chief deliberative body in the state to the imperial councils. By the time of the Severan dynasty, the Senate enjoyed only the purely passive function of registering its approval of decrees drafted by the *princeps* and read to it by his representative. Expansion of the judicial functions of the urban and praetorian prefects resulted in the abolition of the standing courts of the praetors, that indirectly came under the supervision of the Senate, and that body's judicial competence was reduced to the trial of its own members on charges of treason. Even under Severus Alexander there was no real revival of the Senate's power, although concessions were made to its prestige to conciliate its members and win their approbation. One important right remained vested in the Senate—the power to confer or withhold deification. Even here its freedom to act was occasionally hampered by the pressure of the new *princeps*. Although the Senate had lost heavily, both in competence and in prestige, it still remained an influential body, both because of its traditions and because of the standing of its individual members and the class to which they belonged. Interesting changes in the composition of the Senate are observable, organic changes that reflect basic social and economic facts of life in the Empire. Matrimonial connections of the oldest republican families with the Julio-Claudian house had been their own undoing during the various persecutions before A.D. 68, by which date they were almost eliminated. The senatorial order as a whole had never reproduced itself. From the very beginning of the Principate its membership had been rejuvenated by the admission under imperial patronage of equestrian "new men" from Italy and the most Romanized provinces, and, on occasion, individual emperors had strengthened their following by admitting senators from specific provinces. More important in changing recruitment of that body was the occasional difficulty emperors had in finding men in Italy with the wealth, experience, and inclination to pursue a senatorial career. It was natural for the government to look for recruits in those provinces where the *pax Romana* had produced a wealthy and ambitious class eager for senatorial prestige. In the course of the late first and early second centuries A.D., the proportion of senators of western provincial origin thus increased, followed in the second century by recruitment in Africa, and in the late second and early third centuries by an increase of easterners. The Senate nevertheless was strongly Italian in tone, since senators invested in Italian estates and since many of them moved to Italy.

Great as was the extension of the powers of the principate in administration, it was equaled if not surpassed in the field of law. Not only did the *princeps* legislate through controlled decrees of the Senate, but he acquired independent legislative authority through the edictal power he exercised by virtue of his *imperium*. Like other magistrates, he could issue edicts valid during his term of office within the sphere of his *imperium*. He could also hand down *decreta* or judicial verdicts and issue responses to the petitions of his subordinates or private persons under his authority, as well as mandates or instructions to officials who were subject to his orders. Originally, the edicts were valid only during the principate of their author, and the other pronouncements merely applied to specific cases or individuals to whom they were directed. In course of time, however, all these constitutions, as they came to be called, gained recognition as establishing rules of public and private law and remained in force unless they were definitely revoked by another imperial constitution. It was the jurisconsults advising Hadrian who found a constitutional basis for the authority of the *princeps* in legislative matters. Gaius, a legal writer of the middle second century, enumerated the constitutions of the emperors, along with the other sources of Roman law and went on to say: "A constitution of a *princeps* is what an emperor has authorized by decree, edict or letter. Nor is it ever doubted that this has the force of law, since the emperor himself receives his *imperium* by a law."[2] In other words, the act which conferred the *imperium* on a *princeps* transferred to him the legislative authority of the Roman people. By the third century, imperial constitutions had become the regular form for legislation.

The evidence does not support the view that from the time of Augustus the *princeps* had a right of jurisdiction over Roman citizens in Rome and Italy. Strictly speaking, his right to pronounce judgment upon persons of senatorial rank was not recognized even under the Severan emperors. There is no doubt, however, that the *princeps* influenced the administration of justice in the Senate and the other tribunals. Frequently, moreover, emperors with autocratic or tyrannical leanings abused their power by extending their right to hold preliminary investigations (*cognitiones*) to cover pronouncement and execution of sentences, and at times they openly used force at their command to execute their personal orders as if these were legal judgments. Such conduct was always regarded as unconstitutional, however, and provoked great resentment. The case was quite different with the judicial authority that the *princeps* derived from his *imperium*. By virtue of his authority he could pronounce judgment in cases arising in the military establishment, the imperial service, and the provinces under his command. His appointees, the imperial officials, administered justice in their respective spheres only by virtue of authority he delegated to them, and appeals from their decisions might be directed to him. In the time of Hadrian this appellate jurisdiction of the *princeps* was extended by the constitutional lawyers to include appeals from all sources. They argued that, since the emperor derived his powers from the people and hence acted in their place, an appeal to him was the exercise of the age-old citizen's right of appeal from the action of a magistrate to the judgment of the people in assembly. With the extension of the judicial powers of the praetorian prefect, the city prefect, and the prefects of the watch and grain supply, and the consequent disappearance of the courts of the praetors and minor city magistrates, all jurisdiction in Rome and Italy, except for the limited civil jurisdiction of local municipal courts, was exercised by appointees of the *princeps*, subject to appeals to himself. Thus the *princeps* came to exercise the supreme jurisdiction for the whole of the Roman world.

---

[2] *Institutes*, I, 5. Compare the parallel statement in Justinian, *Institutes*, I, 2, 6.

The principate of the third century, then the ultimate source of all administrative, legislative, and judicial activity, was by no means the same office as that organized by Augustus or re-established by Vespasian. It had advanced far along the road to autocracy and assumed many characteristics of monarchy. In theory, in its titulature, its form of investiture, and other features, it still preserved the traditions of its magisterial character. A jurist like Ulpian might declare that the *princeps* was above the laws, but there were still influential circles not prepared to accept a ruler clothed with symbols expressing autocratic power over the Greco-Roman world.

CHAPTER 19

PUBLIC ADMINISTRATION UNDER THE PRINCIPATE

I. Rise of Imperial Bureaucracy

RESPONSIBILITY OF THE PRINCEPS. The necessary counterpart to the assumption of administrative duties by the *princeps* was the development of an imperial civil service, the officials of which were nominated by the *princeps* and promoted or removed at his pleasure. In this Augustus had taken the first steps by the establishment of equestrian procuratorships and prefectures and the creation of an equestrian career, but the number of these posts greatly increased with the extension of the administrative sphere of the *princeps* at the expense of the Senate. The idea of conducting the government through various departments manned by permanent salaried officials was foreign to the Roman Republic, which employed such servants only for clerical positions of minor importance in Rome. The chaotic conditions that obtained under the republican system showed the need for change, and the concentration of administration in the hands of the *princeps* both required and gave the opportunity for the development of an organized civil service. This development was unquestionably stimulated and influenced by the incorporation in the Empire of Egypt, which possessed a highly organized bureaucratic system that continued to function essentially unchanged. As control of the *princeps* over imperial administration widened at the expense of the Senate, imperial officials took over an ever-increasing share of the government, until by the end of the Severan dynasty, it was largely carried on by them.

EQUESTRIANS OR FREEDMEN. At first the imperial civil service lacked system, and there was little or no connection between administrative offices in Italy and in the provinces. Augustus and his immediate successors conducted the administration as part of their private business, keeping in touch with imperial officials through private secretaries of their households, that is to say, their freedmen, who, in another capacity, managed the private estate of the *princeps*. An important change was introduced under Claudius, when these secretaryships were changed into powerful ministries with official titles that indicated the sphere of their duties. Establishment of these ministries in the imperial household tended to centralize the imperial administration more completely and to give it greater uniformity and regularity. The influence of the freedmen who occupied these important positions was also responsible for the admission of freedmen to many minor administrative procuratorships. The freedmen did not maintain indefinitely their hold upon the imperial administrative service, however.

Otho, Domitian, and Trajan chose equestrian secretaries, and Hadrian generalized this practice, so that only occasionally thereafter did any of these important posts fall to freedmen favorites of the emperors. This step transformed what were till then palace offices into civil service positions with a consequent improvement of their official status and the traditions governing the conduct of their holders. Hadrian was also responsible for the removal of freedmen from most of the imperial procuratorships in the provinces.

THE EXPANSION OF THE SERVICE.   The first, second, and early third centuries saw a great expansion of the imperial civil service with the object of promoting administrative efficiency. The number of equestrian procuratorial posts rose steadily from about 23 under Augustus to 170 under Septimius Severus. The more noteworthy increases in numbers of personnel were made by the latter emperor and by Trajan and Hadrian. Hadrian's reforms in the procuratorial bureaucracy in particular and in the equestrian service in general were basic. By his time such officials had control of all branches of the administration that were later characteristic of them. Of particular interest were Hadrian's reforms of tax collection. Under him the system of farming the revenues was virtually abolished, and government employees took the place of private contractors who had handled this branch of the public business. He also created the post of advocate of the *fiscus*, whose holders prosecuted the claims of the state against delinquent taxpayers. When Septimius Severus gave general supervision of the imperial service to the praetorian prefects, the process of centralization reached completion. A bureaucratic system of government had developed, elaborate, highly specialized, and at the same time well coordinated.

Augustus had insisted upon a preliminary military career preceding appointment to administrative procuratorships, and this prerequisite was not formally abandoned under his successors. There was, however, room in the system for equestrians who had had no military service. Hadrian opened careers for such men, which were restricted mainly to the holding of procuratorships at the capital. Especially noteworthy was the promotion to civil and procuratorial careers by Septimius Severus of lowly soldiers who had risen from the ranks—a striking indication of that emperor's favor to the military and of the Romanized state of the army.

SALARY CLASSES IN THE IMPERIAL SERVICE.   The ordinary career of an official in the imperial administrative service included a considerable number of procuratorships in various branches of the administration in Rome, Italy, or the provinces. Although from the time of Augustus a salary was paid to each of these offices, it was not until the end of the second century at the latest that four classes of procurators were recognized on the basis of the relative importance of their offices expressed in terms of pay. These four classes, known as *sexagenarii, centenarii, ducenarii,* and *trecenarii,* who received respectively an annual salary of 60,000, 100,000,

200,000, and 300,000 sesterces, remained unchanged until the close of the third century. At that time the highest class included the imperial ministers of state, whose title was then master (*magister*). The salary of the four chief equestrian prefectures was probably higher still. Although it is surprising that relatively few executives of this type were required to run the Empire, payment of salaries of these procurators—not to mention their numerous subordinates and officials in other branches of government— became increasingly burdensome. It has been estimated that the procuratorial service alone was five times as expensive to run under Septimius Severus as it had been under Augustus.

THE EQUESTRIAN ORDER. It has been pointed out before how the senatorial order was recruited from the upper class of the equestrians. A good example of such advancement is seen in the case of the praetorian prefects. After the time of Trajan they frequently entered the Senate with the rank of ex-consuls and in the third century were generally promoted to the senatorial office of city prefect. The vacancies in the upper ranks of the equestrians caused by this and similar promotions were filled from the lower grades of the order, which in turn were recruited from still lower classes, such as freedmen, soldiers (that is, officers of low commissioned rank), and the municipal and provincial aristocracies. The effect of this process was to transform the equestrians, like the senators, from a national Roman to an imperial cosmopolitan body. After the first century the proportion of admissions from Italy and the West declined, that from Africa and Asia Minor increased in the second century, and that from Syria, Egypt, and Arabia showed a similar advance in the third. This increase in recruits of eastern origin coincides with the period of the maximum number of admissions from the freedman class.

The general tendency of the age, which placed ever-growing emphasis upon official prestige, rank, and precedence, led to the appearance of an hereditary title—that of *clarissimus* (most distinguished or noble)—for members of the senatorial order. At first informal and unofficial, by the second century this title had passed into formal, official usage. Following the example of the senatorial order, the equestrians also acquired honorary titles which depended upon their official rank. From the time of Hadrian the title *vir eminentissimus* (most eminent) was the prerogative of the praetorian prefects. Under Marcus Aurelius appear two other equestrian titles, *vir perfectissimus* (most perfect) and *vir egregius* (honorable). In the third century the latter was held by all the imperial procurators, while the former was reserved for the higher prefectures (apart from the praetorian), the chief officials of the treasury, and the imperial ministers.

ADMINISTRATION OF THE IMPERIAL FINANCES. (*a*) *Fisci*. The most important branch of the civil administration was that of the public finances, which merit special consideration. Under Augustus the traditional treasury of the Republic, the *aerarium Saturni*, remained at Rome as the principal one. Revenue from all provinces flowed into it, and from it the emperor, like any republican magistrate, was voted funds to perform his official functions. There also existed in all the provinces, both senatorial and imperial, local branches of the *aerarium* called *fisci*, where taxes were deposited and whence magistrates, like the emperor, could withdraw funds for local administrative purposes. Little cash actually flowed from the *fisci* to the central *aerarium*, except in the case of certain rich provinces, like Asia and Egypt, that tended always to produce revenue surpluses. In most cases only accounts of balances on hand were sent on to the capital. The *aerarium militare*, established by Augustus to pension off veteran troops, also had the character of a public, as distinguished from an imperial, treasury and was administered by three ex-praetors. Whereas senatorial officials continued to manage the *aerarium Saturni*, the accounts of the *fisci* already under Augustus were prepared by a domestic freedman secretary called *a rationibus*. Augustus acknowledged a strict accountability of such monies to the Senate, and his policy was followed by Tiberius and, for a time, by Caligula, after which the practice completely lapsed. Important changes in this system were made under the Flavians, in particular by Vespasian, who established new *fisci* at Rome, whence flowed the surpluses from rich provinces that had formerly nourished the *aerarium Saturni*. These new *fisci* were placed under the management of imperial procurators rather than senatorial officials. The net result of this change was the progressive impoverishment of the senatorial treasury. Henceforward emperors could bypass that treasury by drawing on the *fisci* at Rome for expenditures in Italy. From a popular viewpoint all the *fisci* under the management of imperial officials came to be regarded as an aggregate of fiscal organizations distinct from the *aerarium*.

(*b*) *Patrimonium*. Roman Emperors beginning with Augustus had, of course, their own fortunes as private individuals, their patrimony, but because of their position in the government the distinction between its administration and that of other monies expended for reasons of state was often blurred. Emperors frequently contributed sums from their immense private fortunes to the *aerarium*, and upon their deaths their extensive estates almost inevitably were regarded and managed as state property. At the latest from the reign of Claudius procurators headed the management of patrimonial estates, and the various treasuries into which patrimonial income flowed were known as *fisci*, just like the various state chests.

(*c*) *Res Privata or Private Purse*. This situation continued until the accession of Septimius Severus, whose enormous confiscations of the property of the adherents of Niger and Albinus were incorporated into his personal estate, known as the *patrimonium privatum*. Septimius Severus then reorganized the financial administration. On the one hand, he consolidated the management of the old patrimonial estates he had inherited from preceding reigns with his own *patrimonium privatum* and placed it under a new department of public administration known officially as the *ratio* or *res privata*, headed by a secretary called *procurator*, later *magister, rei privatae*. On the other hand, he consolidated the administration of the various *fisci* managed by imperial officials into a single treasury under an official called the *rationalis*. Both may be regarded as departments of the imperial Fiscus, a term which, in a pregnant sense, had gradually become the predominant technical term used in speaking of emperors' wealth. The *aerarium Saturni* still existed, but it was of little consequence in the third century.

Under the Republic there had grown up in Rome a class of professional government clerks from whom the various magistrates, including provincial governors, recruited most of their office personnel. After the establishment of the Principate this practice was continued by most of the appointees of the Senate. Imperial officials, however, used imperial freedmen and slaves or, particularly if they exercised military authority, soldiers who were detailed from their units for this type of service. This latter practice, also republican in origin, became especially important by the reign of Hadrian. By the time of the Severans such soldiers had come to constitute an integral part of the lower echelons of the bureaucracy. So widespread was their use that the titles of the various posts in these offices were taken largely from those in the military administration.

II. The Army and Defense of the Frontiers

PROVINCIALIZATION OF THE LEGIONS AND THE PRAETO-RIANS. It will be recalled that the military policy of Augustus aimed at securing the supremacy of the Roman element in the Empire by restricting admission to the legions to Roman citizens and to freeborn inhabitants of provincial municipalities who received citizenship upon entering the service. The gradual provincialization of the recruitment of such professional citizen-soldiers is one of the most significant facts in the military history of the Principate.

Augustus would probably have preferred to recruit his armies as far as possible from citizens in Italy, but he faced what became an increasing Italian reluctance to render military service, and so gradually he instituted recruitment on a territorial basis, recruiting legions stationed in the West from Italy and the Romanized provinces there, the eastern legions from the Greek East and Galatia. By the end of the Julio-Claudian dynasty, provincial citizens accounted for about half the legionary strength, and by the beginning of the second century they outnumbered the Italians by almost five to one. There was not, however, at any time a conscious policy of excluding Italians from the army. Along with the provincialization of manpower there went a parallel and equally organic development, the recruitment of legionaries first from the provinces where they were stationed and then from the immediate vicinity of the garrisons themselves. This was perhaps inevitable, granted the generally defensive nature of the early imperial military establishment, which tended to transform the legions into a garrison force. It was cheaper for the Empire to recruit its soldiers from the immediate hinterland of the various headquarters, and recruits would be easier to find if they could serve close to their homes. Very often a family tradition of military service arose, and, granted the upward social mobility that legionary service offered provincial citizens, many noncommissioned officers upon their discharge retired to their home towns as men of some substance and standing. By the second century the normal term of legionary enlistment had been raised to twenty-five years. Down to the Severan dynasty the Roman army remained the most powerful Romanizing catalyst in the Empire. Recruitment for the praetorian guard followed the same tendencies as those obtaining among the legionaries, except that as an elite corps its provincialization was slower. Provincial praetorians are known from the first century A.D., while Italians remained a heavy majority until the reign of Septimius Severus. Septimius reconstituted the guard by recruiting it from legionary troops. This meant that henceforth the guard was largely provincialized, although Italians continued to serve in it, as they did in the legions themselves.

AUXILIARIES. Organization of the auxiliary corps as troops raised and officered by Romans and for a specified term of twenty-five years was begun by Augustus but was not completed until the reign of Vespasian. Generally speaking, the *auxilia*, like the legions, were recruited in areas where they served, and the removal of the Batavi to a far distant frontier after their revolt in A.D. 69 is merely the exception that proves the rule. At first they were not citizens until their discharge, but already in the first century some of them were citizens while in service and this proportion had risen to half by Hadrian's time. The extension of Roman citizenship to practically the whole Roman world by Caracalla in 212 removed the basic juridical distinction between Romans and auxiliaries. Tactically, they had also been largely assimilated to legionary status by the second century and received the same training and weapons as the legionaries.

NUMERI. As the auxiliary units increasingly approximated the legions, their place was gradually taken in the military establishment, probably beginning with Domitian, by organizations known as *numeri*. National contingents of barbarians or non-Romanized frontier peoples, they kept their own weapons and methods of warfare. They were commanded by Roman officers and used Latin as the language of commands, but the degree of Romanization they attained in service is questionable. Their functions and tactical organization corresponded to that of the original *auxilia* when the latter had been a force supporting the legions.

THE STRENGTH OF THE ARMY. At the death of Augustus the number of the legions was twenty-five, under Nero it was twenty-eight, under Trajan it was thirty, and Severus increased it to thirty-three, comprising over 180,000 men. A corresponding increase was made in the numbers of the auxiliaries. From about 150,000 in the time of Augustus, they had increased to about 220,000 in the second century. The total number of troops in the Roman service at the opening of the third century was therefore about 400,000.

SYSTEM OF FRONTIER DEFENSE. A second momentous fact in the military history of the Principate was the transformation of the army from a field force into garrison troops. This was the result of the system developed for the defense of the frontiers. Augustus, his imperialistic designs having failed, finally decided that the Empire should attain only a frontier protected by natural barriers. Roughly speaking, these natural defenses of the Empire were the ocean on the west, the Rhine and the Danube on the north, and the desert on the east and south. At strategic points behind this frontier, Augustus stationed his troops in large fortified camps, in which both legionaries and auxiliaries were quartered. These camps served as bases of operations, and from them military roads were constructed to advantageous points on the frontier to permit the rapid movement of troops for offensive or defensive purposes. Such military roads were called *limites*, a name which subsequently was used in the sense of frontiers. The *limites* were protected by small forts manned by auxiliary troops. Although Claudius and Vespasian discarded the maxims of Augustus in favor of an aggressive border policy, they adhered to his system for protecting their new acquisitions in Britain and southern Germany. These conquests, however, and that of the Wetterau region by Domitian pushed the frontier beyond the natural boundaries and led to the characteristic Flavian interest in constructing an artificial barrier as a substitute. Another notable feature of Flavian military policy was the use of legionary detachments or *vexillationes* behind the fortified frontier.

GERMANIC AND RAETIAN LIMITES. By the third century the Roman frontier in Germany was protected by a continuous system of fortifications and barriers that followed an irregular line around the area of Roman occupation from Rheinbrohl on the Rhine to Heinheim on the Danube, a distance of about 345 miles. The northwestern section of this line was called the Germanic, the eastern section the Raetian, Limes. The dividing point was near Lorch on the borders of Germania Superior and Raetia. The final form of the Limites was attained only after a long development in which the frontier was frequently changed and the system of defences varied. Domitian laid the foundations of the system by constructing a continuous barrier along these frontiers in the form of a low embankment of earth, which in places gave way to wooden fences. Along this line were placed wooden watchtowers at irregular intervals, and some distance to the rear was a series of earthen forts, each garrisoned by a corps of auxiliaries and linked by roads to the line of the barrier. While the auxiliary troops were thus distributed along the frontiers in small detach-

ments, Domitian broke up the larger legionary cantonments, so that after
A.D. 89 no camp regularly contained more than a single legion. This had
the effect of scattering the legions along the line of the frontiers as support
for the line of auxiliary forts. Trajan strengthened the fortifications of
Domitian but rather stressed improving the system of communication between the border provinces by building military highways along the northern frontier from the Rhine to the Black Sea, as he also did in Arabia and
Africa. The principate of Hadrian marked a new stage in the development
of the Germanic and Raetian Limites. Along their whole length he erected
an unbroken palisade wall, constructed of the split trunks of oak trees set
upright to a height of nine feet in a shallow trench. In order to facilitate
observation and signaling from the watchtowers, he also shortened and
straightened the line of the Limites which now ran in rectilinear sections as
far as possible without regard to the configuration of the ground. The
adoption of the new line brought about the abandonment of some of the
older forts for newer ones of earth or of earth and wood placed close to
the palisade. Antoninus Pius, who carried on Hadrian's policy of strengthening the border defences, converted these advance forts into stone structures; and Commodus reinforced the barrier still more by substituting in
some places a wall of stone for Hadrian's palisade. Finally Caracalla completed the process by providing the Raetian Limes with a wall of stone six
to nine feet high and four feet thick which ran uninterruptedly along its
whole front for about 105 miles, while he also had a wide ditch dug along
the Germanic Limes just behind the palisade. This system of fortifications
was by no means impenetrable and was not intended to serve as a permanent barrier against large forces, but it enabled the Romans to control
communications along the frontier and was a formidable obstacle to raiding
bands, whose entry would be reported quickly to the nearest garrisons and
who would with great difficulty escape with their booty across the Limes
when pursued.

LIMES IN BRITAIN. Hadrian took the first steps to protect Britain
by a continuous barrier such as existed in Germany. In the time of
Domitian, Agricola had built a road guarded by forts placed at irregular
intervals along the seventy-six mile stretch from Newcastle-upon-Tyne to
the Solway Firth. Along this line, under the direction of Hadrian between
122 and 127, the system of fortifications was constructed known as
Hadrian's Wall. It consisted of a stone wall about twenty feet high and
eight feet thick and linked a series of fourteen forts, each accommodating
a detachment of about 1000 auxiliaries. In front of the wall was a deep
V-shaped ditch, thirty feet wide at the top. Incorporated in the wall were
castles for garrisons of 100 men, situated at regular mile intervals. Between the castles were stone turrets likewise spaced at fixed intervals. This
reconstruction of the Limes was completed in 126–127. In contrast to the
Germanic Limes, the wall in Britain had considerable defensive value
against more than mere raiding parties. The Roman sphere of influence

extended northward into Scotland, however, and, in order to protect this outlying territory from the highland tribes, Antoninus Pius in 143 built another wall 36 miles long from the Firth of Forth to the Clyde. This wall was constructed of turf blocks laid like bricks and contained some twenty forts of earth or earth and stone construction. Both the wall of Hadrian and that of Antoninus were partially destroyed by a Pictish invasion in 181. Severus later rebuilt Hadrian's Wall, but the wall in Scotland was permanently abandoned.

DANUBIAN FRONTIERS. Where the Danube marked the northern frontier of the empire, it was defended by a line of auxiliary forts and legionary encampments on the Roman side of the river. Roman advance to the north, particularly the occupation of Dacia, led to the development of frontier delimitation and defense similar to that in Germany and Raetia. Only relatively short stretches of these Limites are traceable today. An earthen wall running west to east for about sixty-three miles from the Danube to the Theiss protected that part of Moesia north of the Danube in the enclave between these two rivers. The line of another Limes-wall has been found on part of the northern frontier of Dacia, and two lines of fortifications roughly parallel to the Aluta river seem to have formed part of the eastern defenses of that province. Of three walls that run from the Danube eastward to the Black Sea near Tomi, one, a large wall of turf, belongs to the time before Trajan and formed a temporary Limes in that part of Moesia; the other two seem to be post-Roman.

LIMITES IN ASIA AND AFRICA. Neither in Asia nor in Africa was there a continuous line of frontier defenses, but the Limites were marked out by roads protected by chains of small forts and guard stations from which patrols operated. Behind the Limites proper, often at considerable distances, were placed large fortified camps at strategic points. The difference in the Limes organization of Britain and Europe from that of Asia and Africa is explained in part by the difference in the physical features of the boundary lands and in part by the difference of the character of the frontier peoples and frontier warfare on the northern from those on the eastern and southern borders of the Empire.

THE IMPERIAL NAVY. The Roman navy played an important if subordinate part in imperial defense. Two main fleets based at Misenum and Ravenna secured communications by sea between Italy and the provinces and served to convoy troops and supplies. Provincial squadrons were maintained in Egypt, Syria, Mauretania, in the Black Sea, on the Danube and its tributaries, the Save and the Drave, on the Rhine, and in the English Channel. In addition to routine police duties, they suppressed piracy, checked barbarian raids, and helped the army in offensive and defensive operations.

CONSEQUENCES OF THE SYSTEM OF FRONTIER DEFENSE. The result of the construction of permanent fortifications along the frontier was the complete immobilization of the auxiliary corps. Stationed continuously as they often were in the same sectors from early in the second century and recruited increasingly from among the children of the camps, in the third century they were granted frontier lands upon condition of their defending them and were so gradually transformed into a border militia (*limitanei*). A semimilitary status was given to the civilian population in certain frontier districts by the Severi, who concentrated them in small castles and other defensible posts. Scattering of the legions along the line of the frontiers slowed assembling any adequate mobile force. The fortifications, while useful in checking predatory raids by isolated bands and in regulating intercourse across the frontiers, proved incapable of preventing the invasion of larger forces. When the barbarians broke through the Limites in the third century, they found no forces capable of checking them until they had penetrated deeply into the heart of the provinces.

The chaos following the death of Severus Alexander was the result of a military policy that had left the richest and most highly civilized parts of the Empire without any means of self-defense; created a huge professional army the rank and file of which had come to place its own vested interest ahead of the good of the state and rendered the army itself incapable of performing the task for which it was organized by often blurring the distinction between soldier and civilian.

THE ROMAN ARMY AS A CIVILIZING AGENCY. On the other hand, the army was one of the most influential agents in the spread of the material and cultural aspects of Roman civilization. The highways of the Empire, bridges, fortifications, and numerous public works of other sorts were constructed by soldiers. Every camp was a center for the spread of the Latin language and Roman discipline, and the number of Roman citizens was augmented continuously by the stream of discharged auxiliaries. In the *canabae*, or towns of civilian camp-followers, sprang up organized communities of Roman veterans with the institutions and material advantages of municipal life. The constant movement of troops from one quarter of the Empire to another facilitated the exchange of cultural, and in particular of religious, ideas. To the ideal of a Roman Empire the army remained loyal throughout the Principate, although this loyalty was generally interpreted in the light of its own vested interest. Not only was the army the support of the power of the *princeps*, it was also the mainstay of the Roman Peace, which endured with two brief interruptions from the battle of Actium to the death of Severus Alexander and was the necessary condition for the civilizing mission of Rome.

III. The Provinces Under the Principate

It is to the provinces that one must turn to have a true appreciation of the beneficial aspects of Roman government during the Principate. As Mommsen[1] said: "It is in the agricultural towns of Africa, in the homes

[1] *Provinces of the Roman Empire,* I, 5, trans. Dickson, Scribner's, 1906.

of the vine-dressers on the Moselle, in the flourishing townships of the Lycian mountains, and on the margin of the Syrian desert that the work of the imperial period is to be sought and found." In this sphere the chief tasks of the Principate were the maintenance of peace and the extension of Greco-Roman civilization over the barbarian provinces of the west and north. How well this latter work was done is attested by the material remains of once flourishing communities and by the extent to which the civilization of Western Europe rests upon the basis of Roman culture.

THE PROVINCES. At the establishment of the Principate there were about thirteen provinces, at the death of Augustus twenty-eight, and under Hadrian forty-five. In the course of the third century the number was considerably increased. New provinces were formed partly by the organization of newly conquered countries as separate administrative districts and partly by subdivision of larger units. At times this subdivision was made to relieve a governor of an excessively heavy task and to improve the administration, at times it proceeded from a desire to lessen the dangers of revolt by breaking up the larger military commands. The provinces were divided into two classes, senatorial and imperial, corresponding to the division of administrative authority between the Senate and the *princeps*. The principle established by Augustus that the garrisoned provinces should come under the authority of the *princeps* was adhered to, and consequently provinces were at times taken over by the emperor in view of military necessities, while others were transferred to the Senate. As a rule, newly organized provinces were placed under imperial governors, so that these soon came to outnumber the senatorial. With the extension of the administrative powers of the *princeps* and his control over senatorial appointments, senatorial provinces inevitably passed more and more under his direction, until in all but outward forms the distinction between the two types of provinces disappeared.

ADMINISTRATIVE OFFICIALS. The governors of the senatorial provinces were called proconsuls, even if they were of praetorian rank. Asia and Africa, however, were reserved for ex-consuls. Following the law of Pompey, a period of five years intervened between holding a magistracy and a promagisterial appointment. Each proconsul was assisted by a *quaestor* and three propraetorian *legati* whose appointment was approved by the *princeps*. Imperial governors were of two classes, legates of Augustus (*legati Augusti*) and procurators. In the time of Hadrian there were eleven proconsuls, twenty-four legates of Augustus, and nine procurators, besides the prefect of Egypt. The subordinates of the legates of Augustus were legates in command of the legions and fiscal procurators. Procuratorial governors, at first called prefects, were equestrians and placed in command of lesser military districts, garrisoned by auxiliaries only. An exception to this practice was made in the case of Egypt, which senators were forbidden to enter except by special permission of the *princeps*. Egypt was governed by a prefect who at first was the highest ranking equestrian in imperial service but later ranked second to the praetorian prefect. He had under his orders at first three and later two legions besides auxiliary corps. In place of the usual senatorial legates, these legions were commanded by equestrian prefects. From the time of Septimius Severus equestrian procurators frequently were appointed to act as deputy governors in imperial provinces normally commanded by senatorial legates. During the second century the title *praeses* (plural *praesides*) came into general use for senatorial governors serving the *princeps*.

ENLIGHTENED IMPERIALISM. As under the Republic, the governors exercised administrative, judicial, and (in the imperial provinces) military authority. With the advent of the Principate, however, the central government often aimed to secure the welfare and not the spoliation of its subjects. Augustus inaugurated a policy of enlightened imperialism with his two edicts of 7–6 B.C., which delivered the non-Roman provincials of Crete and Cyrene from judicial oppression of the Romans residing there, and his sponsorship of the Senate's decree of 4 B.C., which provided a more direct and less expensive method for the redress of wrongs suffered from provincial officials.[2] It is often assumed that higher standards of administration resulted in marked amelioration in the well-being of the provinces during the early Principate. Such a view demands serious qualification. That the provinces by ancient standards flourished in the first two centuries of imperial rule there can be no doubt, and it is obvious that the emperors, as a whole, were sincerely interested in the welfare of their subjects. But it can be argued that the improved economic status of the Empire was due primarily to the Roman Peace following an era of civil wars and that standards of public morality, in spite of the best of imperial intentions, were not much higher than those of the Republic. In spite of the introduction of salaries for provincial governors and other public servants, officials tended to be corrupt, and it was difficult to bring them to justice. The problem of dishonesty in administration increased as imperial bureaucracy expanded. One may say, then, that the Empire flourished in spite of rather than because of the conduct of many of its civil servants.

PROVINCIAL TAXATION. Under Augustus provincial taxation was revised to correspond more closely to taxpaying capacity. Under the Principate these taxes were of two kinds, direct (*tributa*) and indirect (*vectigalia*). The *tributa* comprised a land tax (*tributum soli*) and a personal tax (*tributum capitis*). The land tax was assessed on all land not granted the exceptional status of Italian soil (*ius Italicum*); the personal tax was levied on all property not subject to the land tax. Poll taxes and taxes on special trades and occupations were also collected in certain provinces. In preparing the census returns for the estimation of the land tax,

2 See p. 285.

the following information had to be furnished: (1) title of the property, (2) name of the municipality on whose list it was carried, (3) name of the *pagus* in which it lay, (4) names of the two nearest estates, (5) acreage in ploughland, (6) number of vine stocks, (7) number of olive trees, (8) acreage of meadowland, (9) acreage of pastures, and (10) acreage of woodland. The chief indirect taxes were the customs dues (*portoria*), the 5 percent tax on the value of emancipated slaves, possibly the 1 percent tax on sales, and the 5 percent inheritance tax, levied on Roman citizens only. In imperial provinces the land tax was a fixed proportion of the annual yield, whereas in the senatorial provinces it was a definite sum (*stipendium*) annually fixed for each community. In addition to these regular taxes the provincials were liable to furnish supplies to imperial troops and officials (*annona*), to provide transport animals for the imperial post service, and to perform personal services (*munera*) for the state. Although compensation was provided for both goods and services requisitioned, exactions of this sort proved a heavier burden than the regular taxation, for they often meant serious economic detriment to the taxpayers and gave many opportunities for graft and oppression.

The Principate did not break abruptly with the republican practice of employing associations of *publicani* to collect revenues. They had been excluded from Asia by Julius Caesar, and it is possible that Augustus dispensed with them for raising direct taxes in the imperial provinces, but even under Tiberius they seem to have been active in connection with the *tributa* in some of the senatorial provinces. Their place in the imperial provinces was taken by the procurator and his agents, in the senatorial at first by the proconsul assisted by the taxpaying communities and later by imperial officials.

Indirect taxes long continued to be raised exclusively by the corporations of tax collectors in all the provinces. The operations of these *publicani*, however, were supervised by imperial procurators. In place of the previous custom of paying a fixed sum to the state in return for a right to the total returns from the taxes in question, *publicani* now received a fixed percentage of the amount actually collected. Under Hadrian the companies of *publicani* engaged in collecting customs dues began to be superseded by individual contractors (*conductores*), who, like the companies, received a percentage of the amount raised. About the time of Commodus the system of direct collection by public officials was introduced and contractors gave way to imperial procurators. The 5 percent tax on inheritances and manumissions was also at first farmed out but later (under Hadrian in the case of inheritances) collected directly by agents of the state.

LOCAL GOVERNMENT. Each province comprised many communes (*civitates*), some of which were organized towns while others were tribal or village communities. From the beginning of the Principate it was a principle of imperial policy to convert rural communities into municipalities, which assumed the burden of local administration. Under the Republic provincial communities had been grouped into three classes: free and federate (*liberae et foederatae*), free and immune (*liberae et immunes*), and tributary (*stipendiariae*). In addition to these native communities there began to appear in the provinces Roman and Latin colonies. Toward the close of the Republic and in the early Principate most of the free communities lost their immunity from taxation and became tributary. Some of them exchanged the status of federate allies for that of Roman colonies. During the same period the number of colonies of both types was greatly increased by founding new settlements or planting colonists in provincial towns. Some of the latter also became municipalities. Thus arose a great variety of provincial communities, well illustrated by conditions in the Spanish province of Baetica (Farther Spain) under Vespasian. This province then contained nine colonies and eight municipalities of Roman citizens, twenty-nine Latin towns, six free, three federate towns, and one hundred and twenty tributary communities.

The policy of transforming rural communities into organized municipalities has been noted. How rapidly this transformation took place may be gathered from the fact that in Tarraconensis (Hither Spain) the number of rural districts sank from one hundred and fourteen to twenty-seven between the reign of Vespasian and that of Hadrian. A parallel movement was the conversion of native towns into Roman colonies and municipalities, often through the transitional stage of Latin communities, a status existing in the provinces only. Acquirement of Roman or Latin status brought exemption from the poll tax, while the former opened the way to all civil and military offices. An added advantage went with the charter of a Roman colony, for this usually involved immunity from the land tax. The last step in the Romanization of the provincial towns was Caracalla's edict of 212, which conferred Roman citizenship upon all non-Roman municipalities.

THE THREE GAULS.   From this municipalization of the provinces two districts were at first excluded. These districts were the three Gauls (Aquitania, Lugdunensis, and Belgica) and Egypt. At the time of its conquest Gaul was a rich agricultural country, with sharply defined tribal communities but little or no city development. This condition Augustus judged well adapted, under strict imperial control, to furnishing recruits and money and produce for the army of the Rhine. He therefore continued the division of Gaul into sixty-four tribal units (*civitates*), each controlled by its native nobility. His policy was adhered to in general for about two hundred years, but during the third century the municipal system was introduced into Gaul by converting the chief town of each *civitas* into a municipality with the rest of the *civitas* as *territorium* under its control.

EGYPT.   Although Augustus added Egypt to the Empire as a province, it occupied a peculiar status within his *imperium* and was kept more directly under his control than other provinces. This was primarily due to the wealth of the country and its importance for the grain supply of Rome. In Egypt he appeared as the heir of the Ptolemies by right of conquest and was recognized by the Egyptians as "king of upper Egypt and king of lower Egypt, lord of the two lands, *autocrator*, son of the Sun." For the Greek residents he was an absolute deified ruler of the Hellenistic type. Thus Egypt, although a part of the Empire, was looked upon at times as subject to the rule of the *princeps* alone. As in the theory of government, so in the political institutions of the country, the Romans adapted to their purposes existing conditions.

Under Augustus there were three Greek towns in Egypt, Alexandria the capital, Ptolemais, and Naucratis. To these Hadrian added a fourth, Antinoöpolis. Ptolemais, Naucratis, and Antinoöpolis enjoyed municipal institutions, but Alexandria, because of the turbulence of its population, was ruled by imperial officials, following Ptolemaic practice. The rest of the population lived in villages throughout the Nile Valley, which was divided into thirty-six districts (nomes). The bulk of Egypt was imperial or public domain land, and the great majority of the Egyptian population were tenants on the imperial domain. For collection of the land tax, poll tax, professional and other taxes, for the supervision of irrigation, and for maintenance of public records of the cultivated acreage and the population (for which a census was taken every fourteen years), there had been developed a highly organized bureaucracy with central offices at Alexandria and agents in each of the nomes. This system was maintained by the Romans and profoundly influenced the organization of the imperial civil service. At the head of the administration stood the prefect, an equestrian because of his position as a personal employee of the *princeps* and because the power he wielded would have proved a dangerous temptation to a senator. The chief burden laid upon Egypt was to supply one third of the grain consumed at Rome, or about 5,000,000 bushels annually. This amount was drawn partly from the land tax, paid in kind, and partly from grain purchased by the government.

The first step toward spreading municipal government throughout Egypt was taken in A.D. 200 when Septimius Severus organized a senate, or town council, in Alexandria and in the metropolis or administrative seat of each nome. His object was to create bodies that could be made to be responsible for administration.

THE PROVINCES AND THE IMPERIAL GOVERNMENT. The Principate's greatest service to the provinces was two and a half centuries of peaceful government. This led in many areas to material development unequalled in these regions before or since. In these centuries the history of Rome becomes the history of the provinces. At the opening of the period the Italians occupied a privileged position within the Empire; at its close they and their one-time subjects were on the same level. The army and the senatorial and equestrian orders were increasingly provincialized, and the emperors had come to be usually provincials. Rome was still the seat of administration, adorned with the spoils of Empire, its populace regaled with bread and public entertainments. It remained the center of Roman political traditions, but from the constitutional point of view its status differed little from that of a provincial municipality.

Obviously imperial government had no desire to create or to maintain a spirit of local nationalism in the provinces. Consequently, it never sought to build up any form of provincial self-government. The only institution that served to voice the opinion of a province was the council, which came to direct the provincial cult of Rome and Augustus. Provincial councils had not been unknown under the Republic. More of them were instituted during the Principate, but by no means everywhere. These councils were composed of representatives from the municipalities or other local units who belonged to the most influential classes in their respective communities. They could address petitions, recommendations, and complaints either to the governor or to the *princeps*. They might have been an important factor in the prosecution of governors for maladministration, but such prosecution was difficult and dangerous, and the councils often preferred to flatter outgoing governors who could no longer oppress them but who, as senators, might become their patrons at the capital. The councils themselves never exercised political functions.

It is difficult to estimate the extent to which the provincials had been "Romanized," because the meaning of "Romanization" is debatable. It may fairly be said that, apart from administrative organization, imperial government made virtually no effort to impose uniformity upon its subjects by supplanting local languages, religions, customs, and even laws by those of Rome. This was particularly true of the Hellenistic East, where Western cultural influences made little impression. But even in the African provinces (apart from Egypt and Cyrenaica), in the Danubian areas, in the Rhineland, Gaul, Spain, and Britain, survivals of pre-Roman institutions, customs, and ways of life were numerous and persistent. The rapid and widespread reception of Latin culture in certain areas was due to the influences radiating from Roman colonies and Roman camps, from Roman businessmen and officials, and to the general appeal exerted by the culture of a ruling element rather than to any conscious imperial policy.

Under the Principate, as under the Republic, respect for local prejudices went far to reconcile conquered peoples to Roman rule and develop a feeling of loyalty to the Empire. Perhaps it is here that one should look for the real test of Romanization—namely, the degree to which articulate and therefore upper-class provincials took pride in being "Romans," as citizens of the Empire, and in taking an active share in its defense and its government. Development of this attitude found expression in the participation of provincials in imperial service and their incorporation in the senatorial order, which reflected alike the economic and cultural condition of the areas from which they came and the attitude of leading men toward the Empire.

IV. Municipal Life

Under the Principate the Roman Empire became the greatest state the world had yet seen, surpassing both the old Persian Empire and that of Alexander the Great. Its area was approximtely three and a half million square miles, its population possibly one hundred million. To the Greek rhetorician Aelius Aristides, who in 143 delivered a speech in Rome in praise of Roman rule, this vast empire, coextensive with the civilized world, appeared as an aggregate of cities held together by Roman civil administration and the Roman military establishment. This view is substantially correct, in spite of the existence in many provinces of areas of considerable size, especially imperial domain lands, that did not possess municipal organization. For the most part the Empire consisted of many locally autonomous communities serving as units for taxation, jurisdiction, and conscription and in general relieving imperial administration of the burdens of local government. These communities were the municipalities, each of which was responsible for an area under its jurisdiction and constituting its territory (*territorium*). The municipalities were of two general types: the Hellenic in the East and the Italian in the West.

HELLENIC MUNICIPALITIES. Hellenic municipalities were developments from the *poleis*, or city-states, which existed prior to the Roman conquest in Greece and the Hellenized areas of Asia and Africa. Municipal towns organized in these areas subsequent to Roman occupation were of the same type. Their language was Greek. The characteristic political institutions of the Hellenic municipalities were a popular assembly, a council or *boule*, and annual magistrates. The assembly had the power to initiate legislation; the council and magistrates were elected by it or were chosen by lot. Even under the Republic these democratic institutions were considerably modified in the interests of the wealthier classes. Timocratic constitutions were established, with property qualifications for citizenship and for the council and offices. The Principate accentuated this development. The assemblies lost their right to initiate legislation, a power which passed to the magistrates, while the council tended to become a body of ex-magistrates who held their seats for life. In spite of this approximation to the Italian type, Greek official terminology remained unchanged throughout the first three centuries A.D.

ITALIAN MUNICIPALITIES. The Latin type of municipality was that developed on Italian soil with the extension of Roman domination in Italy and given uniformity by the legislation of Julius Caesar. With the Romanization of the western part of the Empire, it spread to Africa, Spain, Gaul, Britain, Germany, and the Danubian provinces. In spite of the distinctions between Roman and Latin colonies and *municipia*, all these classes of municipalities were of the same general type, which is revealed in the Julian Municipal Law (45 B.C.), the charter of the Roman *Colonia Genetiva Iulia* (44 B.C.), and those of the Latin municipalities of Malaca and Salpensa (A.D. 81–84).

These municipalities were patterned closely after Rome, although certain titles, like those of consul and Senate, were reserved for the capital city. Like Rome, the municipal towns had their officials, their council (*curia, ordo*), and their assembly. The chief magistrates were a pair of duovirs (or at times a college of quattuorvirs), who were assisted by two aediles and two quaestors. The duovirs were in charge of the local administration of justice and in general conducted the public affairs of the community. Every fifth year the duovirs were called *quinquennales* and took the census. The aediles had charge of public works and market and police regulations, while the quaestors were the local treasury officials. All officials were popularly elected, but a property qualification was required of each candidate. If no candidates presented themselves for a particular office, provision was made for the nomination of candidates obliged to serve if elected. At his election each magistrate paid into the treasury, or expended by order of the council, a sum of money (*summa honoraria*), which varied for each office in different communities. Oftentimes these officers did not restrict themselves to the required sum but took this opportunity for philanthropic display. As other prominent citizens followed their example, the municipalities were richly provided with useful and ornamental public works. Thus the municipal offices, being unsalaried, were a heavy drain upon the resources of their holders. They also offered almost the sole opportunity for gratifying the political ambitions of the prosperous middle class in the provinces. In addition to these civil officials, each community had its colleges of pontiffs and augurs.

The members of the *curia* were called *decuriones* and were usually one hundred in number. Their wealth, like that of the imperial senatorial order, was derived almost exclusively from land. They comprised those who had held some local magistracy, and others having the requisite property qualification and enrolled directly (*adlecti*) in the council. The council supervised the work of the magistrates and directed municipal administration. As in early Rome, so in the municipalities, the people were grouped in *curiae*, which were the voting units in the local assembly or *comitia*. This assembly elected the magistrates and had legislative powers like those of the Roman assemblies. In the second century A.D., however, these legislative powers passed into the hands of the council, whose decrees became the sole form of municipal legislation.

GUILDS AND COLLEGES. While the lower classes of Rome and the municipalities had little opportunity for political activity, they found compensation in the social life of their guilds or colleges. These were associations of persons who had some common tie, such as trade or profession, worship, or the humble desire to secure for themselves a decent burial. Thus arose professional, religious, and funerary colleges. Their organization was modeled on that of the municipalities. They had their patrons, presidents (*magistri*, or *quinquennales*), quaestors, and treasury, sustained by initiation fees, monthly dues, fines, contributions, gifts, and legacies. The membership was called plebs or *populus*. The chief factor in the life of the colleges was the social element, and their most important gatherings were for holding a common banquet. The professional colleges in no way corresponded to modern trade unions; they attempted no collective bargaining with regard to wages, prices, or working hours, although they did not altogether neglect the common interests of their profession.

Apparently until late republican times no restrictions were placed upon such collegiate associations. In 64 B.C. all unions of the sort in Rome were abolished because of the disorders occasioned by political clubs. In 58 B.C. complete freedom of association was restored, only to be revoked again by Julius Caesar, who permitted only the old and reputable professional and religious colleges to exist. Under Augustus a law was passed that regulated the character, organization, and activities of these associations. New colleges could be established in Italy or the provinces only if sanctioned by the Senate or an edict of the *princeps*, and membership in an unauthorized college was a treasonable offence. Trajan authorized the unrestricted formation of funerary colleges (*collegia tenuiorum*) in Rome, and Septimius Severus extended this privilege to Italy and the provinces. Under Marcus Aurelius the colleges were recognized as juristic persons, with power to manumit slaves and receive legacies. Not only men of free birth but also freedmen and slaves, and in many cases women, were freely admitted to membership.

V. Beginnings of Economic Decline

In the second century A.D., under the aegis of imperial government, the ancient world reached the height of its material prosperity. This prosperity was due above all to the maintenance of the Roman Peace and had been achieved in the face of government corruption which the imperial system, with all its good intentions, was unable to stamp out. In spite of generally favorable conditions, even in the second century there were signs that all was not well with the economy of the Empire, and before the close of the Severan dynasty these indications had become much more apparent.

BURDEN OF TAXATION. The cost of government had increased to the point that taxes could no longer be met from the income of the taxpayers and began to draw upon their capital wealth so that this in turn became less productive and general income proportionately declined. The maintenance of local government constituted an indirect tax upon property, whereas the superstructure of provincial and imperial government was supported by taxation collected by imperial or local agents in the municipal and other administrative units. In addition, the central government could requisition upon its own terms supplies and services from its subjects, over and above the normal load of taxation. It was the steadily mounting cost of imperial government that was responsible for the increase in the fiscal burden imposed upon the civilian population.

One increasingly expensive item was the army, whose numbers had grown considerably over those established by Augustus. The permanent fortifications constructed on the frontiers and new military highways, although built largely by labor of the troops, added still more to the sum expended for military purposes. A second factor that materially increased the cost of government was the gradual expansion of the imperial administrative service with its numerous departments and its permanent paid officials. Other significant factors were development of the imperial post; construction of public works, including roads, bridges, aqueducts, temples, theaters, amphitheaters, and public baths; the ever more elaborate system of doles, largesses, and entertainments for the populace of the capital; and the expenditures on education, public health, and Italian farm relief. The fundamental causes for this expansion of public services were in most cases the search for efficiency and a corresponding growth of a sense of responsibility on the part of the government toward the governed. Laudable as these motives were, the result rendered the financial situation so precarious that a long war or a spendthrift emperor threatened to cause, and at times actually did cause, bankruptcy of the treasury. There is ample evidence to show that the cost of defending and governing the Empire strained to the utmost the taxpaying power of its population. One of the chief reasons for giving up the attempt to occupy the region between the Rhine and the Elbe and for relinquishing to the Parthians the conquests of Trajan in Armenia and Mesopotamia was inability to meet the cost of conquering and defending these areas. The heavy burden of taxation played a large part in the rebellion in Judaea in A.D. 66. Both Hadrian and Marcus Aurelius were obliged to remit arrears of taxation that had accumulated over the years, and the latter received repeated requests from municipalities for financial aid or reduction of taxes. Marcus Aurelius expressed with brutal frankness the desperate condition of the public finances when he answered the petition of his victorious troops for an increase in pay with the words: "Anything you receive over and above your regular wages must be exacted from the blood of your parents and relations."[3] Financial stringency led to the debasement of coinage in order to secure a temporary profit for the treasury. Nero reduced the silver content of the denarius by 10 percent. Under Trajan the debasement with copper increased to 15 percent, under Marcus Aurelius to 25 percent, and under Septimius Severus to almost 40 percent. Caracalla issued a new silver coin, the Antoninianus, supposedly equal to two denarii, but it also contained scarcely 60 percent silver. Not only the denarius but also the standard gold coin, the aureus,

[3] Cassius Dio, *Epitome*, LXXI, 3.

was reduced in weight. These inflationary expedients brought no permanent relief, however.

FISCAL OPPRESSION. From Egypt comes the most striking evidence of the burden of maintaining the Empire imposed upon the provinces. It is true that for a long time conditions in Egypt were not typical for all provinces, because the absence of municipal autonomy, the extent of the public domain, and the highly developed bureaucratic administration there made possible fiscal exploitation that would have been difficult elsewhere. Ultimately, however, the fiscal situation in other provinces came to approximate closely that of Egypt. Even in Egypt it was not the intention of the imperial government to ruin its subjects, but rather to make them prosperous so that they might produce more revenue. If taxation proved too heavy, it meant that the combined weight of imperial and local administration constituted a load greater than even this rich area could support. As early as the principate of Nero the peasantry and poorer townspeople were complaining of oppression to which they were subjected by local tax collectors. Since the government held the properties of the collectors themselves as security for the total sum of taxes they were supposed to collect, these officials used every means, legal or illegal, to force individual taxpayers to contribute the full amount. If anyone was unable to meet his obligations, his relatives or, in default of these, fellow townsmen and villagers were forced to make good the deficit. The demands of the tax collectors were enforced brutally, at times with the aid of police and soldiers. When harvests failed, farmers who could not pay their assessments fled, leaving their lands untilled for the next season. The result was that, by A.D. 60 a serious decline had taken place in the population of many villages even in so rich a part of Egypt as the Fayum.

Despite attempts made by some prefects and emperors to curb illegal exactions and to improve the condition of the peasants, the situation gradually grew worse, because the necessities of government prevented any lightening of the load. More and more peasants refused to lease public lands, since the burdens involved were too heavy. To prevent loss of revenue from this cause, officials assigned the unleased plots to adjacent villages or to individual private landholders, who thereby became responsible for the cultivation of these lands and the payment of the taxes assessed against them. This made heavier the burden on those who remained on the land, and more and more peasants sought refuge in flight. These runaways were mainly responsible for the armed revolts of A.D. 152 and 172, as well as for the appearance of brigandage on a wide scale under Septimius Severus.

Although tenant farmers were the first to suffer, it was not long before landholders and well-to-do townspeople were also affected. At first, following the Ptolemaic custom, Roman government employed salaried officials in the lower administrative posts throughout Egypt. In the second half of the first century A.D. these were displaced by officials drafted from the propertied classes of communities in the nomes. These appointees served without salary, and their service constituted an additional property tax. This practice was not altogether new in the Hellenistic East, for it originated in the well-known Greek institution of the liturgy, or obligatory personal service imposed on persons who possessed certain property qualifications. The Romans, however, applied the principle on a hitherto unexampled scale. As the officeholders remained responsible with their properties for any deficiencies in tax returns, they were more merciless than ever in exacting full payment from helpless peasants. When the latter deserted their villages, the burden fell back upon the officials. The fear under which men lived is reflected in the standard questions addressed to temple oracles in the second century A.D.: whether the petitioner should run away, or whether the government was going to sell his property to settle tax accounts.

DECLINE OF MUNICIPAL AUTONOMY. The prosperity of the municipalities was a gauge of the prosperity of the Empire as a whole, and their condition was watched with anxiety by the government. By the second century A.D. many of these communities were in financial difficulties. The causes of this condition are not everywhere easy to trace. Among them were the ruin of some of the wealthier families by the requirements of office holding, the withdrawal from municipal life of individuals who entered imperial service, overtaxation, bad management of local finances, and at times decline of the rural population that furnished a market for manufacturers and merchants of the towns. This situation invited imperial interference, and Trajan appointed curators and other commissioners to rehabilitate the finances of individual municipalities or those of a whole province. These officials were chosen from senators and equestrians and at first were appointed for emergencies. By the time of Severus Alexander they had become a fixture in many municipalities and were appointed from the local decurions. Here government paternalism, which at first sought to guide the towns through particular economic crises, ended in placing the operation of municipal finances under the control of the central administration. For this the apathy of the municipal governing classes was largely to blame.

Another aspect of the decline of municipal autonomy is seen in the change that took place in the character of the local magistracies and the relationship of municipal councils to the imperial authorities. In the second century A.D. the magistracies were still looked upon as positions of honor, for which candidates presented themselves voluntarily, although there were unmistakable signs that in some districts they were regarded as a burden. Since in default of voluntary candidates for the magistracies, eligible citizens could be forced to be candidates, public office was an inescapable obligation for the propertied class. By the third century, magistrates came to be appointees of the decurions, and membership in municipal councils likewise became obligatory for those with enough property. The principle also developed that municipal councils or their representatives were responsible to the state for the revenues due from the municipal territories. In the eastern provinces committees of ten, called *decaprotoi* or "first ten," were nominated by the councils and put in charge of collecting imperial taxes. These *decaprotoi* had to make good from their personal properties whatever taxes they failed to collect. Because of this new function of the municipal councils Septimius Severus organized them in the nome capitals of Egypt, where they were charged with responsibility for local financial administration and for nominating and acting as sureties for both municipal officials and local agents of the provincial administration.

The municipalities had thus lost control over their own finances and also had become agents of the imperial government for raising public revenues.

THE STATE AND THE PROFESSIONAL GUILDS. The loss of municipal independence was accompanied by an encroachment upon the freedom of the voluntary professional colleges. From the beginning of the Principate, the government depended largely upon private initiative for the performance of many necessary services in connection with provisioning the city of Rome, which became increasingly complicated when the state undertook the distribution of oil under Septimius Severus. Therefore such colleges as those of the shipowners (*navicularii*), bakers (*pistores*), pork merchants (*suarii*), wine merchants (*vinarii*), and oil merchants (*olerarii*) received official encouragement. Their members individually assumed public contracts and came to receive exemption from certain municipal obligations, since it was recognized that they were performing necessary services. Marcus Aurelius, Severus, and Caracalla were emperors who thus fostered the professional guilds. Gradually the idea developed that these services were public duties (*munera*) to which the colleges were obligated, and under Severus Alexander the initiative in organizing new professional guilds passed to the state. The same *princeps* appointed judicial representatives from each guild and placed them under the jurisdiction of certain courts. The colleges henceforward operated under governmental supervision and really formed a part of the administration, although they had not yet become compulsory and hereditary organizations.

The history of the colleges in the municipalities paralleled that of the Roman guilds, although it cannot be traced so clearly in detail. The best known of the municipal colleges are those of the artificers (*fabri*), the makers of rag cloths (*centonarii*), and the woodcutters (*dendrophori*). The organization of these colleges was everywhere encouraged because their members had the obligation of acting as a local fire brigade, although in the exercise of their trades they were not in the service of their communities.

CHAPTER 20

SOCIAL, INTELLECTUAL, AND RELIGIOUS LIFE UNDER THE PRINCIPATE

I. Social and Economic Conditions

IMPERIAL ROME. Roman society under the Principate was generally similar to that of the last century of the Republic. Rome itself was a cosmopolitan city, where the concentration of wealth and political power attracted the ambitious, the adventurous, and the curious from all lands. Whole quarters were occupied by various nationalities, most prominent among whom were the Greeks, Syrians, and Jews, speaking their own languages and plying their native trades. With the freeborn population mingled the thousands of slaves and freedmen of every race and tongue. During the first and second centuries the population of Rome must have been nearly one million, but in the third century it began to decline as a result of pestilence and the general bankruptcy of the Empire. Inevitably in such a city there were the sharpest contrasts between riches and poverty. Luxurious palaces of the wealthy were at one end of the scale, squalid tenements of the proletariat were at the other. In outward appearance Rome underwent a transformation that made her worthy to be the capital of so vast an Empire. This was largely due to the many public buildings erected by various emperors and to the lavish employment of marble in public and private architecture from the time of Augustus. The temples, basilicas, fora, aqueducts, public baths, theaters, palaces, triumphal arches, statues, and parks combined to arouse the admiration of travelers and the pride of its inhabitants. After the great fire of A.D. 64 many improvements were made in the plan of the city, restrictions were placed on the height of buildings, and fireproof construction required for the lower stories, but the streets remained narrow and dingy, the lofty tenements were flimsy, in perpetual danger of collapse, and devastating conflagrations occurred periodically.

The task of feeding the city mob and providing for their entertainment was a ruinous legacy left by the Republic to the Principate. Augustus and his successors maintained the number of recipients of free grain at 200,000. There were also frequent distributions of money (*congiaria*) by the emperors, and public spectacles became ever more numerous and magnificent. Under Tiberius eighty-seven days of the year were regularly occupied by these entertainments, and by the time of Marcus Aurelius there were one hundred and thirty-five such holidays. In addition there were extraordinary festivals, such as the one-hundred-and-twenty-three-day carnival given by Trajan at his second Dacian triumph in A.D. 106. The spectacles were of three main types: chariot races in the circus, gladiatorial combats and animal baiting in the amphitheater, and dramatic and other performances in the theater. The expense of these celebrations fell upon senators and the *princeps*. The most important function of the consulship, praetorship, and, until its disappearance in the third century, the aedileship, came to be the celebration of the regular festivals. The sums provided for such purposes by the state were inadequate, so the cost had to be met largely from the magistrates' private resources. Extraordinary spectacles were all given by the *princeps*, who also at times granted subventions to favored senators from the imperial purse. Financing of the public shows placed as heavy a drain on the fortunes of the senatorial order, as did the office fees and local expenditures on those of the decurions.

A new feature of Roman society under the Principate was the growth of the imperial court. In spite of the wishes of Augustus and some of his successors to live on a footing of equality with the rest of the nobility, it was inevitable that the exceptional political power of the *princeps* should give a corresponding importance to his household organization. Specific offices developed within the imperial household not only for the conduct of public business but also for the control of slaves and freedmen in the domestic service of the *princeps*. The chief household officials were the chamberlain (*a cubiculo*) and the chief usher (*ab admissione*). Because of their intimate personal association with the *princeps* their influence over him was great, and as a rule they used their position to enrich themselves at the expense of those seeking imperial favor. From among the senators and equestrians the *princeps* chose a number of intimate associates and advisers who were called his "friends." When forming part of his cortege away from Rome, they were known as his companions (*comites Augusti*). In connection with imperial audiences a ceremonial developed, with fixed forms of salutation differentiating the rank and station of those in attendance. In the society of the capital the personal tastes of the *princeps* set the fashion.

CLIENTS. Characteristic of the times was a new form of clientage, a voluntary association of master and paid retainer. Under the Republic eminent men had throngs of adherents to greet them at their morning reception and accompany them to the forum. Custom now demanded that virtually every man of wealth maintain such a retinue, to be at his beck and call at all hours of the day and prepared to serve him. In return the patron helped to support his clients with fees, food, and clothing, and rendered them other favors. The clients were recruited partly from freedmen, partly from citizens of low birth, and partly from genteel but impoverished persons. In general, the lot of these pensioners was not very happy—even their patrons' slaves despised them—and their large numbers are attributed to the relative lack of industrial employment in Rome.

SLAVES AND FREEDMEN. In the early Principate slaveholding continued on as large a scale as in the late Republic. The palaces of the wealthy in Rome could count slaves by hundreds; on the larger plantations they were numbered by thousands. Trained slaves were also employed in great numbers in trades and industries. Their treatment varied according to their employment and the character of their owners, but there was a steady progress toward greater humanitarianism, largely due to the influence of philosophic doctrines. In the age of the Antonines this produced legislation limiting the power of the master over his slave. As time went on the number of slaves steadily diminished, in part because of the cessation of foreign wars after Augustus, in part because of a great increase in manumission. Not only were many set free at their owners death as a final act of generosity, but also many found it profitable to liberate their slaves and provide them with capital to engage in business. Many slaves also had good opportunities for accumulating a small store of money (*peculium*) with which they could purchase their freedom.

The result of these wholesale manumissions was a tremendous increase in the freedmen class. Augustus foresaw the effect this would have upon the Roman citizen body[1] and endeavored to restrict the right of emancipation. Even freedmen who became Romans lacked the right to vote or hold office in Rome or the municipalities, unless they received from the *princeps* the right to wear the gold ring which gave them the privileges of freeborn citizens. In spite of these laws the number of freedmen grew, and there is no doubt that during the Principate the ethnic makeup of the population of Rome, and of the whole peninsula of Italy, was profoundly transformed as a result of the infusion of new elements and the emigration of Italians to the provinces.

The importance of the role played by freedmen in Roman society corresponded to their numbers. From them were recruited some of the lower ranks of the civil service, they filled every trade and profession, the commerce of Italy was largely theirs, and they became managers of estates and of business undertakings. An eager pursuit of money was their common characteristic, and "freedman's wealth" was a proverbial expression for riches quickly acquired. The more successful of their class became landholders in Italy and aped the life and manners of the nobility. Their sons often attained equestrian rank, and their more remote descendants sometimes became senators. Their lack of good taste, so common to the *nouveaux riches* of all ages, afforded a good target for the jibes of satirists and is caricatured in the novel of Petronius written under Nero. A few among them attained positions of political importance and great influence through the favor of emperors. Despise the freedmen though they might, the Romans found them indispensable for the conduct of public and private business.

[1] Above, p. 282.

COMMERCE AND INDUSTRY. Restoration of peace within the Empire, the suppression of piracy, extension of military highways throughout all the provinces, establishment of a single currency valid for the whole Empire, and low duties levied at the provincial customs frontiers combined to produce an unprecedented development of commerce. Traders from all parts of the Empire thronged the ports of Italy, and one merchant of Hierapolis in Phrygia has left a record of his twenty-two voyages between Asia Minor and Italy. Puteoli on the Bay of Naples was Italy's chief port, Ostia at the mouth of the Tiber its second. Generally speaking, the government's attitude toward the economy was one of laissez faire, but the production and distribution of certain strategic commodities were regulated. Sea-borne trade was not left entirely to individual enterprise, since the imperial government supervised the guilds of shipowners both of Italy and the provinces to maintain the grain supply of Rome and the transportation of supplies for the armies.

Roman commerce was not confined within the borders of the Empire; it also flourished with foreign peoples, particularly those of the East. A brisk caravan trade through the Parthian Empire from Mesopotamia across the Iranian plateau to Turkestan and thence to China brought the products of that country, especially silk and silk goods, to Syrian ports. From the Egyptian harbors on the Red Sea large merchant fleets sailed for southern Arabia and thence across the Arabian Sea to India and Ceylon. Numerous finds of Roman coins in India, evidence of the presence of Greek merchants from Egypt there, and the visits of ambassadors of Indian princes to Rome bear witness to the regularity and importance of the Empire's Indian trade. Roman traders did not stop at India. They crossed the Bay of Bengal to the Malay Peninsula, passed through the Strait of Malacca, and followed the coast of Indochina until some of them finally reached the southern ports of China. Chinese sources even record the presence of a Roman embassy in China in the time of Marcus Aurelius, but this was probably not an official mission. Active trade relations were maintained with the interior of Russia through the cities on the north shore of the Black Sea, and Roman traders and their wares crossed Germany to the Baltic. In Africa, isolated Roman officials ventured far into the Sahara Desert and followed the Nile deep into the Sudan, but traffic with these regions remained in the hands of natives who brought their wares to the Roman frontiers.

Among all the peoples of the Empire, the most active merchants were the Syrians, whose presence may be traced not only in the commercial centers of the East but also in the ports of Italy and all the western provinces. The increased opportunities for trading stimulated the development of manufacturing, for not only could raw materials be more easily procured but towns favorably situated for the manufacture of particular goods could find a wider market for their products.

In the history of Italian industry the first two centuries of the Principate form a single epoch with the last century of the Republic. In this period the industrial development of Italy reached its height, largely owing to two factors: concentration of free capital in the hands of the emperors and the abundant supply of slave labor at low cost. The preference for investing capital in lands, loans, and trading ventures rather than in industrial enterprises joined with the competition of provincial products to check the growth of Italian manufacturers. Usually the wealthy tried to make their town and country establishments self-sustaining by employing their slaves and tenants in making articles for farm use and by having among their slaves craftsmen trained as bakers, weavers, dyers, shoemakers, masons, smiths, carpenters, and even jewelers and glass blowers. They were able to make themselves independent of outside production, for which poor land-holders and city dwellers provided a larger and steadier market. Among the important industries catering to more than local trade were bronze-working and ironworking, manufacture of pottery, lamps, bricks, and tiles, glass blowing, and the weaving of linen and woolen textiles. These industries tended to be concentrated in special centers, determined by the presence of raw materials or a situation advantageous for distribution. Thus the centers for ironworking were Como in Cisalpine Gaul and Puteoli in Campania. Capua was the leading center for bronze work, and Arretium in Etruria for pottery. Certain industries, such as brick, tile, and pottery making, were frequently carried on in rural districts, oftentimes as an adjunct to a plantation. A peculiar feature of industrial life was the activity of the *princeps*, i.e., the State, in certain manufactures competing with private enterprise. This rivalry, however, was limited largely to the production of materials for the construction and maintenance of public works, such as bricks, tiles, cement, lead pipes, and the like, and did not drive private concerns out of business. Large- and the small-scale production flourished side by side, but the latter was by far more general. As a result industrial organization never attained a high degree of development. In the production of articles of bronze, silver, glass, and pottery, an approach to a true factory system developed in that successive steps in the manufacture of each article were performed by different specialists. In general, however, this was not so; a finished article was usually the product of one man's labor. The workers fell into several categories: free hired laborers, freedmen working for their patrons or for others, and slaves employed by their owners or leased out to other employers. The evidence bearing upon the relative numbers in these classes is very incomplete, but it seems that most workers in large and small industries alike were slaves, that freedmen were numerous, and that the proportion of freeborn persons engaged in industry was not nearly so great as in agriculture. A majority of the slaves and freedmen were Greeks and Hellenized Orientals, and their presence explains why technically and artistically Italian industry in this period could hold its own with that of the eastern provinces.

The large-scale development of some Italian industries was due to the opening up of an export trade to the provinces in the first century of the Principate. Among the leading Italian exports were bronze work to trans-alpine countries, Arretine pottery in great quantities to the West and North and to some extent to the East, pottery lamps to the same regions, and glass to Spain, Gaul, and the Danubian lands. The development of Gallic pottery drove Arretine ware from the western provinces by the time of the Flavians; by the end of the first century A.D. Gallic bronze and silver work was able virtually to exclude Italian imports; and from about the same time the glass industry of Gaul and Germany, with its final center at Cologne, monopolized the trade of the western half of the Empire. In the products just mentioned, Italian industry dominated the home market, however, while in woolen manufactures it at least met foreign competition.

The balance of trade was heavy against Rome and Italy, for Italy demanded foodstuffs, raw materials, and manufactured articles of use and luxury far beyond the value of her exports. Each province exported wares to Italy. From Egypt, Italy imported glassware, linens, paper, jewelry, and ointments; from Syria, glass, purple dyestuffs, and silk goods; from Asia Minor, woolens, iron, and steel. Greece supplied the best olive oil, besides figs, and marble for sculpture and building; Africa sent oil, fruit, grain, fish, and marble; Spain exported tin, lead, copper, gold, silver, cloth, wool, flax, wine, oil, and fish; Gaul contributed agricultural products, meat, wool, and woven goods; from Britain came gold, silver, iron, hides, fleeces, cattle, slaves, poultry, and oysters; and the Danubian regions furnished both raw and worked iron, hides, wild beasts for the games, and slaves. The products of the Far East reached Rome through Alexandria and Syrian ports, where raw materials were often converted into finished products. The bulk of these Eastern imports came from India, or at least through India, whence the Romans procured linens, cottons, silk, ivory, precious stones, spices, tortoiseshell, and rare wild animals. In return the Empire sent to India copper, lead, tin, silverware, glass, wine, clothing, musical instruments, slaves, and above all gold and silver coins. This steady flow of coinage eastward was noticed by the Romans and constituted a drain upon the supply of precious metals in the Empire.

Although the expansion of commerce and industry was an outstanding feature of the economic life of the Principate, agriculture still remained the basic occupation engaging the activities of the vast majority of the population and constituting the bulk of invested wealth. This was the result of several factors. In the first place, landholding enjoyed greater social prestige than other forms of business activity and was in the long run a safer form of investment, so that the profits of commercial and industrial enterprises were largely devoted to the development of rural properties and not reinvested in the activities that had produced them. Secondly, from the standpoint of technology industry showed no advance over the Hellenistic Age. Its expansion therefore, consisted in exploiting hitherto underdeveloped areas within the Empire and the concentration of more workers at particular centers rather than in any improvement in efficiency or productivity by individual industries. Continued preference for the small shop over the large unit and failure to invent and apply machinery to replace manual labor in industrial processes and lower the cost of production reflect the static condition of industry. Owing to the extensive use of slaves in Italian industries and the abundance of cheap free labor in the eastern provinces, there was little incentive to develop labor-saving devices. The lack of legal recognition of patent rights removed a powerful stimulus to invention. Neglect of scientific investigations made unlikely any revolutionary discoveries that might have had practical uses in industry. A third factor that militated against progress in industrial organization was that Roman law, while recognizing corporations with limited liability for shareholders to undertake public contracts, forbade them in private business enterprises. In this area the only legal form of organization was a partnership in which each partner was responsible for all the firm's obligations and where the association was dissolved when one of the partners died. Lastly, a most potent deterrent to industrial progress lay in the conditions that governed available markets. Owing to slow transportation by land and the risks and delays attending transportation by sea, it was cheaper to produce articles locally, provided that the raw materials and an adequate supply of labor were available, than to import them from any distance. Thus, although at first underdeveloped districts within the Empire absorbed the surplus manufactures of developed areas, with the advance of civilization they began to provide an ever-increasing share of their own necessities, and the regions formerly supplying them had to rely more and more upon local consumption. When the Empire ceased to expand, no new areas were opened up to take the place of self-supplying markets. Furthermore, the Empire never succeeded in creating wealth in depth or a mass class of consumers, except for the most basic necessities of life, which meant that production could never develop beyond a fairly primitive level in most cases. Industry and commerce thus stagnated after reaching a certain level and failed to create new sources of wealth that might have kept pace with the increasing cost of government. Economic decline set in when, as a result of overtaxation, the peasant population began to decrease and become more impoverished, so that its ability to consume the products of the towns grew progressively less. Local production and imports shrank correspondingly.

AGRICULTURE. Like industry under the Principate, agriculture made practically no technical advances over the Hellenistic period. As might be expected, conditions of land tenure and farm economy varied greatly with varying soil and climate in different parts of the Empire. New areas were opened up for agricultural enterprise in Gaul, Britain, Germany, the Danubian provinces, Africa, and on the Arabian and Syrian frontiers. Of soil exhaustion resulting from overcropping or erosion there is little evidence, except as to certain parts of Greece and Italy, where this condition had existed previously and apparently did not grow much worse. If agriculture declined toward the close of this period, the causes lay elsewhere.

Agriculture in Italy remained on the whole in a flourishing condition during the first and second centuries A.D. It was carried on with great skill, as we know from Columella, an agricultural writer of the reign of Nero, whose work shows a good knowledge of the principles of fertilization and crop rotation. Just as under the late Republic, great estates (*latifundia*) dominated agricultural economy, but small peasant holdings persisted in many districts, particularly in north central Italy and the Po valley. On the *latifundia* there was a strong tendency to replace slave labor by free tenant farmers called *coloni*. This was brought about by the drying-up of the chief sources of the supply of slaves through the suppression of piracy and the cessation of aggressive foreign wars, by generous manumissions, by the growth of humanitarian tendencies that checked ruthless exploitation of agricultural slave labor, and by the growing realization that the employment of free labor was in the long run more profitable, particularly when slaves were becoming more expensive. To a certain extent, the breeding of domestic slaves replenished the supply, but not sufficiently to check the trend towards tenant farming. The *coloni*, many doubtless freedmen or the descendants of freedmen, were sharecroppers tilling their holdings for a fixed proportion of the harvest. In Italy agricultural prosperity probably reached its height about A.D. 100. Signs of weakness in the Italian agricultural economy became apparent toward the end of the first century, when Domitian sought to protect cereal farming and viticulture from provincial competition, and it seems that simultaneously Italy faced a shortage of working capital and the beginnings of a decline in population.

In Africa, at the beginning of the Principate, the cultivable land, outside of the municipal territories, fell into three classes: public land, private estates of wealthy Romans, and imperial domains. Under the early emperors, particularly Nero, most private estates passed by legacy or confiscation to the *princeps* and were incorporated in imperial domains. Administration of public land, in so far as this was not absorbed into new municipal territories, rested likewise with the *princeps*. Domain land was divided into large districts (*tractus, regiones*) administered by imperial procurators. Each district comprised a number of estates (*saltus, fundi*). Whatever slave labor had at one time been used in African agricultural operations was, by the early Principate, largely displaced by *coloni*. These *coloni* were either Italian immigrants or tributary native holders of public land.

Estates were usually managed as follows. Procurators leased them to tenant contractors (*conductores*), who retained a part of their leaseholds under their own supervision and sublet the remainder to tenant farmers (*coloni*). The relation of these *coloni* to the contractors, as well as to the owners of private estates or their bailiffs (*vilici*), was regulated by an edict of a certain Mancia, apparently a Flavian procurator. By this edict the *coloni* were obliged to pay part of their crop as rental and to render a certain number of days' work, personally and with their teams, on the land of the leasor. The *coloni* were both landless residents on estates and small landholders from neighboring villages. They were encouraged to occupy vacant domain land and cultivate it. Over plowland thus cultivated they obtained a life tenancy, but orchard land became an hereditary possession, while in both cases the occupant was required to pay rent in kind to the state. Hadrian also tried to further the development of peasant landholdings by permitting *coloni* to occupy any land not tilled by middlemen and giving them possession over all types of land. Forced service still remained and constituted the chief grievance of the *coloni*. The government was on the horns of a dilemma; if the middlemen were restrained from undue exactions often large areas remained untilled, and if the *coloni* were oppressed they absconded and left their holdings untenanted.

The land system in Asia Minor during the Principate reflected conditions established prior to the Roman occupation. Most of the land was incorporated in the territories of the Greek cities. There were also numerous large estates, which were private property. There is little evidence for agricultural slavery, and farm labor was carried on by free peasants who lived in villages on municipal lands or private properties. At first imperial estates were not very extensive in this area. Their increase was gradual, and it was not until the great confiscations made by Septimius Severus at the expense of the faction supporting his defeated rival, Pescennius Niger, that they became a major factor in agricultural life. Although we do not have much evidence for their management, it seems probable that they were operated along much the same lines as imperial estates in Africa.

In Gaul and Britain, farming was intensified under Roman rule, but the land system shows a development conditioned by Celtic origins and customs. Throughout Gaul, the unit of agriculture was generally the *fundus* or farm, with an isolated farmstead as the home of the proprietor or tenant. On the larger estates, the farmstead was a villa comprising the residence of the owner, quarters for laborers, and other buildings necessary for the care of livestock and other operations. Smaller farms, whether operated by their owners or by free or servile tenants, had correspondingly modest accommodations. With the development of town life, under Roman influence in the first and second centuries A.D., the wealthier proprietors moved to the cities to share in municipal life and government, leaving their properties to the care of bailiffs or tenants. The villa system flourished in Britain, especially among the wealthier and more deeply Romanized landholders. Most of the agricultural population, however, seems to have been free peasants who lived on small fenced farms surrounded by fields which they tilled for themselves.

Agriculture in Egypt, like the administration of that province, had an exceptional character, owing to the survival of conditions developed under the Pharaohs and the Ptolemies. All agricultural life depended upon the Nile, with its annual floods, and the irrigation system that distributed the flood water. The government regulated and maintained this system and therefore had greater control over crops and agricultural labor than in other provinces. Under the Ptolemies most of the land had been royal or state property, and much of this remained public land after the Roman conquest. The Roman government did, however, encourage the development of private properties particularly on waste or marginal land not normally inundated by the Nile but irrigated by artificial methods. In order to facilitate such development and maintain production at the highest possible level, the administration improved and extended the system of irrigation canals. As a result, there was for a time an increase in prosperity and population. Increasing taxation gradually undermined this prosperity, however, and brought about a decline in agriculture. In their attempts to control the activities of tenants of public land, the Romans accepted the practice of the Ptolemies in compelling the inhabitants of village communities to perform corvées, such as work on canals and dykes and the cultivation of royal lands not let out on contract, within the boundaries of the community in which each was registered (his *idia*). Under Roman rule, this practice was applied with greater precision. All land registered in each village had to be cultivated by the residents of that village, either as owners or tenants. At times, the inhabitants might also be forced to work distant vacant lands. During sowing and harvest the presence of every villager was required in his *idia*. Compulsion and regimentation were widespread by the end of the Severan dynasty.

II. The Intellectual World

EDUCATION.   Roman education under the Principate followed lines already established at the close of the Republic. From primary school a pupil passed at about the age of thirteen to the *grammaticus*, and about three years later he entered the school of the *rhetor* or professor of oratory. Advanced studies, as in philosophy, usually were pursued in Greece. The outstanding feature of this system was the universality of training in oratory, which was the preparation alike of the jurist, the civil administrator, the army officer, and the man of letters. Its effect upon contemporary literature was inevitable and not altogether wholesome, since it rather stressed effective presentation and verbal cleverness than depth and originality of thought. A new feature in educational organization was state support for schools and teachers. Vespasian originated this policy by providing a salary for Greek and Latin rhetors, but it is unknown how many benefited thereby. Trajan went further by providing public instruction for five thousand poor boys. Hadrian made still more important changes. He provided retirement allowances for needy teachers and founded schools in the provinces aided by grants of money. He also furnished suitable quarters for the rhetorical schools of Rome. His successor Antoninus Pius continued this general policy by increasing the salaries of teachers and exempting some of them in each municipality from burdensome taxes. By the close of the Principate there existed a system of municipally supported schools under the supervision of the state, that is, the emperor.

LITERATURE. The Principate had two literatures—one Greek, the other Latin. The forms of literary production were the same in each, and Roman authors ranked with those of Greece in their respective fields. The Romans could boast that they had adapted the Latin tongue to the literary types of the older culture, while preserving a spirit genuinely Roman.

THE SILVER AGE. The outburst of literary creativity that accompanied the establishment of the Principate showed unmistakable symptoms of weakening with the passing of the great poets, even before the end of Augustus' reign. At the same time the popularity of the rhetorical training was increasing among the educated classes and was to become an important factor in determining the development of both poetry and prose. The educated believed that anyone who knew rhetorical rules could write, and the result of this attitude was literary dilettantism of questionable value. The century following Augustus is often called the Silver Age, a period which was less great than the "Golden Age," even though it did produce some of the most characteristic and famous works of Latin literature.

Until after A.D. 50 there are few names of note in Roman letters. One may mention in passing a second-rate survey of Roman history by Velleius Paterculus, and Q. Curtius' *History of Alexander the Great*, the first example of a Latin prose work whose orientation was not Roman. There were also various technical treatises, like those of Celsus on medicine and Columella's agricultural handbook, and the satires of Persius, echoing the work of Horace.

The reign of Nero saw the production of literary works in some ways most typical of the Silver Age. Rhetorical emphasis had made the "pointed" style fashionable, one which strove for clever, epigrammatic effects, overemphasized the emotional element, and created prose and poetry that were increasingly artificial and allusive. At the center of this movement stood Lucius Annaeus Seneca (4 B.C.–A.D. 65), one of the most important Latin authors of any epoch, a Spaniard from Corduba, Nero's tutor, minister, and victim. Seneca is best known as the only Roman tragedian whose works have survived and as an exponent of the practical Stoic religion. His tragedies find their source of inspiration among the Greeks, especially Euripides, but Seneca was interested primarily in describing intense emotion, not the conflict of man with his destiny. His philosophical writings express the ideal equanimity of the Stoic sage who rises above emotional disturbances. Seneca's nephew, Lucan (39–65) wrote the only Silver Age epic that was more than a Vergilian imitation. This work, the *Pharsalia*, is the story of the civil wars between the republicans and Julius Caesar. It is well composed and enthusiastic, although rhetorical and tending to dwell on the harrowing, and it rises well above the level of other epic poems of the period. Another of Nero's courtiers, Petronius Arbiter (d. 66), deserves mention as the author of the *Satyricon*, a work that survives as a fragment, the first picaresque novel in European literature. This is a very realistic, ribald, and highly entertaining tale of low life among freedmen in the Greek municipalities of south Italy. Its most famous section, Trimalchio's Banquet, is a broadly humorous commentary on the attitudes of the *nouveaux riches* of any epoch.

The Silver Age also produced learned, encyclopaedic works, the most famous of which was the *Natural History* of Pliny the Elder (Gaius Plinius Secundus, 23–79), composed toward the end of his life. The *Natural History* is a monumental work and a remarkable collection of miscellany, but it is a catalog rather than the result of scientific research, training, or critical acumen. It bespeaks Pliny's lack of discrimination in collecting evidence and his belief, typical of the age, in the marvelous and supernatural. Of greater literary and intellectual merit was Pliny's younger contemporary, the Spaniard Quintilian (M. Fabius Quintilianus, ca. 35–ca. 95), who was appointed by Vespasian as the first salaried teacher of rhetoric at the capital. The influence of Quintilian was powerful, since he numbered among his students sons of the great and near great, and it is accordingly fortunate that his educational theories, expressed in the *Institutes of Oratory*, have survived. The work reveals Quintilian as a kindly professor, not lacking in a sense of humor. Although a rhetorician writing in a highly rhetorical age, Quintilian insisted that the ideal orator have something worthwhile to say and that he not overemphasize form to the detriment of substance.

The Flavian dynasty also witnessed the continued production of poetry. Epic themes still tempted writers, although this genre tended to be imitative rather than inspired. Following Lucan, Statius (ca. 45–95) is the only interesting epic poet, although, his *Thebais*, based on Greek mythology, lacks dramatic unity and vivid characterization. Perhaps the best-developed, and in some ways most typically Roman, genre of the Silver Age was satire. The Spaniard Martial (M. Valerius Martialis, ca. 40–102), whose wide acquaintance with writers and intellectuals included his countrymen Seneca and Lucan, wrote epigrammatic satire of great merit during Domitian's reign. His observations on the meaner aspects of human nature are all the more convincing as caricatures because he was able to keep his essentially good temper.

TACITUS AND HIS CONTEMPORARIES. The advent of the good emperors saw the flowering of one of the most unusual literary geniuses to write in Latin, the historian Tacitus (ca. 56–ca. 120), whose family, of recent senatorial rank, probably came from Narbonese Gaul. Like other members of his circle, Tacitus gained advancement under the tyrant Domitian. He profited by the more liberal regimes of Nerva, Trajan, and Hadrian to write on the traditional subjects befitting a Roman senator: oratory and history. Tacitus was a master of innuendo; his style is both epigrammatic and elusive. His works are impregnated with distrust of the imperial system as such, a feeling that stemmed in part from his experience of the Domitianic terror, and one that was not assuaged by the more benevolent, if potentially as autocratic, reigns of Trajan and Hadrian. If his judgment of the Principate is understandably prejudiced, his narrative sets a high standard of accuracy, and he is justly ranked next to Thucydides as the most representative of artistic historical writing in antiquity. His first work, published under Nerva, was his *Life of Agricola*, an apologia for his father-in-law, who had governed Britain under Domitian. This was followed under Trajan by his *Treatise on Orators*, a rather frank discussion of the reasons for the decline of forensic oratory under the Caesars, and by the *Germania*, a derivative account of the Germanic peoples. Then came his masterpieces, the *Histories*, covering the reigns of emperors from Galba to Domitian, and the *Annals*, the history of Rome under the Julio-Claudian dynasty. He apparently finished the *Annals* early in Hadrian's reign. A friend of Tacitus, the younger Pliny (62–113), imitated Cicero in collecting and publishing his own letters. This correspondence is valuable as an illustration of the life and literary dilettantism of educated circles of the day, as also for the light it throws on the administrative policies of Trajan. The tranquility and rather smug self-satisfaction of Pliny contrast with the bitter criticism of society under the first good emperors of Juvenal of Aquinum (D. Junius Juvenalis, ca. 50–130), who ranks with Martial as a satirist. Juvenal returned to Rome from exile under Domitian and remained thereafter a bitter and poverty-stricken man. His poems rarely abandon their high emotional pitch. His first nine satires give a vivid picture of the ugly aspects of life at the capital, a crass, venal, and even perverted world. His later ones, which are really epistles to his friends, pursue ethical themes of a stoical nature. A younger contemporary of Juvenal's, Gaius Suetonius Tranquillus (ca. A.D. 70–140), possibly a native of Hippo in Africa, produced early in Hadrian's reign his gossipy *Lives of the Caesars* (from Julius to Domitian), which set the style for future historical writing at Rome. His approach to history was journalistic, and he made uncritical use of biased sources. His work is important, however, since he had access, as a bureaucrat under Trajan and Hadrian, to archival material which he incorporated. After falling from grace under Hadrian, he retired to write, among other things, the first literary history of Rome.

THE LATER SECOND CENTURY. The stress on rhetoric had developed into sterile antiquarianism by the second century, a spiritless imitation of past models of literary art that became canonical. The period witnessed the first important classicizing renaissance in European literature, one that was encouraged by no less a personage than the Emperor Hadrian himself. The artificial return to the Latin of Cato, Ennius, and Plautus was an unmistakable symptom of intellectual sterility, however, illustrated by the jejune correspondence of Fronto (ca. 100–167), tutor to Marcus Aurelius and Verus. Disdainful of philosophy, Fronto claimed fame solely as an expert in Latin rhetoric, but his prose was lifeless. The archaizing tendency of the second century is also evident in the work of one of Fronto's pupils, Aulus Gellius (ca. 123–165), who wrote *Attic Nights*, a rambling collection of antiquarian notes on 275 authors, a work important more for its preservation of excerpts from works since disappeared rather than for any stylistic or artistic excellence.

LATIN PROVINCIAL LITERATURE. The progress of Romanization in the provinces is clearly marked by the participation of provincials in the literary life of Rome. From the Cisalpine, from Narbonese Gaul, and from Spain, men with literary instincts and ability were drawn to the capital as the sole place where their talents could find recognition. Gradually some of the provinces developed a Latin culture of their own. Although Spain may have taken the lead in this development, the first real evidences of such a movement came from the province of Africa, where a Latin literature made its appearance under the Antonines. Its earliest representative was the sophist Lucius Apuleius (ca. 125–180), whose work, although archaizing and rhetorical, had greater artistic merit than that of his contemporaries. He is best known for the *Golden Ass*, an adventure story of the transformation of a traveler into a donkey with human intelligence.

CHRISTIAN LITERATURE. It was in Africa also that a Latin Christian literature first arose, and it was the African Christian writers who made Latin the language of the Church in Italy and the West. Of these Christian apologists, the earliest and most influential was Tertullian of Carthage, whose literary activity belongs to the period of the Severi. Cyprian and Arnobius continued his work in the third century. In Minucius Felix, a contemporary of Tertullian, the Christian community at Rome found an able defender of the faith.

JURISPRUDENCE. In all other sciences the Romans learned from the Greeks, although in that of jurisprudence they displayed both independence and originality. The growth of Roman jurisprudence was furthered by the Principate, for the development of a uniform administrative system for the Empire necessitated a corresponding development of a uniform system of law. In a sense Augustus and his successors sought to restore jurisprudence to the respected position it had occupied in the early Republic by limiting the right of publicly giving legal opinions (*ius publice respondendi*) to relatively few senatorial jurists of prominence. It was these jurists who were the productive force behind classical Roman law.

As during the late Republic, however, there continued to be many un-authorized jurisconsults, many of them from outside the governing estab-lishment. The great service of the jurists of the Principate was the introduction of the principles of equity founded on a philosophic concep-tion of natural law and a systematic organization and interpretation of the civil law. Roman jurisprudence reached its height between the accession of Hadrian and the death of Severus Alexander. The chief legal writers of this period were Salvius Julianus under Hadrian, Gaius under the Antonines, his contemporary Scaevola, three celebrated jurists of the time of the Severi—Papinian, Paul, and Ulpian—and lastly their younger con-temporary Modestine, who closes the long line of classic jurisconsults.

GREEK LITERATURE. The Roman Peace evoked a revival of Greek literature, which was patronized by philhellenic emperors like Hadrian. Even Augustus had recognized Greek as the language of govern-ment in the eastern half of the Empire, and with the gradual abandonment of his policy of preserving the domination of Italians over provincials, Greeks came to have the same standing as Latin-speaking provincials in the eyes of the imperial government. In Rome a Greek author received the same recognition as his Roman *confrère*. Greek historians, geographers, scientists, rhetoricians, and philosophers wrote not only for Greeks but for the educated circles of the whole Empire. And it was in Greek that the *princeps* Marcus Aurelius chose to write his *Meditations*. Nor should it be forgotten that Greek was the language of early Christian writers, begin-ning with the Apostle Paul. By the beginning of the third century the champions of the new faith had begun to rank among significant authors of the day in either language.

PLUTARCH: CA. A.D. 50–120 AND LUCIAN: CA. A.D. 125–200. The best-known names in Greek literature of the Principate are Plutarch and Lucian. Plutarch, a voluminous essayist, is deservedly popular as the author whose *Parallel Lives* of famous Greeks and Romans possess a perpetual freshness and charm. Lucian was essentially a writer of prose satires, a journalist who was "the last great master of Attic eloquence and Attic wit." In the realm of science, Claudius Ptolemy of Alexandria, the astronomer and geographer, and Galen of Pergamon, the student of medi-cine, both active in the second century, profoundly influenced their own and subsequent times.

PHILOSOPHY. The doctrines of Stoicism continued to appeal to the highest instincts of Roman character. Besides Seneca and Marcus Aurelius, this creed found a worthy exponent in the ex-slave Epictetus, who taught between 90 and 120 at Nicopolis in Epirus.

ART AND ARCHITECTURE. The first two centuries of the Princi-pate saw Roman art, especially officially inspired art, attain its highest development. The stimulus to production came in the great demand for public buildings, for monuments to be erected in honor of emperors and private persons, for statuary, and for the construction and decoration of countless private mansions and villas. Rome was transformed into a magnificent and imposing city by the interest and generosity of Augustus and his successors. Each of the new municipal towns sought to imitate the capital, in so far as its resources or private and imperial philanthropy permitted. Each of these towns had its forum, surrounded by temples, basilicas, and colonnades, its theater (often an amphitheater as well), its public baths, and frequently a monumental arch, an imposing aqueduct, a great bridge, or some other outstanding work of architecture that proclaimed community pride or imperial generosity. Countless statues of gods, emperors, and magistrates adorned the temples and public squares. This imperial art drew heavily upon the riches of the classical Greek and the Hellenistic periods, as seen especially in the classicizing artistic tastes of the Emperor Hadrian, which created a fashion, but it also exhibited distinctively Roman contributions. Roman art found its chief inspiration in, and remained in close contact with, public life. The artists of the Principate may well have been Greeks, but they worked for Romans and had to satisfy Roman tastes. Realism and careful attention to details are two great characteristics of Roman art. The spirit of Roman art is revealed best in the historical reliefs that adorned altars, arches, columns, and sarcophagi, and in portrait statuary. The power of characterization in Roman portraiture is attested not only by surviving statues but also by the imperial likenesses on coins. New architectural forms and methods of construction also characterized the period. Among the former belong the imposing monumental arches erected by emperors from Augustus to Septimius Severus in Rome, Italy, and the provinces, and columns with shafts decorated in relief, of which the columns of Trajan and Marcus Aurelius are the outstanding examples to survive. The Principate was the great age of brick and concrete. The Golden House of Nero was one of the first important buildings of brick-faced concrete. The utilitarian nature of such construction was quickly realized under the Flavians, and by the second century its use in apartment houses revolutionized urbanistic development in the Western world. Marble, of course, was used extensively in colonnades, architraves, interior columns, and as the stone veneer applied to some of the more elaborate public buildings, decorative reliefs, arches, and altars. The use of cement reached its greatest development in the construction of the vast domes and vaults of buildings like the Pantheon and the Baths of Caracalla in Rome.

The most striking testimony to the grandeur of Rome are the remains of architecture in the provinces—from such imposing ruins as the Porta Nigra of Trèves, the theater at Orange, the Pont du Gard near Nîmes, the bridge over the Tagus at Alcantara, and the amphitheaters of Nîmes in France and El-Djemm in Tunisia. The field of interior decoration is represented by mural frescoes, stucco moldings, and mosaics that have survived in the ruins of public and private buildings of Rome, Pompeii, Ostia, and numerous provincial towns. At Pompeii in particular, changing styles of wall painting may be traced. Artists at times sought to create the illusion of depth by painting scenes of nature or achitectural vistas in an occasionally impressionistic style. At other times they respected walls as flat surfaces by decorating them with panels. The minor arts of gem cutting, the manufacture of ornamental gold, silver, and bronze work, and the ornamentation of pottery exhibit the same skill and tendencies seen in works on a grander scale. It is in this period that Christian art, like Christian literature, first arose. In the East, the mural paintings of the Christian church at Dura on the Euphrates from the time of Severus Alexander show that Christian artists adopted the oriental style which emphasized the spirituality of human figures to the neglect of their physical characteristics. Their subjects were selected from the Gospel narratives, of course, just as the Jews decorated their synagogue at Dura with scenes drawn from the Old Testament. In the West, Christian art found its first humble mission in the adornment of underground tombs, catacombs, and chapels. Here it imitated the technique of pagan mural decorations, but for subject matter drew largely on the narrative literature, oral traditions, and religious symbolism of early Christianity.

CULTURAL CHANGES IN THE PRINCIPATE.   Except in a few very Roman fields like law and architecture, the classical Greco-Roman world had apparently exhausted its artistic self-expression by the second century A.D. At first glance it may seem paradoxical that the artistic productivity of the classical world became less original just as the Roman Empire reached the height of its political and economic development. Certainly in some fields of creative activity, like that of forensic oratory, political conditions tended to affect adversely that synthesis of cultures we call Greco-Roman. Political limitations on the development of literature were only part of the story, however. The rhetorical nature of Roman education increasingly tended to favor the development of showy style at the expense of substance. Educated gentlemen were supposed to be writers and even poets, and this resulted in a vast production by dilettantes of works with little claim to inspired art. The archaizing tendency in belles-lettres, in which classic works, even when genuinely appreciated, were rather slavishly copied, was symptomatic of widespread literary ennui. What was new and dynamic in literature and art came increasingly from classes and areas outside the mainstream of the Greco-Roman tradition and with other standards of creativity.

III. Pagan Cults of the Empire Under the Principate

PUBLIC CULTS.   Pagan religion had two contrasting aspects. On the one hand were the public official cults, both imperial and municipal; on the other were the private cults, practised by individuals and unofficial religious associations. Throughout the period under consideration there was

Ampitheater at Nimes

no neglect of most of the state gods worshipped under the Republic, particularly Jupiter Capitolinus with his associates Juno and Minerva, Mars, and other divinities of the Greco-Roman pantheon. Worship of these gods was spread with the organization of Roman and Latin colonies and municipalities in the provinces. With the Romanization of the native populations, Greco-Roman deities usually displaced or assimilated local gods. Druidism, a religion widespread among the Celts of Gaul and Britain, was suppressed, chiefly because it fostered resistance to Roman rule, but other tribal and racial religious practices suffered little interference. Some native gods even found adherents among officials and soldiers. In the East, there was little change from Hellenistic times. The Greek city communities retained their old state gods, the towns and temples of Asia Minor and Syria maintained their ancient cults. In Egypt the native priesthood kept up the temple rites, dating from the Pharaohs, although under the supervision of Roman officials. Even the Phoenician towns of Africa worshipped some of the old Semitic deities.

A few provincial gods even found a place among the official deities of Rome, either because of the devotion of certain emperors and their families to gods of their native lands or because others gave official recognition to deities whose worship they had first adopted privately. For example, Gaius sanctioned the cult of the Egyptian goddess Isis, whose worship together with that of her associate god Serapis, was given more formal status by Vespasian and Domitian. Septimius Severus built temples to the Punic Bacchus and to Hercules. Elagabalus tried to place the Baal of Emesa in the place of Jupiter Capitolinus as the chief god of the Empire, which was one of the chief reasons for his removal.

The most important innovation in the official religion of the Empire was the establishment of the imperial cult of Roma and Augustus. As we have seen, this cult was a visible expression of the loyalty of the provincials and their acknowledgment of the authority of Rome. When provincial councils were given the responsibility of maintaining and directing this cult, a new sphere of activity was presented to provincial notables, and as priests of Rome and Augustus, they were linked more closely with the *princeps* and the principate. This effect was increased whenever the councils communicated directly with the *princeps* on provincial matters. After the death of Augustus, the imperial cult in the provinces gradually came to include worship of both the ruling Augustus or Augusti and the Divi, that is, deceased emperors whom the Senate had deified. This practice was in vogue in all the eastern provinces after the reign of Claudius, and in the West from the time of the Flavian dynasty. In Rome, where the cult of the ruling *princeps* did not receive official standing, Domitian converted the temple of Divus Augustus into a temple for all the Divi.

The imperial cult played an important part in laying the foundations of autocracy. In general, imperial authority came to be looked upon as created and sustained by the will and favor of the gods, and each *princeps* was regarded as obtaining and exercising it through divine providence. Even a weak ruler could not impair the dignity and authority of the office of *princeps*. In harmony with the idea that the *princeps* ruled by divine favor was the emphasis laid by the Severi on descent from former deified rulers, as when Severus proclaimed himself a descendant of Nerva through a succession of Divi. The official deification of deceased empresses, and at times other imperial women, contributed to the idea of the "divinity" of the imperial house. Further recognition of the divinity inherent in the emperor is seen in the value attributed to oaths taken in his name or his genius, which were considered more binding than those in the name of other deities, and in the cult of his image in army camps, where he was given precedence over the other official divinities. Coins issued from the imperial mints in the late second and early third centuries proclaimed to Roman subjects the close association of the *princeps*, as an earthly deity, with the gods. Certain of the latter are represented as guardians, protectors and even companions of the emperors. Particularly significant was the emphasis placed on the connection with Sol, the unconquered Sun-god, lord of heaven, who was represented on coins of the Severi as the emperor's comrade and preserver.

ORIENTAL RELIGIONS. The most striking phenomenon of pagan religious life during the first three centuries of the Principate was the penetration of the western provinces of the Empire by a group of cults from the Near East, generally styled "Oriental" religions. These faiths were ancient among the native populations of Egypt and western Asia but had been greatly modified by contact with Greek civilization after Alexander the Great's conquest of the Persian Empire. As a result of their Hellenization they had become rationalized in their theology and so better adapted for general acceptance. During the Hellenistic Age they were readily received in many of the Greek cities, pressed, however, into the mold of the civic cults. It was not until the establishment of the Roman Empire, with its facilities for, and stimulus to, intercourse between all peoples within its frontiers that they were able to gain a foothold in Italy and the West. Their penetration of Italy began with the official reception of the cult of the Great Mother at Rome in 205 B.C., but Roman society as a whole held aloof from them until the close of the Republic.

Expansion of the Oriental cults followed trade routes, along which they were carried by travelers, merchants, and colonies of Oriental traders. The army cantonments were also centers for their diffusion, not only through the agency of troops recruited in the East, but also through detachments that had served there during numerous wars on the eastern frontiers, and oriental slaves were active propagandists of their native faiths.

The explanation of the ready reception of these cults by all classes of society is that they guaranteed their adherents a satisfaction the official religions were unable to offer. The state and municipal cults were mainly political, and with the disappearance of independent political life they lost their hold upon men who needed a refuge from the miseries of the present world in a world of the spirit and the promise of a future life. This need the Oriental cults were able to meet with the doctrines of a personal religion far different from the formal worship of the Greco-Roman deities.

Certain characteristics of doctrine and ritual were common to Oriental cults. They had an elaborate ritual which appealed both to the senses and to the emotions of the worshippers. By witnessing certain symbolic ceremonies, the believer was roused to spiritual ecstasy and communion with the deity, while by the performance of sacramental rites he felt cleansed from earthly defilements and fitted for a purer spiritual existence. A professional priesthood had charge of the worship, ministered to the needs of individuals, and conducted missionary work. In an age when men gave over an attempt to solve the riddles of the universe by scientific methods, they spoke with the authority of revelation, giving a comforting theological interpretation of life. They appealed to the conscience by imposing a rigid rule of conduct, observance of which would fit the believer for a happier existence in a future life.

The most important of these Oriental divinities were the Great Mother (Magna Mater) of Pessinus, otherwise known as Cybele, worshipped with the male deity Attis; the Egyptian pair Isis and Serapis; Atargatis, the chief female divinity of North Syria; a number of Syrian gods (Ba'als) named from the site of their Syrian shrines; and finally Mithra, a deity whose cult had long formed a part of the national Iranian religion. Toward all these cults the state displayed wide toleration, or rather indifference, only interfering with them when their orgiastic rites came into conflict with standards of public conduct. In spite of this indifference, it was a long time before the conservative prejudices of the upper classes of Roman society were sufficiently undermined to permit of their participation in these foreign rites. For a hundred years after the introduction of the worship of Magna Mater, Romans were prohibited from enrolling themselves in the ranks of her priesthood. A determined but unsuccessful attempt was made by the Senate during the last century of the Republic to drive out the cult of Isis, the second of these religions to find a home in Italy. In 42 B.C. the triumvirs were authorized to erect a temple to this goddess. Augustus, however, banished her worship beyond the *pomerium*. This restriction was not enforced by his successors, and by A.D. 69 the cult of the Egyptian goddess was firmly established in the capital. The various Syrian deities were of less significance in the religious life of the West, even though Elagabalus set up the worship of one such, the Sun God of Emesa, as an official cult at Rome.

The Oriental cult that overshadowed all the rest in importance was Mithraism, one of the latest to cross from Asia into Europe. In the Zoroastrian religion of ancient Persia, Mithra appears as the chief spiritual agent of the supreme god of light Ormuzd in his struggle against Ahriman, the god of darkness. He was a beneficent force in the natural world and in the moral world the champion of righteousness against the powers of evil. Under Babylonian and Greek influences Mithra was identified with the Sun-god and appeared in Rome with the title Unconquered Sun-god Mithra (*deus invictus sol Mithra*). Toward the close of the first century A.D. Mithraism arrived in Rome and the western provinces, and from that time it spread rapidly. Mithra, as the god of battles, was a patron deity of soldiers, who became his zealous missionaries in frontier camps. Unlike other Oriental cults, Mithraism was a religion for men only and lacked a professional clergy.

The Oriental cults were a substantial addition to Roman paganism, but they did not dominate it, nor did they alter its traditional character. In spite of the fact that some of them received official recognition and support from various emperors, they generally remained the religions of individuals or private religious associations and did not assume a political character. Their influence was felt mainly in the cities, where there were many Easterners. Notwithstanding the popularity of Mithra among the soldiery, he had no place in the roster of the army's official gods.

PHILOSOPHY.   Attention has already been called to the value of Stoicism in supplying its adherents with a moral code of conduct. Other philosophical systems, notably Epicureanism, also inculcated particular rules of life. But the philosophical doctrines best able to hold their own with the new religions were those of Neoplatonism and Neopythagoreanism, which came into vogue during the second century and exhibited a combination of mysticism and idealism well suited to the spirit of the age.

ASTROLOGY AND MAGIC.   Throughout the Principate all classes of society were deeply imbued with a superstitious fatalism and placed implicit belief in astrology and magic. Chaldean and Egyptian astrologers were popular and were consulted on all important questions. They were frequently banished by the emperors who feared that their predictions might give encouragement to their enemies. These very emperors, however, kept astrologers in their own service, and banishment never remained long in force. The almost universal belief in miracles and oracles led to the appearance of many impostors, who throve on the credulity of their clients. One of the most celebrated of these was the Alexander who founded a new oracle of Aesculapius at Abonoteichus in Paphlagonia, whose fame spread throughout the whole Empire and even beyond its borders. In his exposé of the methods employed by this false prophet, the satirist Lucian gives a vivid picture of the depraved superstition of his time.

At the close of the Principate the pagan world presented a great confusion of religious beliefs and doctrines. But the various pagan cults were tolerant of one another, for the followers of one god were ready to acknowledge the divinity of the gods worshipped by their neighbors. The refusal of the Jews and Christians to recognize the pagan gods placed them in irreconcilable opposition to the whole pagan world.

IV. Judaism and Christianity in Their Relation to the Roman State

THE JEWS IN THE ROMAN EMPIRE. Alexander the Great's conquest of the Near East had thrown open to the Jews the whole Greco-Macedonian world, and Jewish settlements soon appeared in all its important commercial centers. Jewish colonies were encouraged by Hellenistic monarchs, who granted them immunity from military service, protection of their religion, and a privileged judicial status in the cities where they were established. Gradually the number of Jews of the dispersion became much greater than those who remained in Judaea itself. Although Jews resident outside of Syria adopted Greek and were influenced in many ways by their contact with Hellenistic culture, they still formed part of the religious community presided over by the High Priest at Jerusalem. In addition to the annual contribution of two drachmas to the temple of Jehovah, every Jew was expected to visit Jerusalem and sacrifice in the temple at least once in his life. Moreover, they were active in proselytizing and made many converts among Greeks and other peoples. Their connection with Judaea was purely religious, however, not political in character.

The privileged status the Jews enjoyed in the Hellenistic states was recognized by the Romans and specifically confirmed by Augustus because of their earlier cooperation with Rome against the Seleucids and the support they had given him in his war with Antony and Cleopatra, although this policy caused considerable dissatisfaction among their Greek fellow townsmen. In deference to their peculiar religion, the Jews were not required to participate in the imperial or state cult. Because of its positive attitude, the Romans could not be indifferent toward Judaism and so tolerated it. The imperial government made no attempt to foster settlements of Jews in the western provinces, however, and during the early Principate the only considerable Jewish colony west of the Adriatic was that in Rome. With the exception of Caligula, who tried to force the imperial cult on the Jews, the successors of Augustus did not interfere with Judaism except to forbid its propaganda. Expulsions of the Jews from Rome under Tiberius and Claudius were not religious persecutions but police measures taken for the maintenance of order. After the close of the Jewish war and the disruption of the Jewish religious community, Vespasian made Judaism a licensed religion by establishing the two drachma head tax for all who professed it. The subsequent Jewish revolts under Trajan and Hadrian did not alter the status of the Jews in their relation to the government.

CHRISTIANITY AND JUDAISM. The Christian religion had its origin in Judaea as a result of the teachings of Jesus of Nazareth, who was crucified by the Roman authorities about A.D. 33, during the principate of Tiberius, after having been condemned for blasphemy by the Sanhedrin, the Jewish high court for the enforcement of the law of Moses. From Judaea, Christianity spread to the scattered Jewish communities through the missionary activity of the disciples and other followers of Jesus, particularly the Apostle Paul. Although Christian propaganda was not confined to these Jewish communities, it was among them that the first Christian congregations arose. This, and the Jewish origin of the new faith, caused the Christians to be regarded by the Roman government as a Jewish sect. It is not known for sure whether Claudius' banishment of the Jews from Rome in 49 was because of disorders between Christians and adherents of the older faith. Initial persecution of the Christian sect came not from the Roman authorities but from the orthodox and conservative Jewish elements. The early Christians benefited on the whole from the Roman attitude toward their sect, for it gave them the benefit of the immunities Jews enjoyed. It seems that after 64 the Christians no longer enjoyed these privileges, even if it is true that Domitian exacted the Jewish license tax from Christians. After the destruction of Jerusalem in 70, however, and the resulting predominance of the non-Jewish element in Christian ranks, it was impossible for confusion between the two sects to be long-lived.

POPULAR ANTAGONISM TOWARD THE CHRISTIANS. The earliest relations between Christians and representatives of the Roman government arose in the cities of the East, where popular hostility toward adherents of the new faith made them victims of hostile demonstrations, mob violence, and denunciation on criminal charges before local courts. This atmosphere of general hostility is explained by the attitude of the Christians toward society. The early Church believed sincerely in the near approach of the Kingdom of Christ and set no store by the things of this world, concentrating its efforts upon preparation for the future life. The refusal of Christians to have anything to do with pagan divinities caused them to withdraw from participation in public festivals and to refuse to share in the public life of their communities by holding magistracies or priesthoods. The practice by some Christians of community of goods among the brethren and their advocacy of celibacy ran counter to the accepted social practices. In both municipal and family life the Christians thus became a disturbing factor which threatened to grow more dangerous because of their proselytizing activity. Another of their customs, for which they were viewed with extreme suspicion by their contemporaries, was the exclusion of non-Christians from certain of their gatherings, particularly the sacrifice of the Mass. This gave rise to the accusation that they practiced criminal rites, such as child murder, in their gatherings and met together to plot against their pagan neighbors. So far were the Roman officials from being influenced by the popular attitude, however, that up to 64 they protected the Christians from the widespread antagonism toward them.

NERONIAN PERSECUTION AND ITS CONSEQUENCES. Because of scanty evidence, it is impossible to state definitely why the ministers of Nero selected the Christians as a fit group to accuse of having set fire to Rome. It seems a logical inference, however, that the Christians were known to be unpopular with the mob in the city. They were brought to trial on the technically criminal charge of arson, probably before the city prefect, who had jurisdiction over common criminals, and they were punished by burning, crucifixion, and being hunted as wild beasts in the arena— penalties fixed for magicians and sorcerers. The explanation of the conviction is that, in the course of the trial, the charge was changed from arson to that of "hatred of mankind" (*odium generis humani*) because of the interpretation of what was known of Christian beliefs and practices. Thereafter the Roman government regarded the Christians as persons who harbored views dangerous to state and society, so that the confession of being a Christian exposed an individual to the punishment of outlaws. So far as is known, however, no general edict was passed forbidding the belief and practice of Christianity or ordering a general search for and punishment of Christians. It was left to provincial magistrates and others with the proper judicial and police authority to deal with Christians accused before them of being responsible for public disturbances or criminal acts. Under the Flavians the same policy prevailed, and the report of persecution at Rome in the time of Domitian lacks satisfactory evidence, although during his principate the Christian communities of Asia Minor seem to have suffered at the hands of local authorities.

CHRISTIANS AND THE LAW. Conflict with secular power was inevitable in the very nature of Christianity, which was non-Roman, non-national, and monotheistic, refusing to recognize the cults of the state and denying the divinity of the ruler. The Romans regarded worship of the state gods, including participation in the imperial cult, from a political standpoint and considered refusal to share in such worship as treason (*maiestas*). For this the punishment was death. It was furthermore a proof of atheism, which might also be regarded as treasonable. On the other hand, the Christians looked upon the question as a matter involving their souls' salvation. They felt that to worship the state gods and acknowledge the divinity of the *princeps* would be to commit idolatry and sacrilege. They could pray for the emperor but not to him. These attitudes could not be reconciled. On another ground the Christians were for a time liable to punishment under the law of treason, namely, as forming unauthorized religious associations. In Rome, however, after the time of Hadrian and in the provinces after Septimius Severus, their religious communities might be regarded as funerary colleges and so held to be licensed burial societies. This concession would not secure them immunity from prosecution on other grounds. The obstinate refusal of the Christians to conform to the political religion of the state convinced Roman officials that they were public enemies, hostile to society in general and to the Empire in particular.

IMPERIAL POLICY FROM TRAJAN TO SEVERUS ALEXANDER. The attitude of the government toward the Christians in the early second century is clearly seen from the correspondence between Trajan and Pliny the younger, governor of Bithynia in 112. This correspondence fails to reveal any law prohibiting Christianity but shows that the admission of the name of Christian, accompanied by the refusal to worship the gods of the state and the *princeps*, constituted sufficient grounds for punishment. A great deal of discretion was left to the governor, who was directed to pay no attention to anonymous accusations but expected to repress Christianity whenever its spread caused conflicts with the non-Christian element under his authority. A rescript of Hadrian to Minucius Fundanus, proconsul of Asia, questioned but probably genuine, ordained that Christians should receive a regular trial and that they should not be condemned for the name, but for some definite crime, e.g., treason. The persecution of the Christian community at Lyons under Marcus Aurelius was no exception to general imperial policy of the second century, although he did lay greater stress than the others upon the performance of the state cults. The Severans continued to follow the precepts laid down by Trajan. Under Septimius Severus there was a local persecution of Christians by the governor of Syria in 202, but the emperor apparently did not, as is occasionally alleged, forbid Jewish proselytizing and conversions to Christianity, nor did he order that both the converts and those who made them be sought out and prosecuted. Severus Alexander is said to have been well disposed to the sect, and under him its adherents enjoyed a respite from local official persecution.

ORGANIZATION OF THE CHRISTIAN CHURCH. The early Christians formed a number of small, independent communities, united by ties of common interest, belief and continual intercourse. Although the majority were humble people, they were by no means confined to the proletariat. In their organization these communities were all of the same general type, resembling the Roman religious *collegia*, but local variations were common. Each church community was directed by a committee, whose members were called at times elders (presbyters), at times overseers (bishops). These were assisted by deacons, who, like themselves, were elected by the congregation to which they belonged. Among the presbyters or bishops one may have acted as president. The functions of the bishops were primarily administrative, including the care of funds and of the poor, the friendless, and traveling brethren, and of discipline among the members of the community. The deacons were subordinates of the bishops and assisted in the religious services and the general administration of the community. Besides these local church officers, there were itinerant prophets or apostles who devoted themselves to evangelical teaching.

In the course of the second and third centuries this loose organization was gradually changed as a result of separatist tendencies among the Christians themselves and the increasing official oppression to which they were exposed. Opposition to these forces resulted in a strict formulation of evangelic doctrine and a firmer organization of church communities. This organization came to be centralized in the hands of the bishops, now representatives of the communities. The episcopate, at first collegiate, became monarchical, and claimed authority by virtue of apostolic succession, by which power to administer the sacraments of the Church was transmitted. The president of the committee of bishops or presbyters tended to become the sole bishop, and presbyters became priests subject to his authority, although at times presiding over separate congregations. Bishops were by the third century regularly nominated by the clergy, approved by the congregation, and finally inducted into office by the ceremony of ordination. Besides their administrative powers, the bishops guarded the traditions and doctrines of the Church. The clergy became salaried officers, sharply distinguished from the laity, who gradually ceased to participate actively in the government and regulation of worship of their respective communities. These communities developed into corporations organized on a juristic basis, promising redemption to their members and withholding it from deserters.

In the third century a movement took place to organize separate churches in larger unions, and so provincial synods arose. In these the metropolitan bishops, that is, those from the provincial administrative centers, assumed the leadership. Among the churches of the Empire as a whole, two rival tendencies emerged. One was to accord equal authority to all the bishops, the other to recognize the supremacy of the bishop of Rome. The claim for primacy of the Roman see was based upon the imperial political status of Rome and the special history of the Roman Church. It was strongly pressed by certain bishops of the second century, who laid emphasis upon the claim that the Roman bishopric had been established by the Apostle Peter.

DISINTEGRATION AND RECOVERY: A.D. 235–285

During the half century between 235 and 285, the Roman Empire and ancient civilization passed through a great crisis. The causes of this crisis are in large measure ultimately attributable to basic defects in the reorganization of the state undertaken by Augustus: reliance of the emperors on military force to maintain their power against rivals; creation of a government that, in the long run, could not be supported by the human and natural resources of the Empire; and perpetuation of a class structure that failed to give the producing classes rewards commensurate to the tax burdens imposed upon them. Within the Empire disorder reigned as a result of continuous mutinies of the soldiery and struggles between their leaders for imperial authority. From without came wave after wave of barbarian invaders, accompanied by repeated invasions from the aggressive rulers of the revived Persian Empire. In the wake of devastation caused by war and plundering, epidemics ravaged the population. Commerce and industry declined and the economic foundations of ancient civilized life were badly shaken. Despairing of the ability of the Empire to cope with the disasters, men set up independent states, both in the East and the West, to protect themselves. In the hope of rallying all elements of the population to present a united front against their enemies, certain emperors tried to force the Christians to conform to the state religion. Eventually, the soldiery were brought under control, the soil of the Empire was cleared of its foreign foes, and its political unity was reestablished. Victory was achieved only at great cost. Politically, economically, and culturally the Roman World that emerged from the ordeal was far removed from what it had been. Greco-Roman civilization had received a mortal blow, and the dawn of the Middle Ages was at hand.

Unfortunately the sources of information about this period are by no means commensurate with its importance. Herodian's history stops at 238, and for the years that follow there is no continuous contemporary narrative. Conditions did not stimulate historical writing, and, of the little that was produced, hardly anything has survived. Biographical sketches of the emperors are given in the fourth century *Augustan History*, but these are of poor quality and full of falsifications. Additional information is supplied by the epitomators and chroniclers of the fourth and fifth centuries and by those of the Byzantine period. A new source of information for the relations of the Christians and the Roman government is to be found in contemporary Christian writings and in the earliest historical works by Christian authors, the *Ecclesiastical History* of Eusebius, bishop of Caesarea, and the pamphlet *On the Death of the Persecutors* by Lactantius, both dating from the early fourth century. The dearth of literary sources renders all the more valuable contemporary inscriptions, papyri, coins, and archaeological remains. Unfortunately the prevailing poverty caused a great falling-off in the number of inscriptions, both of public and private character.

I. Mutiny of the Soldiery

SOLDIER EMPERORS. With the murder of Severus Alexander in 235 and the nomination of Maximinus the Thracian as *princeps* by the mutinous soldiery there began a fifty-year-long repetition of the shorter epochs of civil war from 68 to 69 and 193 to 197. In the resulting turmoil, the Roman Peace, greatest achievement of the Principate, came to an end. Between 235 and 285 no less than twenty-six Augusti, including colleagues in the imperial power, obtained recognition in Rome. Of these only one escaped violent death. Although five of the Augusti were nominated by the Senate and about the same number by emperors already in office, the great majority were revolutionary officers who engineered their acclamation as emperors by their own soldiers. In addition to those who had their authority confirmed by the Senate and so could boast a legal right to the *imperium*, there were a number of unsuccessful claimants defeated and killed by their rivals. In the language of the day, usurpers who failed to make good their claims to the principate were called "tyrants." One emperor alone, Gallienus, had to suppress no fewer than eighteen such rivals. For the most part the soldier emperors were men of superior military capacities and achievements. Successful generalship was in fact the main criterion applied by the soldiers in their support of candidates for the principate. As a rule, once in office, they conscientiously devoted themselves to restoring peace and order in the Empire, but all too often their efforts were nullified by the treachery of their own subordinates or the rise of more powerful rivals.

CAUSES AND CHARACTER OF THE REVOLTS. The causes of these chaotic conditions lay principally in the ambition of the members of the officer class, abetted by the greedy and undisciplined spirit of the rank and file of the professional soldiery. Such an attitude had been displayed by professional armies even under the Republic, and under the Empire it had been manifested on numerous occasions by the praetorians, and to some extent by the legionaries also in the crises of 68–69 and 193, but disorder now became chronic and permeated all branches of the military establishment. The general loss of a sense of loyalty to the Empire is not easy to explain. Provincialization of the legions had led gradually to recruitment first on a territorial and then a local basis, which meant that by the early third century the bulk of the army came from the immediate vicinity of frontier garrisons in what were the most rustic but by no means un-Romanized provinces. At least down to the beginning of the Severan dynasty, the military establishment was generally loyal to the civilizing ideals of Rome and a not insignificant number of soldiers were sons of the municipal gentry of frontier provinces, scarcely types to form a revolutionary soldiery. A partial explanation may be the granting of citizenship to virtually all Roman subjects in 212, which, by removing an important incentive that attracted the better type of recruit, led to the enlistment of least Romanized subjects. More important, however, in the barbarization of the army was the scramble by the numerous revolutionary commanders to recruit troops in the chaos following 235. Revolutionaries showed no compunctions against enlisting the roughest types from within the Empire and barbarians from outside it. At the same time, particularly because of the policy of the Severi in emphasizing the degree to which their authority was based on the army, the soldiers felt themselves more than ever a vested interest and lost all feeling of duty or obligation towards the state they served. Their appetite whetted by generous donations distributed by previous emperors, they determined to enrich themselves at the expense of the civilian population and the public treasury. Mutual jealousy between the frontier armies and the praetorians and the rivalries between the various corps long stationed in different parts of the Empire prevented the soldiery from acting as a single unit, however. Armies of different provincial commands, and at times formations brought together for a specific campaign, sought separately to force the recognition of their nominees to the principate. Each hailed as Imperator the commander who led them to victory over foreign foes or other mutinous troops and forced him, often against his will, to lead a march on Rome, in the expectation of receiving increases in pay and fresh largesses. It has been suggested that these mutinies be regarded in the light of a social revolution, in which the soldiers headed a rise of the peasantry against the municipal aristocracy of landholders and merchants who formed the *bourgeoisie* of the Empire. For this theory evidence is lacking. Soldiers plundered impartially both the rural population and the townfolk through whose territories they marched and showed no indication of sharing with the former whatever spoils they wrested from the latter. There is no sign of any attempt to alter the conditions of land ownership or land tenure in the interests of the peasantry or to alleviate the taxes and other burdens pressing heavily upon them.

II. Collapse of the Imperial Defenses

NORTHERN BARBARIANS. The Roman world was simultaneously exposed to all the horrors of barbarian invasion. This does not seem to have been caused merely, or even primarily, by the appearance of new and more aggressive barbarian nations along the frontiers. It was the direct result of the old policy of recruiting barbarians to serve in the Roman army. Such recruitment, by no means unknown even under the first emperors, increased notably in the second century and reached a flood in the third, as various pretenders to the throne sought to make good their claims with the use of barbarian contingents. The Roman frontiers had thus long acted as a magnet for warlike bands looking for the material advantages offered them in Roman military service. Now the way was open for such bands, already attracted to the frontier, to find the rewards of plunder and booty through invasion, since certain sectors of the borders were now denuded of troops, withdrawn to meet attacks from other quarters, and since armies were being diverted from frontier defense to engage in civil war.

These bands placed themselves in the service of barbarian nations, some now appearing for the first time on Rome's borders, and encouraged them to engage in a series of raids designed to plunder rather than win territory for permanent settlement. These nations included the Saxons who occupied the coast of the North Sea between the Rhine and the Weser and whose fleets raided the shores of Britain and Gaul; the Franks, who were at home across the lower Rhine; and the Alamanni, who threatened the Limes in Upper Germany and Raetia. Further east, the Marcomanni and Quadi still held their former position on the Upper Danube, and Dacia and Lower Moesia were menaced by their old neighbors the Sarmatians and Carpi, as well as by the Vandals, who occupied part of the Hungarian plain. Potentially more dangerous than the latter tribes, however, were the Goths, who had made their way from the Baltic to the fertile plains on the north shore of the Black Sea, where they were joined by the Heruli. It is well to remember that in no case do the names given these nations reflect any great degree of ethnic unity in so far as they affected the Empire. Each "nation" was the result of an amalgamation between barbarians moving to the frontiers and those already there. Once the frontier defense system was broken through, the invaders met with little serious opposition, for the emperors had no adequate mobile forces ready to deal with such attacks and required a considerable length of time to organize field armies able to cope with them. It is inaccurate to speak of barbarian invasions in terms of "hordes." Their effective strength was, in general, surprisingly small, and most nations could field armies no larger than several tens of thousands of men.

GOTHIC INVASIONS.   By a successful campaign against the Alamanni in 235, the emperor Maximinus secured a period of tranquility on the Rhine frontier, but under him and his successors the Danubian provinces were subjected to continual invasions by Sarmatians, Dacian Carpi, and Goths, who suffered numerous defeats but could not be forced to keep the peace. It was found necessary to buy off the Goths by paying them annual subsidies. It was during the principate of Decius (249–251) that the seriousness of the Gothic menace was first clearly realized. In 249 a

Gothic host crossed the Danube into Lower Moesia and, although defeated by the emperor, moved southward into Thrace. When Decius followed them he was surprised and defeated with heavy losses (250). As the Goths withdrew with their plunder and captives, Decius attacked them again. After some initial success, his army was trapped and annihilated by the barbarians. Both Decius and his son, whom he had made coemperor, fell in the battle. Thereafter the Danubian provinces were subjected to continuous incursions of Gothic and other tribes, against whom no effective resistance could be offered.

The main Gothic activities then shifted further to the east. In 253 began a series of raids by sea against the coasts of Asia Minor and the Aegean, the chronology of which is uncertain. That of 256 or 257 passed through the Bosporus and brought wholesale devastation to the leading cities of Bithynia. Particularly disastrous was the assault on Asia Minor some years later. The Goths, descending into the Aegean by way of the Bosporus and Hellespont, ravaged the coastal cities of Ionia. They then marched inland as far east as Galatia and Cappadocia, plundering as they went. They finally turned north to Heraclea on the Black Sea, whence they sailed home with their booty. In 267 a large fleet manned by the Heruli and a great land force of Goths and associated tribes skirted the west shore of the Black Sea and descended upon Greece, which they devastated as far south as Sparta. Among other cities, Athens was seized and plundered. This time the raiders did not escape scot-free. An imperial army led by the Emperor Gallienus (253–268) cut off their retreat and defeated them in a bloody battle at Naissus in Moesia. Fifty thousand barbarians allegedly fell on the field. The rest sought refuge in a fortified encampment. Gallienus was forced to return to face a usurper in Italy, where he was assassinated by his own staff officers. His successor, Claudius (268–270), took over the command in the Balkans. His troops won several victories and forced the surrender not only of the survivors of the former Gothic invasion but also of fresh bands that crossed the Danube to aid them. The captives were partly settled in depopulated areas and partly incorporated in the Roman army. His victories brought Claudius the well-deserved surname of Gothicus. Although Gothic inroads did not cease entirely, none of their subsequent incursions was comparable to those of 267. The Gothic peril was averted for over a hundred years.

FRANKS AND ALAMANNI.   In the meantime the western barbarians added to the desolation and disintegration of the Empire. Between 254 and 258 Gallienus was occupied in clearing Gaul and the Rhineland of Franks and Alamanni who had overrun the frontier defences in that area. At about the same time Pannonia was raided by the Marcomanni, Quadi, and Iazyges. The Marcomanni even reached Italy, advancing as far as Ravenna (254). In order to stop their attacks Gallienus had to grant them certain districts in Upper Pannonia. In 259/260 when Gallienus had to withdraw part of his forces from the Rhine to meet a revolt in Pannonia, the Franks again crossed the Rhine. Traversing the whole of Gaul they entered Spain and, obtaining ships in the harbors of Hispania Tarraconensis, crossed over to Mauretania. Meanwhile the Alamanni descended into the Rhone valley, which they occupied for three years and from which they raided other parts of Gaul. One of their bands crossed the Alps into Italy and threatened Rome. Gallienus hastily returned to Italy to meet the raiders, whom he defeated decisively near Milan. As a result of these invasions the Romans lost their hold upon outposts across the middle Rhine and were also forced to give up their positions in the angle between the Rhine and the Danube. Even Raetia, south of the Danube, could not be adequately protected, for the Emperor Claudius had to cope with another Alamannic band that pushed through the Alps to the borders of Italy (269).

Even the African provinces suffered from invasions of border tribes. A league of desert peoples called the Five Nations (*Quinquegentiani*), as well as other tribes from Mauretania, fell upon Numidia, which was successfully defended by the Roman garrison, however.

PERSIAN WARS. The new Persian Empire under its Sassanian dynasty raised claims to the eastern provinces of the Roman Empire and initiated a policy of action that led Severus Alexander to undertake an invasion of Persia. A period of almost continuous conflict between the two powers then ensued, but the chronology of the various wars is difficult to establish because of our meager sources. Although the Roman attack resulted in failure, the Persians were held in check for a time, and it was not until 237–238 that they again took the offensive. King Ardaschir invaded Roman Mesopotamia and took the fortresses of Nisibis and Carrhae. Ardaschir's son, Shapur I, who succeeded him about 240, at once opened a much more vigorous offensive. Syria was overrun and Antioch endangered. Emperor Gordian III (238–244) took the field, and his able praetorian prefect and father-in-law Timesitheus drove the Persians out of Syria in 243 and recovered both Carrhae and Nisibis. The death of Timesitheus late that year, followed by the murder of Gordian—possibly by the new prefect, Philip the Arabian, who himself became emperor—prevented the Romans from following up their victory. Philip was content to make peace with Shapur, who accepted the former Roman boundary, but the Persian king merely shifted the direction of his attack. After taking Media Atropatene, he secured the assassination of Chosroes, king of Armenia, who had been a loyal Roman ally, and then set a Persian nominee on the Armenian throne (252). The way to Asia Minor was now open. Shapur began a series of raids into Mesopotamia, Syria, and Cappadocia, which brought the Emperor Valerian to the East to retrieve the situation. Valerian won successes over the Persians in 257 and 259, but his army was weakened by disease. When he tried to relieve the siege of Edessa in 259 he was forced to open negotiations with Shapur, who enticed him to a conference and treacherously took him prisoner. This was a tremendous blow to Roman prestige in the East and a great triumph for the Persian king, who commemorated his exploit in a series of rock reliefs still to be seen in Persia. Shapur at once marched into Syria and seized Antioch, while other Persian armies overran Cilicia and Cappadocia. When Persian forces scattered on plundering raids, the Romans began to organize resistance and to cut off isolated detachments. Shapur began a retreat laden with booty and captives. Before he reached his own territory, however, he was robbed of part of his spoils by the Arabs of Hatra and, in the neighborhood of Carrhae, suffered a serious defeat from Odenathus, the Roman client prince of Palmyra. This disaster ended Persian aggression for many years but could not repair the damage done to the population of the devastated provinces.

III. Gaul and Palmyra

ROMAN EMPIRE OF THE GAULS. The inability of the Emperor Gallienus to protect Gaul from barbarian invasion and his occupation with usurpers elsewhere, coupled with the capture of his father and senior colleague Valerian by the Persians, led to the temporary creation of an independent state in the West. In 259 Roman troops under the orders of Marcus Cassianus Latinius Postumus, after a victory over the Franks, proclaimed him Emperor and murdered the young Caesar Saloninus (Valerianus), who had been left by his father Gallienus in nominal command on the Rhine. For the moment Postumus contented himself with securing his position in Gaul and made no attempt to extend his authority over all the Empire. By 263 Gallienus was able to proceed against the usurper, but he was unable to overthrow him, owing to the treachery of one of his own generals and a serious wound that forced him to abandon the campaign. Left to himself, Postumus won over both Spain and Britain and set up an imperial government with his capital at Trèves (*Augusta Treverorum*). There he appointed a Senate and annual consuls, issued a coinage, and maintained his own Praetorian Guard. When Gallienus was called to the Balkans in 267 to cope with the great Germanic invasion of that year, the general Aureolus, whom he had left to guard Italy, turned traitor and went over to Postumus. The latter received only brief recognition in North Italy for Aureolus was besieged in Milan by Gallienus, whose successor Claudius forced him to surrender and executed him.

In Gaul, however, Postumus was able to keep the barbarians at bay and maintain internal peace, which enabled the country to effect a partial recovery from its disasters. His troops proved disloyal, however, and in 268 forced him to accept as colleague one of his officers, Victorinus, to fight against a rival emperor, Laelianus. Postumus defeated Laelianus at

Mainz (Mogontiacum), but when he refused his victorious soldiers the right to sack the city they mutinied and killed him. Victorinus also fell a victim to the rebellious soldiery in 270. He was succeeded by Tetricus, governor of Aquitania and member of the Gallo-Roman aristocracy, who reigned until the collapse of the Gallic Empire in 274.

RISE OF PALMYRA. Palmyra, ancient Tadmor, situated in an oasis of the Syrian desert, owed its importance to its strategic position at the junction of the main caravan routes between the Mediterranean ports of Syria and the Euphrates, as well as those connecting Arabia with North Syria and upper Mesopotamia. Its significance was early recognized by the Romans who gradually obtained control over it in the course of the first century A.D. Hadrian granted it the right of Italian soil (*ius Italicum*), and under the Severi its ruling family were Roman citizens, some of senatorial rank. Detachments of Palmyrene archers served as Roman auxiliaries on the Syrian frontier. When the invasion of Shapur called Valerian to the East in 256, the prince of Palmyra was Septimius Odenathus, whose adherence to the Roman cause was rewarded by consular rank. The capture of Valerian and the Persian march to the sea gave Odenathus an opportunity to play a more decisive and more independent role in eastern affairs. After inflicting severe losses on Shapur's army on its retreat through Mesopotamia, he turned upon and defeated the usurper Quietus, one of two emperors proclaimed in the East in 260, while the other, Macrianus, was making an unsuccessful attempt to secure recognition in the West. Gallienus rewarded Odenathus for his exploit by entrusting him with command of operations against the Persians as Commander of the Romans (*dux Romanorum*). This mission Odenathus successfully accomplished. Roman Mesopotamia was recovered and the war carried to the Persian capital, Ctesiphon. When the Goths swarmed over Asia Minor in the 260s, Odenathus hurried to the rescue, although he was too late to prevent their withdrawal by way of Heraclea. In 267 or 268 he was murdered, along with his eldest son and chosen successor Herodian, by one of his own relatives, Maeonius, who himself soon was assassinated. By the close of his career, Odenathus was very influential in the Orient. For his victories over the Persians, Gallienus had conferred upon him the title Imperator. To this was added that of *corrector totius Orientis*, which gave him general supervision of the region between Egypt and Asia Minor. After his first victory over Shapur, Odenathus had taken the title of King of Palmyra and after his later ones styled himself King of Kings, although he was still a Roman subject, in fact the highest Roman official in the Near East.

PALMYRA'S CHALLENGE TO ROME. With the death of Odenathus, real power in Palmyra passed to his beautiful, gifted, and ambitious widow, Septimia Zenobia. Zenobia secured the crown of Palmyra for her son Vaballathus, who was his mother's willing tool. Conscious of the momentary weakness of Rome and the military successes of Odenathus, she became convinced that Palmyra should seize the opportunity to become independent and establish its rule over the East. She devoted her unusual energy and ability to realize this aim. The break with Rome was not immediate. Throughout the brief principate of Claudius Gothicus, Palmyra still remained nominally part of the Empire, although its rulers gradually strengthened their hold upon Syria and extended it over eastern Asia Minor. When Claudius died of plague in 270, Palmyra refused to recognize the authority of his brother and successor Quintillus, and its troops proceeded to occupy Egypt and western Asia Minor. When Quintillus, after about three months' reign, gave place to the able general Aurelian, Zenobia and Vaballathus returned, nominally at least, to their allegiance, without, however, giving up control of territories they had seized. For the moment Aurelian was obliged to temporize and recognized Vaballathus as Imperator and general of the Romans but not as a colleague. In 271 Zenobia decided that the moment had come for Palmyra to declare its independence. Vaballathus assumed the title Augustus, while Zenobia became Augusta. The East, like Gaul and the adjacent western provinces, had now separated from the central government, and it seemed probable that the disintegration of the Empire would become permanent.

IV. Imperial Unity Restored

AURELIAN, "RESTORER OF THE WORLD": A.D. 270–275. At this critical moment the choice of the soldiery had fallen upon Lucius Domitius Aurelianus, commander of the imperial cavalry under Claudius, who had contributed greatly to the crushing of the Goths in the Balkan peninsula. By birth a humble Illyrian, Aurelian had risen from the ranks to high command by virtue of his soldierly qualities. Of great physical strength and outstanding courage, a natural leader and a skillful general, he was stern in enforcing discipline, unyielding, undiplomatic, and hot-tempered. "Hand on Steel" (*manu ad ferrum*) his soldiers called him, and this epithet well expressed his character. Such was the emperor destined to reestablish the political unity of the Roman world.

Aurelian's first task was to free the heart of the Empire from new waves of northern barbarians. While on his way to Rome from the middle Danube, he was forced to return to Pannonia to cope with an invasion by Vandals and Sarmatians. After a severe struggle, the invaders were defeated and allowed to return home upon condition of supplying a strong cavalry force to the Roman army. Then came word of a devastating invasion of northern Italy from the upper Danube by the Juthungi, apparently a group of Germanic peoples who had been subsidized as Roman allies. Aurelian met this enemy in the Po valley. After several battles, in which the barbarians at times gained victories, the emperor was able to drive them north beyond the Danube. A conspiracy among the senators called

Aurelian to the capital, where he had to suppress a serious revolt of employees of the imperial mint, who resented attempts to check their profiteering on debased coins. He also ordered the fortification of Rome as a protection against future barbarian inroads. Rome had not been in danger of attack by foreign enemies since Hannibal's invasion of Italy, and the city had outgrown its old defences, which had fallen into decay. It was now surrounded by a brick wall twenty feet high, twelve feet wide, and twelve miles in circuit. This wall, begun in 271, was not completed until after Aurelian's death.

RECONQUEST OF THE EAST. Once Italy was secured by the defeats of the Juthungi and Vandals, Aurelian undertook the recovery of the East, where Vaballathus and Zenobia had proclaimed their independence. On his march eastward in 271 the emperor crossed the Danube and inflicted a severe defeat upon a Gothic king. He then abandoned the province of Dacia because of the shortage of troops to defend so exposed an area. Gallienus had already given up the northern part of the province, and now Aurelian began the withdrawal of its garrison and such of the civilian population as wished to retreat south of the Danube. There he organized a new Dacian province at the expense of Moesia and Thrace. Resuming his march, he passed rapidly through Asia Minor and entered Syria, where the Greek population went over to him. Near Antioch he encountered the Palmyrene army, which included both the famous mounted archers and equally formidable lancers whose heavy horses, like the men, were protected by armor. Here and again at Emesa, Aurelian's superior generalship won decisive victories, and Zenobia withdrew to Palmyra. Aurelian followed and, overcoming the difficulties presented by the desert and its nomads, besieged the city. Zenobia, trying to flee to Persia, was caught, and Palmyra surrendered (272). Zenobia, Vaballathus, and other Palmyrene notables were taken to Rome; Palmyra itself received lenient treatment. When Aurelian was engaged in a campaign against the Carpi later in the same year, the people of Palmyra rebelled and massacred their Roman garrison. Without delay Aurelian marched again to the East and retook the city (273). This time it was sacked and destroyed. Meantime a rebellion had broken out in Alexandria, which cut off the supply of wheat for Rome. Aurelian easily suppressed the revolt and dismantled the fortifications of Alexandria.

RECOVERY OF GAUL. The time was now ripe for Aurelian to direct his attention to Gaul. There the elderly Emperor Tetricus was with great difficulty warding off the barbarians and repressing rebellions among his own commanders. He was both unwilling and unable to offer serious opposition to the reunion of Gaul with the Empire, and perhaps he was already acting in collusion with Aurelian when the latter attacked (273 or 274). He allowed Aurelian to cross the Alps unhindered, and, when his troops compelled him to offer battle near Chalons, he deserted them and surrendered to his opponent. Aurelian's victory was complete. Both Gaul and Britain returned to their allegiance as parts of the Empire. Reestablishment of imperial unity was achieved, and Aurelian returned to Rome to celebrate a splendid triumph graced by his captives Zenobia and Tetricus. Both of these received honorable treatment, the latter being placed in charge of the administration of Lucania. On his coins Aurelian assumed the title "Restorer of the World" (*restitutor orbis*).

AURELIAN AND THE SOLAR CULT. In Rome Aurelian erected a temple to the Unconquered Sun God whom he established as the protective deity of the Empire. In this he was influenced by his belief that Elagabalus, the Sun God of Emesa, had aided him in his victory over Palmyra. He did not transplant to Rome the form of the cult practised at Emesa, however, as the Emperor Elagabalus had tried to do. In Roman fashion a priestly college of senatorial pontiffs supervised the ritual of the new "lord of the Roman Empire." The Sun God of Aurelian was no mere local divinity but was looked upon as the highest of the gods, whom all who recognized any solar divinity could unite in worshipping. The Sun God was then thought of as the source of imperial authority and in a special sense the protector of the emperor. This view supported the autocratic position of the ruler and the idea of his divinity. It is not surprising that one of the imperial mints issued coins of Aurelian with the inscription "born Lord and God," *dominus et deus natus*.

Aurelian did not confine his attention to purely military or political matters but also interested himself in economic questions. He may have made some change in the status of the professional guilds in the city of Rome, where he substituted a dole of baked bread for the former public distribution of grain and also issued allowances of pork, oil, and salt to the population. He attempted a rehabilitation of the imperial silver coinage on the basis of the sestertius instead of the denarius, which was hopelessly inflated, but the reform was not sufficiently far-reaching to be effective. Like so many of his predecessors, Aurelian fell victim to military conspiracy. Early in 275, while on his way to the East to deal with the Persian question, he was murdered by a group of his officers who had been falsely informed by his secretary—himself in danger of punishment—that they were going to be executed.

PROBUS, EMPEROR: A.D. 276–282. At the death of Aurelian the principate was bestowed upon Marcus Claudius Tacitus, an elderly senator, nominated by the Senate at the request of the army. Tacitus was killed by his troops after a war-filled rule of six months and was succeeded by his brother Florianus, who seized the *imperium*. He found a rival in Probus, the nominee of armies in Egypt and Syria. In less than three months Florianus was struck down by his own troops, and Probus was recognized as sole emperor. Marcus Aurelius Probus, like Aurelian, was Illyrian. Possessed of outstanding military and administrative qualities, he devoted himself unsparingly to completion of the work Aurelian had so well begun, by restoring order throughout the provinces and reestablishing military discipline. He cleared Gaul of Franks and Alamanni, who had resumed their incursions, and subdued the rebellious Isaurians in the mountains of Asia Minor. Everywhere he successfully upheld imperial authority, suppressing usurpers and holding foreign enemies in check. Not the least of his services was the reclamation of abandoned or hitherto un-exploited lands, which he accomplished in part by the settlement of many conquered barbarians within the Empire. In this he was motivated largely by a desire to assure adequate provisions for the military establishment. In many of his enterprises he also used the labor of his soldiers, and this demand upon their services in peace time, as well as his strict discipline, led to a mutiny which cost his life.

CARUS, CARINUS, AND NUMERIANUS: A.D. 282–285. Marcus Aurelius Carus, praetorian prefect under Probus, had been forced by his troops to accept their salutation of Imperator while Probus was still alive. Apparently a native of Narbonne in Gaul, he was a very able and energetic general. Upon his accession, he appointed his sons Carinus and Numerianus as Caesars. His chief exploit was a successful campaign against the Persians, which recovered upper Mesopotamia, and the capture of Ctesiphon. In the midst of his success he died mysteriously, probably a victim of the ambition of his praetorian prefect Aper (283). At his death Carinus and Numerianus were proclaimed Augusti. Carinus had been left in Rome to supervise the government of the West, where his cruelty made him detested. Numerianus had accompanied his father to the East. As the army was returning through Asia Minor, Aper had him assassinated. Instead of Aper, the army acclaimed as emperor Diocles, commander of the imperial bodyguard, who promptly put Aper to death (284). Carinus at once rallied the troops under his command and met the army of Diocles at the river Margus in Moesia. There the western soldiers prevailed, but Carinus was murdered by one of his own officers (285). His leaderless army accepted Diocles as their Imperator, who then adopted the name Diocletian. With the consolidation of imperial power in his hands a new period of Roman history began.

V. Christianity in Danger

PROBLEM OF THE CHRISTIANS. By about 250 the Christian Church was flourishing. With adherents in all classes and professions, it was nevertheless a religion that appealed mainly to the urban lower and middle classes, and it still had many more converts in the East than in the West. Its leaders were increasingly men of culture and ability, and, aban-doning the attitude of the early church toward the Kingdom of Heaven, Christians were taking an active part in society. The number of the Chris-tians was so great as to disquiet the government, since they were still traitors in the eyes of the law, in view of their attitude toward the cults of the state. Individual congregations were bound in a strong organization under the leadership of the bishops and seemed to form a state within the state. Christian spokesmen, while willing to give moral support to the Roman government, condemned the participation of believers in public office and military service, although in practice their admonitions were often disregarded. The Christians were generally looked upon as enemies within the gates, and the calamities of the time were often attributed to the anger of the gods at the toleration extended to them. These considerations help in understanding why, in their struggle against the forces threatening the dissolution of the Empire, a few of its rulers sought to stamp out Christianity to restore religious and political harmony and loyalty among their subjects.

Under Maximinus the Thracian, the Christians experienced a brief persecution explained by his conscious reversal of the policies of Severus Alexander. Maximinus seems to have directed his attack against the higher clergy as the ones responsible for propagation of Christian doctrines. He did not initiate a general persecution of the Church, and the effects of his hostility were mainly limited to Rome and Palestine. After the death of this emperor (238), the old policy of Trajan was resumed, and under the Emperor Philip in particular the Christians enjoyed general immunity. This respite was merely a lull before the storm.

PERSECUTION OF DECIUS: A.D. 250–251. Under the Emperor Decius, the successor of Philip, the first attempt was made to abolish Christianity throughout the Empire. In 250 Decius issued an edict ordering all the citizens of Italy and the provinces, according to their municipalities, to perform public acts of worship to the state gods. Those who refused were liable to the death penalty. This edict threatened the destruction of all the church communities, for it was directed against lay as well as clerical members. It also meant that Christians were to be sought out and revealed by compelling universal public registration for sacrifices. Many of the certificates of conformity granted to those who performed the sacrifices before the authorities have been found among the papyri recovered in Egypt. They are all of the same type, of which the following is an example. In the handwriting of a petitioner: "To the Superintendents of Sacrifices, from Aurelius Akis, from the village of Theoxenis, with his children Aion and Heras, all being of the village of Theadelphia. It was always our practice to sacrifice to the gods and now in your presence, in accordance with the regulations, we have sacrificed, have made libations, and have tasted the offerings, and we request you to certify this. Farewell," and in the handwriting of the Superintendent of Sacrifices: "We, Aurelius Serenus and Aurelius Hermas, saw you sacrificing."—"The first year of the Emperor Caesar Gaius Messius Quintus Traianus Decius, Pius, Felix, Augustus, Pauni 23rd."[1]

[1] P. Mich. III, 157.

PERSECUTION OF VALERIAN: 257–259. The persecution of Decius was terminated by his death in 251, but his policy was renewed by Valerian in 257. In that year Valerian required the Christians to sacrifice publicly, forbade their reunions, and closed their cemeteries. The next year he ordered the immediate trial of bishops, priests, and other officers and set penalties for the various grades of the clergy who persisted in their beliefs. Valerian's persecution also was brief, ending with his defeat and capture by the Persians in 259. Naturally, in so large a body as the Christians now were, not all were animated by the zeal and sincerity of the early brethren. Under threat of punishment many abjured or pretended to abjure their faith. Many others cheerfully suffered martyrdom and furthered the Christian cause by their example. Truly, "the blood of the martyrs was the seed of the church." The persecutions tried the church terribly, but it emerged triumphant from the ordeal.

Valerian's son Gallienus, who in many respects did not sympathize with his father's policies, permitted the Christians the use of their religious buildings and cemeteries and even issued an edict forbidding their further persecution. The church then enjoyed more than a generation of peaceful development.

VI. End of the Principate

PRINCEPS AND SENATE. In the period between 235 and 285 the Principate, as the form of government established by Augustus for Rome and the Empire, came to an end. Its termination was marked by the complete elimination of the Senate as a factor in government and as the authority that legally conferred the powers of the *princeps* upon a new emperor. An accompanying and closely related development was the exclusion of the senatorial order from military command and to a large extent from the civil administration of the provinces. These changes were the logical, perhaps the inevitable, outcome of trends that were manifest before the close of the Severan dynasty. They were effected gradually and were not the work of any one emperor. On certain occasions the Senate displayed much independence and initiative, but it did not command the armed forces, and any influence it exerted was only temporary. It recognized Gordian I and his son Gordian II as emperors while Maximinus was still alive and took over the defence of Italy for them. At their death it declared them Divi and appointed as their successors Balbinus and Pupienus, but it was unable to protect these latter against the praetorians, who murdered them and forced the Senate to accept their own choice, the infant Gordian III (238). Later, when the army called upon the Senate at the death of Aurelian to name the new *princeps*, it declined to take the responsibility and referred the decision back to the soldiers only to yield and make the appointment when they insisted. Although the Senate resented the actions of emperors like Gallienus and Aurelian, who deprived it of some of its remaining prerogatives or failed to respect its dignity, it could do nothing to protect its interests. If, as alleged, the senatorial order recovered some of its former privileges under Tacitus, it was too late for it to regain its earlier position, and what it gained by the good will of one emperor it lost as readily under his successor.

Until Carus, however, the emperors all recognized that their constitutional right to rule depended upon acceptance by the Senate and its conferment upon them of the *imperium* and other powers, honors, and titles. It did not matter whether the Senate took this action voluntarily or under pressure, but it had to be taken. When Carus was acclaimed emperor by the soldiers, he regarded himself as in full and legal possession of imperial authority by virtue of the action of the army alone, and he so informed the Senate. Diocletian followed his example in disregarding the Senate's traditional role in confirming an emperor, and henceforth it was admitted that the right to confer *imperium* had passed from the Senate to the army.

The Senate's loss of the right to make emperors found a counterpart in the increased emphasis laid upon the divinity of the imperial office. This doctrine found its clearest expression under Aurelian, who, besides being styled "god" on some of his coins, also appeared as the god Aurelian in contemporary inscriptions. The same idea was expressed when Hercules was called the "consort" of Aurelian. In harmony with this was Aurelian's adoption of the diadem, long the symbol of deified autocracy in the ancient world, and his declaration to his troops that not they but God alone decided the choice of an emperor and the length of his rule. Aurelian's example was generally followed by his successors, whose coins also bear the legend, "god and lord," besides showing at times the emperor and a god side by side as two divinities.

RISE OF THE EQUESTRIANS.   The exclusion of senators from a military career and from the command of the legions was effected by Gallienus, who believed that by this step he would secure more efficient officers among equestrians of military origin. Beginning with Hadrian, and especially under the Severans, both senatorial and equestrian officials had tended to specialize in either civil or military careers. With the Empire in a state of siege in the 250s, preference was given to men whose background and training were predominantly military. It was natural for Gallienus to favor the equestrians, who, unlike the senators, were mostly ex-soldiers. Even under Augustus the legions stationed in Egypt had been commanded by equestrian prefects, and this had also been true of the three new legions created by Septimius Severus. Following these precedents, all the legionary commanders now became equestrian prefects. Gallienus also replaced most of the senatorial legates who governed imperial provinces by equestrian officials who took the legates' title of *praesides*. He found a precedent in the practice of the early third century by which equestrians acted as temporary substitutes for senators in imperial and senatorial provinces. The successors of Gallienus continued his policy, although a few of the imperial provinces still retained governors of senatorial rank as late as the accession of Diocletian. It is uncertain to what extent equestrians supplanted proconsuls in the senatorial provinces, but it seems probable that they did so very often. A sign of the new spirit was the appointment of curators to administer different parts of Italy, a prelude to its division into provincial districts. Symbolic also of the rise of equestrians was the continued extension of the powers of the praetorian prefect. Although the judicial development of the office ceased with Philip, prefects were given control of the imposts in kind levied in support of the army (the military *annona*). They also acquired the right to issue general regulations, provided that these were in conformity with existing laws. In their military capacity they commanded all the troops stationed in Italy, and when they accompanied the emperors in the field they were the highest general officers. It is not surprising that the praetorian prefecture became in several instances a steppingstone to the principate. The militarization of the equestrian order, a process greatly accelerated under the Severi, became still more pronounced under Gallienus, who conferred equestrian rank at birth upon the sons of the legionary centurions and officers of subordinate rank.

MILITARY REFORMS. The failure of the system of frontier defences developed in the second century to check barbarian invasions caused a regrouping of the armed forces. This was essentially a return to the practice of the early Principate, when mobile forces of considerable strength were stationed at strategic points well back of the frontiers, ready to move rapidly against an enemy that broke through the border fortifications and garrisons. Units remaining on the frontiers increasingly assumed the character of militia troops, particularly since, owing to the increasing shortage of man-power, they were reinforced by many barbarian captives and sometimes client tribes given lands along the Limites upon condition of their supplying troops to defend them. Other significant changes, dictated by the changing character of warfare in the third century, occurred in the equipment and training of the legions. The need for greater mobility both on the march and on the field of battle led to the abandonment of the custom of constructing fortified camps at the end of each day's march, and also to replacement of the breastplate by a leather jacket, sometimes covered with metal scales, and of the heavy shield by a small, round buckler. Since the age-old weapons of the legionary, the javelin and the short straight sword, proved ineffective against the cavalry of the day, they were given up in favor of lances and the long sword used by the auxiliaries. Of far-reaching consequence was the gradual disappearance of the Romanized element in the officer class, whose place was taken by provincials of inferior culture and education. Under these conditions a marked decline resulted, not only in the knowledge of military traditions and organization among the lower officers but also of training and discipline among the rank and file. Until about 250, however, the legions constituted the élite troops in Roman service, and the legionary formation determined the Roman order of battle. Under Gallienus the Romans began to look upon cavalry as more important than infantry and developed a cavalry force, organized independently and able to take the field without support of the legions. This consisted of the already famous Moorish cavalry, the cavalry troops formerly attached to the legions, and new units recruited in Dalmatia. In equipping their cavalry, the Romans displayed traditional readiness to adapt to their own use their enemies' weapons. They had already used Osrhoënian and Palmyrene mounted archers armed with the powerful Asiatic laminated bow and to a lesser extent heavy-mailed lancers of the Persian type (*cataphractarii*). Many of the European cavalry regiments were now also organized as archers or heavy cavalry. The cavalry corps, which had its headquarters at Milan, was further strengthened by Aurelian, himself a great leader of horse, who increased the number of *cataphractarii*. The importance of the cavalry was shown by its being placed on a par with the praetorians, and from the date of its organization its commander rivalled, if he did not eclipse, the praetorian prefect. Both Claudius Gothicus and Aurelian advanced from the command of the cavalry directly to the principate.

An important stage in the barbarization of the army was the inclusion of German soldiers, not merely in irregular corps called *numeri* or as allies (*foederati*), but also in regular units of the auxiliaries. Following earlier precedents Aurelian enrolled new auxiliary corps recruited among the Vandals, Alamanni, and Juthungi. In this period also the term *dux* (duke) became a formal military title, used of generals commanding special corps like the field armies and the cavalry or forces grouped in particular areas not corresponding to older provincial commands.

ECONOMIC DECLINE. It was inevitable that foreign invasions and civil strife over so long a period should result in a disruption of agriculture, industry, and commerce. Apart from the destruction of property and the interruption of communication, movable wealth of all sorts was carried off as spoils of war by Persians and barbarians. There was also an increasingly acute shortage of agricultural and military manpower, although the causes and development of what was undoubtedly an absolute decline in numbers are difficult to describe, granted the almost complete lack of reliable statistics in surviving sources. Certainly the barbarian invasions and revolutions, and probably the plague that began in 251, contributed to the phenomenon. The peasant classes in particular, on whom the entire economy of the Empire finally rested, seem not to have reproduced themselves in sufficient numbers, since they had little sustenance left after they had paid taxes to support the numerous unproductive classes like the soldiers, urban proletariat, bureaucrats, and estate holders with their numerous retinues.

The confusion in finances is revealed in the complete collapse of the silver coinage. Under Gallienus the Antoninianus, then the standard silver coin, retained only 2 percent of its silver content; the rest was copper. This meant that the revenues of the state were completely inadequate to meet its outlays and that, since the production of the silver mines declined, its only recourse was to issue masses of debased coins with their old nominal value. The result was a tremendous rise in prices. In Egypt, a province for which we have considerable documentary evidence, the rise amounted to between fourteen and twenty times the original values. Faced with diminishing revenues because of general depopulation and impoverishment, the government became even more exacting than before in its demands for services and extraordinary contributions. The only means the imperial government had at its disposal to assure its own survival was the tightening up of controls and the increasing use of force, which meant an expansion of bureaucracy and the use of the military to enforce obedience. Such compulsion, by no means unknown earlier in the Principate and increasingly evident in the second and early third centuries, now became general. The associations of businessmen and tradesmen were forced into public service and put under stricter control, while municipal obligations pressed more and more heavily on propertied townspeople, who formed the middle class. From its ruin in the third century this class as a whole never recovered. The emperors were not unaware of the danger that threatened the state from increasing impoverishment, but they were unable to find a way out of the difficulties. Aurelian's attempt to rehabilitate the coinage was a step in the right direction, and this is also true of the efforts of Probus to establish new proprietors on vacant lands. The remedies adopted merely extended control of the state over the private citizen and his activities, so that both opportunity and incentive were gradually removed from the field of private enterprise.

LITERATURE AND ART. The political and economic disorder prevailing between 235 and 285 affected unfavorably both literary and artistic pursuits. Only a few had time or inclination to engage in literary activity, and among these writers of note were extremely rare. Latin authors were eclipsed by Greek, both in numbers and in quality. Among the latter was the historian Herodian, whose work has been mentioned already, and the Athenian Dexippus, famed for his defeat of Gothic raiders who plundered his native city in 267. Dexippus composed a *Universal History*, now lost, and a *History of the Scythians*, preserved only in fragments. The outstanding philosopher of the age was the Neoplatonist Egyptian Plotinus, a friend of the emperor Gallienus, who taught at Rome from about 253 to 270. With him Greek philosophy became definitely religious in character, resting upon revelation and belief, not upon reason. A Syrian Greek named

Cassius Longinus, like Plotinus a product of Alexandria, became a distinguished teacher of rhetoric and philosophy at Athens and a leading literary critic. At the invitation of Zenobia he left Athens for Palmyra, where he was one of the queen's trusted advisers, a position which cost him his life upon Aurelian's reconquest of the East (272).

Many of the bishops of the Christian Church were men of high education, distinguished as orators, theologians, and moralists. Outstanding among them was St. Cyprian, bishop of Carthage, a writer of real merit, who met a martyr's death in the persecution of Valerian (258).

Architecture in particular suffered from the prevailing poverty. Only the emperors were able to construct buildings of any size, and these were almost exclusively of a public character: amphitheaters, triumphal arches, public baths, or temples, in Rome and in the provinces. For the most part these followed traditional types, but some new contributions were made to the solution of the problem of vaulting in buildings of circular form. There were several interesting developments in styles of sculpture, as seen especially in portrait busts and in reliefs on sarcophagi. At mid-century there was a temporary reaction to a certain baroque fussiness apparent in official art produced during the Severan dynasty. The consequent reversion to a quieter, more classical style is generally referred to as the "Gallienic Renaissance." The reversion to classicism was only temporary, however, and throughout the third century there was an increasingly strong movement, originating in the East, toward an art whose canons were more abstract than those of the Greco-Roman tradition.

The third century, the age of the great persecutions, was also the age of the greatest expansion of the Catacombs near Rome, the secret burial places of the Christians. There were many of them, each a complicated underground network of narrow passages lined with niches for the dead. Here and there the passages widened into chambers, which served as the tombs of distinguished persons or whole families. Mural paintings, stucco reliefs, and inscriptions constituted the decoration. In execution, they show the technical skill of the trained workmen of the period; in subject matter, they continued to draw their inspiration from the Scriptures and to make use of the conventional figures and symbols of earlier Christian art.

PART

IV

AUTOCRACY OR LATE EMPIRE: A.D. 285–565

THE EMPIRE STANDS
UNITED: A.D. 285-395

The political history of the Roman Empire from 285 to 565 falls into three main periods. During the first of these, from 285 to 395, the Empire remained united and able to maintain its integrity against barbarians from without and rebellion from within. During the second period, from 395 to 518, the Empire split into a Roman Empire in the East and a Roman Empire in the West; the latter gradually crumbled and gave way to a number of Germanic kingdoms, while the former succeeded in surviving the forces of disintegration, eventually as the Byzantine Empire. The third period, from 518 to 565, is characterized by the attempt, only partially successful, made by the East to reestablish imperial authority in the lost western lands and so preserve the ideal of a universal Roman Empire. Although the second and third periods will be treated in later chapters, it will be convenient to survey here our principal sources for the whole epoch.

For the fourth century the most valuable sources are the surviving books, 14 to 31, of the history of Ammianus Marcellinus, which give a detailed account of the years 353 to 378. This is paralleled and supplemented by the *New History* of Zosimus, covering the period from 270 to 410. There are also the brief manuals referred to in preceding chapters. Sextus Aurelius Victor's *Caesars*, a series of short lives of the emperors from Augustus to 360; the so-called *Epitome of the Caesars*, which runs to 395; Eutropius' *Breviary* of Roman History to 364; and the work of Paulus Orosius entitled *Against the Pagans*, ending with 417. For most of the fifth century, however, there exists no important historical literature. The events of Justinian's reign, however, are recorded in the noteworthy *History* of Procopius, whose work, ending with 554, emphasizes the Vandal, Gothic, and Persian Wars. Procopius has left a valuable account of Justinian's building activities. A continuation of Procopius is to be found in Agathias' *On the Reign of Justinian*, in which he narrates the events of the years 552 to 558. The gaps in the narrative history are partially filled by various chronicles of the fourth, fifth, sixth, and later centuries. Of these, one of the most important is the Greek chronicle of Eusebius, which ran to 325 and is partly preserved in the Latin version of St. Jerome, who brought it down to 378. This chronicle was continued by others in both Latin and Greek until nearly 600. Another valuable work of similar kind is the Greek *Pascal Chronicle*, a chronological record from the creation of the world to 629.

Among the more specialized historical works are the various Church Histories by Eusebius and others and the already mentioned tract of Lactantius, *On the Death of the Persecutors*. Useful also are the histories of the Goths, Franks, and other Germanic peoples written by Romans or others who carried on the traditions of Roman culture in lands lost to the barbarians. There is also a wealth of material in contemporary nonhistorical writings of churchmen, panegyrics addressed to the emperors, collections of speeches and letters, and other forms of literature. Invaluable source material is also presented in the compilations of imperial constitutions, the *Theodosian Code* of 438; its supplement the *Novellae* or "New Constitutions" dating between 438 and 472; and the *Code* of Justinian of 534, together with his *Novellae*. These collections are paralleled by those compiled at the orders of Visigothic and Burgundian kings for their Roman subjects. A document of prime importance for the administrative organization of the Late Empire is the *Notitia Dignitatum* of the early fifth century. This is an official list of the chief civil and military officials with their departmental staffs and in some cases the spheres of their competence. Inscriptions, although not very numerous, with coins and archaeological remains, supplement literary sources. For Egypt, papyrus documents continue to throw light upon all aspects of the life of that province.

I. Diocletian and the Tetrarchy: A.D. 285–305

DIOCLETIAN'S IMPERIAL POLICY.   When Diocletian became sole emperor in 285, he was in advanced middle age. By birth a Dalmatian, he had had a distinguished military career. He was dominant, courageous and strong-willed. Lacking in statesmanlike imagination and breadth of vision, Diocletian proceeded cautiously but with determination in effecting significant reforms. Like preceding Illyrian emperors, he saw as his prime obligation the preservation of the Empire as the home of civilization, and he sought to defend it against external attack and internal disorder. In his attempt to realize this goal, in spite of a decline in manpower and in economic prosperity, lies the clue to all of his important innovations. Foremost among them were an exaltation of imperial authority and a strengthening of the military forces. The autocratic tendencies that had grown ever stronger during the late Principate became completely triumphant with Diocletian. Acclaimed by the army, he considered confirmation of its action by the Senate as superfluous. Even his selection by the soldiers he regarded as an expression of the will of Jupiter, and in this way claimed divine sanction for his authority. The army could not be ignored, however, and its support remained an essential base of imperial power.

AGAINST REVOLTS AND INVASIONS.   In 286 Diocletian was faced by a serious rebellion in Gaul, where the peasants, impoverished by barbarian invasions and heavy taxation, had abandoned their fields. These dispossessed, known as Bagaudae, were terrorizing the countryside in formidable armed bands. To restore order in Gaul and rebuild the Rhineland defences, Diocletian dispatched one of his trusted officers, a Pannonian named Valerius Maximianus, whom he raised to the rank of junior colleague as Caesar and Son of Augustus (*filius Augusti*). Maximian easily suppressed the Bagaudae. He then strengthened the Rhine frontier, which in the years 286 to 288 he successfully defended against attacks by Franks, Alamanni, and Burgundians. In 286 a more serious rebellion occurred. Carausius, an able officer entrusted with the protection of the coasts of the North Sea and English Channel against piratical raids, occupied Britain and proclaimed himself Augustus. Diocletian then elevated Maximian from Caesar to Augustus. Owing to the loss of his fleet in a storm, Maximian failed to recover Britain and depose Carausius. This forced the two emperors to come to terms with the usurper and recognize his authority in the area actually under his control (290). Carausius claimed the status of Augustus equal to Diocletian and Maximian. His control of the chief Gallic channel port, Gesoriacum (Boulogne), and his alliance with barbarian tribes across the Rhine threatened Gaul, so Diocletian decided to attack again and entrusted the military operations to Flavius Valerius Constantius, a tried Illyrian officer whom he made a Caesar early in 293. Constantius captured Gesoriacum and then defeated the barbarian allies of Carausius, many of whom he transplanted to till the vacant lands of Gaul and furnish recruits for Roman armies, and Carausius was murdered by one of his own officials. In 296 the forces of Constantius landed in Britain, and the island was reunited to the Empire. This victory gave the Romans mastery of the seas off Britain and Gaul and enabled them to check Frankish pirates who had been raiding the coasts of Spain and North Africa. Serious disturbances in the North African provinces were then suppressed by Maximian (297).

The eastern parts of the Empire were being threatened at the same time by barbarian tribes along the Danube, by the Persians on the Asiatic frontier, and by raids of the Blemmyes into upper Egypt. On the Danube, Gaius Galerius, another Caesar who received this title in 293, severely defeated the Iazyges and Carpi with Diocletian's support and improved the system of defence. Captured barbarians were settled in great numbers in the Danubian provinces. In 296 a rebellion broke out in Egypt under a usurper named Domitianus as the result of heavy taxation and inflation. The rebels were no match for the imperial troops. Diocletian blockaded Domitianus in Alexandria, which he took in March 297, thus ending the revolt. To hold the Blemmyes in check, Diocletian gave up some border territory south of the First Cataract of the Nile, settling it with an allied tribe. The revolt in Egypt appeared all the more serious in view of the hostility of Narses, King of Persia, who launched an offensive in 297, overrunning the Roman protectorate of Armenia and defeating the Caesar

Galerius. Later in the year Galerius beat him decisively, and he was obliged to accept peace on Roman terms (298). Rome recovered her province in Upper Mesopotamia; the Roman nominee in Armenia regained the throne; and some border districts north of the Tigris became a Roman protectorate. All along the eastern frontier new military installations were constructed.

THE TETRARCHY. Diocletian had no male heir, and the experience of his predecessors had taught him the danger of entrusting serious military operations to a potential rival. For this reason, when confronted by military necessity, he appointed Maximian as his colleague, first as Caesar and then as Augustus. Military necessity again forced him to appoint two new Caesars, Constantius and Galerius, in 293. In this way a Tetrarchy, or rule of four, was created; "four princes of the world," as a later writer called them. To bind them more closely to each other, Diocletian gave his daughter in marriage to Galerius, while Constantius married the daughter of Maximian. Diocletian extended the claim to divine support for his authority to his colleagues. He himself assumed the title of Jovius, indicative of his being the choice of Jupiter, and he bestowed on Maximian that of Herculius, since Hercules appeared in mythology as the helper of Jupiter. When the two Caesars were appointed, Constantius became a Herculius, and Galerius a Jovius. Neither Diocletian nor his associates proclaimed themselves gods, but they did claim divine sanction and inspiration in exercising of imperial power. From this point of view, any opposition to their ordinances amounted to defiance of divine will.

The Tetrarchy was held together by the dominance of Diocletian over his colleagues, which was based on his seniority and his strength of personality. It was he who formulated and directed imperial policy in all fields. Correspondingly, there was no fourfold administrative division of the Empire, although the armed forces were divided into four great commands, each under an Augustus or a Caesar. Each of the four rulers selected as residence a city strategically placed with respect to the frontiers under his particular supervision. Diocletian chose Nicomedia in Asia Minor, on the Sea of Marmora, well adapted for directing the defence of Egypt, the Asian provinces, and Thrace. Galerius, whose forces guarded the Danubian frontier, took up his quarters in Sirmium on the lower Save; Maximian established himself at Milan, in command of Raetia, Italy, North Africa, and Spain; and Constantius, to whom fell Gaul and Britain, resided at Trèves (Augusta Treverorum) in northern Gaul. Rome accordingly ceased to be the imperial residence and administrative capital of the Empire, a change that reflected the decline in the importance of the Senate. The Eternal City continued to enjoy a privileged status, however, and its citizens were still fed and amused by the state.

Implicit in the organization of the Tetrarchy was the idea that ultimately the two Caesars should succeed the two Augusti as senior rulers and should in turn appoint successors. There is no evidence that Diocletian set any number of years as the term during which the Augusti should hold office, or that he decided any long time in advance upon the date of the transfer of authority.

DIOCLETIAN'S REFORMS. Diocletian's reforms profoundly affected nearly all branches of government. Many of them will be discussed in the following chapter, but it will be convenient to indicate here something of their scope and character. In strengthening the system of imperial defence, Diocletian increased considerably the size of the army, which consisted of an expanded frontier guard and the nucleus of a mobile reserve in attendance at the emperor's court. Since Roman subjects could not furnish all of the new units, many recruits were barbarian captives or volunteers. Frontier provinces were divided into smaller units, largely in order to provide closer supervision of border garrisons and weaken the power of commanders. The provinces were grouped into new administrative districts called *dioceses*. These changes greatly increased the number of civilian and military personnel in the service of the state. Mistrustful of his own bureaucracy, Diocletian reorganized the imperial secret service (*frumentarii*), now called the *agentes in rebus*, and used it to inform on governmental operations.

The resulting increase in expenses, coupled with the economic decline of the third century and the inadequacy of the old taxes, led Diocletian to establish a new and in general uniform system of taxation for all the Empire. Realizing that economic instability was due in part to the great depreciation of the coinage, he attempted to introduce a new, stable gold and silver currency. His devaluation of the copper coins then in circulation unfortunately resulted in widespread inflation, accentuated by shortages in production. This situation created hardships for soldiers and bureaucrats, and led Diocletian to try to control prices by law. His Edict of Prices of 301 fixed a uniform price for each commodity and every form of labor or professional service for the Empire. Death was the penalty for all who demanded or offered more than the legal price. This law took no account of the variations of supply and demand in various parts of the Empire and made no distinction between wholesale and retail trade or between good and poor workmanship. In spite of the severe penalty prescribed, the law was disregarded so generally that the government gave up its enforcement. The prices fixed by the Edict continued for many years, however, to serve as the government standard for buying or assigning a monetary value to taxes collected in kind.

PERSECUTION OF CHRISTIANS: A.D. 303. Diocletian's reputation has suffered from his responsibility for initiating the last great persecution of the Christians. They had enjoyed immunity from repressive legislation for nearly half a century after Valerian's death. They had also increased greatly in number, including at this time perhaps as much as one tenth of the population. They were prominent in all walks of life, including government service. The organization of the Church had been strengthened greatly, until it constituted a veritable "state within a state." Owing to the emphasis Diocletian placed upon the divine sanction of imperial power and upon worship of the state gods, a conflict between the state and the Christians was almost inevitable. It was only after nearly twenty years of rule, however, that Diocletian decided to make the Christians conform to the state religion. His reasons for doing so are not clear. He may have come to regard them as a potentially disloyal element or his pagan susceptibilities may have been offended by acts of certain Christians. Christian tradition ascribes his decision to the pressure of Galerius, the most superstitious and ruthless member of the Tetrarchy, but while the Caesar's attitude is clear, he was not the leader in determining the new policy. An indication of Diocletian's attitude toward a cult he considered a menace to religious and political unity is to be found in his edict of 297 against the Manicheans, followers of the third century prophet Mani. They not only rejected Roman paganism but were suspected of being political agents of Persia.

The first of Diocletian's three edicts against the Christians was issued early in 303. It called for destruction of Christian churches and Christian books. The second and third edicts ordered, respectively, that Christian clergy of all ranks be imprisoned and that they be compelled to sacrifice to the state gods. A fourth edict prescribed in 304 that all persons make the customary sacrifices upon pain of death. These edicts were not enforced everywhere with equal vigor. Constantius, in whose sphere the Christians were relatively few, contented himself with carrying out the first edict only, whereas Maximian and Galerius were zealous persecutors. The persecution was still in progress when Diocletian's reign ended in 305.

ABDICATION OF DIOCLETIAN AND MAXIMIAN: A.D. 305. At the celebration of the twentieth anniversary of his accession, in Rome in 303, Diocletian seems to have induced Maximian to abdicate with him. While returning to the East early in the next year, the senior Augustus became seriously ill, perhaps suffered a stroke, and for some months was unable to perform his duties. Upon his recovery he determined to abdicate on May 1, 305, and forced Maximian to divest himself of his authority at the same time. Constantius and Galerius became the new Augusti. In the appointment of the new Caesars, the sons of Maximian and Constantius were passed over, and the choice fell on Severus and Maximin Daia, both favorites of Galerius. Diocletian retired to his magnificent palace near Salonae in Dalmatia, and Maximian, much against his will, to his estate in Lucania.

*II. Collapse of the Tetrarchy and the Reign of
Constantine I, the Great: A.D. 305–337*

COLLAPSE OF THE TETRARCHY: A.D. 305–310. Diocletian's tetrarchic system did not long survive his abdication. Lacking the forceful and unifying leadership of its organizer, it was wrecked by dynastic loyalty and personal ambition. When the Emperor Constantius died in Britain in 306, his army at once acclaimed his son Constantine, then twenty-one years old, as Augustus. This Galerius refused to accept, but, while he advanced the Caesar Severus to the rank of Augustus, he acknowledged Constantine as Caesar, in order to avoid civil war. Almost immediately another claimant to imperial power arose. This was Maxentius, son of Maximian, who capitalized on the discontent in Rome and Italy over new taxes imposed by Severus and his dissolution of the Praetorian Guard to have himself proclaimed *princeps*, in the hope of being made Caesar. Galerius refused him recognition and ordered Severus to depose him. Thereupon Maximian came out of retirement to support his son and soon resumed his old title Augustus. Approaching Rome, Severus was deserted by his troops and surrendered to Maximian, who put him to death (summer, 307). Maxentius then declared himself Augustus.

Galerius prepared to intervene in the West; Maximian tried to strengthen his position by an alliance with Constantine, whom he named Augustus and to whom he gave his daughter, Fausta, in marriage (307). Constantine in return recognized him as Augustus. Galerius failed in his invasion of Italy, owing to the disloyalty of his soldiers, and called upon Diocletian to return to power. This the old emperor refused, although he did meet Galerius and Maximian at Carnuntum (308). There Maximian was induced to abdicate again. Licinius, a protege of Galerius, was made junior Augustus, and Maxentius was treated as an outlaw. The response of Maximin Daia and Constantine was to demand from Galerius the title of Augustus, but they only received that of Son of Augustus (*filius Augusti*), which Constantine never accepted and Maximin soon ignored. Maximian, who had quarreled earlier with his son Maxentius and failed in an attempt to depose him, now took refuge with Constantine and appeared once more as an Augustus. Maximian soon engaged in an intrigue against his son-in-law, which led to the former's execution. At the close of 310 five Augusti, including Maxentius, ruled the Empire.

EDICT OF TOLERATION: A.D. 311.   The persecution of the Christians initiated by Diocletian had not produced the desired result. Many leading Christians suffered martyrdom, far more suffered mutilation or were sentenced to prison or the mines; many had yielded and met the formal requirements of pagan sacrifice; many churches were destroyed, but the majority of the Christian community held steadfastly to their faith. The truth was that persecution did not have the solid backing of the pagan population. Civilians and officials alike connived to protect their Christian neighbors from the laws. Persecution slackened or ceased, except where it was stimulated by fresh edicts, as in the sphere of Maximin Daia. Finally in 311, Galerius, then mortally ill, issued an edict as senior Augustus that gave Christians the right to practice their religion and rebuild their churches, provided that they not offend public order. For the first time since Nero's persecution a man could be both a loyal Roman and a good Christian.

CONSTANTINE CONQUERS MAXENTIUS: A.D. 312. With the death of Galerius the remaining Augusti became rivals rather than colleagues. Constantine sought possession of Italy as the next step in winning the whole Empire. He allied himself with Licinius, who anticipated trouble with Daia, and declared war on Maxentius, invading Italy early in 312. He defeated his rival's forces in north Italy and pressed on to Rome. Maxentius, relying on Roman gods, risked a battle not far from the Milvian bridge across the Tiber. There his army was completely defeated, and he, with many of his troops, was drowned in the rout. Just before this battle Constantine, as the result of a vision, ordered his soldiers to mark their shields with a monogram resembling a combination of chi and rho, the first two letters of the Greek word *Christos*, meaning Christ. It was an appeal to the God of the Christians, and Constantine regarded his victory as the answer to this appeal. With the death of Maxentius not only Rome and Italy but also Spain and North Africa fell into Constantine's hands. The Senate declared him to be senior Augustus. In Rome, he disbanded the *equites singulares* and the praetorian guard and dismantled their barracks.

CONSTANTINE AND LICINIUS: A.D. 312–324. Early in 313, Constantine and Licinius met at Milan and agreed to grant Christians unrestricted freedom of worship and to restore confiscated properties to the respective church communities. The alliance between the two emperors was cemented by the marriage of Constantine's daughter to Licinius, but the latter got no share of the territories of Maxentius and was left to expand his own part of the Empire at the expense of Daia. Endangered, Daia took the offensive, crossed the Bosporus, and marched against Licinius. The latter defeated him, pursued him into Asia Minor, and when Daia fell ill and died, annexed all of the Roman East (autumn, 313). Letters that Licinius wrote to the governors of his newly subdued provinces explain the policy toward the Christians formulated at Milan, which does not seem to have been expressed in any general edict.

Elimination of Daia brought out the latent rivalry between Constantine and Licinius, widely different men. Constantine sought to create a buffer out of territories to be ceded by each of them to a Caesar, but Licinius tried to instigate an army revolt against Constantine, and this led to war. Military operations were inconclusive, although Constantine had the advantage and Licinius ceded to him all his European territories except Thrace, while Constantine gave up his right as senior Augustus to legislate for all the Empire. In 317 the two emperors jointly recognized as Caesars and their future successors Crispus and Constantine, the elder sons of Constantine, and Licinianus, son of Licinius. Harmony did not long prevail, and growing tension was reflected in the religious policy of the rivals. While Constantine granted ever greater privileges and advantages to the

Christians, Licinius gradually reversed his toleration and initiated repressive measures. It became obvious that Constantine aimed at being sole emperor, while Licinius sought a definite partition of the Empire. Finally in 323 Constantine, pursuing a band of Gothic raiders, led his army into Thrace, and Licinius' resentment of this trespass led to war. In 324 Constantine routed Licinius at Adrianople, and Crispus destroyed his fleet in the Hellespont. Licinius withdrew to Asia Minor where in the same year he suffered a final defeat at Chrysopolis. He surrendered to Constantine, who at first spared his life but not long after executed him for fresh intrigues. Constantine thus reigned alone over a united Empire.

FOUNDING OF CONSTANTINOPLE: A.D. 324–330. One of the early decisions of Constantine as sole emperor was to establish a new residence, Constantinople, on the site of Byzantium, the Greek city situated where the Bosporus joins the sea of Marmora. The choice of this site was determined by its strategic importance with reference to the Persian and Danubian frontiers and its command of the crossing from Europe to Asia Minor and of the exit from the Black Sea to the Mediterranean. Before long the site began to prove equally advantageous for the growth of a world market. Construction was begun as early as 324, but the city plan evolved slowly, and it was not until 330 that formal dedication of the new imperial residence was celebrated. In retrospect, the foundation of Constantinople appears as one of the more epochal of Constantine's innovations, but he could not have foreseen the effects that the fateful and eventually permanent shift eastward of the administrative center of gravity would entail, or that his city would become the nerve center of a new world. Constantinople was a second Rome, not a new one. Upon his death he did not even designate it as the residence of his eldest son, but rather assigned it to the least important of his successors. Old Rome on the Tiber kept its first rank among cities, even though it was not Constantine's home. He certainly did not intend it to be a new, exclusively Christian residence symbolizing a break with the pagan past associated with Rome in the West. Although predominantly Christian from the very beginning, Constantinople contained pagan temples, administrators, and philosophers. It was given many of the institutions and appurtenances characteristic of an imperial city on the model of old Rome. These included a Senate, a palace, public buildings, *objets d'art* ransacked from other cities, even traditional Roman festivals and distribution of free grain to the populace.

CONSTANTINE, THE CHRISTIAN EMPEROR. By birth and early training Constantine was a pagan. His father, Constantius, was a devotee of the Sun God, and Constantine, who followed his monotheistic example, accepted at first Hercules and later the Sun God as his protective deity. His mother Helena, in later life a zealous Christian, does not appear to have adopted Christianity before her son. Constantius was tolerant toward Christians, and prior to his march on Rome in 312, Constantine must have been fairly well acquainted with the doctrines and organization

Basilica of Constantine at Treves

of the Church in his dominions. It is clear that on the eve of the final encounter with Maxentius he placed both himself and his army under the protection of the Christian God and that he was convinced that his victory then and his later success in winning the Empire were due to the power and favor of this divinity. After 312 he looked upon himself as designated by God to rule the Roman World. In return for this divine recognition, he felt obliged to promote Christianity in all possible ways. This meant that Christianity must receive official recognition as a state religion and that it must eventually become the only state religion, for Christians could recognize no other gods. Thus Constantine must have seen in Christianity the only religion that could and should provide a spiritual bond among his subjects, as well as a moral basis for political loyalty to himself as the elect of God. It is true that as late as 324 Constantine's coins bore non-Christian devices and legends, that he tolerated the imperial cult and other pagan practices, and continued to bear the title Pontifex Maximus, but this attitude is largely a tribute to his political astuteness. Even up to the time of his death, a majority of his officials, soldiers, and civilian subjects were still pagans. He realized his need of their support and could not afford to antagonize them by forcing them to abandon abruptly the ideas and symbols of the past. When he declared Sunday a general holiday, in 321, he had in mind both Christians and pagans, for while the former celebrated it as "the Lord's Day," the latter could regard it as the "day of the Sun-god." In calling himself "the bishop of those without" he may have regarded himself as responsible for the conversion of the pagan elements, by direct and indirect pressure, although he did not interfere with private, and in some cases public, practice of pagan rites.

Symbolic of Constantine's acceptance of Christianity was his adoption in 317 of a new spiritual standard, the Labarum. This was a long-handled cross, having at the upper end a gold wreath enclosing the monogram chi-rho, below which, from the crossbar, hung a square silk cloth with the likenesses of Constantine and his two sons, the Caesars. Constantine only received Christian baptism on his deathbed. At that time this was not uncommon, and, in spite of his declared Christianity, it may well be that the emperor, conscious of the wrongs his violent temper had led him to commit, doubted his ability fully to measure up to the ethical standards that baptism implied. Following the example of pagan emperors, Constantine assumed responsibility for the religious welfare of the state. Having decided to favor Christianity, he also felt obligated to take the initiative in ensuring the unity of the Christian community. This decision had far-reaching consequences and raised in a new form the problem of relations between church and state.

CONSTANTINE'S IMPERIAL POLICY. In many respects Constantine's imperial policy followed that of Diocletian, whose ideas he developed and perfected. A convinced autocrat, he based his claim to rule upon hereditary right, confirmed by divine sanction, a claim Christians as well as pagans could accept. As the outward symbol of his authority, he assumed in 325 the diadem, a narrow band around the head which had been the accepted emblem of autocratic power for both Persian and Hellenistic kings. He completed the separation of military and civil authority by depriving the praetorian prefects of the right of command, and by abrogating the authority of provincial governors over commanders of border garrisons. Whereas Diocletian had greatly increased the strength of the frontier forces, Constantine weakened them by transferring many of their units to an enlarged mobile field army strategically stationed well back of the frontiers. The place of the prefects as general officers was taken by newly created masters of horse and masters of foot. In recruiting soldiers Constantine displayed a strong partiality for barbarians and opened even the higher commands to barbarian officers. He continued the policy of transplanting tribes of barbarians into depopulated areas of the Empire, under perpetual obligation to furnish recruits for the army. For administrative purposes Constantine divided the Empire into four prefectures, each under a resident praetorian prefect. He also created new ministers of state called counts (*comes* or Companion), who formed a new council of state.

Constantine's expansion of the bureaucracy and the army, the building of Constantinople, the erection of many new and magnificent churches, and state support for the Christian clergy materially increased government expenditures and necessitated increased revenues. These were met by the imposition of new and burdensome taxes. To help ensure their payment and to provide manpower for the maintenance of public services and essential economic activities, Constantine made full use of his autocratic power to develop a totalitarian regime, for which the foundations had been laid by earlier emperors. He regimented the activities of practically all classes of the population, which were divided into hereditary occupations. Constantine continued Diocletian's attempt to stabilize the coinage by issuing a standard gold coin equal to one seventy-second of a pound of gold, with coins of silver and copper of smaller denominations. Metal needed to strike the new issue seems to have come from the confiscated treasures of pagan temples, but not enough coins could be issued to supply demand. Payment of salaries in allowances continued, and shortages of silver and copper led the state to debase coinage, with consequent and costly inflation. Constantine devoted great attention to justice. By directives issued to judges he sought to secure greater protection for the poor, the weak, and the defenseless. Christian, Stoic, and Hellenistic Greek influences can be traced in his legislation. He forbade crucifixions and branding on the face because of resemblance of the face to heavenly beauty, humanely ordered that prisoners should be taken out of doors each day, but at the same time he prescribed excessively cruel punishments for various offences. Under Christian influences he annulled the long-standing disabilities imposed upon bachelors.

CONSTANTINE AND HIS CAESARS. Like Diocletian, Constantine realized the necessity of having partners in imperial power, but his own experience and inclination led him to choose associates as soon as possible from his own household. Following Crispus and Constantine the younger, his younger sons Constantius and Constans were made Caesars in 323 and 333 respectively. A possible rival was removed by the brutal murder of young Licinianus. In 326 Constantine executed his oldest son Crispus, and in the same year his wife Fausta, the mother of his three younger sons, both allegedly on charges of adultery. By 335 the remaining three Caesars had been entrusted with the government of major portions of the Empire. Constantine the Younger had Britain, Gaul and Spain; Constans was in charge of Italy, Africa, and Pannonia; to Constantine fell Asia and Egypt. One of Constantine's nephews, Dalmatius, was appointed a fourth Caesar, with the intention that he should govern the dioceses of Thrace and Macedonia. Another, Annibalianus, was designated as future ruler of Pontus and Armenia with the title of King of Kings.

CONSTANTINE'S ACHIEVEMENT. Constantine died in May, 337. His had been an epoch-making reign. Although deficient in formal education and lacking in administrative training, his tremendous energy and force of character led him to sole dominion over the Roman World. He was a great military genius and leader of men. Unquestionably his greatest achievement was initiating the process of transforming the Roman Empire from a pagan to a Christian state, a process that, but for him, might have been delayed indefinitely. Quite properly Christian historians honored him with the title of "the Great," and the Eastern Orthodox Churches have made him a saint and hailed him as an "equal of the Apostles." Actively participating in all phases of imperial government, Constantine completed the work of Diocletian, giving to the autocracy, bureaucracy, army, and hereditary class system the forms they preserved with few changes until the collapse of the Empire in the West and the transition to the Byzantine Empire in the East. It cannot be denied, however, that many of his policies hastened rather than delayed the disintegration, which he strove so hard and so conscientiously to arrest.

III. Dynasty of Constantine the Great: A.D. 337–363

THREE EMPERORS, CONSTANTINE II, CONSTANTIUS, AND CONSTANS: A.D. 337–340. Constantine the Great's plan for succession was thwarted by the troops at Constantinople. Allegedly instigated by Constantius, they refused to accept any other rulers than the sons of the deceased emperor and put to death his other male relatives, with the exception of two young nephews, Gallus and Julian. The three brothers then assumed the title Augusti and divided the Empire. Constantine II, the elder, whose seniority was recognized by the others, retained the West, and Constantius accepted the East with the addition of Thrace. To Constans, the youngest, were assigned the central dioceses—Africa, Italy, and Illyricum—apparently under the supervision of Constantine II. Constans soon grew weary of playing a subordinate role. He asserted his right to legislate independently of his brother, who then invaded Italy in 340. Constans met and defeated him at Aquileia. Constantine II was killed in the battle, and Constans took over the western dioceses.

RULE OF CONSTANTIUS AND CONSTANS. Constantius acquiesced in the extension of his younger brother's sphere. He himself, from 338 onward, was engaged in a continuous but indecisive war with Sapor II of Persia, who sought to reestablish Persian control over Armenia and Upper Mesopotamia. Constans was energetic in defending the Rhine and British frontiers against the barbarians and in restoring discipline among his soldiers. His strictness made him unpopular with the army, and his reputation for drunkenness and other vices added to his disfavor. A conspiracy among his civil and military officials capitalizing on widespread discontent among the lower classes, who were suffering because of the inflation of small change in everyday use, led to the recognition of a barbarian officer, Magnentius, as Augustus. Constans was executed and Magnentius was recognized in all of the territory of Constans except Illyricum, where the master of foot, Vetranio, was saluted as emperor (350). A cessation of the Persian offensive enabled Constantius to return to Europe to face the usurpers. Vetranio, who had been encouraged to assume the purple by Constantius' sister in order to save Illyricum from Magnentius, abdicated at a meeting with the eastern Augustus. He was allowed to retire on a state pension, while his army joined Constantius. Magnentius failed to obtain recognition from Constantius, and he invaded Illyricum, although the forces of his opponent were twice as large as his own. After some initial successes he was soundly beaten in a battle at Mursa, which was won by the mail-clad cavalry of Constantius (351). Magnentius escaped to northern Italy, where Constantius followed him the next year, meanwhile using his control of the sea to recover Africa, peninsular Italy, and Spain. Magnentius then withdrew to Gaul and, after another defeat, committed suicide to avoid being surrendered to the victor by his own soldiers.

CONSTANTIUS SOLE AUGUSTUS: A.D. 353–360. In the course of his campaign against Magnentius, Constantius had appointed as Caesar his elder cousin Gallus, who had been spared in the massacre of 337, married him to his sister Constantia, and sent him to guard the eastern frontier (351). Gallus proved unworthy, cruel and licentious. His execution of officials sent by the emperor to recall him convinced Constantius that he must be removed, and the death of Constantia deprived him of her influential support. Gallus was induced to return to Europe, where he was arrested, condemned to death, and beheaded (354). Constantius himself was occupied in repelling barbarian threats along the Rhine and the Danube. A brief revolt of a Frankish general, Silvanus, in Gaul was due to a false accusation of treason brought against him by a rival. The death of Silvanus was followed by a disastrous invasion of the Rhineland by Franks and Alamanni, and made the emperor realize the need of having a loyal colleague in the imperial power. On the advice of the empress Eudoxia, Constantius summoned to Milan his younger and sole surviving cousin, Julian, from his studies in Athens and appointed him Caesar, to the acclamation of his troops. Julian was married to Helena, the daughter of Constantius, and then dispatched to Gaul (355). He lacked military authority, but, owing to the incompetence of the commanding general, Julian was given the command in 357. In that year he defeated an invading force of Alamanni near Strassburg, pursued them across the Rhine, and recovered many prisoners. During the next two summers he conducted successful campaigns in barbarian territory and restored the Rhine defenses. The Salian Franks, who earlier had settled south of the lower Rhine, were confirmed in their territory as Roman allies.

JULIAN'S USURPATION AND DEATH OF CONSTANTIUS: A.D. 360–361. In 359 Sapor II, having defeated the Asiatic peoples who disturbed his northern frontier, invaded Roman Mesopotamia and destroyed the important city of Amida. The situation called for the presence of Constantius, who set out for the East early in 360. On the way he received the news that Julian had been saluted as Augustus by his army in Gaul, but he proceeded to the front where Sapor was continuing his offensive. Julian's usurpation was the direct result of Constantius' ordering him to dispatch many of his best troops for service in the East. For this the Persian menace was a valid excuse, but the real reason was a desire to undermine Julian's position, and possibly to do away with him. From the beginning Constantius had surrounded Julian with spies and sought to hamper his activities. When he gained remarkable military success in spite of them, and showed himself honest and capable, popular both with the army and the civilians, Constantius decided upon more direct action. Under protest, Julian was prepared to carry out the orders of Constantius to send troops to the East, but some of his supporters persuaded the soldiers, who were reluctant to leave Gaul, to refuse to march. Julian sought to check the mutiny, but the troops saluted him as Augustus and he yielded to their acclaim (360). In 361, when he learned that Constantius refused to recognize him and was preparing to attack, Julian took the initiative and marched on Constantinople. Constantius was on his way from the East to meet him when he died at Tarsus, naming Julian as his successor. Julian ruled alone.

POLICY OF CONSTANTIUS. Like his brothers, Constantius grew up a Christian, but he was an Arian. He zealously sought to stamp out paganism and used his authority to bring about doctrinal unity within the

Church. Of mediocre ability, undistinguished as a general, and unduly influenced by his palace officials and attendants, he nevertheless worked hard and conscientiously in the service of the state. Although he enlarged the civil service, strengthened the secret police, and maintained a luxurious court, he seems to have been aware of the dangers inherent in a corrupt bureaucracy, and toward the end of his reign he tried by legislation to correct the most flagrant governmental abuses. He also defended civil authority against encroachments of the military, and profiting by the experience of Magnentius' revolution, he sought to check inflation.

JULIAN THE APOSTATE. In his early youth Julian had been given a Christian education but had also received training in Greek classical literature. As a young man he studied rhetoric and philosophy, the latter under pagan teachers at Pergamon and Athens. Under the influence of Hellenism even before he became Caesar, and disgusted with the bloodbaths within the imperial family instituted by the first Christian emperor, Julian had become a secret convert to paganism and had been initiated into pagan mysteries. After Constantius' death he openly proclaimed his apostasy. At first he announced a policy of religious toleration, but before long he issued edicts against the Christian church. He ordered the restitution of temple property appropriated to Christian uses, deprived Christian clergy of state support, and forbade Christians to interpret classical literature in the schools. By recalling bishops exiled by his predecessor for religious nonconformity, he caused dissension within the Church, and he stimulated literary attacks upon Christian doctrine and practice, which he himself led. Not content with persecuting Christians, Julian endeavored to make paganism a living religion. Himself a monotheist, he regarded paganism as a unified system of religious beliefs, and sought to infuse a moral character into its doctrine and ritual. Following the example of Maximin Daia, he tried to set up a pagan church organized on the Christian model. Julian's early death put an end to his pagan reaction, but even had he lived much longer, it is doubtful whether his attempt could have had any lasting success—Christianity was too firmly established, the pagan cults had too far lost their meaning for the mass of the people, and most of those who abandoned Christianity did so in order to gain material advantages. Julian's emphasis on classical studies did, however, strengthen the position of Hellenic culture in the civilization of the Empire.

JULIAN'S ADMINISTRATION. Julian was a man of fine qualities, abstemious, just, and courageous, although he was unrealistic and at times displayed poor judgment. He took as his models the great emperors of the past—Augustus, Trajan, and Marcus Aurelius. His devotion to the past led him into a display of respect for Roman republican practices inconsistent with his own autocratic position. His reforms affected the operation rather than the structure of the bureaucratic administration. He continued and intensified the antibureaucratic and deflationary policies pursued by

Constantius at the end of his reign. He cut down extravagant expenditures, reduced the numbers and power of the secret police, corrected abuses in the public post, and tried to infuse new life into depopulated and bankrupt municipal councils (*curiae*). He also restored the metallic content of the alloy and copper coins issued by Constans and Constantius. Like Constantine and Constantius, he took a keen interest in the administration of justice, although he tended to restore older legal rules canceled by their decrees. He also favored the selection of government officials from men trained in schools of rhetoric.

JULIAN'S PERSIAN EXPEDITION AND DEATH: A.D. 363. Julian inherited the Persian problem from Constantius and determined to solve it by placing a pro-Roman prince on the Persian throne. By invading Persia, he seems to have looked upon himself as a second Alexander the Great. Early in 363 he crossed the Euphrates with an army of 65,000. He detached a division to join his ally, the King of Armenia, at Ctesiphon, the Persian capital. He himself, with the rest of his forces, followed the Euphrates to Babylonia, then crossed to the Tigris, and won a great victory under the walls of Ctesiphon. On the approach of the main Persian army under Sapor, he decided to march up the Tigris to join reinforcements whose route Sapor had barred. The Persians harassed the Roman army on the march, and in the course of one attack Julian was mortally wounded, possibly by one of his own soldiers, many of whom resented his paganism (June, 363). With his death ended the dynasty of Constantine the Great.

REIGN OF JOVIAN: A.D. 363–364. The army at once asserted its right to choose a new emperor, and rival factions finally agreed upon Jovian, commander of the imperial bodyguard. In order to extricate his army and return to Roman soil to secure his position as emperor, Jovian agreed to a humiliating peace with Sapor. He surrendered to Persia the Roman districts beyond the Tigris, the eastern frontier of Roman Mesopotamia with the great fort of Nisibis, which had defied three Persian attacks, and the Roman protectorate over eastern Armenia. The peace was for thirty years, and Rome was to pay an annual subsidy to help Persia close the Caucasus to barbarian raiders.

Jovian was a Christian, and, once he regained Roman territory, he annulled Julian's anti-Christian legislation. He was not a persecutor and proclaimed freedom of worship. He died in Bithynia after a reign of eight months. A new dynasty began with his successor.

IV. The House of Valentinian and Theodosius the Great: A.D. 364–395

VALENTINIAN I AND VALENS: A.D. 364. After some delay following the death of Jovian, the chief military and civil officials selected as his successor Flavius Valentinianus, a veteran Pannonian officer although not of the highest rank. Yielding to demands of the army for a second emperor, Valentinian soon afterwards appointed his younger brother Valens as his colleague as Augustus. In contrast to Diocletian and Constantine, Valentinian chose the West as the sphere of the senior Augustus, making his capital at Milan. Dissatisfaction with the new rulers was widespread among the Gallic troops loyal to Julian's memory, among former adherents of the house of Constantine I, among pagans, and in other circles. These elements gave their support to a usurper, Procopius, an official under Constantius and a favorite of Julian, who seems to have regarded him as a possible successor. Procopius, feeling himself suspect, declared himself emperor at Constantinople late in 365 and occupied Thrace and Bithynia. Early in 366, however, his generals deserted him for Valens. Procopius was executed, but the rebellion was continued for a short time by a relative, Marcellinus, who was soon suppressed.

WARS OF VALENTINIAN I: A.D. 365–375. Valentinian considered his chief duty to be defense of the Empire, all the frontiers of which were either under attack or threatened. The situation in Gaul was particularly dangerous and required the presence of the emperor in person from 365 to 375. He and his generals defeated the Alamanni, Franks, and Saxons. Rhineland fortresses were rebuilt from Raetia to the North Sea, and strong bridgeheads established to guard the crossings. For a long time thereafter Gaul enjoyed immunity from invasion. In the meantime, Valentinian's able general Theodosius cleared Britain of Picts, Scots, and other invaders and suppressed an attempted revolt by a Pannonian named Valentinus. Upon recovering from a serious illness in 367, Valentinian appointed his nine-year-old son, Gratian, as a third Augustus, in order to forestall intrigues over the succession. Valentinian also gave his attention while in Gaul to the Danubian frontier, where he strengthened the defenses of Raetia and Pannonia. In the wake of a serious incursion of the Quadi in 375, he visited Pannonia. In the course of an interview with a Quadian embassy, he fell into a violent rage and suffered a fatal stroke. During his reign the African provinces had suffered from invasions, misgovernment, and, ultimately, revolt. In 372 or 373 a rebellion broke out in Mauretania and Numidia, led by a Moorish chief named Firmus, who was supported by many of the Roman population. In 374 Firmus was defeated by Theodosius and committed suicide. Theodosius uncovered the intrigues of corrupt Roman officials, however, and the influence of their friends at court led to his summary execution (375 or 376), either by order of Valentinian or of Gratian, his successor in the West.

VALENS AND THE EAST: A.D. 365–378. From the beginning of his reign Valens had to cope with repeated Gothic invasions of Thrace. A Roman victory in 369 forced these barbarians to accept peace on Roman terms. In the meantime, Sapor II brought Armenia and Iberia under his control. In 371 Valens moved to the East and reestablished Roman influence in both countries. A Persian invasion of Mesopotamia was repelled, but no satisfactory settlement had been reached by 377, when Valens was obliged to return to Europe to meet a new Gothic peril.

The new crisis in relations of the Goths to the Empire is traceable to the westward movement of the Huns, a nomadic people of Mongolian origin, whose advance from Asia into the area north of the Black Sea led to a series of great migrations among the Germanic peoples of eastern and central Europe. In 373 the Huns fell upon the powerful kingdom of the East Goths (Ostrogoths) in the Ukraine and overwhelmed it. Then they attacked the West Goths (Visigoths) on the Dniester. Unable to resist, many of the latter retreated to the Danube and, joined by other Germanic refugees, sought permission to settle in Moesia or Thrace. Valens granted this, in the expectation of using them as army recruits, but required them to surrender their arms. Roman officials in charge of their settlement allowed them to keep their arms in return for bribes, while they issued food to the starving Goths only at high prices. The Goths then took to plundering, and, when the Romans failed in an attempt to murder the Gothic leaders, war broke out (377). In spite of reinforcements from the West, the generals of Valens failed to keep the Goths north of the Balkans. In 378 Valens personally took command of his forces and marched to meet the enemy, whose strength had been increased by Ostrogothic and other invaders. Gratian sent word that he was coming to help his uncle and begged him not to risk battle until his arrival, but Valens decided against delay and attacked the Goths, who numbered perhaps 20,000, with inferior forces near Adrianople. The battle was decided by the superiority of the Goths' cavalry. The Roman army was cut to pieces, Valens was killed, and the Goths overran the Balkans.

GOVERNMENT OF VALENTINIAN AND VALENS. In relation to Valens and later Gratian, Valentinian was senior Augustus. Unity of the imperial government was emphasized by the issuance of legislation in the name of all the emperors, as well as by other means. Although a very forceful person, Valentinian was neither refined nor well educated, and regarded with suspicion and even hostility the cultured classes. For the most part he selected as his officials and advisers cronies whose cruelty and misgovernment became notorious. Although they betrayed his confidence, he was reluctant to remove them from office. The senatorial aristocracy of Rome was treated with special severity. On charges of practicing secret magical rites, which the superstitious emperor feared and regarded as treasonable, many prominent senators were tortured, executed, or punished by exile and loss of property.

Yet, Valentinian seriously tried to lighten the burdens of the poor, both farmers and townspeople, particularly by correcting abuses in tax collection and the administration of justice. Although he reduced extravagance at his court, his need for money to defray the costs of his new fortifications, to repair cities, and enlarge the army compelled him to increase taxes and partly accounts for his confiscation of senatorial properties. By harsh measures he restored discipline among his troops, and he rewarded his higher officers, particularly Germans, with privileges and honors. He continued the practice of settling barbarians on depopulated lands.

Valens was much weaker than Valentinian. He lacked courage and resolution, was hot tempered, inclined to cruelty, and possessed neither military nor civil education. In general his policy followed his brother's and resulted in an expansion of the system of bureaucratic administration and strictly regulated occupation classes. Like Valentinian he sought to alleviate the burdens of the poor and tried, though vainly, to control the rapacity and corruption of officials. An incompetent commander, he nevertheless maintained discipline among his troops, to whom he added many Goths and other barbarians. Following the earthquake of 365 which devastated the eastern Mediterranean, Valens gave liberal financial aid to the ruined cities. In spite of the better economic condition of the eastern as compared to the western provinces, the high cost of wars and military and civil installations on a large scale caused a heavy drain on the treasury and prevented any effective lightening of tax burdens in this part of the Empire.

Valentinian was an orthodox Christian, but he followed a policy of religious toleration. He refused to be concerned with doctrinal matters, restricting himself in his legislation affecting the Christian clergy to maintenance of public order, preservation of the fiscal interests of the state, and orderly administration of justice. Pagans enjoyed religious freedom except in the practice of specifically prohibited rites. The right to teach and to learn was made independent of religious belief. In contrast, his brother Valens, although proclaiming freedom of religion, was very active in dogmatic strife within the Church. He was an adherent of the Arian heresy, which he sought to make the orthodox doctrine, and engaged in violent persecution of its opponents. Toward pagans he, too, was tolerant, except for his suppression of secret and magical practices.

THEODOSIUS I AND THE GOTHS: A.D. 379–382. At the death of Valentinian I government of the West passed to his son, Gratian, Augustus since 367 but only in his seventeenth year. He had received a careful education but was weak, lacking in military and administrative capacity. His policy was determined by his advisers. Perhaps in order to forestall any action by the Gallic soldiery, some of the higher officials nominated Gratian's younger brother, Valentinian, at the age of four, as Augustus in Illyricum, where he received the sanction of the troops. Gratian was obliged to accept him as a colleague but allocated to him only the diocese of Illyricum, which he governed under the guidance of his mother and of the Frankish general Merobaudes. Following the death of Valens, Gratian summoned from retirement in Spain Theodosius, son of the like-named general who had been executed about three years before, and appointed him first master of cavalry, then Augustus (379). Theodosius was thirty-four years old and had gained distinction as an officer. Gratian entrusted him with the government of the East and the solution of the Gothic problem. Avoiding any general engagements with barbarians, Theodosius weakened them by playing rival factions among the Goths against each other, while he strengthened his own forces by taking many Goths into Roman service. Finally in 382 peace was made upon the following terms: the Goths were allowed to settle on vacant lands between the Danube and the Balkans as a nation having its own ruler and its own laws but bound to Rome by an alliance; as federate allies they received from Rome annual supplies of food, in return for which they furnished soldiers. Having found it impossible to destroy or drive out the Goths, Theodosius resigned himself to the best alternative: to use them to defend the Empire.

REVOLT OF MAXIMUS AND DEATH OF GRATIAN: A.D. 383. In the West, Gratian revealed himself as a feeble administrator, more interested in hunting than ruling, leaving the government to incompetent favorites. Discontent spread among soldiers and civilians. The troops in Britain saluted their commander Magnus Maximus as emperor, and he crossed over to Gaul. Because of his indecision, he was deserted by his army. Gratian took flight, was captured, and executed. The authority of Maximus was accepted in Britain, Gaul, and Spain. He demanded and received recognition from Theodosius, who did not feel strong enough to attack him. Valentinian II, however, remained in control of Italy and Illyricum. The legislation of Gratian was unimportant except in the sphere of religion. A devoted Christian, he at first proclaimed religious toleration but later, influenced by orthodox advisers, he suppressed both Christian heresies and pagan practices.

OVERTHROW OF MAXIMUS: A.D. 388. The ambition of Maximus led to his downfall. He appointed his son Victor as Caesar, and in 387, when Valentinian II accepted his aid against a barbarian invasion of Pannonia, he seized the opportunity to obtain control of Italy. Valentinian fled to Thessalonika. Soon afterward Theodosius married Valentinian's sister, Galla, and decided to avenge the death of her half-brother, Gratian, and to restore Italy to Valentinian. A treaty with Sapor II of Persia resulted in a partition of Armenia between Rome and Persia, greatly to Sapor's advantage, and an Ostrogothic attempt to cross the Danube was repulsed, so that Theodosius was able to concentrate his forces against Maximus. Maximus made the Caesar Victor an Augustus and invaded Illyricum. He was forced to withdraw to Italy, however, by the fleet of Theodosius, which succeeded in landing Valentinian at Ostia. Theodosius defeated the army of Maximus in two engagements in Illyricum and advanced to Aquileia at the head of the Adriatic. There Maximus was surrendered by his troops to Theodosius, who had him executed (388). Theodosius's general Arbogast recovered Gaul and put Victor to death. Maximus had governed in the tradition of the Roman emperors, but his need for money led him to persecute the wealthy and confiscate their goods. His withdrawal of troops from Britain resulted in the evacuation of Hadrian's Wall and other northern defences of Britain, which were never reoccupied.

THEODOSIUS AND ST. AMBROSE.   Theodosius took up residence at Milan, sending Valentinian II to Gaul under the protection of Arbogast. His own elder son Arcadius, whom he had proclaimed Augustus in 383, remained at Constantinople. In 388 the monks of Callinicum in Meso-potamia incited a Christian mob to burn a Jewish synagogue. Theodosius ordered the bishop to restore the building. But Ambrose, the strong-willed bishop of Milan, interfered and threatened to withhold the sacrament from the emperor until he rescinded his order. Theodosius yielded but refused to accept Ambrose as his adviser, to the latter's displeasure. In 390 a riot occurred in Thessalonika in which the mob killed the general Butheric, who had refused to release from prison a favorite charioteer. In a fit of anger Theodosius ordered the garrison to massacre the citizens, three thousand of whom were killed. The emperor countermanded his order, but too late. On this occasion Ambrose notified Theodosius that he would exclude him from the Church services until he did public penance for his crime. For eight months the emperor's pride prevented his yielding, but at length his guilty conscience made him humble himself and publicly acknowledge his guilt. In this affair Ambrose appears in a much more favorable light than in that of Callinicum. He courageously asserted, not the supremacy of the Church over the secular authority, but the right of a priest to hold even an emperor responsible for obedience to Christian moral law.

REVOLT OF ABROGAST AND EUGENIUS: A.D. 392-394. In 391 Theodosius returned to the East. Arcadius was at odds with his mother-in-law, the Empress Galla; the Goths had been raiding and plun-dering in Thrace; and there was friction among high civil officials. An end was put to the Gothic raids, partly by the skill of the Roman generals, partly because of factional strife among the Goths themselves, and an all-out war was avoided. Among the favorites of Theodosius, the greatest influence was wielded by the praetorian prefect Rufinus and the half-barbarian general Stilicho, who had married a niece of the emperor. In the West, Theodosius was betrayed by one of his trusted commanders. Arbogast, who had been left as adviser and protector of Valentinian II, tried to prevent the young Augustus, who displayed much energy and ability, from pursuing an independent policy. The conflict became so bitter that Valentinian dismissed Arbogast, who refused to vacate his post. In May, 392 Valentinian was found dead, almost certainly murdered by fol-lowers of Arbogast. Ambitious though he was, Arbogast, by birth a Frank, dared not make himself emperor, but proclaimed as Augustus a prominent Roman official, the rhetorician Eugenius.

Eugenius tried to obtain recognition, but Theodosius refused. He made his younger son Honorius an Augustus in 393, and Eugenius, whose policy was dictated by Arbogast, occupied Italy. He was welcomed by the pagan senatorial faction in Rome, was acknowledged in Spain, and was supported by the commanding general in Africa. Finally in 394 Theodosius took the offensive. Arbogast and Eugenius awaited him with superior forces at the river Frigidus in northeastern Italy. In the ensuing battle, however, Theodosius won a complete victory. Eugenius was captured and beheaded, Arbogast escaped but killed himself. Once more the Empire was united, but Theodosius did not long survive his triumph. He died at Milan early in 395.

THEODOSIUS "THE GREAT." Theodosius succeeded in maintaining the unity of imperial authority throughout the Empire. In many areas the internal difficulties confronting the government—depopulation, growing impoverishment, corrupt administration, growth of great private estates, decline of the cities—increased rather than diminished, however, during his reign. His attempted settlement of the Gothic question, although perhaps finding a precedent in the treatment of the Franks in Gaul, left a legacy of trouble for his successors. His desperate need of manpower for the army probably forced him to adopt a policy here detrimental in the long run to the state's interest. Theodosius maintained a magnificent and costly court and enhanced the magnificence of Constantinople by erecting new buildings and monuments. His chief interest and activity was in religious spheres. A convinced orthodox Christian, he conceived it his duty to unite the Empire in this creed, and so he took drastic steps to stamp out both pagan and Christian heresies, although he protected the rights of the Jews. His religious policy was the result of his own convictions, not due to the influence of others. More vigorously than any of his predecessors, he asserted the right of the emperor to exercise authority in Church matters. To his resolute championship of orthodoxy is due his later title "the Great."

CHAPTER 23

THE PUBLIC
ADMINISTRATION
UNDER THE AUTOCRACY

I. The Autocrat and His Court

THE EMPEROR. The third century saw the completion of the transformation of the principate of Augustus into an undisguised autocracy that received its definitive form under Diocletian and Constantine I. All the sovereign powers of the Roman people were considered as transferred to the emperor, who based his right to rule upon the grace of God revealed in his election by a human agency. An emperor could speak of the *imperium* as having been conferred upon him by the heavenly majesty. The emperor was no longer "First" of Roman citizens (*primus inter pares*); all Romans were equally his subjects. He was the sole authority in all spheres of government, legislative, military, administrative, judicial. In keeping with his exalted state, the emperor's person and everything in any way belonging to him were called "sacred" or "divine," and "the imperial divinity" was a common expression.

As sole author of the laws, the emperor was also their final interpreter. Since he acted under divine guidance, those who questioned his decisions and those who neglected or transgressed his ordinances were guilty of sacrilege. The emperor was held to be above the laws in the sense that he could not be held responsible for his legislative and administrative acts; and yet he was bound by the laws in that he had to respect their general principles and institutions and had to abide by his own edicts, for his own authority rested upon obedience to them.

IMPERIAL TITLES AND REGALIA. The emperors continued to bear the titles Imperator, Caesar, and Augustus. Until Theodosius I they also counted the years of their tribunician power and styled themselves proconsuls. The new order found expression in the regular use of *Dominus* or *Dominus noster*,[1] of Victor and Triumpher, the latter two qualified as "eternal." The wearing of the "purple" (red) military cloak, formerly the right of Roman generals celebrating a triumph, had become an imperial prerogative, and the robe of "purple" silk interwoven with gold, called *paragauda*, was also reserved for the emperor. The white diadem of earlier times had become a purple silk band adorned with pearls. Purple became a symbol of imperial power, in fact, and its manufacture and use were

---

[1] From which comes the term Dominate, often used to describe the Autocracy in contrast to the Principate.

under government control. The privilege of "adoring the purple," i.e., of kissing the emperor's robe, was an honor reserved for favored officials. All persons entering the imperial presence had to kneel in reverence. The imperial costume and regalia, as well as the prescribed salutations, were partly the result of a natural evolution in Rome since the days of Augustus, partly adoptions from the courts of Hellenistic autocrats. There is little to indicate direct borrowing from the contemporary Persian court.

SUCCESSION. There was no hereditary right to the purple. An emperor had either to be elected or appointed by another emperor. Election regularly took the form of selection by high military officers with or without participation by civilian dignitaries, followed by a presentation of the nominee to a part of the army, which saluted him as Imperator and Augustus. He was then considered duly elected and was clothed in the imperial robes and crowned with the diadem. In Constantinople, from the fifth century, the presentation was made to the soldiers and populace assembled in the Hippodrome. The acclamation of an emperor was regarded as an expression of Divine selection. "Almighty God and your decision, most valiant fellow soldiers, have chosen me ruler," declared the emperor Leo I. At this presentation to the soldiers, an emperor first was crowned with a soldier's golden neckpiece (*torques*), afterwards with the diadem. In time the torque came to be placed around the ruler's neck, and, from the time of Leo I (457–474), he was crowned with the diadem by the Patriarch of Constantinople, acting as the representative of the people. An Augustus could appoint a colleague, as Caesar or as Augustus, anyone whom he wished to succeed him. In case he coopted a son in this manner, however, the latter became emperor by virtue of his father's will and not by right of birth. As history shows, the right of election might be exercised at any time. In this way usurpers arose, but a victorious usurper became a legitimate ruler. Thus the Autocracy, as has been remarked, was tempered by a legal right of revolution.

IMPERIAL PALACE. The organization of the imperial household became much more elaborate than ever before. Palace employees—ushers, chamberlains, grooms, and the like—were formed as quasi-military corps with definite regulation of uniforms, pay, terms of service, and promotion under the direction of an official called the *castrensis*. The formal court ceremonies were the culmination of a long development under the Principate. Their object was to emphasize the gulf separating the emperor from his subjects and to protect his person by rendering it inaccessible except to a favored few. This seclusion enhanced the influence of those permitted to come into contact with him, in particular the higher palace officials. Of these the most influential was the grand chamberlain, who had charge of the attendants of the imperial bedchamber. Before the close of the fourth century, the chamberlain, who, like most of his underlings, was often a eunuch, had become one of the great ministers with a seat in the

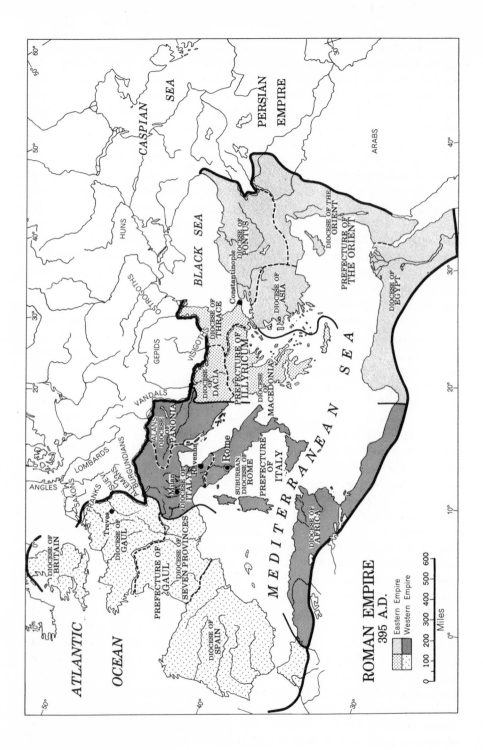

ROMAN EMPIRE
395 A.D.

Eastern Empire
Western Empire

Miles

0 100 200 300 400 500 600

ATLANTIC OCEAN

DIOCESE OF BRITAIN

Treves

DIOCESE OF GAUL

PREFECTURE OF GAUL

DIOCESE OF SEVEN PROVINCES

DIOCESE OF SPAIN

ANGLES

SAXONS

FRANKS

SUEVI

BURGUNDIANS

LOMBARDS

HUNS

OSTROGOTHS

GEPIDS

VISIGOTHS

VANDALS

ALANS

DIOCESE OF PANONIA

Milan

DIOCESE OF ITALY

Ravenna

Rome

SUBURBAN DIOCESE OF ROME

PREFECTURE OF ITALY

DIOCESE OF AFRICA

MEDITERRANEAN SEA

DIOCESE OF DACIA

PREFECTURE OF ILLYRICUM

DIOCESE OF MACEDONIA

DIOCESE OF THRACE

Constantinople

BLACK SEA

DIOCESE OF PONTUS

DIOCESE OF ASIA

PREFECTURE OF THE ORIENT

DIOCESE OF THE ORIENT

DIOCESE OF EGYPT

ARABS

PERSIAN EMPIRE

CASPIAN SEA

imperial cabinet. In addition to its civilian staff the palace had its armed guard. This was formed by the scholarians, organized by Constantine I when he disbanded the praetorians in 312. The scholarians took their name from the *scholae* or palace halls to which they were assigned. Recruited from barbarians, they eventually formed five *scholae* of 500 each in the West, seven in the East.

II. Military Organization

GENERAL CHARACTERISTICS. The military organization of the late Empire was the work of Diocletian and Constantine. Its chief characteristics were an initial and almost complete elimination of officers with both civil and military authority, a policy abandoned, however, whenever military emergency demanded unified command; a sharp distinction between mobile field forces and the frontier garrisons; and a large proportion of cavalry. During the fourth century the barbarian element increased both among the soldiers and also among the officers, including those of highest rank. Beginning about 400, however, this situation was reversed in the eastern half of the Empire, which found sufficient indigenous sources of military manpower, while the West fell increasingly under the control of a barbarian soldiery.

SIZE AND RECRUITMENT OF THE ARMY. The size of the Roman army at the end of the troubles of the third century is not known, but it is certain that Diocletian increased it considerably. It is doubtful that he raised its numbers to much over 450,000. Of these some 200,000 constituted the field army, about equally divided between the eastern and western parts of the Empire. Almost one fourth of this number were cavalry. The maintenance of armed forces at their authorized strength proved very difficult, owing to the decline of population. Recruits came from four sources. Beginning with the reign of Constantine at least, sons of veterans, if physically fit, were required to enter the army, while members of the hereditary occupation classes were forbidden to do so. There were still civilians, unencumbered by obligations of caste or occupation, who might volunteer for military service. Both these sources failed to satisfy military needs, and the imperial government instituted a draft that fell chiefly on the peasants. Farm land was divided into units called *capitula*, each of which was expected to furnish a specified number of recruits. The proprietors of the *capitula* contributed money with which the recruits could be hired either by themselves or by army agents. Valens sought to modify this system by requiring the landlords of each *capitulum* to furnish from among their own tenants recruits whose masters received monetary compensation for the loss of labor, although it still remained common to accept money instead of men from the proprietors. The scarcity of Roman recruits and their generally inferior military qualifications led the army in the fourth century to depend often upon barbarian volunteers for replacements. There were three main sources for recruiting barbarians. Some joined individually as volunteers. Many more were drafted from conquered peoples already settled within the Empire (*laeti, dediticii, gentiles*). Others were raised among the free tribes outside the frontiers, which were enlisted as allies in the Roman service. In return for subsidies in money and food, these allies, who came to be called *foederati*,[2] agreed to aid the Romans against other enemies. In the case of the Franks and Visigoths, during the fourth century allied peoples of this type were settled in Roman territory. Retaining their political autonomy and serving under their own chiefs, they were not regarded as part of the Roman armed forces. In the case of other threatening neighbors, the Romans purchased immunity from attack by regular payments in money which the recipients regarded as tribute.

In spite of all efforts, the army could not be maintained at full strength. Every campaign was preceded by an intensive drive for recruits, and the size of the Roman forces in critical battles was surprisingly small. Julian had only 13,000 men at Strassburg in 357, and the forces of Valens at Adrianople in 378 were not much larger. The strength of the barbarians in these engagements was not appreciably greater. Julian mustered some 65,000 for his invasion of Persia, but these included western as well as eastern field forces and also barbarian allies. During the invasions of the early fifth century, an appeal was made to slaves to volunteer for military service under promise of freedom.

ORGANIZATION AND COMMAND OF THE ARMY. Diocletian's policy was to provide for the defence of the Empire by greatly strengthening the forces stationed along the frontiers. He also formed the nucleus of a mobile field army, although he dispersed the great cavalry corps built up by Gallienus and his successors. Constantine I reversed this plan. He created a large field army by detaching the more mobile units from the border garrisons and grouping them at strategic points well within the borders. Since these troops formed the escort (*comitatus*) of the emperor, they received the name *comitatenses*. Certain elite units among them were further honored by being called palace troops (*palatini*). The frontier troops were called "borderers" (*limitanei* or *riparienses*). They were attached to the border defences, and many of them received land for cultivation in the vicinity of the fortifications they manned. The borderers ranked below the field troops, their physical standards were lower, their pay was less, and they had to serve twenty-four years instead of the twenty of the *comitatenses*. They degenerated into a border militia.

Constantine I deprived the praetorian prefects of military authority. In their place he created a master of horse and a master of foot as generals

---

[2] In the fifth and sixth centuries *foederati* in the eastern part of the Empire were no longer exclusively barbarian corps, but also included indigenous manpower.

of the field army directly subordinate to himself. The later stationing of large corps of field troops at a distance from the capital brought about the appointment of other masters who, since they commanded both classes of troops, were called masters of horse and foot or masters of either service and finally masters of the soldiers, a title also given to the original masters. At the death of Theodosius I, there were in the East two masters of the soldiers stationed at Constantinople, and one each in Illyricum, Thrace, and Asia (the Orient). In the West at this time there were two masters of the soldiers (still technically called master of horse and master of foot) at the court, and a master of horse in Gaul. The frontiers were divided into military districts that corresponded in general to the border provinces, and the garrison in each was commanded by an officer called duke (*dux*). In certain areas several *duces* were under the orders of a general of higher rank known as a count (*comes*). Select young officers called *protectores* were assigned for training to the imperial court. There they served as a bodyguard for the emperor and received the title *domestici*.

Whereas in the East the several masters of the soldiers enjoyed independent commands, by 395 there had developed in the West a concentration of supreme military power by the master of foot at the court, who outranked the master of horse. The master in Gaul and the dukes and counts in the provinces were all under his orders. This subordination was emphasized by the fact that the heads of the office staffs (*principes*) of the counts and dukes were appointed by the master of foot at court. In the East these *principes* were appointed by a civil official, the master of the offices, who was also charged with inspecting the frontier defences and, from the opening of the fifth century, exercising judicial authority over the dukes. The latter remained subordinate to the masters of the soldiers. Thus the concentration of military power in the West in the hands of a single commander in chief prepared the way for the rise of the kingmakers of the fifth century, while the division of the higher command in the East prevented a single general from completely dominating the situation.

MILITARY EQUIPMENT, PRIVILEGES, AND DISCIPLINE. The desire to secure greater mobility, the necessity of coping with great numbers of mounted raiders as well as mass cavalry attacks, and the influence of barbarians enrolled in Roman service brought about changes in arms and armor. Infantry units gave up the javelin for lighter darts and lances. Longer swords came into use. No longer was the characteristic Roman fortified camp in use. The soldier's heavy pack was discarded, and under Gratian heavy body armor and metal helmets were generally abandoned. Among the cavalry appeared heavily armored lancers, light horse, and archers. Barbarian units recruited on a tribal basis were armed in their native fashion. Considerable use was made of artillery in the form of heavy catapults and slings, particularly in siege operations.

Three fourths of the soldiers' pay was in allowances, the rest in money.

In the fourth century they had the privilege of defending themselves against criminal charges in the courts of their military commanders; in the fifth this right was extended to civil cases also. False muster rolls and other devices for making personal profit at the expense of the state indicate widespread corruption among army personnel. Requisitioning and quartering of troops among the civilian population gave rise to many abuses. With increasing barbarization of the army, traditional Roman discipline and methods of training tended to break down, and now the only advantages Roman armies possessed over their enemies were their carefully preserved traditions of strategy, their fortifications, and their supply services. Over and above their pay, the soldiers, and in particular the veterans, received advantages in the form of reduced taxation for their families, land grants, and the like. Officers enjoyed high social status because of the military power they wielded and became the patrons of less fortunate civilian land-lords, defending them against the demands of imperial tax collectors. Among the Romans there had come to be a great aversion to military service, and many prospective recruits mutilated themselves to avoid it. Desertion and absenteeism were chronic, and bands of soldiers became sometimes veritable brigands, plundering and terrorizing defenseless rural populations.

NAVAL FORCES. The strength and organization of the navy of the late Empire are not known. To guard against the North Sea raiders, there was a fleet based on harbors in Britain and Gaul. There were also flotillas on the Rhine and on the middle and lower Danube. No great naval force was apparently maintained in the western Mediterranean, but a fleet of considerable strength was stationed near Constantinople. The navy of the East was employed effectively in operations against western usurpers.

III. Civil Administration

ADMINISTRATIVE FRAMEWORK. The administrative machinery of the Autocracy was simply an outgrowth from, and a more elaborate form of, the bureaucracy developed under the Principate. All state officials were now servants of the emperor, appointed by him and subject to dismissal at his pleasure. The administration was based upon the division of the Empire into prefectures, dioceses, and provinces. At the close of the fourth century there were one hundred and twenty provinces, of which most had been created by subdivision of the originally large provincial units, in order to weaken the governors, to ensure closer supervision of administrative details and, in a few cases, to place more administrative appointments at the emperor's disposal. The provinces were grouped in fourteen dioceses, which in turn made up the four prefectures of Gaul, Italy, Illyricum, and the Orient. In the fourth century the Illyrian prefecture was at times partly or wholly merged with the Italian, but from 395 on it acquired separate states permanently and with the prefecture of the Orient, made up the Empire in the East. The two other prefectures, those of Italy and Gaul, then constituted the Empire in the West.

GOVERNMENT OF PREFECTURES, DIOCESES, AND PROVINCES. At the head of each prefecture stood a praetorian prefect, the highest civil official of the Empire. He was in charge of the collection, storage, and distribution of taxes paid in kind and of the administration of justice for the civilian population of his prefecture. Subordinate to the prefect were vicars, who were the chiefs of the several dioceses, and under the vicars were the civil governors of the provinces. They bore various titles—proconsul, consular, corrector, *praeses*—depending upon their relative importance. Subordination of vicars to prefects was only superficial, for they reported directly to the emperor, and appeals from their judgments were made to him. The proconsuls of Asia, Africa, and Achaia were also under the immediate authority of the emperor. Italy was merged into the provincial system and was divided into several provinces. Those north of the Apennines were united with Raetia in the diocese of Italy; those of the peninsula, with Sicily, Sardinia, and Corsica, formed the suburban region (*regio suburbicaria*), which had the obligation of supplying Rome.

CENTRAL ADMINISTRATIVE DEPARTMENTS. Branches of the administration not under the control of the Prefects were directed by a number of ministers resident at the eastern and western capitals, many of whom had subordinates in the dioceses and provinces. Of these ministers the chief were the master of the offices, the quaestor, the count of the sacred largesses, and the count of the private purse. The master of the offices exercised control over the secretarial bureaus of the palace, oversight over the public post and the imperial arsenals, direction of the imperial intelligence service (the *agentes-in-rebus*), command of the scholarians, supervision of several branches of the palace administration, and jurisdiction over practically all the personal attendants of the emperor. In the East, he also enjoyed some authority over the *duces*. The quaestor (not to be confused with urban quaestorships) was the emperor's judicial adviser, and played a large part in preparing imperial legislation. The office of count of the sacred largesses had grown out of that of the *rationalis* who had been head of one branch of the imperial Fiscus under the Principate. He was charged with the collection and disbursement of taxes paid in money, and his title derived from the fact that salaries of government employees paid in coin, and other objects of value distributed on various jubilee occasions, were regarded as imperial donations or largesses, just like distributions of money on the accession of an emperor or other special occasions. This minister likewise supervised imperial workshops engaged in the manufacture of silks, other textiles, and purple dye. The count of the private purse was head of the department of the *res privata*, which included the imperial properties attached to the office of emperor, as well as those forming the ruler's private estate. These four ministers, together with the grand chamberlain, formed the council of state or consistory (*consistorium*), so called because its members had to stand in the imperial presence. They were attended there by notaries or secretaries. Under the direct orders of the emperor, these notaries were entrusted frequently with important missions and from their ranks came many of the higher officials.

Rome and Constantinople were not under the praetorian prefects, each being administered by an urban prefect. Two consuls were nominated annually, one in each of these cities. They gave their names to the year but their duties were limited to furnishing entertainments for the city populace. The consulship was still regarded as one of the highest honors and frequently was held by the emperor himself. Of the older city magistracies only the praetorship and quaestorship survived. They were filled by imperial appointment on recommendation of the urban prefects, and their functions paralleled those of the consuls.

LESSER BUREAUCRATS.   Each official directing an administrative department, civil or military, was aided by an office staff (*officium*), whose members were called *officiales*. These subordinate government employees were freemen and, generally speaking, were institutionally descended from the military *officiales* of the Principate, which accounts for the quasi-military nature of their organization and nomenclature. The numbers, terms of service, promotion and discharge of these minor bureaucrats were regulated by imperial edicts. Since each *officium* was a permanent organization staffed by long-term civil servants, the burden of routine administration fell upon them rather than upon the department head whose term was short, at times annual, and for whose acts they were jointly responsible. This responsibility applied particularly to the bureau chief (*princeps*), who regularly was appointed from the retiring *agentes-in-rebus* and served as a *liaison* with and at times a spy for the palace administration. Like the soldiers, civil servants enjoyed exemption from the ordinary courts and the privilege of defending themselves before their ministers-in-chief. The favorable conditions of service on the staffs of the central ministries made admission to them popular, but the situation was different in the provincial bureaus. Difficulty in recruiting employees for the latter brought about the imposition of an hereditary obligation for sons of civil servants.

CHARACTER OF THE BUREAUCRACY.   The elaborate bureaucracy was cumbersome, expensive, and none too efficient, although it did assure order and regularity in collecting revenues and in judicial procedures. For the civilian population the operation of the administration became a great source of oppression. In order to increase their meager salaries, the purchasing power of which was less in the fourth century than in the third, the *officiales* demanded gratuities from those who had to deal with their offices. The emperors at first tried to prevent this sort of extortion, but they had to compromise by authorizing the demands within limits. The *officiales* themselves were obliged to make certain donations to other members of their offices with each promotion in rank and, at times, upon enrollment in the office. In like manner their superiors, the governors and other administrators, frequently paid large sums for their appointments to higher officials and even to the imperial treasury.

The attitude of emperors toward their officials was marked by mistrust and suspicion. It was largely for this reason that they weakened many of the more powerful offices by separating civil and military authority and subdividing larger administrative units. They also built up a highly developed system of espionage. In spite of the efforts of most emperors to secure an honest and efficient administration, the elaborate bureaucratic system nullified their efforts. An almost impassable barrier had been built up between the ruler and his subjects. Their complaints seldom reached his ears, and his ordinances for their relief remained ineffective because officials of all grades cooperated with one another to conceal their misdeeds and to enrich themselves at the expense of the civilians. So thoroughly had the spirit of graft and intrigue permeated all ranks of government services that in order to gratify their personal ambition persons in positions of highest responsibility did not hesitate to compromise the safety of the Empire. The increased burden imposed on the taxpayers by the enlarged civil and military establishments was thus aggravated immensely by the extortion practised by representatives of both services, whose rapacity knew no bounds.

IV. The Nobility and the Senate

SENATORIAL ORDER. In the course of the third century senators had come to be excluded from nearly all of the administrative offices that had been their prerogatives in the early Principate. This tendency was reversed after Diocletian, who used senators in only a few posts and relied mainly on equestrians. With the loss of any claim to authority by the Senate as a body, there was no longer any objection to their entering the service of the emperor, and Constantine and his successors expanded the number of senatorial positions in government and enlarged the order by promoting into it many equestrians. The senatorial order of the Late Empire was therefore a mixed body of only recent distinction, most senators then being men who had risen in the imperial service during and after the reign of Constantine.

The distinguishing mark of this new senatorial order was the right to the title *clarissimus*, acquired by inheritance, by imperial grant, or by the attainment of an office conferring the clarissimate either during the term of service or upon retirement. Practically all higher officials in the imperial service were *clarissimi*, and there was consequently a great increase in the number of senators in the course of the fourth century. As many equestrian posts became senatorial, equestrian status became an inferior order of rank conferred upon lower imperial officials and municipal senators.

HIGHER ORDERS OF NOBILITY. Throughout the Republic and the Principate, nobility in the Roman world had been dependent upon membership in the senatorial order and the holding of higher public offices. This situation continued under the Autocracy, but development of an elaborate court ceremonial prescribed a fixed order of precedence among those admitted to imperial audiences. The great increase in the number of important civil and military officials necessitated a classification of official posts from the point of view of rank, and led to the creation in the second half of the fourth century of new and more exclusive orders of nobility within the class of *clarissimi*. These were, in ascending order, the Respectables (*spectabiles*) and the Illustrious (*illustres*), also called Most Illustrious (*illustrissimi*). By 400 the praetorian prefects, masters of the soldiery, masters of the offices, quaestors, counts of the sacred largesses and private purse, and the grand chamberlains all held the rank of Illustrious. Under Justinian in the sixth century, these important officials were promoted to a still higher grade, that of the Glorious (*gloriosi*). The official positions to which these titles of rank were attached were called dignities (*dignitates*), and the great demand for admission to these classes of rank, which entitled their members to valuable privileges, led to many honorary dignities, i.e., titles of official posts with appropriate rank but sinecures. The titles Caesar and Most Noble (*nobilissimus*) were reserved for members of the imperial household.

COUNTS AND PATRICIANS. Constantine I revived the use of the title Count (*comes*), which had been used irregularly of the chief associates of the *princeps* in his suite during the Principate, and used it as the title of many new officials. This led to the creation of three classes of rank among the counts. In time the title Count became a permanent part of the title of certain higher civil and military officials and also a title of nobility automatically attained by lesser bureaucrats in office or on retirement. Far different was "patrician," a title also revived, with a new meaning, by Constantine I. This became the highest title conferred upon persons not born into the imperial family. It was granted very sparingly, and in the fifth century in the West was monopolized by the senior master of the soldiers.

INEQUALITY BEFORE THE LAW. Nothing illustrates more clearly the importance of official position than the division of the citizens of the Empire into two classes—the *honestiores* (more honorable) and the *humiliores* (more humble or "little people"). Unlike the latter, the former class, which included imperial and municipal senators, soldiers, and veterans, were exempt from execution except with the emperor's consent, from penal servitude, and, with some limitations, from torture in judicial investigations.

SENATE. The Senate at Rome was not abolished but continued to function both as a municipal council and as the mouthpiece of the senatorial order. After the founding of Constantinople, a similar Senate was established there by Constantius II, probably in 340. At first all *clarissimi* had a right to participate in meetings, and their sons were expected to fill the quaestorship. After the middle of the fifth century, only those ranking as *illustres* were admitted to the senate chamber, and sessions became a gathering of the highest officials and ex-officials. In addition to their functions as municipal councils, the Senates made recommendations for the quaestorship and praetorship, discussed with imperial officials the taxes affecting the senatorial order, and even participated sometimes in drafting imperial legislation.

The most important privilege enjoyed by senators was their exemption from the control of officials of the municipalities within whose territories their estates were situated. This was one of the chief reasons for the extension of their power in the provinces.

V. Totalitarian State

NEW ECONOMIC ORDER. While the government of the Roman Empire was gradually being transformed politically into an autocracy, the economic policies which it had pursued paved the way for a condition in which the activities of the individual were prescribed and limited by state regulation. The ultimate result was a form of totalitarian state. This did not come into being in its entirety as a set plan or as the embodiment of a social theory of Diocletian or Constantine. It matured as the result of reforms initiated by them and carried to their logical conclusion by the legislation of their successors. The immediate economic problem that confronted the government was the need to raise revenues large enough to maintain the expensive military establishment, the enlarged bureaucracy, and the imperial court. Since income produced from a diminishing and impoverished population by the old tax system was inadequate, the emperors carried to extremes the practices of the late Principate by demanding more and more public service of different classes of the population and in circumscribing their freedom of activity. There was no doctrinaire attempt to eliminate freedom of initiative in industrial, agricultural, or commercial activities, and private enterprise continued to exist in spheres in which the state was uninterested. Landlords in Italy, for example, after they had paid their taxes in kind to the state, could sell their surplus agricultural produce, if any, on a very active free market. Such landlords also commonly engaged in the type of speculation in commodity markets traditionally associated with the free-enterprise system.

It would be a mistake to regard the Late Empire as a period of uninterrupted and universal economic decline. There were great differences in the degrees of prosperity maintained by various provinces, so that it is very difficult to generalize regarding prevailing economic conditions. Restoration of internal peace and stabilization of the coinage did something to stimulate recovery after the chaos of the third century, even if that recovery was by no means continuous. Trade within provincial areas and to a lesser degree between province and province was resumed or became more active. There was even some commerce with India and the Far East, partly through Persia but mainly by the Red Sea route. Certain parts of the Empire prospered more than others. In Egypt, following the restoration of the irrigation system, which had fallen into decay, agriculture made a partial recovery. The commerce and industry of the Syrian cities also experienced a revival, and Antioch and its environs in particular seem to have been reasonably prosperous. Residence of the emperors at Trèves for long periods and successful defence against the German tribes gave rise to a temporary rehabilitation of agriculture and industry in Gaul and along the Rhine, as did similar conditions near Milan and Ravenna. The large landed proprietors, who were an extremely prosperous class of the population, tended in some areas like Gaul and Africa to withdraw to their estates tilled by serfs, a development that prefigured the manorial social system of the early Middle Ages. Elsewhere, as in northern Italy, near Rome, and in some parts of the East, they were absentee landlords and maintained until a late date their city residences and thereby the traditional urban cultural interests that had characterized them throughout antiquity. Technically, agriculture was carried on less intensively and became less productive than previously, while industry, owing to the loss of skilled workmen and the failure to train others to take their places, resorted to more primitive practices and sometimes produced articles of inferior quality. An exception was the glass industry, which enjoyed particular advantages under imperial protection. Britain was the only province that seems to have been as prosperous in the first half of the fourth century as before the debacle of the third, if not more so, mainly because it had largely been spared the devastations of civil strife and barbarian raids that produced such havoc elsewhere. In Britain, as in Gaul, the towns declined, however, and rural villas became centers of economic life. The Danubian provinces in particular experienced a continuous decline in population and prosperity. Generally speaking, conditions throughout the Empire as a whole fell far short of those characteristic of the first and second centuries A.D. and became steadily worse, especially in the west, from the latter part of the fourth century. There can be no doubt that a general manpower shortage, already manifest in the third century, became increasingly acute during the fourth and fifth. This was not only because the state demanded more from the productive classes of the population; it also reflected a decline in their numbers. The peasant classes, on whom the entire economy of the Empire rested, either failed to reproduce themselves, or sought refuge from their burdens by fleeing to cities that had programs of social assistance, the bread and circuses that some urban governments then maintained on an expanded scale. Such cities remained reasonably populous, at least for a time, as the result of migration, but in most cases they did not attain the demographic levels they had enjoyed under the Principate. Such cities were few, however, and most municipalities, at least in the West, were rapidly decaying.

Except for luxury articles, industrial production beyond local needs was largely for the state, and the movement of such goods took place under its direction. The government itself had become a large producer. Apart from the vast imperial domains, there were imperial factories that produced arms and equipment for the troops, besides articles designed for the court.

MONEY AND BARTER. Wholesale debasement of the coinage after 250 had led to a tremendous rise in prices. Whereas Aurelian had sought to combat this tendency by stabilizing the depreciated billon (copper and silver) coins of low value, Diocletian reformed the gold and silver coinage. Although the gold coins had remained pure in content, they had been made lighter and irregular in weight, and Diocletian in 286 fixed the weight of the standard gold coin (the *aureus*) at 1/60 of a pound. In 295 he issued an improved silver coin. The final reform was made by Constantine I, however, who reduced the gold coin, now called the *solidus*, to 1/72 of a pound and issued a new silver coin called the *siliqua*, 1/24 of a *solidus*. From this time on the *solidus* retained a constant weight and purity. But owing to the shortage of both gold and silver, great use was made of billon coins of small denominations known by different names. In spite of attempts at reform, this small change suffered a continuous depreciation, which was responsible for price fluctuations, although not comparable to the great inflation of the time of Gallienus. Imperial bureaucrats whose job it was to determine the relation between this inflated billon coinage and the stable *solidus* did so at rates advantageous to themselves and the state, and the population at large, which very rarely used the gold coins, benefited little by Constantine's currency reform.

It has been held that, owing to lack of an adequate gold and silver coinage and depreciation of the billon, payment in kind, both for goods and services, had taken the place of payment in money by the fourth century. Such was not the case, however. The Late Empire was based on a money economy and on the gold standard. It inherited from the Principate a system of tax collection and salary disbursements in kind, and these certainly became more extensive and important than before, but the development was evolutionary. The commutation of payments in kind into payments in coin (*adaeratio*) was provided. Given the uncertain value of inflated billon coinage, different elements in the state viewed *adaeratio* in terms of their own particular economic advantage. The state, its functionaries, and soldiers preferred to receive taxes and wages in coin when such commutations evaluated the commodities concerned above the real or market price. The producing classes, landlords of great or moderate substance, preferred to pay in coin only when the value of their crops was set below the market price.

NEW TAX SYSTEM.   Confronted by complete disorganization in the public finances due to the inflation and economic decline of the third century, Diocletian revised drastically the system of taxation. The old land taxes were abolished, and their place was taken by the *annona*, a tax collected in kind. This amounted to a regularization of the extraordinary levies that had become so important in the Late Principate. The resort to a land tax in kind rather than to an increase in monetary taxes is probably explained by a desire to protect the state against future inflation. Not only was the land tax revised but also in some provinces the method of assessment. The new land taxes in some provinces were based on a division of productive land, agricultural workers, and livestock into units of equal taxpaying liability. The system as a whole was called *capitatio*, and the term *caput* (pl. *capita*) could be applied to land, personal, and animal units. A special term *iuga* (sing. *iugum*) was applied to the unit of land, and the land tax was often called *iugatio*. Naturally the *iugum* varied in size according to productivity. When the new tax was introduced into Egypt in 297, the prefect announced "the quota of each aroura ($\frac{5}{8}$ acre) with respect to the quality of the soil and the quota of each head of the agrarian population." In Syria a *iugum* of plough land comprised twenty acres of first-class, forty of second-class, or sixty acres of third-class soil; a *iugum* of vineland, five acres; and a *iugum* in olive groves, 225 trees in lowlands, 450 in uplands. Apparently the *caput* of farm labor was one man or two women. Thus the land was taxed and also the labor to work it. A new survey and census of the rural areas was required to calculate the new tax units. This was carried out apparently between 298 and 312.

INDICTION.   The total amount of the land tax to be raised was announced in an annual proclamation called an indiction (*indictio*), which also specified the amount assessed against each province, and a revaluation of the tax units was made periodically. The term indiction was also used of the period between two reassessments, which occurred at first every five years and after 312 every fifteen years. The indictions thus furnished a new system of chronology.

MONETARY TAXES.   In addition to the land tax raised in kind on the basis of *iuga* and *capita*, there were other taxes payable in money. Chief of these were: the *chrysargyrum*, a tax levied on all trades and professions; the *aurum coronarium*, a nominally voluntary but really compulsory contribution paid by municipal councillors every five years to enable the emperor to distribute largesses to officials and troops; the *aurum oblaticium*, a similar payment made by the senatorial order; and the *collatio glebalis* or *follis senatoria*, a special tax imposed upon senatorial lands by Constantine I.

FORCED PUBLIC SERVICES.   Besides the taxes, the government laid upon its subjects the burden of performing public services without compensation. The most expensive of these charges (*munera*) were the upkeep of the public post and the furnishing of quarters (*hospitium*) and rendering other services in connection with movement of troops, officials, and supplies. So heavy was the burden of the post that it denuded of draught animals the districts it traversed and had to be drastically curtailed in the sixth century. In connection with exaction of these charges, collection of revenue in kind, and administration of justice imperial officials found opportunity to practise extortions which weighed perhaps more heavily upon the taxpayers than the taxes themselves.

CURIALES. The class that suffered most from the new fiscal system was that of the municipal councillors, now called *curiales* from the *curia* (senate or council) to which they belonged. These landholders, once the prosperous middle class, had been severely reduced in numbers and brought in many cases to the verge of ruin between Severus Alexander and Diocletian. Here, too, one cannot generalize; the economic decay of this class was by no means universal. In some areas, certainly more often in the East than in the West, they survived into the Late Empire as a reasonably flourishing class, their traditional pride in status and in service to their cities intact. In the course of the third century, membership in the *curia* had become an obligation upon all who possessed sufficient property, which amount varied from place to place. When the local senates became agents of the *fiscus* in collecting revenues from their municipal territories, the *curiales*, through the municipal officers or committees of the local council, had to apportion them among landholders, collect them, and be responsible for the payment of the total amount to the public officers. They were also responsible for maintenance of the public post and performance of other services. Inevitably the *curiales* sought to protect themselves by shifting the burden of taxation as much as possible on to the lower classes in the municipal territories, who regarded them as oppressors. "Every *curialis* is a tyrant" (*quot curiales, tot tyranni*), says a fourth-century writer.

The exactions of imperial officers proved more than the *curiales* could meet, and they attempted to withdraw from their order and its obligations. The government required responsible landholders as its agents, for they alone could offer security for taxes assessed against their communities and so guarantee the government against loss. The status of *curialis* was therefore made hereditary, and, to prevent men from escaping its obligations by giving up part or all of their properties, they were forbidden to alienate them and were not allowed to leave their home towns without permission. They tried to find exemption from their inherited obligations by entering the imperial senatorial order, the military or civil service, or the clergy, but these avenues of escape were also closed. Only those who had filled all the municipal offices might become *clarissimi* and immune from curial obligations, and only clergy of the rank of bishops were excused, while the lower orders had to supply a substitute or surrender two thirds of their property before they could leave the *curia*. The legal limitations on the social mobility of the curial class were more restrictive on paper, however, than they were in reality. In particular, the wealthier and better connected municipal gentry seem to have contravened imperial regulations on a mass scale and bought their way into the imperial Senate or into the bureaucracy, where they were protected against the fiscal demands of the state. They left behind a dwindling number of the less well-to-do members of their own class, whose financial responsibilities for their order increased proportionally

Valentinian I attempted to aid the municipalities by making the so-called "defenders of the cities" (*defensores civitatium*), now known as "defenders of the plebs" (*d. plebis*), public officials whose duty it was to check unjust exactions and protect the common people against officials and judges. These *defensores* were at first persons of influence, chosen by the praetorian prefects and approved by the emperor. They were empowered to try certain cases and had the right to report directly to the emperor and to bypass the provincial governor. The *defensores* accomplished little, and in the fifth century this office became an additional obligatory service resting upon the *curiales*. By the fifth century, at least in the West, this class of municipal landholders had dwindled alarmingly, and by the sixth century it had practically disappeared.

HEREDITARY CORPORATIONS. The associations of businessmen, tradesmen, and craftsmen throughout the Empire were now called corporations (*corpora*), rather than colleges, and their members were known as *corporati*. Like the *curiales*, the *corporati* were required to devote much time, energy, and resources to serving the state or their municipalities. The idea that such duties constituted an obligation developed gradually during the Late Principate and was accepted as axiomatic under the Autocracy. It became more important with the introduction of the general land tax in kind, for the transportation, warehousing, and distribution of such revenues necessitated the employment of many more persons than heretofore. The first step taken by the state to insure the performance of these services was to make this duty a charge that rested permanently upon the property of members of the corporations, no matter into whose possession it passed. Men as well as money were needed for the performance of these charges, and, to prevent a decline in the numbers of the *corporati*, the state made membership in their associations hereditary. This was really an extension of the principle that a man was bound to perform certain services in the community in which he was enrolled (his *origo*). Finally, the emperors exercised the right of conscription and attached to various corporations in need of recruits persons engaged in less essential occupations.

The burden of their charges led the *corporati*, like the *curiales*, to seek refuge in some other profession. They tried to enroll in the army or among the *officiales* or to become *coloni* of the emperor or senatorial landholders. All these havens of refuge were officially closed by imperial edicts. When discovered, the truant *corporati* were supposed to be dragged back to their associations. Such was the corruption and inefficiency of the bureaucracy enforcing these regulations that, in fact, many *corporati* undoubtedly remained undisturbed among the privileged orders of society in which they found refuge.

Although the corporations probably retained their former organization and officers, their heads were now called patrons (*patroni*), who directed their public services. In Rome and Constantinople corporations were under the supervision of the city prefects; in the municipalities, under that of local magistrates and provincial governors. The professional corporations were the only ones to survive during the late Empire. Religious and funerary associations vanished with the spread of Christianity and the impoverishment of the lower classes.

COLONATE. Just as the *curiales* were bound to the *curia* and the *corporati* to their associations, so were many tillers of the soil bound to the estates they cultivated. These agricultural workers were known generally as *coloni*, and their status was called the colonate. This condition arose as a result of forces operative under the Principate and still continuing to affect agricultural conditions, plus the consequences of the new system of taxation introduced by Diocletian. The growing weight of taxes and public services demanded of the peasants increased their poverty, and the decline in the rural population made these burdens press more heavily upon survivors, with the result that there was little incentive for them to take up leases on either public or private land. Many captive barbarians had been settled on vacant land as state tenants under obligation not to leave their holdings. With the imposition of the land and labor tax in kind, proprietors had to maintain crop returns from their estates at a sufficiently high level. Naturally they leased their plots in return for rents in kind, with or without obligation to do additional work on the unleased portion of the estate. When tenants were unable to fulfill their obligations and became indebted to their landlords, they threw up their leases and left their land untenanted. This threatened the public revenues, and the government stepped in and attached the *coloni* to the estates where they had been working. It is not known when this step was taken or whether the obligation was extended to all such tenants at the same time. It seems clear, however, that the obligation had become virtually universal for such tenants by 325. At the same time there existed a free, independent peasantry, owning and tilling their own farms. In some areas, like northern Italy during the fourth century, this population was gradually reduced to the status of serfs, as their properties were absorbed by the great landlords of the senatorial aristocracy. Elsewhere, however, probably more often in the eastern than in the western provinces, they were able to resist senatorial patronage and keep their lands and their completely free status, as for example in the vicinity of Antioch.

The status of the *coloni* became hereditary, like that of the *corporati*.

Mosaics from the Fourth Century Villa at Piazza Armerina

Mosaics from the Fourth Century Villa at Piazza Armerina

Their condition was halfway between that of free men and that of slaves. They were bound to the estate upon which they resided and passed with it from one owner to another, although they were not absolutely under the power of the owner and could not be disposed of by him apart from the land. They had also other rights that slaves lacked, but as time went on their condition tended to approximate servitude more and more closely. "Slaves of the soil," they were called in the sixth century. As this status of serfdom was hitherto unknown in Roman law, many imperial enactments were issued defining the rights and duties of *coloni*.

Crushed by the weight of their obligations, the *coloni*, like the *curiales* and *corporati*, tried to change their status by entering public service or attaining admission to another social class. They also found themselves legally excluded from all other occupations and classes. Only the fugitive *colonus* who had managed to remain undetected for thirty years (in the case of women twenty years) could escape being sent back to the land he had deserted. As in the cases of the *curiales* and *corporati*, many of these peasants, at least in the fourth century, apparently did escape from their legal obligations by migrating to cities and losing themselves among the proletariat recipients of the dole.

GREAT LANDHOLDERS. The growth of immense private estates at the expense of public and imperial domains, and of the smaller proprietors, was an outstanding phenomenon. This was due in part to the inability of the state to check the spread of wastelands, in part to the ability of the rich landholders to buy up or occupy illegally the properties of their weaker neighbors. Faced by the need to maintain production for the sake of revenue, the government permitted great proprietors to take over deserted lands under various forms of heritable lease or in freehold tenure. In accordance with Roman tradition and under prevailing economic conditions, acquisition of landed property was both the most respectable and the most secure form of investment. Although the small landowner and the tenant farmer found it hard to gain a livelihood from their lands, particularly in view of the heavy taxation and extortionate methods of tax collecting, owners of big estates could operate them profitably in spite of low productivity.

The immunities of the senatorial order and the power of high civil and military officials tended to give an almost manorial character to the position of the great landed proprietors now called the *potentiores* or "more powerful." These inherited judicial powers of the procurators on imperial estates and transferred this authority to themselves. Over their slaves and *coloni* they exercised powers of police and jurisdiction. Not subject to the municipal authorities and, during the greater part of the fourth century, also exempt from the jurisdiction of the provincial governors, they assumed an independent position and did not hesitate to defy municipal magistrates and even minor agents of the imperial government. Their power made their protection extremely valuable and led to a new type of patronage. Individuals and village communities, anxious to escape the exactions to which they were subject in their municipal districts, placed themselves under the patronage of a senatorial landholder, becoming his tenants. He did not hesitate to afford them protection, albeit extralegal, against the local authorities. Complaints by the latter to higher officials obtained little redress, for these officials were themselves proprietors and sided with their own class. The power of the state was thus nullified by its chief servants, and the landed aristocracy became the heirs of the Empire.

RESUME.   The transformation society underwent during the Empire may be aptly described as the transition from a regime offering some degree of social mobility to all classes to one in which such mobility was largely destroyed, in theory at least, by class ascription. The population of the Empire came to be legally divided into a number of sharply defined castes, each of which was supposed to play a definite role in the life of the state. The state demanded that the sons of senators, soldiers, *curiales*, *corporati*, and *coloni* follow in their fathers' walks of life, while a great number sought to escape from the tasks to which they were born. In the eyes of the government *collegiati*, *curiales*, and *coloni* existed solely to work or to pay taxes for the support of the bureaucracy and the army. In contrast was the widespread attempt to find any refuge from fiscal obligations in the urban proletariat, senatorial order, army, civil service, church, or wilderness. The corruption of administration helped them escape. There was much more social mobility than the law allowed, and the tightly regimented caste system, erected on the principle of compulsion, operated inefficiently. The traditional picture of the Late Empire is one of languishing private industry, declining commerce, untilled fields, and a feeling of hopelessness that paralyzed initiative. Such an interpretation is well grounded in fact, but striking local economic differences existed. In particular there were subtle forces at work differentiating the western and eastern halves of the Empire. As yet too little is known about these forces, but it would appear that the East was better able to maintain a reasonably prosperous urban tradition and that it was better able to resist the manorializing tendencies of the landlord class, which, in the West, increasingly escaped from the control of the central government.

CHAPTER 24

GERMANIC OCCUPATION OF ITALY AND THE WESTERN PROVINCES: A.D. 395–493

I. General Characteristics of the Period

PARTITION OF THE EMPIRE. With the death of Theodosius the Great the Empire passed to his sons, Arcadius a youth of eighteen, whom he had left in Constantinople, and Honorius a boy of eleven, whom he had designated as Augustus for the West. However, in the East the government was really in the hands of Rufinus, the praetorian prefect of Illyricum, while an even greater influence was exercised in the West by Stilicho, the Vandal master of the soldiers, whom Theodosius had selected as regent for young Honorius. The rivalry of these two ambitious men and the attempt by Stilicho to secure for Honorius restoration of eastern Illyricum, which had been seized by the eastern administration for Arcadius, were the immediate causes of the complete and formal division of the Empire into an eastern and a western half, a condition which had been foreshadowed by the division of imperial power throughout most of the fourth century.

The fiction of imperial unity was preserved by the nomination of one consul in Rome and one in Constantinople, by the joint display of the statues of both Augusti throughout the Empire, and by the issuance of imperial enactments under their joint names. There was, in fact, however, a complete separation of administrative authority. Before A.D. 395 edicts issued by one emperor required the sanction of the other before attaining validity within his own territory. After that date, the two parts of the Empire increasingly tended to separate legislatively, since edicts issued in one half were frequently not republished in the other. Furthermore, upon the death of one Augustus, the actual government of the whole Empire did not pass into his survivor's hands. The Empire had really split into two independent states.

GERMANIC INVASIONS. In addition to the partition of the Empire, the period between 395 and 493 is marked by the complete breakdown of Roman resistance to barbarian invasion and the penetration and occupation of the western provinces and Italy by Germanic peoples. The position of Romans and barbarians was reversed: the latter became the rulers, the former their subjects, and the power passed from Roman officials to Germanic kings. A barbarian soldier finally sat himself on the throne of the western emperor, when a Germanic kingdom was established in Italy.

MILITARY DICTATORS. During this period of disintegration, the real power in the western Empire was in the hands of military dictators who, with the office of senior master of the soldiers, secured the position of commander in chief of the imperial armies and the title patrician. The emperors exercised only nominal authority. As these dictators were either barbarians or depended upon barbarian troops for their support, they were continually intrigued against and opposed by the Roman or civilian element, headed by the civil officers of the court. The fall of one "kingmaker" was always followed by the rise of another, for by their aid alone could the Romans offer any effective resistance to the flood of barbarian invasion.

THE EMPIRE MAINTAINED IN THE EAST. But while the western Empire was thus absorbed by Germanic invaders, the East survived the crisis of the fifth century with its institutions and, generally speaking, its frontiers intact. This is in part accounted for by the ability of the central government in the East better to resist the decentralizing tendencies of the great landholders and of barbarian armies and their generals. In the West the greatest civil offices were held by members of the senatorial oligarchy, who encouraged the development of the vested economic interest of their own class and the spread of manorializing tendencies injurious to the imperial treasury. In the East, in contrast, important ministers of state were frequently civil servants of rather low social origin who, even if they were often corrupt, nevertheless owed a primary allegiance to the bureaucratic system that had produced them rather than to senatorial vested interest as such. The civil administration in the East held the army in check more effectively because of the division of supreme military authority among several masters of soldiers. The East also successfully solved the problem of barbarization of the army rank and file by purging it of barbarians on two notable occasions and by recruiting indigenous manpower from the Balkans, Asia Minor, and Armenia to take their place. The strength of the eastern Empire caused the West to come to look to it for support, and western emperors upon several occasions were nominated, and at other times given the sanction of legitimacy, by those in the East.

II. Visigothic Migrations

REVOLT OF ALARIC: A.D. 395. Seizing the opportunity created by the death of Theodosius and the absence of the army of the East, which he had drawn into Italy, Alaric, a prince of the Visigothic *foederati*, began to ravage Thrace and Macedonia with a band of his own people, aided by other tribes from across the Danube. He was opposed by Stilicho, who was leading back the troops of the eastern emperor and intended to occupy eastern Illyricum. The latter was ordered by Arcadius to send the army of the East back to Constantinople, and he complied. This gave Alaric access to southern Greece, which he systematically plundered. Stilicho intervened again, transporting an army by sea to the Peloponnesus. He maneuvered Alaric into a precarious situation but came to terms with him, possibly because of a revolt that had broken out in Africa. Stilicho was declared an enemy by Arcadius, while Alaric, after devastating Epirus, settled there with his Goths and extorted the title of *magister militum* from the eastern court.

DEATH OF STILICHO: A.D. 408. In 401, when Stilicho was occupied with an inroad of Vandals and Alans into Raetia, Alaric invaded Italy. Stilicho forced him to withdraw and foiled a second attempt at invasion in 403. Alaric did not long remain inactive. He now held the title of master of the soldiers from Honorius and agreed to help Stilicho accomplish his designs upon Illyricum. When the western Empire was embarrassed by new invasions and the appearance of a usurper in Gaul, however, he made his way into Noricum, and demanded an indemnity and employment for his troops. On the advice of Stilicho his demands, which included a payment of 4,000 pounds of gold, were met. Shortly afterwards, Stilicho fell victim to a plot hatched by court officials who were jealous of his influence (408).

VISIGOTHS IN ITALY. The death of Stilicho removed the only capable defender of Italy, and, when Honorius refused to honor the agreement with Alaric, the latter crossed the Alps. Honorius shut himself up in Ravenna, and the Goths marched on Rome, which was ransomed at a heavy price. As Honorius still refused to give him lands and supplies, Alaric returned to Rome and set up a new emperor, Attalus. Honorius, supported by troops from the eastern Empire, remained obdurate, and a disagreement between Alaric and Attalus led to the latter's deposition. Rome was then occupied by the Goths, who plundered it for three days (410). Alaric's next move was to march to south Italy with the intention of crossing to Sicily and Africa, but his flotilla was destroyed by a storm. While retracing his steps northward he fell ill suddenly and died.

GOTHS IN GAUL AND SPAIN. Alaric's successor was his brother-in-law, Ataulf, who led the Visigoths into Gaul (412), where he at first allied himself with a usurper, Jovinus, but soon deserted him to serve the Romans. When Honorius failed to furnish him supplies, he seized Narbonne and other towns in southern Gaul and married the emperor's sister, Galla Placidia, whom the Goths had captured in Rome. He again attempted to come to terms with the Romans but failed, and Constantius, the Roman master of the soldiers, who had succeeded to the position and influence of Stilicho, forced him to abandon Gaul. Ataulf and his Goths crossed the Pyrenees into Spain, where he died in 415. His successor Wallia, facing famine and failing in an attempt to invade Africa, came to terms with the Romans. He surrendered Placidia and in the name of the emperor attacked the Vandals and Alans who had occupied parts of Spain. Alarmed by his success, Constantius recalled the Goths to Gaul, where they were settled in southern Aquitania (418).

VISIGOTHIC KINGDOM IN GAUL. The status of the Goths in Gaul was that of *foederati*, bound to render military aid to Rome but governed by their own kings. The latter, however, had no authority over the Roman population among whom the Goths settled. This condition was unsatisfactory to the Gothic rulers, who sought to establish an independent Gothic kingdom. Theodoric I, the successor of Wallia, forced the Romans to acknowledge his complete sovereignty over Aquitania but failed in his attempt to conquer Narbonese Gaul. Subsequently he joined forces with the Romans against Attila the Hun and was largely responsible for checking the latter at the battle of the Mauriac plain near Troyes (451) in which he was killed. For a time the Goths remained on friendly terms with the Empire. Under Euric, who became king in 466, the anti-Roman faction was in the ascendant, and they embarked upon a policy of expansion. In 475 Euric, after a protracted struggle, occupied the district of Auvergne, and the Roman emperor acknowledged his sovereignty over the country between the Atlantic and the Rhone, the Loire, and the Pyrenees, besides some territory in Spain. Two years later the district between the Rhone and the Alps, south of the Durance, was added to the Visigothic kingdom.

III. Vandals

INVASIONS OF A.D. 406. In 405 an invading band of Vandals and Alans had descended upon Italy, and were utterly defeated by Stilicho. In the following year fresh swarms of the same peoples, united with the Suevi, crossed the Rhine near Mainz and plundered Gaul as far as the Pyrenees. For a time they were held in check by the usurper Constantine, who held Gaul and Spain. Later, when he was involved in a struggle with a rival, Gerontius, they found an opportunity to make their way into Spain (409).

OCCUPATION OF SPAIN. They quickly made themselves masters of the whole Iberian peninsula. In spite of their successes against Roman troops, lack of supplies forced them to terms with the Empire. In 411 they became Roman *foederati* and were granted lands for settlement. Under this agreement the Asdingian Vandals and the Suevi occupied the northwest part of Spain, the Alans the center, and the Silingian Vandals the south. The Roman government made peace with the Vandals and their allies only under pressure and seized the first opportunity to be rid of these unwelcome guests. In 416 Constantius authorized the Visigoths under Wallia to attack them in the name of the emperor. Wallia was so successful that he utterly annihilated the Silingian Vandals and so weakened the Alans that they united with the Asdingian Vandals, who escaped destruction only through the recall of the Visigoths to Gaul. The Vandals quickly recovered from their defeats, waged successful war upon the Suevi, who had reached an agreement with the Romans, and occupied the whole of southern Spain.

VANDAL KINGDOM IN AFRICA. In 429 the Vandals under their king Gaiseric crossed into Africa, attracted by its richness and its importance as one of the granaries of the Roman world. Their invasion was facilitated by war between Count Bonifacius, the military governor of Africa, and the western emperor. The number of the invaders was estimated at 80,000, of whom probably 15,000 or 20,000 were fighting men.

In spite of a reconciliation between Bonifacius and the imperial government and their united opposition, Gaiseric was able to overrun the open country, although he failed to capture the chief cities. In 435 peace was concluded, and the Vandals were allowed to settle in Numidia, once more as *foederati* of the Empire. In 439, Gaiseric broke the peace and treacherously seized Carthage. This step was followed by the organization of a fleet, which harried the coasts of Sicily. In 442 the western emperor acknowledged the independence of the Vandal kingdom. Peace continued until 455, when the assassination of the emperor Valentinian III gave Gaiseric the pretext to attack Italy and seize Rome, which was systematically plundered of its remaining treasures, although its buildings and monuments were not wantonly destroyed. Among the captives was Eudoxia, widow of the late emperor, and her daughters, who were valuable to Gaiseric as hostages.

Lack of cooperation between the eastern and western Empires enabled the Vandals to extend their power. Their fleets controlled the whole of the Mediterranean and ravaged both its western and its eastern coasts. A powerful expedition fitted out by the eastern emperor Leo I in 468 for the invasion of Africa ended in utter failure, and in 476 his successor Zeno was compelled to come to terms and acknowledge Vandal authority over the territory under their control. At the death of Gaiseric in 477, the Vandal kingdom included all Roman Africa, the Balearic Islands, Corsica, Sardinia, and the fortress of Lilybaeum in Sicily.

IV. Burgundians, Franks, and Saxons

BURGUNDIAN INVASION OF GAUL. The invasion of Gaul by the Vandals and Alans in 406 was followed by an inroad of the Burgundians, Ripuarian Franks, and Alamanni. The latter two peoples established themselves on the left bank of the Rhine, while the Burgundians penetrated farther south. In 433 the Burgundians were at war with the Empire and were defeated by Aetius, the Roman master of the soldiers in Gaul. Subsequently they were settled in Savoy. From there, about 457, they began to expand until they occupied the valley of the Rhone as far south as the Durance.

On the whole they remained loyal *foederati* of the Empire. They fought under Aetius against Attila in 451, and their kings bore the title of *magister militum* until the reign of Gundobad (473–516), who was given that of patrician by the emperor Olybrius.

SALIAN FRANKS. The Salian Franks—as those who had once dwelt on the shores of the North Sea were called in contrast to the Ripuarians, whose home was along the Rhine—crossed the lower Rhine before 350 and occupied Toxandria, the region between the Meuse and the Scheldt. They were defeated by Julian, who left them in this district as *foederati*. The disturbances of the early fifth century enabled the Salian Franks to assert their independence and extend their territory as far south as the Somme. They fought as Roman allies against the Huns in 451, and their king Childeric, who began to rule shortly afterwards, remained a faithful *foederatus* until his death in 481.

In 486 Clovis, the successor of Childeric, overthrew the Gallo-Roman state south of the Somme and extended his kingdom to meet the Visigoths on the Loire. Thus the whole of Gaul passed under the rule of Germanic peoples.

SAXONS IN BRITAIN. After the decisive defeat of the Picts and Scots by Theodosius, father of Theodosius the Great, in 368 and 369, the Romans were able to maintain the defence of Britain until the close of the fourth century. In 402, however, Stilicho was obliged to recall part of the garrison for the protection of Italy, and in 406 Constantine, who claimed the imperial crown in Britain, took with him the remaining Roman troops in his attempt to obtain recognition on the continent. The ensuing struggles with the barbarians in Gaul prevented the Romans from sending officials or troops across the channel immediately, and the Britons for the time being had to fend for themselves.

The Roman garrison was eventually restored to the island under the command of a *comes Britanniarum*, but it was unequal to stemming the tide of Saxons, Angles, and Jutes, who made permanent settlements beginning in 428. Toward 442 the Roman garrison evacuated the island forever. Four years later the inhabitants directed one last appeal to the Roman government for help, but it went unheeded. Because Roman civilization in Britain had been a relatively thin veneer, the subsequent struggle for possession of the island resulted in the obliteration of the Latin language and the disappearance of what material civilization had developed under four centuries of Roman rule.

V. Fall of the Western Empire

HONORIUS: A.D. 395–423. After the murder of Stilicho in 408, Honorius was faced with the problem of restoring his authority in Gaul, where for a time he was forced to acknowledge the rule of the rival emperor Constantine, who had donned the purple in Britain in 406. Constantius, a Roman noble who succeeded Stilicho as master of the soldiers, was dispatched to Gaul in 411 and soon overthrew the usurper. Two years later another rival, Jovinus, was crushed with the help of the Visigoths.

Constantius, leader of the antibarbarian faction of the court, was now the mainstay of Honorius' power and used his influence to further his own ambitions. After the Visigoths returned the princess Placidia, he induced the emperor to make her his wife (417). In 421 Honorius appointed him coemperor, but he was not recognized as an Augustus at Constantinople. His death the same year was followed by a quarrel between the emperor and his sister, as a result of which Placidia and her son took refuge with the eastern emperor, Theodosius II.

VALENTINIAN III: A.D. 425–455. Honorius died in 423, leaving no children, and Castinus, the new commander in chief, secured the nomination of John, a high officer of the court, as his successor. Theodosius refused him recognition, however, and his authority was defied by Bonifacius, an influential officer in Africa. Valentinian, the five-year-old son of Placidia and Constantius, was escorted to Italy by forces of the eastern Empire, and John was deposed. His chief supporter Aetius, who had brought an army of Huns to his aid, was induced to dismiss his troops and accept a command in Gaul with the rank of count. Placidia, who had returned to Italy with Valentinian, became regent with the title of Augusta.

AETIUS. During the reign of Valentinian III interest centered about the career of Aetius, "last of the Romans." In 429, after getting rid of his enemy Felix, who had succeeded to the position of Castinus, Aetius himself became master of the soldiers and the real ruler in the West. Fearing his influence, the Augusta Placidia endeavored to engineer his downfall by an appeal to Bonifacius, who, after his revolt of 427, had fought with the Empire against the Vandals. In 432 Bonifacius returned to Italy and was appointed master of the soldiers in place of Aetius. The latter took to arms, was defeated near Ariminum, and forced to flee to his friends the Huns. Bonifacius died not long after his victory; Aetius, with the backing of the Huns, was able to force the emperor to reappoint him to his command as patrician in 433. From that time until his death in 454 he directed imperial policy in the West. He received embassies from foreign peoples, and the latter made treaties with him and not with the emperor.

ATTILA'S INVASION OF GAUL: A.D. 451. The chief efforts of Aetius were directed toward the preservation of central and southeastern Gaul for the Empire. In this he was successful, holding in check the Franks on the north, the Burgundians on the east, and the Goths in the southwest. Gaul was saved, but Africa was lost to the Vandals, Britain to the Saxons, and the greater part of Spain to the Suevi. The success of Aetius in Gaul was due principally to his ability to draw on large numbers of Hunnish troops, through the influence he had acquired with the leaders of that people while a hostage among them. At this time the Huns occupied the region of modern Hungary, Rumania, and South Russia. They comprised many separate tribes, which were united in 444 under the strong hand of King Attila, who extended his sway over neighboring Germanic and Scythian peoples.

At first Attila remained on friendly terms with Aetius, but his ambitions and his interference in Gaul led to friction and to his demand for the hand of Honoria, sister of Valentinian III, with half of the western Empire as her dowry. When the emperor refused to comply, Attila led a great army across the Rhine into Gaul and besieged Orleans. Their common danger united the Romans and the Germans of Gaul, and Aetius was able to face the Huns with an army strengthened by the kings of the Visigoths and the Franks. Repulsed at Orleans, Attila withdrew to the Mauriac plain, where, in the vicinity of Troyes, a memorable battle was fought between the Huns and the forces of Aetius. Although the result was indecisive, Attila did not risk another engagement and recrossed the Rhine. The next year he invaded Italy, but famine and disease among his own forces and the arrival of troops from the eastern Empire induced him to listen to a Roman embassy led by the Roman bishop Leo and to withdraw from the peninsula without occupying Rome. Upon his death in 453 his empire fell to pieces, and the power of the Huns declined.

MAXIMUS AND AVITUS: A.D. 455–456. The death of Attila was soon followed by that of Aetius, who was murdered by Valentinian at the instigation of his chamberlain Heraclius (454). This rash act deprived him of his best support, and the next year Valentinian himself fell victim to the followers of Aetius. With him ended the dynasty of Theodosius in the West. The new emperor, a senator named Petronius Maximus, compelled Valentinian's widow, Eudoxia, to marry him, but when the Vandal Gaiseric appeared in Italy in answer to her appeal, Maximus offered no resistance and died in flight. He was succeeded by Avitus, a Gallic follower of Aetius, whom he had made master of the soldiers. After ruling about a year, Avitus was deposed by his own master of the soldiers, Ricimer (456).

RICIMER. Ricimer, a German of Suevic and Gothic ancestry, succeeded to the power of Aetius and was the virtual ruler of the western Empire from 456 until his death in 472. Backed by his mercenaries, he made and unmade emperors at will and never permitted his nominees to be more than puppets. Majorian, who was appointed emperor in 457, was overthrown by Ricimer in 461 and followed by Severus. After the death of Severus in 465 no emperor was appointed in the West for two years. Imperial power was nominally exercised by the eastern emperor, Leo, while Ricimer was in actual control of the government in Italy. In 467 Leo sent to Rome as emperor Anthemius, a prominent dignitary of the eastern court, whose daughter was married to Ricimer to secure the latter's cooperation in a joint attack of the two empires on the Vandal kingdom. In 472 Ricimer broke with Anthemius, who had endeavored, with the support of the Roman Senate, to free himself from the powerful barbarian. Athemius was besieged in Rome and executed following the capture of the city. Ricimer then raised to the purple Olybrius, a son-in-law of Valentinian III. Both the new emperor and his patron died in the course of the same year (472).

LAST YEARS OF THE WESTERN EMPIRE. In 473 Gundobad, the nephew of Ricimer, had Glycerius proclaimed emperor. But his appointment was not recognized by Leo, who nominated Julius Nepos. The next year Nepos invaded Italy and overthrew his rival, only to meet a like fate at the hands of Orestes, his master of the soldiers (475). Orestes did not assume the imperial title but bestowed it upon his son Romulus Augustulus. Orestes was unable to maintain his position for long. Germanic mercenaries in Italy—Heruli, Sciri, and others—led by Odovacar demanded lands in Italy such as their kinsmen had been granted as *foederati* in the provinces. When they were refused, they mutinied and killed Orestes. Romulus was forced to abdicate, and Odovacar assumed the title of king (476). His soldiers were settled in Italy, and barbarians acquired full control of the western Empire.

KINGSHIP OF ODOVACAR: A.D. 476–493. With the deposition of Romulus Augustulus, the commander in chief of the barbarian soldiery, long virtual ruler in the western Empire, was legally confirmed in his power. Imperial authority was united again, nominally through the eastern emperor, who sanctioned the rule of Odovacar by granting him the title of patrician, which had been held already by Aetius, Ricimer, and Orestes.

It was only in Italy that Odovacar obtained authority. The last remnants of Roman authority vanished in Gaul and Spain, while Raetia and Noricum were abandoned to the Alamanni, Thuringi, and Rugii.

OSTROGOTHIC CONQUEST OF ITALY: A.D. 488–493. In 488 the position of Odovacar was challenged by Theodoric, king of the Ostrogoths. This people, after having long been subject to the Huns, recovered their freedom at Attila's death and settled in Pannonia as *foederati* of the eastern Empire. Theodoric, who became sole ruler of the Ostrogoths in 481, proved himself a troublesome ally of the emperor Zeno, who mistrusted him. When Theodoric demanded an imperial commission to attack Odovacar in Italy, Zeno readily granted him authority, together with the office of patrician in the special western sense, in order to remove him far from Constantinople. In 488 Theodoric set out to invade Italy. Odovacar was defeated in two battles and, in 490, blockaded in Ravenna. After a long siege he agreed to surrender, upon condition that he and Theodoric should rule jointly. Shortly afterward he and most of his followers were treacherously assassinated by the Ostrogoths (493). Theodoric was proclaimed king by his army and later received the royal insignia from the new eastern emperor, Anastasius.

VI. Survival of the Empire in the East

ARCADIUS: A.D. 395–408. The year Theodosius the Great died the Asiatic provinces of the Empire were overrun by Huns, who ravaged Syria and Asia Minor, while the Visigoths under Alaric devastated the Balkan peninsula. The presence of the eastern troops in Italy prevented the government from offering any effective opposition to either foe. When Stilicho came to the rescue from Italy and was holding the Visigoths in check, his rival, the praetorian prefect Rufinus, regent to the young Arcadius, induced the emperor to order Stilicho to withdraw and send the troops of the East to Constantinople. This order resulted in the death of Rufinus, who was killed by the returning soldiery at the orders of their commander, the Goth Gaïnas.

The influential position of Rufinus at the court devolved upon the grand chamberlain Eutropius, who had been an enemy of his predecessor. He had induced Arcadius to marry Eudoxia, a daughter of a Frankish chief, instead of the daughter of Rufinus, as the latter had desired. The fall of Eutropius in turn was brought about by Gaïnas, now a master of the soldiers, who sought to play the role of Stilicho in the East, and by the empress Eudoxia, who chafed under the domination of the chamberlain. In 399, when the Gothic troops in Phrygia revolted, Gaïnas held aloof, and the failure of a nominee of Eutropius to crush the movement gave Gaïnas the opportunity to recommend to the emperor the latter's dismissal. The bitter complaints of Eudoxia against the eunuch finally brought about his fall from power and eventually his death.

Gaïnas' aspirations to become an eastern Stilicho were not to be realized. He and his troops were unpopular at Constantinople because of their Arianism, and, upon the removal of Eutropius, preponderant influence at court fell to an anti-barbarian faction supported by the empress .and led by the praetorian prefect, Aurelian. A massacre of thousands of Gothic soldiers in Constantinople followed, and, with the aid of a loyal Goth, Fravitta, Gaïnas was driven north of the Danube, where he was killed by the Huns (400). Units composed of indigenous troops were soon raised by Arcadius to replace the barbarians. This was the first step taken by the eastern court to combat the barbarization of the army and to rely on a predominantly "national" military establishment.

Eudoxia, of course, was more influential than ever following the fall of Eutropius. But she herself found a critic in the eloquent bishop of Constantinople, John Chrysostom, who inveighed against the extravagance and dissipation of the court and censured the empress in particular. Ultimately, in 404, Eudoxia was able to have him deposed from his see. Four years later Arcadius died, leaving the Empire to his eight-year-old son Theodosius II.

THEODOSIUS II: A.D. 408–450. At the beginning of the reign of Theodosius II, the government was in the hands of the praetorian prefect Anthemius, who had shown himself an able administrator during the last years of Arcadius. In 414, the emperor's elder sister, Pulcheria, was made regent with the title of Augusta. She was strong-willed and for many years completely dominated the emperor, who lacked independence of character and energy. In 421 Pulcheria selected as a wife for Theodosius, Athenais, the daughter of an Athenian sophist, who took the name Eudocia upon accepting Christianity. After a lapse of some years differences arose between the empress and her sister-in-law, which led to the latter's withdrawal from court (after 431). About 440 Eudocia lost her influence over the emperor, and she was compelled to retire from Constantinople and reside in Jerusalem, where she lived until her death in 460. Power then passed to the grand chamberlain Chrysaphius, whose corrupt administration rivalled that of Eutropius.

During the reign of Theodosius II the peace of the eastern Empire was broken by war with Persia and by inroads of the Huns. The Persian war, which began in 421 as a result of persecutions of the Christians in Persia, was concluded victoriously in the next year. A second war, following a Persian invasion in 441, ended with Persian defeat in 442. With the Huns the Romans were not so fortunate. In 424 King Rua, the ruler of the Huns in Hungary, had extorted from the Empire payment of an annual tribute. At the accession of Attila and his brother in 433, this tribute was raised to 700 pounds of gold, and the Romans were forbidden to give shelter to Hunnish defectors. Payment of tribute failed to win a permanent respite, for Attila was bent on draining the wealth of the Empire and reducing it to helplessness. In 441–443 the Huns swarmed over the Balkans and defeated the imperial armies. An indemnity of 6,000 pounds of gold was exacted and the annual payment increased to 2,100 pounds. Another disastrous raid occurred in 447. The Empire could offer no resistance. Chrysaphius plotted the assassination of Attila, but the plot was detected; Attila claimed to regard himself as the overlord of Theodosius.

Although Theodosius was undeniably a weak ruler, his reign was important historically for three events. One was the erection of a new city wall in 413 under the administration of Anthemius. The new wall stretched from the Sea of Marmora to the Golden Horn, and its circuit was much greater than the old wall of Constantine, which the city had outgrown. Theodosius' wall made Constantinople virtually impregnable, and its ruins remain to this day one of the notable landmarks of the city. Possibly influenced by the philosopher-empress Eudocia, Theodosius refounded the school of higher learning in the capital. Originally an establishment of Constantine's, now after 425 it was endowed with ten chairs of Greek and ten of Latin grammar, five of Greek and three of Latin rhetoric, two of law, and one of philosophy. Of great importance for the development of law was the publication in 438 of the Theodosian Code, which was supposed to contain for purposes of ready reference all the still valid imperial ordinances, beginning with the reign of the first Christian emperor.

MARCIAN: A.D. 450–457. Choice of a new emperor was left to the Augusta Pulcheria. She selected Marcian, a tried officer, whom she married. Marcian proved himself able and conscientious. He refused to continue the indemnity to Attila and was able to adhere to this policy, since the latter invaded the West and subsequently died. He also permitted the Ostrogoths to settle as *foederati* in Pannonia (454).

LEO I: A.D. 457–474. At the death of Marcian in 457, imperial authority was conferred upon Leo, an officer of Dacian origin, who was appointed because of the support of the Alan, Aspar, one of the masters of the soldiers. Aspar's power rivalled that of Ricimer in the West. Since the breakup of the Hunnish Empire, the number of Gothic barbarians in East Roman armies had tended to increase, a tendency the would-be barbarian kingmaker furthered. Leo was alive to the danger of becoming the puppet of the powerful general, who was unpopular and even suspected of treason when he failed to give proper support to the unsuccessful expedition against the Vandals. What happened was not unlike the events of 400 surrounding the fall of Gaïnas and the massacre of his Gothic troops. As a counterpoise to Gothic mercenaries and *foederati*, the mainstay of Aspar's power, Leo enlisted in his military service the Isaurians, warlike mountaineers of southern Anatolia, who, if they were little better than barbarians themselves, were good fighting material and imperial subjects. The emperor's eldest daughter was married to Zeno, an Isaurian, who was made master of the soldiers in the East. In 470 Aspar was still strong enough to force Leo to marry his second daughter to his son Leontius and to appoint the latter Caesar, but in the following year when Zeno returned to Constantinople, Aspar and his eldest son were assassinated in the palace. The second notable attempt by barbarians to take over the army of the East thus failed; thereafter indigenous elements predominated heavily among the officer cadres and rank and file of East Roman armies.

LEO II: A.D. 473–474. In 473 Leo took as his colleague and destined successor his grandson, also called Leo, the son of Zeno. The elder Leo died early in 474, and the younger soon crowned his father Zeno co-emperor. When Leo II died before the close of the same year, Zeno became sole ruler.

ZENO: A.D. 474–491. The reign of Zeno was an almost uninterrupted struggle against usurpers and revolting Gothic *foederati*. In 474 occurred an outbreak of the latter led by their king Theodoric the son of Triarius, called Strabo or "the Squinter," who ruled over the Goths settled in Thrace as master of the soldiers. Before this revolt was put down, unpopularity of the Isaurians induced Basiliscus, brother-in-law of Leo I, to plot a *coup d'état*. He was supported by his sister, the ex-empress Verina, and Illus, the chief Isaurian officer in Zeno's service. The conspirators seized Constantinople and proclaimed Basiliscus emperor in 475. His heretical religious views aroused strong opposition, however, and he was deserted by both Verina and Illus. Zeno reentered the capital, and Basiliscus was executed.

During the revolt Zeno had been supported by Theodoric the Amal, a Gothic prince who was a rival of Theodoric, son of Triarius. The emperor tried to crush the latter with the former's help, whom he made a master of the soldiers with patrician rank, but the two Theodorics came to an agreement and acted in concert against Zeno in 478. In 479 peace was made with the son of Triarius, but hostilities continued with the Amal. At this time a brief insurrection broke out in Constantinople, under the leadership of Marcian, a son-in-law of Leo I, in protest against the predominance of Isaurians, Illus in particular.

Theodoric, son of Triarius, was killed in 481, and in 483 Zeno made peace with Theodoric the Amal, restoring his office of master of the soldiers and granting him lands in Dacia and lower Moesia. These concessions were made because of the antagonism that had developed between the emperor and his all-powerful minister Illus. This ill feeling culminated in 484, when Illus, who was master of the soldiers in the East, induced the dowager empress Verina to crown a general, Leontius, as emperor. Outside of Isauria the movement found little support. After a long siege in an Isaurian fortress, the leaders of the revolt were taken and put to death (488). In the meantime Theodoric the Amal had asked and received permission to attack Italy. With the departure of the Goths the eastern Empire was delivered from the danger of Germanic invasion. Zeno died in April 491.

ANASTASIUS: A.D. 491–518. Choice of a successor was left to the empress Ariadne, who selected as emperor and husband an experienced officer of the court, Anastasius. The first act of Anastasius was to remove the Isaurian officials and troops from Constantinople. This led to an Isaurian rebellion in southern Asia Minor, which was not stamped out until 498. The power of the Isaurians was broken, their strongholds were captured, part of their population was transported to Thrace, and they ceased to menace the peace of the Empire.

In place of the Goths, new enemies appeared on the Danubian border— Slavic Getae and Bulgars, who overran the depopulated provinces of the northern part of the Balkan peninsula. Their ravages were widespread. So utterly did the imperial troops fail to hold them in check that Anastasius was obliged to repair a protective wall built some years before outside the city across the peninsula upon which Constantinople stood. Anastasius had also to cope with a serious Persian war, which began with an invasion of Roman Armenia and Mesopotamia by King Kawad in 502. After four years of warfare, in which the Persians gained initial success but were ultimately defeated by the master of the offices Celer, peace was reestablished on the basis of the *status quo ante*.

Anastasius' reign is noteworthy for the abolition of the tax called *chrysargyrum* (498) and for his relief of the *curiales* from responsibility for the collection of the municipal taxes. The former step was taken because the impoverishment and numerical decline of tradesmen and workers had made the raising of the *chrysargyrum* both a crushing burden and unprofitable, and the latter because the virtual disappearance of municipal landholders had rendered their councils useless as tax-collecting agencies. A land tax paid in money replaced the tax on the urban populace. A testimony of the increasing influences of Christian morality was the abolition of certain pagan festivals and of combats between gladiators and wild beasts.

In spite of the justness and efficiency of his administration, the reign of Anastasius was marked by several popular uprisings in Constantinople and in other cities of the Empire. The cause lay in his sympathy for the Monophysite doctrine, which was vigorously opposed by orthodox Christians. In 512 the appointment of a Monophysite bishop at Constantinople provoked a serious rebellion that almost cost Anastasius his throne.

Although the emperor was able to quiet the city by a display of courage, the prevailing religious discord encouraged Vitalian, the commander of the Bulgarian *foederati* in the Thracian army, to revolt in 513. He defeated all forces sent against him and endangered the capital, but he was induced to withdraw by a ransom of 5,000 pounds of gold and the office of master of the soldiers in Thrace. The truce was only temporary, and in 515 he again advanced on Constantinople. This time his forces were crushingly defeated on land and sea, and the rebellion ended. Three years later Anastasius died, leaving an immense treasury surplus, which was to be the economic basis for the program of expansion soon to be undertaken by Justinian.

CHAPTER 25

AGE OF JUSTINIAN:
A.D. 518-565

I. Germanic Kingdoms in the West to A.D. 533

GERMANS AND ROMANS. The passing of Italy and the western provinces under the rule of Germanic kings was the result of the settlement of many barbarians in the conquered territories. This necessitated a division of land and a definition of the status of the Romans with respect to the invaders, who were everywhere less numerous than the native population. These questions were settled in different ways.

UNDER THE VISIGOTHS. In the Visigothic kingdom in Gaul, the Goths and the Romans lived side by side as separate peoples, each enjoying its own laws, and the Romans were not regarded as subjects without rights, although intermarriage between the two races was forbidden. The law that applied to the Romans was published by King Alaric II in 506 and is known as the *Lex Romana Visigothorum*, or the Breviary of Alaric. His predecessor Euric sponsored the compilation of a code of Gothic customary law, in imitation of the Theodosian Code.

The settlement of Goths on the land took the form of *hospitium* or quartering. By this arrangement Roman landholders gave up to the Goths two thirds of their property, both land and cattle, *coloni*, and slaves. What the Goths received was not taxable.

For purposes of administration the Roman provincial and municipal divisions were retained (*provinciae* and *civitates*), the former being placed under dukes and the latter under counts of the cities (*comites civitatium*). The Goths settled within these districts formed their own national associations of tens, hundreds, and thousands, under Gothic officers. Adoption of a more settled form of life deeply affected Gothic tribal institutions. Their national assembly could no longer be easily assembled and came to exist in the army alone. In the division of the land, the more influential warriors and friends of the king received the larger shares, and this stimulated the rise of a landed nobility. The government was established at Toulouse, where central ministries were set up, modeled on those of the Roman court. This led to a considerable strengthening of royal power. The language of government remained Gothic for the Goths, Latin for the Romans, but the leading Goths appear to have been bilingual.

UNDER THE VANDALS. In the Vandal kingdom of Africa the position of the Romans was much less favorable. They were treated as conquered subjects. As under the Goths, intermarriage between them and the conquering race was prohibited. In the province of Zeugitana (old

Roman Law (*Lex Romanum Burgundiorum*) which appl
subjects and to Burgundians in their disputes with Roma
of their advance to the Seine the Franks had annihilated t
lation of northern Gaul. In the region between the Seine
however, they left the Romans in possession of their propert
kings making no distinction between their Frank and Roma

THE RELIGIOUS QUESTION. In addition to ethn
there was also a religious line of demarcation between Goths, ...dals, and
Burgundians on the one hand, and the Roman population on the other.
The Goths and neighboring Germanic peoples had been conve ed to
Christianity in the latter half of the fourth century, largely thrc   the
missionary activities of Ulfila, who translated the Bible into Goth   Inder
his influence they had been won to the Arian and not the Nic?   creed,
and consequently they were regarded as heretics by the orthodox Romans,
who never became reconciled to rulers of another confession. This hostility
led frequently to government intervention and persecution, but in this
respect the policy of the Germanic kingdoms varied.

In general the Visigoths pursued a tolerant policy, leaving the orthodox
clergy undisturbed except when the latter were politically disloyal. At the
time of their settlement in Zeugitana the Vandals confiscated the property
of the orthodox Church and turned it over to their own Arian clergy. Elsewhere in Africa the Catholics remained unmolested during the reign of
Gaiseric but were persecuted by his successors. Generally speaking, Vandal
occupation dealt a mortal blow to orthodoxy in Africa. In the Ostrogothic
kingdom in Italy Theodoric, although an Arian, gave complete freedom to
the orthodox Church throughout most of his reign, but his policy changed
in 523 when the emperor Justin began to persecute the Arians in the East.
The ban against Arianism was supported by the Romans in Italy, particularly by the orthodox clergy and senators. This led Theodoric to suspect
that the emperor's action had been stimulated by a faction in the Roman
Senate. Realizing the effect that imperial proscription of Arianism would
produce upon relations between his Roman and Gothic subjects, Theodoric
sent a delegation to Constantinople, headed by the bishop of Rome, to
secure the annulment of the anti-Arian decree. Although Justin apparently agreed to this, Theodoric was angered by the favor shown the pope
by the emperor, which emphasized the solidarity of eastern and western
orthodoxy. Theodoric died in 526 before religious peace had been restored
in Italy.

The Burgundians were also Arians, and this prevented their winning the
loyal support of the orthodox clergy, who recognized the authority of the
Burgundian kings. Although Sigismund, son of Gundobad, who came to
the throne in 516, was converted to orthodoxy, it was too late to heal the
religious breach before the fall of Burgundian power.

Unlike their neighbors, the Visigoths and Burgundians, the Franks were agans when they established themselves in Roman territory and remained so until toward the close of the fifth century. In 496 the Frankish king Clovis was converted to Christianity, to the orthodox belief, a fact of great importance in his conquests in Gaul.

EXPANSION OF THE FRANKS. The foreign policy of Theodoric was directed toward strengthening his position in Italy by establishing friendly relations with western Germanic kingdoms and maintaining peace and a balance of power among them. To this end he contracted a series of family alliances with the rulers of these states. In 492 he married a sister of Clovis the Frank and gave his own sister in marriage to the Vandal king Thrasamund. One of his daughters became the wife of Sigismund, king of the Burgundians; and another was married to Alaric II, who succeeded Euric as Visigothic king.

Theodoric's scheme was rudely disturbed by the ambitions of Clovis. In 496 Clovis conquered the Alamanni. He next forced the Burgundians to acknowledge his overlordship, and with these as his allies he attacked the Visigothic kingdom in 507. The conquests of Euric in Gaul and Spain had overtaxed the strength of the Visigoths and weakened their hold upon the territory they occupied, and their Roman subjects gave active aid to the orthodox Clovis. In a battle near Poitiers the Visigoths were defeated and their king, Alaric II, was killed. Theodoric was prevented at first from intervening personally by the emperor Anastasius, who sanctioned the action of Clovis and sent him the insignia of the consulship. In 508, however, the Ostrogothic king came to the aid of the Visigoths. He repulsed the Franks and Burgundians before Arles and recovered Narbonese Gaul. The greater part of Aquitania remained in the hands of the Franks. Theodoric established his grandson Amalaric as Visigothic king and exercised a regency in his name (510). Clovis died in 511, and expansion of the Franks ceased for a time, but the death of Theodoric in 526 led to fresh disturbances. The Visigothic king Amalaric at once asserted his independence in southern Gaul and Spain. Not long afterward, in 531, he fell in battle against the Franks, who seized the remaining Visigothic possessions in Gaul except Septimania—the coast district between the Pyrenees and the Rhone. Three years later the Franks overthrew the Burgundians and so brought under their sway the whole of Gaul outside of Septimania and Provence.

In 533 the situation in the West was as follows. Gaul was mainly in the hands of the Franks, Spain was under the Visigoths, the Vandals were still established in Africa, and the Ostrogoths in Italy. Both of the latter kingdoms, however, were showing signs of internal weakness. In addition to hostility between Germanic conquerors and the subject Roman population, factional strife had broken out over the succession to the throne. Evidence of the declining power of the Vandals was the success of the Moorish tribes in winning independence. By 525 both Mauretania and Numidia had been lost to them, and the tribes of Tripolis had shaken off the Vandal yoke. In 530 the Moors of southern Byzacene inflicted a severe defeat on the Vandals, which led to the deposition of the king. The weakness of these states seemed to offer a favorable, opportunity for the reestablishment of imperial authority in the West.

II. Restoration of Imperial Power in the West: A.D. 533–554

JUSTIN I: A.D. 518–527. Anastasius died in 518 and was succeeded by Justin, a lowly Illyrian who had risen to the post of commander of the imperial bodyguard (*comes excubitorum*). Unlike his predecessor, Justin was orthodox, and at the beginning of his reign an exceedingly influential position was held by the general Vitalian, who had been the champion of orthodoxy against Anastasius. He became master of the soldiers at Constantinople and in 520 was honored with the consulship. His power and ambitions constituted a real menace to the emperor, and induced the latter to arrange his murder. Justin reigned for nine years. He was an experienced soldier but personally unequal to imperial government. The guiding spirit of his administration was his nephew Justinian, who was largely responsible for Vitalian's removal. In fact the reign of Justin was a brief introduction to the long rule of Justinian himself, whom his uncle crowned as his colleague in 527 and who became sole emperor at the latter's death in the same year.

JUSTINIAN'S IMPERIAL POLICY. Justinian was by birth a Latin peasant probably from near Scupi (modern Uskub) in Upper Moesia, but through his uncle he had been able to enjoy all the educational advantages offered by the schools of Constantinople. In public life he showed himself a laborious and careful administrator, extremely autocratic and yet rather vacillating. He was a devout Christian, zealous for the propagation of orthodoxy, with a strong liking for, and considerable learning in, questions of dogmatic theology. He regarded religious and secular affairs as equally subject to imperial will, and in each sphere he exercised absolute authority. In him the autocratic ideal found its most perfect embodiment.

The goal of Justinian's imperial policy was the recovery of the western Empire from its Germanic rulers and the reestablishment of imperial unity in his own person. The attainment of unity of belief throughout the Christian world he regarded as no less important than political unity: one empire, one law, one church was his motto.

RECONCILIATION WITH THE WESTERN CHURCH: A.D. 519. The way was paved for the reconquest of the Roman West by a reconciliation with the Roman bishop Hormisdas, as a result of which orthodoxy was once more formally established at Constantinople and persecution of the Monophysites and other heretics was inaugurated in the eastern Empire (519). Although this ecclesiastical union with ʃ   ʷas brought about while the influence of Vitalian was predominant, it had the cordial support of Justinian, who recognized that the good will of the clergy and the Roman population of the western provinces would be won for the eastern emperor in this way. Such proved to be the case, and the subsequent wars for the recovery of the West assumed the aspect of crusades for the deliverance of orthodoxy from Arian domination.

OUTBREAK OF THE VANDAL WAR: A.D. 533. The deposition of Hilderic, who had been on friendly terms with the eastern Empire, and the accession of Gelimer, who reverted to an anti-Roman policy, gave Justinian a pretext for intervention in the Vandal kingdom. In conformity with his policy of treating Germanic kings as vassal princes of the Empire, he demanded the reinstatement of Hilderic. When this was refused, he prepared to invade Africa. An expeditionary force of ten thousand foot and five thousand horse, accompanied by a powerful fleet, was placed under the command of the able general Belisarius and dispatched from Constantinople in 533. An alliance concluded with the Ostrogoths forestalled the possibility of their coming to the aid of the Vandals.

MILITARY CONDITION OF THE EMPIRE. The trends in the military establishment of the eastern Empire during the fifth century continued during Justinian's reign. Constantinople had by then created an army predominantly "national" and indigenous, and even corps of *foederati* included some Byzantine subjects among the barbarians. The government was particularly interested in keeping Armenia within the Roman sphere of interest, because of its importance as a recruiting area along with the Balkans and Isauria. The army was kept up to its normal strength of about 150,000 men by recruiting volunteers and the sons of veterans, and the draft or its commutation through money payments was applied only sporadically. Most units were indifferently called *numeri* in the sixth century, and their strength varied from about two hundred to more than five hundred men. Mounted troops and units of the field army (*comitatenses*) were still valued higher than infantry and the border militia (*limitanei*). Crack units were found among the *foederati* and *bucellarii*. These latter were really private armies, developed in the course of the latter fourth and fifth centuries, that were enlisted in the service of important generals and other ministers of state. These *bucellarii* took oaths of loyalty to their commanders and to the emperor. They were usually taken into the service of the state and maintained at public expense. Justinian's armies were in general greedy for plunder and impatient of discipline, and both officers and men displayed a singular lack of sympathy for the civilian population. The actual size of individual field armies fighting Justinian's wars was remarkably small, since the emperor's aims outran his resources. Justinian was in fact on the point of abandoning the invasion of Africa for financial reasons when the favorable prophecy of an eastern bishop induced him to persevere.

RECONQUEST OF AFRICA: A.D. 533–534. The landing of Belisarius in Africa (September, 533) completely surprised the Vandals. Gelimer was defeated in battle, and Belisarius occupied Carthage. A second defeat before the close of the year doomed the Vandal kingdom. Early in 534 Gelimer surrendered, and all resistance ended. The Vandal insular possessions—Sardinia, Corsica, and the Balearic Islands—fell to the Romans without further opposition.

REVOLTS OF THE MOORS. The Moors, who had managed to assert their independence against the Vandals, were not disposed to pass under the Roman yoke peacefully. A revolt broke out in 535 and was not finally crushed until 539. Another, which was complicated by a mutiny of the imperial troops, raged between 546 and 548. Roman authority was finally reestablished over all the African provinces except Mauretania Caesariensis and Tingitana. The previous system of civil administration was restored and elaborate measures taken to defend the frontiers. Unfortunately, the ravages of the Moors and the war of restoration had played such havoc with conditions in Africa that, despite government assistance, its former prosperity was never revived. Africa had been recovered for the Empire, nevertheless, and was destined to remain a part of it until the Saracen invasion nearly a century and a half later.

RECOVERY OF ITALY. *First Phase:* A.D. 535–540. The overthrow of the Vandal kingdom had scarcely been accomplished when events in Italy gave Justinian the desired pretext for its invasion. Upon the death of King Athalaric in 534, Theodoric's grandson and successor, his mother, the regent Amalasuntha, married Theodahad, whom she made her consort. Shortly afterward he had her imprisoned and put her to death when she appealed to Justinian for aid. As avenger of his former ally, Justinian attacked the Gothic king. The possession of Africa gave the Romans an excellent base of operations against Italy. In 535 Belisarius invaded Sicily with 7,500 men and speedily reduced the island, while another Roman army marched on Dalmatia. From Sicily Belisarius crossed into south Italy, where he found little resistance. The inactivity of Theodahad produced a revolt among his own people. He was deposed, and Witiges became king. Witiges was able to purchase the neutrality of the Franks, who were allied with Justinian, by ceding to them the Ostrogothic possessions in South Gaul. Belisarius meanwhile continued his advance and occupied Rome (December, 536). There he was besieged for a year (March, 537–March, 538) by the Goths, who in the end were forced to abandon the blockade and fall back upon north Italy. The eunuch Narses arrived in Italy at this time at the head of a new Roman army. His presence was largely due to Justinian's mistrust of Belisarius, and he failed to cooperate with the latter, accomplishing nothing before his recall in 539. The last episode of the campaign was the siege of Ravenna (539–540), which was defended by the Gothic king. With its fall and his capture in 540, the resistance of the Goths

MAXIMIANVS·

Mosaics of Justinian and his entourage from the Church of San Vitale at Ravenna

ended. Italy was declared a Roman province, the civil administration was reestablished, and Belisarius was recalled to assume the command against Persia.

Second Phase: A.D. 541–554. The withdrawal of Belisarius with his best troops led to a revolt of the Goths under the leadership of the brave and energetic Totila (or Baduila) in 541. Within the next three years he drove the Roman garrisons from most of Italy, including Rome. Belisarius was sent to the West again but given inadequate support and accomplished nothing beyond the recovery of Rome, which he held until recalled at his own request in 548. The drain of a fresh Persian war upon the resources of the Empire forced Justinian to abandon temporarily Corsica, Sardinia, Sicily, and Italy, apart from Ravenna, and a few other fortresses. At last in 552 he was able to resume the struggle and entrusted conduct of the war to Narses, whose ability as a commander was superior even to that of Belisarius. Narses' army numbered over 30,000 and consisted chiefly of auxiliaries, including contingents of Lombards, who had been settled as *foederati* in Noricum since 547. He marched upon Italy by way of Illyricum and reached the Roman base at Ravenna. Thence he advanced toward Rome and met and defeated the Goths in a decisive engagement in Umbria (552). Totila fell in the battle. A second victory in Campania in the following spring forced the surviving Goths to come to terms. They were allowed to leave Italy and seek a new home beyond the Roman borders. A fresh enemy appeared in the Franks, who were then nominal allies of the Goths. A band of Alamanni and Franks swept down upon Italy and penetrated deep into the peninsula. Narses annihilated one of their divisions at Capua (554); the remainder were decimated by disease and forced to withdraw. Roman sway was firmly established over Italy as far as the Alps, but Raetia, Noricum, and the Danubian provinces remained lost to the Empire.

The long and bitter wars of restoration severely damaged the material welfare of Italy, and the heavy financial burdens imposed by the Roman administrative system aroused bitter protests. Relief measures proved insufficient, the middle class disappeared, the richer landed proprietors left the peninsula, and, as in Africa, the former prosperity was never restored.

ATTEMPTED RECOVERY OF SPAIN: A.D. 554. Following the conclusion of hostilities in Italy, Justinian seized an opportunity that presented itself for intervention in Spain. He sent an army to support the rebel Agila against Athanagild, king of the Visigoths (554). Roman forces occupied Corduba, Carthagena, and other coast towns. On the death of Athanagild, Agila succeeded to his throne and led the Visigothic opposition to the Romans, who were unable to advance further. They were able to retain what they had already conquered, however.

EXTENT OF THE ROMAN RECONQUESTS. Justinian's policy resulted in the overthrow of the Vandal and Ostrogothic kingdoms and the

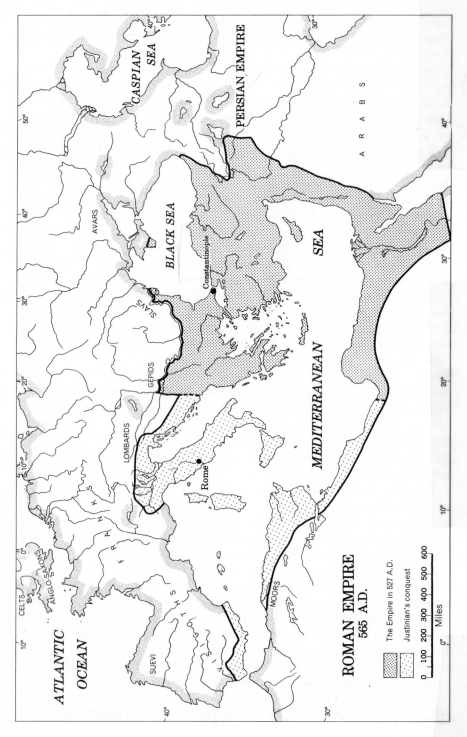

CASPIAN SEA

PERSIAN EMPIRE

A R A B S

50°

ATLANTIC

OCEAN

CELTS

ANGLO-SAXONS

AVARS

BLACK SEA

SLAVS

Constantinople

GEPIDS

LOMBARDS

SUEVI

Rome

MEDITERRANEAN SEA

MOORS

ROMAN EMPIRE
565 A.D.

The Empire in 527 A.D.

Justinian's conquest

0 100 200 300 400 500 600
Miles

recovery for the Empire of Africa, Italy, the Mediterranean islands, and a strip of the Spanish coast. The Empire was too weak to accomplish more.

III. Justinian's Frontier Problems and Internal Administration

BARBARIAN INVASIONS OF THE BALKAN PENINSULA. The strain imposed by the policy of expansion in the West on the strength of the Empire is clearly seen in the failure to defend the Danubian frontier and the ineffective conduct of the Persian wars. Time after time bands of Bulgars and Slavs poured into the Balkans. Especially destructive were the inroads of 540 and 559. In 540 the invaders penetrated as far as the Isthmus of Corinth; in 559 they threatened the capital itself but were driven off by the aged Belisarius.

PERSIAN WARS. In 527 the Persian king Kawad declared war on the Empire. The struggle was indecisive, but, on the death of Kawad in 532, Justinian, who wished to be free at any price to pursue his western policy, concluded peace with Kawad's successor, Chosroes I, upon paying an annual indemnity. The successes of Justinian in the West aroused the jealousy and ambitions of Chosroes in 539. The Persians overran Syria and captured Antioch in 540, carrying off its population. They failed, however, to take Edessa (544). In Mesopotamia an armistice was concluded in 545, although war continued between the Arab dependents of both states, and in the district of Lazica (ancient Colchis), a Roman protectorate that transferred its allegiance to Persia. Finally a fifty-years' peace was concluded in 561. Roman suzerainty over Lazica was acknowledged by the Persians, but the Romans promised to pay the Persians a heavy annual subsidy, in return for which the Persians undertook the defence of the Caucasus. In this way the Persians became technically Roman *foederati*, although, as in the case of the Visigoths in the fourth century, this was equivalent to a confession that the Romans were unable to subdue their enemy, who regarded subsidy as tribute.

EMPRESS THEODORA. In 525 Justinian had married Theodora, a former professional pantomime actress from the purlieus of the Hippodrome, and when he became emperor in 527, Theodora was crowned with him as Augusta. From that time until her death in 548 Theodora tried to influence public policy. Whatever the character of her previous career, her private life as empress was beyond reproach. She was fond of power, jealous of her influence with the emperor, and unforgiving toward those who crossed her. Both Belisarius and John of Cappadocia, the powerful praetorian prefect, were driven from the emperor's service by her enmity. She was a woman of great courage, possessed of remarkable political ambition.

THE "NIKA" RIOT: A.D. 532. The courage of the empress was conspicuously displayed when the factions of the Hippodrome—the

Greens and the Blues—rioted in 532. These factions had been organized in Constantinople in imitation of the circus factions of Rome but had acquired a different character and a greater importance. They appear to have served as an urban militia organized for the defence of the city walls. The two factions divided between them the entire urban population and had their regularly appointed leaders, who enjoyed a recognized place in the administrative organization of the city. It also appears that their leadership represented two different political, social, and religious points of view, the Blues tending to be conservative, upper class, and orthodox, the Greens, radical, lower class, and monophysitic. These parties may be regarded as the last survival of city-state democracy, and, owing to the extreme centralization of the administration at Constantinople, they exercised considerable pressure on the government.

The emperor and the court regularly supported one or the other of the parties. Anastasius had favored the Greens, Justinian was a partisan of the Blues. Factional rivalry was intense and culminated, in the early years of Justinian's reign, in open warfare. The punishment of notorious criminals of both factions in 532 led to their uniting in a revolt which overthrew the emperor. At first the mob demanded the release of their partisans and the dismissal of John, the praetorian prefect, whose financial policy was extremely oppressive, of Tribonian, the able but unscrupulous quaestor, and of the prefect of the city. Later emboldened by their success, they crowned as emperor Hypatius, a nephew of Anastasius. The situation became extremely critical, when the whole city with the exception of the palace fell into the hands of the rebels, whose battle cry was "Nika" or "Conquer!" Justinian and his councillors had already resolved upon flight when Theodora, declaring that she would die before abandoning the capital, encouraged them to stay and resist. By a judicious use of bribes they induced the Blues to desert the Greens, and imperial troops exacted a bloody vengeance from the rebellious populace. For the time being the population of the capital became politically a negligible quantity.

CODIFICATION OF THE ROMAN LAW. One of the greatest monuments to the reign of Justinian is the *Corpus Iuris Civilis*, a codification of Roman law by a commission of expert jurists, headed by Tribonian. The object of this codification was to collect in a convenient form all the sources of law then in force and to settle controversies in interpretative juristic literature. The compilation was divided into three parts: the *Code of Justinian*, the *Digest* or *Pandects*, and the *Institutes*. The *Code* was a collection of all valid imperial constitutions; it was first published in 529, a revised edition being issued in 534. The *Digest*, issued in 533, consisted of abstracts from writings of the most famous Roman jurists systematically arranged so as to present the whole civil law not contained in the *Code*. The *Institutes* was a brief textbook for law students. From the time of their promulgations these compilations constituted the sole law of the Empire, alone carried validity in the courts, and formed the only material for instruction in recognized law schools—those at Rome, Constantinople, and Berytus (Beirut). Provision was made for the publication of future legislation in a fourth compilation—the *Novels* or *New Constitutions*.

BUILDINGS. Justinian's administration was characterized by great building activity. He was zealous in the construction of frontier defences, the rebuilding of ruined cities, the founding of new ones, and the erection of religious edifices. Among the latter the most famous was the great Church of the Holy Wisdom (St. Sophia), which took the place of a building destroyed in the Nika riot. Transformed into a mosque, it remained for centuries the greatest architectural monument of the eastern Roman Empire. Currently it is a museum.

The execution of grandiose works of this sort increased the heavy expenditures necessitated by Justinian's foreign policy and required the continual wringing of fresh contributions from the already overburdened taxpayers. In raising revenues needed to meet fiscal demands, the emperor found the prefect John an invaluable agent.

JUSTINIAN'S RELIGIOUS POLICY. Throughout the whole of his reign Justinian strove to secure a united Christian Church. To this end he did not hesitate to use the autocratic power he claimed in religious as well as secular affairs. The degree to which he was able to dominate the eastern Church is revealed in the significant reminder of the Patriarch Menas to some of the members of the Synod of 536 that "Nothing whatsoever may be done in the Church contrary to the wish and order of the emperor." Justinian's interference in ecclesiastical matters was due largely to his interest in theological discussions, and he did not hesitate to write on questions of church doctrine. The reconciliation with Rome in 519, so necessary for the recovery of the West, had alienated the Monophysites, who were predominant in Egypt, Syria, and Mesopotamia, especially among the lower classes. At the outset of his reign Justinian strove to heal this breach, a policy in which he was largely influenced by Theodora, who sympathized with the Monophysites and saw the danger to the Empire in the continued hostility of the eastern peoples. This attempt however, was defeated by the energetic action of the Pope Agapetus, but Justinian resumed his efforts, and an ecumenical council convoked by him at Constantinople in 553 condemned the writings of three Church Fathers of whose teachings the Monophysites disapproved. The bishops who refused to agree were persecuted and exiled, and Pope Vigilius, then held as a prisoner in Constantinople, was forced to approve. Justinian failed to attain the unity he desired, for the clergy of Italy and Africa challenged the decision of the Council, while the Monophysites still refused to be conciliated. Toward the close of his reign Justinian moved even closer to the Monophysite point of view and began to persecute the clergy who ventured to oppose him. His death in 565 removed all danger of the Monophysite doctrines becoming the orthodox belief of the Eastern Empire.

A far harsher treatment was meted out to the Arians, who were treated as heretics and punished as criminals. A rebellion of the Samaritans, occasioned by their persecution, was stamped out savagely. A determined effort was made to eradicate the last remains of the old Hellenic faith, which still claimed adherents of note. In 529 the endowment of Plato's Academy was confiscated and the teaching of philosophy forbidden at Athens. The persecution of heretics and unbelievers was accompanied by a vigorous missionary movement to carry the Christian gospel to the peoples of southern Russia, the Caucasus, Arabia, the Sudan, and the oases of the Sahara.

THE CONDITION OF THE EMPIRE AT THE DEATH OF JUSTINIAN. Justinian died on November 14, 565. He left the Empire exhausted by the conquest of the western provinces. The national antagonism between Greeks and Romans, which was becoming more and more evident, was not effectively bridged by formal church unions, and a mistaken religious policy had fostered the growth of national ambitions among the native populations of Syria and Egypt and led to further disunion within the Empire. Under Justinian the annual consulship, for a thousand years identified with the life of the Roman state, was abolished in 540. When driven by military necessity, individual emperors had occasionally abandoned the principle of the division of civil and military authority, which had been so marked a feature of Diocletian's organization. Justinian departed still further from that organization in important reforms of provincial administration undertaken in 535 and 538–539, in which military commanders in many areas became the heads of civil government as well. Although Justinian later partially retracted these reforms, they survived in some provinces and foreshadowed the establishment of *themes*, military districts characteristic of the medieval Byzantine Empire.

It was in Justinian's reign also that the culture of the silkworm was introduced into the Empire by Persian monks, who learned the jealously guarded secrets of this art and brought some eggs of the silkworm out of central Asia concealed in hollow canes. The weaving of silk goods had long been a flourishing industry in certain cities of the Greek East and was made an imperial monopoly by Justinian. The introduction of the silkworm made this industry largely independent of the importation of raw silk from the Orient.

Justinian was the last emperor to stress Latin as the language of government at Constantinople and to uphold the old traditions of Roman imperial policy.

CHAPTER 2 6

RELIGION, LITERATURE, AND ART IN THE LATE EMPIRE

I. End of Paganism

PAGANISM OF THE LATE EMPIRE. In spite of the tremendous impulse given to Christianity by Constantine's policy of toleration and by its adoption as the religion of the imperial house, the extinction of paganism was by no means rapid. The chief pagan religions during the fourth century were the Oriental cults and the Orphic mysteries of Eleusis, which strongly resembled each other, but the worship of the Greco-Roman Olympian divinities still attracted numerous followers. Although paganism persisted in many forms, these had come to find their place in a common theological system by a process of religious syncretism. This development was based on the common characteristics of mystery religions, each of which inculcated the belief in a supreme deity, and was stimulated by the conscious opposition of all forms of paganism to Christianity, which they came to recognize as their common, implacable foe. The chief characteristic of later paganism was its tendency to monotheism—a belief in one abstract divinity of whom the various gods were but separate manifestations. The development of a harmonious system of pagan theology was greatly aided by Neoplatonic philosophy, which may be regarded as the ultimate expression of ancient paganism. Neoplatonism was more than a philosophical system; it was a religion and, like the Oriental cults, preached a doctrine of salvation. It was essentially a pantheism, in which all forms of life were regarded as emanations of the divine mind. Such was the paganism that confronted the Christians of the Late Empire and which, because of its many points of resemblance to their own beliefs and practices, they admitted to be a dangerous rival. This similarity also made the task of conversion less difficult.

CAUSES OF THE PERSISTENCE OF PAGANISM. There were several reasons for the persistence of paganism. Oriental and Orphic cults exercised a powerful hold over their votaries and their appeal resembled that of Christianity. Stoicism, with its high ideal of conduct, remained a strong tradition among the upper classes of society; Neoplatonism had a special attraction for men of intelligence and culture. Municipal patriotism, where it still existed, also fostered at least nominal worship of the traditional city gods, especially among the local curial class. Roman patriotism encouraged loyalty to gods who had made Rome great, and until the close of the fourth century pagan influences in the Roman Senate made it an indefatigable champion of the ancient faith. More potent was the fact that the Greco-Roman literature of the past was utterly pagan. This was the only material available for instruction in the schools and formed the basis of the rhetorical and philosophical studies that constituted higher education. The whole contemporary system of organized education thus subjected the minds of youth to pagan influences. To the intelligentsia Christianity was also repulsive, because it had been traditionally regarded as vulgar in both language and class. Generally speaking, in the East articulate opposition to Christianity was intellectual and came from the schools of higher learning and from professors rather than from the governing establishment, since the Senate at Constantinople had been thoroughly Christian since its foundation.

PERSECUTION OF PAGANISM. Constantine I sought to convert all of his subjects to Christianity and to make it eventually the official religion of the Empire, although for political reasons he did not place any severe restrictions upon the practice of pagan cults. It was not until the reign of Theodosius I (379–395) that Christianity in fact became the state religion. In converting the classes that mattered, Constantine and his successors were aided by the heterogeneous nature of the new imperial service-nobility which, in contrast to the paganism of urban West Roman senators, was not a firmly entrenched aristocracy hostile to religious changes. The new ruling classes of the Late Empire were dependent upon imperial patronage for their advancement, and they tended to be subservient to the court in matters of religion. Christianity soon became fashionable and respectable in the East through imperial support. The gradual conversion of the urban senatorial aristocracy in West Rome was not smooth; often relations between it and the court were embittered because of religious antagonism.

Constantine's sons, Constantius and Constans, initiated Christian persecution of paganism. They prohibited public sacrifices, forbade the adoration of statues of the gods, removed these from temples, closed many of the latter and turned them over to the Christian clergy. Nevertheless, they continued to appoint pagans to high administrative offices. Under Julian the antipagan laws were abrogated, restrictions were placed upon Christians, and a vain attempt made to create a pagan state church. This pagan reaction ended with Julian's death and his successors, Jovian, Valentinian I, and Valens, restored Christianity to its former status, but adhered to a policy of toleration of paganism much in the spirit of Constantine I.

With Gratian and Theodosius I official persecution of paganism was renewed. Theodosius was the first emperor to refuse the title of Pontifex Maximus at his accession, and he probably influenced his colleague Gratian to abandon its use. In 382 Gratian withdrew all official recognition of pagan worship, deprived the Roman priesthoods of public support, confiscated temple properties, and abolished the privilege of pagan priests. He also removed from the Senate house in Rome the altar and statue of Victory, which Julian had replaced after its removal by Constantius. For many senators, this altar was the symbol of the state, and their spokesman Symmachus made an eloquent plea for its restoration. Under the influence of his Christian advisers, Gratian remained obdurate. Later appeals to Valentinian II and Theodosius were equally vain. Although the brief reign of Eugenius produced a revival of pagan influence in Rome, the cause of paganism was already lost in the imperial city. After his victory over Arbogast and Eugenius, Theodosius pardoned their supporters in the Roman Senate on condition that they accepted Christianity. By the fifth century, the Senate was thoroughly Christian.   As early as 380 Theodosius had ordered all his subjects to accept the Christian creed formulated at the Council of Nicaea in 325. In 391 he ordered the destruction of the image and temple of Sarapis in Alexandria, a step that sounded the death knell of paganism in the eastern part of the Empire. The following year he unconditionally forbade pagan worship under the penalties for treason and sacrilege, and in 393 he ended the Olympic Games and their traditional pagan associations. Theodosius II continued the vigorous persecution of pagans. Adherence to pagan beliefs was declared criminal, and in the Theodosian Code, laws against pagans were included among those regulating civic life.

Many prominent persons continued to be secret devotees of pagan beliefs, and pagan philosophy was taught in the schools of Athens until they were closed by Justinian. Acceptance of Christianity was more rapid and complete in the cities than in the country. This gave rise to the use of the term pagan (*paganus*, "rural" in the sense of "barbarian") to designate non-Christian, a usage that became official by 370. Between the fifth and ninth centuries paganism virtually disappeared within the Empire.

The long association between pagans and Christians and the rapid incorporation of new converts into the Church exercised a profound influence upon Christian beliefs and practices. Pagan belief in magic contributed largely to Christian belief in miracles, and the development of the cult of saints was stimulated by pagan concepts of inferior divinities, demigods and daemons. Many pagan festivals were transformed into festivals of the Church.

II. The Church in the Christian Empire

THE CHURCH AND THE EMPEROR.   The right of emperors to legislate for the religious welfare of their subjects was inherent in imperial power and was accepted by the Christians, clergy and laity alike. Constantine established the procedure regularly followed by the emperors in dealing with problems that arose within the body of the Church. He was willing to accept the decision of the clergy in determining the correct or orthodox position in matters of dogma and discipline, but he took the responsibility of enforcing such decisions. His view was that, since he had been selected by divine will to rule the Roman World, it was his duty to God to prevent the spread of errors and strife within the Church.

In order to obtain the judgment of the clergy on disputed matters, Constantine adopted the Christian practice of calling synods or councils to settle controversies. These councils had already been organized on a provincial basis; Constantine simply made them representative of larger areas, even of the whole Empire. His first council was the Synod of Arles called in 314 to settle the Donatist controversy in Africa. Bishop Donatus and his followers had taken the position that clergymen who had yielded to the edicts of Diocletian's persecution and handed over Christian religious works should not be readmitted to their offices. Their opponents, headed by the bishop Cecilian, advocated pardon and restitution in office for those who repented. Strife between the two groups became so bitter and widespread that two sets of clergy appeared in almost all the towns of Africa and Numidia, and public order was endangered. When Constantine obtained control of Africa in 312, he recognized the Cecilianists as the orthodox party and reserved to them the benefits granted to the Christian clergy and congregations. The Donatists appealed to the emperor. After a small council of bishops, acting by imperial authority, had decided against them, they made a second appeal. Constantine then convoked the Synod of Arles, a council of western bishops, to settle the controversy. This synod condemned the Donatists anew and defined the Orthodox position in the matter. The Donatists refused to accept the Synod's verdict and for more than a century violently opposed Church and state alike, but the Synod of Arles set a precedent for future church councils. The first ecumenical or Empire-wide council was summonded by Constantine in 325 to deal with the Arian heresy.

Procedure in the councils was modeled upon that of the Roman Senate; meetings were presided over by the emperor or his deputy; all the bishops who attended had the right to speak and to vote; decisions were accepted and approved by the emperor, who transmitted them to the appropriate parties with his sanction that gave them legal validity.

Constantine's successors followed his example of summoning church councils to settle sectarian controversies, although, unlike him, many like Constantius sought to influence the decisions of the councils in favor of doctrines they supported. Since the general councils seemed to accentuate rather than allay sectarian strife, the emperor Zeno substituted a referendum of bishops by provinces, but his example was not followed by his successors. Justinian was the emperor who most effectively asserted his authority over the Church. He issued edicts upon purely theological questions and upon matters of church discipline without reference to councils, and he received from the populace of Constantinople the salutation "High Priest and King."[1] The decision of the Council of 553, influenced by Justinian, favored the heretical sect of the Monophysites, and provoked an attack upon the sacerdotal power of the emperor by Facundus, bishop of Hermiania in Africa, who declared that the priests and not the emperor should rule the Church. This opposition, however, had no immediate effect, and Justinian remained the successful embodiment of "Caesaro-papism." The attitude of the Church toward the emperor's right to intervene in the religious sphere was generally consistent: that the clergy acknowledged the emperor's sole right to call ecumenical councils, but that in these councils the bishops alone had the right to speak and vote, that the emperor had the right and duty to enforce their decisions and the right to legislate in religious matters on his own initiative, provided that such legislation conformed to orthodoxy established by the councils.

RISE OF THE PAPACY.   The Late Empire witnessed a rapid extension of the authority of the bishopric of Rome, which had even previously laid claim to primacy among the episcopal sees. In the West the title "pope" (from the Greek *pappas*, "father") became the exclusive prerogative of the bishop of Rome after the fourth century. The papacy was the only western patriarchate or bishopric with jurisdiction over metropolitan and provincial bishops, and it was the sole representative of the western Church in dealings with eastern bishops. At ecumenical councils the seniority of the Roman see over other bishoprics was recognized. The ideal of the papacy became the organization of the Church on the model of the Empire, with the pope as its religious head. In spite of appeals by eastern bishops to the pope on questions of orthodoxy, the eastern Church never fully admitted the papal authority, however.

The claim of the papacy was pushed with particular vigor by Innocent I (402–417) and Leo I (440–461). Leo laid particular stress upon the primacy of Peter among the Apostles and taught that this had descended to his successors in the Roman see. On this ground he induced the emperor Valentinian III in 455 to order the whole western Church to obey the bishop of Rome. Pope Gelasius (492–496) wrote to Anastasius that the power of priests was superior to imperial authority, but the establishment of the Ostrogothic Kingdom in Italy and then reconquest of the peninsula by Justinian weakened papal independence. Justinian forced the popes to submit to his authority in certain religious controversies.

PATRIARCHATE OF CONSTANTINOPLE.   A papal rival developed in the patriarchate of Constantinople, which, at the Council of Constantinople in 381, was recognized as taking precedence over the other eastern bishoprics and ranking next to that of Rome. This council also established the authority of other eastern patriarchates, Alexandria,

---

[1] *Archiereus basileus.* The title Basileus (King) was in common use in the eastern part of the Empire from the fourth century, but it was not assumed officially by the emperors until 629.

Antioch, Ephesus, Caesarea of Cappadocia, and Heraclea in Thrace, over the dioceses where they were situated. The primacy of Constantinople was not readily accepted by Alexandria, Antioch, and Ephesus, all apostolic foundations, whereas the claims of Constantinople to that honor were more than dubious. Between 381 and 451 the patriarchs of Alexandria successfully challenged the doctrinal authority of Constantinople, but in the latter year the Council of Chalcedon reasserted the primacy of the latter. This council also recognized the bishopric of Jerusalem as a patriarchate. The patriarch of Constantinople was made equal to the pope, a decision against which Pope Leo I protested in vain. But the patriarchs of Constantinople never acquired the power and independence of the popes, however, situated as they were in the shadow of the imperial palace and owing their ecclesiastic authority as well as their appointments to the secular authority. They rarely offered strong opposition to the emperors. The position of the patriarch under Justinian has been described as that of a "minister of state in the department of religion."

TEMPORAL POWER OF THE CLERGY. When Christianity became the favored and then the state religion, it was inevitable that the clergy should occupy a privileged position. Constantine the Great exempted them from personal services (*munera*) in 313 and from taxation in 319. Those who became clerics were expected to abandon all worldly pursuits, and an imperial edict of 452 excluded them from all employment. In addition to their authority in dogma and church discipline, the bishops also acquired considerable power in secular affairs. During persecution the Christians had regularly submitted legal differences among themselves to the arbitration of their bishops, rather than resort to tribunals of state. Constantine the Great gave legal sanction to episcopal arbitration in civil cases; Arcadius restricted its use to cases in which the litigants voluntarily submitted to the bishop's judgment. Bishops enjoyed no direct criminal jurisdiction, although the right of sanctuary was accorded to the churches, and they were frequently able to intercede for those seeking asylum with them. In enforcing moral and humanitarian legislation, the state called for cooperation of the bishops.

The influential position of the bishops as religious heads of municipalities led to their being accorded a place in the municipal administration. In protecting impoverished taxpayers against imperial officers, they were more effective than the *defensores plebis*. During the barbarian invasions, when the representatives of imperial authority were driven from the provinces, the bishops became the leaders of the Roman population in their relations with the barbarian conquerors.

It seems clear that the growth of the Church contributed materially to the decline of the Empire and to its extinction in the West. The Church hierarchy was a magnet that attracted ambitious and able men who might otherwise have served the state in civil capacities. The Church also attracted funds that might otherwise have contributed to shoring up ancient institutions. Monasticism provided an important alternative to city life and helped to undermine the military and political structure of the state. The Church in the West contributed to the feeling of defeatism that aided imperial collapse. Western Church fathers, by searchingly criticizing imperial institutions, seemed to imply that the Empire was not worth saving. They collaborated with the barbarians when the latter displaced Roman imperial leadership. In the East, however, the Church seems to have recognized the greater vitality of imperial institutions, to have thought of them as worth saving, and to have stood by New Rome in its struggle with its enemies.

III. Sectarian Strife

SECTARIANISM. The history of the Church from Constantine to Justinian is largely the history of sectarian strife, which had its origin in doctrinal controversies. While the western Church generally abstained from bitter theological discussions, adhered strictly to the orthodox or established creed, and devoted its energies to the development of church organization, the Church of the East, imbued with the Greek philosophic spirit, tried to solve the mysteries of the Christian faith and was a fruitful source of heterodoxy. Strife between the adherents of the various sects was waged bitterly and frequently culminated in riots and bloodshed. Toleration was unknown, and heretics, like pagans, were classed as criminals and excluded from communion with the orthodox Church. Of the many sects that arose in the fourth and fifth centuries, two were of outstanding importance. These were the Arians and the Monophysites.

ARIANISM. Arianism was an attempt to express precisely the relation of the three members of the Holy Trinity: God the Father, the Son, and the Spirit. About 318 Arius, a presbyter of Alexandria, taught that God was eternal but that the Son and the Spirit were his creations. A controversy arose over the teaching of Arius that threatened the unity of the Church. Constantine intervened and summoned the ecumenical council of Nicaea to decide on the orthodoxy of Arianism. The council accepted the formula that the Son was of the same substance (*homo-ousion*) as the Father, begotten but not created, which was the doctrine of the West. Arius was exiled.

The struggle was by no means over, for the Nicene creed found many opponents among eastern bishops who did not wish to exclude the Arians from the Church. The leader of this party was Eusebius of Nicomedia. In 335 they brought about the deposition of Athanasius, chief opponent of Arius, who had been bishop of Alexandria since 328. After the death of Constantine, Athanasius was permitted to return to his see, only to be expelled again in 339 by Constantius, who was influenced by Eusebius.

He took refuge in the West, where Pope Julius gave him his support. At a council of the Church held at Serdica (Sofia) in 343, there was a sharp division between East and West. The supporters of Athanasius were in the majority, and he and the other orthodox eastern bishops were reinstated in their sees (345).

When Constantius became sole emperor (353), the enemies of Athanasius once more gained the upper hand. The emperor forced a general council, convoked at Milan in 353, to condemn and depose Athanasius, while Pope Liberius, who supported him, was exiled to Macedonia. A new council, held at Sirmium in 357, tried to secure religious peace by forbidding the use of the word "substance" in defining the relation of the Father and the Son and sanctioned only the term *homoios* (like). Adherents of this creed were called Homoeans. Although they were not Arians, their solution was rejected by conservatives in both East and West. In 359 a double council was held, the western bishops meeting at Ariminum, the eastern at Seleucia. The result was the acceptance of the Sirmian creed, although the western council almost had to be starved into yielding. Under Julian and Jovian the Arians enjoyed full toleration; Valentinian I pursued a similar policy, while Valens went further and supported Arianism.

In the meantime the labors of three great Cappadocians—Basil of Caesarea, Gregory of Nazianzus, and Gregory of Nyssa—had already done much to reconcile the eastern bishops to the Nicaean confession, and, with the accession of Theodosius I, the fate of Arianism was sealed. A council of the eastern Church met at Constantinople in 381 and accepted the Nicene creed, adding a definition of the nature of the Holy Spirit as one of the Trinity. The Arian bishops were deposed and assemblies of heretics forbidden by imperial edicts. Arianism rapidly died out among the subjects of the Empire, although it existed for a century and a half as the faith of several Germanic peoples.

MONOPHYSITE CONTROVERSY. While the point at issue in dogmatic controversies of the fourth century was the relation of God to the Son and the Holy Spirit, the burning question of the fifth and sixth centuries was the nature of Christ. Like the former, the latter dispute arose in the East, originating in divergent views of the theological schools of Antioch and Alexandria. The former stressed the two natures in Christ—the divine and the human; the latter emphasized his divinity to the exclusion of his humanity, and hence its adherents were called Monophysites. The Diophysite Antiochene position was the orthodox view held universally in the West, where the duality of Christ was accepted without any attempt to define logically the relationship of his divine and human qualities. Beneath doctrinal controversy lay the rivalry between the patriarchates of Alexandria and Constantinople and the awakening national antagonism of native Egyptians and Syrians toward the Greeks. The conflict began in 429 with an attack of Cyril, patriarch of Alexandria, upon the teachings of

Nestorius, the patriarch of Constantinople. Cyril, believing that the nature of Christ was human made fully divine, justified the use of the word *Theotokos* (Mother of God), which was popularly applied to the Virgin Mary. Nestorius criticized its use and argued in favor of the term Mother of Christ. In the ensuing controversy, Cyril won the support of the bishop of Rome, who desired to weaken the authority of the see of Constantinople, and Nestorius was condemned at the council of Ephesus in 431.

The next phase of the struggle opened in 448, when Dioscorus, Patriarch of Alexandria, assailed Flavian, the patriarch of the capital, for having deposed Eutyches, a Monophysite abbot of Constantinople. At the so-called "Robber Council" of Ephesus in 449, Dioscorus succeeded in having Flavian deposed. Pope Leo I pronounced in favor of the duality of Christ, and in 451 the new emperor Marcian called an ecumenical council at Chalcedon, which reasserted the primacy of the see of Constantinople in the East, approved the use of *Theotokos*, and declared that Christ was of two natures. The attempt to enforce the decisions of this council provoked disturbances in Egypt, Palestine, and eastern countries. In Palestine armed force was required to suppress a usurping Monophysite bishop. In Egypt, enforcement led to a split between the orthodox Greek and the Monophysitic Coptic Churches.

As opposition to the decree of Chalcedon still disturbed the Church, the emperor Zeno in 482, instigated by patriarchs Acacius of Constantinople and Peter of Alexandria, tried to settle the dispute by exercise of imperial authority. He issued a letter to the church of Egypt called the *Henoticon*, which, while acknowledging the councils of Nicaea and of Constantinople, condemned that of Chalcedon and declared that "Christ is one and not two." This doctrine was at once condemned by Pope Silvanus. The rupture with Rome lasted until 519, when a reconciliation was effected at the price of complete submission by the East and rehabilitation of the council of Chalcedon. This in turn antagonized the Monophysites of Syria and Egypt and led Justinian to embark on his hopeless task of reestablishing complete religious unity by holding the western and winning back the eastern Church.

Justinian hoped to reconcile the Monophysites by an interpretation of the discussions at the council of Chalcedon acceptable to them. This led him (544) to condemn the so-called Three Chapters, doctrines of the Monophysites' opponents. Although this step implied a condemnation of the council of Chalcedon and was consequently opposed in the West, he forced the fifth ecumenical council of Constantinople in 553 to sanction it. Neither this concession nor still greater ones at the very end of his reign availed to win back the extreme Monophysites of Egypt and Syria, where opposition to the religious jurisdiction of Constantinople had taken a national form. Religious disunion in the East continued until these lands were lost to the Empire.

IV. Monasticism

ORIGIN OF MONASTICISM. Monasticism (from the Greek *monos*, "alone,"), which became so marked a feature of the religious life of the Middle Ages, originated in the ascetic tendencies of early Christianity, which harmonized with eastern religious and philosophical ideals of a purely contemplative life. It also gave expression to a widespread feeling of despair over social and economic conditions. The chief characteristics of early Christian monasticism were celibacy, fasting, prayer, surrender of worldly goods, and the adoption of a hermit's life.

MONASTICISM IN EGYPT. Monastic life first developed on a large scale in Egypt in the late third and early fourth centuries, when many men and women renounced a worldly life and began living on the edge of the desert or in oases. A leading figure in this movement was St. Anthony, whose monastic career began in 285. His life, written by Athanasius, had a great influence on the expansion of monasticism. The reputation for sanctity acquired by Anthony and others attracted numerous monks. In this way the earliest monastic communities arose—gatherings of monks living in separate cells entirely independent of their neighbors.

From these unregulated colonies gradually evolved monastic communities whose members lived a common life within a walled enclosure under the direction of a single head, the abbot, who enforced rules governing their religious life and daily labor. The first such truly cenobitic monastery was established in upper Egypt about 325 by Pachomius, whose "rule" of monastic life was widely adopted.

SPREAD OF THE MONASTIC MOVEMENT. During the fourth century monasticism spread rapidly throughout the eastern dioceses, partly under Egyptian influence, partly as the result of parallel developments elsewhere. A peculiar feature of Syrian monasticism were the pillar hermits, who passed many years on the tops of high columns. Eastern monks were noted for their fanaticism, and they participated prominently in religious disorders. Everywhere the abuses of early, unregulated monastic life led to the formulation of cenobitic rules and attempts to subject those monks who were not regular clergy to the authority of bishops. The most influential organizer of monasticism in Asia Minor was St. Basil, who founded a monastery at Neocaesarea in 360. His rule, which discouraged excessive asceticism and stressed study and useful labor, became very popular.

WESTERN MONASTICISM. Athanasius brought monks with him from Egypt when he took refuge in Rome in 341. Monasticism then found a foothold in Italy, whence it spread to Gaul and other western dioceses. The great organizer of western monasticism was Benedict, founder of the monastery at Monte Cassino about 520. The Benedictine rule for cenobitic life required monks to read as well as to work and to worship. This stimulated the collection of libraries in the monasteries and made the monks the guardians of classical and biblical literature through the Middle Ages. As yet no distinct monastic orders had developed, each monastery being autonomous under its abbot.

MONASTICISM AND THE STATE. The spread of monasticism created a situation disquieting to the government. For one thing, adoption of celibacy by many thousands of men and women helped to accelerate depopulation—a trend already well established. For another, withdrawal of such numbers of able-bodied persons from the ranks of agricultural workers, craftsmen, and other occupational groups lessened productivity and accentuated the manpower shortage felt in both public and private services.

V. The World of Letters and Art

FROM PAGAN TO CHRISTIAN CULTURE. The Late Empire saw the transition from the old pagan Greco-Roman culture of the Late Republic and Early Empire to a new, Christian culture. The transition was gradual, and the older pagan culture was by no means completely destroyed. Some elements were preserved intact, although far more were modified and adopted to serve the needs of Christian society. Great change was inevitable, for a fundamental difference between paganism and Christianity lay in the fact that the former was concerned primarily with life in this world, whereas Christianity regarded this life merely as a preparation for life hereafter. This new Christian spirit was expressed in late Roman literature, art, and architecture.

EDUCATION IN THE LATE EMPIRE. The general decline of the municipalities, increasing impoverishment of the middle and lower classes, and the influx of barbarian settlers, led to a gradual decrease in literacy among the inhabitants of the Late Empire. The old system of education culminating in the schools of rhetoricians was still available to a narrowing circle of those who could afford it and was a status symbol for the upper classes. Competing with the schools of rhetoric were academies teaching more technical subjects like law and stenography. All three disciplines could lead to careers in the civil service, and law and stenography were especially popular with those of limited means interested in improving their status by pursuing bureaucratic careers. The emperors were patrons of education because the schools produced their administrators. Constantius especially furthered stenography, Julian supported rhetoric, while his successors were interested equally in rhetoric and law.

Instruction in rhetorical schools followed the principles laid down by the great rhetoricians of the past from Isocrates to Quintilian. It sought to develop character and to produce eloquent speakers, but the curriculum was based wholly on the Greek and Latin classics. Educated circles were thus steeped in the masterpieces of pagan classical literature. When they came to write, they used language, illustrations, and ideas derived from the great Greek and Roman writers of the past. Their works therefore suffered from a conscious archaism in vocabulary and style and from a lack of original ideas. Intensive training in rhetoric, with its emphasis on form rather than content, on cleverness rather than intellectual honesty, tended also to discourage constructive thinking. Whatever their defects, the schools of the rhetoricians were very effective in preserving the traditions of pagan intellectualism, and in these schools there were Christian as well as pagan teachers.

Inevitably, the Christian clergy would also develop a system of Christian education. This was limited, however, to training of Christian children in their early years in the Holy Scripture and other religious writings, to instructing converts from paganism in the history and principles of Christianity, and to giving more advanced religious education to persons who wished to pursue a career within the Church. No attempt was made to provide Christian schools that would displace those of the grammarian and the rhetor. Many Christian writers denounced the study of the classics as dangerous to Christian morality or at best useless for Christians. The majority conceded, however, that it was a practical necessity for those whose careers required advanced training in letters and, while pointing out the dangers latent in pagan writings, declared that much good could be derived from them. Virtually all the notable Christian authors and many outstanding preachers were in fact products of the traditional educational system. With the collapse of the West Roman Empire what survived of pagan Latin literature owed its preservation to the Church, and especially to the monasteries.

Knowledge of Greek was maintained in educated circles in the West during the fourth century through the schools. It disappeared in the course of the fifth. This was due in part to barbarian occupation of the western Empire, but it was also due to the fact that Latin became the language of western Christianity, and the western clergy with rare exceptions had neglected the study of Greek. In the East, with the expansion of bureaucracy and establishment of Constantinople as an imperial capital where Latin was the official language, there probably was an increase in the knowledge and use of Latin for government purposes at least until the division of the Empire in 395. Latin literature was generally neglected in Greek literary circles, and the knowledge of Latin rapidly died out during the fifth and early sixth centuries. Justinian might issue his code of Roman Law in Latin, but he had to resort to Greek in his later legislation to make it intelligible.

LATIN SECULAR LITERATURE IN THE FOURTH CENTURY. Literate upper-class Romans remained the guardians of the cultural heritage of the classical world during the Late Empire. Guardianship of this heritage consisted primarily of literary interests conditioned by rhetorical and other trends apparent in the world of Roman letters since the Principate, and the production of prose and poetry that were excessively antiquarian, pompous, and basically uncreative. The literary developments of the Late Empire were complicated by the emergence of Christianity as the most vital social and intellectual force. The subsequent history of belles lettres is essentially the story of the efforts of a narrowing circle of pagan *literati* to defend their traditional cultural interests, while certain Christian writers, confronted with the storehouse of classical learning, letters, and art, sought to salvage and adapt at least some of the pagan past to the service of the Church.

The average literary and intellectual interests of late Roman aristocrats were by no means profound. On the contrary, they were rather superficial, as is indicated by the widespread popularity among the educated reading public of diluted abridgements and epitomies of history and historical biography in imitation of Suetonius. Many such works were written by members of an important circle of pagan senatorial intellectuals living and writing at Rome in the last decades of the fourth century.

This circle deserves attention, since it was composed of aristocrats who drew together to defend their paganism against two generations of steady attack by Christian writers and against the tightening persecution of the Theodosian dynasty. They did so in part by assiduous cultivation of antiquarian and therefore pagan literary and intellectual interests. The most famous person in this circle is the younger Symmachus (ca. 340–402), a leader of the pagan party in the Roman Senate under Gratian and Valentinian II. Symmachus was a typical representative of educated society of his time. He left a collection of letters that are vapid and verbose. Those written in an official capacity when he was prefect of Rome (384–385) are of considerable historical interest though of no literary value. An able orator, Symmachus delivered the unsuccessful appeal of the Senate for the restoration of the Altar of Victory in 384. At the center of the circle was Macrobius, whose *Saturnalia* records the learned and antiquarian conversation of his pagan friends and was inspired by Cicero's *De Republica*. The *Saturnalia* reveals late Roman aristocrats at their best, men who cultivated the traditional classical virtues of *urbanitas* and *gravitas* in the midst of a rapidly changing world. Perhaps the most important accomplishment of members of this circle and the one that bears witness to the sincerity of their literary convictions was their preservation and scholarly emendation for posterity of the manuscripts of significant earlier Latin authors like Juvenal, Livy, and Tacitus.

Closely affiliated with this circle, although he was a Greek from Antioch and therefore an outsider, was Ammianus Marcellinus (ca. 330–400), who retired from a military career, moved to Rome, and, at the end of the century, turned to writing history in Latin. This work was no mere epitome in the contemporary style but history in the grand manner, since Ammianus conceived of himself as the literary heir of Tacitus. Although Ammianus' style is crabbed and rhetorical, his work was a first-rate achievement, truthful and unusually objective. Himself a pagan, he treated Christianity fairly. He ranks deservedly with Livy and Tacitus as one of the best Roman historians. His work covered the years 96–378. Fortunately the most detailed parts, and those he wrote as a contemporary and even as an eyewitness of events (353–378), have survived.

POETRY IN THE FOURTH CENTURY. Stylistically the poetry of the period was as empty of true feeling as the prose, and there are few notable figures. The first Christian poet was Ausonius of Bordeaux (ca. 310–395), tutor to Gratian, and a powerful minister of state. Ausonius wore his Christianity lightly and was favorably disposed toward the old pagan aristocracy. His one work that rises above the pedestrian was the *Mosella*, a description of a voyage on the River Moselle, which is not without a feeling for natural beauty. A younger contemporary of Ausonius was Claudian (Claudius Claudianus, ca. 370–405), a Greek born in Alexandria, who, like Ammianus, wrote in Latin. He attached himself to the court of Honorius and was patronized by the general Stilicho. Most of his poems were written in praise of the emperor and his officials and of Stilicho's exploits. They accordingly have historical as well as artistic interest. Some of his poems are not merely "potboilers." Claudian had genuine epic gifts and, at his best, he could produce work not unworthy of Virgil. Like Ausonius, Claudian was only nominally a Christian, and his poetic style and allusions are those of educated pagan circles. A pagan contemporary of Claudian was Rutilius Namatianus, a native of southern Gaul but a resident of Rome, where he held the highest civic offices. His literary fame rests upon a poem in which he described his journey home from Rome in 416, a work similar to Ausonius' *Mosella* but of greater intrinsic poetic merit.

GREEK SECULAR LITERATURE IN THE FOURTH CENTURY. Greek secular literature of the Late Roman Empire displays the same general characteristics as the Latin. Both were products of the rhetorical system of education, and both were archaic and artificial. There was, however, a greater interest in philosophy in the Greek-speaking East. The Syrian Neoplatonist Iamblichus (d. ca. 330) deserves mention not because of the importance of his philosophic thought but because of his contamination of philosophy with mysticism and magic, and because of the influence his pupil Maximus had in converting the emperor Julian from Christianity to paganism. Julian the Apostate, Neoplatonist emperor (361–363) and dabbler in the occult, was also an active writer. His works included orations, letters, satires, and pagan hymns. His satirical pamphlet "Against the Christians" has not survived, but his letters and orations are valuable historical sources. Standing in the East for the cultural and educational ideals of the vanishing classical Greek world, the *paideia* inherited from Hellenistic times, were the pagan sophists and rhetoricians Themistius (320–388) and Libanius (314–393). Themistius held important appointments at Constantinople under Constantius, Valens, and Theodosius I, and many of his orations and some of his correspondence survive. More important was Themistius' friend, Libanius, the most distinguished man of letters of his age. Libanius taught for a time at Constantinople, but he spent most of his career at Antioch. For over a generation the sons of decurions and bureaucrats flocked to take the traditional rhetorical curriculum with him, despite occasionally serious competition from schools of stenography and law. Libanius' scores of orations and his hundreds of letters to important personages throughout the Empire are important historical sources. They also bespeak his intense and genuine municipal patriotism for Antioch and show, even as antiquity was dying, how men could still be motivated by concern for the well-being of the cities that had been traditional homes of civilization.

CHRISTIAN LITERATURE IN THE FOURTH AND EARLY FIFTH CENTURIES. In the field of religious literature writers of outstanding merit appeared. The Late Empire may be regarded as the golden age of patristic literature in both Latin and Greek. Unlike their pagan contemporaries, Christian writers had new things to tell the world, and their message was forcefully and creatively expressed. Their literature derived its inspiration from the new offensive undertaken against paganism after 312, from the need to stamp out heresies within the Church, and from the need to provide religious and historical literature to edify the Christian community.

The strident and vengeful voice of triumphant Christianity was first raised at the beginning of the fourth century by an African, Lactantius, who became a teacher of rhetoric and tutor of one of Constantine's sons, Crispus. In his most famous work, *On the Death of the Persecutors*, written about 316, he described with relish the divine retribution that had befallen the recent enemies of the Church. Although Lactantius was too biased an observer to be a true analyst of political and social trends, his forceful style has earned him the title of "the Christian Cicero."

The offensive against the pagans was maintained vigorously by St. Ambrose (Aurelius Ambrosius, d. 397), talented aristocrat and minister of state, who, like so many of his contemporaries, abandoned a career in the civil service for one in the Church. As Bishop of Milan he championed ecclesiastical rights against encroachment by the imperial court. Although a close friend of many of the senators affiliated with Symmachus' circle, he bitterly resisted the pagan counteroffensive launched in the 380s, as seen in his opposition to the restoration of the Altar of Victory in the Senate House in Rome. The bulk of his surviving literary work consists of sermons dealing with pastoral and political problems and written in the current rhetorical style. These works reveal Ambrose as a learned man, conversant with Plato and not unaffected by Neoplatonic thought. More familiar and of greater artistic merit are his hymns, and he is deservedly called "the father of church song."

A younger contemporary of Ambrose, the Spaniard Prudentius (fl. ca. 400), maintained the antipagan literary offensive in poetry and became the first great ecclesiastical Latin poet. His most famous work is *Against Symmachus*, in which he refuted the argument that the troubles befalling the Empire were attributable to defection from worship of the old gods. He also produced two collections of first-rate lyrical poems imbued with deep religious feeling. One work, the *Cathemerina*, dealt with the teachings of Christianity, the other, the *Peristaphanon*, celebrated the deaths of Christian martyrs.

This period of Latin patristic writing culminated in two literary giants, Jerome and Augustine. Jerome (Hieronymus, 335–420), a native of northern Dalmatia, was the most learned of the Christian Latin writers. His inspiration by pagans, especially Cicero, disturbed him because it contradicted his ascetic ideals. He spent the latter part of his life as head of a monastery at Bethlehem, and he did much to popularize ascetic monastic values in the West, especially among aristocratic ladies of Rome. Jerome was learned in Greek and Hebrew and, in addition to dogmatic writings and a collection of brilliantly satirical letters, he made the first Latin translation of the Old Testament directly from the Hebrew, which became the basis of the later Vulgate. He also translated the Greek *Church History* of Eusebius and part of the latter's *Chronicle*, which he continued from 325 to 378. Not the least of his classical qualities was his great pride in literary craftsmanship.

A more subtle thinker who made a cleaner break with the classical tradition was St. Augustine (354–430), Bishop of Hippo. He closed a long line of notable figures of the African church when he died during the siege of his city by the Vandals in 430. Augustine started life as a pagan, rhetorically trained for a civil-service career. Upon his eventual conversion to orthodox Christianity he wrote on almost every conceivable aspect of Christian theology, philosophy, and morality. Of his numerous works the two most famous are the *Confessions* and *On the City of God*. The *Confessions* are a moving and even lyrical narrative of his spiritual life, the struggle of the good and evil in his own soul. *On the City of God* is a monumental work, one of the most important our civilization has produced. It was inspired by the reaction to the sack of Rome by Alaric, after which some people questioned whether the disaster was not, in fact, a sign that Christianity was bad for the Empire. In meeting this attack, Augustine developed a philosophical interpretation of history as the conflict between good and evil, in which the Heavenly City is destined to triumph over that of this world. Thoughtful persons could see in this allegory a searching criticism of the Roman state and could draw the conclusion that the Empire in the West was not worth saving.

Greek religious literature resembled its Latin counterpart in many ways, not the least of them being the creation of Christian historical works with a providential orientation. Corresponding to Lactantius in the West was Eusebius (265–339?) of Caesarea, whose *Church History* was the first work of its kind. It covered the period from the birth of Christ to 323 and set a model for later church historians by emphasizing the importance of the remote past and of doctrinal controversies and by its lavish use of documents, which distinguished this genre from the work of pagan historians. Eusebius' *Chronicle*, in which he corrected and coordinated the work of his predecessors in this field, consists of parallel columns of dates of the chief events recorded in pagan and Jewish sources, preceded by a brief outline of world history. A biography of Constantine is also attributed to Eusebius, but this type of work was unique in Christian literature. Christian writers preferred to leave biographies of generals and politicians to the pagans. They were also uninterested in reinterpreting ordinary literary, political, or diplomatic history in Christian terms.

As in the West, orthodox reaction to heresy produced polemical books and pamphlets, some of them written by churchmen of note. Such, for example, were many of the works of Athanasius (295–373), the great foe of Arianism. Athanasius also produced the first biography of a saint with his celebrated life of St. Anthony. A younger contemporary of Athanasius and defender of orthodoxy was Basil of Caesarea (330–379), author of a famous monastic "rule" observed to this day in many parts of the Greek Orthodox world, and he was noted for his published sermons and letters. His brother, Gregory of Nyssa (341?–395), was an even abler defender of orthodoxy. Another champion of the true faith was Gregory of Nazianus (330–390), an eloquent preacher and a charming letter writer and prolific poet, who in certain poems introduced the use of rhythm into Greek Christian verse.

If Greek churchmen had much in common with their Latin colleagues, many of them differed in one important respect: they believed that the Empire in the East was worth saving from barbarism. This is seen especially in the attitudes of John Chrysostom (344–407) and Synesius of Cyrene (370–413), both of whom took an active role in leading the anti-barbarian faction at the imperial court when Gaïnas and his army were eliminated in 400. Both these men are also interesting for other reasons. Chrysostom ("Golden Mouth"), a pupil of Libanius, was the most eloquent of the fourth-century preachers and one of the most famous patriarchs of Constantinople. Synesius, although possibly born of a Christian family, was exposed to predominantly pagan influences in his youth. He received a Neoplatonic education at Alexandria, and even after becoming Bishop of Ptolemais in Cyrenaica he was noted rather for his administrative and soldierly qualities than for any depth of piety. He has left poems, personal letters, and hymns of some artistic merit.

THE FIFTH AND SIXTH CENTURIES.   After about 400 the literary history of the Roman Empire shades gradually into the medieval period in the West and the Byzantine in the East. The pessimistic attitude of Augustine toward the Empire was maintained in the West in works of his disciple, Orosius, and of Salvian. The latter's *On the Governance of God*, written about 450, contrasted what he thought were fine Germanic qualities with imperial degeneracy. There are few other figures of literary note in the West during the fifth century. One may mention in passing Sidonius Apollinaris (431–487), a Gallo-Roman aristocrat who attained high civil office in Rome before returning to Gaul, where he became Bishop of Clermont. Like other members of his class, Sidonius attempted poetry, but he lacked any real talent. Of some historical, if not literary, interest is his correspondence, which reveals conditions in his province during the initial stages of the barbarian occupation. In Rome itself the tradition of scholarly emendation of classical works of Latin literature was continued by the now Christian descendants of the circle of Symmachus and Macrobius.

The last interesting literary figures in the West having any real claim to classical affinities flourished during the Ostrogothic regime in Italy. One of the noblest and most tragic of all Latin writers is Boethius (d. 524), minister of state to Theoderic. Boethius in a very real sense was the last Roman from a literary point of view. He translated and commented on Aristotle and, while in prison and awaiting execution by Theoderic, he wrote *On the Consolation of Philosophy* to explain why just deserts are not meted out to good and bad men alike. Boethius' knowledge of ancient philosophy was profound, and the effect of his premature death on medieval intellectual history is inestimable. A long-lived contemporary was Cassiodorus (480–575), a quaestor and master of the offices under Theoderic, who has left valuable historical material in his *Variae*, a stylistically turgid collection of official correspondence prepared by him in the king's service. His chief literary work was a history of the Goths, of which unfortunately only a few excerpts remain. In his later years, Cassiodorus founded two monasteries organized according to the Benedictine rule and wrote an important manual called *Institutes of Divine and Secular Letters*. In this he urged monks to copy manuscripts, and so performed a great service in fostering the preservation of secular as well as ecclesiastical knowledge.

In the Greek East the disasters that had beset the Empire in the early years of the fifth century evoked the same sorts of attack on Christianity that had produced defenses of the Church by Augustine, Prudentius, Orosius, and others. In the East the attack brought about a revival of Greek pagan historiography, which had lagged behind its Latin counterpart in the fourth century. In general, although differing greatly in ability, these historians maintained a tradition of objectivity, but much of their work has been lost.

The Age of Justinian witnessed the production of outstanding historical works by Procopius of Caesarea in Palestine (fl. 527–563), the most distinguished historian writing in Greek since Polybius, whom he resembled in his approach to history. Procopius used the language of Herodotus and Thucydides rather than living Byzantine Greek. Trained as a lawyer, he became Belisarius' private secretary and thus was an eyewitness to many of the events he described. He has left a valuable and objective narrative of the Vandalic, Gothic, and Persian wars of Justinian (533–552) and an account of Justinian's great building program. Procopius was also the author of the *Anecdota* or *Secret History*, a grossly satirical attack on Justinian, Theodora, Belisarius, and the latter's wife, Antonina. Although a malicious work, the *Secret History* contains important facts and, when properly used, is an important source for the social, administrative, and economic history of Justinian's reign.

Worthy of passing mention are two other historical writers of Justinian's reign: Peter the Patrician, a diplomat whose treatise on court ceremonies is excerpted in part in a work of the tenth century, and Agathias, an inferior historian who continued Procopius' work for the years 552 to 558. Agathias was also a poet and published numerous epigrams, many of which have survived.

ARCHITECTURE.   Public architecture of the Late Empire evolved from that of the Principate but displayed new forms, most of which were inspired by the needs of Christianity. Many buildings were still built to serve secular needs—city walls, aqueducts, reservoirs, hospitals, palaces, and prisons; but there were no more pagan temples, and, after Constantine's buildings in Constantinople which duplicated those of Rome, there were few new theaters, amphitheaters, hippodromes, or great public baths built for entertaining the public at government expense. Constantine I took the initiative in building churches and urging their construction on Christian congregations. Money for these was provided from the public treasury, and building materials were often mined from confiscated or abandoned temples, although many of the latter were not destroyed but modified to meet the requirements of Christian worship.

Earlier Christian buildings had been relatively small. Now churches were erected on a scale befitting the position of Christianity as the imperial religion and the tremendously increased number of worshippers. It was inevitable that the architects should at first use forms and methods of construction employed in monumental pagan architecture, but in so doing they displayed great originality and eventually came to develop new architectural types. For church services they needed buildings with spacious, well-lighted interiors. So the emphasis shifted from exterior beauty of form and ornamentation to the interior effects of space, light, and color.

Four important types of churches came into use: basilicas, churches with central domes, domed basilicas, and cruciform churches. The basilica was adapted from the like-named Roman building. It was a long, rectangular hall divided by rows of columns into a central nave and two side aisles. The walls of the nave rose above the roofs of the aisles and gave space for windows. In the West the roofs were of wood, flat or gabled, but in the East stone or vaulted roofs were in general use. Usually one end of the basilica terminated in an apse, but apses also occurred at both ends. Central domed churches had their forerunners in circular buildings with masonry domed roofs like the Pantheon at Rome. But many churches of this type had octagonal rather than circular walls. Domed basilicas and domed cruciform churches were made possible by the solution of the architectural problem of placing a circular dome on a square building, through the development of the triangular pendentive to carry the weight across the corner angles. Once this was achieved, one or more sides of the square could be extended to form a rectangular nave, as in a basilica, or a rectangular nave crossed by another at right angles (a transept), as in a cruciform church. These basic types and their various combinations greatly influenced later church architecture in the East and West.

Many examples of late Roman churches still stand, and of these the most magnificent by far and the most famous is the previously mentioned Church of the Holy Wisdom (Santa Sophia) in Constantinople. St. Sophia is a domed basilica with a nave 250 feet long and 110 wide, with aisles and galleries above them. The great dome 108 feet in diameter and 179 feet in height with forty windows at its base is flanked by two halfdomes, all supported by eight enormous piers. Its architects were Anthemius and Isidore, both from Asia Minor. St. Sophia was dedicated in 537, but part of its original dome was destroyed by an earthquake in 558 and was replaced by the present one, the work of another Isidore. Many Turkish mosques are copies, more or less modified, of Justinian's great church.

ART. The art of the Late Roman Empire, while owing much to that of the preceding age, had a new spirit and certain new techniques. Although traditional canons of Greco-Roman art with its idealism and naturalism never disappeared, they lost ground before or blended with certain nonclassical standards during the Late Empire. These standards seem to have had their origins in the Semitic Near East, and their spread was due partly at least to Christianity, which found them amenable to its outlook. The new art, which was especially at home in the eastern Empire, intended to convey ideas forcefully rather than be merely pretty or pleasing. Like modern art, it resorted to extremes to achieve its purpose. It was characterized by a starkness verging on the abstract, a preference for frontality, and an enlargement of important figures out of scale for the sake of effect. The nature of this art may be seen in certain panels on the Arch of Constantine (315) that stand out in sharp contrast to other reliefs on the same arch appropriated from monuments of much earlier date. It is misleading to say that late imperial artists were technically less competent than their

The Church of St. Sophia at Constantinople

predecessors. Many of them simply were choosing to express in a different manner the reality of their world.

The major creations in decorative art were mosaics and wall paintings adorning the interiors of churches and other religious edifices, and of these the mosaics were more important and more costly. During the Principate, mosaics had been widely employed as floor decorations but rarely on walls. Now they were raised from the floor to cover the walls and at times the vaulting of the churches. They no longer served a purely decorative purpose. Along with paintings, they portrayed Biblical scenes that impressed on spectators the great events in the stories of the Old and New Testaments. Their rich colors and elaborate designs gave to the interior of churches an impressive magnificence. Mosaics and paintings alike reveal a blending of artistic influences, Hellenic and Eastern. Out of these contrasting elements a new Christian decorative art arose. It appears also in the miniature paintings that decorated manuscript books, in the sculptured reliefs on coffins, in sculptured ivories, and other forms of minor art.

SCIENCE. The intellectual climate of the Late Empire was not favorable to science. A stultifying respect for traditional ideas was inculcated by the educational system, and the tightening of autocratic controls discouraged freedom of thought. Christian leaders taught that the Bible had spoken the final word on all questions in the natural and physical sciences, and that further speculation was useless if not impious. The widespread belief in magic was also detrimental to scientific studies. In medicine, as in law, scholarship was limited to commenting on, or making excerpts from, works of earlier authors. Arithmetic and geometry were still studied, largely for their practical aspects. In industry there was only one important new development, the adaptation of the water wheel to provide power for milling grain, which apparently was introduced during the fourth century.

EPILOGUE

LOMBARD AND SLAVIC INVASIONS. In 568, three years after Justinian's death, the Lombards descended on Italy from Pannonia and wrested from the Empire the Po Valley and part of central Italy. The Romans were confined to Ravenna, Rome, and the southern part of the peninsula. Toward the close of the sixth century (after 581) Bulgars and Slavs migrated across the Danube, resulting in the Slavic occupation of Illyricum and the interposition of a barbarous, heathen people between the eastern Empire and western Europe. Early in the seventh century the Roman possessions in Spain were lost to the Goths.

THE PAPACY AND THE HOLY ROMAN EMPIRE. The weakness of imperial authority in the West led to the strengthening of the papacy and its acquisition of political power in Italy. It was the papacy that kept alive in western Europe the ideal of a universal imperial Church, for the whole of western Christendom came to acknowledge the supremacy of the Roman see. Nor was the concept of a reestablished western Empire lost to view; it was destined to be realized in the Holy Roman Empire of Charlemagne and his successors. Of great future importance for the development of European civilization was the fact that the western part of the Roman world passed to peoples either already Christianized or soon to become so and that the Church, chiefly through the monasteries, was thus able to become the guardian of the remnants of ancient culture.

THE BYZANTINE EMPIRE. The loss of the western provinces and Illyricum transferred the center of gravity in the Empire from the Latin to the Greek element and accelerated the transformation of the eastern Roman Empire into an essentially Greek state—the Byzantine Empire. The Byzantine Empire inherited from the Roman its organization and the name Romaioi (Romans) for its citizens, but before 600 Greek had supplanted Latin as the language of government. This transformation further accentuated the religious differences between East and West, which led ultimately to the separation of the Greek Orthodox and Roman Catholic Churches.

THE MOSLEM INVASION. Before 650 Egypt and Syria were occupied by the Moslems, whose conquest was facilitated by the animosity of Monophysite natives toward the rule of an orthodox emperor. The loss of these territories gave fresh solidarity to the Empire in the East by restricting its authority to the religiously and linguistically homogeneous and thoroughly loyal population of Asia Minor and the eastern part of the Balkan peninsula. This solidarity enabled the Byzantine Empire to fulfill its historic mission of forming the eastern bulwark of Christian Europe against the Moslems throughout the Middle Ages.

For the student of Roman history, the major problem is to find the causes of the political, economic, and cultural changes that overtook the Roman World by the third Christian century and led ultimately to the collapse of the Roman Empire and classical culture in the West. An allied problem is to understand why it simultaneously survived in the East and later revived. In the preceding chapters attention has been drawn to various phenomena indicative of these historical processes and their interpretation. It is plain that there is no simple explanation of these developments in terms of a single cause such as soil exhaustion, moral "decadence," or the like. Rather there were a number of interacting factors that operated to reduce the vitality of the Roman state and its inhabitants. Among them high place must be given to the following. Rome failed to develop an economic system that could give to the working classes of the Empire living conditions sufficiently advantageous to encourage them to support it devotedly and to reproduce in adequate numbers. Rome failed to develop a broad system of liberal and scientific education that would have fostered progressive technical developments in industry and agriculture and led to greater production and greater prosperity for all the population. Rome failed to evolve a political system that would have assured liberty of thought and action to its citizenry and so provided greater incentives to intellectual and economic efforts. Rome came to pursue a fallacious military policy that ultimately placed the civilian population at the mercy of a lawless professional army. These failures were themselves due to the political, social, and economic outlook which had been typical of the governing circles of Rome during the Republic, an outlook which imperial rule did nothing to change. Its results began to be felt in the latter part of the second Christian century. In the early third century the weaknesses were revealed clearly in cultural stagnation, a decline in population, and a decline in productivity. The half century of disorders that followed dealt a mortal blow to the Empire's human and material resources. If the Empire had enjoyed healthier political, economic, and cultural conditions at the close of the Severan dynasty, it is conceivable that it could have weathered these storms without suffering crippling losses. As it was, the Empire that emerged was so weak that it would have required exceptionally favorable conditions for it to have regained the stability and morale necessary for its survival. Unfortunately, however, it was one of the fateful coincidences of history that it had to face the great wave of barbarian invasion, coupled with continuous assaults from Persia. The exigencies of the military situation imposed upon the government of the Late Empire the necessity of creating an organization for defense that proved too heavy for its subjects to support. The desperate measures taken to save the state, which under other circumstances might have succeeded, proved so unsuccessful that most of the central and western parts of the Empire were lost beyond recovery. In this loss of the West errors of statesmanship also played a considerable role. All aspects of the imperial survival in the East have not as yet been clarified, but here greater economic vitality, a healthier urban tradition, less highly developed manorialism, greater cooperation from important forces like the Church, coupled with superior statesmanship and a stronger will to survive, obviously were factors of the highest significance. Perhaps the general problem that faced the Romans—to construct a stable and enduring world state of the heterogeneous racial and cultural elements once included within their Empire—was a task beyond human capacity. Nevertheless, they made a valiant effort deserving of respect and gratitude from later ages that have benefited in so many ways from the Roman achievement.

APPENDIX

APPENDIX

CHRONOLOGICAL TABLE

B.C.	To ca. 9000	Palaeolithic Age. Cro-Magnon Culture.
	ca. 9000–3500	Mesolithic Age.
	ca. 3500–2500	Opening of the Neolithic Age and Introduction of Agriculture.
	ca. 2000	Earliest Palafitte lake villages.
	ca. 2000–1800	Copper-Stone Age.
	ca. 1800–1300	Beginning of the Bronze Age.
	ca. 1700	Terremare villages.
	ca. 1000–800	Transition to the Iron Age.
	Early VIII Cent.	Etruscan settlement in Etruria.
	Early or Middle VIII Cent. ?	Iron Age settlement on Palatine Hill.
	Late VIII Cent.	Greek colonization of Sicily and south Italy begins.
	ca. 725–700	Foundation of Carthage.
	VII–VI Cent.	Etruscan expansion in Latium, Campania, and the Po Valley.
	VII Cent.	Rome of the Four Regions.
	ca. 509	Overthrow of Etruscan supremacy at Rome. End of the early monarchy. The first consuls appointed. Dedication of the Capitoline temple.
ca. 493 (486) ?		Alliance of Rome and the Latins.
ca. 450		Foundation of plebeian Tribunate.
ca. 451–449 (444–442)		The Decemvirate. Codification of the Law.
ca. 445 (437)		Lex Canuleia.
ca. 444 (436)		Office of military tribune with consular powers established.
	ca. 435	Censorship established.
	ca. 400	Celtic migration into Po Valley.
	ca. 392	Capture of Veii.
390 (387)		Battle of the Allia. Sack of Rome by the Gauls.
367 (363)		Sextio-Licinian Laws.
366 (362)		Praetorship established.
	343–341	First Samnite War.
340 (338)– 338 (336)		The Latin War.
	340 ?	Alliance of Rome and the Campanians.
	339	Lex Publilia
326 (324)–304		Second Samnite War.
321 (319)		The Caudine Forks.
	309–308	War with the Etruscans.
312 (310)		Appius Claudius Censor.

300	Lex Ogulnia.
298–290	War with Samnites, Etruscans, and Gauls.
295	Battle of Sentinum.
290	Subjugation of Samnium.
287	Secession of the Plebs. Lex Hortensia.
285	Occupation of the Ager Gallicus. Defeat of Gauls and Etruscans at Lake Vadimo.
281–272	War with Tarentum and Pyrrhus.
280	Battle of Heraclea.
279	Battle of Asculum. Alliance of Rome and Carthage.
278	Pyrrhus invades Sicily.
275	Battle of Beneventum.
264–241	First Punic War.
263	Alliance of Rome and Syracuse.
260	Naval Victory at Mylae.
256–255	Roman invasion of Africa.
250	Roman naval disaster at Drepana.
242	Battle of the Aegates Is. Office of *praetor peregrinus* established.
241	Sicily ceded to Rome.
241/40	Reform of the Centuriate Assembly.
241–238	Revolt of Carthaginian mercenaries. Sardinia and Corsica ceded to Rome.
237	Hamilcar in Spain.
232	Colonization of Ager Gallicus.
229–228	First Illyrian War.
229	Hasdrubal succeeds Hamilcar in Spain.
227	Provinces of Sicily, and Sardinia and Corsica organized.
226	Roman treaty with Hasdrubal.
225	Gauls defeated at Telamon.
224–222	Conquest of Boii and Insubres.
221	Hannibal Carthaginian commander in Spain.
220–219	Second Illyrian War.
219·	Siege of Saguntum.
218–201	Second Punic War.
218	Hannibal's passage of the Pyrenees and Alps. Roman invasion of Spain.
217	Battle of Trasimene Lake. Q. Fabius dictator.
216	Cannae. Revolt of Capua.
215	Alliance of Hannibal and Philip V of Macedon. First Macedonian War.
214	Revolt of Syracuse.
211	Syracuse and Capua recovered. Roman Alliance with the Aetolians. Roman disasters in Spain.
210	P. Cornelius Scipio Roman commander in Spain.
207	Battle of the Metaurus.
205	Peace between Philip of Macedon and Rome.
204	Scipio invades Africa.
202	Zama.

201	Annexation of Carthaginian Spain.
200–196	Second Macedonian War.
197	Battle of Cynoscephalae. Provinces of Hither and Farther Spain organized.
196	Flamininus proclaims the "freedom of the Hellenes."
192–189	War with Antiochus the Great and Aetolians.
191	Antiochus defeated at Thermopylae.
190	Battle of Magnesia.
186	Dissolution of the Bacchanalian societies.
184	Cato the Elder censor.
180	*Lex Villia annalis.*
171–167	Third Macedonian War.
168	Battle of Pydna.
167	Achaean political prisoners held in Italy.
149–146	Third Punic War.
149	Calpurnian Law.
149–148	Fourth Macedonian War.
148	Macedonia a Roman province.
147–139	War with Viriathus in Spain.
146	Revolt of the Achaeans. Sack of Corinth. Dissolution of the Achaean Confederacy. Destruction of Carthage. Africa a Roman province.
143–133	Numantine War.
136–132	Slave War in Sicily.
133	Kingdom of Pergamon willed to Rome. Tribunate of Tiberius Gracchus.
129	Province of Asia organized.
123–122	C. Gracchus tribune.
113	Siege of Cirta.
111–105	Jugurthine War.
105	Romans defeated by Cimbri and Teutones at Arausio. Province of Gallia Narbonenis organized.
104–100	Successive consulships of Marius. Slave war in Sicily.
104	Domitian Law.
102	Teutones defeated at Aquae Sextiae.
101	Cimbri defeated at Vercellae.
100	Affair of Saturninus and Glaucia.
91	Tribunate of Livius Drusus.
90–88	Italian or Marsic War.
90	Julian Law.
89	Plautian Papirian Law. Pompeian Law.
89–85	First Mithradatic War.
88	Massacre of Italians in Asia. Mithradates invades Greece.
87	Marian revolt at Rome.
87–86	Siege of Athens and Peiraeus.
86	Seventh consulship of Marius. Chaeronea and Orchomenus.
83	Sulla's return to Italy.

82–81	Sulla dictator.
77–71	Pompey's command in Spain.
75	Bithynia a Roman province.
74–63	Second Mithradatic War.
74–66	Command of Lucullus in the East.
73–71	Revolt of the gladiators.
70	First consulate of Pompey and Crassus. Trial of Verres.
67	Gabinian Law.
66	Manilian Law.
63	Cicero consul. Conspiracy of Catiline. Annexation of Syria. Death of Mithradates.
60	Coalition of Pompey, Caesar, and Crassus (First Triumvirate).
59	Caesar consul. Vatinian Law.
58	Cicero exiled.
58–56	Subjugation of Gaul.
57	Cicero recalled. Pompey Curator of the Grain Supply.
56	Conference at Luca.
55	Second consulate of Pompey and Crassus.
55–54	Caesar's invasions of Britain.
53	Death of Crassus at Carrhae.
52–51	Revolt of Vercingetorix.
52	Pompey sole consul.
49–46	War between Caesar and the Optimates.
48	Pharsalus. Death of Pompey.
48–47	Alexandrine War.
47	War with Pharnaces.
46	Thapsus.
45	Munda. Julian Municipal Law.
44	Assassination of Julius Caesar (March 15).
44–43	War at Mutina.
43	Octavian consul. Coalition of Antony, Lepidus, and Octavian (Second Triumvirate).
42	Battles of Philippi.
41	War at Perusia.
40	Treaty of Brundisium.
39	Treaty of Misenum.
37	Treaty of Tarentum. Second term of the Triumvirate begins.
36	Defeat of Sextus Pompey. Lepidus deposed. Parthian War.
31	Battle of Actium.
30	Death of Antony and Cleopatra. Annexation of Egypt.
27	Octavian princeps and Augustus.
27 B.C.–A.D. 14 AUGUSTUS	
25	Annexation of Galatia.
23	Second Imperial Act of Settlement by Augustus.
20	Agreement with Parthia.

	18	Julian Law on Marriage.
	16	Conquest of Noricum.
	15	Subjugation of the Raeti and Vindelici.
	14–9	Conquest of Pannonia.
	12	Augustus Pontifex Maximus. Altar of Rome and Augustus at Lugdunum. Invasion of Germany. Death of M. Agrippa.
	9	Death of Drusus.
	6	Subjugation of the Alpine peoples completed.
A.D.	6–9	Revolt of Pannonia.
	9	Revolt of Arminius. Papian Poppaean Law.
	14–37	TIBERIUS.
	14–17	Campaigns of Germanicus.
	19	Death of Germanicus.
	26	Tiberius retires to Capri.
	31	Fall of Sejanus.
	37–41	GAIUS CALIGULA.
	40	Annexation of Mauretania.
	41–54	CLAUDIUS.
	43	Invasion and annexation of southern Britain.
	48	Aedui receive admission to magistracies and the Senate.
	54–68	NERO.
	58–63	Parthian War.
	59–60	Rebellion of Boudicca.
	64	Great Fire in Rome.
	65	Conspiracy of Piso. Death of Seneca.
	66–67	Nero in Greece.
	66	Rebellion of the Jews.
	68	Rebellion of Vindex.

68 (June)–69 (January) GALBA.
69 January–March. OTHO.
69 April–December. VITELLIUS.
69 (December)–79 VESPASIANUS.

	69	Revolt of Civilis and the Batavi.
	70	Destruction of Jerusalem. End of the Jewish Rebellion.
	79–81	TITUS.
	79	Eruption of Vesuvius. Destruction of Pompeii and Herculaneum.
	81–96	DOMITIANUS.
	83	Battle of Mons Graupius. War with the Chatti.
	84	Domitian perpetual censor.
	85–89	Dacian Wars.
	88–89	Revolt of Saturninus.
	96–98	NERVA.
	98–117	TRAIANUS.
	101–102	First Dacian War.
	105–106	Second Dacian War. Annexation of Dacia.
	106	Annexation of Arabia Petrea.

114–117	Parthian War.
114	Occupation of Armenia and Upper Mesopotamia.
115	Jewish Rebellion in Cyrene.
116	Annexation of Assyria and Lower Mesopotamia. Revolt in Mesopotamia.
117–138	HADRIANUS.
117	Abandonment of Assyria and Mesopotamia. Armenia a client kingdom.
121–126	Hadrian's first tour of the provinces.
129–134	Second tour of the provinces.
132–134	Revolt of Jews in the East.
138–161	ANTONINUS PIUS.
161–180	MARCUS AURELIUS.
161–169	LUCIUS VERUS.
161–166	Parthian War.
166	Plague spreads throughout the Empire.
167–175	War with Marcomanni, Quadi, and Iazyges.
175	Revolt of Avidius Cassius.
177–192	COMMODUS.
177–180	War with Quadi and Marcomanni.
180	Death of Marcus Aurelius, Commodus sole emperor.
193 January–March.	PERTINAX.
193 March–June.	DIDIUS JULIANUS.
193	Revolts of Septimius Severus, Pescennius Niger, Clodius Albinus.
193–211	SEPTIMIUS SEVERUS.
194	Defeat of Pescennius Niger.
195–196	Invasion of Parthia.
197	Defeat of Albinus at Lugdunum.
197–199	Parthian War renewed. Conquest of Upper Mesopotamia.
208	Caledonians invade Britain.
211–217	CARACALLA and
211–212	GETA.
212	Antoninian Constitution.
214	Parthian War.
217–218	MACRINUS.
218–222	ELAGABALUS.
222–235	SEVERUS ALEXANDER.
227	Establishment of Persian Sassanid Kingdom.
230–233	War with Persia.
234	War on Rhine frontier.
235–238	MAXIMINUS.
238	GORDIANUS I and GORDIANUS II. BALBINUS and PUPIENUS.
238–244	GORDIANUS III.
243–249	PHILIPPUS ARABUS.
247–249	PHILIPPUS JUNIOR.

249–251	DECIUS.
249	Persecution of the Christians.
251–253	GALLUS and VOLUSIANUS.
253	AEMILIANUS.
253–260	VALERIANUS and
253–268	GALLIENUS.
257	Persecution of the Christians renewed.
258	Postumus establishes Roman Empire in Gaul.
259	Valerian defeated and captured by the Persians. Gallienus sole emperor.
267	Sack of Athens by the Goths.
268–270	CLAUDIUS GOTHICUS.
270	QUINTILLUS.
270–275	AURELIANUS.
271	Revolt of Palmyra.
272	Reconquest of Palmyra and the East.
274	Recovery of Gaul and Britain.
275–276	TACITUS.
276	FLORIANUS.
276–282	PROBUS.
282–283	CARUS.
283–285	CARINUS.
284–305	DIOCLETIANUS and
286–305	MAXIMIANUS.
286	Revolt of Carausius in Britain.
293	Galerius and Constantius Caesars.
296	Recovery of Britain.
297	Persian invasion.
301	Edict of Prices.
303–304	Edicts against the Christians.
305	Abdication of Diocletian and Maximian. GALERIUS and CONSTANTIUS. Severus and Daia Caesars.
306	GALERIUS and SEVERUS. Constantinus Caesar. Revolt of Maxentius.
307	GALERIUS, LICINIUS, CONSTATINUS, DAIA, and MAXENTIUS.
311	Edict of Toleration.
312	Battle of Saxa Rubra.
313	Edict of Milan. Fall of Daia.
324	Battle of Chrysopolis.
324–337	CONSTANTINUS sole Augustus.
325	Council of Nicaea.
330	Constantinople the imperial residence.
337–340	CONSTANTINUS II.
337–350	CONSTANS.
337–361	CONSTANTIUS.
342	Council of Serdica.
350	Revolt of Magnentius.

351	Gallus Caesar. Battle of Mursa.
354	Death of Gallus.
355	Julian Caesar.
357	Julian's victory over the Alamanni at Strassburg.
359	War with Persia.
360–363	JULIANUS.
363	Invasion of Persia. Death of Julian.
363–364	JOVIANUS.
364–375	VALENTINIANUS I.
364–378	VALENS.
367–383	GRATIANUS.
375–392	VALENTINIANUS II.
376	Visigoths cross the Danube.
378	Battle of Hadrianople.
379–395	THEODOSIUS I.
380–382	Settlement of Visigoths as allies (*foederati*) in Moesia.
381	Council of Constantinople.
382	Altar of Victory removed from the Senate.
383	Revolt of Maximus in Britain. Death of Gratian.
383–408	ARCADIUS.
388	Maximus defeated and killed.
390	Massacre at Thessalonica.
391	Edicts against Paganism. Destruction of the Serapaeum.
392	Revolt of Arbogast. Murder of Valentinian II. Eugenius proclaimed Augustus.
393–423	HONORIUS.
394	Battle of Frigidus. Death of Arbogast and Eugenius.
395	Death of Theodosius I. Division of the Empire. ARCADIUS emperor in the East, HONORIUS in the West. Revolt of Alaric and the Visigoths.
396	Alaric defeated by Stilicho in Greece.
406	Barbarian invasion of Gaul. Roman garrison leaves Britain.
408	Murder of Stilicho. Alaric invades Italy.
408–450	THEODOSIUS II eastern emperor.
409	Vandals, Alans, and Sueves invade Spain.
410	Visigoths capture Rome. Death of Alaric.
412	Visigoths enter Gaul.
415	Visigoths cross into Spain.
418	Visigoths settled in Aquitania.
423–455	VALENTINIANUS III western emperor.
427	Aetius Master of the Soldiers.
429	Vandal invasion of Africa.
438	The Theodosian Code.
439	Vandals seize Carthage.
450	MARCIANUS eastern emperor.
451	Battle of the Mauriac Plains. Council of Chalcedon.
453	Death of Attila.

454	Aetius assassinated. Ostrogoths settled in Pannonia.
455	MAXIMUS western emperor. Vandals sack Rome.
455–456	AVITUS western emperor. Ricimer Master of the Soldiers.
457–474	LEO I eastern emperor.
457–461	MAJORIANUS western emperor.
461–465	SEVERUS western emperor.
465–467	No emperor in the West.
467–472	ANTHEMIUS western emperor.
472	OLYBRIUS western emperor. Death of Ricimer.
473–474	GLYCERIUS western emperor. LEO II eastern emperor.
474–475	(480) NEPOS western emperor.
474–491	ZENO eastern emperor.
475–476	ROMULUS AUGUSTULUS western emperor.
476	Odovacar king in Italy.
477	Death of Gaiseric.
486	Clovis conquers Syagrius and the Romans in Gaul.
488	Theodoric and the Ostrogoths invade Italy.
491–518	ANASTASIUS eastern emperor.
493	Defeat and death of Odovacar.
506	Roman Law of the Visigoths.
507	Clovis defeats the Visigoths.
518–527	JUSTINUS I eastern emperor.
526	Death of Theodoric.
527–565	JUSTINIANUS eastern emperor.
532	The "Nika" riot.
533–534	Reconquest of Africa.
534	Franks overthrow the Burgundian kingdom.
529–534	Publication of the *Corpus Iuris Civilis*.
535–554	Wars for recovery of Italy.
554	Reoccupation of the coast of Spain.
565	Death of Justinian.

GENEALOGICAL TABLES

TABLE I. THE JULIO-CLAUDIAN LINE

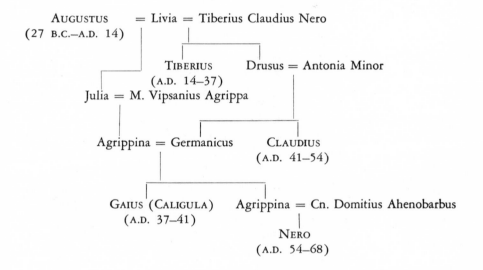

TABLE II. THE DYNASTY OF THE SEVERI

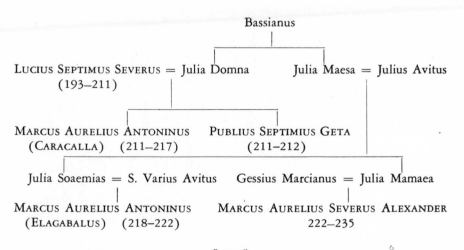

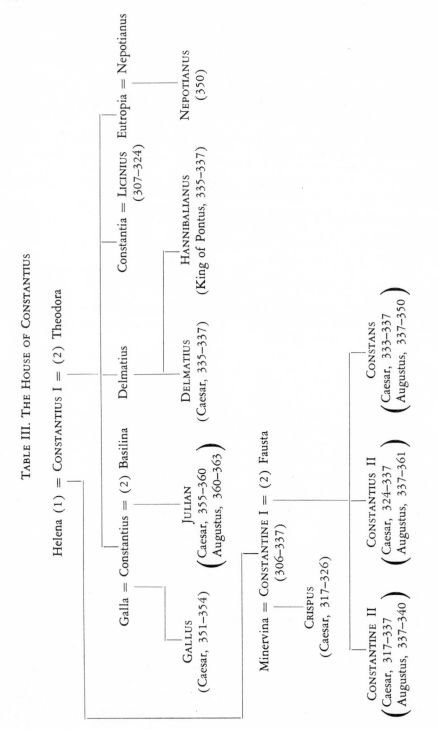

TABLE III. THE HOUSE OF CONSTANTIUS

TABLE IV. THE DYNASTY OF VALENTINIAN AND THEODOSIUS

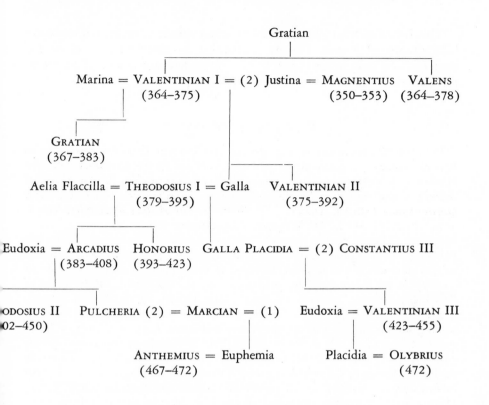

Gratian

Marina = VALENTINIAN I = (2) Justina = MAGNENTIUS   VALENS
(364–375)   (350–353) (364–378)

GRATIAN
(367–383)

Aelia Flaccilla = THEODOSIUS I = Galla   VALENTINIAN II
(379–395)   (375–392)

Eudoxia = ARCADIUS   HONORIUS   GALLA PLACIDIA = (2) CONSTANTIUS III
(383–408) (393–423)

ODOSIUS II   PULCHERIA (2) = MARCIAN = (1)   Eudoxia = VALENTINIAN III
02–450)   (423–455)

ANTHEMIUS = Euphemia   Placidia = OLYBRIUS
(467–472)   (472)

SUPPLEMENTARY READINGS

This list of supplementary readings is not meant to be a comprehensive bibliography of Roman History. Rather, it is conceived as a guide for students who wish to find basic and/or up-to-date discussions of problems and periods in the field.

Bibliography and Sources

Detailed bibliographies of the sources and modern literature pertaining to Roman History are given in the pertinent volumes of the *Cambridge Ancient History* (12 Vols., 1924–1939; currently being rewritten). Roman historical writing is also treated in B. Niese, *Grundriss der römischen Geschichte nebst Quellenkunde* (5th ed., 1923); J. T. Shotwell, *The History of History*, Vol. I, 1939, Part iv; M. L. W. Laistner, *The Greater Roman Historians*, 1947; M. Cary, "Historiography, Roman," *Oxford Classical Dictionary*, 1949; and H. Bengtson, *Einführung in die alte Geschichte* (4th ed., 1962). Recent trends in the literature of the field are surveyed in two important articles in Vol. 50 (1960) of the *Journal of Roman Studies*: A. H. McDonald, "Fifty Years of Republican History," and C. G. Starr, "The History of the Roman Empire, 1911–60." Bibliographies and/or discussions of source problems are found in leading surveys and texts of Roman history such as M. Cary, *A History of Rome* (2nd ed., 1954); F. Heichelheim and C. Yeo, *A History of the Roman People* (1962), A. Piganiol, *Histoire de Rome* (5th ed., 1962); and especially A. Heuss, *Römische Geschichte* (1960), Chap. 12. The most important current bibliography of research on all phases of classical antiquity, including Roman History and Civilization, published yearly, is J. Marouzeau and Juliette Ernst (eds.), *L'année philologique* (1924–   ). The most important encyclopedia of classical antiquity, now approaching completion, is Pauly-Wissowa-Kroll et al., *Realencyclopädie der klassischen Altertumswissenschaft* (1894–   ). A recent, first-rate atlas is A. A. M. van der Heyden and H. H. Scullard, *Atlas of the Classical World* (1959).

Early Italy and the Foundation of Rome
Alföldi, A., *Early Rome and the Latins* (1964).
Altheim, F., *Der Ursprung der Etrusker* (1950).
Bloch, R., *The Origins of Rome* (1960).
Boëthius, A., et al., *Etruscan Culture, Land and People* (1962).
Cary, M., *The Geographic Background of Greek and Roman History* (1949).
Ducati, P., *Etruria antica* (2nd ed., 1927).
Dunbabin, T. J., *The Western Greeks* (1948).
Etruscan number of *Historia*, Vol. 6 (1957).
Fell, R. A. L., *Etruria and Rome* (1924).
Fraccaro, P., *La storia romana arcaica* in *Opuscula*, Vol. 1 (1956), 1ff.

Gerkan, A. von, "Zur Frühgeschichte Roms," *Rheinisches Museum* (1957), 82ff.

Gjerstad, E., *Early Rome* (1953–1960).

Holland, L. A., *Janus and the Bridge* (1961).

"Italy: Topography," *Encyclopaedia Britannica* (14th ed.).

Johnstone, M. A., *Etruria Past and Present* (1930).

Momigliano, A., "An Interim Report on the Origins of Rome," *Journal of Roman Studies*, Vol. 53 (1963), 95ff.

Mueller-Karpe, H., *Vom Anfang Roms* (1959).

Pallottino, M., *The Etruscans* (1955).

Piganiol, A., *Essai sur les origines de Rome* (1917).

Pulgram, E., *The Tongues of Italy: Prehistory and History* (1958).

Randall-MacIver, D., *Greek Cities in Italy and Sicily* (1931).

———, *The Iron Age in Italy* (1927).

———, *Italy Before the Romans* (1928).

———, *Villanovans and Early Etruscans* (1924).

Richardson, E., *The Etruscans. Their Art and Civilization* (1964).

Rose, J. H., *The Mediterranean in the Ancient World* (1933).

Ryberg, I. Scott, *An Archaeological Record of Rome from the Seventh to the Second Century B.C.* (1940).

Schachermeyr, F., *Etruskische Frühgeschichte* (1929).

Siegfried, A., *The Mediterranean* (1948).

Thompson, J. O., *History of Ancient Geography* (1948).

Werner, R., *Der Beginn der römischen Republik* (1963).

Whatmough, J., *The Foundations of Roman Italy* (1937).

The Republic

Aymard, A., *Les premiers rapports de Rome et de la confédération Achaienne (198–189 avant J.-C.)* (1938).

Badian, E., *Foreign Clientelae 264–70 B.C.* (1958).

———, "From the Gracchi to Sulla (1940–59)," *Historia*, Vol. II (1962), 197ff.

———, *Studies in Greek and Roman History* (1964).

Baker, G. P., *Sulla the Fortunate* (1927).

Bennett, H., *Cinna and his Times* (1923).

Bleicken, J., *Das Volkstribunat der klassischen Republik* (1955).

Boren, H. C., "The Urban Side of the Gracchan Economic Crisis," *American Historical Review*, Vol. 63 (1958), 890ff.

Broughton, T. R. S., *Magistrates of the Roman Republic* (2 vols. with supplements, 1951/52, 1960).

Brunt, P. A., "The Army and the Land in the Roman Revolution," *Journal of Roman Studies*, Vol. 52 (1962), 69ff.

Burkert, W., "Caesar und Romulus-Quirinus," *Historia*, Vol. 11 (1962), 356ff.

Carney, T. F., *A Biography of C. Marius* (1962).

Carpenter, R., "Phoenicians in the West," *American Journal of Archaeology* (1958), 35ff.

Cassola, F., *I gruppi politici romani nel 3. secolo a. C.* (1962).

Cowles, F. H., *Gaius Verres* (1917).

Dickinson, J., *Death of the Republic: Politics and Political Thought at Rome, 59–44 B.C.* (1963).

Fowler, W. W., *Julius Caesar* (1919).

Frank, T., *Roman Imperialism* (1914).

Gabba, E., *Appiano e la storia delle guerre civili* (1956).

Gelzer, M., *Caesar der Politiker und Staatsmann* (6th ed., 1960).

———, *Die Nobilität der römischen Republik* (1912).

———, *Pompeius* (2nd ed., 1949).

Hadas, M., *Sextus Pompey* (1930).

Hampl, F., "Das Problem der Datierung der ersten Verträge zwischen Rom und Karthago," *Rheinisches Museum*, Vol. 101 (1958), 58ff.

———, "Römische Politik in republikanischer Zeit und das Problem des Sittenverfalls," *Historische Zeitschrift*, Vol. 188 (1959), 497ff.

———, "Stoische Staatsethik und frühes Rom," *Historische Zeitschrift*, Vol. 184 (1957), 249ff.

Hardy, E. G., *The Catilinarian Conspiracy* (1924).

Haywood, R. M., *Studies on Scipio Africanus* (1933).

Henderson, M. I., "The Establishment of the *Equester Ordo*," *Journal of Roman Studies*, Vol. 53 (1963), 61ff.

Heuss, A., "Der erste Punische Krieg und das Problem des römischen Imperialismus," *Historische Zeitschrift*, Vol. 169 (1949), 457ff.

———, "Der Untergang der römischen Republik und das Problem der Revolution," *Historische Zeitschrift*, Vol. 182 (1956), 1ff.

Hoffman, W., "Catalina und die römische Revolution," *Gymnasium*, Vol. 66 (1959), 459ff.

———, *Rom und die griechische Welt im 4. Jahrhundert* (1934).

———, "Die römische Kriegserklärung an Karthago i. J. 218," *Rheinisches Museum*, Vol. 94 (1951), 69ff.

———, "Die römische Politik des 2. Jahrhunderts und das Ende Karthagos," *Historia*, Vol. 9 (1960), 309ff.

———, "Hannibal und Rom," *Antike und Abendland*, Vol. 6 (1957), 7ff.

Holmes, T. R., *Caesar's Conquest of Gaul* (1911).

Kienast, D., *Cato der Zensor* (1954).

Liddell-Hart, B. H., *A Greater than Napoleon, Scipio Africanus* (1927).

Marsh, F. B., *A History of the Roman World from 146 to 30 B.C.* (3rd ed., 1963).

Meier, C., "Zur Chronologie und Politik in Caesars erstem Konsulat," *Historia*, Vol. 10 (1961), 68ff.

Meyer, E., *Caesars Monarchie und das Principat des Pompejus* (3rd ed., 1922).

Münzer, F., *Römische Adelsparteien und Adelsfamilien* (1920).

Ooteghem, P. van., *Pompée le Grand* (1954).

Petersson, T., *Cicero* (1920).

Picard, G. and C., *La vie quotidienne à Carthage au temps d'Hannibal* (1958).

Scullard, H. H., *From the Gracchi to Nero: A History of Rome from 133 B.C. to A.D. 68* (2nd ed., 1963).

———, *History of the Roman World 753–146 B.C.* (3rd ed., 1961).

———, *Scipio Africanus in the Second Punic War* (1930).

Sihler, E. G., *Cicero of Arpinum* (1914).

Smith, R. E., *The Failure of the Roman Republic* (1955).

Stavely, E. S., "Cicero and the Comitia Centuriata," *Historia*, Vol. 11 (1962), 299ff.

Stier, H., *Roms Aufstieg zur Weltmacht und die griechische Welt* (1957).

Strasburger, H., *Concordia Ordinum* (1931).

Suolahti, J., *The Roman Censors* (1963).

Taylor, L. R., "Forerunners of the Gracchi," *Journal of Roman Studies*, Vol. 52 (1962), 19ff.

———, *Party Politics in the Age of Caesar* (1949).

Volkmann, H., *Kleopatra* (1953).

———, *Sullas Marsch auf Rom* (1958).

Walbank, F. W., *Historical Commentary on Polybius* (1957–   ).

———, "Polybius and Rome's Eastern Policy," *Journal of Roman Studies*, Vol. 53 (1963), 1ff.

Warmington, B. H., *Carthage* (1960).

Principate

Balsdon, J. P. V. D., *The Emperor Gaius* (1934).

Boddington, A., "Sejanus. Whose Conspiracy?" *American Journal of Philology*, Vol. 84 (1963), 1ff.

Brunt, P. A., "Charges of Provincial Maladministration under the Early Principate," *Historia*, Vol. 10 (1961), 189ff.

Buchan, J., *Augustus Caesar* (1937).

Charlesworth, M. P., *Five Men: Character Studies from the Roman Empire* (1936).

Chilver, G. E. F., "The Army in Politics, A.D. 68–70," *Journal of Roman Studies*, Vol. 47 (1957), 29ff.

———, "Augustus and the Roman Constitution," *Historia*, Vol. 1 (1950), 408ff.

Crees, J. H. E., *The Reign of the Emperor Probus* (1911).

Damereau, P., *Kaiser Claudius II Gothicus* (1934).

Dudley, D. R., and Webster, G., *The Rebellion of Boudicca* (1962).

Farquharson, A. S. L., *Marcus Aurelius* (1951).

Fuchs, A., "The Jewish Revolt A.D. 115–117," *Journal of Roman Studies*, Vol. 51 (1961), 98ff.

Gsell, S., *Essai sur le règne de l'empereur Domitien* (1894).

Hainsworth, J. C., "Verginius and Vindex," *Historia*, Vol. 11 (1962), 86ff.

Hammond, M., *The Augustan Principate* (1933).

Hasebroek, J., *Untersuchungen zur Geschichte des Kaisers Septimius Severus* (1921).

Hay, J. S., *The Amazing Emperor Elagabalus* (1911).

Henderson, B. W., *Civil War and Rebellion in the Roman Empire A.D. 69–70* (1908).

———, *Five Roman Emperors* (1927).

———, *Life and Principate of the Emperor Hadrian A.D. 76–138* (1923).

———, *Life and Principate of the Emperor Nero* (1903).

Holmes, T. R., *The Architect of the Roman Empire* (1928–31).

———, *The Roman Republic and the Founder of the Empire* (1923).

Homo, L., *Essai sur le règne de l'empereur Aurélien* (1904).

———, *Vespasien, L'empereur du bon sense* (1949).

Hopkins, R. V. N., *The Life of Alexander Severus* (1907).

Huettl, W., *Antoninus Pius* (2 vols., 1933–36).

Jardé, A., *Etudes critiques sur la vie et la règne de Sévère Alexandre* (1925).

Jones, A. H. M., "The Decline and Fall of the Roman Empire," *History*, Vol. 40 (1955), 209ff.

Lepper, F. A., *Trajan's Parthian War* (1948).

Levi, M. A., *Nerone e i suoi tempi* (1949).

Marsh, F. B., *The Founding of the Roman Empire* (2nd ed., 1927).

———, *The Reign of Tiberius* (1931).

Mattingly, H., *Roman Imperial Civilisation* (1957).

Meloni, P., *Il regno di Caro, Numeriano e Carino* (1948).

Momigliano, A., *Claudius* (repr. 1961).

Moreau, J., "Krise und Verfall: Das dritte Jahrhundert n. Chr. als historisches Problem," *Heidelberger Jahrbücher* (1961), 128ff.

Orgeval, B. d'., *L'empereur Hadrien* (1950).

Paribeni, R., *Optimus Princeps* (2 vols. 1926–27).

Parker, H. M. D., *A History of the Roman World from A.D. 138 to A.D. 337* (2nd ed., 1958).

Platnauer, M., *Life and Reign of Septimius Severus* (1918).

Premerstein, A. von, *Vom Werden und Wesen des Prinzipats* (1937).

Reinhold, M., *Marcus Agrippa* (1933).

Rogers, R. S., *Criminal Trials and Criminal Legislation under Tiberius* (1935).

———, *Studies in the Reign of Tiberius* (1943).

Salmon, E. T., "The Evolution of Augustus' Principate," *Historia*, Vol. 5 (1956), 456ff.

———, *A History of the Roman World from 30 B.C. to A.D. 138*, (4th ed., 1963).

Scramuzza, V. M., *The Emperor Claudius* (1940).

Scullard, H. H., *From the Gracchi to Nero* (2nd ed., 1963).

Sedgwick, H. D., *Marcus Aurelius, A Biography* (1921).

Syme, R., *The Roman Revolution* (repr. 1951).

———, *Tacitus* (2 vols., 1958).

Timpe, D., *Untersuchungen zur Kontinuität des frühen Prinzipats* (1962).

Vittinghoff, F., *Kaiser Augustus* (1959).

———, *Römische Kolonisation und Bürgerrechtspolitik unter Caesar und Augustus* (1952).

Vitucci, G., *L'imperatore Probo* (1952).

Walser, G., and Pekáry, T., *Die Krise des römischen Reiches* (1962).

Walser, G., "Zu den Ursachen der Reichskrise im 3. Jahrhundert," *Schweizer Beiträge zur allgemeinen Geschichte* (1960/61), 142ff.

Weber, W., *Untersuchungen zur Geschichte des Kaisers Hadrian* (1907).

Wright, F. A., *Marcus Agrippa* (1937).

Late Empire

Alföldi, A., *A Conflict of Ideas in the Late Roman Empire* (1952).

———, *The Conversion of Constantine and Pagan Rome* (1948).

Baynes, N. H., and Moss, H. S. L. B., *Byzantium. An Introduction to East Roman Civilization* (1948).

Bidez, J., *La vie de l'empereur Julien* (1930).

Boak, A. E. R., *Manpower Shortage and the Fall of the Roman Empire in the West* (1955).

———, *The Master of the Offices in the Later Roman and Byzantine Empires* (1924).

Burckhardt, J., *The Age of Constantine the Great* (1956 ed.).

Bury, J. B., *History of the Later Roman Empire from the Death of Theodosius I to the Death of Justinian* (2 vols., 1923).

Charanis, P., *Church and State in the Later Roman Empire* (1939).

Chastagnol, A., *La préfecture urbaine à Rome sous le Bas-Empire* (1960).

Dill, S., *Roman Society in the Last Century of the Western Empire* (1899).

Doerries, H., *Konstantin der Grosse* (1958).

Downey, G., *Antioch in the Age of Theodosius The Great* (1962).

Ensslin, W., *Theoderich der Grosse* (1947).

———, *Zur Geschichtsschreibung und Weltanschauung des Ammianus Marcellinus* (1923).

Gardner, A., *Julian, Philosopher and Emperor* (1901).

Gibbon, E., *Decline and Fall of the Roman Empire* (7 vols., 1896–1900, ed. J. B. Bury).

Gordon, C. D., *The Age of Attila: Fifth Century Byzantium and the Barbarians* (1960).

Hampl, F., "*Die Gründung von Konstantinopel*," Südostforschungen, Vol. 14 (1955), 9ff.

Harmand, L., *Libanius, Discours sur les patronages* (1955).

Holmes, W., *The Age of Justinian and Theodora* (2nd ed., 1912).

Jones, A. H. M., *The Later Roman Empire 284–602* (3 Vols., 1964).

Laistner, M. L. W., *Christianity and Pagan Culture* (1951).

———, *Thought and Letters in Western Europe, A.D. 500–900* (1957 ed.).

Liebeschuetz, W., "Did the Pelagian Movement have Social Aims?", *Historia*, Vol. 12 (1963), 227ff.

Martin, E., *The Emperor Julian* (1919).

Mazzarino, S., *Aspetti Sociali del quarto secolo* (1951).

Meer, F. van der, *Augustine the Bishop: The Life and Work of a Father of the Church* (1961).

Momigliano, A. (ed.), *The Conflict between Paganism and Christianity in the Fourth Century* (1963).

Ostrogorsky, G., *History of the Byzantine State* (English ed. 1957).

Pack, R. A., *Studies in Libanius and Antiochene Society under Theodosius* (1935).

Petit, P., *Libanius et la vie municipale à Antioche au IVe siècle après J. C.* (1955).

———, *Les étudiants de Libanius* (1957).

Piganiol, A., *L'empereur Constantin* (1932).

———, *L'empire chrétien* (1947).

Quasten, J., *Patrology*, Vol. 3: *The Golden Age of Greek Patristic Literature From the Council of Nicaea to the Council of Chalcedon* (1960).

Rubin, B., *Das Zeitalter Justinian* (1960–).
Ruggini, L., *Ebrei e Orientali nell'Italia settentrionale fra il IV e il VI secolo D. Chr.*, in *Studia et Documenta Historiae et Iuris* (1959), 186ff.
———, *Economia e società nell'Italia Annonaria* (1961).
Saunders, J. J., *"The Debate on the Fall of Rome," History* (1963), 1ff.
Schmidt, L., *Geschichte der deutschen Stämme bis zum Ausgang der Völkerwanderung* (2nd ed., 1934–38).
Seeck, O., *Geschichte des Untergangs der antiken Welt* (6 vols., 1901–20).
Seston, W., *Dioclétien et la Tétrarchie* (Paris, 1947).
Sirago, A., *Galla Placidia e la trasformazione dell'Occidente* (1961).
Stein, E., *Histoire du bas-empire* (2 vols., 1949–59).
Stroheker, K., *Der senatorische Adel im spätantiken Gallien* (1948).
Ure, P. N., *Justinian and His Age* (1951).
Vasiliev, *History of the Byzantine Empire* (1952).
———, *Justin the First* (1950).
Vogt, J., *Constantin der Grosse und sein Jahrhundert* (2nd ed., 1960).

Politics and Government

Abbott, F. F., *A History and Description of Roman Political Institutions* (3rd ed., repr. 1963).
Adocock, F. E., *Roman Political Ideas and Practice* (1959).
Alföldi, A., *Die Ausgestaltung des monarchischen Zeremoniells am römischen Kaiserhofe* (1934).
Boissier, G., *L'opposition sous les Césars* (4th ed., 1900).
Botsford, G. W., *The Roman Assemblies* (1909).
Brunt, P., "Lex Valeria Cornelia," *Journal of Roman Studies*, Vol. 51 (1961), 71ff.
Crook, J., *Consilium Principis* (1955).
Earl, D. C., *Tiberius Gracchus: A Study in Politics* (1963).
Grant, M., *From Imperium to Auctoritas* (1946).
Greenridge, A. H. J., *Roman Public Life* (1901).
Hammond, M., *The Antonine Monarchy* (1959).
Hirschfeld, O., *Die kaiserlichen Verwaltungsbeamtem bis auf Diocletian* (2nd ed., 1905).
Homo, L., *Roman Political Institutions from City to State* (repr. 1962).
Jones, A. H. M., *Studies in Roman Government and Law* (1960).
Kornemann, E., *Doppelprinzipat und Reichsteilung im Imperium Romanum* (1930).
Lacey, W. K., "Nomination and the Elections under Tiberius," *Historia*, Vol. 12 (1963), 167ff.
Laet, S. J. de, *Portorium* (1949).
Lambrechts, P., *La composition du sénat romain de l'accession d'Hadrien à la mort de Commode* (1936).
———, *La composition du sénat romain de Septime Sévère à Diocletien (193–284)* (1937).
Larsen, J. A. O., *Representative Government in Greek and Roman History* (1955).

Magdelain, A., *Auctoritas principis* (1947).

Millar, F., "The Fiscus in the First Two Centuries," *Journal of Roman Studies*, Vol. 53 (1963), 29ff.

Oliver, J. H., *The Ruling Power. A Study of the Roman Empire in the Second Century after Christ Through the Roman Oration of Aelius Aristides* (Transactions of the American Philosophical Society, Vol. 43, Part 4, 1953).

Pflaum, H. G., *Les carrieres procuratoriennes équestres sous le haut empire romain* (4 vols., 1960–61).

———, *Les procurateurs équestres sous le haut-empire romain* (1950).

Scullard, H. H., *Roman Politics, 220–150 B.C.* (1951).

Sherwin-White, A. N., *The Roman Citizenship* (1939).

———, "Violence in Roman Politics," *Journal of Roman Studies*, Vol. 46 (1956), 1ff.

Sinnigen, W. G., "The Roman Secret Service," *The Classical Journal*, Vol. 67 (1961), 65ff.

Taylor, L. R., *Voting Districts of the Roman Republic* (1960).

Regional Studies and Municipalities

Abbott, F. F., and Johnson, A. C., *Municipal Administration in the Roman Empire* (1926).

Arnold, W. T., *The Roman System of Provincial Administration* (3rd ed., 1914).

Bouchier, E. S., *Life and Letters in Roman Africa* (1913).

———, *Sardinia in Ancient Times* (1917).

———, *Spain under the Roman Empire* (1914).

———, *Syria as a Roman Province* (1916).

Broughton, T. R. S., *The Romanization of Africa Proconsularis* (1929).

Chilver, G. E. F., *Cisalpine Gaul* (1941).

Collingwood, R., *Roman Britain* (1923).

———, *Roman Britain and the English Settlements* (2nd ed. 1937; Oxford History of England, Vol. 1).

Debevoise, N. C., *A Political History of Parthia* (1938).

Graham, A., *The Roman Provinces of Africa* (1905).

Grenier, A., *Les Gaulois* (1945).

Gwatkin, W., *Cappadocia as a Roman Procuratorial Province* (1930).

Haverfield, F., *The Romanization of Roman Britain* (rev. ed., 1924).

Jones, A. H. M., *Cities of the Eastern Roman Provinces* (1937).

———, *The Herods of Judaea* (1938).

Jullian, C., *Histoire de la Gaule* Vol. 2 (4th ed., 1921).

Magie, D., *The Roman Rule in Asia Minor* (1950).

Milne, J., *A History of Egypt under Roman Rule* (3rd ed., 1924).

Mommsen, Th., *The Provinces of the Roman Empire* (1909).

Parvan, V., *Dacia* (1928).

Powell, T. G. E., *The Celts* (1958).

Reid, J. S., *The Municipalities of the Roman Empire* (1913).

Richmond, I. A., "Palmyra under the Aegis of the Romans," *Journal of Roman Studies*, Vol. 53 (1963), 43ff.

————, *Roman Britain* (1960).
Romanelli, P., *Storia delle provincie romane dell'Africa* (1959).
Stevenson, G., *Roman Provincial Administration* (1939).
Sutherland, C. H. V., *The Romans in Spain* (1939).
Welch, G. P., *Britannia; The Roman Conquest and Occupation of Britain* (1963).
Wheeler, M., *Rome Beyond the Imperial Frontiers* (1954).
Witt, N. J. de, *Urbanization and the Franchise in Roman Gaul* (1940).

Law

Cramer, F., *Astrology in Roman Law and Politics* (1954).
Jolowicz, H. F., *Historical Introduction to the Study of Roman Law* (2nd ed. 1952).
————, *Roman Foundations of Modern Law* (1957).
Kunkel, W., *Herkunft und soziale Stellung der römischen Juristen* (1952).
————, *Römische Rechtsgeschichte* (2nd ed., 1948).
Martino, F. de, *Storia della costituzione romana* (1951).
Schulz, F., *Classical Roman Law* (1951).
————, *History of Roman Legal Science* (2nd ed., 1953).
————, *Principles of Roman Law* (1936).
Sherwin-White, A. N., *Roman Society and Roman Law in the New Testament* (1963).

Society

Abbott, F. F., *Society and Politics in Ancient Rome* (repr. 1963).
André, J., *L'alimentation et la cuisine à Rome* (1961).
Balsdon, J. P. V. D., *Roman Women: Their History and Habits* (1962).
Barrow, R. H., *Slavery in the Roman Empire* (1928).
Berchem, D. van, *Les distributions de blé et d'argent à la plèbe romaine sous l'empire* (1939).
Carcopino, J., *Daily Life in Ancient Rome* (1940).
Corte, M. della, *Case ed abitanti a Pompeii* (2nd ed., 1954).
Cowell, F. R., *Cicero and the Roman Republic* (1948).
————, *Everyday Life in Ancient Rome* (2nd ed., 1962).
Dill, S., *Roman Society from Nero to Marcus Aurelius* (1905).
Duff, A. M., *Freedmen in the Early Roman Empire* (1928).
Fowler, W., *Social Life in Rome in the Days of Cicero* (1909).
Friedlaender, L., *Roman Life and Manners under the Early Empire* (1908).
Hill, H., *The Roman Middle Class in the Republican Period* (1952).
Jennison, G., *Animals for Show and Pleasure in Ancient Rome* (1937).
Mattingly, H., *The Man in the Roman Street* (1947).
Tanzer, H. H., *The Common People of Pompeii* (1939).
Taylor, L. R., "Freedmen and Freeborn in the Epitaphs of Imperial Rome," *American Journal of Philology*, Vol. 72 (1961), 113ff.
Tucker, T. G., *Life in the Roman World of Nero and St. Paul* (1910).
Westermann, W. L., *Slave Systems in Greek and Roman Antiquity* (1955).
Winter, J., *Life and Letters in the Papyri* (1933).

Economy

Adams, L., *A Study in the Commerce of Latium from the Early Iron Age through the Sixth Century B.C.* (1921).

Bolin, S., *State and Currency in the Roman Empire to 300 A.D.* (1958).

Cary, M., and Warmington, E. H., *The Ancient Explorers* (1929).

Casson, L., *The Ancient Mariners: Seafarers and Sea Fighters of the Mediterranean in Ancient Times* (1959).

Charlesworth, M. P., *Trade Routes and Commerce of the Roman Empire* (2nd ed., 1926).

Frank, T., *Economic History of Rome* (2nd ed., 1927).

———, *Economic Survey of Ancient Rome* (5 vols., 1933–40).

Grant, M., *Roman History from Coins* (1958).

Hatzfeld, J., *Les trafiquants italiens dans l'orient hellénique* (1919).

Heichelheim, F., *An Economic History of the Ancient World* (1958–   ).

Heitland, W. E., *Agricola, A Study of Agriculture and Rustic Life in the Greco-Roman World from the Standpoint of Labour* (1921).

Klausing, R., *The Roman Colonate* (1925).

Loane, H. J., *Industry and Commerce of the City of Rome (50 B.C.–200 A.D.)* (1938).

Louis, P., *Ancient Rome at Work* (1927).

Mattingly, H., *Roman Coins* (2nd ed., 1960).

Maxey, M., *Occupations of the Lower Classes in Roman Society* (1938).

Meiggs, R., *Roman Ostia* (1960).

Milne, J. G., *The Development of Roman Coinage* (1937).

Robertis, F. M. de, *Il diritto associativo romano dai collegi della repubblica alle corporazioni del basso impero* (1938).

Rostovtzeff, M., *Caravan Cities* (1932).

———, *Social and Economic History of the Roman Empire* (2nd ed., 1957).

———, *Studien zur Geschichte des römischen Kolonats* (1910).

Sutherland, C. H. V., *Coinage in Roman Imperial Policy, 31 B.C.–A.D. 68* (1951).

Sydenham, E. A., *The Coinage of the Roman Republic* (1952).

Thomsen, R., *Early Roman Coinage* (3 vols., 1957–61).

Walbank, F. W., *Decline of the Roman Empire in the West* (1946).

Waltzing, J. P., *Etude historique sur les corporations professionnelles chez les Romains* (4 vols. 1895–1900).

Warmington, E. H., *The Commerce between the Roman Empire and India* (1928).

Roman Civilization

Adcock, F. E., *Caesar as a Man of Letters* (1956).

Allbutt, T., *Greek Medicine in Rome* (1921).

Anderson, W. S., *Pompey, His Friends, and the Literature of the First Century* (1963).

Arnold, E. V., *Roman Stoicism* (1911).

Bailey, C., *Lucretius* (3 vols., 1947).

Bardon, H., *Les empereurs et les lettres latines d'Auguste à Hadrien* (1940).

Baynes, N. H., *The Historia Augusta, Its Date and Purpose* (1926).

Beare, W., *The Roman Stage* (1950).

Bieber, M., *The History of the Greek and Roman Theater* (2nd ed., 1961).

Boissier, G., *Cicero and His Friends* (1929 ed.).

Bonner, S. F., *Roman Declamation* (1949).

Butler, H. E., *Post-Augustan Poetry* (1909).

Ciaceri, E., *Cicerone e i suoi tempi* (2 vols., 1926–30).

Clarke, M. L., *Rhetoric at Rome: A Historical Survey* (1963).

Duff, J. W., *A Literary History of Rome from the Origins to the Close of the Golden Age* (repr., 1953).

————, *A Literary History of Rome in the Silver Age* (rev. ed., 1959).

————, *Roman Satire* (1937).

Earl, D. C., *The Political Thought of Sallust* (1961).

Fraenkel, E., *Horace* (1957).

Frank, T., *Life and Literature in the Roman Republic* (1930).

Fuchs, H., "Ciceros Hingabe und die Philosophie," *Museum Helveticum*, Vol. 16 (1959), 1ff.

————, *Der geistige Widerstand gegen Rom in der antiken Welt* (1938).

Glover, T., *Life and Letters in the Fourth Century* (1901).

Grant, M., *The World of Rome* (1959).

Gwynn, J., *Roman Education* (1926).

Haarhoff, T. J., *The Schools of Gaul* (1920).

Hadas, M., *History of Latin Literature* (1952).

————, *Stoic Philosophy of Seneca* (1958).

Haffter, H., "Neuere Arbeiten zum Problem der humanitas," *Philologus*, Vol. 100 (1956), 287ff.

Hamberg, P., *Studies in Roman Imperial Art* (1945).

Haskell, H. J., *This was Cicero* (1942).

Havelock, E. A., *The Lyric Genius of Catullus* (1939).

Heitland, W., *The Roman Fate* (1922).

Highet, G., *Poets in a Landscape* (1957).

Hunt, H. A. K., *The Humanism of Cicero* (1954).

Jones, T., *The Silver Plated Age* (1962).

Klingner, F., *Römische Geisteswelt* (4th ed., 1961).

Kroll, W., *Die Kultur der ciceronischen Zeit* (1933).

Laistner, M. L. W., *The Greater Roman Historians* (1947).

Latte, K., et al., *Histoire et historiens dans l'antiquité* (1956).

McDonald, A. H., "The Roman Historians," *Fifty Years of Classical Scholarship* (ed. M. Platnauer 1954), chap. 13.

Mackail, J. W., *Latin Literature* (1915).

Marrou, H. L., *A History of Education in Antiquity* (1956).

Pohlenz, M., *Die Stoa* (2 vols., 1948–49).

Rose, H. J., *A Handbook of Latin Literature* (2nd ed., 1949).

Seel, O., *Cicero* (1953).

Sihler, E. G., *Cicero of Arpinum* (1914).

Sikes, E. E., *Lucretius, Poet and Philosopher* (1936).

Sinclair, T. A., and Wright, F. A., *A History of the Later Latin Literature* (1931).

Singer, C., ed., *A History of Technology*. Vol. 2, *The Mediterranean Civilizations and the Middle Ages, c. 700 B.C. to c. A.D. 1500* (1956).

Starr, C., *Civilization and the Caesars: the Intellectual Revolution in the Roman Empire* (1954).

Syme, R., *Sallust* (1964).

———, *Tacitus* (2 vols., 1958).

Ussani, V., *Guida allo studio della civiltà romana antica* (2 vols., 1952–53).

Vogt, J., *Ciceros Glaube an Rom* (1935).

Walsh, P. G., *Livy: His Historical Aims and Methods* (1961).

Wilkins, A. S., *Roman Education* (1905).

Wilkinson, *Horace and his Lyric Poetry* (2nd ed., 1951).

———, *Ovid Recalled* (1955).

Art and Architecture

Boëthius, A., *The Golden House of Nero* (1960).

———, *Roman and Greek Town Architecture* (1948).

Brown, F. E., *Roman Architecture* (1961).

Cumont, F., *Recherches sur le symbolisme funéraire des Romains* (1942).

Dalton, O. M., *East Christian Art* (1925).

Encyclopaedia of World Art (1959–   ); Articles: "Etrusco-Italian" (M. Pallottino), "Hellenistic-Román," (O. Vessberg), "Italo-Roman Folk Art" (G. Mansuelli).

Maiuri, A., *Roman Painting* (1953).

Morey, C. R., *Early Christian Art* (1942).

Nash, E., *Pictorial Dictionary of Ancient Rome* (2 vols., 1961–62).

Richter, G. M. A., *Ancient Italy* (1955).

Robertson, D. S., *Greek and Roman Architecture* (2nd ed., 1943).

Schober, A., "Zur Entstehung und Bedeutung der provinzial-römischen Kunst," *Jahreshefte des öst. arch. Instituts* (1930), 9ff.

Strong, E., *Art in Ancient Rome* (2 vols., 2nd ed., 1930).

———, *Roman Sculpture from Augustus to Constantine* (1907).

Toynbee, J. M. C., *The Hadrianic School: A Chapter in the History of Greek Art* (1934).

Walters, H. B., *Art in Ancient Rome* (2nd ed., 1930).

Religion

Altheim, F., *History of Roman Religion* (1938).

Bailey, C., *Phases in the Religion of Ancient Rome* (1932).

Cumont, F., *Oriental Religions in Roman Paganism* (repr. 1956).

Fowler, W. W., *Religious Experience of the Roman People* (1911).

Glover, T. R., *The Conflict of Religions in the Early Roman Empire* (2nd ed., 1909).

Halliday, T. R., *Roman Religion* (1922).

Latte, K., *Römische Religionsgeschichte* (1960).

Lewis, M. H. L., *The Official Priests of Rome under the Julio-Claudians* (1955).

Rose, H. J., *Ancient Roman Religion* (1948).

———, "Roman Religion, 1911–1960," *Journal of Roman Studies*, Vol. 50 (1960), 161ff.

Scott, K., *The Imperial Cult under the Flavians* (1936).
Taylor, L. R., *The Divinity of the Roman Emperor* (1931).
Turchi, N., *La religione di Roma antica* (1939).

Judaism and Christianity

Angus, S., *The Mystery-Religions and Christianity* (1925).
Baynes, N. H., *The Early Church and Social Life* (1927).
Burrows, M., *More Light on the Dead Sea Scrolls* (1958).
Farmer, W. R., *Maccabees, Zealots, and Josephus: An Inquiry into Jewish Nationalism in the Greco-Roman Period* (1956).
Grant, R. M., *Gnosticism and Early Christianity* (1959).
Halliday, W. R., *The Pagan Background of Early Christianity* (1925).
Harnack, A., *Mission und Ausbreitung des Christentums in den ersten drei Jahrhunderten* (2 vols., 4th ed., 1924).
Jaeger, W., *Early Christianity and Greek Paideia* (1962).
Juster, J., *Les Juifs dans l'empire romain* (2 vols., 1914).
Kidd, B. J., *History of the Church to 461 A.D.* (1922).
Leon, H. J., *The Jews of Ancient Rome* (1960).
Merrill, E. T., *Essays in Early Christianity* (1924).
Moore, G. F., *Judaism in the first Centuries of the Christian Era* (2 vols., 1930–32).
Moreau, J., *La persécution du christianisme dans l'empire romain* (1956).
Mowry, L., *The Dead Sea Scrolls and the Early Church* (1962).
Nock, A. D., *Conversion: the Old and New in Religion from Alexander the Great to Augustine of Hippo* (1933).
———, *Early Gentile Christianity and Its Hellenistic Background*, in *Essays on the Trinity and the Incarnation* (1928) (ed. A. Rawlinson).
Oesterly, W. O. E., *A History of Israel*, Vol. 2, (1932).
Walker, W., *A History of the Western Church* (1918).

Army and Navy

Adcock, F. E., *The Roman Art of War under the Republic* (1940).
Baillie-Reynolds, P. K., *The Vigiles of Imperial Rome* (1926).
Berchem, D. van, *L'armée de Dioclétien et la réforme Constantinienne* (1952).
Birley, E., *Roman Britain and the Roman Army* (1953).
Cheesman, G. L., *The Auxilia of the Roman Imperial Army* (1914).
Durry, M., *Les cohortes prétoriennes* (1938).
Forni, G., *Il reclutamento delle legioni da Augusto a Diocleziano* (1953).
Gabba, E., "Le origini dell'esercito professionale in Roma," *Athenaeum* (1949).
Grosse, R., *Römische Militärgeschichte von Gallienus bis zum Beginn der byzantinischen Themenverfassung* (1920).
Karayannopulos, J., *Die Entstehung der byzantinischen Themenordnung* (1959).
Kraft, K., *Zur Rekrutierung der Alen und Kohorten an Rhein und Donau* (1951).
MacMullen, R., *Soldier and Civilian in the Later Roman Empire* (1963).
Mann, J. C., "A Note on the Numeri," *Hermes*, Vol. 82 (1954), 501ff.
Parker, H. M. D., *The Roman Legions* (2nd ed., 1958).

Salmon, T. E., "The Roman Army and the Disintegration of the Roman Empire," *Transactions of the Royal Society of Canada, Third Series, Section II,* Vol. 52, (1956).

Smith, R. E., *Service in the Post-Marian Roman Army* (1958).

Starr, C. G., *The Roman Imperial Navy* (2nd ed., 1959).

Suolahti, J., *The Junior Officers of the Roman Army in the Republican Period* (1955).

Thiel, J. H., *A History of Roman Sea-Power Before the Second Punic War* (1954).

————, *Studies in the History of Roman Sea-Power in Republican Times* (1946).

Wallinga, H., *The Boarding Bridge of the Romans: Its Function in the Naval Tactics of the First Punic War* (1956).

Yoshimura, T., "Die Auxiliartruppen und die Provinzialklientel in der römischen Republik," *Historia,* Vol. 10 (1961), 473ff.

INDEX

NOTE: All Romans, except emperors and men of letters, are to be found under their *gens* name: *e.g.* for Cato see Porcius. All others are indexed under the name most commonly used in English: *e.g.* Trajan, Horace, Alaric.

E DUE

NOV 1 1 '68

Sweoringen

DEC 1' '69

APR 27 71

OCT 25 72

JUN 2 7 '73

DEC 1 6 74

DEC 1 6 1977

SEP 1 1 1978

DEC 17 1979

DEC 17 1982

NOV 28 83

OC 14 '85

FE 22 '88

MR 7 '88

MAY 1 1989